A DREAM OF
RED MANSIONS

A DREAM OF RED MANSIONS

Volume III

TSAO HSUEH–CHIN
and KAO HGO

FOREIGN LANGUAGES PRESS BEIJING

First Edition 1978
Third Printing 1995

Translated by
YANG HSIEN-YI and GLADYS YANG

Illustrated by
TAI TUN-PANG

ISBN 7-119-01548-6
© Foreign Languages Press, Beijing, 1978

Published by Foreign Languages Press
24 Baiwanzhuang Road, Beijing 100037, China

Distributed by China International Book Trading Corporation
35 Chegongzhuang Xilu, Beijing 100044, China
P.O. Box 399, Beijing, China
Printed in the People's Republic of China

CONTENTS

CONTENTS

CHAPTER 81

Four Beauties Fish in the Pond
to Try Their Luck
Pao-yu's Father Orders Him Back
to the Family School

After Ying-chun's departure, Lady Hsing behaved just as if nothing had happened. Lady Wang, however, who had brought Ying-chun up, was bitterly distressed. She was sighing to herself in her room when Pao-yu came in to pay his respects. Noticing the tear-stains on her cheeks he did not venture to take a seat, simply standing on one side till she urged him to mount the *kang* and sit beside her.

His mother saw from the dazed look on his face that he had something on his mind.

"What's worrying you now?" she asked.

"It's nothing really. But after hearing yesterday what poor Ying-chun has to put up with, I feel it's truly too much for her to bear! I didn't dare tell grandmother, but it kept me from sleeping all night. How can girls from a family like ours stand such cruel treatment? Ying-chun especially, who's always been too timid to answer anyone back. Yet now *she* of all people is up against such an inhuman monster, who has no idea how sensitive a girl is." As he spoke his eyes brimmed with tears.

"There's no help for it," Lady Wang answered. "As the saying goes, 'A married daughter — spilt water.' So what can I do about it?"

"Last night I had an idea. Suppose we talk grandmother into having Cousin Ying-chun fetched back? Then she can go on staying in Purple Caltrop Isle, eating and playing with us just like in the old days, instead of being bullied by that scoundrel Sun. When he sends to fetch her back we won't let her go,

1

not even if he sends a hundred times! We'll just tell him this is the old lady's decision. Don't you think that's a good plan?"

Both amused and exasperated, his mother exclaimed, "There you go again — talking nonsense! Sooner or later a girl has to leave home, and once she's married off what can her mother's family do for her? If she happens to get a good husband, fine; if not, there's no help for it — that's fate. Surely you know the saying, 'Marry a cock and follow the cock; marry a dog and follow the dog'? How can every girl be like your eldest sister, chosen as an Imperial Consort? Besides, Ying-chun's newly married; her husband's still young. People's temperaments differ, and just at the start she's bound to feel a bit awkward. A few years from now, when they know each other better and have a child or two, things should work out all right.

"Mind you don't breathe a word about this to the old lady. If I find you have, you'll catch it! Go and see to your own affairs now. Don't stay here talking nonsense."

Pao-yu sat there a little longer in subdued silence, then listlessly took his leave. Thoroughly depressed and not knowing how to work off his feelings, he went back to the Garden, straight to Bamboo Lodge. Once inside, he burst out crying.

Tai-yu, who had just finished dressing, was most alarmed to see the state he was in.

"What's happened?" she asked. "Who's been annoying you?"

Although she repeated her questions several times, Pao-yu just went on sobbing, his head bent over the table, unable to speak. She sat on a chair in bewilderment to watch him.

"Has someone else provoked you? Or have I offended you?" she asked presently.

"No, neither!" he blurted out with a sweep of one hand.

"Well, what's upset you then?"

"I can't help thinking that the sooner we all die the better! Life is really so meaningless."

"What are you talking about?" she asked, more puzzled than ever. "Have you taken leave of your senses?"

"No, I haven't. If I tell you, it will upset you too. You saw how wretched Ying-chun looked yesterday, and heard all that she said. Why must a girl get married when she grows up? That's what I'd like to know. Why put up with such bad treatment from her husband? I still remember what fun we had when we started our Begonia Club, making up poems and acting as host in turn. Now Cousin Pao-chai has gone home, even Hsiang-ling can't come here any more; and on top of that, Ying-chun has left us to get married. With these congenial spirits gone, what's to become of us? I wanted to ask grandmother to have Ying-chun fetched back, but mother won't hear of it. She called me silly, said I was talking nonsense, and I dared not argue with her. Such a short time, and just see how the Garden has changed! If this goes on a few years more, goodness knows what it will be like. The more I think about it, the sadder I feel."

Tai-yu, while he was speaking, had gradually lowered her head and withdrawn to the *kang*. Now, without saying a word, she heaved a sigh and lay down with her face to the wall.

Tzu-chuan, who had just brought in tea, was puzzled to find the two of them like this. And now Hsi-jen arrived.

"So here you are, Second Master," she said to Pao-yu. "The old lady's been asking for you, and I guessed you'd be here."

Tai-yu rose at this to offer Hsi-jen a seat. Pao-yu noticed that her eyes were red from weeping.

"Cousin, I was only talking nonsense just now. Don't let it upset you," he pleaded. "Take my advice and look after your health. Have a rest now. I'll be back when I've seen what the old lady wants me for."

After he had gone, Hsi-jen asked what had happened.

"He was upset on account of Cousin Ying-chun," Tai-yu answered. "I was rubbing my eyes because they itched — that's all."

Hsi-jen made no comment but hurried out after Pao-yu, then went on her own way while he proceeded to his grandmother's quarters. As she was already having her siesta, he returned to Happy Red Court.

That afternoon when Pao-yu got up from his nap, feeling

thoroughly bored he picked up a book at random. Hsi-jen
seeing this went out to brew him some tea. The book he had
happened to take was an anthology of ancient songs, and leafing
through it he came upon Tsao Tsao's verse:

> Facing the wine let us sing,
> For life is short.

In dismay, he put it down and picked up a collection of Tsin
Dynasty prose. After turning a few pages only, however, he
closed the book abruptly and rested his chin on his hands, lost
in thought. This was how Hsi-jen discovered him when she
brought in the tea.

"Why have you stopped reading?" she asked.

Instead of answering, he merely took the bowl from her,
putting it down again after one sip. Hsi-jen stood beside him
watching in mystification till he suddenly stood up.

" 'Transported beyond the earthly form' — fine!" he muttered.

Hsi-jen was amused but afraid to ask what he meant.

"If you don't enjoy reading these books, why not take a
stroll in the Garden?" she suggested. "Don't make yourself
unwell by moping."

Pao-yu agreed to this and walked out, still deep in thought.
Soon he reached Seeping Fragrance Pavilion, but found it looking desolate and deserted. Going on to Alpinia Court, he was
even more dismayed to see its plants as luxuriant as before but
the doors and windows closed. Turning past Scented Lotus
Pavilion, he saw a few girls in the distance who were leaning
over the railings at Smartweed Bank. On the ground beside
them several young maids were squatting down as if to search
for something. He tiptoed behind a rockery to hear what they
were saying.

"Let's see whether it rises to the bait," said one girl — it
sounded like Li Wen.

"Good, it's gone!" laughed Tan-chun. "I knew it wouldn't
rise."

"That's right, cousin. Don't move, just wait, and it's bound
to surface."

"Here it comes!"

The last two speakers were Li Chi and Hsing Hsiu-yen.

Pao-yu could not resist picking up a stone and tossing it into the pool. The splash it made startled the four girls.

"Who's this practical joker?" they cried. "Giving us such a fright!"

He bounded out laughingly then from behind the rockery.

"You're having such a good time — why didn't you let me know?"

"I knew it couldn't be anyone else," said Tan-chun. "Only Second Brother would play such a trick. All right, to make up for that you must catch us some fish. One was rising to the bait just now, but before we could hook it you frightened it away."

"You enjoy yourselves here, leaving me out," he chuckled. "By rights I should penalize *you*!"

They all laughed at that.

"Let's all fish to try our luck," proposed Pao-yu. "Whoever catches a fish will have good luck this year. Whoever doesn't will have bad luck. Who'll start?"

Tan-chun urged Li Wen to take the lead, but she declined.

"In that case I'll start off." Tan-chun turned to Pao-yu. "If you drive away my fish again, Second Brother, I shan't let you off!"

"I was trying to scare you for fun just then. But you can go ahead now," he assured her.

Tan-chun cast the line and, in less time than it takes to say ten sentences, a minnow swallowed the bait and the float bobbed down. With a swing of the rod she landed the little fish alive and thrashing. Tai-shu grabbed for it on the ground, then with both hands dropped it into a small porcelain jar filled with clear water.

Tan-chun passed the rod to Li Wen, who cast in turn. When the line twitched she raised the rod, but there was nothing on the hook. She cast again, but when presently the line tautened again and she pulled it in she once more drew a blank. She examined the hook then, and found it was bent inwards.

"No wonder I caught nothing," she said with a smile, then told Su-yun to adjust the hook and bait it with another worm on which a reed had been fixed. Not long after she cast, the reed submerged, and she hastily landed a tiny carp two inches long.

"Now it's your turn, Cousin Pao-yu," she said with a smile.

"Let the other two girls try first," he urged.

Hsiu-yen said nothing, but Li Chi demurred, "No, Cousin Pao, you try first."

"Stop deferring to each other!" cried Tan-chun, who had just seen a bubble on the water. "Look, the fish have all gone over to your side. Go on!"

Li Chi took the rod then and very soon made a catch. When Hsiu-yen had followed suit and returned the rod to Tan-chun, she handed it to Pao-yu.

"I'm going to fish like Chiang Tai Kung,"[1] he announced as he walked down the stone steps and sat down by the pool. But his reflection frightened the fish away. Though he waited there a long time holding the rod, the line still did not move. And when bubbles rose from one side of the pool, he swung his rod there so fast that the fish made off quickly.

"I'm impatient but they're slow coaches! What shall I do? Good fish, come quick to my rescue!" he exclaimed so frantically that the four girls laughed.

While Pao-yu was still talking, the line twitched. In delight, he yanked so hard that the rod knocked against a rock and broke into two. The line snapped as well, so that the hook was lost. A roar of laughter went up.

"I've never seen anyone so clumsy!" teased Tan-chun.

Just then Sheh-yueh hurried towards them, in a great fluster.

"The old lady's woken, Master Pao," she cried. "She wants you to go there at once."

This startled all five of them.

---

[1] Chiang Shang of the eleventh century B.C. was said to fish by the Weishui River (present-day Shensi) holding a line, with no hook or bait, three feet above the water, and saying at the same time: "Whoever is ordained, come and take the bait."

"What does she want him for?" Tan-chun inquired.

"I don't know," the maid answered. "I heard say some scandal's come to light and she wants to ask Pao-yu about it. She's going to question Madam Lien as well."

Pao-yu was petrified.

"Which maid is going to catch it this time?" he wondered.

"We've no idea what it's all about," said Tan-chun. "You'd better go immediately, Second Brother. If there's any news, send Sheh-yueh to let us know."

Then the four girls went off.

When Pao-yu entered the Lady Dowager's room, he was relieved to find her playing cards there with his mother as if nothing were amiss.

At sight of him she said, "The year before last when you fell ill you were cured by a crazy monk and a lame Taoist. When you had that fit, how did you feel?"

Pao-yu cast his mind back.

"I remember standing up feeling quite all right before the fit came on. Then it seemed as if someone had clubbed my head from behind, and it hurt so badly that everything went black. Still, I saw green-faced, long-fanged devils all over the place, who were swinging swords and clubs. When I lay down on the *kang*, my head felt as if clamped in a vice. I passed out from the pain. When I came round, I remember seeing a shaft of golden light in the hall which shone on to my bed. All the devils ran away from it and vanished. My head stopped aching too and my mind cleared."

"That sounds like it," observed the old lady to Lady Wang.

At this point Hsi-feng came in and paid her respects to both her seniors in turn.

"What did you want to know, Old Ancestress?" she asked.

"Do you still remember what it was like when you were seized by that fit of madness that year?"

"I can't remember too clearly," was Hsi-feng's answer. "But I felt I couldn't control myself, as if someone was pushing and tugging me to kill people. I tried to seize every weapon I could lay hands on and kill everyone I saw. Even when I was exhausted, I couldn't stop."

"And when you got better?" prompted the old lady.

"I thought I heard a voice in the air — just what it said I can't remember."

"Judging by this, it was her all right," said the Lady Dowager. "The way they felt during their fits coincides with what we've just heard. How could that old witch be so vicious! And to think that we chose her to be Pao-yu's godmother! It was that monk and priest — Buddha be praised! — who saved his life, yet we never thanked them for it."

"Why are you interested in our illnesses, madam?" Hsi-feng wanted to know.

"Ask your aunt. I'm too tired to tell you."

Then Lady Wang explained, "Just now the master was here. He told us that Pao-yu's godmother was actually a witch who practised black magic. Now that her secret's out, she's been arrested by the police and taken to prison to be put to death.

"A few days ago some fellow — Pan San-pao I think his name was — brought evidence against her. He sold a house to the pawnshop across the street for several times what it was worth, but still wanted more. The pawnbroker naturally refused this demand. Then Pan bribed that old witch, as she was for ever calling in at the pawnshop and knew everybody there, to cast a spell so that all their women fell ill and their homes were topsy-turvy. Thereupon she went there claiming that she could cure them, and burnt paper offerings which proved effica-cious. She got several dozen taels from them as well.

"But all-seeing Buddha meted out retribution. She left in such a hurry that day that she let fall a silk bundle, which the shop assistants picked up. On opening it, they found inside a whole lot of paper figures as well as four pills with a pungent smell. They were wondering what these could be when the old witch went back for them, and they caught and searched her. They found on her a box with two carved ivory naked devils inside, one male and one female, besides seven red embroidery needles. At once she was haled to the police court, where she disclosed many secret affairs of ladies in big official families. This being reported to the garrison, a search was made of her house and a whole lot of clay devils were brought to light together with some boxes of knockout scent. In addition, in an unoccupied room behind her *kang* hung a seven-star lamp, and under it were straw effigies — some with iron bands round their heads, some with nails stuck in their chests, some fastened with locks. In the cupboard was a great stack of paper figures. And below were account books listing the families which had employed her and the amounts of silver due to her. She had also collected a good deal of money as donations for oil and incense."

"Yes, she must have been our jinx!" Hsi-feng exclaimed. "After we got well, I remember, that old witch called several times to ask Concubine Chao for money. When she saw me, she changed colour and her eyes blazed. I couldn't guess the reason at the time. Now it's clear what they were up to! In my case, of course, running the household I'm bound to get myself hated by certain people, and it's not to be wondered at if they try to kill me. But what reason has anyone to hate Pao-yu? How could they be so vicious?"

"I suppose it's because I prefer Pao-yu to Huan," said the old lady. "That sowed the seeds of hatred."

"The old creature's already been sentenced," observed Lady Wang, "so we can hardly bring her here as a witness. But without her evidence, how are we to get Concubine Chao to confess? And if such a scandal got out, our reputation would suffer. We'd better give her rope to hang herself — she's bound to give herself away one of these days."

"You're right," agreed the Lady Dowager. "A case of this kind can't be proved without a witness. But Lord Buddha is all-seeing! Haven't Hsi-feng and Pao-yu recovered? Never mind, Hsi-feng, let's forget about the past. You and your aunt must have dinner here before you go." She told Yuan-yang and Hu-po to serve the meal.

"Why trouble to order the meal yourself, Old Ancestress?" asked Hsi-feng with a twinkle.

Lady Wang also smiled. And as some serving-women were waiting outside for instructions, Hsi-feng told a young maid to order dinner, informing her that they would both be dining there.

At this moment, however, Yu-chuan arrived with a message for Lady Wang:

"The master wants you to find something for him, madam, after the old lady's meal."

"You'd better go now," urged the Lady Dowager. "It may be important."

Lady Wang assented. Leaving Hsi-feng there, she went back to her room to chat with Chia Cheng and find him the things he wanted.

"Has Ying-chun gone back?" he asked. "How's she making out with the Sun family?"

"The poor child kept shedding tears and saying her husband's a tyrant." She repeated what Ying-chun had told her.

Chia Cheng sighed.

"I knew it wasn't a good match," he recalled, "but what could I do once my brother had settled on it? The pity is, Ying-chun's the one to suffer."

"She's newly married. We can only hope that later they'll get on better." This said, his wife suddenly tittered.

"What's there to laugh at?"

"It's Pao-yu — he came here specially first thing this morning and talked like a silly boy."

"What did he say?"

When she repeated their son's remarks Chia Cheng started laughing too.

"Speaking of Pao-yu, this reminds me," he said. "It's no good leaving that boy all the time in the Garden. If a daughter turns out badly, she'll go to another family anyway; but having a bad son is serious. The other day someone recommended a tutor to me. His scholarship and moral character are excellent, and he's a southerner too. But I feel that teachers from the

south are too lenient. Our young rascals here all have enough
low cunning to get away with slacking. Besides, they're so
unruly that a teacher who isn't strong on discipline and just
humours them may let them waste their time. That's why the
last generations never engaged a teacher from outside but just
picked some elderly, fairly scholarly kinsman to run the family
school. Uncle Tai-ju now, though he's no great shakes as a
scholar, knows how to keep these boys under control and isn't
soft with them. I don't think we should let Pao-yu go on idling.
We'd better send him back to the family school."

"I quite agree," approved his wife. "While you were away
at your post he often fell ill, so he hasn't studied properly these
last few years. It will be good for him to go over his lessons
again in the family school."

Chia Cheng nodded. The rest of their talk can be passed
over.

The next morning when Pao-yu had finished his toilet, his
pages announced that the master wanted him. He hastily
straightened his clothes and went over to Chia Cheng's study.
Having paid his respects he stood waiting for instructions.

"What have you been studying recently?" asked his father.
"Though you've done some calligraphy, that doesn't amount to
much. In these last few years, I can see, you've grown wilder
than ever; and I've often heard that you refused to study on
the pretext of poor health. But aren't you in good health now?
I've also heard that you spend all your time in the Garden
playing about with your girl cousins and even fooling about
with the maids, forgetting your studies completely. You may
write a few lines of poetry but it's not up to much, nothing to
boast about. After all, when you come to take the examinations, it's essay-writing that counts; but you've neglected that.
Here's what you're to do from now on. Stop versifying and
writing couplets, and concentrate on studying eight-section
essays. I give you one year. If you've made no progress by the
end of that time you can stop studying, and I shall disown you!"

He called for Li Kuei then and told him, "Tomorrow morning Pei-ming is to accompany Pao-yu to the family school, after first getting ready the books he needs and bringing them to show me."

To Pao-yu he said sternly, "You may go now. Come back here tomorrow morning."

Pao-yu had nothing to say to this and went back to Happy Red Court, where Hsi-jen was anxiously waiting. She was pleased by the news that he was to go back to school. He, however, sent word at once to his grandmother in the hope that she would put a stop to this scheme; and on receiving his message she sent for him.

"Don't worry," she told him. "Go to school, or your father will be angry. Anyone who makes it difficult for you will have me to reckon with."

As there was no more Pao-yu could do, he went back.

"Call me early tomorrow morning," he ordered his maids. "The master's taking me to the family school."

Hsi-jen and the others assented, and she and Sheh-yueh took turns keeping watch that night.

Hsi-jen woke Pao-yu early the next day and, having helped him dress, sent a young maid to tell Pei-ming to be ready waiting by the inner gate with his books and other school things. But she had to urge Pao-yu twice before he would leave. On reaching Chia Cheng's study, he asked whether his father had arrived or not.

The page on duty told him, "Just now one of his secretaries came to see him, but they said the master was still getting dressed and asked him to wait outside."

Feeling slightly relieved Pao-yu hurried to Chia Cheng's apartment, arriving just as his father was sending for him. Pao-yu went in and listened to his instructions, after which they mounted the carriage and, with Pei-ming carrying the books, drove to the family school. A servant had gone on ahead to announce their arrival.

Tai-ju stood up as Chia Cheng entered the classroom and greeted him. Taking him by the hand, the teacher asked after his health and that of the old lady. Then Pao-yu went over to pay his respects, while his father waited for Tai-ju to take a seat before sitting down himself.

"I have brought my son here myself today because I have a request to make," said Chia Cheng. "He's no longer a child and it's time for him to study for his career, so as to establish himself and win a name in future. At home nowadays he just fools around with the children. He may have a smattering of poetry, but the verses he writes are nonsensical; and even if they were good, those effusions about the wind and rain, moonlight and dew have no bearing on his life-work."

"He looks a handsome, intelligent lad," Tai-ju answered. "Why should he just play about instead of studying? Poetry is all very well, but he'll have plenty of time to take that up after passing the official examinations."

"Quite so," agreed Chia Cheng. "All we want him to study now is the classics. He must learn how to expound them and how to write essays. If he is disobedient, I hope you will discipline him thoroughly, so that his life won't be wasted for lack of solid learning."

He stood up then, made a bow, and after a few more civilities took his leave. Tai-ju saw him to the gate and asked him to convey his respects to the Lady Dowager. Then Chia Cheng, assenting, mounted his carriage and left.

Re-entering the classroom, Tai-ju saw that Pao-yu had a small hardwood desk in a corner by the southwest window. On the right side of the desk he had piled two sets of old books and one slim volume of essays. Pei-ming, on his instructions, was arranging his writing materials in the drawers.

The teacher said, "Pao-yu, I heard you were unwell some time ago. Have you recovered completely?"

Pao-yu stood up to answer, "Yes, sir."

"Well, the time has come now for you to study hard. Your father is very anxious that you should turn out well. First revise, right from the beginning, all those books you studied before. Spend every morning on that. After lunch you can practise calligraphy. In the afternoon, you'll expound texts and read essays."

Pao-yu assented respectfully, then sat down and looked around, perceiving that several old classmates such as Chin Jung were missing, while the few younger boys who had joined since he left appeared a coarse, common lct. Recalling Chin Chung, it struck him with dismay that he had no friend now with whom to exchange confidences. But not venturing to speak, he moodily started reading.

The teacher told him, "As this is your first day, I'll let you go home early. Tomorrow I want to hear you expound a text. You're by no means stupid. When you've analysed a few passages for me tomorrow, I shall be able to see how much you've read recently and what standard you've reached."

This set Pao-yu's heart thumping. To know how he made out, read the following chapter.

CHAPTER 82

An Old Teacher Expounds the Classics
to Warn Against Mischief
The Queen of Bamboos Falling III
Has a Fearful Nightmare

Pao-yu, home from school, went to call on his grandmother.

"Good! Now the wild colt's muzzled," she said with a smile. "Report to your father, then go and amuse yourself."

Pao-yu, having assented, presented himself to Chia Cheng.

"Back from school so early?" his father asked. "Did the teacher assign your lessons?"

"Yes, sir. In the morning I'm to revise the Four Books; after lunch, practise writing; in the afternoon, expound texts and read essays."

Chia Cheng nodded.

"Go and keep your grandmother company for a while. Instead of just fooling around you must learn some manners. Go to bed early, and get up early to go to school every day. Do you hear?"

"Yes, sir. Yes, sir."

Pao-yu, withdrawing, hurried to call on his mother and then to report to his grandmother, very soon leaving her again to rush to Bamboo Lodge. Once inside the gate, he clapped and crowed with laughter.

"Here I am back safe and sound!"

Tzu-chuan raised the portière and he went in and sat down.

"I thought I heard you'd gone to school," said Tai-yu, startled by his sudden return. "How come you're back so early?"

"Ah, it's too bad!" he exclaimed. "When my father made me go to school today, I thought I'd never set eyes on you all again. But I survived it somehow, and now that we're together again I feel as if I'd just risen from the dead! 'One day apart seems three autumns' — how true that old saying is."

"Have you paid your duty calls?"

"Yes, all of them."

"Called anywhere else?"

"No, I haven't."

"You should drop in to see your other cousins too."

"I can't be bothered right now. I'd rather just sit here and chat with you for a while. 'Early to bed and early to rise' — those are my father's orders; so I'll have to leave calling on them till tomorrow."

"After sitting here a bit you must go back to rest."

"I'm not tired, only dying of boredom. Sitting here with you I don't feel bored, yet now you're trying to shoo me away again!"

With a faint smile Tai-yu told Tzu-chuan, "Brew a cup of my *Lungching* tea for the Second Master. Now that he's studying we must treat him with more respect."

Tzu-chuan laughingly fetched the tea leaves and told one of the younger maids to make tea.

"Don't mention studying!" Pao-yu continued. "I can't stand such moral talk. And those eight-section essays are still more ridiculous. Using them to wangle a degree and make a living — that's not so bad; but how can you claim they 'voice the views of the sages'? The better ones are nothing but a hotch-potch of classical tags, while the most ludicrous ones are written by ignoramuses who drag in this, that and the other to make up a monstrous mishmash, yet boast of their erudition! How can this be called expounding the views of the sages? When father insists on my studying these essays, I can't oppose him; but here are *you* talking about study too."

"We girls don't have to write essays," Tai-yu answered. "Still, when I was young and your kinsman Mr. Chia Yu-tsun was my tutor, I read a few essays too. Some of them showed good sense, some were quite subtle. Though I didn't altogether understand them, I thought quite highly of them. I don't see

how you can condemn them so sweepingly. Besides, If you
want an official career, this is the scholarly way to go about it."

Pao-yu was disgusted by talk of this kind.

"Tai-yu never used to be like this," he reflected. "What's
made her so worldly-wise all of a sudden?" But not wanting
to argue with her, he simply snorted.

Just then they heard the voices of Chiu-wen and Tzu-chuan
outside.

"Sister Hsi-jen said I'd find him in the old lady's place, but
instead he's here," said Chiu-wen.

"We've just made tea," Tzu-chuan told her. "Wait till he's
drunk it before fetching him back."

Then the two of them came in.

"I'll be coming presently," Pao-yu promised Chiu-wen. "I'm
sorry you had the trouble of looking for me."

When Chiu-wen made no answer, Tzu-chuan said, "Drink
up quickly and go. They've been longing for you all day."

"Shut up, you bitch!" cried Chiu-wen.

Amid general laughter he rose to take his leave, and Tai-yu
saw him to the door while Tzu-chuan waited at the foot of the
steps, not re-entering the house until he had gone.

Pao-yu soon reached Happy Red Court. As he went in, Hsi-
jen emerged from the inner room.

"Is he back?" she called out.

"Long ago," Chiu-wen answered. "I found the Second
Master with Miss Lin."

"Did anything happen today?" Pao-yu wanted to know.

"Nothing much," said Hsi-jen. "Only Her Ladyship sent
Sister Yuan-yang over just now with a message: The master
has set his mind on your studying hard, and if any maids dare
fool about with you they'll be dealt with in the same way as
Ching-wen and Ssu-chi. After serving you all this time, I must
say I find a warning like that uncalled for!" She was looking
most put out.

"Good sister, don't worry," he cried. "I'll have to study
hard so that the mistress doesn't scold you again. In fact, I
must do some reading this evening, as tomorrow I've got to

expound texts to the teacher. If I need anything, Sheh-yueh
and Chiu-wen can attend to it. You'd better go and rest."

"If you're really going to study hard, we'll be glad to wait
on you," was her reply.

Pao-yu had a hasty supper, then made them light the lamp
so that he could revise the Four Books. But where to start?
When he leafed through one volume, the text seemed clear
enough; yet when he thought it over carefully, he was not too
sure of the meaning. He consulted the notes and then the
commentaries, until the first watch had sounded.

"I find poetry very easy, but with this I'm getting nowhere,"
he reflected as he sat there, his mind in a whirl.

"Go to bed now," urged Hsi-jen. "You can't digest all that
in just one night."

When Pao-yu mumbled agreement she and Sheh-yueh helped
him to bed, then turned in themselves. But Hsi-jen, waking
later, heard him still tossing about.

"Are you still awake?" she asked. "Stop racking your
brains! You must get some rest if you're going to study well
tomorrow."

"I know, but I can't sleep. Will you come and take off one
of these quilts for me?"

"Better keep it on — it's not hot."

"Well, I feel hectic."

He started kicking off one of his quilts.

Hsi-jen promptly got up to stop him, and laying one hand
on his forehead found it a little hot.

"Don't move," she coaxed. "You're rather feverish."

"I know."

"How come?"

"Don't worry. It's because I'm feeling frantic. But don't
raise an alarm, or my father's bound to say I'm shamming to
get out of going to school — or why else should I fall ill now
of all times? I'll be well enough to go back to school tomorrow;
then everything will be all right."

Taking pity on him she said, "I'll come and sleep with you."
She massaged his back for a while, then they both dozed off,

not waking until the sun was high in the sky.

"Confound it, I've overslept!" exclaimed Pao-yu.

He hastily dressed, paid his respects to his elders and hurried to school. Already the teacher was glowering.

"No wonder your father is angry and calls you good-for-nothing — you start slacking on your second day at school! What time is it now?"

Pao-yu excused himself by explaining about his feverish night, then settled down again to study.

That afternoon Tai-ju set him a passage to analyse from the *Analects,* beginning with the line "Respect the young." He thanked his lucky stars that it was not from the *Great Learning* or the *Doctrine of the Mean.*

"How am I to analyse it?" he asked.

"Carefully explain the passage and the gloss."

Pao-yu read it aloud, then began, "In this passage the sage is encouraging young people, exhorting them to work hard while there is time, so as not. . . ."

He broke off here and glanced up at the teacher, who smiled.

"Just go ahead. In expounding the classics, as the *Book of Ceremony* says, nothing is taboo. Go on. 'So as not . . .' — what?"

"So as not to grow old without achieving anything. First he says 'respect' to encourage young people, then warns them not to grow into men whom nobody would respect."

He looked up expectantly.

"That's more or less right," said Tai-ju. "Now paraphrase the whole text."

"The sage said: When people are young, their intelligence and talents all seem quite formidable. Who can be sure that in future they won't equal me today? But if they let things slide until they are forty or fifty and still not known, however promising they may have been when young, by that time nobody will ever fear them."

The teacher smiled.

"When you summarized the meaning just now, it was fairly clear," he said. "But your paraphrase was rather childish. The words 'not known' don't mean failure to attain officialdom. Here 'knowing' refers to understanding the truth, which doesn't depend on becoming an official. Didn't some sages of old turn hermit and remain unknown? They weren't officials, were they? But does that mean they were no good?

"When he said that such cases were 'not to be feared,' he meant that people knew the limitations of their understanding; so this is in direct contrast to the previous idea — it doesn't imply fearing their power. You should examine such points carefully to grasp their subtlety. Do you understand now?"

"Yes, sir."

"Then here's another passage for you to expound."

He turned to a page and pointed out for Pao-yu the line, "I have never yet seen anyone who loved goodness as much as beauty."

Feeling rather sensitive on this score, Pao-yu objected with a smile, "There's nothing worth expounding here."

"Nonsense! If this subject were set in the examinations, would you say it wasn't worth writing about?"

Then Pao-yu had to comply.

"The sage noticed that men didn't love goodness but were enraptured with beauty when they saw it. Actually, goodness is something inherent in human nature, yet people don't hanker after it. As for beauty, though it's also born not made, and everybody loves it, it is a human desire whereas goodness is a law of nature. However, people don't love the law of nature as much as human desire. Confucius both deplored this and hoped that men would change their ways. He also noticed that though some men loved goodness, that love didn't go very deep. Only when they came to love goodness as much as beauty could that be considered true love."

"That is more or less correct," commented Tai-ju. "Now tell me this. If you understand the sage's teachings, why are you having trouble on both scores? Though I don't stay in your family and your father has never spoken to me of this, I am well aware of your shortcomings. Why don't you want to make progress? You're young now, just at the 'formidable' age.

Whether you turn out well or not is entirely up to you. I'm going to give you a month to revise all the classics you studied before, then another month to read essays. After that I'll set you subjects to write about. And I shan't tolerate any slacking! As the proverb says, 'Men must choose between progress and comfort.' Keep what I've told you in mind!"

Pao-yu promised to do so, and from that day on he had to apply himself harder to his studies.

After Pao-yu went back to school, Happy Red Court was so quiet that Hsi-jen had more time for embroidery. As she stitched a pouch for betel-nuts one day, she reflected that his return to school had made life less complicated for his maids; indeed, had he gone back earlier, Ching-wen might never have come to such a sad end. Grieving over her friend's death, she sighed. Then it occurred to her that although at present she could control Pao-yu, as she was not destined to be his wife but only a concubine, if his wife proved a termagant she herself would share the same fate as Second Sister Yu and Hsiang-ling. Judging by the attitude of Their Ladyships as well as certain remarks let fall by Hsi-feng, it seemed as if their choice would be Tai-yu — who could be difficult. Flushing at this thought, her heart beat so fast that she plied her needle at random. Finally, laying down her embroidery, she went to Tai-yu's place to sound her out.

Tai-yu, engrossed in reading when she arrived, got up to offer her a seat.

"Are you much better these days, miss?" asked Hsi-jen stepping forward.

"How could I be? A bit better, that's all. What have you been doing at home?"

"Since Master Pao went back to school we've had very little to do. So I dropped in here for a chat to see how you are."

Tzu-chuan brought in tea at this point.

"You mustn't trouble, sister!" Hsi-jen rose to her feet, then added with a smile, "I heard the other day from Chiu-wen that you'd been gossiping behind our backs!"

"Don't you believe her," Tzu-chuan laughed. "All I said was that with Master Pao away at school, Miss Pao-chai gone and even Hsiang-ling staying away, you must be feeling lonely."

"Don't talk about Hsiang-ling!" cried Hsi-jen. "Poor thing! She must be having a hard time of it with her mistress such a martinet, a worse terror even than *her*." She held up two fingers to indicate the Second Mistress — Hsi-feng. "She doesn't even care for appearances."

"She's no less hard-hearted," put in Tai-yu. "Remember how Second Sister Yu died?"

"Of course," agreed Hsi-jen. "We're all women, only a bit different in status, so I can't think why anyone should be so cruel. It spoils our reputation outside as well."

Tai-yu guessed there was something behind this, as it was not Hsi-jen's habit to gossip in such a way behind people's backs.

"Well, it's hard to say," she answered. "In every family, if the east wind doesn't prevail over the west wind, then the west wind is bound to prevail over the east wind."

"But a concubine is diffident to start with. How dare she take advantage of the wife?"

Just then a serving-woman called from the courtyard, "Is this Miss Lin's house? Is anybody in?"

Hsueh-yen went out and, thinking she recognized one of Aunt Hsueh's servants, asked her business.

"Our young lady sent me to bring something to Miss Lin."

Telling her to wait, Hsueh-yen came back to report this, and Tai-yu made her fetch the woman in. The latter curtseyed to Tai-yu, but instead of explaining her errand just stared at her.

Embarrassed by her scrutiny Tai-yu asked, "What did Miss Pao-chai tell you to bring me?"

"A jar of lichees preserved in honey." Catching sight of Hsi-jen then, the woman added, "Isn't this Miss Hua from the Second Master's place?"

"How did you know, aunty?" asked Hsi-jen.

"We stay in mostly to keep an eye on the house, not going out much with our mistress or young ladies, so you other young ladies wouldn't be likely to know us. But as you sometimes come to our place, we have a faint recollection of you all."

Having given the jar to Hsueh-yen she turned back to look at Tai-yu again, then observed with a smile to Hsi-jen, "No wonder our mistress says that Miss Lin here and your Master Pao would make a perfect pair. She's as pretty as a goddess, indeed she is!"

To put a stop to such foolish talk, Hsi-jen hastily interposed, "You must be tired out, aunty. Take a rest and have some tea."

"We're all very busy over there preparing for Miss Pao-chin's wedding," the woman chuckled. "And there are two more jars of lichees which Miss Pao-chai wants sent to Master Pao."

She took her leave then and started to hobble away. Tai-yu, though annoyed by her impertinence, could hardly reprove a messenger sent by Pao-chai. When the woman had stepped outside she called:

"Thank Miss Pao-chai for me."

The old creature was still exclaiming, "Such good looks — too good for anyone but Pao-yu!"

Tai-yu could only pretend not to have heard.

Hsi-jen remarked with a smile, "When people grow old they talk so foolishly, one doesn't know whether to be angry or laugh."

Hsueh-yen showed Tai-yu the jar of fruit.

"I don't want it now. Put it away," said Tai-yu, then talked a little longer with Hsi-jen until the latter left.

That evening when Tai-yu went into the inner room to get ready for bed, the sight of the jar of lichees reminded her of the old woman's maundering and she felt a pang. In the quiet dusk, her heart filled with forebodings.

"My health's poor and I've reached the age to marry," she reflected. "Judging by Pao-yu's behaviour, he isn't interested in anyone else; but my grandmother and aunt haven't yet indicated their preference. If only my parents were still alive, or had fixed this match in advance!" Then it occurred to her, "Even if they'd lived they might have promised me to someone else, who couldn't possibly be up to Pao-yu. This way there may still be a chance."

Her heart was in a turmoil, distraught as a pulley swinging up and down. After many a sigh and tear, she flung herself listlessly down on her bed fully dressed.

She was lying there in a daze when a young maid approached to report that Mr. Chia Yu-tsun had asked to see her.

"It's true that I studied under him," said Tai-yu. "But I'm not a boy; why should he want to see me? Besides, though he's my uncle's friend my uncle's never mentioned him to me; so it would be inappropriate to receive him."

She told the maid, "I'm not well enough to go out. Give him my greetings and apologies."

"I think he's here to offer congratulations," said the girl. "Some people have just come from Nanking to fetch you."

That same moment in walked Hsi-feng, Lady Hsing, Lady Wang and Pao-chai.

"We've come to congratulate you and to see you off!" they cried.

"What do you mean?" asked Tai-yu in alarm.

"Don't play the innocent," teased Hsi-feng. "Surely you know that your father has been promoted to be the Grain Commissioner of Hupeh and has taken another wife, a most suitable match. They don't feel it would be right to leave you here, so they asked Mr. Chia as go-between to arrange for you to marry a relative of your stepmother, a widower. Now they've sent to fetch you back, and the wedding will probably take place as soon as you get home. It's all been decided by your stepmother. We're sending your Second Cousin Lien to escort you and look after you on the road."

At this, Tai-yu broke out in a cold sweat. She did seem to have a hazy recollection of her father's appointment to an official post there.

"This can't be true!" she protested frantically. "Cousin Hsi-feng must be joking."

She saw Lady Hsing wink at Lady Wang, then say, "She still doesn't believe it. Let's go."

With tears in her eyes Tai-yu begged, "Dear aunts, please wait!"

But in silence, smiling coldly, they all went away.

Tai-yu had no means to express her desperation. Sobbing bitterly, she seemed through her tears to see the Lady Dowager standing before her. Thinking, "If I beg my grandmother, she's the only one who may save me," she fell on her knees and clasped the old lady's waist.

"Save me, madam!" she pleaded. "I'd rather die than go south. Besides, she's my stepmother, not my own mother. Do let me stay with you, madam!"

But with a look of indifference the old lady said, "This has nothing to do with me."

"What does that mean, madam?" she sobbed.

"Marrying a widower is good: you'll get two sets of wedding presents."

"If I can stay with you, madam, I promise not to put you to extra expense. I just implore you to save me!"

"It's no use. All girls must get married sooner or later. You ought to know that, child. You can't stay here for ever."

"I'd rather be a bondmaid here, earning my keep. Please, please speak up for me, madam!"

Still the old lady said nothing.

Tai-yu caught hold of her again and cried, "Madam, you were always so kind, so fond of me, how can you leave me in the lurch like this? Even if I'm only your grand-daughter, removed by one generation, my mother was your own daughter — won't you protect me for her sake at least?" She gave way to a storm of weeping in the Lady Dowager's lap.

"Yuan-yang, take her out to calm down," ordered the old lady. "She's wearing me out, making such a scene."

Tai-yu knew then that appealing for help was useless. Determining to kill herself instead, she stood up and started out. How bitterly she grieved that she had no mother! For though her grandmother, aunts and cousins had always seemed so good to her, this now appeared to be nothing but a pretence.

"How is it I haven't seen Pao-yu?" she wondered. "*He* might be able to help."

And just then Pao-yu suddenly appeared.

"Congratulations, cousin!" he said with a smile.

This made Tai-yu even more frantic. Forgetting all reserve she seized him by the arm.

"Fine!" she cried. "Now I know how heartless you are, Pao-yu!"

"In what way am I heartless? Now that you're engaged, we must each go our own way."

Feeling yet more angry and helpless, she gripped his arm.

"Good cousin, to whom do you want me to go?" she sobbed.

"If you don't want to leave, you can stay here. You were originally promised to me: that's why you came to live here in the first place. And just think how close we've been."

Then it seemed to Tai-yu that she had indeed been engaged to Pao-yu. Her sorrow turned to joy.

"My mind's made up even if I die!" she cried. "Tell me honestly, do you want me to leave or to stay?"

"I want you to stay. If you doubt me, I'll show you my heart!"

He drew a small knife and plunged it into his chest so that blood spurted out. In terror, she thrust one hand over his heart.

"How can you do that!? You'd better kill me first!"

"Don't be afraid," he said. "I'll show you my heart."

He groped around with his hand in the gaping wound while Tai-yu trembled and wept, fearful lest others see them. Racked by sobs she held him close.

Then Pao-yu exclaimed, "I'm done for! Now I've lost my heart I must die!"

He turned up his eyes and slumped with a thud to the ground.

As Tai-yu started screaming she heard Tzu-chuan calling her.

"Miss! Miss! Have you had a nightmare? Wake up! Undress and go to bed properly."

Tai-yu turned over and found it was all a dream. She was

still sobbing, her heart beating wildly. Her pillow was drenched and she felt icy cold.

She thought, "My parents both died long ago and never engaged me to Pao-yu, so how could such ideas occur to me?" Recalling the dream and her helplessness, she wondered what would become of her if Pao-yu were really to die. Her mind in a turmoil of anguish, she burst out weeping again until soon she was perspiring. Struggling up to take off her robe, she told Tzu-chuan to tuck in her quilt and lay down again, but toss and turn as she might she could not sleep. There was a rustling outside like wind or rain, and presently some way off she heard heavy breathing — it was Tzu-chuan, fast asleep and beginning to snore. She sat up again with an effort, wrapping the bedding around her; but a cold draught through the window cracks made her shiver, so once more she lay down. As she was dozing off, she heard sparrows twittering on the bamboo; and although the blinds were drawn, light gradually filtered through the window-paper.

By now Tai-yu was wide-awake. She started coughing, waking up Tzu-chuan.

"Still not asleep, miss?" she asked. "And coughing again! You must have caught cold. Look, the window's light and it will soon be dawn. You must rest properly, not let your thoughts wander."

"I *want* to sleep, but I can't. You can go back to sleep." Talking set her coughing again.

But Tzu-chuan was too upset by Tai-yu's fit of coughing to sleep any longer. She hastily got up to fetch the spittoon. By now it was light.

"Are you getting up?" Tai-yu asked.

"It's already bright. How can I go on sleeping?"

"In that case, you may as well change the spittoon."

Tzu-chuan, assenting, hurried out to fetch a clean spittoon, placing the used one on the table in the outer room. Having closed the door behind her, she let down the soft flowered portière before going to wake Hsueh-yen. When she came back to empty the spittoon, she was shocked to find the sputum in it flecked with blood.

"Oh!" she exclaimed. "Heaven help us!"

"What's the matter?" called Tai-yu from the inner room.

Aware of her gaffe Tzu-chuan hedged, "It's the spittoon — it nearly slipped from my hand."

"It wasn't because there's something in the sputum?"

"Oh no!" But her voice was quavering with distress and tears gushed from her eyes.

Tai-yu's suspicions had been aroused by the sweet-salty taste in her throat, and now they were confirmed by Tzu-chuan's exclamation of dismay as well as the catch in her voice.

"Come in!" she called. "It's cold out there."

"Yes, miss." Tzu-chuan sounded even more woeful, and the sadness in her voice set Tai-yu shivering.

She came in, wiping her eyes with a handkerchief.

"Why are you crying for no reason so early in the morning?" Tai-yu asked.

"Who's crying?" She forced a smile. "When I got up my eyes felt itchy. You must have slept even less than usual last night, miss. I heard you coughing half the time."

"That's right. The harder I tried to sleep, the more wide-awake I felt."

"You're so delicate, miss, I don't think you should worry so much. Health is what counts. As the saying goes, 'As long as the mountain's there we shan't lack fuel.' Besides, everyone here from Their Ladyships down is ever so fond of you."

Unfortunately, this last remark reminded Tai-yu of her dream. Her heart missed a beat, all turned dark before her eyes, and the colour drained from her face. Tzu-chuan hastily held up the spittoon for her while Hsueh-yen patted her back, and after retching she spat out some dark, bloody mucus. Her two maids turned pale with fright. As they stood there gaping, she fell back in a faint. In dismay, Tzu-chuan signalled to Hsueh-yen to go for help.

As soon as Hsueh-yen went out she saw Tsui-lu and Tsui-mo approaching.

"Why hasn't Miss Lin come out yet?" asked Tsui-lu with a smile. "Our young lady and Miss Tan-chun are in Miss Hsi-chun's place, discussing that painting she's done of the Garden."

Hsueh-yen waved her hands to stop them.

"What does this mean?" they asked in astonishment.

When she explained what had happened they thrust out their tongues in dismay.

"This is no joking matter. You must report it at once to the old lady. Heavens! How can you be so stupid?"

"I was on my way there when you turned up," she countered.

Just then Tzu-chuan called from the house, "Who's that out there Miss Lin would like to know."

They hurried in, and the two newcomers saw Tai-yu lying in bed covered with a quilt.

"Who told you to make such a fuss over nothing?" she asked them.

Tsui-mo said, "Our young lady and Miss Hsiang-yun are in Miss Hsi-chun's place discussing that painting she's made of the Garden. They told us to invite you over, miss. We didn't realize you were unwell."

"It's nothing serious: I just feel a bit limp. I shall get up after I've rested. Go back and tell Miss Tan-chun and Miss Hsiang-yun I'd like them to drop in if they've time after lunch. Has Master Pao gone there too?"

"No."

Tsui-mo added, "Master Pao's going to school these days. The master checks up on his lessons every day, so he can't run around the way he used to."

When Tai-yu made no response, after waiting a little the two maids slipped away.

Let us turn now to Tan-chun and Hsiang-yun in Hsi-chun's room. Commenting on her painting of Grand View Garden, they found it rather overcrowded in parts and rather empty in others. When it came to discussing a suitable inscription, they sent to invite Tai-yu over to consult her. And now they saw Tsui-lu and Tsui-mo return looking thoroughly disconcerted.

"Why hasn't Miss Lin come?" asked Hsiang-yun.

"Last night her illness flared up again, and she coughed all night," Tsui-lu answered. "We heard from Hsueh-yen that she spat out a whole lot of blood."

"Is that true?" exclaimed Tan-chun in consternation.

"Of course it's true," Tsui-lu insisted.

"Just now when we went in to see her," Tsui-mo added, "she looked in a very bad way, hardly able to talk."

"If she's in a bad way of course she can't talk," said Hsiang-yun.

"How can you be so dense?" cried Tan-chun. "If she can't speak, that means. . . ." Her voice trailed away.

Hsi-chun said, "Cousin Lin is very intelligent but I think she takes things too much to heart — she's so serious about even the least little thing. How can one take everything so seriously?"

"Well, if that's the case," said Tan-chun, "we should all go and see her. If she's so very ill, we must get our sister-in-law to report it to the old lady and send for a doctor, so that we'll know how to cope."

"That's right," agreed Hsiang-yun.

"The two of you go on ahead," said Hsi-chun. "I'll go over later on."

Then Tan-chun and Hsiang-yun, helped along by some young maids, went to Bamboo Lodge. Their arrival upset Tai-yu, reminding her of her dream.

"What can I expect of them, when even my grandmother cold-shouldered me like that?" she wondered. "Besides, they wouldn't have come unless I'd invited them." But instead of showing what was in her mind, she made Tzu-chuan help her to sit up and offered them seats.

Tan-chun and Hsiang-yun sat down, one on either side of her on the edge of the bed, distressed to see her so ill.

"What brought on this relapse, cousin?" Tan-chun asked.

"It's nothing serious. I just feel very limp."

Tzu-chuan standing behind her pointed surreptitiously at the spittoon. And Hsiang-yun, being young and straightforward, picked it up to have a look. What she saw horrified her.

"Did you bring this up, cousin?" she exclaimed. "Heaven help us!"

Tai-yu had been too dazed before to look carefully at her sputum. At Hsiang-yun's ejaculation she turned to look, her heart already sinking.

To cover up Hsiang-yun's tactlessness, Tan-chun hastily put in, "This is nothing out of the usual — it's just that a hot humour in the lungs made her bring up a drop or two. But Hsiang-yun is so silly, the least little thing always makes her fly off the handle."

Hsiang-yun, regretting her blunder, blushed at this.

Seeing how listless and tired Tai-yu seemed, Tan-chun got up and said, "You must rest well, cousin. We'll call again later on."

"Thank you both for your concern."

Tan-chun urged Tzu-chuan, "Look after your young lady well!"

As Tzu-chuan assented Tan-chun turned to leave; but just then somebody outside started shouting.

To know who it was, read on.

CHAPTER 83

The Imperial Consort Falls Ill and
Her Relatives Call at the Palace
Chin-kuei Makes a Scene and Pao-chai
Has to Swallow Her Anger

Tan-chun and Hsiang-yun, on the point of leaving, heard an old woman shouting outside, "You good-for-nothing little bitch! Who are you to come and fool around in our Garden?"

At this Tai-yu pointed outside. Showing the whites of her eyes she exclaimed, "I shall have to leave here!"

For ever since moving into Grand View Garden, though able to rely on her grandmother's partiality Tai-yu had always watched her step with other people. When she heard this abuse shouted outside her window, she was sure it must be aimed at nobody else but her. Reflecting that she was a finely brought up young lady but now had lost her parents, she wondered who had sent this old creature to insult her. This was too much to bear! With a heart-rending cry she fainted away.

"What's come over you, miss?" wailed Tzu-chuan. "Wake up, quick!"

Tan-chun called her too, and after a while Tai-yu regained consciousness. Still she could not speak, just kept pointing out of the window.

Tan-chun caught her meaning and opening the door went out. She saw an old woman with a stick chasing after a grubby little girl.

"I'm here to look after the flowers and fruit trees," the old crone was shouting. "Why should *you* come too? Wait till we get home and I'll give you a good thrashing."

The child looked round, sucking one finger, and laughed at her.

Tan-chun scolded, "You people are getting too out of hand! Is this the place for you to bawl abuse?"

When the old woman saw who it was she said sheepishly, "It's my grand-daughter who followed me here. I was afraid she'd make a noise, so I told her to go back. I wouldn't dare bawl her out here."

"That's enough. Hurry up and go, the two of you. Miss Lin's not feeling well. Hurry!"

"Yes, miss."

The old woman made off, the small girl running after her. Going back inside Tan-chun found Hsiang-yun in tears, holding Tai-yu's hand. Tzu-chuan supported the invalid with one arm and massaged her chest till, slowly, she opened her eyes.

"What did you think that old woman meant?" Tan-chun asked her with a smile.

Tai-yu just shook her head.

"She was scolding her grand-daughter. I heard her just now. Such creatures talk nothing but nonsense. They don't understand that some things aren't allowed."

"Cousin . . ." sighed Tai-yu, then broke off, clasping her hand.

"Don't fret yourself. It's only right that we should come to see you as you haven't anyone to look after you. If you'll just rest, take your medicine and look on the bright side of things, you'll gradually get well enough for us all to start the poetry club again. Wouldn't that be nice?"

"That's right," chimed in Hsiang-yun. "That would be fun."

"You want me to cheer up," sobbed Tai-yu. "But how can I? I shan't live to see that day."

"That's taking too gloomy a view!" protested Tan-chun. "Who doesn't fall ill or have trouble from time to time? How can you think in that way? Now just have a good rest while we go to see the old lady. We'll look in again by and by. If there's anything you want, tell Tzu-chuan to let me know."

"Dear Cousin!" cried Tai-yu, in tears. "When you see the old lady, please give her my respects and tell her I'm a bit poorly, but it's nothing serious — she's not to worry."

"I know. You just have a good rest."

When Tan-chun had gone off with Hsiang-yun, Tzu-chuan helped her young mistress to lie down again and stayed by her side while Hsueh-yen saw to other things. Her heart ached but she dared not weep. Tai-yu lay there awhile with closed eyes but could not sleep. Normally she found the Garden very quiet, but now lying in bed she was conscious of the soughing of the wind, the chirr of insects, the chirping of birds, and the sound of passing footsteps. She seemed to hear children, too, crying in the distance. Disturbed by these noises, she told Tzu-chuan to let down her bed-curtains.

Presently Hsueh-yen brought in a bowl of bird's-nest soup which she passed to Tzu-chuan.

"Will you have some soup, miss?" asked Tzu-chuan outside the curtain.

When Tai-yu assented faintly she gave the bowl back to Hsueh-yen to hold while she helped the patient sit up. Having tested the temperature of the soup herself, still supporting Tai-yu she raised the bowl to her mouth. Tai-yu, her eyes half-closed, took two or three sips, then shook her head and would not drink any more. Tzu-chuan handed the bowl back to Hsueh-yen and gently laid her young mistress down once more. After a little rest, feeling slightly better, Tai-yu heard a low voice outside asking:

"Is Sister Tzu-chuan at home?"

Hsueh-yen hurried out and saw it was Hsi-jen.

"Come in, sister," she said softly.

"How is your young lady?"

As they started in Hsueh-yen described what had happened just now and the night before.

"No wonder Tsui-lu just came to our place and said Miss Lin was ill!" exclaimed Hsi-jen in dismay. "Master Pao was so alarmed, he told me to come and see how she is."

While they were whispering, Tzu-chuan lifted the portière of the inner room and beckoned Hsi-jen over.

"Is she asleep?" asked Hsi-jen tiptoeing towards her.

Tzu-chuan nodded. "Have you only just heard about it?"

Hsi-jen inclined her head with a worried look. "How is this going to end? I was nearly scared to death too last night by the other!"

Tzu-chuan asked what had happened.

"He was all right when he went to bed in the evening," Hsi-jen told her. "But in the middle of the night he suddenly yelled that he had a pain in his heart, and raved that someone seemed to have cut it out! He kept up this rumpus quite a time, not quieting down till after the last watch had sounded. Wouldn't you call that frightening? Today he couldn't go to school, and we're sending for a doctor to prescribe medicine."

Just then they heard Tai-yu coughing behind her bed-curtains, and Tzu-chuan hurriedly took her the spittoon. Tai-yu languidly opened her eyes.

"Whom were you talking to?"

"Sister Hsi-jen has come to see you, miss."

By now Hsi-jen had come over to her bed. Tai-yu made Tzu-chuan help her sit up, then indicating the edge of the bed invited Hsi-jen to be seated. Perching sideways, Hsi-jen urged her with a smile:

"You'd better lie down, miss."

"I'm all right. Don't be such alarmists. What was that you were saying just now about someone having a pain in the heart in the middle of the night?"

"Master Pao had a nightmare, nothing of consequence."

Tai-yu was touched and at the same time distressed, knowing that Hsi-jen had said this for fear she might be anxious.

"Did you hear him talk in his sleep?"

"He didn't say anything."

Tai-yu nodded. After a while she sighed.

"Don't tell Master Pao that I'm ill. It would make him waste time, and his father would be angry."

"Yes, miss. You'd better rest now."

Tai-yu nodded and asked Tzu-chuan to lower her to her pillow. Hsi-jen stayed to say a few more encouraging words, then took her leave and went back to Happy Red Court where she simply told Pao-yu, to his great relief, that Tai-yu was a little unwell but not in any danger.

Tan-chun and Hsiang-yun, leaving Bamboo Lodge, had set off to call on the Lady Dowager. On the way Tan-chun warned her cousin:

"When you see the old lady, mind you don't talk in that wild way you did just now!"

Hsiang-yun lowered her head. "I know. It's because just now I was frightened out of my wits!"

When they arrived, Tan-chun's report that Tai-yu was unwell worried the old lady.

"That precious pair are always falling ill," she said. "Now that Tai-yu's growing up she should pay more attention to her health. I think the child broods too much." When no one ventured to make any comment she ordered Yuan-yang, "Go and tell them: After the doctor's seen Pao-yu tomorrow he must go to Miss Lin's place too."

Yuan-yang assented and withdrew to pass on these instructions to serving-women, who went off to relay the message. Tan-chun and Hsiang-yun took dinner with the old lady before going back to the Garden, where we will leave them.

The next day the doctor came. He diagnosed Pao-yu's upset as a slight one, a mild case of indigestion and a chill which sweating would put right. Lady Wang and Hsi-feng sent servants with his prescription to report this to the old lady, at the same time sending word to Bamboo Lodge that the doctor was on his way. Tzu-chuan promptly tucked Tai-yu's quilt round her and put down the bed-curtains, while Hsueh-yen hastily tidied up the room.

Soon Chia Lien arrived with the doctor.

"This gentleman often comes to our house," he said, "so there's no need for all the maids to hide."

An old nurse raised the portière, the doctor was invited in and they took seats. Then Chia Lien suggested that Tzu-chuan should first describe her young lady's symptoms.

"Wait a bit," said Doctor Wang. "Suppose I first feel the

pulse to make my own diagnosis. If these girls think it wrong or there's something I've omitted, then they can let me know."

Tzu-chuan drew one of Tai-yu's hands out from the curtain, rested it on a cushion, and gently pulled her sleeve and bracelet up out of the way. Doctor Wang felt the pulse for some time, then that of the other wrist, after which he and Chia Lien withdrew to take seats in the outer room.

"All six pulses[1] are tense," he announced, "due to bottled up emotion."

At this point Tzu-chuan came out too and stood in the doorway, and Doctor Wang, addressing her, continued:

"I would expect this illness to give rise to constant dizzy spells, loss of appetite as well as frequent dreams; and no doubt she wakes several times in the night. She must be hypersensitive, taking offence at remarks which don't even concern her. People not knowing the truth may think her cross-grained, when in fact it's all due to this illness which has upset her liver and weakened her heart. Am I right?"

Tzu-chuan nodded and said to Chia Lien, "The gentleman is absolutely right."

"So that's how it is," said the doctor.

He got up and went with Chia Lien to the study to write out a prescription. The pages there had already prepared a sheet of pink stationery. After Doctor Wang had sipped some tea he took a brush and wrote:

> The six pulses are tense and slow owing to pent-up grief. The feebleness of the left *tsun* pulse shows debility of the heart. The strength of the *kuan* pulse shows an over-heated liver. When the liver humour cannot disperse, it is bound to invade the spleen, causing loss of appetite and inevitably affecting the lungs too. The humours, failing to turn into vital force, will congeal as phlegm and agitate the blood, so that naturally there will be coughing.
>
> The treatment should calm the liver, protect the lungs and strengthen the heart and the spleen. But invigorants must not be rashly administered. I suggest starting off with thorowax boiled with turtle-blood, followed with medicine to soothe and strengthen the lungs. This is my humble proposal for your wise consideration.

---

[1] According to the *Yellow Emperor's Manual of Medicine,* in each wrist there are three pulses, the *tsun,* the *kuan* and the *chi,* which show the state of the internal organs.

He then listed seven drugs and an adjuvant.

Chia Lien reading this asked, "When the blood is agitated, is it safe to use thorowax?"

Doctor Wang smiled.

"I see you know, sir, that thorowax is a stimulant, not to be used in cases of vomiting blood or nose-bleed; but actually, boiled with turtle-blood, this is the only drug which will stimulate the digestive system and release the humour from the gall. Instead of agitating the blood it can strengthen the liver and keep down hot humours. This is why the *Yellow Emperor's Manual of Medicine* says, 'Use stimulants for a haemorrhage, occludents for a blockage.' This method is similar to 'using Chou Po's strength to stabilize the Liu's dynasty'[1] — applying turtle-blood to mitigate the stimulating function of the thorowax."

Chia Lien nodded. "So that's how it is. Very well, then."

"Let her take two doses first, after which we can add or cancel certain ingredients or perhaps try a different prescription. I still have a little business to attend to and mustn't stay longer, sir. I shall come to pay my respects some other day."

As Chia Lien saw him out he asked, "What about Cousin Pao's prescription?"

"There's nothing much wrong with Master Pao. I think another dose should set him right."

The doctor mounted his carriage then and left.

Chia Lien, having ordered servants to get the medicine, had just gone back to tell Hsi-feng about Tai-yu's illness and the doctor's prescription, when Chou Jui's wife arrived to report on some matters of no great consequence.

"Tell the mistress that," he cut in halfway. "I'm busy." With that he left.

"Just now I went to Miss Lin's place," said Chou Jui's wife after transacting her business. "She seems in a very bad way!

---

[1] Chou Po was a Han general who assisted Liu Pang (247-195 B.C.) to found the Han Dynasty. Knowing that his wife, Empress Lu, and her nephews schemed to usurp the throne after his death, Liu Pang predicted that "Chou Po will be the man who'll stabilize the Liu's dynasty."

Her face has no colour at all; she's nothing but skin and bones. And when I asked how she felt, not a word did she say — simply cried. Later Tzu-chuan told me, 'Our young lady's ill, yet when she needs something she won't ask for it. So I mean to ask Madam Lien to advance us a couple of months' allowance. Although we get issued medicine, we need some cash for incidental expenses.' I promised to pass on this request to you."

Hsi-feng lowered her head in thought.

"I'll tell you what," she said presently. "I'll give her a few taels to use, and you needn't let Miss Lin know. I can't very well advance the monthly allowance. If once the precedent was set and everyone else followed suit, what should we do? Remember how Concubine Chao quarrelled with Miss Tan-chun — all because of the monthly allowance? Besides, as you know, our outlay exceeds our income these days and we've never got around this. Those not in the know think me a bad manager. Some gossips even accuse me of spiriting stuff away to my own family. But you as a stewardess, Mrs. Chou, must naturally know better."

"The injustice of it!" exclaimed Mrs. Chou. "A big household like this can only be run by someone with your forethought, madam. No ordinary woman could manage it; no, not even a man with three heads and six arms! Yet people still talk such rubbish." She suddenly laughed. "You haven't heard the even more stupid things they say outside, madam. The other day when Chou Jui came home, he told me outsiders imagine we're *made* of money. They talk of the Chia family having so many storerooms for gold, so many for silver, and of using nothing but golden utensils studded with gems!

"Some say, 'When their daughter became an Imperial Consort, naturally the Emperor would give half his things to her family. That time Her Highness paid a visit home, we saw with our own eyes the cartloads of gold and silver that she brought, which is why the house is fitted out like the crystal palace of the Dragon King. And that day they went to give offerings in the temple, they spent tens of thousands of taels, but to them that's just one hair from the hide of an ox.'

"Other people say, 'The lions outside their gate must be made of jade. In their Garden they had two gold unicorns, but one got stolen so now there's only one left. Not to say the mistresses of the house, even the maids have nothing to do except drink, play chess, strum the lyre or paint — they have attendants to wait on them anyway. The silks and gauzes they wear, all their food and ornaments too, are things that common folk never even heard of. As for the young masters and mistresses, of course it goes without saying that if they want the moon from the sky someone will pluck it down for them to play with!'

"Then, madam, there's a song:

> The House of Ning, the House of Jung,
> Treat silver and gold as clay;
> No end to their victuals and clothing,
> But at last. . . ."

She broke off here because the final line ran:

> But at last all will vanish away.

Mrs. Chou had been rattling on, only pulling up short when she suddenly remembered how ominous this sounded. And Hsifeng, guessing this, did not press her to finish.

"Well, never mind that," she said. "But where did they get that story about the gold unicorn?"

"That was the small gold unicorn presented to Master Pao by the old Taoist priest of that temple." Mrs. Chou smiled. "Later it was lost for a few days, but Miss Shih found it and returned it to him. Then they made up this story outside. Ridiculous, isn't it, madam?"

"Not ridiculous, actually, but rather alarming! Things are getting harder for us every day, and yet we still keep up such an outward show. 'Bad for a man to be famed, bad for a pig to grow fat,' the proverb says. Especially as with us this is empty fame. Goodness knows what the end will be."

"You have reason to worry, madam. Still, for years now that has been the talk of the town — in teashops, taverns and every least little alley. And how can you stop people talking?"

Hsi-feng nodded, then asked Ping-erh to weigh out a few ounces of silver for Mrs. Chou.

"Take this to Tzu-chuan," she instructed her, "Just tell her I'm giving her this for sundries, and she mustn't hesitate to ask for things that are their due, but let's have no more talk of advancing the monthly allowance. She's quite clever enough to catch on. When I've time, I shall call to see Miss Lin."

Mrs. Chou, assenting, took the silver and left. No more of this.

Now as Chia Lien was on his way out a page had approached and reported, "The Elder Master wants you, sir."

He hurried over and Chia Sheh informed him, "We've just had word that an Imperial Physician and two assistants were summoned to the Palace to attend a patient — it can hardly be one of the maids-of-honour or attendants. Has there been any news from the Imperial Consort's palace these last few days?"

"None, sir."

"Go and ask the Second Master and your brother Chia Chen, or send to find out from the Academy of Imperial Physicians."

Accordingly, Chia Lien dispatched a man to the Academy of Imperial Physicians, then went over to see Chia Cheng.

"Where did you hear that?" asked Chia Cheng when he had explained his errand.

"From the Elder Master just now."

"You and your brother Chen had better go to the Palace to find out."

"I've already sent to the Academy of Imperial Physicians."

Chia Lien then withdrew to find Chia Chen and, meeting him, told him about this.

"I heard the same news," said Chia Chen. "I was on my way to tell Their Lordships."

Both went together to Chia Cheng, who said, "If it's *our* Imperial Consort, we're bound to be sent some word."

Chia Sheh joined them then and they waited till the afternoon, but the messengers sent out had still not returned. Then in came a gatekeeper.

"Two Imperial eunuchs have come, asking to see Your Lordships," he announced.

"Invite them in," said Chia Sheh.

Servants led in the eunuchs, who were met by Chia Sheh and Chia Cheng at the inner gate. Their Lordships first inquired after the health of Her Highness, then ushered the eunuchs into the hall and invited them to sit down.

"The other day the Imperial Consort from your house became indisposed," the eunuchs informed them. "Yesterday we received the order to summon four of her female relatives to the Palace to see her. Each may bring one maid, no more. As for male relatives, they may send in their cards at the gate to pay their respects and await further orders there; but they must not enter the Palace. You are to go between eight and ten tomorrow morning and leave between four and six in the afternoon."

Chia Cheng and Chia Sheh had risen respectfully to hear these injunctions. When they had resumed their seats tea was offered to the eunuchs, who then took their leave. Their Lordships escorted them out of the main gate, returning to report this to the Lady Dowager.

"Four female relatives," she said. "Naturally there's myself and your wives, but who's to be the fourth?"

No one venturing to answer her, she thought it over.

"It will have to be Hsi-feng," she concluded. "She always knows how to cope. You menfolk go and discuss which of you will go."

Their Lordships assented and withdrew. They decided that apart from Chia Lien and Chia Jung, who would be left in charge at home, all the other men of the family should go. They ordered four green sedan-chairs and some dozen carriages to be made ready by dawn, and servants went to carry out these instructions. Then Chia Sheh and Chia Cheng went in again to report:

"You are to enter the Palace between eight and ten in the morning and leave between four and six in the afternoon; so you'd better retire early, madam, in order to make an early start tomorrow."

"I know," she said. "You may go."

After their withdrawal Lady Hsing, Lady Wang and Hsi-feng stayed behind a little longer to talk of Yuan-chun's illness and other things, then went back to their own quarters.

The next day at dawn, the maids in the different houses lit the lamps, their mistresses washed and dressed, and the masters made ready too. It was about six when Lin Chih-hsiao and Lai Ta came to the inner gate to announce:

"The sedan-chairs and carriages are ready outside the gate."

Presently Chia Sheh and Lady Hsing came over. When all had breakfasted Hsi-feng escorted the old lady out first, followed by the other ladies, each supported by one maid, advancing slowly. Li Kuei and another steward were ordered to ride ahead, followed by their wives, to the outer gate of the Palace. Their Lordships and the gentlemen of lower generations rode in carriages or on horseback, with a great retinue of servants, leaving Chia Lien and Chia Jung at home in charge.

The Chia family's carriages, sedan-chairs and horses had halted for some time outside the gate of the outer west wall when at last two eunuchs emerged.

"The Chia ladies come to see their noble relative can enter the Palace now," they announced. "The gentlemen are to pay their respects outside the inner gate, but may not go in."

Guards at the gate cried, "Make haste!"

The four sedan-chairs were borne in behind some young eunuchs, while the gentlemen followed on foot. All the men-servants had been ordered to wait outside. When they approached the inner gate, some old eunuchs sitting there rose to their feet.

"No further, gentlemen!" they ordered.

Then Chia Sheh, Chia Cheng and the rest ranged themselves at attention in order of seniority while the ladies alighted from their chairs which had also stopped at the gate and, each supported by her maid, were led in by the young eunuchs. Soon they came to the bed-chamber of Imperial Consort Yuan-chun, its walls dazzling with gleaming glazed tiles. Two young maids-of-honour told them:

"You need only pay your respects. Other formalities can be dispensed with."

The Lady Dowager's party, having thanked the Imperial Consort, went over to the bed and paid their respects. The Imperial Consort told them to sit down, which they did with murmured thanks.

"How has your health been recently?" she asked her grandmother.

The old lady stood up, leaning on her maid's arm.

"By grace of Your Highness, my health is still good."

Lady Hsing and Lady Wang were questioned next, and they rose to answer too.

Then Hsi-feng was asked, "How are you managing at home?" Rising she replied, "We are managing all right."

"It's not been easy for you all these years working so hard."

Before Hsi-feng could answer, a maid-of-honour brought in a list for Her Highness to inspect. When she saw on it the names of Chia Sheh, Chia Cheng and others, her heart ached and she could not hold back her tears. The maid passed her a handkerchief.

"I'm a little better today," she said wiping her eyes. "Tell them to rest outside."

Her relatives rose to their feet again to give thanks for her graciousness.

With tears in her eyes she told them, "We are less fortunate than humble folk whose daughters can keep close to their fathers and brothers."

Suppressing their own grief they answered, "Don't grieve, Your Highness. Our family has benefited so much from your grace!"

"How is Pao-yu these days?"

"Working much harder at his books," said the old lady. "Because his father makes strict demands on him, he can write essays now."

"That's good."

She ordered a feast to be served to them outside. Then two maids-of-honour and four young eunuchs led them to another palace where the feast was already laid, and they sat down in due order. But we need not dwell on this.

After dining, the old lady led the three others back to thank the Imperial Consort for the feast, and they kept her company until nearly five when, not daring to stay any longer, they took their leave. The Imperial Consort ordered her maids-of-honour to show them to the inner gate, outside which the same four young eunuchs escorted them. When the ladies had seated themselves once more in their chairs, Chia Sheh and the other gentlemen followed them home, where similar arrangements were made for visiting the Palace on the two following days. No more of this.

Let us turn back now to Chin-kuei in the Hsueh family. After driving Hsueh Pan away she had no one to squabble with as Chiu-ling had gone to stay with Pao-chai, leaving only Pao-chan with her. And Pao-chan since becoming Hsueh Pan's concubine showed more spirit than before, so that Chin-kuei found in her an even worse rival and repented — too late — of having made her a secondary wife.

One day after drinking a few cups alone Chin-kuei, lying on the *kang*, decided to work off her spleen on Pao-chan.

"Where did the master go when he left home the other day?" she asked. "You must of course know."

"How should I?" answered Pao-chan. "If he wouldn't tell even *you*, madam, who can possibly know what he's up to?"

Chin-kuei laughed scornfully.

"Are you still calling me 'madam'? You two have it all your own way. *She's* untouchable because she has a protectress, and I dare not catch the lice on a tiger's head, but *you* are still my maid. Yet when I ask you a question you scowl at me and snap back! If you're so powerful, why not strangle me? Then either you or Chiu-ling could be the mistress — wouldn't you like that better? It's too bad that I'm not dead yet, blocking your path!"

Unable to stomach this, Pao-chan glared at her.

"Save that talk for someone else, madam!" she retorted. "*I* haven't said anything wrong. Why should you work off your

anger on someone weaker because you daren't challenge *her*?   If
someone really offends you, you pretend not to hear so as to
keep out of harm's way." She burst out crying.

More enraged than ever, Chin-kuei scrambled down from the
kang to beat her. But Pao-chan had also acquired the Hsia
family ways, and she would not give an inch   While Chin-kuei
smashed cups and saucers and overturned tables and chairs, Pao-
chan paid no attention, just bewailing her unjust fate at the top
of her voice.

Aunt Hsueh in Pao-chai's room heard this commotion.

"Hsiang-ling," she said, "go over and see what's happening.
Tell them to calm down."

"That won't do, mother. Don't tell *her* to go," said Pao-chai.
"How could she stop them? It would simply pour oil on the
flames."

"In that case, I'll go myself."

"I don't think you need go either. Let them make a scene.
There's nothing we can do about it."

"But this is outrageous!"

With that Aunt Hsueh took a maid and headed for Chin-
kuei's room. Pao-chai, impelled to go with her, told Hsiang-ling
to stay behind. As mother and daughter reached Chin-kuei's
door they heard unabated shouting and sobbing inside.

"What are you doing?" cried Aunt Hsueh. "Turning the
house upside-down again! What way is this to behave? The
walls are so thin, aren't you afraid our relatives may hear and
laugh at you?"

Chin-kuei called back from inside, "Of course I don't want
people to laugh at us. But things here are topsy-turvy, with no
distinction between mistress and maid, between wife and concubine — this whole household's a mix-up! That's not how we
behave in our Hsia family. I really can't stand your household
any longer!"

"Sister-in-law," put in Pao-chai, "mother came because you're
making too much noise. Even if she spoke a little hastily, lump-
ing mistress and maid together, never mind. Let's first clear

things up, so that we can live in peace and mother can stop worrying about us."

"That's right," said Aunt Hsueh. "Let's first clear everything up. You'll have plenty of time to grouse about me later."

Chin-kuei sneered, "Dear sister, good sister! What a paragon you are! You're bound to marry into a good family and get yourself a good husband. You certainly won't be a grass-widow like me, lone and lorn, trampled on and bullied by everyone. I'm a foolish creature but all I beg of you, sister, is not to twist my words like that so as to run me down! My parents never taught me properly. Besides, what goes on here between wife and husband, wife and concubine, is hardly the business of an unmarried girl!"

Pao-chai was mortified and enraged by such talk, but what rankled most was the affront to her mother.

Suppressing her anger she said, "Watch your tongue, sister-in-law. Who's run you down? Who's bullied you? Why, not to say you, not even Chiu-ling has ever had a single harsh word from me."

This only made Chin-kuei pound the edge of the *kang*.

"How can *I* compare with Chiu-ling?" she wailed. "I'm not even as good as the dirt beneath her feet. She's been here so long, she's in your confidence and knows how to make up to you. I'm a newcomer and no good at flattery. How can I compare with her? Why be so hard on me? How many girls are fated to be Imperial Consorts? Do a few good turns, or else you'll end up like me — married to a fool, a grass-widow and a disgrace to the family!"

By now Aunt Hsueh could contain herself no longer. She sprang up.

"I'm not defending my own child," she cried. "She was advising you for your own good, yet you keep taunting her. If you have grievances, don't quarrel with her. Better strangle me instead!"

Pao-chai hastily intervened, "Mother, don't be angry. we came here to calm her down, but by losing our own tempers we're making things worse. Let's go now, and wait till sister-in-law feels better before we say any more." She told Pao-chan, "You stop your rumpus too."

As she and her mother went out to cross the courtyard, they saw one of the Lady Dowager's maids approaching with Hsiang-ling.

"Where have you come from?" asked Aunt Hsueh. "Is the old lady well?"

"Yes, madam, she is. She sent me to give you her greetings and thank you for those lichees the other day, as well as to congratulate Miss Pao-chin."

"How long have you been here?" asked Pao-chai.

"Quite a while now."

Aunt Hsueh flushed, aware that she must have overheard them.

"Nowadays we have these disgraceful scenes — not like a respectable family," she said. "It must sound ridiculous to you over there."

"Don't say that, madam! What family doesn't have a few tiffs and squabbles? You are over-sensitive."

The maid followed them to their room and after sitting there for a while went off. Pao-chai was just giving Hsiang-ling some instructions when Aunt Hsueh suddenly let out a cry:

"I've such a pain in my left side!"

To their consternation, she collapsed on the *kang*. To know the upshot of this, read the next chapter.

CHAPTER 84

Pao-yu's Writing Is Tested and
His Marriage Considered
Chia Huan Visits an Invalid and
Arouses Fresh Resentment

Aunt Hsueh's anger over the scene with Chin-kuei upset her liver, bringing on a pain in her left side. Pao-chai, knowing the cause, did not wait for the doctor to come but first sent out to buy a little *Ourouparia rhynchophylla* and brewed a strong bowlful of this for her to drink. Then she and Hsiang-ling massaged the patient's legs and rubbed her chest until presently she felt better.

Aunt Hsueh was both angry and sad: angry with Chin-kuei who had proved such a shrew, and sorry for Pao-chai who was so forbearing. Pao-chai soothed her till she drifted off to sleep, and her liver gradually ceased to trouble her.

"You mustn't take these quarrels to heart, mother," Pao-chai urged her. "In a few days, when you feel up to it, why not go and enjoy a chat with the old lady and Aunt Wang. After all, Hsiang-ling and I are here to see to things at home, and I don't suppose she'll dare try anything."

Aunt Hsueh nodded. "I'll wait a couple of days and see."

The Imperial Consort's recovery restored the whole household's good humour. Especially when, a few days later, some old eunuchs came with gifts and silver from her, announcing that Her Highness wished to express her gratitude for the family's concern, and apportioning each one's share. Chia Sheh and Chia Cheng sent word of this to the Lady Dowager, and together they returned thanks to Her Highness. After some tea the eunuchs left, and Their Lordships went to the old lady's

49

room to chat until one of the serving-women outside reported:
"The pages say someone has come to see the Elder Master on important business."

The old lady urged him to go, and Chia Sheh withdrew.

Struck by a sudden thought then, she remarked cheerfully to Chia Cheng, "Her Imperial Highness is really very concerned about Pao-yu. The other day she asked after him specially."

"But the scamp has fallen short of her kind expectations," he answered. "He won't study properly."

"Well, I put in a good word for him. I told her that recently he'd learned to write essays."

"No, he still isn't up to that, madam."

"You're always sending him to write poems and essays outside, and doesn't he do all right? He's only a child; you have to teach him slowly. As the saying goes, 'No one grows fat on just one mouthful.' "

"Quite right, madam," he agreed at once with a smile.

"Talking of Pao-yu," she went on, "I want to consult you on something. Now that he's growing up, you should look out for some nice girl for him. After all, marriage is for life — it's very important. Whether she's a distant relative or a close one, wealthy or poor, is immaterial. Provided we know for sure that she has a good temper and is nice-looking, that will do well enough."

"That's very true, madam, but I'd just like to add this: Before we find a good girl for him he must learn better ways himself. Otherwise, if he turned out a ne'er-do-well and spoilt some girl's life, that would be deplorable."

This answer vexed the old lady.

"Of course," she said, "with his father and mother at hand, why should I worry my head over this? I suppose, as Pao-yu's been with me since he was small, I may have spoilt him a bit and held up his progress. Still, he seems to me quite handsome and, what's more, he has a good heart. How can you be so sure he's a good-for-nothing, bound to spoil some girl's life? Or am I prejudiced? I think he's better anyway than Huan. What's your opinion?"

Disconcerted by this, Chia Cheng answered with a smile, "You have so much experience of people, madam, if you approve of him and think him promising, you can't be wrong. I was just a little too anxious for him to grow up quickly. This may be the reverse of that old saying, 'No man recognizes his son's good qualities.'"[1]

The old lady laughed at this and the others joined in.

"Now that you're getting on in years and have an official post you're naturally growing more diplomatic," she chuckled. She turned to tell Lady Hsing and Lady Wang, "When I think of him as a boy, with his cranky ways, he was twice as bad as Pao-yu! It was only after his marriage that he began to learn a little sense. Now he's for ever complaining about his son, but to my mind Pao-yu shows a bit more understanding than *he* does!"

Both her daughters-in-law laughed, "You will have your little joke, madam!"

Some young maids came in then to ask Yuan-yang to announce that dinner was ready.

"What are you whispering about over there?" the old lady asked. When told by Yuan-yang she said, "In that case the rest of you had better all go and have dinner, leaving just Hsi-feng and Chen's wife to eat with me."

Chia Cheng and Their Ladyships agreed to this but waited none the less till the meal was served and she dismissed them again before withdrawing, Lady Hsing returning to the other mansion.

Chia Cheng and Lady Wang went back to their own quarters, where he reverted to his mother's proposal.

"The old lady dotes on Pao-yu," he said. "But he must have some solid learning if he's to get an official rank in future. Then all her affection for him won't have been wasted, and he won't ruin some girl's life."

---

[1] Here he is twisting a line from *The Great Learning*: "There is an old saying: No man recognizes his son's shortcomings."

"Of course you are right, sir," agreed Lady Wang.

He sent one of the maids to Li Kuei with the message: "When Pao-yu gets back from school and has had his dinner, I want him to come here at once. I have something to ask him."

"Very good," was Li Kuei's answer.

So when Pao-yu, back from school, was about to pay his duty calls, Li Kuei told him, "There's no need for that, Second Master. You're to go to see your father after dinner. I hear he has some questions to ask you."

Pao-yu was thunder-struck. Having called on his grandmother he went back to the Garden for a hasty meal, then rinsed his mouth and hurried over to see his father, whom he found sitting in his inner study. Pao-yu paid his respects, then stood there at attention.

"These days I have had other things on my mind, so there's something I forgot to ask you," said Chia Cheng. "Earlier on, you said your teacher had told you to expound the classics for a month, after which he would start you off on essay-writing. Nearly two months have passed since then. Have you started writing essays?"

"I've only written three, sir. The teacher said, there was no need to tell you until I can write better. That's why I didn't venture to report it."

"What were the subjects?"

"One was 'At fifteen I set my mind on study,' one was 'When people do not know him he bears no resentment,' one was 'Then they followed the Mohists.' "[1]

"Do you have the drafts?"

"I copied them all out and the teacher corrected them."

"Did you bring them home or leave them at school?"

"They are at school."

"Have them fetched for me to see."

Pao-yu promptly sent word to Pei-ming that he was to fetch him quickly from the school a thin bamboo-paper copybook

---

[1] The first two quotations are from *The Analects*, the third is from *Mencius*.

labelled Class Work, which was in the drawer of his desk.

Soon Pei-ming brought in the exercise book and gave it to Pao-yu, who handed it to his father. Opening it he read the first essay entitled "At fifteen I set my mind on study." Pao-yu had started off, "Even as a child the sage had already set his mind on study." Tai-ju had crossed out "child" and substituted "at fifteen."

Chia Cheng commented, "Your use of 'child' doesn't make the meaning clear, because childhood lasts until the age of sixteen. In this passage the sage explained how his learning and understanding improved with the years; that is why he specified clearly his attainments at fifteen, thirty, forty, fifty, sixty and seventy, to show different stages of development. By changing your 'child' to 'at fifteen' your teacher made it much clearer."

Going on to read the exegesis he saw that the original, which had been crossed out, started, "Now it is common for people not to be bent on study." He shook his head.

"Not only is this childish, it shows you have no desire to become a scholar."

He read on, "For the sage to set his mind on it at fifteen was surely very rare."

"This is even greater nonsense!" he exclaimed.

Then he read Tai-ju's correction, "Who is there who does not study? But few set their minds on it. This was why the sage had faith in himself when he was fifteen."

"Do you understand his corrections?" he asked.

"Yes, sir."

His father then turned to the second essay on "When people do not know him he bears no resentment." First he read the teacher's correction: "One who does not grieve because other people do not recognize his merits will remain well content." Then strained his eyes to read what had been crossed out.

"What is this? 'When one is not annoyed with people, he is truly a scholar.' First you tackle only the idea of 'no resentment.' Then you confuse the definition of a gentleman. Of course that had to be changed to fit the subject. Besides, to be logical, the second part should refer to what precedes it. You need to think things over more carefully."

"Yes, sir."

Chia Cheng read on, " 'Now all men grieve if their talents go unrecognized, yet he was an exception. How could he have achieved this unless he was well content?' " And Pao-yu's conclusion read, "Wasn't he a true scholar?"

Chia Cheng commented, "This has the same fault as the opening. The correction, though a little flat, will pass muster."

The third essay was on "Then they followed the Mohists." After reading the title he looked up thoughtfully to ask Pao-yu, "Have you studied *Mencius* already?"

"The teacher said *Mencius* was easier to understand, so he taught me that first, sir. We finished three days ago and are on the first half of *The Analects* now."

Chia Cheng saw that the opening was virtually unaltered. "It seems there was no other course to follow apart from that of Yang Chu."

"That's not too bad for you," he commented, then read on, "It is not that men wanted to follow the Mohists, but as Mo Tzu's teachings swayed half the world, apart from Yang Chu who else was there to follow?"

"Did you write this?" he asked his son.

"Yes, sir."

Chia Cheng nodded. "It's nothing very brilliant; still it's not bad for a beginner. The other year at my post I set the subject 'Only a knight is capable of this.'[1] Those candidates had all read essays on this theme, and instead of writing something original they could only plagiarize. Have you studied that passage?"

"Yes, sir."

"I want you to introduce some ideas of your own. Don't imitate earlier writers. Just broach the theme and that will be enough."

---

[1] This is a quotation from *Mencius*: "To have no fixed estate and yet remain steadfast — only a true knight is capable of this."

Pao-yu, forced to accept this assignment, lowered his head and cudgelled his brains while his father, his hands clasped behind his back, also stood by the door thinking. Just then a young page came dashing towards the gate. At sight of the master he pulled up and stood respectfully with his arms at his sides.

"What are you doing?" Chia Cheng asked.

"Madam Hsueh has called on the old lady, and Madam Lien has told us to order dinner."

As Chia Cheng made no comment, the page withdrew.

Now ever since Pao-chai had left the Garden, Pao-yu had missed her acutely. On hearing that Aunt Hsueh had called, he assumed that Pao-chai must be with her. He braced himself to say:

"I've broached the subject, sir, but don't know whether it will do or not."

"Read it out."

"Not all men in the world are knights. If one without property can remain steadfast, that is quite exemplary."

Chia Cheng nodded. "That will do. In future when you write essays, you must first make clear the definitions and grasp the meaning and logic. Does the old lady know that you're here?"

"Yes, sir."

"In that case, you had better go now to her place."

Pao-yu assented. Controlling his impatience he slowly withdrew. However, once past the screen by the moon-gate at the end of the corridor, he ran like the wind to the Lady Dowager's compound, paying no attention to Pei-ming who called frantically after him:

"Mind you don't fall! The master's coming!"

As soon as he entered the gate, Pao-yu heard his mother and Hsi-feng laughing and chatting with Tan-chun and some others. At sight of him the maid who lifted the portière whispered:

"Your aunt is here."

Pao-yu hurried in to greet Aunt Hsueh, then paid his evening respects to the old lady.

"How is it you're so late back from school?" she asked.

He explained that his father had been reading his essays and had made him broach a new theme. His grandmother beamed. Then he asked the others, "Where is Cousin Pao-chai?"

"She didn't come," answered Aunt Hsueh with a smile. "She's doing needlework at home with Hsiang-ling."

Pao-yu, disappointed as he was, could hardly leave at once. As they were chatting dinner was served, and naturally the Lady Dowager and Aunt Hsueh took the seats of honour, with Tan-chun and the others in lower seats.

"How about Pao-yu?" asked Aunt Hsueh.

"Pao-yu, come and sit with me," said the old lady.

"When I came back from school," he countered quickly, "Li Kuei said my father wanted to see me after my meal; so I asked at once for one dish and one bowl of rice with some tea, then went over there. Please go on with your meal, ladies."

"In that case, Hsi-feng can sit with me. Your mother just told me that this is one of her fast days, so she'll be eating separately."

Lady Wang also told Hsi-feng, "Go ahead and eat with the old lady and Aunt Hsueh. You needn't wait for me, I'm fasting today."

Hsi-feng acquiescing, a maid set a cup and chopsticks before her. She rose to take the wine-pot and fill the others' cups before resuming her seat.

As they drank the Lady Dowager remarked, "Just now, aunt, you mentioned Hsiang-ling. The other day I heard the maids speak of Chiu-ling, and had no idea whom they meant. When I asked, I discovered it was Hsiang-ling! Why should the child change a perfectly good name?"

Aunt Hsueh flushed crimson and sighed.

"Don't mention that, madam!" she said. "Since Pan married that senseless wife of his they bicker all day long, not like a proper family at all. I've spoken to her several times, but she's too stubborn to listen and I haven't the energy to wrangle with them; so I just let them do as they please. It was *she* who disliked the maid's name and must needs change it."

"Why, what was wrong with it?"

"I'm ashamed to speak of it, madam. But you over here know all that goes on in our household. Of course it wasn't because the name was no good but because it was chosen by Pao-chai — or so I've heard. That's why she wanted to change it."

"But why should that be?"

Aunt Hsueh wiped her tears with her handkerchief. Before going on she sighed.

"You've no idea, madam! Nowadays my daughter-in-law keeps picking on Pao-chai. The other day when you sent someone to see me, we were in the middle of a family row."

"Yes, the other day I heard you had liver trouble and meant to send someone to ask after you; but then I didn't, because they said you were better. My advice to you is: Don't take such things to heart. The young couple are newly married; they'll get straightened out in time. Not everyone can have Pao-chai's sweet disposition — young as she is, she's much better than most older folk. The other day when the maid came back to report, we all lauded her to the skies as one in a hundred, so broad-minded and sweet-tempered! I'm willing to guarantee that, once she marries, her in-laws are bound to love her and high and low in their house will look up to her."

Pao-yu, who had been listlessly waiting for an excuse to leave, sat down again now to listen carefully.

"It's no use," said Aunt Hsueh. "However good she is, she's only a girl. And Pan's grown up such a fool, he really causes me endless anxiety. I'm always afraid he'll drink too much outside and land himself in trouble. Luckily he's often with the gentlemen here: That makes me feel easier in my mind."

Pao-yu put in, "Don't worry, aunty. All his friends are big merchants and respectable people. How could he get into trouble?"

Aunt Hsueh smiled at him. "If you're right, then I needn't worry."

The meal at an end, Pao-yu excused himself on the pretext that he had to study that evening. And while some maids were

serving tea, Hu-po came in with a whispered message for the
old lady, who turned to tell Hsi-feng:

"You must go home at once to see to Chiao-chieh."

Hsi-feng did not know what had happened, and the others
were mystified too until Hu-po explained:

"Just now Ping-erh sent a girl to report that Chiao-chieh is
poorly. She hopes you'll go back at once, madam."

"Go on," urged the Lady Dowager. "You don't have to
stand on ceremony with your aunty."

Hsi-feng promptly assented and took her leave of Aunt Hsueh.

"You go first," put in Lady Wang. "I'll be coming presently. Poor little soul! Don't let the maids make a commotion,
and tell them to keep your pet dogs and cats quiet too. A
delicately nurtured child like her is bound to have these little
upsets."

Murmuring assent, Hsi-feng went off with her maid.

Aunt Hsueh asked now about Tai-yu's illness.

"She's a good child, only too sensitive," said the old lady.
"That's undermined her health. As far as intelligence goes,
she's a match for Pao-chai; but regarding consideration for other
people, she hasn't her thoughtfulness and unselfishness."

After a little more idle talk Aunt Hsueh said, "You should
rest now, madam, and I must get back to see how things are
doing, as there are only Pao-chai and Hsiang-ling at home. And
from there I must go with my sister to see Chiao-chieh."

"That's right. You've had a great deal of experience. Tell
them if you notice anything amiss, so that they'll know what to
do."

Thereupon Aunt Hsueh took her leave, accompanying Lady
Wang to Hsi-feng's quarters.

Chia Cheng, pleased by the results of Pao-yu's test, brought
the subject up when he went out to chat with his secretaries.
One of them was the relative newcomer Wang Erh-tiao, a good
chess-player whose courtesy name was Tso-mei.

"We can see that Master Pao has made great progress in
learning," he observed.

"Progress? No," said Chia Cheng. "He's only just making a start. And it's too early by far to talk of 'learning.' "

Chan Kuang demurred, "You are too modest, sir. This is the opinion of us all, not only Mr. Wang. Master Pao is sure to distinguish himself in the examinations."

"You are too partial to him, gentlemen."

"I have a proposal to make, sir," added Wang Erh-tiao, "if you don't think it presumptuous."

"What is it?"

With a deferential smile Wang answered, "Some acquaintances of mine, the family of Old Mr. Chang the former Governor of Nanshao, have a daughter who is said to be a paragon of virtue and a beauty, and she is not yet bespoken. The Changs have no son, and a property worth millions; but they won't agree to a match until they can find a young man from a rich and noble house who is himself outstanding. After two months here I can see that Master Pao, with his disposition and scholarship, will go far. And your family, sir, is of course unexceptionable! If I propose the match, I can vouch for it that they will agree at once."

"Yes, Pao-yu has reached the right age, and the old lady often speaks of this," Chia Cheng answered. "But I know very little about this Old Mr. Chang."

"I know this family Brother Wang means," said Chan Kuang. "The Changs are related to the Elder Master. You can ask him about them, sir."

After a moment's reflection Chia Cheng remarked, "I have never heard him speak of this connection."

"You wouldn't know of them, sir, because they are related to his brother-in-law Mr. Hsing," Chan Kuang explained, whereupon Chia Cheng realized that they were relatives of Lady Hsing.

After sitting there for a' while he went in to pass on this proposal to his wife and get her to make inquiries of Lady Hsing. But his wife had gone with Aunt Hsueh to see Chiao-chieh, and she did not come back till the evening when Aunt Hsueh had left. Only after telling her what his secretaries had said did Chia Cheng ask:

"How is Chiao-chieh?"

"She seems to have had some kind of fit."

"Is it serious?"

"It looks like epilepsy, but she hasn't had convulsions."

He simply coughed by way of comment, after which both of them retired for the night.

The next day, when Lady Hsing came over to pay her respects, Lady Wang told her mother-in-law of this proposal and asked her sister-in-law about the Chang family.

"Though we are relatives from way back, these last few years we've been out of touch," was the answer. "I don't know what that girl is like. But the other day Ying-chun's mother-in-law Mrs. Sun sent an old woman to ask after us and she mentioned this Chang family, saying they wanted Mrs. Sun to find a suitable husband for their daughter. I hear she's an only child and very pampered. She has studied a little, but being shy of company she always stays at home. Because she's the only daughter, Old Mr. Chang won't hear of her leaving home to be married, for fear her in-laws are too strict with her. They want a son-in-law who will live with them and help to manage the household."

"That would never do!" cried the old lady, not waiting for her to finish. "Our Pao-yu needs people to look after *him*: how can he manage someone else's household?"

"Quite so, madam," agreed Lady Hsing.

The old lady turned to Lady Wang. "When you go back, tell your husband from me: This match with the Chang family is out of the question."

Lady Wang promised to do so.

"And how did you find Chiao-chieh yesterday?" the old lady asked them next. "Just now Ping-erh came over and said she's in a bad way. I intend to go and see her too."

"We know how fond you are of her, but you shouldn't trouble, madam," they demurred.

"No, it's not just to see her. I need a bit of exercise to loosen my joints."

They went off then, on her instructions, to have their meal, after which they escorted her to Hsi-feng's compound. Hsi-feng, hurrying out to meet them, invited them in.

"How is Chiao-chieh?" asked the old lady.

"We're afraid it's epilepsy," was the reply

"In that case why don't you send for a doctor at once?"

"We already have, madam "

Their Ladyships went into the inner room where the nurse was holding the child wrapped up in a peach-red silk-padded quilt. Her face was deathly pale, her forehead contorted and her nose feebly twitching. After looking at her they went back to the other room and had just sat down to have a consultation when a young maid came in.

"His Lordship has sent to ask after Chiao-chieh," she announced.

"Tell him from me that we've sent for the doctor," answered Hsi-feng. "We'll let the master know what prescription he makes out."

The old lady, recollecting the Changs' proposal, reminded Lady Wang, "You should go and let your husband know what we decided. Otherwise the Changs may send a matchmaker and their request." She asked Lady Hsing, "How is it you have nothing to do with the Chang family these days?"

"Because their stingy ways don't suit us, madam. They're not good enough for Pao-yu!"

From this Hsi-feng inferred what was afoot.

"Are you talking about Brother Pao's marriage, madam?" she asked.

Lady Hsing having confirmed this, the old lady explained the conclusion they had reached.

"Excuse my presumption, Old Ancestress," said Hsi-feng with a twinkle. "But there's an ideal match *here*. Why look elsewhere?"

The old lady, chuckling, asked what she meant.

"One 'precious jade' and one 'gold locket' — how could you forget that, madam?"

"Why didn't you propose it yesterday when your aunt was here?" countered the old lady, laughing.

"In the presence of our Old Ancestress and Their Ladyships, how could we young people presume? Besides, how could I bring that up when it was our Old Ancestress aunty came to see? The way to do it is for Their Ladyships to call on her and make a formal proposal."

The Lady Dowager smiled, as did both her daughters-in-law.

"Yes, that was stupid of me," she conceded.

Just then the doctor was announced. The old lady remained in the outer room while Lady Hsing and Lady Wang went inside. The doctor, led in by Chia Lien, paid his respects to the Lady Dowager before going into the sickroom. Returning after examining the patient, he bowed to the old lady and standing before her reported:

"The child's trouble is half owing to hot humours, half to some external shock. First we should dose her to clear up the cold and phlegm, then give her Four-Spirit Powder, because this illness is quite serious. Nowadays the cow bezoar sold in the market is usually counterfeit. We'll have to find the genuine article."

When the old lady had thanked him the doctor went out with Chia Lien to write his prescription, then left.

"We usually keep a stock of ginseng," said Hsi-feng. "But I doubt if we have any cow bezoar. If we buy some outside we must make sure it's genuine."

"Let me send to Aunt Hsueh for some," proposed Lady Wang. "Hsueh Pan does so much business with overseas merchants, he may have some genuine bezoar. I'll send to ask them."

At this point the girls of the family came to ask after Chiao-chieh, and after a short visit left with the old lady.

When the medicine was ready they forced it down Chiao-chieh's throat and, gagging, she brought it up with some phlegm, much to her mother's relief. And now one of Lady Wang's young maids came in with a small red package.

"Here's the bezoar, madam," she said. "Her Ladyship wants you to weigh it yourself to make sure the amount is correct."

Hsi-feng took it, assenting, and told Ping-erh to make haste and brew the pearl powder, baroos camphor and cinnabar while she herself used a small steelyard to weigh out the required amount of cow bezoar. This had just been mixed with the other ingredients, ready to dose Chiao-chieh when she woke up, when Chia Huan raised the portière and came in.

"What's the matter with Chiao-chieh, Second Cousin?" he asked. "My mother sent me to see her."

"She's better," answered Hsi-feng, who had an aversion to both him and Concubine Chao. "Go back and thank your mother for her concern."

Chia Huan, while agreeing to this, kept staring around.

"I hear you've got cow bezoar here. What's it like?" he asked. "Can I have a look?"

"Don't be such a nuisance!" she scolded. "Chiao-chieh's only just on the mend. The bezoar is being brewed."

Chia Huan reaching out for the skillet bumped against it. It overturned with a splash, dousing the fire, and ashamed of his bungling he took to his heels.

Beside herself with fury Hsi-feng cursed, "Our true sworn enemy, aren't you! Why play such dirty tricks here? Your mother tried to do me in before; now you come to do for Chiao-chieh! What cause have I given you to make you hate us so?" She swore at Ping-erh too for not stopping him.

As she was raging a maid came in looking for Huan.

"Go and tell Concubine Chao to stop trying so hard!" snapped Hsi-feng. "Chiao-chieh's done for: she needn't worry!"

Ping-erh was hastily brewing a fresh lot of medicine, and the maid not knowing what was amiss asked in a whisper why Madam Lien was so angry. Ping-erh told her how Huan had upset the skillet.

"No wonder he dared not go home!" exclaimed the maid. "He must be hiding somewhere. Goodness knows what he'll be up to next! Let me clear up for you, sister."

"There's no need. Luckily there was still a bit of cow bezoar left, and it's ready now. You'd better go."

"I'm going back to tell Concubine Chao," said the maid. "This should stop her singing his praises every day."

On her return she was as good as her word. Concubine Chao

sent angrily for her son, and the maid found him skulking in an outer room.

"You good-for-nothing!" scolded his mother. "Why spill their medicine, giving them a chance to curse us? I told you to call to ask after her, not to go in. But in you went, and instead of leaving at once you had to 'catch lice on the tiger's head.' Just wait till I tell your father, and see what a thrashing he'll give you!"

As Concubine Chao was storming, Chia Huan in the outer room made an even more startling statement. To know what it was, read on.

CHAPTER 85

Chia Cheng Is Promoted to the Rank
of Vice-Minister
Hsueh Pan Is Involved in Another
Manslaughter Case

As Concubine Chao in her room was raging at Chia Huan in the outer room, he suddenly blurted out:

"All I did was upset the skillet and spill some medicine — I didn't kill the brat! Why should everyone curse me as if I were a monster? Do you want to hound me to death? Some day I'll kill that little bitch, and let's see what you do then! Just tell them to watch out."

His mother hurried out to stop his mouth.

"Still raving!" she cried. "Do you want them to kill me first?"

Mother and son wrangled for a time. And Hsi-feng's taunts so rankled with Concubine Chao that she sent her no further condolences. Although in a few days Chiao-chieh recovered, their two households were on even worse terms than before.

One day, Lin Chih-hsiao reported to Chia Cheng, "Today is the birthday of the Prince of Peiching. What are your instructions, sir?"

"Just send presents as we did in the past, after letting Lord Sheh know."

The steward accepted these orders and went to carry them out.

Presently Chia Sheh came over and they decided to take Chia Chen, Chia Lien and Pao-yu with them to offer congratulations. The others took this as a matter of course, but Pao-yu was most eager to see more of the prince whose distinguished appearance and manners had so impressed him. He changed hastily into ceremonial dress and went with his father to the prince's mansion, where Their Lordships sent in their cards, then waited to be summoned. Soon a eunuch came out, a chaplet in his hand, and beamed at the sight of them, asking:

"How are you two gentlemen?"

Chia Sheh and Chia Cheng greeted him in return, and the three young men followed suit.

"His Highness asks you to come in," said the eunuch.

The five of them followed him in past two gates and one court to the inner palace gate, where they halted while he went in to announce their arrival and the young eunuchs there stepped forward to greet them.

Before long, the eunuch returned to invite them in, and they followed him respectfully. The Prince of Peiching in ceremonial robes had come out to the corridor to meet them. First Their Lordships stepped forward to pay their respects, and after them Chia Chen, Chia Lien and Pao-yu.

The prince took Pao-yu by the hand. "It's so long since I saw you," he said, "I've been thinking of you." With a smile he asked, "Have you kept that jade of yours safe?"

Pao-yu bowed and bent one knee as he replied, "By the grace of Your Highness, yes."

"I've no rich fare to offer you today, but let us have a chat," the prince proposed.

Some eunuchs raised the portière and he led the way in, followed by Chia Sheh's party with bowed heads. First Chia Sheh asked to pay homage and knelt down even while the prince was declining. Then Chia Cheng and the others made obeisance too.

As they were withdrawing respectfully, the prince ordered eunuchs to take them — all but Pao-yu — to join his relatives and friends and to entertain them well. He offered Pao-yu a seat so that they could talk, and the boy kowtowed his thanks. Then seated on the edge of an openwork porcelain stool near the door he launched into a description of his studies and essay-writing, to which the prince listened with sympathetic interest.

"Yesterday," the prince told him after tea had been served,

"Governor Wu came to court and spoke of your honourable father's probity as an examiner, and the great respect in which all the candidates held him. His Majesty asked about this when he received him, and the governor commended your father most highly. This augurs well for him."

Pao-yu who had stood to hear this replied, 'Your gracious Highness and Governor Wu are most kind."

At this point a young eunuch entered to report, "The gentlemen in the front court thank Your Highness for the feast."

He presented the cards on which the guests paid their respects, and the prince after glancing at them handed them back, remarking with a smile:

"I have put them to undue trouble."

"And the special meal Your Highness is conferring on Chia Pao-yu is ready now."

He received orders then to take Pao-yu to a small courtyard, a charming place where attendants waited on him at his meal. On his return to offer thanks, the prince spoke to him kindly again and suddenly remarked with a smile:

"Last time I was so intrigued by that jade of yours that on my return I had a replica made. I'm glad you have come today — you can take it back for your amusement."

He made the young eunuch fetch it and gave it to Pao-yu, who received it with both hands, thanked him and then withdrew. Two young eunuchs escorted him out on their master's orders and he went back with Chia Sheh and the rest.

While Chia Sheh went home, Chia Cheng took the three young men to call on the old lady and tell her whom they had met in the prince's mansion, after which Pao-yu reported to his father how Governor Wu had recommended him to the Emperor.

"This Governor Wu is an old family friend," observed Chia Cheng. "He is one of our sort, a man of integrity."

After a little more casual talk the Lady Dowager urged them to go and rest. Chia Cheng took his leave but told his three juniors, who were following him to the door, to stay and keep the old lady company. Back in his room he had barely sat down when a maid announced:

"Lin Chih-hsiao is outside with something to report, sir." She presented Governor Wu's red visiting-card.

Realizing that Governor Wu had called in his absence, Chia Cheng told her to bring the steward in, and went out to the corridor to see him.

Lin Chih-hsiao reported, "Today Governor Wu came to call, and I told him where you had gone, sir. I also heard that a vacancy for a vice-minister has come up in the Ministry of Works, and people outside and in the ministry are all saying that you are to be appointed, sir."

"That remains to be seen," replied Chia Cheng.

Lin Chih-hsiao reported then on a few other matters and left.

Now Pao-yu, the only one of the three young men to have stayed with his grandmother, described how the prince had entertained him and displayed the jade given him. When it had been admired by all, the old lady ordered the maids to put it away so that he would not lose it.

"Mind you keep your own jade safely," she warned Pao-yu. "Don't mix them up!"

Taking his jade from his neck he rejoined, "*This* is mine — how could I lose it? They're quite different when you compare them. Impossible to confuse them. And there's something else I've been meaning to tell you, madam. The other night when I went to bed and hung my jade on the curtain, it started glowing, making the whole curtain red!"

"You're talking nonsense again," she said. "The valance of the canopy is red, so naturally when it catches the light the curtain seems red too."

"No, the light was out by then. The whole room was pitch dark, and yet I saw it clearly."

Lady Hsing and Lady Wang exchanged meaning smiles.

"It's a lucky sign," Hsi-feng assured him.

"A lucky sign? What do you mean?"

"You wouldn't understand," said his grandmother. "You've had an exciting day, so go and rest now. Don't stay here talking nonsense."

Pao-yu hung around for a while before going back to the Garden, and as soon as he had gone the old lady said:

"That reminds me, when you went to see Aunt Hsueh did you broach that business?" ˙

"We only went today," replied Lady Wang, "because Hsi-feng was held up for two days by Chiao-chieh's illness. We told Aunt Hsueh, and she was only too willing. However, she says she must first consult Hsueh Pan — as his father's gone — and Pan's still away from home."

"Quite right too," agreed the old lady. "We'd better not make it public, in that case, until Aunt Hsueh has decided."

But no more of their discussion about Pao-yu's marriage.

Pao-yu back in his own quarters told Hsi-jen, "Just now my grandmother and Cousin Hsi-feng were talking so cryptically, I'd no idea what they meant."

Hsi-jen reflected, then smiled.

"I can't guess either," she said. "Was Miss Lin there at the time?"

"No, she hasn't been over there recently — she's only just left her bed."

Just then they heard a quarrel break out in the outer room between Sheh-yueh and Chiu-wen.

"What are you two scrapping about now?" called Hsi-jen.

"We were playing cards," said Sheh-yueh, coming in. "When she won she took my money, but when I won she wouldn't pay. To make it worse, she grabbed my whole bank too."

"What does a little money matter?" chuckled Pao-yu. "Stop making such a noise, you silly things."

The two girls went off then and sat down to sulk while Hsi-jen helped Pao-yu to bed.

Hsi-jen had realized from Pao-yu's remark that his marriage was under discussion. She had not told him this, however,

for fear that his senseless notions would make him burst out
again with a flood of foolish talk. But as she too was deeply
concerned about his marriage, she lay awake that night thinking
and decided to go to see if Tzu-chuan knew of any developments which might shed light on the matter. The next day
she rose early. Having seen Pao-yu off to school, she spruced
herself up and walked slowly to Bamboo Lodge. Tzu-chuan,
whom she found picking flowers, invited her to go in and take
a seat.

"Thanks, sister, I will," said Hsi-jen. "Picking flowers are
you? Where's your young lady?"

"She's just finished dressing and is waiting for her medicine
to be heated."

She led Hsi-jen inside, where Tai-yu was reading.

"No wonder you wear yourself out, miss, reading as soon
as you get up," said Hsi-jen cheerfully. "I only wish our
Master Pao would study as hard as you do!"

Tai-yu smilingly put down her book. By now Hsueh-yen
had brought in a small tray on which were one cup of medicine,
another of water, while a young maid behind her was holding
a spittoon and rinse-bowl.

Hsi-jen had come to size up the situation. But although she
sat there for a while she found it impossible to approach the
subject; and she did not like to risk upsetting Tai-yu, sensitive
as she was, by fishing for information. So presently she made
some excuse to leave. Approaching Happy Red Court, she
halted at sight of two people standing outside. One of them,
spotting her, ran over and Hsi-jen saw it was Chu-yao.

"What are *you* doing here?" she asked.

"Just now Master Yun came with a note for Master Pao.
He's waiting here for a reply."

"Surely you know that Master Pao goes to school every day.
Why wait for a reply?"

"I told him that, but he wanted me to tell *you*, miss, so that
you can give him an answer."

Before Hsi-jen could make any comment she recognized the
other person as Chia Yun, now sidling sheepishly towards her.

"Tell him I've got the note and I'll give it to Master Pao later," she told Chu-yao.

Chia Yun had been hoping to engage Hsi-jen in conversation in order to ingratiate himself with her, but for fear of seeming presumptuous he had come over slowly. Being close enough now to hear this remark, he could hardly come any further. And as Hsi-jen now turned her back on him and went in. he had to leave dejectedly with Chu-yao.

When Pao-yu came home that evening Hsi-jen told him, "Today young Master Yun who lives in the lane called."

"What did he want?"

"He left a note."

"Where is it? Let me see it."

Sheh-yueh fetched it from the bookcase in the inner room, and Pao-yu saw that the envelope was inscribed "Respected Uncle."

"Why has this boy stopped calling me father?" he demanded.

"What do you mean?" asked Hsi-jen.

"The other year when he sent me those white begonias, he called me his god-father. Now on this envelope he's written 'uncle.' Evidently he no longer considers me as his father."

"He has no sense of shame, and neither have you!" she scolded. "A big fellow like him calling a boy like you father — isn't that shameless? Why, you're not even. . . ." She broke off, blushing and smiling.

Pao-yu knowing what she meant rejoined, "That doesn't follow. As the saying goes, 'A childless monk may have many filial sons.' I agreed to it only because he struck me as clever and pleasant. If he backs out, what do I care!" While saying this he opened the letter.

"There's something shifty about young Master Yun," observed Hsi-jen. "At times he insists on seeing you, at others he looks around slyly; it shows he's up to no good."

Pao-yu concentrating on his letter ignored her comments, and Hsi-jen saw that its contents made him frown, smile and shake his head by turns. He ended up looking exasperated.

"Well, what does he say?" she asked.

By way of answer he tore the note into pieces.

To change the subject she asked, "Will you be studying again after dinner?"

Leaving her question unanswered he exclaimed, "What a swine this young Yun is — ridiculous!"

"What's the matter anyway?" she asked with a smile.

"Why ask? Let's eat now, then we can rest. I'm fed up." He told a young maid to light a fire and burned the scraps of the letter. But when the meal was ready presently, he sat down in a daze and Hsi-jen had to coax him to get him to eat one mouthful. Soon he pushed aside his bowl and flung himself down moodily on the couch. Then he suddenly burst into tears.

Hsi-jen and Sheh-yueh were nonplussed.

"Why carry on like this for no reason at all?" cried Sheh-yueh. "It's all that Chia Yun's fault! Why should he send such a stupid note to addle Master Pao's wits and send him into hysterics. If he goes on bottling up his feelings like this, what are we to do?" She started sobbing too.

Hsi-jen could hardly help laughing.

"Cut that out, good sister!" she urged her. "It's bad enough him making a scene without *your* joining in. What has that letter got to do with you?"

"That's crazy talk," Sheh-yueh countered. "Who knows what rubbish he wrote? Why pin it on me? Come to that, his note may have had to do with *you*!"

Before Hsi-jen could answer Pao-yu burst out laughing and, scrambling off the couch, smoothed out his clothes.

"Stop squabbling and let's sleep now," he said. "I must get up early tomorrow to go to school."

So they went to bed, passing an uneventful night.

The next morning when Pao-yu had dressed he set off to school. But as he was leaving his compound, struck by a thought he told Pei-ming to wait, then turned to call Sheh-yueh.

"What brings you back?" she asked him, coming out.

"If Chia Yun comes again today, tell him not to fool about here. If he does, I'll tell the old lady and the master."

Sheh-yueh agreed to this. But Pao-yu had no sooner started off again than he saw Chia Yun hurrying towards him. At sight of Pao-yu he swept him a bow.

"Congratulations, uncle!"

"You've got a nerve!" Pao-yu retorted, remembering his note of the previous day. "Disturbing me when I have other things on my mind."

"You can have a look, uncle, if you don't believe me. The heralds are already here at the main gate."

More exasperated than ever Pao-yu cried, "What are you talking about?"

Just then they heard shouting outside.

"Listen, uncle, to that!"

This set Pao-yu wondering.

"Have you no manners?" they heard someone shout. "How dare you make such a row here?"

Another voice answered, "Your master has been promoted! How can you stop us proclaiming the good news? Other families would be only too pleased to hear us!"

Then Pao-yu realized with delight that they were announcing his father's promotion to be vice-minister. He started off.

Chia Yun caught up with him, saying, "Are you pleased, uncle? Once your marriage is fixed, that'll be double happiness for you!"

Pao-yu flushed and spat. "Clear off, you oaf!"

"What have I said wrong?" Chia Yun reddened. "Wouldn't you . . . ?"

"Wouldn't I what?" demanded Pao-yu sternly.

Then Chia Yun dared say no more, and Pao-yu hurried off to school.

"What brings you here today?" asked Tai-ju beaming. "I just heard of your father's promotion."

"I came to see you, sir, before going to my father," said Pao-yu respectfully.

"You need not study today, you can have a holiday. But don't spend it playing in the Garden. You're no longer a child, remember. Though you can't handle affairs yet, you should learn from your elder cousins."

Pao-yu assented and went home. At the inner gate he met Li Kuei coming out.

"So here you are, young master!" The steward halted, smiling. "I was just going to the school to fetch you."

"On whose instructions?"

"The old lady sent to find you, and your maids said you'd gone to school. So just now she sent again to tell me to ask for a few days' leave for you — I hear operas will be put on to celebrate. You've turned up just in time, Master Pao."

Passing through the gate, Pao-yu observed that all the maids and matrons in the court were beaming.

"Why so late, Master Pao?" they cried. "Go in and congratulate the old lady, quick!"

Pao-yu entered his grandmother's room and his face lit up when he saw Tai-yu sitting on her left, Hsiang-yun on her right. All the ladies of the house had assembled there except for Pao-chai, Pao-chin and Ying-chun. Beside himself with joy, he offered congratulations to his grandmother and then to Their Ladyships, after which he greeted his cousins one by one.

"Are you better, cousin?" he asked Tai-yu.

"Yes, much better," she answered with a smile. "I heard you were unwell too. Are you all right now?"

"Oh yes. That night I suddenly had a pain in my heart, but these last few days I've been well enough to go back to school. That's why I've had no time to call on you."

While he was still speaking Tai-yu turned away to talk to Tan-chun. Hsi-feng standing near them smiled.

"You two are behaving like guests, not like inseparables," she teased. "All these civilities! Well, as the saying goes, 'you show each other respect as to a guest.'"[1]

---

[1] Meng Kuang and Liang Hung of the Eastern Han Dynasty (25-220) were a loving couple. They were described as showing each other respect as to a guest.

The others laughed while Tai-yu blushed furiously, not knowing whether to let this go or not. After some hesitation she blurted out:

"What do *you* know about it?"

That set the company laughing even more loudly. Hsi-feng, conscious of her gaffe, was wondering how to change the subject when Pao-yu suddenly exclaimed to Tai-yu:

"Cousin Lin, you never saw anyone as *boorish* as Chia Yun...." He broke off without finishing the sentence.

This provoked a fresh gale of mirth.

"What *is* all this?" others asked.

Tai-yu, also in the dark, smiled shyly too.

Pao-yu hedged, "Just now I heard that some operas are to be presented. When will that be?"

All looked at him, still laughing.

"If you heard that outside," quipped Hsi-feng, "you should come and tell us, not ask *us* about it."

"I'll go and find out," he offered.

"Don't go running around outside," warned the old lady. "For one thing, the heralds would laugh at you. For another, your father's in a good humour today, but if he saw you outside he would be angry."

"Yes, madam," said Pao-yu, then slipped away.

The old lady asked Hsi-feng, "Who's talked of presenting operas?"

"Uncle Wang. He said that the day after tomorrow, which is an auspicious day, he'll send over a new company of actresses to congratulate you, madam, as well as the master and mistress." She added with a twinkle, "It'll not only be an auspicious day but a happy occasion too. That day...." She winked at Tai-yu, who smiled back.

"Why, of course!" exclaimed Lady Wang. "It's our niece's birthday."

The old lady thought for a second and then said, "It shows I'm growing old, I get so muddled. It's lucky I have Hsi-feng as my mentor. All right then. If Pao-yu's uncle wants to offer congratulations, Tai-yu's uncle's family can celebrate her birthday too."

Everybody laughed.

"Whatever our Old Ancestress says is so aptly put, no wonder she has such good fortune!" someone exclaimed.

Pao-yu coming back just then was in raptures when he heard about Tai-yu's birthday. Presently they all had a meal there and made merry with the old lady.

After the meal, Chia Cheng came back from thanking the Emperor and kowtowed to the ancestors, then to his mother. Standing before her, he spoke to her briefly before going out to entertain his guests. A constant stream of kinsmen was coming and going now, with a great noise and bustle. Carriages and horses thronged the gate; silks and sables filled the hall. Truly:

Bees and butterflies converge on flowers in bloom;
Sea and sky stretch boundless under the full moon!

These visits continued for two days till the time for the celebration. Early that morning Wang Tzu-teng and other kinsmen had sent over a company of actresses, and a stage was set up in front of the Lady Dowager's main hall. Outside it waited the men of the family, in official robes. More than ten tables of feasts had been prepared for relatives; and as the actresses were new and the old lady was in high spirits, they set up a glass screen in the inner hall to feast the ladies there. At the table of honour sat Aunt Hsueh accompanied by Lady Wang and Pao-chin. Opposite was the table for the old lady accompanied by Lady Hsing and Hsiu-yen. The two lower tables were vacant, and the old lady urged the girls to seat themselves there quickly.

Presently Hsi-feng, a troop of maids behind her, escorted in Tai-yu. Dressed in new clothes and made up, she appeared like the moon goddess come down to earth as she greeted the others with a bashful smile. Hsiang-yun, Li Wen and Li Chi invited her to take the best seat at their table, but she declined.

"You must sit there today," insisted the old lady, smiling.

Aunt Hsueh rose to ask, "Is this a happy occasion for Miss Lin too?"

"Yes, it's her birthday."

"How could I have forgotten!" Aunt Hsueh went over to Tai-yu. "Excuse my bad memory, child! I'll send Pao-chin over presently to offer her congratulations."

"You are too kind." Tai-yu smiled. While every one took a seat, she looked around and seeing Pao-chai was not there, she asked Aunt Hsueh, "How's Cousin Pao-chai? Why hasn't she come today?"

"She should have come, but we have no one to keep an eye on things at home, so she has to stay in," Aunt Hsueh explained.

"But now she has a sister-in-law, aunty, surely you don't need Pao-chai to mind the house? I suppose she doesn't like joining in noisy parties, but I do miss her so!"

"It's good of you to think of her," said Aunt Hsueh. "She longs to see you all too. One of these days I'll send her over to have a chat with you."

Now maids came in to pour wine and bring in dishes, while outside the performance had started. The first two items, of course, had propitious themes. When it came to the third, they saw fairy pages and maids with flags and pennons lead in a girl dressed as a goddess, with black gauze on her head, who sang an aria and then left the stage. No one knew what opera this was till they heard it said outside that this was the scene "Returning to Heaven from Hell" from the new opera *The Tale of Jui-chu*.[1] The girl was the moon goddess who descended to earth and became betrothed to a mortal; luckily the goddess Kuan-yin had shown her the right course and she died before her marriage took place. She was now going back to the moon. That was why she sang:

---

[1] The playwright is unknown.

> Sweet they say is the love of mortals,
> Yet autumn moon and spring flowers are soon abandoned,
> And I nearly forgot the palace of the moon.

The fourth item was "Eating Husks" from *The Tale of the Lute*.[1] The fifth was about Bodhidharma leading his disciples back across the river — a fantastic and most spectacular performance.

At the height of their enjoyment, one of the Hsueh family servants came rushing in, pouring with sweat.

"Go back quickly, sir!" he panted to Hsueh Ko. "And ask madam to go back too. There's bad trouble at home!"

"What's happened?" Hsueh Ko demanded.

"I'll tell you when we get back, sir."

Hsueh Ko went off without stopping to take his leave. And when maids took word of this to Aunt Hsueh, she turned pale with alarm. After a hasty leave-taking she mounted her carriage with Pao-chin to go back, amid general consternation.

"We must send someone over to find out what's amiss and to show our concern," said the Lady Dowager.

The others approved this, then went on watching the opera.

Aunt Hsueh, reaching home, saw court runners standing by the inner gate. Some assistants from the pawnshop were telling them:

"Wait till the mistress comes home, then everything can be settled."

The runners, at the arrival of an old lady attended by so many servants, knew that this must be Hsueh Pan's mother. And as she looked someone of consequence they kept themselves in check, standing at attention to let her pass. She went to the back from whence came sounds of wailing, and discovered Chin-kuei there. As she hurried forward Pao-chai came out to meet her, her face wet with tears.

"So you've heard the news, mother," she said. "Don't worry. We must find some way to square things!"

---

[1] By Kao Tse-cheng of the Ming Dynasty.

Aunt Hsueh went inside with her daughter, trembling with fright after having heard from the servants in the court what her son had done.

"Whom had he been quarrelling with?" she asked tearfully.

"Don't try to get to the bottom of it now, madam," they urged her. "Taking a life is a capital offence regardless of persons. We had better discuss what to do."

"What is there to discuss?" she sobbed.

"What we propose is this," they said. "We'll get ready some silver tonight and go straight with Master Ko to see Master Pan. We can find some shrewd scrivener there and pay him to tear up that capital offence charge; then we can ask the Chia family to intercede with the magistrate of the yamen. There are those runners waiting outside too. First give them a few taels of silver to get rid of them, madam, and then we can get started."

"Better find the other man's family," was Aunt Hsueh's counter-proposal. "Promise them some money for the funeral as well as for compensation. If they drop the charge, the matter can be hushed up."

"That won't do, mother!" called Pao-chai from the inner room. "In a business like this, the more money you pay them the more trouble they'll make. What the servants suggested was right."

"I wish I were dead!" wailed Aunt Hsueh. "I'll go and see my son for the last time, then die together with him!"

Pao-chai urged her to be of good comfort and called to the servants in the outer room, "Quickly go with Master Ko to deal with this business."

Maids helped Aunt Hsueh inside.

"If you have any news, cousin, send word at once!" called Pao-chai to Hsueh Ko who was starting out. "But stay there yourselves to cope."

Hsueh Ko assented and left. And Chin-kuei seized this chance, while Pao-chai was consoling her mother, to round upon Hsiang-ling.

"You used to boast that this family came to the capital after getting away scot-free with murder!" she raged. "Now he's really gone and killed a man! And for all your bragging about the Hsuehs' wealth and powerful connections, look at the panic everybody's in now! If my husband's for it and can't come back, you'll all clear off leaving me to bear the brunt!" She burst out storming and sobbing.

Aunt Hsueh hearing this nearly fainted away with anger and Pao-chai, though frantic, was helpless. At the height of this scene, one of Lady Wang's trusted maids came from the Chia Mansion to ascertain what had happened. Pao-chai knew she was going to marry into their household, but as this had not yet been announced, and she was feeling desperate, she did not hide herself as etiquette demanded but told the maid:

"At present this business isn't very clear. All we've heard is that my brother has been arrested by the county yamen for killing a man outside. We don't know what the verdict will be. Hsueh Ko has just gone to make inquiries. As soon as we have definite news, we'll send word to your mistress. Go back now and thank her for her concern. We shall be asking later for help from your master."

The maid accepted these instructions and left.

Aunt Hsueh and Pao-chai stayed at home in suspense until, two days later, a page came back with a letter which a young maid brought in. Pao-chai opened it and read:

> This case involving Brother Pan was inadvertent manslaughter, not murder. This morning I sent in a plea in my name, but it has not yet been approved. Brother Pan's first confession was most unfortunate. Once my plea is ratified, we shall ask to go to court again to retract it, and then he may be let off. Five hundred more taels of silver to cover expenses are needed at once from our pawnshop. There must be no delay! Tell Aunt not to worry. For the rest you can question the page.

Having perused this, Pao-chai read it out again in full for her mother.

"So it seems his fate is still in the balance!" cried Aunt Hsueh, wiping her tears.

"Don't be upset, mother," urged Pao-chai. "Let's first call in the page and find out the details."

She sent a maid to fetch him in, and Aunt Hsueh asked him to tell them just what had happened.

"When I heard what Master Pan told Master Ko the other evening, I was frightened out of my wits!" he began.

To know his account of the matter, read the next chapter.

CHAPTER 86

An Old Magistrate Takes a Bribe
to Re-open a Case
A Young Girl, to While Away Time,
Explains a Lute Score

After listening to Hsueh Ko's letter, Aunt Hsueh called in the page who had brought it.

"You heard what Master Pan said. How did he come to kill a man?" she asked.

"I didn't get it too clear, madam. That day he told Master Ko. . . ." The page looked round to make sure they were alone before continuing, "Master Pan said he was so sick of all these rows at home that he made up his mind to go south to buy goods. He decided to ask somebody to go with him — a certain Wu Liang who lives more than two hundred *li* south of this city. On his way to find him he met that Chiang Yu-han who used to be such a friend of his, bringing some young actors to town. While they were having a meal and drinking together in his inn, Master Pan was annoyed by the way the waiter kept staring at Chiang Yu-han. But then Chiang left.

"The next day, while drinking with Wu Liang, Master Pan remembered what had happened the day before and, when the waiter was slow in bringing fresh wine, he started cursing him. When the fellow answered back, he threatened him with his wine bowl. The rogue craned his neck, daring our master to hit him. Then Master Pan brought the bowl down on his head. Blood spurted out and he dropped to the ground swearing — but very soon he fell silent."

"Why did no one stop him?" scolded Aunt Hsueh.

"That, Master Pan didn't say and I dare not make anything up."

"You go and rest now."

"Yes, madam."

When the page had gone Aunt Hsueh went to see Lady Wang, to enlist her husband's help. Learning what had happened, he hedged. They must wait to see the magistrate's response to Hsueh Pan's petition, he said, before deciding on a course of action.

Aunt Hsueh sent the page back with more money from the pawnshop, and three days later received another letter. She sent to tell Pao-chai, who came at once and read it out as follows:

> With the money you sent we have squared the yamen officers. Brother Pan is not being ill-treated in jail; don't worry. Only the local people are cutting up rough. The dead man's family and the witnesses are holding out, and even that friend invited by Brother Pan is taking their side.
>
> I and Li Hsiang are strangers here, but luckily we found a good pettifogger, and after his palm was greased he came up with a plan. He advised us to get hold of Wu Liang who was drinking with Brother Pan and bail him out, then offer him money to enlist his help. If he wouldn't agree, we could say he was the one who killed Chang San then laid the blame on an outsider. If that scared him, then it should be easy to handle.
>
> I took his advice and got Wu Liang out; then we bribed the dead man's relatives and the witnesses; and the day before yesterday I sent in another petition. Today the answer has come, and I enclose a copy for you to see.

Pao-chai next read out the petition:

> Petitioner....
> Petition on behalf of his brother, a victim of foul play who has been unjustly accused.

> My elder brother Hsueh Pan, a native of Nanking now resident in the capital, set off on such and such a day to go south on business. A few days after he left home, a family servant brought the news that he had been involved in manslaughter. I came immediately to Your Honour's county and learned that he had accidentally injured a man named Chang. When I went to the jail, he told me with tears that this Chang was a stranger to him and there had been no enmity between them. An accidental quarrel had broken out when my brother, asking for wine, spilt some on the ground. Chang San happened to be stooping to pick something up, and my brother, whose hand slipped, struck the top of his head with the wine bowl and killed him. During interrogation, for fear of torture, he confessed that he had killed the man in a fight. But Your

Honour, in your infinite goodness, realized that this could not have been the case and deferred giving a verdict. As my brother in jail is forbidden to send in a plea, on account of our close relationship I am venturing to intercede for him. I hope Your Honour will graciously permit another trial. This will be a great act of mercy, and my whole family will for ever remember your ineffable goodness. This is my earnest petition.

The magistrate's rescript read:

Investigation at the scene of the crime uncovered definite proof; and your brother, without being tortured, confessed in writing to killing a man in a brawl. Coming from far away and not being an eye-witness, how can you trump up a case? By law you should be punished, but in view of your brotherly concern I shall pardon you. Your petition is rejected.

"He's done for, then!" exclaimed Aunt Hsueh. "What shall we do?"

"Wait till you hear the end of Brother Ko's letter," said Pao-chai, then read it out.

What really matters, the messenger can tell you.

Then Aunt Hsueh questioned the page.

"The magistrate knows that our family is well off, madam," he said. "If we get help from people of consequence in the capital, then send him a handsome present, he can hold another trial and lighten the sentence. There's no time to be lost. Any delay, and the master will suffer for it."

Aunt Hsueh dismissed the page and went straight to the Chia Mansion to tell Lady Wang of this and appeal to her husband. Chia Cheng agreed only to send someone to speak to the magistrate — not to send him a bribe. And doubting the use of this, Aunt Hsueh prevailed on Hsi-feng to send Chia Lien with several thousand taels to buy off the magistrate, while Hsueh Ko at the same time squared the others involved.

Then the magistrate held a fresh trial, to which he summoned the local bailiff, witnesses and dead man's relatives as well as Hsueh Pan, who was fetched from the jail. When the secretaries of the criminal department had checked the roll of names, the magistrate ordered the bailiff to identify the original deposition, then called forward the dead man's mother Mrs. Chang and his uncle Chang Erh for questioning.

Mrs. Chang, weeping, testified, "My husband, Chang Ta, lived in the southern suburbs and died eighteen years ago. My first and second sons died too, leaving me only Chang San — who has been killed. He was twenty-three this year and not yet married. Because our family is poor, with no means of livelihood, he worked as a waiter in Li Family Inn. That afternoon, they sent from the inn to tell me he had been killed. I was frightened to death, Your Honour! I rushed there and saw him lying on the ground, at his last gasp, bleeding from a gash on his head. When I called him he could not answer, and soon he died. I must have it out with that young devil!"

The runners raised an intimidating shout.

Then she kowtowed, pleading, "Your Honour, avenge me! He was the only son I had left."

The magistrate waved her aside and called for the inn-keeper. "Was Chang San a workman in your inn?" he asked.

"Not a workman but a waiter," Li Erh replied.

"At the autopsy, you said that Hsueh Pan killed Chang San with a bowl. Did you see him do it?"

"I was serving at the bar. I heard a customer call for wine, and soon after that someone cried, 'Confound it! He's knocked out!' I ran there and saw Chang San flat on the ground, unable to speak. I lost no time in summoning the bailiff and sent word to Chang's mother too. But as to how the fight started, I really have no idea. The man who was drinking with him must know that, Your Honour."

"In your testimony at the first trial you said you witnessed the fight," said the magistrate sternly. "How is it you're now retracting?"

"The funk that I was in made me muddle things up."

Once more the runners raised a warning shout.

Next the magistrate asked Wu Liang, "You were drinking with Hsueh Pan, weren't you? How did he come to strike the waiter? Out with the truth!"

"I was at home that day when this Mr. Hsueh asked me out to drink with him. Not liking the wine, he called for a different kind; and when Chang San refused to fetch it, he flared up. He dashed the wine over the waiter's face, and somehow or other the bowl struck his head. This I saw with my own eyes."

"Rubbish! At the autopsy, Hsueh Pan admitted to killing him with the bowl, and you confirmed that. Why are you eating your words now? Slap his face!"

With an answering shout the runners raised threatening hands.

"Hsueh Pan didn't fight Chang San — truly!" faltered Wu Liang. "His hand slipped — that's how the wine bowl hit Chang San's head. Please have the goodness to ask Hsueh Pan, Your Honour!"

The magistrate summoned Hsueh Pan.

"What feud was there between you and Chang San?" he demanded. "How did he die? Tell the truth!"

"Be merciful, Your Honour!" begged Hsueh Pan. "I truly never hit him. Because he wouldn't bring us better wine, I was emptying my bowl on the ground when my hand slipped and the bowl smashed in his head. I tried to stem the bleeding, but couldn't. Blood came pouring out, and presently he died. At the autopsy that day, for fear Your Honour would have me beaten, I said I'd struck him with the bowl. I beg Your Honour's pardon."

"You dolt!" bellowed the magistrate. "When first I asked why you struck him, you said you were angry because he wouldn't fetch fresh wine. But now you say it was an accident!"

Glaring, he threatened to have him beaten and tortured. But Hsueh Pan stuck to his statement.

The magistrate ordered the coroner, "Give me an honest report of the wounds you recorded in the autopsy that day."

"When I examined Chang San's corpse," said the coroner, "the only wound on the body was one gash on the skull caused by a porcelain object. Half an inch deep and 1.7 inches long, it had broken the skin and fractured 0.3 inch of the parietal bone. This wound was undoubtedly caused by a blow."

The magistrate checked this with the post-mortem record. Although knowing that the secretaries had altered this he did not dispute it but ordered them, hugger-mugger, to sign the new confession.

"Your Honour!" sobbed Mrs. Chang. "Last time, I heard there were other wounds. How are there none today?"

"You are talking nonsense," he fumed. "Here is the post-mortem record. Can't you read?"

He then summoned the dead man's uncle Chang Erh to ask him, "How many wounds were there on your nephew's body?"

"One on the head," replied Chang Erh hastily.

"Quite so," said the magistrate.

He made a secretary show Mrs. Chang the record, and told the bailiff and Chang Erh to point out the testimony of all the eye-witnesses that there had been no fight and that this was not murder but simply an accident. Having made them append their signatures, he consigned Hsueh Pan to jail until further notice, ordered the bailiff to take the others away, and declared the court adjourned. When Mrs. Chang wept and clamoured, he told runners to throw her out.

"It really was an accident," Chang Erh assured her. "How can we hold him to blame? Now His Honour has decided the case, don't make a scene."

Hsueh Ko, outside, was pleased when he heard the upshot. He sent word home but stayed there himself, waiting to pay the plaintiffs compensation once the verdict was announced. Then he overheard several passers-by in the street saying that an Imperial Concubine had died, and the Emperor had suspended court for three days. As this place was not far from the Imperial Sepulchres, the local magistrate had to prepare for the funeral and would probably be occupied for some time. Hsueh Ko, knowing that waiting there would serve no purpose, went to see Hsueh Pan in prison.

"Just wait with an easy mind, cousin," he urged him. "I'm going home but will be back before long."

To allay his mother's anxiety, Hsueh Pan gave him a note for her in which he had written:

> I am all right now. After a few more payments to the yamen I'll be able to return home. Don't begrudge spending money!

Then, leaving Li Hsiang to attend to things there, Hsueh
Ko went home. When he saw Aunt Hsueh, he told her how
the magistrate had been suborned and decided the case in their
favour, returning a verdict of death by misadventure.

"After paying the dead man's family more compensation, we
should have no further trouble," he concluded.

Aunt Hsueh said with relief, "I was hoping you'd come back
to see to our family affairs. I ought to go to thank the Chia
family. Besides, now that Imperial Concubine Chou has died
they have to go to court every day, leaving the house empty.
I was thinking of going over to help see to things and keep
your aunt company, but we have no one at home. You've
come just at the right time."

"It's because I heard outside that Imperial Consort *Chia* had
died that I hurried back. I did wonder, though, how that could
be, as she had been in good health."

"Last year she had one bout of illness, then recovered. This
time we hadn't heard that she was unwell, but we were told
that for several days the old lady in the Chia Mansion had been
poorly, and whenever she closed her eyes she saw Her Highness — that had everyone worried! Yet when they sent to
make inquiries, it seemed nothing was amiss. Then three nights
ago the old lady asked, 'How could Her Highness come all by
herself to see me?' No one took her seriously, thinking this
another hallucination brought on by illness. 'You don't believe me,' she said, 'but Yuan-chun herself just told me:
Prosperity and splendour soon run out; some way of escape
must be found!'

"Still no one paid much attention, thinking it natural for
an old soul of the worrying sort to have such notions. But the
very next morning, word came from the Palace that the Imperial Consort was mortally ill and all ladies of rank were
to go to pay their respects. That threw them into a fluster,
and they hurried to the Palace. Before their return, though,
word reached us here that it was Imperial Concubine *Chou*
who died. Just fancy, isn't it remarkable the way these rumours
outside and our suspicions at home coincided!"

Pao-chai put in, "It wasn't just the rumours outside that misled us, but the mere words 'Her Highness' set her family in a tizzy, and only afterwards did they find out the truth. The last couple of days their maids have come and told us that they knew earlier on it couldn't be *their* Royal Highness.

"'How can you be sure?' I asked.

"The answer was, 'A few years ago at New Year, someone in the provinces introduced to us a fortune-teller, said to be infallible. The old lady told us to put Her Highness' horoscope in with the maids' for him to work out.

"'He said, "There must be some mistake in the hour of birth of that girl born on the first of the first month. Otherwise, she must be of high degree — she couldn't be in this house."

"'Lord Cheng said, "Never mind whether there's a mistake or not. Just predict her fortune."

"'"She was born in the year *chia-shen*, the month *ping-yin*," he said. "Three of these characters signify 'demotion' and 'bankruptcy.' Only *shen* augurs well for officialdom and wealth; still that doesn't hold good for a girl who has to leave home. The day of her birth is *yi-mao*. In early spring the 'wood' element is in the ascendant. Although the two signs clash, the bigger the clash the better, just as in the case of good wood — the more you polish it, the greater its value. But most auspicious of all is the hour sign *hsin-ssu, hsin* meaning precious as gold, *ssu* high rank and wealth. Combined, they make up the 'winged horse' sign, and the day in this combination is so exceptionally auspicious that she should soar up like the moon in the sky and rank high in the Emperor's favour. If the hour of her birth is correct, she must be a sovereign lady."

"'Wasn't that an accurate forecast?' said the maids. 'We also remember his saying that unluckily her splendour would be short-lived. If a *mao* month happened to fall in a *yin* year, there would be a double clash and that would undermine her strength, just as in the case of good wood if it's carved too intricately. They forgot all those predictions and got worked up over nothing. But we remembered the other day and told our mistress. This isn't the *yin* year nor the *mao* month, is it?' "

Before Pao-chai could finish, Hsueh Ko said excitedly, "Never mind about other people. If you know of such a miraculous fortune-teller, quickly give me Hsueh Pan's horoscope — I'm sure he's under some evil star this year to have such a bad stroke of luck — and I'll get him to work out what's going to happen."

"That man came from the provinces," said Pao-chai. "We don't know whether he's still in the capital this year or not."

Pao-chai then helped her mother get ready to go to the Chia Mansion. At the time of Aunt Hsueh's arrival, the only ones of the family at home were Li Wan, Tan-chun and Hsi-chun, who asked her about Hsueh Pan's case.

"It won't be settled till the court has reported it to the higher-ups," Aunt Hsueh told them. "But it looks as if it won't be too serious."

They were relieved to hear this.

Tan-chun remarked, "Yesterday evening Her Ladyship, thinking back, said, 'Last time we had trouble at home, Aunt Hsueh rallied round. But now, with troubles of our own, we're in no position to help her.' This has been preying on her mind."

"I've been feeling bad myself," answered Aunt Hsueh. "But with your Cousin Pan in this fix and your Cousin Ko away to sort things out, there was only Pao-chai at home — and what could *she* do? I couldn't leave her before, especially not with my daughter-in-law so senseless. At present the magistrate there is so busy preparing the funeral of Imperial Concubine Chou, he has no time to wind up Pan's case. So your Cousin Ko has come back, making it possible for me to come over."

"Won't you stay here for a few days, aunt?" urged Li Wan.

"I'd like to stay and keep you company for a bit." Aunt Hsueh nodded. "But that would be rather lonely for Pao-chai."

"If that's what worries you, aunty, why not bring her over too?" suggested Hsi-chun.

Aunt Hsueh smiled.

"No, that wouldn't do."

"Why not?" asked Hsi-chun. "Didn't she stay here before?"

"You don't understand," put in Li Wan. "She has work to
do at home. How could she come?"

Hsi-chun, thinking this the truth, did not press the point.

As they were chatting, the Lady Dowager's party returned.

At sight of Aunt Hsueh, without stopping to exchange greetings, they asked her for news of Hsueh Pan, which she gave
them in full. When she described his encounter with Chiang
Yu-han, Pao-yu — though he could not ask in front of the
rest — knew that this was his friend the actor. He wondered,
"If he's back in the capital, why hasn't he come to see me?"
Pao-chai's absence puzzled him too, and he remained lost in
thought till Tai-yu's arrival cheered him up and stopped him
thinking about her. He and the girls stayed to dine with the
old lady, after which they dispersed, Aunt Hsueh staying on to
sleep in the old lady's annex.

Once home again, Pao-yu was changing his clothes when he
remembered the sash given him by Chiang Yu-han.

He asked Hsi-jen, "Do you still have that red sash which
you refused to wear the other year?"

"I put it away," she said. "Why do you ask?"

"Oh, for no special reason."

"Didn't you hear how Master Pan got charged with murder
through mixing with such riffraff? Why bring that up again?
You'd better study quietly and forget about such trifles, instead
of worrying your head over nothing."

"I'm not doing anything wrong, am I?" he demanded. "It
just happened to cross my mind. What does it matter whether
you have it or not? I ask one little question, and listen to the
way you run on!"

"I didn't mean to nag." She smiled. "But someone who
studies the classics and knows the rules of propriety ought to
aim high. Then, when the one you love comes, she'll be pleased
and respect you."

This reminded Pao-yu of something.

"Botheration!" he exclaimed. "There was such a crowd with
the old lady just now that I wasn't able to talk with Cousin

Lin. She paid me no attention either. By the time I left, she'd already gone. She must be in her place now. I'll drop in to see her." With that he started out.

"Don't be too long," said Hsi-jen. "I shouldn't have said that, getting you all worked up."

Pao-yu made no reply but went off with lowered head to Bamboo Lodge where Tai-yu, bending over her desk, was reading. He approached her with a smile.

"Have you been back long?"

"You cut me, so why should I stay there?" She asked archly.

"There were so many people talking, I couldn't get a word in. That's why I didn't speak to you."

He had been eyeing Tai-yu's book, but could not recognize the characters in it. Some looked familiar, others were combinations of various radicals and numerals.

In puzzled surprise he observed, "You're getting more erudite, cousin, all the time, reading something so esoteric!"

Tai-yu burst out laughing.

"What a scholar!" she teased. "Have you never seen a lute score before?"

"Of course I have. But how come I don't know any of those characters there? Do you understand them, cousin?"

"Would I read it if I didn't?"

"I don't believe you. I've never seen you playing a lute. We have several hanging in our study. The other year a scholar called, Chi Hao-ku I think his name was. My father asked him to play, but when he took the lutes down he said none of them was any good and proposed, 'If you like, sir, I'll bring my own lute some day to play for you.' But he never turned up again, probably because my father's no connoisseur. Why have you been hiding this accomplishment from me?"

"I'm no good at it really," she said. "The other day, feeling a bit better, I rummaged through the books on the big bookcase and found a set of lute scores which looked intriguing. It gives a lucid account of musical theory and clear instructions for playing. Luting was truly an art the men of old cultivated to

achieve tranquillity and integrity. In Yangchow, I heard it explained and learned to play, but then I gave up and that was the end of that. As the saying goes, 'Three days without playing, and fingers become thumbs.'

"The other day when I read those scores, there were no words to the music, only titles. Then I found a score somewhere else with words set to the music, which made it more interesting. It's really hard to play well. We read that when the musician Kuang played the lute, he could summon up wind and thunder, dragons and phoenixes. Even the sage Confucius learned from the musician Hsiang, and as soon as he played a piece he realized that this was King Wen's music. Then there was the musician who, playing of mountains and streams, met a man of true understanding. . . ." Here her eyelashes fluttered and, slowly, she lowered her head.

By now Pao-yu's enthusiasm was aroused.

"Dear cousin, how fascinating you make it sound!" he exclaimed. "But I can't read any of those characters. Won't you teach me a few of them."

"You don't have to be taught. Once I explain, you'll catch on."

"I'm a stupid fellow, so tell me what that character like 'big' (大) with a hook to it means, and the one that has a 'five' in it."

Tai-yu rejoined gaily, "The one made up of 'big' and 'nine' means that you must thumb the ninth note of the lute. The hook combined with 'five' means that you must pluck the fifth string with your right hand. They're not characters actually but musical signs, which are very easy to follow. Then there are various methods of fingering: whirring, stroking, plucking, damping, tapping, sliding, gliding, pushing and so forth."

Pao-yu was delighted.

"Good cousin, since you understand all about it, why don't we learn to play the lute?" he proposed.

"No," she said. "The men of old made music to induce self-restraint, curb passion, and suppress licence and extravagance. So anyone wanting to play the lute should choose some quiet, lofty studio either in some attic among forests and rocks, or on the summit of a hill or the bank of a stream. A fine, mild day should be chosen too, with a cool breeze and bright moon. Then one should burn incense and sit quietly, one's mind a blank, one's breathing regular, to become one with the spirit world and the Way. This is why the ancients said 'Hard to meet one who understands music.' When there are no understanding listeners, one should play to the cool breeze and bright moon, green pines and rugged rocks, wild monkeys and hoary cranes, conveying one's emotions in solitude so as not to do injustice to the lute.

"Then again, good fingering and execution are needed. Before playing one must dress fittingly in a loose cape or long robe like the men of old, to be worthy of this instrument of the sage's. This done, the hands should be washed, incense lit, and the lutist should sit lightly on the couch with the lute on his desk, its fifth note facing his heart. Only then, when mind and body are well-regulated, can the two hands be raised slowly. And whether soft or loud, fast or slow, the playing must be natural and dignified."

"We're only learning for fun!" exclaimed Pao-yu. "If you're so particular, it'll be too hard."

While they were talking Tzu-chuan had come in. She smiled at the sight of Pao-yu.

"So you're in good spirits today, Master Pao!" she remarked.

"My cousin's conversation is so illuminating, I could never tire of listening," he told her.

"That's not what I meant," said the maid. "You must have been in good spirits today to come here."

"While she was unwell, I was afraid to disturb her; besides, I had to go to school. That's why I gave the impression of keeping away. . . ."

"Miss Lin's only just better," Tzu-chuan interrupted. "As you know that, Master Pao, you should let her rest now and not wear her out."

"I was so intent on listening, I forgot that she might be tired."

"It's not tiring but fun to discuss such things," said Tai-yu with a smile. "I'm only afraid you may not understand."

"Well, anyway, I'll get it clear gradually." With that he stood up saying, "Really you'd better rest now. Tomorrow I'll ask Tan-chun and Hsi-chun to learn to play the lute for me too."

"You're too spoilt!" chuckled Tai-yu. "If we all learn to play but you don't understand, won't that be a case of playing a lute to an...."[1] Here she recollected herself and broke off.

"So long as you can play, I'll be only too glad to listen," said Pao-yu cheerfully. "I don't care if you think me an ox."

Tai-yu blushed and smiled while Tzu-chuan and Hsueh-yen laughed.

Pao-yu was on his way out when along came Chiu-wen with a younger maid carrying a small pot of orchids.

"Someone sent four pots of orchids to Her Ladyship," she announced. "They're too busy to enjoy them, so Her Ladyship told us to take one pot to Master Pao, one to Miss Lin."

Tai-yu saw that a few sprays had double blooms. The sight stirred her, but whether with joy or with grief she did not know as she stared at them blankly. Pao-yu's mind, however, was still set on the lute.

"Now that you have these orchids, cousin," he said, "you can play that tune *The Orchid*."[2]

This remark upset Tai-yu. Going back to her room she gazed at the orchids, reflecting, "In spring, plants put out fresh blooms and luxuriant leaves. I'm still young, yet already I'm like a plant in late autumn. If my wish comes true, I may gradually grow stronger. If not, I fear I'll be like a fading flower — how can I stand buffeting by rain and wind?" She could not hold back her tears.

---

[1] The phrase "playing a lute to an ox" has the same meaning as "casting pearls before swine."

[2] Confucius while on his travels through different states was often reviled. He was said to have played this tune to assert his integrity.

Tzu-chuan seeing this could not understand the reason. She thought, "Just now with Pao-yu here she was so happy. Why has looking at orchids made her sad again?"

She was anxiously wondering how to comfort her mistress when a maid arrived with a message from Pao-chai. To know what it was, read on.

CHAPTER 87

Moved by an Autumn Poem,
a Lutist Mourns the Past
One Practising Yoga Is
Possessed Through Lust

Pao-chai's maid, called in by Tai-yu, presented her young lady's greetings and letter, then was sent off to have some tea. Opening the letter, Tai-yu found written there:

> Born on an unlucky day in an ill-fated family, I have no sister and my mother is failing. Day and night there is bickering and brawling here, on top of which fearful disasters have assailed us thick and fast. At dead of night I toss and turn, overwhelmed by anxiety. Surely you who understand me must sympathize with me?
>
> I recall the Begonia Club we formed in autumn and how we enjoyed chrysanthemums and crabs in happy harmony. When I remember those lines:
>
> > Proud recluse, with what hermit are you taking refuge?
> > All flowers must bloom, what makes you bloom so late?
>
> I cannot but feel that the chrysanthemum's cold fragrance is like the two of us! Moved by these thoughts I have scribbled out four stanzas. Though simply an empty lament, they voice my distress.

I

Sad to see the passing of seasons,
Cool autumn is here once more;
My family is ill-fated,
Alone I dwell, my heart sore.
Day-lilies in the northern hall
Cannot make me forget my cares.
With no means to banish grief,
My heart despairs.

2

Low hang the clouds,
The autumn wind makes moan;
I pace the court
Through withered leaves turned roan.
Where can I go?
Lost, my past happiness.

Remembered joys
But fill me with distress.

3

The sturgeon has its tarn,
The crane its nest,
One lurking within scales,
One with long plumage dressed!
At my wit's end
I ask infinity:
High heaven, vast earth,
Who knows my misery?

4

The Milky Way is twinkling,
The atmosphere strikes chill;
The moon is sloping down the sky,
The jade clepsydra's still.
There is no sleep for aching hearts,
My grief I must impart;
Chanting again and yet again
For one who knows my heart.

Tai-yu after reading these lines was plunged in grief. She reflected, "The fact that Cousin Pao-chai didn't send these to anyone else, only to me, shows that we are kindred spirits."

She was lost in thought when someone outside called out, "Is Cousin Lin at home?"

Putting Pao-chai's letter away she asked who was there, even as Tan-chun, Hsiang-yun, Li Wen and Li Chi trooped in. They exchanged greetings while Hsueh-yen brought them tea, after which they chatted. Remembering the poems they had written that year on chrysanthemums, Tai-yu remarked:

"Pao-chai came over twice after moving out, yet these days — even when something happens — she doesn't come. Isn't that odd? I wonder whether she'll ever come back or not!"

"Why shouldn't she?" asked Tan-chun with a smile. "She's bound to eventually. . . . Just now, of course, she has too much to see to, what with her sister-in-law's cranky ways, aunty getting on in years, and on top of everything this trouble of Cousin Pan's. She hasn't the time to spare that she used to have."

Just then a gust of wind sprang up, dashing fallen leaves

against the window paper. By and by they smelt a faint
fragrance.

"Where does this scent come from?" they wondered. "What
can it be?" •

"It's like fragrant osmanthus," observed Tai-yu.

"Cousin Lin is talking like a southerner," teased Tan-chun.
"How could fragrant osmanthus bloom in the ninth month?'

"Quite so." Tai-yu laughed. "That's why I said it's *like*
fragrant osmanthus."

"You'd better pipe down, Tan-chun," put in Hsiang-yun.
"Don't you remember the lines:

> Ten *li* of lotus blooms,
> And in late autumn fragrant osmanthus seeds.

This is the season for it to blossom down south, only you've
never seen it. When you go south in future, you'll find out."

"Why should I go south?" asked Tan-chun. "Besides, I
knew that without your telling me."

Li Wen and Li Chi said nothing, only smiled.

"Don't be so sure about that, cousin," said Tai-yu. "As
the saying goes, 'Man is a wanderer, here today but gone tomorrow.' For example, how did *I* get here, when I'm a southerner?"

Hsiang-yun clapped her hands and laughed.

"Today Cousin Lin's floored Cousin Tan-chun!" she crowed.
"Not only is Tai-yu here from the south, the rest of us come
from different places too. Some are northerners, others were
born in the south and brought up in the north, still others were
brought up in the south and then came north. Our coming
together now in one place shows that everyone's fate is fixed.
Each individual is destined for different places."

The others nodded approval while Tan-chun merely smiled.
And after more casual talk the visitors left. When Tai-yu saw
them to the door they said, "You've only just got a bit better,
don't come out. We don't want you to catch cold."

She stood in the doorway exchanging civilities with them
until they left the compound, then went back to her room and

sat down. It was sunset now, birds were winging back to the hills. And Hsiang-yun's talk about the south filled Tai-yu's mind with fancies.

"If my parents were still alive . . . the south with spring flowers and autumn moonlight, limpid streams and lucent hills, Yangchow's twenty-four bridges and Six Dynasties' relics . . . no lack of maids to wait on me, and freedom to do as I pleased without worrying . . . a scented carriage and a painted barge, the red apricots and green signs of country taverns, my own mistress, respected by all. . . . Now, living with another family, although they treat me so well I have to watch my step all the time. . . . What sins did I commit in my last life to be so wretched now? In the words of the deposed king of Southern Tang,[1] 'Here I can only bathe my face in tears every day'. . . ." She lost herself in these reflections.

Tzu-chuan coming back supposed that her melancholy had been induced by the talk about south and north, which Tai-yu had taken to heart.

"The young ladies were here so long chatting, you must be tired, miss," she said. "I just told Hsueh-yen to get the kitchen to prepare you a bowl of cabbage soup with ham and dried shrimps, as well as some bamboo shoots and laver in it. Is that all right?"

"It will do."

"There'll be congee too."

Tai-yu nodded, then said, "I'd like you two to cook it, not leave it to the kitchen."

"Yes, we will," Tzu-chuan assured her. "I was afraid, too, that the kitchen wouldn't be clean enough. As for the soup, I asked Hsueh-yen to tell Mrs. Liu that it must be very clean. And Mrs. Liu said she'd get together the ingredients, then ask their Wu-erh to cook it on the small stove in their own room."

"It's not that I think them dirty," said Tai-yu. "But all this time I've been unwell I've had to depend on them for everything. So now they may resent these special instructions

---

[1] 937-975.

about soup and congee." Her eyes brimmed with tears again.

"Don't go imagining things, miss," urged Tzu-chuan. "You're the old lady's grand-daughter and she dotes on you. They're only too glad of a chance to please you. How can they possibly complain?"

Tai-yu nodded. Then she asked, "That Wu-erh you mentioned just now, isn't she the girl who was with Fang-kuan in Master Pao's place?"

"That's the one."

"Didn't I hear say she'd be coming to work in the Garden?"

"Yes, miss. But she fell ill, and when she got over it and was to come, there was all that trouble over Ching-wen and the rest, and so it got delayed."

"She looked to me a neat girl," Tai-yu said.

Now a serving-woman outside delivered the soup, Hsueh-yen went out to fetch it.

The woman reported, "Mrs. Liu says to tell your young lady that this was prepared by her Wu-erh. She didn't dare have it prepared in the big kitchen for fear your young lady might think it not clean enough."

Hsueh-yen voiced approval and brought the soup in. Tai-yu, who had heard this exchange, made Hsueh-yen tell the woman to thank them for their trouble, after which the latter left. Then Hsueh-yen set Tai-yu's bowl and chopsticks on the small table.

"We've those five-spice pickles from the south too," she said. "Would you like some with sesame oil and vinegar?"

"All right, if it's not too much trouble."

When the congee was served, Tai-yu ate half a bowl and two spoonfuls of the soup, but then gave up. Two maids cleared and wiped the table, took it away, then brought in the small table which she liked to use.

Tai-yu, having rinsed her mouth and washed her hands, asked Tzu-chuan, "Have you added fresh incense?"

"I'll do it now, miss."

"You two may as well finish up the congee and soup; they

taste quite good and they're clean. I'll see to the incense myself."

The two maids agreed and sat down to supper in the outer room.

After adding fresh incense, Tai-yu settled down to read when a west wind sprang up and set all the trees rustling. Presently the iron chimes swinging from the eaves raised a loud tinkling too. Hsueh-yen, her supper finished, now came back.

"It's grown cold," Tai-yu told her. "Have you aired my fur clothes, as I asked you the other day?"

"Yes, all of them."

"Bring me something to put over my shoulders."

Hsueh-yen fetched in a bundle of fur-lined clothes and unwrapped it for Tai-yu to make her choice. The first thing her eye fell on was a silk wrapper. Undoing this, she found the old handkerchiefs Pao-yu had sent her when he was ill, on which she had written poems — they still had her tear-stains on them. Wrapped inside were the scented pouch which she had cut up, a fan-case and the tassel from Pao-yu's Jade of Spiritual Understanding. These had been in the chest when it was opened to sun the clothes, and Tzu-chuan for fear that they might get mislaid had put them in the bundle.

The sight of these things made Tai-yu forget about putting on something warmer. She picked up the two handkerchiefs and gazed blankly at her old poems, then started weeping. Tzu-chuan coming in now saw Hsueh-yen standing there stock-still, holding a felt wrapper of clothes. The mutilated pouch, the fan-case in two or three pieces and the snipped off tassel were on the little table; and Tai-yu, clutching two old handkerchiefs with writing on them, was gazing at them in tears. Truly:

> When the sad meet with sadness,
> New tears mingle with the old!

Tzu-chuan realized that these things had re-opened old wounds, making her young mistress grieve over the past, and guessed it would be useless to reason with her.

"Why look at those, miss?" she asked, smiling. "They'll only remind you of the pranks Master Pao and you got up to when you were young, quarrelling one day and making it up the next. If he'd been as well-mannered then as he is now, these things would never have got spoilt."

To Tzu-chuan's surprise, this banter reminded Tai-yu even more of her first years here. Big tears streamed down her cheeks.

"Hsueh-yen's standing waiting," Tzu-chuan reminded her. "Do put on something warmer."

Then at last Tai-yu put down the handkerchiefs. Tzu-chuan promptly picked them up to wrap them up with the pouch and other things and whisk them away.

Tai-yu, draping a fur-lined jacket over her shoulders, went disconsolately to the outer room to sit down. Turning her head she noticed that she had not yet put away Pao-chai's poems. She picked them up, re-read them twice, then sighed:

"Though our positions are different, we're one in our distress. I may as well write four verses too and set them to music, to sing them to a lute accompaniment. Tomorrow I'll copy them out and send them to her by way of reply."

She told Hsueh-yen to fetch the brush and ink-stone from her desk, then wrote four stanzas, after which she got out the lute scores and set her verses to the melodies *Quiet Orchid* and *Longing for a Worthy Man*. She made a copy to send to Pao-chai, then told Hsueh-yen to fetch from the chest the short lute she had brought north with her. Having tuned the strings she practised some finger exercises. And as Tai-yu was so intelligent and had learned to play a little in the south, although out of practice she soon regained her old skill. She played until it was late, then called Tzu-chuan in to clear up and went to bed.

To return to Pao-yu. He got up and dressed the next morning and was on his way to school with Pei-ming when Mo-yu came running towards them, grinning from ear to ear.

"Master Pao, you've got off cheap today!" cried Mo-yu.

"The tutor's not at school; it's a holiday."

"Is that true?" demanded Pao-yu.

"If you don't believe me, look! Can't you see Master Huan and Master Lan coming?"

Sure enough, Pao-yu saw the two boys accompanied by their pages laughing and chatting together as they approached. At sight of him they stood at respectful attention.

"Why are you coming back?" he asked.

Huan answered, "The tutor has some business today, so he's given us one day's holiday. We're to go back tomorrow."

Pao-yu went to report this to his grandmother and father, then returned to Happy Red Court.

"Why are you back?" asked Hsi-jen.

He told her the reason, and after sitting down for a short time started out.

"Where are you off to?" she wanted to know. "What's the hurry? You've just been given a day off. I advise you to have a rest."

He halted then with lowered head and said, "You're right, of course. But it's so seldom I get a free day, why shouldn't I have some fun? Do have a heart!"

He looked so pathetic that Hsi-jen chuckled, "All right, go wherever you like, sir!"

Just then lunch was served, however, and Pao-yu had to eat. But after gobbling his food and rinsing his mouth he dashed off to find Tai-yu. When he reached her gate, he saw Hsueh-yen hanging out some handkerchiefs in the courtyard.

"Has your mistress had her meal?" he asked.

"She had half a bowl of congee in the morning, but didn't want any lunch. She's taking a nap now. You'd better come back later, Master Pao."

Pao-yu had to turn back. He did not know where to go until it occurred to him that he had not seen Hsi-chun for several days; so he strolled over to Smartweed Breeze Cot. Stopping outside her window, he discovered that all was quiet and thought he had better not enter as she must be having a siesta too. He was on the point of leaving when he heard a faint sound inside, but could not make out what it was. He stopped to listen, and after some time heard a chinking sound. Still he could not make out what it was.

"If you move that piece here," said a voice inside, "what about your position *there*?"

At that he realized they were playing draughts, but could not identify the voice. Then he heard Hsi-chun say, "What do I care? If you take that piece of mine, I'll move here. If you take this piece, I'll move there. I shall still be able to encircle that place in the end."

"What if I do this?" asked the other.

"Ah!" exclaimed Hsi-chun. "I didn't guard against a thrust like that!"

The second voice sounded familiar, but Pao-yu knew it was not one of his cousins'. Assuming that the other player could not be an outsider, he softly raised the portière and went in, only to discover that the visitor was no other than the "outsider" Miao-yu of Green Lattice Nunnery. Seeing this, he dared not disturb them; and the two girls, intent on their game, did not notice him. Pao-yu stood beside them watching.

Miao-yu, her head lowered, asked, "Don't you want this corner?"

"Of course I do," said Hsi-chun. "But your pieces there are all dead, so what have I to fear?"

"Don't be so sure," said Miao-yu. "Wait and see."

"I'll attack here and see what you can do."

Miao-yu, smiling, linked her pieces in one continuous border and counter-attacked, threatening Hsi-chun's corner.

"This is called 'pulling off the boot,'" she chuckled.

Before Hsi-chun could reply Pao-yu burst out laughing, making the two girls start.

"Why do such a thing?" exclaimed Hsi-chun. "Coming in without a word to startle us! How long have you been there?"

"Quite a while. I've been watching you fight for that corner."

He greeted Miao-yu and said to her with a smile, "It's rarely that you leave your saintly abode. Why have you descended today to the mundane world?"

Miao-yu flushed up but said nothing, lowering her head to keep her eyes on the board. Conscious of his gaffe, Pao-yu tried to cover it up.

"You who have renounced the world are not like us vulgar worldlings," he said with a conciliatory smile. "First of all, your hearts are at peace, so you are more spiritual and have quiet perception. . . ."

He was running on like this when Miao-yu glanced up at him, then lowered her head again, blushing furiously. Pao-yu, cold-shouldered like this, sat down sheepishly at one side.

Hsi-chun wanted to finish the game, but after a while Miao-yu said, "Let's play some other time." She stood up to smooth down her clothes, but then sat down again and asked Pao-yu fatuously, "Where did you come from?"

He had been waiting for her to address him so that he could make up for his earlier tactlessness. However, it occurred to him that she might be testing his understanding. He reddened and could not answer. With a faint smile Miao-yu turned to talk to Hsi-chun.

"Is that so hard to answer, Second Brother?" chuckled Hsi-chun. "Have you never heard the saying, 'I came from where I've been'? Why blush like that as if she were a stranger?"

Miao-yu took this dig personally. Her heart misgave her and her cheeks burned — she knew she must be red in the face too. In her embarrassment she stood up and said, "I've been here so long, I must be getting back to my nunnery."

As Hsi-chun knew her ways, instead of pressing her to stay she saw her to the door.

"It's so long since last I was here," said Miao-yu, "I may not be able to find my way back with all those twists and turns."

"Why not let me show you the way?" Pao-yu volunteered.

"Thank you, sir. Please lead on!"

Taking their leave of Hsi-chun, they left Smartweed Breeze Cot and followed a winding path which took them near Bamboo Lodge. Suddenly they heard a twanging.

"Where does that luting come from?" Miao-yu asked.

"It must be Cousin Lin playing the lute."

"Can she play too? Why did she never mention it?"

Pao-yu repeated what Tai-yu had said to him.

"Let's call on her," he proposed.

"One can only listen to luting, not look at it — that's always been the rule," she objected.

"I'm a vulgar person, I know," he said with a grin.

Being outside Bamboo Lodge now, they seated themselves on an artificial hill to listen quietly to the clear music. Tai-yu was chanting softly:

> The wind is soughing, the days drawing in,
> Far away, lost in thought, the lovely maid;
> I gaze towards my home — where is it?
> Tears stain my dress beside the balustrade.

After a pause she continued:

> Far-stretching hills, long rivers,
> Bright moonlight shining on my window-sill;
> Sleepless I lie beneath faint Milky Way,
> Clad in thin silk; the wind and dew are chill.

As she paused again, Miao-yu remarked, "The first stanza used the *chin* rhyme, the second the *yang* rhyme. Let's hear what follows."

Then they heard fresh chanting inside:

> Your lot is not of your choosing,
> And mine is filled with care;
> You and I are kindred spirits,
> Revering the ancients that we may not err.

Miao-yu commented, "Another stanza, but how mournful!"

"Though I don't understand music, it *does* sound too sad," Pao-yu agreed.

Inside, they heard the strings being re-tuned.

"The main string is too high!" Miao-yu exclaimed. "It may not fit that scale."

Inside, Tai-yu resumed:

> Life in this world is but a speck of dust,
> Karma ordains all mortals' destiny;
> If Karma rules, then why repine?
> Would that my heart were pure as the moon in the sky!

The colour draining from her face Miao-yu exclaimed, "Why did she suddenly play such a high note? It's enough to crack metal or stone! This is too extreme."

"What do you mean?"

"I doubt if she can keep it up."

Even as she said this, they heard the main string snap. Miao-yu stood up and hastily started off.

"What's the matter?" Pao-yu asked.

"You'll know later; don't talk about it."

With that she left, and Pao-yu went back to Happy Red Court feeling puzzled and depressed.

Miao-yu returned to the nunnery, and the old deaconess waiting for her there closed the gate. She sat down for a while to chant the sutra for the day, and after supper burned incense and worshipped Buddha. This done, she dismissed the deaconess for the night. As her couch and back-rest were ready, she quietly let down the curtain and sat cross-legged to meditate, banishing all frivolous thoughts to concentrate on the truth.

Some time after midnight, she heard a thud on the roof. Suspecting a thief, she left her couch and went out to the veranda. She saw cloud streamers in the sky and moonlight limpid as water. As it was not yet too cold, she stood there alone for a while by the balustrade till a sudden caterwauling broke out on the roof. Abruptly recalling Pao-yu's remarks that day, her heart started beating faster and her face burned. Hastily suppressing her feelings, she returned to her cell and sat down again on the couch.

But her fancy, now running as wild as galloping horses, made her imagine that the couch was rocking and she was no longer in the nunnery. Many young lordlings had come to ask for her hand and, against her wishes, go-betweens were tugging and pushing her into a carriage. Then brigands kidnapped her and threatened her with swords and clubs, so that she screamed for help.

This aroused the novices and deaconess, who came with

torches to see what was the matter. Finding Miao-yu with outflung arms, frothing at the mouth, they hastily woke her up.

Her eyes staring, crimson in the face, she shouted, "How dare you thugs attack one under Buddha's protection!"

Frightened out of their wits they assured her, "It's us! Wake up!"

"I want to go home," she cried. "If there's any kind soul among you, take me back!"

"You're here in your own cell," said the deaconess, then told the novices to pray to Kuan-yin and ask for an oracle. They opened the book of oracles at a passage indicating that she had "offended a spirit in the southwest corner."

"That's right!" one of them exclaimed. "No one lives in the southwest corner of Grand View Garden, so there are bound to be evil spirits there."

They busied themselves getting soup for her and boiled water. And the novice who took the best care of Miao-yu, being a southerner herself, sat on the couch and put one arm around her.

Miao-yu turned to her and demanded, "Who are you?"

"Don't you know me?"

Miao-yu looked more carefully. "So it's you!" she cried, hugging the novice to her. "If you don't save me, mother," she sobbed, "I'm done for!"

The novice tried to bring her to her senses. She massaged her while the deaconess brought tea, and not till dawn did Miao-yu fall asleep. They sent for doctors then. One diagnosed her trouble as debility of the spleen brought on by worry; one attributed it to a hot humour in the blood; another to offending evil spirits; and yet another diagnosed a chill. They could not reach agreement.

Later they called in another doctor who after examining the patient asked, "Did she practise yoga?"

"Yes, every night," answered the deaconess.

"Was this a sudden fit last night?"

"That's right."

"Then it came on because evil thoughts crossed her mind and kindled a hot humour."

"Is it dangerous?"

"It can be cured, as luckily she did not meditate very long, so the evil did not penetrate too deep."

He prescribed some medicine to alleviate the hot humour in her heart, and after taking it Miao-yu felt some relief.

When young dandies heard this story, they spread all manner of rumours and commented, "She's too young — romantic and intelligent too — to stand such an austere life. Who knows what lucky man will get hold of her in future?"

After a few days, although Miao-yu felt better, she was still not back to normal, her mind remaining confused.

One day, Hsi-chun was sitting quietly when Tsai-ping came in to ask, "Do you know, miss, what happened to Sister Miao-yu?"

"No. What?"

"I heard Miss Hsing and Madam Chu discussing it yesterday. The night after she went back from playing chess with you, some evil spirit took possession of her, and she started raving that bandits had come to kidnap her! Even now she hasn't recovered. Isn't that extraordinary?"

Hsi-chun remained silent, thinking, "Though Miao-yu is so chaste, she's not severed all earthly ties yet. It's too bad that I live in a family like this and can't become a nun. If *I* renounced the world, how could evil thoughts assail me? Not one would cross my mind — all desires would be stilled!" Then, suddenly struck by an idea, she chanted:

> In the beginning Creation had no abode;
> Where, then, should we abide?
> Since we come from the void
> We should return to the void.

She told a maid to burn incense and sat quietly for a while, then looked up the treatises on draughts by Kung Jung,[1] Wang Chi-hsin[2] and others. After reading a few pages, she was not

---

[1] 153-208.
[2] Of the Tang Dynasty.

impressed by such gambits as "thick foliage enfolds crabs" and "yellow hawks seize a hare," while the "thirty-six ways to enclose a corner" struck her as too hard to remember. She was intrigued, however, by "ten galloping dragons" and was thinking this over when someone entered her compound calling "Tsai-ping!"

If you want to know who it was, read the following chapter.

CHAPTER 88

Pao-yu, to Please His Grandmother, Praises a Fatherless Boy
Chia Chen, to Uphold Household Discipline, Has Unruly Servants Whipped

As Hsi-chun was studying the treatise on draughts, she heard Tsai-ping's name called in the courtyard and recognized Yuan-yang's voice. Tsai-ping went out to usher in Yuan-yang, who had brought a young maid carrying a small yellow silk bundle.

"What brings you here?" asked Hsi-chun with a smile.

"The old lady will be eighty-one next year, miss. As that's nine times nine, she's going to offer sacrifices for nine days and nine nights, and she's vowed to have three thousand six hundred and fifty-one copies of the *Diamond Sutra* made. This work has been given to copyists outside. But as people say this sutra, like Taoist canons, is only the shell of truth whereas the *Prajnaparamitra Sutra* is the kernel, this second sutra must be included as well to make the offering more meritorious. Since the *Prajnaparamitra Sutra* is the more important, and Kuan-yin is a female bodhisattva, the old lady wants some mistresses and young ladies of the family to make three hundred and sixty-five copies of it, as an act of reverence. In our family — except for Madam Lien who's too busy with household affairs and, besides, can't write — all the ladies are going to write copies, some more, some less. Even Madam Chen and the concubines of the East Mansion will be doing their share. So of course all the ladies over here must join in."

Hsi-chun nodded. "Other tasks may be beyond me, but I've every confidence when it comes to copying sutras. Just put your things down, and now have some tea."

Yuan-yang placed the little bundle on the table and sat down with her. Tsai-ping brought them tea.

"Will you do some copying too?" Hsi-chun asked Yuan-yang.

"You must be joking, miss! In the past I might have managed, but these last three or four years have you ever seen me with a brush in my hand?"

"Still, it would be a meritorious deed."

"Well, I'm doing something else. Every night after helping the old lady to bed, I pray to Buddha and set aside a grain of rice for each time I invoke his name. I've been doing that for more than three years, and saved the rice. When the old lady makes her sacrifice, I shall add my rice to it for alms as an offering to Buddha, to show my devotion."

"In that case," joked Hsi-chun, "when the old lady becomes Kuan-yin you'll be her Dragon Maid."[1]

"How could I aspire to that? It's true, though, that it's the old lady and nobody else that I want to serve. I don't know if this was predestined!"

Making ready to go, she told the little maid to unwrap the bundle and take out its contents.

"This stack of paper is for copying the sutra. And this" — she held up a bundle of Tibetan incense — "is for you to light while copying."

Hsi-chun agreed to this.

Yuan-yang, leaving her, went back with the little maid to make her report to the Lady Dowager. Finding her playing *shuang-lu*[2] with Li Wan, she stood and watched. Li Wan made some lucky throws and captured several of the old lady's pieces, at which Yuan-yang inwardly chuckled.

Then in came Pao-yu with two miniature cages made of thin bamboo splints, containing green crickets.

"I heard you're not sleeping well at night, madam," he

---

[1] The daughter of a legendary Dragon King. She was said to have gone at the age of eight to pay her respects to Sakyamuni Buddha, and then to have become a bodhisattva.

[2] A dice game for two players using a special board and sixteen counters apiece.

said. "So I'll leave you these to amuse you."

"Don't go fooling around now your father's away!" she warned him with a smile.

"I haven't been fooling around."

"If you haven't been playing truant from school, how did you get hold of these?"

"I didn't get them myself. This morning, our teacher set Huan and Lan some couplets to write. Huan couldn't do them, so I secretly helped him. When he recited them the teacher was pleased and commended him. He bought these for me to show his gratitude. That's why I'm making you a present of them."

"Doesn't he study every day? Why can't he write a couplet? If he can't, your Grandad Ju should slap his face to shame him! You're bad enough yourself. Remember, when your father was at home, how devilish scared you were every time he made you write poems. But now you're bragging again. Of course, Huan is even worse, getting other people to do his work for him, then thinking up ways to bribe them. A child of his age up to such dirty tricks, and with no sense of shame either! What sort of creature will he grow up to be?"

Everyone in the room burst out laughing.

"What about young Lan?" the old lady asked. "Did he manage to write the couplets? Or did Huan do them for him, as Lan's smaller?"

"No," said Pao-yu with a smile. "Lan did them himself."

"I don't believe you. You must have been up to more monkey business. You're getting above yourself nowadays — a camel in a flock of sheep — being the eldest and the one who can write!"

"He really wrote them himself," insisted Pao-yu, smiling. "And our teacher praised him, saying he'll go far in future. If you don't believe me, madam, you can send for him and test him yourself; then you'll know."

"Well, if that's truly the case I'm very glad. I was just afraid you were fibbing. If he's up to writing couplets, the boy should get somewhere in future." Her eye fell on Li Wan, reminding her of Chia Chu. "That means your sister-in-law hasn't brought him up in vain since your brother Chu died. He'll become the mainstay of the house some day in place of his father." She could not refrain from tears.

Li Wan was very moved too, but held back her own tears to comfort the old lady.

"This is all owing to the virtue of our Old Ancestress," she said with a smile. "We all benefit from your good fortune. If he lives up to your expectations, madam, how lucky we shall be! You should be pleased, Old Ancestress, not sad." She turned to tell Pao-yu, "You mustn't praise your nephew like that in future. What does a child of his age understand? I know you just meant to be kind, but he has no sense. If he gets conceited and cocky, he won't make any progress."

"Quite right," the old lady agreed. "Still, he's too small to be driven too hard. A little boy is timid. If you force him too hard his health may suffer and he won't be able to study. Then all your efforts would be wasted."

At this, Li Wan could no longer restrain herself. Tears streamed down her cheeks, and she hastily wiped her eyes.

Chia Huan and Chia Lan now came in to pay their respects to the old lady. Lan greeted his mother too, after which he came over and stood at attention beside his great-grandmother.

"Just now," she said, "I heard from your uncle that your teacher commended you for writing a good couplet."

Lan said nothing, only smiled. Then Yuan-yang came to announce that dinner was ready.

"Ask Aunt Hsueh to come over," ordered the old lady.

Hu-po sent to Lady Wang's place to deliver this message. Pao-yu and Huan withdrew then while Su-yun and some young maids cleared away the dice game. Li Wan stayed to wait on the old lady, and Lan remained by his mother.

"You two had better eat with me," said the old lady.

Li Wan assented, and the table was laid.

Then a maid came in to announce, "Her Ladyship told me to report that Madam Hsueh has been shuttling back and forth these days and can't come to see you today, madam, because after lunch she went home."

Thereupon the old lady made Lan sit beside her.

Dinner at an end, the old lady washed and rinsed her mouth, then lay down on the couch. They were chatting together when a young maid came in and whispered to Hu-po. The latter reported to the Lady Dowager:

"Master Chen of the East Mansion has come to pay his respects."

"Tell him not to trouble, and thank him. As he must be tired out with family business, he should go and rest."

This message passed on by a maid to the serving-woman outside was relayed to Chia Chen, who withdrew.

The next day, Chia Chen came over to attend to certain business. Servants at the gate reported on several matters, one of them announcing, "The bailiff of our farm has brought some produce."

"Where's the list?" demanded Chia Chen.

The man presented it, and he saw that it comprised simply fresh fruits, vegetables, game and the like.

"Which is the steward in charge of these things?" he asked.

One of the gate-keepers replied, "Chou Jui."

Then Chia Chen ordered Chou Jui, "Check the list and take the produce inside. I'll have a copy of the list made later, to see that the accounts tally. Tell the kitchen to add a few dishes to the lowest-grade meal for the fellow who brought these things, and tip him according to the usual practice."

Chou Jui assented and had the things delivered to Hsi-feng's compound. After handing over the list and the produce he left. Before long he returned to ask Chia Chen, "Have you checked the amounts of the things that just arrived, sir?"

"What time do I have? I gave you the list to check."

"I have, sir. There's nothing short, and of course nothing extra. As you've kept a copy, sir, please call the messenger in to ask whether this is the genuine list or faked."

"What are you driving at? Only a little fruit, what does it

matter? And I'm not doubting your word."

Just at this point, Pao Erh came in and kowtowed.

"Please, sir, let me go back to working outside," he requested.

"What have the two of you been up to now?" demanded Chia Chen.

"I can't speak out here," said Pao Erh.

"Who's asking you to speak?"

"Why should I stay here — getting in people's way?"

Chou Jui cut in, "I handle the rents and the income and expenditure of the farm — a matter of three to five hundred thousand a year — and the master and mistresses have never found fault, not to say over a few trifles like these. Yet, judging by Pao Erh, we've eaten up all our masters' farms and properties!"

It was clear to Chia Chen that Pao Erh had been making trouble and he had better dismiss him.

"Clear off, quick!" he ordered, then turned to Chou Jui. "You needn't say any more either. Go and attend to your business."

Then the two men went away.

Chia Chen was relaxing in his study when he heard a great uproar at the gate. He sent to find out what had happened and the gate-keepers reported:

"Pao Erh is fighting with Chou Jui's adopted son."

"And who may that be?" he asked.

"A rascal called Ho San, who gets drunk and brawls every day at home and often comes to sit at our gate. When he heard Pao Erh scrapping with Chou Jui he joined in."

"Outrageous!" swore Chia Chen. "Have Pao Erh and that fellow Ho San tied up. Where is Chou Jui?"

"When they started fighting, he slipped away."

"Bring him here! This is the limit!"

The servants assented.

In the midst of this commotion Chia Lien came back and his cousin described what had happened.

"Scandalous!" exclaimed Chia Lien.

He sent more servants in search of Chou Jui, who came, knowing he was in for it.

"Tie them all up!" Chia Chen ordered.

Chia Lien fumed at Chou Jui, "Your earlier dispute could have been overlooked, and the master had already dismissed you both. Why start another fight outside? The two of you fighting was bad enough, but you dragged in that bastard Ho San as well to make trouble. And instead of checking them, you cleared off!" He gave Chou Jui several kicks.

"Just beating Chou Jui is not enough," said Chia Chen.

He ordered his men to give Pao Erh and Ho San fifty lashes apiece, then drive them out, after which he and Chia Lien discussed other business.

The servants, in private, aired different views about this. Some said Chia Chen was biased, unable to settle disputes, others that he was a debauchee.

"Earlier on, when the Yu sisters were carrying on in that shameless way, wasn't it he who persuaded Master Lien to take Pao Erh on?" one pointed out. "Now it must be because he's lost interest in Pao Erh's wife that he's found fault with Pao Erh."

Thus they argued the matter at length.

Now Chia Cheng's post in the Ministry of Works enabled his domestics to enrich themselves. And Chia Yun, getting wind of this, hoped to procure some lucrative job himself. He approached contractors outside, and after coming to terms with them bought some fashionable embroidery with which to persuade Hsi-feng to secure him a commission.

Hsi-feng, at home, heard from the maids that Chia Chen and her husband, angry with some of the servants, were having them beaten. She was about to send to find out what had happened, when Chia Lien came in and told her the whole story.

"It's a small matter in itself," was Hsi-feng's comment, "but we'll have to put a stop to such behaviour. Our family still counts as enjoying good fortune, but even so these underlings dare fight! Later on, when the younger generation takes over, they'll get quite out of hand. The other year, in the East Mansion, I saw Chiao Ta lying as drunk as a lord at the foot of the steps cursing wildly. Swearing at high and low he was, quite regardless! He may have served his first master well, but still he's only a servant and ought to show some respect. Your Cousin Chen's wife — if you don't mind my saying so — is so easy-going that all her staff are spoilt and quite above themselves. And now there's this fellow Pao Erh! I understood that he was a favourite with you and your Cousin Chen, so why did you beat him today?"

Embarrassed by this question, Chia Lien sheepishly changed the subject, then left her on the pretext that he had business.

Hung-yu came in next to report that Chia Yun was outside asking to see her.

"Invite him in," said Hsi-feng, wondering why he had come.

Hung-yu went out and smiled at Chia Yun, who hastily stepped closer.

"Did you give her my message, miss?" he asked.

Blushing she said, "You seem to have a lot of business, sir!"

"How often have I troubled you before?" he protested. "Only once, the other year when you were in Uncle Pao's place. . . ."

For fear of detection she cut him short by asking, "Did you see the handkerchief I left you that time, sir?"

Chia Yun was overjoyed by this question. But before he could answer a young maid came out, and he and Hung-yu hurried towards the house, walking side by side, not keeping their distance from each other.

"When I come out presently," whispered Chia Yun, "I want you to see me out. I've something amusing to tell you."

Hung-yu blushed and glanced at him, but did not answer. When they reached Hsi-feng's room, she went in first to announce him, then came out again and raised the portière. She beckoned him in, but said deliberately, "Madam Lien asks you to come in, Master Yun."

Smiling, he followed her into the room and paid his respects to Hsi-feng.

"My mother sends her greetings," he added.

Hsi-feng inquired after his mother too, then asked, "What can I do for you?"

"I've never forgotten your past goodness to me, aunt, and have always wished I could show my gratitude. Only I was afraid you might suspect I had ulterior motives. Now I've brought you a little gift for the Double-Ninth Festival. Of course you lack for nothing here, but this is just to show your nephew's respect. I only hope you'll condescend to accept it."

Hsi-feng smiled. "Sit down if you have something to say."

Chia Yun perched on the edge of a chair, hastily placing his present on the table beside him.

"You're not all that well off," said Hsi-feng. "Why waste money on this? And I don't need such things. So tell me honestly what you've come here for."

"I didn't have anything special in mind, just wanted to show how I appreciate your kindness to me, aunt," he said with a smirk.

"That's no way to talk," she answered. "You're badly off, I know that perfectly well; so why should you spend money on me for nothing? If you want me to accept this, you must tell me your reason clearly. If you beat about the bush like this, I won't take it."

Chia Yun had no choice but to come out with the truth. Standing up with an obsequious smile he said, "Well, it's not too high-flown, what I'm hoping. The other day I heard that Lord Cheng was in charge of the construction of the Imperial Sepulchres. I have several friends who have done work of this kind and are most reliable; so please, aunt, will you recommend us to the master? If you get us a couple of contracts, I'll be eternally grateful! And if you need me for anything at home, I'll serve you to the best of my ability."

"On other matters I have some say," she replied. "But these government jobs are fixed by officials above and seen to by the secretaries and runners under them, so that other people can hardly get a look-in. Even our servants only go along to wait on the master. Your uncle Lien too only goes there in connection with family business — he can't interfere with public works.

"As for our family affairs, as soon as one trouble's settled another crops up. Not even Master Chen can keep order here. So how could you, young as you are and junior in status, possibly cope with these people? Besides, those cushy government jobs are nearly finished: they're simply spinning them out. Can't you make do by finding other commissions at home? This is honest advice. Go back and think it over and you'll see that. I appreciate your offer, but take these things back and return them to whomever you got them from."

Just then in came some nannies with little Chiao-chieh, tricked out in embroidered silks, her arms filled with toys. She went up to her mother, smiling, to prattle to her. At once Chia Yun sprang to his feet.

Beaming, he asked, "Is this my younger sister? Do you want something nice?"

The child burst out crying, and he quickly stepped back.

"Don't be frightened, darling," said Hsi-feng, taking Chiao-chieh on her lap. "This is your big Cousin Yun. Why be shy?"

"What a pretty child!" he exclaimed. "She's another who's destined to enjoy great good fortune."

Chiao-chieh turned to look at him, then started crying again. When this had happened several times, Chia Yun saw that it was impossible to stay and got up to take his leave.

"Take those things with you," Hsi-feng reminded him.

"They're only trifles, aunt. Won't you do me the honour of accepting them?"

"If you won't take them, I'll have them sent back to your place. Don't behave this way, Yun. It's not as if you were an outsider. When there's some opening I'll certainly send for you; but if there's none, what can I do about it? These things are quite superfluous."

Seeing her so adamant he reddened and said, "In that case,

aunt, I'll look for something more acceptable to show my respect."

Hsi-feng told Hung-yu, "Take those things and see Master Yun out."

Chia Yun left thinking to himself, "People call her a martinet, and she certainly is one! There's no chink in her armour — she's as hard as nails. No wonder she's never had a son. And this Chiao-chieh is even odder, treating me as if we'd been enemies in some past life. I'm really out of luck — all this trouble for nothing!"

As Chia Yun had been rebuffed, Hung-yu was upset too as she followed him out. Chia Yun took the bundle from her and unwrapped it, then chose two pieces of embroidery to slip to her. But Hung-yu thrust them back.

"Don't, sir!" she said. "If the mistress knew, it would look bad for both of us."

"Just take them. What is there to be afraid of? How could she possibly know? If you refuse, that means you look down on me."

Hung-yu accepted then with a smile but said, "Why should I want these things of yours? What is this anyway?" She blushed crimson again.

"It's the thought that counts," he chuckled. "Besides, these aren't worth much."

They had now reached the compound gate, and Chia Yun tucked the rest of the embroidery inside his jacket while Hung-yu urged him to leave.

"If there's anything you want, just come and ask me," she said. "Now that I'm working here it's easy to find me."

Chia Yun nodded. "It's too bad your mistress is such a martinet that I can't call too often. Anyway you must understand what I meant just now. I've something more to tell you when I have the chance."

Blushing all over her face she answered, "Go now. You must call more often in future. You shouldn't have kept at such a distance from her."

"Right."

Then Chia Yun left the compound. Hung-yu stood at the gate watching till he was out of sight before finally turning back.

Hsi-feng in her room now ordered dinner and asked the maids if they had prepared any congee. Some went to ask, returning with the answer, "Yes, we have."

"Get a couple of southern dishes preserved in liquor."

"Very good, madam," said Chiu-tung, and sent some young maids for these.

Ping-erh now stepped forward and said, "It had slipped my mind, but at noon today while you were with the old lady, the abbess of Water Moon Convent sent a nun to ask for two jars of southern pickles, madam. She wants a few months' allowance advanced too, because she isn't well. I asked the nun what was wrong, and she said the abbess has been unwell for four or five days. The other night some acolytes and novices refused to blow out the light when they went to bed. She scolded them several times, but they paid no attention. When she saw that the lamp was still burning after midnight, she told them to blow it out; but as they were all asleep no one answered, so she had to get up herself to put it out. When she went back to her room, she saw a man and a woman sitting on the *kang*. And when she asked who they were, they fastened a rope round her neck! She screamed for help. That roused the others who lit lamps and hurried over. They found her lying on the ground, foaming at the mouth. Luckily they managed to bring her round. But she still has no appetite; that's why she asked for the pickles. As I couldn't give her any in your absence, I told the nun you were busy with the old lady and I would tell you after you came back. Then I sent her away. Just now that talk about preserves from the south reminded me; otherwise I'd have forgotten."

Hsi-feng digested this in silence.

"We still have some of those preserves from the south, don't we?" she said. "Send her some. As for the money, tell Master Chin to come in a day or so to take it."

Then Hung-yu came and reported, "Just now Master Lien

sent a messenger to let you know that he has business to see to outside town and won't be back tonight."

"Very well," said Hsi-feng.

Just then they heard a young maid screaming at the back and come panting to the courtyard. Ping-erh, going out to investigate, found several maids chattering there.

"What's all the excitement?" Hsi-feng called out.

Ping-erh, returning, told her, "One girl who's scary was talking about ghosts."

"Which one?"

The girl came in and was asked, "What's this about ghosts?"

"I went just now to the back to get a servant to put more coal on the stove, and I heard a scuffling in those three empty rooms. First I thought it was a cat chasing rats, but then I heard a sound like someone sighing. I got scared and ran back."

"Nonsense!" Hsi-feng scolded. "We don't allow talk about ghosts and spirits here. I never believe such tales. Hurry up and get out!"

At once the young maid withdrew.

Next Hsi-feng made Tsai-ming check their account for that day. By the time this was done it was nearly the second watch and after sitting up for a while to chat she sent them all to bed, then retired herself.

Towards midnight, sleeping fitfully, Hsi-feng found herself shivering and woke with a start. Her trepidation growing as she lay there, she surprised Ping-erh and Chiu-tung by calling them over to keep her company. Chiu-tung had formerly often defied Hsi-feng, but she had become more obedient after Chia Lien began to slight her owing to her treatment of Second Sister Yu, and Hsi-feng had done her best to win her over. Still, she lacked Ping-erh's devotion to their mistress, making only a show of complaisance. Now that Hsi-feng was unwell, she brought her some tea.

"Thank you." Hsi-feng took a sip. "Go back to bed now. It's enough if just Ping-erh stays here."

To please her, however, Chiu-tung said, "If you can't sleep, madam, we can take it in turns to sit with you."

Hsi-feng talked with them for a while, then dozed off. By the time she was sound asleep they heard cocks crowing in the distance; so they lay down fully dressed till dawn, when they got up to help her with her toilet.

Hsi-feng was on edge and upset after her bad night, but not wanting to show this she forced herself to get up. She was sitting there listlessly when she heard a maid in the courtyard asking for Ping-erh.

"I'm in here," Ping-erh called.

The girl lifted the portière and came in, having been sent by Lady Wang to find Chia Lien.

She reported, "Someone outside has come on urgent official business. As the master has just gone out, Her Ladyship wants Master Lien to go over at once."

Hsi-feng was startled by this. To know what this business was, you must read the next chapter.

CHAPTER 89

A Memento of a Dead Maid Leads Pao-yu
to Write a Poem
A False Suspicion Makes Tai-yu
Abstain from Food

Hsi-feng, in low spirits that morning, was shocked by the young maid's announcement.

"Official business!" she exclaimed. "What is it?"

"I don't know, ma'am. Just now a page from the inner gate reported that urgent business has come up at His Lordship's ministry, so Her Ladyship sent me to ask Master Lien to go over."

Relieved to know that the matter concerned the Ministry of Works, Hsi-feng told her, "Go and tell Her Ladyship that Master Lien left town on business last night, and hasn't yet returned. But first send someone to let Master Chen know."

The maid assented and left.

Before long, Chia Chen came over to question the messenger from the ministry. Then he went in to inform Lady Wang, "Word has come from the Ministry of Works that yesterday they heard from the Yellow River Commission that the dyke in Honan has been breached, flooding several prefectures and districts. State funds have been allocated for repair work, and this will be keeping the whole ministry busy. So they sent specially to report this to His Lordship." This said he withdrew, and on Chia Cheng's return relayed this message to him.

From then on right up till winter, as Chia Cheng was busy every day and constantly in his yamen, Pao-yu grew more slack in his studies, although for fear of his father he still attended school. He dared not call on Tai-yu too often either.

One morning in the middle of the tenth month, a sudden drop in the temperature made Hsi-jen prepare a bundle of warm clothes for him before he set off to school.

"It's so cold today," she said, "you must dress more warmly first thing and in the evening."

She took out a coat for him to wear, and wrapped up a cape for a young maid to give Pei-ming with the message, "Now that it's cold, you must keep this ready for Master Pao."

The page assented, took the bundle, and followed Pao-yu to school.

Pao-yu was doing his lessons when a wind sprang up, buffeting the window paper.

"The weather is changing," remarked Tai-ju and, opening the window, he saw that tiers of black clouds in the northwest were bearing slowly southeast.

Pei-ming now came in. "Master Pao, it's getting colder; better put on more clothes," he advised.

When Pao-yu nodded, Pei-ming brought in a cape. At sight of it Pao-yu became lost in thought. All the other boys stared at it too. For it was the peacock-feather cape which Ching-wen had mended.

"Why bring this?" demanded Pao-yu. "Who gave it to you?"

"The girls in your place brought it out in a wrapper," said Pei-ming.

"I'm not too cold; I won't wear it. Wrap it up."

Tai-ju imagined that Pao-yu thought the cape too good to wear, and was pleased by this evidence of frugality.

But Pei-ming urged, "Do put it on, Master Pao. If you catch cold, I'll be the one who's blamed. Please wear it for my sake!"

Pao-yu had to comply then. He sat staring at his book in a dazed fashion; but the tutor paid no attention, thinking he was studying.

That evening, when the class was dismissed, Pao-yu asked for a day's sick leave. And as old Tai-ju simply coached these boys to while away the time when he himself was not ailing, as often happened, he was glad to have one less to worry about the next day. Knowing, moreover, that Chia Cheng was busy and that Pao-yu's grandmother doted on the boy, he nodded his consent.

Pao-yu on his return reported this to his grandmother and mother, who naturally believed him. After sitting there for a while he went back to the Garden to join Hsi-jen and the others. He was not his usual cheerful and talkative self, however, for he lay down, still wearing the cape, on the *kang*.

"Supper's ready," Hsi-jen announced. "Would you like it now, or a bit later?"

"I don't want any, I'm not feeling well," he answered. "You go ahead and have yours."

"In that case, you'd better take your cape off. You'll spoil it if you crumple it like that."

"Never mind."

"It's not just that it's flimsy, but look at that stitching on it — you shouldn't spoil it."

Touched to the quick by this he sighed, "All right then, wrap it up carefully for me and put it away. I'll never wear it again!"

He stood up to take off the cape and folded it up himself before Hsi-jen could take it.

"Well, Master Pao!" she exclaimed. "Why are you putting yourself out like this today?"

Instead of answering he asked, "Where is the wrapper?"

Sheh-yueh quickly passed it to him and while he wrapped the cape up turned to wink at Hsi-jen.

Pao-yu sat down by himself then, in low spirits, ignoring them. When the clock on the shelf struck, he looked down at his watch and saw it was half past five. By and by a young maid came in to light the lamp.

"If you don't want supper," said Hsi-jen, "at least have half a bowl of hot congee. If you go without food that may arouse hot humours; then we shall have more trouble."

He shook his head. "I'm not hungry. If I force myself to eat, I shall feel worse."

"Then you'd better go to bed early."

She and Sheh-yueh prepared the bed, and Pao-yu lay down. He tossed and turned but could not sleep, only dozing off when it was nearly dawn. But after no more than the time it takes for a meal, he was awake again.

By now Hsi-jen and Sheh-yueh were up.

Hsi-jen said, "I heard you tossing about last night till the fifth watch, but I didn't like to disturb you. And then I dropped off myself. Did you get any sleep or not?"

"A little, but then somehow I woke up again."

"Aren't you feeling well?"

"I'm all right, just rather edgy."

"Are you going to school today?"

"No, yesterday I asked for a day's leave. I'd like to amuse myself in the Garden today, but just now I feel cold. Get them to clean up a room for me, and put ready some incense, paper, ink and a brush; then you can get on with your work while I sit there quietly for a bit. I don't want to be disturbed."

"If you want to study quietly," Sheh-yueh said, "who'd dream of disturbing you?"

"That's a good idea," agreed Hsi-jen. "You won't catch cold, and sitting quietly by yourself you won't be distracted either. But what will you eat today, if you've lost your appetite? Let us know in good time so that we can tell the kitchen."

"Anything will do; don't fuss. But I'd like some fruit put in that room to scent it."

"Which room would be best?" Hsi-jen wondered. "The only clean one, really, is Ching-wen's old room. As no one goes there nowadays, it's quite tidy. Only it may be chilly."

"That's all right," he said. "Just put a brazier in there."

She readily agreed to this.

While they were talking a young maid had brought in a saucer, bowl and pair of chopsticks, which she handed to Sheh-yueh saying:

"Just now Miss Hsi-jen asked for these, and the old woman from the kitchen has brought them."

Sheh-yueh saw that it was a bowl of bird's-nest soup.

"Did you order this?" she asked Hsi-jen.

"He had no supper yesterday evening and passed a sleepless night," Hsi-jen explained. "I thought he must be feeling hollow inside this morning; so I got the girls to ask the kitchen for this."

She told the younger maids to bring a table, and Sheh-yueh waited on Pao-yu while he finished the soup and rinsed his mouth. Then Chiu-wen came in.

"The room's been tidied," she said. "But Master Pao had better wait till the charcoal is red before going there."

Pao-yu nodded, too preoccupied by his own thoughts to talk.

Soon a young maid came to announce, "The writing things have been put ready."

"Good," he said.

Yet another girl announced, "Breakfast is ready. Where will you have it, sir?"

"Just bring it here; that's simplest."

She assented and went out to fetch the food.

Pao-yu remarked with a smile to Hsi-jen and Sheh-yueh, "I'm feeling so depressed, I doubt if I can eat anything alone. Why don't you have breakfast with me? If I see you enjoying it, I may eat more."

"You may like the idea, Master Pao," chuckled Sheh-yueh. "But that would never do!"

"Actually it doesn't matter," countered Hsi-jen. "We've drunk together more than once before. But we can only do this occasionally to cheer you up, young master. If it wasn't in fun, that would be against all the rules of propriety!"

So the three of them sat down, Pao-yu in the top place, the two girls on either side. After they had finished the meal, a young maid brought them tea to rinse their mouths and they had the table removed.

Pao-yu holding his cup sat silent, lost in thought.

"Is that room ready?" he asked presently.

"We told you it was," said Sheh-yueh. "Why ask again?"

After a while he went to Ching-wen's old room, lit a stick

of incense and set out some fruit. Then he sent the others away and closed the door. Hsi-jen and the other girls outside took care to keep very quiet.

Pao-yu chose a sheet of pink paper with a gilded border and floral designs on one of the top and bottom corners.

After a short invocation he picked up his brush and wrote:

> The Master of Happy Red Court burns incense to Sister Ching-wen, and presents tea with a sweet fragrance. Pray come to the sacrifice!

He then penned the verse:

> My close companion, you alone
> My inmost thoughts could share;
> A sudden storm out of the blue
> Cut short your life of care.
> Who is there now to speak so sweet and low?
>
> Streams flowing east can no more westward flow.
> I long for you, but have no herb[1]
> To bring you back again.
> Glimpsing the cape — a turquoise cloud —
> Fills me with endless pain.

This written, using the incense stick as a taper, he burned his poem to ashes, then sat quietly till the incense was burnt up, whereupon he left the room.

"Why are you coming out?" Hsi-jen asked. "Were you feeling bored again?"

"I was in the dumps and wanted a quiet place where I could sit for a bit," he prevaricated, smiling. "Now that I've got over it, I'm going to have a stroll outside."

He went out, making straight for Bamboo Lodge, and on reaching the courtyard called, "Is Cousin Lin in?"

"Who is it?" asked Tzu-chuan, raising the portière. "Oh, Master Pao. She's in her room. Please come in."

As Pao-yu followed her in, Tai-yu called from the inner room, "Tzu-chuan, bring Master Pao in here."

---

[1] Legend had it that Emperor Wu of Han, after the death of his favourite Lady Li, kept longing to see her again. Tungfang Shuo presented him with a magic herb; and when he wore this at night, Lady Li appeared to him in his dreams.

Flanking the door of her room, Pao-yu saw a newly written couplet on purple paper with gilded cloud-dragon designs. It read:

> Green casement and bright moon remain,
> But the men of old annals are gone.

He smiled and walked in, asking, "What are you doing, cousin?"

She rose to meet him and said with a smile, "Sit down. I'm copying a sutra, and have only two lines left. Let me finish it and then we can talk." She told Hsueh-yen to bring tea.

"Don't trouble," said Pao-yu. "Just go on with your copying."

He noticed in the middle of the wall a scroll painting of the Moon Goddess Chang Ngo and another goddess, each with an attendant, the second one carrying what looked like a long clothing bag. There were only a few clouds surrounding them, with no other decorations. It was done in the style of Li Lung-mien's[1] outline drawings. The inscription "Contending in the Cold" was written in the old official script.

"Have you just put this painting up, cousin?" he asked.

"That's right," said Tai-yu. "Yesterday when they were tidying up, I thought of it and took it out for them to hang."

"What's its story?"

"Surely everybody knows it," she said with a smile. "Why ask?"

"I can't for the moment remember. Do tell me, cousin."

"You must know the lines:

> The Green Nymph and Chang Ngo, both able to stand cold,
> Are vying in beauty in the frosty moon."[2]

"Of course!" he exclaimed. "How original and cultured! And this is the right season, too, to hang this up."

He strolled around looking at this and that till Hsueh-yen

---

[1] 1049-1106, an eminent Sung painter.

[2] From *Frosty Moon* by the Tang poet Li Shang-yin.

brought him some tea.   And soon Tai-yu, her copying finished, stood up.

"Excuse me for neglecting you," she said.

"Always so polite, cousin!" he chuckled.

He noticed now that Tai-yu was wearing a pale-blue embroidered fur-lined jacket under a short white squirrel tunic, and a pink embroidered silk padded skirt of the kind worn by Lady Yang. With no flowers in her cloudy tresses, which were loosely knotted and clasped with a flat gold pin, she was truly like:

> A jade tree standing gracefully in the breeze.
> Or sweet dewy lotus in bloom.

"Have you been playing the lute these days, cousin?" he asked.

"Not for the last two days, because I found copying made my fingers too cold."

"It's just as well not to play. Though the lute is a refined instrument, I don't think much of it. No one ever won wealth, nobility or long life from playing it, only grief and longing. Besides, to play, you have to memorize the score which is rather an effort. As you're so delicate, cousin, it seems to me you shouldn't waste energy on it."

Tai-yu simply smiled and said nothing.

Then, pointing at a lute on the wall, he asked, "Is this yours? Why is it so short?"

"Because when I first learned to play, being small I couldn't reach the strings of regular lutes, so this was specially made for me. Though it's not anything exceptional, its parts are well fitted and it's well proportioned. See the grain of the wood. Isn't it as fine as yak hair? So it has quite a clear timbre."

"Have you written any poems these days?"

"Hardly any since the last poetry club."

Pao-yu smiled and said, "Don't try to hide it from me! I heard you chanting something like 'Why repine? Would that my heart were pure as the moon in the sky.' You accompanied it on the lute, and the sound seemed exceptionally clear. Can you deny that?"

"How did you happen to hear?"

"I heard it the other day on my way back from Smartweed Breeze Cot, and not wanting to disturb you I just listened quietly then went away. I've been meaning to ask you: Why did you start with level rhymes, then at the end change suddenly to an oblique one?[1] What was the reason for that?"

"Music comes naturally from the heart," she answered. "There are no set rules — you just play as you feel."

"So that's the reason. It's too bad I don't understand music and so it was wasted on me."

"How many understanding people have there been since of old?" she replied.

At that, Pao-yu realized that he had been tactless, and feared he had hurt her feelings. He sat there with so much he longed to say, yet not knowing how to word it. Tai-yu also felt that her last remark had been thoughtless, and must have sounded cold; so she too was silent. This convinced Pao-yu that she took this personally, and he rose sheepishly to say:

"I'll leave you to rest now, cousin. I'm off to see Tan-chun."

"When you see her, give her my regards."

He agreed to this and went out.

After seeing him off, Tai-yu came back and sat down dejectedly.

"Nowadays Pao-yu talks in such an ambiguous way, blowing hot and cold by turns, I can't tell what he means," she thought.

Just then Tzu-chuan came in to ask, "Have you finished copying, miss? Shall I put away the brush and inkstone?"

"Yes, you can. I shan't be doing any more."

She went into the inner room then to lie down, turning the problem over in her mind.

Tzu-chuan came in again to ask if she would like some tea.

---

[1] Chinese characters have four tones: one level and three oblique ones. Since the Tang Dynasty most poems have used level tone rhymes.

"No, I just want to rest a bit. You needn't stay here."

Tzu-chuan going out found Hsueh-yen all alone in a brown study.

"What's worrying *you*?" she asked, going up to her.

Hsueh-yen gave a start, then said, "Don't make such a noise! Today I heard something very strange. I don't mind telling you, but you mustn't pass it on!" She signed towards the inner room, then started out, beckoning Tzu-chuan to follow. At the foot of the steps she said softly, "Did you know, sister, that Pao-yu is engaged?"

Tzu-chuan was flabbergasted.

"Who says so?" she demanded. "Surely not!"

"It's true, I assure you. Most likely, apart from us, all the others know."

"Where did you hear this?"

"From Tai-shu. She says the girl's father is a prefect. It's a wealthy family, and she's good-looking too."

Just then Tzu-chuan heard Tai-yu coughing as if she had got up. Afraid she had come to the outer room and overheard them, she caught hold of Hsueh-yen and signed to her to keep quiet. But when she looked into the room there was no one there.

She whispered to Hsueh-yen, "What exactly did she say?"

"The other day wasn't I sent to Miss Tan-chun's place to thank her?" said Hsueh-yen. "She wasn't in. Tai-shu was the only one there. As we sat chatting we happened to speak of Master Pao's mischievous ways. 'He's really a problem!' she said. 'Just playing about, not at all like a grown man. Already engaged, yet still so muddle-headed!'

" 'Is it settled?' I asked.

"She said, 'Yes. Some Mr. Wang was the go-between — he's related to the East Mansion; so without making further inquiries they accepted out of hand.' "

Tzu-chuan cocked her head, thinking this extremely strange.

"Why has nobody in the house mentioned it?" she pressed.

"Tai-shu explained that too. It was the old lady's idea. She was afraid that if Pao-yu knew about it he'd start running wild. That's why it's never mentioned. And after telling me this Tai-shu told me on no account to pass it on — she said that I like to blab." She pointed at the house. "That's why I didn't tell *her* a word about this. Since you asked me today, I couldn't hide it from you."

At this point they heard the cockatoo, which had learned this from them, call out, "The young lady's back! Bring tea! Quick."

Startled, they turned to look, and seeing no one there they scolded the bird. Going back inside, they discovered Tai-yu just about to sit down on a chair, panting for breath. Tzu-chuan asked in confusion if she wanted a drink.

"Where have you two been?" gasped Tai-yu. "I called but nobody came."

She went back to the *kang* and sank down with her face to the wall, telling them to let down the curtain. Having done this, the two maids went out, each wondering whether she had overheard them, but neither liking to express her misgiving.

Now Tai-yu had been brooding anxiously, then eavesdropped on her two maids' conversation. Though she did not hear everything, she caught the main gist and felt as if plunged into a raging sea. Thinking it over, it bore out the ominous dream she had so recently had. Frustration and grief filled her heart. Die and be done with it, she thought, rather than have a blow like this sprung upon her. She also reflected bitterly that she had no parents to turn to. Well then, she would let her health run down, and in half a year or so leave this sea of troubles. Having reached this resolve, she closed her eyes and pretended to be asleep, without covering herself with the quilt or putting on more clothes.

Tzu-chuan and Hsueh-yen came in several times to see if she needed anything, but as she lay motionless they did not like to call her. She went without supper that evening. After the lamps were lit, Tzu-chuan raised the curtain and found her asleep, her quilt kicked to the bottom of the bed. She covered her gently to stop her from catching cold, and Tai-yu did not move; but as soon as the maid had left she kicked off the bedding again.

Tzu-chuan felt constrained to ask Hsueh-yen, "Was it really true what you told me earlier on?"

"Of course it was."

"How did Tai-shu get to know?"

"She heard it from Hung-yu."

Then Tzu-chuan confided, "I'm afraid our young lady overheard us. Look at the state she was in just now; that must be the reason for it. We mustn't ever mention it again."

They got ready to go to bed then. But first Tzu-chuan went in to have another look at their young mistress, and found that she had kicked off her bedding again. Once more she gently tucked the quilt around her. But no more about that night.

The next day Tai-yu rose early, and instead of calling her maids sat there alone lost in thought. When Tzu-chuan woke and saw her already up, she exclaimed in surprise:

"You're up very early, miss!"

"I know," said Tai-yu. "I went to bed early, that's why I woke early."

Tzu-chuan hastily got up and roused Hsueh-yen to help Tai-yu with her toilet. She just stared blankly, however, at the mirror and soon was weeping so copiously that her silk handkerchief was drenched. Truly:

> Gazing into the mirror at her emaciated face,
> Both she and her reflection pitied each other!

Tzu-chuan refrained from trying to comfort her, for fear of making matters worse. Some time passed before Tai-yu set about her toilet, but listlessly, her tears still flowing. She then sat there a little longer.

"Light a stick of that Tibetan incense," she told Tzu-chuan presently.

"You had hardly any sleep, miss. What do you want incense for? To copy more sutras?"

Tai-yu nodded.

"You woke up too early, miss," protested Tzu-chuan. "If you copy sutras now, I'm afraid you'll wear yourself out."

"Don't worry. The sooner I finish the better. Besides, it's not the sutra I'm thinking about, but writing will help distract me. And later, when you see my calligraphy, it'll be like seeing me again." She shed tears anew.

Knowing that it was useless to reason with her, Tzu-chuan could not hold back her own tears.

Now that Tai-yu had made up her mind to ruin her health, she wanted no nourishment and ate less every day. Pao-yu often made time to visit her after school; but although she had so much she longed to tell him, now that they were no longer children she could hardly tease him playfully as before or express her pent-up feelings. He, too, wanted to bare his heart to her to console her, yet he feared this might offend her and make her illness worse. So when they met they could only express their concern in the most superficial way. Truly, theirs was a case of "devotion leading to alienation."

The Lady Dowager and Lady Wang, fond as they were of Tai-yu, simply called in doctors to attend her as she was so often ill, with no inkling that she was wasting away for love. And though Tzu-chuan knew the truth, she dared not reveal it. So for a fortnight Tai-yu ate daily less, till her appetite had so diminished that she could not even swallow a mouthful of congee. Any talk she heard she suspected concerned Pao-yu's marriage. Anyone from Happy Red Court, whether master or maid, made her think of his impending marriage too. When Aunt Hsueh called on her without Pao-chai, this made her still more suspicious. She even wished everyone would keep away, and refused to take any medicine in the hope of hastening her death. In her dreams, she kept hearing people refer to "Madam Pao." Suspicion poisoned her mind. And at last the day came when, refusing both rice and congee, she was at her last gasp, at death's door.

To know what became of her, read the chapter which follows.

CHAPTER 90

The Loss of a Padded Jacket Involves
a Poor Girl with a Scold
A Gift of Sweetmeats Perturbs
a Young Gentleman

After Tai-yu had resolved on self-destruction she went into a decline, until there came a day when she could eat nothing. For the first fortnight or so, when the old lady and others took it in turn to call, she had still been able to say a few words, but these last two days she remained virtually silent. Sometimes she lay in a coma, sometimes she had lucid spells. Wondering what had brought on this illness, her grandmother questioned her maids a couple of times. But how dared they tell her the truth?

Tzu-chuan wanted to ask Tai-shu to confirm the report but feared that would only hasten her young lady's death, and so when she saw Tai-shu she held her tongue. And Hsueh-yen, as she knew that her tattling was the root of this trouble and only wished she could grow a hundred tongues to deny it, was of course even more afraid to speak out.

The day that Tai-yu abstained completely from food, Tzu-chuan felt that the end had come and, for a while, remained weeping at her side.

Then she came out and whispered to Hsueh-yen, "Go in and look after her carefully while I go to tell the mistresses. She's never been as bad as this before."

Hsueh-yen agreeing to this, Tzu-chuan went off.

Hsueh-yen stayed watching over Tai-yu, now in a coma. Too young to have seen anything like this before, she thought her young mistress was dying and, torn between grief and alarm, longed for Tzu-chuan's return. Then the frightened girl heard footsteps outside the window. It must be Tzu-chuan, she thought with relief. As she sprang up to raise the portière for her, the outside portière swished and in came Tai-shu, sent by Tan-chun to inquire after the invalid.

Seeing Hsueh-yen waiting there Tai-shu asked, "How is she?"

Hsueh-yen nodded and beckoned her in. Tai-shu noticed Tzu-chuan's absence, and was terrified by the sight of Tai-yu apparently at her last gasp.

"Where's Sister Tzu-chuan?" she asked.

"Gone to tell the mistresses."

Under the impression that Tai-yu was unconscious, and as Tzu-chuan was away, Hsueh-yen took Tai-shu's hand and asked her in a low voice, "Was it true what you told me the other day about some Mr. Wang proposing a match for our Master Pao?"

"Of course it was."

"When was the engagement fixed?"

"How could it be fixed? What I told you that day was what I heard from Hung-yu. Later I went to Madam Lien's place when she was talking it over with Sister Ping-erh. She said, 'This is just a pretext for those protégés to suck up to His Lordship, so that he'll help them in future. Not to say Lady Hsing didn't approve of the girl, even if she did what does *her* judgement count for? Besides, unknown to her, the old lady long ago decided on one of the girls in our Garden. She just made a show of consulting her because His Lordship mentioned this proposal.'

"I also heard Madam Lien say, 'For Pao-yu, the old lady's bound to choose some relative. No other proposals, no matter from whom, would even be considered.'"

Hsueh-yen, forgetting herself, blurted out, "Why, then, our young lady's dying for no reason!"

"What do you mean?"

"You wouldn't know, but she overheard me telling Sister Tzu-chuan about this the other day. That's why she's wasting away."

"Keep your voice down, or she may hear us!"

"She's already unconscious. Look! She can hardly last more than a day or two now."

Just then Tzu-chuan lifted the portière and stepped in.

"What's all this?" she exclaimed softly.   "If you want to talk, talk outside instead of here.   You'll be the death of her!"

"This is so extraordinary," cried Tai-shu, "I simply can't believe it!"

"Good sister, don't take offence," retorted Tzu-chuan, "but really you have no sense!   You should have known better than to spread such gossip."

As they were talking they heard Tai-yu cough.   Tzu-chuan ran to the *kang* to attend to her while the two other girls fell silent.

Bending over Tai-yu, Tzu-chuan asked her softly, "Do you want some water, miss?"

"Yes," was the faint reply.

Hsueh-yen at once poured half a cup of boiled water which Tzu-chuan took from her.   Tai-shu stepped forward too, but Tzu-chuan shook her head to make her keep quiet.   They stood there until Tai-yu coughed again.

"Do you want some water, miss?" Tzu-chuan asked again.

Once again Tai-yu murmured her assent and tried to raise her head, but this was beyond her.   Tzu-chuan clambered on to the *kang* beside her, the cup in her hand.   First she made sure that the water was neither too hot nor too cold, then held it to Tai-yu's lips, supporting her head while she sipped.   As she looked eager for more, instead of removing the cup Tzu-chuan held it there while she took another sip.   Then Tai-yu shook her head, declining more, and lay down again with a sigh.   After a while, half opening her eyes, she asked:

"Was that Tai-shu talking?"

"Yes, miss," said Tzu-chuan.

Tai-shu, who had not yet left, came over to greet her.   Tai-yu opened her eyes to look at her and nodded.

After a pause she said, "When you go back, give my regards to your mistress."

Guessing that she wanted to be left in peace, Tai-shu quietly slipped away.

Now Tai-yu though so gravely ill had been clear in her mind.

She had caught a sentence here and there of the conversation between Tai-shu and Hsueh-yen, but she lay as if unconscious, owing partly to sheer weakness. From what she overheard she realized that the match proposed had not been agreed to. And then Tai-shu had quoted Hsi-feng as saying that the old lady had decided on choosing some relative from the girls in the Garden. Who could this mean if not her? At this thought, her despair gave way to joy and her mind became clearer too. That was why she had drunk some water and why she had wanted to question Tai-shu.

Just then the old lady arrived with Lady Wang, Li Wan and Hsi-feng who had hurried over after hearing Tzu-chuan's report. Tai-yu, her fears set at rest now, naturally no longer wanted to die. Though still weak and lacking in energy, she managed to answer their inquiries briefly. Seeing this, Hsi-feng called Tzu-chuan over.

"What do you mean by frightening us like that?" she demanded. "Your young lady's not in such a bad way after all."

"She really looked bad," replied Tzu-chuan. "Otherwise I wouldn't have presumed to disturb you. Now, coming back, I'm quite amazed to find her so much better."

"Don't listen to her. What does she know?" said the old lady with a smile. "When something's wrong, it shows good sense to report it. I like a girl who's not too lazy to use her tongue and feet."

They stayed talking a little longer, then believing Tai-yu to be in no danger they left. Truly:

> The cure for a broken heart is heartening news;
> The knot must be untied by the one who tied it.

So by degrees Tai-yu recovered, and her two maids secretly gave thanks to Buddha.

Hsueh-yen remarked to Tzu-chuan, "Thank goodness she's better now! Her falling ill was odd, and so was her recovery."

"Her falling ill wasn't odd," replied Tzu-chuan, "but her recovery is. I suppose she and Pao-yu must be destined for each other. As people say, 'The way to happiness is never smooth' and 'Nothing can prevent a match made in Heaven.' So it seems human wishes are willed by Providence, and they are fated to marry. Another thing: remember that year when I told Pao-yu Miss Lin would be going back south? He flew into such a frenzy, he nearly turned the whole household upside-down! This time another casual remark nearly cost our young lady her life. What is this if not a case of predestined fate?"

They had a good laugh in secret, after which Hsueh-yen said again, "Well, thank goodness she's better. We must be careful not to gossip in future. Even if Pao-yu marries some other girl and I see the wedding myself, I won't breathe a word about it."

"That's right," agreed Tzu-chuan, smiling.

These two were not the only ones to be talking this business over. All the domestics knew of Tai-yu's strange illness and strange recovery, and in twos and threes they canvassed the matter together, till very soon this came to Hsi-feng's ears. Lady Hsing and Lady Wang also found it puzzling. Only the Lady Dowager had a good inkling of the reason.

One day Their Ladyships and Hsi-feng, chatting with the old lady in her room, brought up the subject of Tai-yu's illness again.

"I was just going to tell you something," said the old lady. "Pao-yu and Tai-yu have been inseparable since they were small, and I didn't think it mattered as they were children. Since then, though, there's been all this talk about her sudden illness and sudden recovery — just because they are growing up now. So I don't think it proper to leave them together all the time. What do you say?"

Taken aback, Lady Wang could only answer, "Tai-yu is a bright, intelligent girl. As for Pao-yu, he's such a simpleton he may get himself talked about sometimes. On the face of it, though, they're both of them still children. If we move one of them out of the Garden now, all of a sudden, won't that give people ideas? As they say: When the time comes do not tarry; boys must wed and girls must marry. Don't you think it would be better, madam, to lose no time in arranging their marriages?"

Frowning, the old lady said, "Tai-yu is over-sensitive, and though that's not a bad thing in a way it's also the reason why I don't want to marry her to Pao-yu. Besides, she's so delicate, I doubt whether she's long for this world. The most suitable choice is Pao-chai."

"We all agree with you there, madam," said Lady Wang. "But we must arrange a marriage for Tai-yu too. A growing girl is bound to get ideas into her head. If she's really set her heart on Pao-yu and hears that he's engaged to Pao-chai, we're going to have a problem on our hands."

"But we can't marry her off before Pao-yu," objected the old lady. "Who ever heard of arranging a marriage for someone else's child before one's own? Especially as she's two years younger than he is. Still, there's truth in what you said, so we'll just have to see to it that there's no talk about Pao-yu's engagement."

At once Hsi-feng turned to the maids.

"Did you hear that? Mind you don't gossip about Master Pao's engagement. I'll flay anyone who blabs!"

"Hsi-feng," said the old lady, "since that illness of yours you've stopped paying much attention to what goes on in the Garden. I want you to keep your eyes open, and not just with regard to this. The way the servants there were drinking and gambling the other year was disgraceful. You have sharper eyes than the rest of us, so we must trouble you to keep them under stricter control. Besides, I think they're more obedient to you."

Hsi-feng promised to do her best, and after a little further talk they dispersed.

After that, Hsi-feng often went to check up in the Garden. One day she had just gone in when she heard an old woman at Purple Caltrop Isle raising a rumpus. As soon as the old woman saw her approaching, she stood at attention and greeted her.

"Why are you making such a noise here?" demanded Hsi-feng.

"The mistresses put me in charge of the flowers and fruit here, madam. I've done nothing wrong, yet Miss Hsiu-yen's maid says we're thieves!"

"Tell me what happened."

"Yesterday our Hei-erh came here with me to play for a bit. Having no sense, she went to Miss Hsiu-yen's place to peek around, and then I sent her home. This morning, her maid told me something was missing. When I asked what it was, she started questioning *me*!"

"That's nothing to get so worked up about."

"Well, this Garden belongs to our mistress' family, not to theirs. It's our mistress who put us in charge here; so how dare they call us thieves?"

Hsi-feng spat in her face. "Don't give me that talk!" she said sternly. "You're here to keep an eye on things. When a young lady loses something, you should look into it. How can you maunder in this senseless fashion?"

She ordered her maids to fetch Lin Chih-hsiao's wife to drive the woman away. At once Hsiu-yen came out to greet her with a smile.

"Please don't," she said. "It's of no account — over and done with."

"That's not the point, cousin," said Hsi-feng. "Quite apart from your losing something, she's gone too far, forgetting her place like that."

Seeing that the woman was kneeling to beg for pardon, Hsiu-yen invited Hsi-feng in to sit down.

"I know these creatures," Hsi-feng went on. "I'm the only one of the mistresses they treat with any respect."

Still Hsiu-yen begged her to let the woman off, saying her own maid was to blame.

"Well, for Miss Hsing's sake then, I'll overlook it this time," conceded Hsi-feng.

The woman kowtowed her thanks to them both and went off, whereupon they sat down.

"What have you lost?" asked Hsi-feng with a smile.

"Nothing much, just a red jacket, an old one. When I told them to look for it and they couldn't find it, I said it didn't matter. But my maid is so silly she asked that woman about it, and of course that put her back up. It's all this silly girl's fault, and I've given her a scolding, so that's that. We may as well forget about it."

Hsi-feng looked her up and down and saw that though she had on some fur-lined and padded clothes, they were rather worn and could not be too warm. Her quilts too were on the thin side. But the knick-knacks in the room and on the desk, all provided by the Lady Dowager, were neatly set out and spotless. Impressed by this and drawn to her, Hsi-feng said:

"Of course a jacket isn't all that important, but now that it's cold you need something snug to wear. Naturally you should try to trace it. The insolence of that old slave, talking back!"

After a little more chat Hsi-feng took her leave, and having paid various other calls she went home. There she told Ping-erh to fetch a red crepe inner jacket, a deep green satin jacket lined with sheepskin, a sapphire blue embroidered padded skirt and a bright green gown lined with white squirrel. When these had been wrapped up she had them sent to Hsiu-yen.

Hsiu-yen was still upset after the old scold's tirade, even though Hsi-feng had put a stop to it. She thought, "No one dares to offend any of the other girls here except me. With me, though, they keep making snide remarks — and now Hsi-feng knows about it." The more she brooded the more wretched she felt, but there was nobody in whom to confide. She was choking back her sobs when Feng-erh brought in the clothes sent by Hsi-feng. Hsiu-yen most resolutely declined the gift.

"My mistress says that if you think these too worn, she'll send new ones later," said Feng-erh.

"It's very kind of your mistress." Hsiu-yen smiled. "She's sent me these because I lost a jacket, but I really can't accept them. So take them back and be sure to thank her for me. I do appreciate her thoughtfulness."

She gave Feng-erh a pouch, and with that the girl had to leave.

Before long, Feng-erh came back again with Ping-erh. Hsiu-yen welcomed them and asked them to sit down.

Ping-erh told her with a smile, "Our mistress says you're treating us like strangers."

"Oh no!" exclaimed Hsiu-yen. "But I really can't accept such a handsome gift."

"Our mistress says that if you won't accept, it must be either because you think these clothes too shabby or because you look down on her. Just now our mistress insisted that if I were to bring back the clothes the way Feng-erh did, she'd be really angry with me."

Blushing, Hsiu-yen said gratefully, "Well then, I dare not refuse." Then she urged them to have some tea.

On their way back, Ping-erh and Feng-erh were accosted by one of the old women who worked for Aunt Hsueh.

"Where have you been?" Ping-erh asked her.

"Our mistress and young lady sent me to give their regards to all the ladies here," the woman replied. "Just now I asked Madam Lien where you were, and she said you'd gone to the Garden. Have you come from Miss Hsing's place?"

"How did you know?"

"I just heard about it. And, truly, no one can help admiring your mistress and you, the way you both behave!"

Ping-erh laughed and invited her back to rest for a while.

"I have something else to do now," said the woman. "I'll call some other day."

She went off, and Ping-erh returned to report on her errand to Hsi-feng. No more of this.

Now Aunt Hsueh's household had been turned upside-down by Chin-kuei. When the woman went back and told them about Hsiu-yen, Pao-chai and her mother shed tears.

"It's all because brother's away that Hsiu-yen has to go on putting up with these slights," said Pao-chai. "I'm glad Cousin Hsi-feng is so considerate. In future we must see what we can do too as, after all, she'll be marrying into our family."

Just then Hsueh Ko came in.

"The friends Brother Pan has been making these years!" he
fumed. "There's not a single decent sort among the whole foxy
lot. They're a pack of curs! I don't believe they feel any concern for him. They just come to ferret out news. The last
couple of days I've sent the whole lot packing. I've told the
gateman, too, not to admit such scoundrels fiom now on."

"Are they Chiang Yu-han's lot?" asked Aunt Hsueh.

"No, Chiang Yu-han hasn't come. These are some others."

Hsueh Ko's outburst had further lowered Aunt Hsueh's spirits.

"Though I have a son, it's as if I had none," she sighed.
"Even if the authorities let him off, he'll be useless. Though
you're my nephew, and not so close, I can see that you have
more sense than Pan and will be my only prop in my old age.
It's up to you to make a success of your life. Especially as the
family of your betrothed isn't as well off as before. It's hard
for a girl to leave home and get married, and all she hopes for
is an able husband who will provide for her. If Hsiu-yen were
like that creature..." — she pointed towards the inner rooms
— "well, enough said! But Hsiu-yen is truly modest, sensible
too. She can put up with poverty, and wealth wouldn't spoil
her either. Once this trouble blows over we must hurry up and
arrange your wedding, and that will be one less thing on my
mind."

"There's still Sister Pao-chin's marriage which must be on your
mind, aunt," he said. "As for mine, don't worry about it."

After some more talk Hsueh Ko went back to his room for
supper. He thought to himself, "Hsiu-yen's living in the Chias'
Garden as a dependent, and being a poor relation she must be
having a thin time of it. As we travelled here together, I know
her character and what she's like. Heaven is really unjust,
giving a spoilt bitch like Hsia Chin-kuei money while a girl like
Hsiu-yen is so badly off. How does the King of Hell decide
these things,[1] I wonder?"

---

[1] It was believed that it was the King of Hell who decided the next
life of a dead person.

He wanted to write a poem to vent his frustration, but as he had no training in versification he could only pen the following doggerel:

> A dragon stranded, a fish high and dry;
> Apart we think of each other, you and I.
> In mud and slime our bitter days are passed;
> When will we find clear water at long last?

This written, he read it through and was tempted to paste it on the wall but diffidently told himself, "I don't want people seeing it to laugh at me." After a second reading he thought, "Never mind! I may as well paste it up for my own amusement." Reading it once more, however, he decided it really was no good and put it between the pages of a book.

"I'm no longer a boy," he mused, "but now our family's run into this bad trouble and there's no knowing when it will blow over. It's keeping that sweet, gentle girl so sad and lonely!"

His reflections were cut short by the arrival of Pao-chan with a hamper which she put on the table, smiling. Hsueh Ko got up and invited her to be seated.

"Here are four dishes of sweetmeats and one small pot of wine," she announced archly. "My mistress told me to bring them to you."

"Please thank my sister-in-law. But why didn't she send a young maid instead of troubling you?"

"That's all right. We're one family, so why stand on ceremony? Besides, you've put yourself out so much over Master Pan's business, our mistress has long been wanting to show her appreciation, but she was afraid people might suspect her motives. You know how it is in our family — all sweet talk hiding inward disagreement. It shouldn't matter sending you a small present, but it might give rise to a whole lot of gossip. So today she simply prepared a couple of dishes and a pot of wine and told me to bring them to you secretly." She glanced at him with a meaningful smile and added, "You mustn't talk in that formal way again, sir, or you'll embarrass me. I'm only a servant. If I can wait on Master Pan, what's to stop me from waiting on you, sir?"

Hsueh Ko was a simple, honest young fellow. He had never been treated like this by Chin-kuei and Pao-chan before; yet as the latter said it was to thank him for helping Hsueh Pan, this seemed to him quite natural.

"Leave the dishes, sister," he said. "But please take back the wine. I really can't drink much, just a cup occasionally when I'm forced to, but ordinarily I never drink. Surely your mistress and you knew that?"

"I can use my own discretion in other matters," she replied, "but I can't obey you in this. You know what our mistress is like. If I took it back, she wouldn't think it's because you don't drink but because I'd been remiss."

So Hsueh Ko had to let her leave the wine. Then Pao-chan went to the door and peeped outside. Turning back to smile at him, she pointed towards the inner rooms.

"I daresay she'll be coming herself to thank you," she said.

Not knowing what she meant, he felt rather put out.

"Please thank her for me, sister," he rejoined. "I don't want her to catch a chill in this cold weather. Besides, as we're relatives, there's no need to be so polite."

Pao-chan made no answer to this but went away smiling.

At first Hsueh Ko had believed that Chin-kuei had sent him these things out of gratitude for his services to Hsueh Pan. But Pao-chan's secretive ways and meaning glances made him afraid there was more to it than that.

"But what other designs could she have on me?" he wondered. "After all, she's my sister-in-law. Maybe this hussy Pao-chan, not liking to make advances herself, is using Chin-kuei's name. Still, she's Cousin Pan's concubine too, so how could she. . . ." Then it occurred to him, "Chin-kuei has never shown the least sense of propriety. When the fancy takes her she gets herself up like a vamp, preening herself on her beauty; so for all I know she *may* have designs on me. Or maybe, because she bears Sister Pao-chin some grudge, she's playing this dirty trick to get me into hot water and give me a bad name — that's possible too."

The likelihood of this alarmed him, and he was in a quandary when he heard someone giggling outside his window. Hsueh Ko gave a start. But to know who it was you must read the following chapter.

CHAPTER 91

Wanton Pao-chan Lays a Cunning Plot
Pao-yu Makes Extravagant Answers
When Catechized

Hsueh Ko was in a quandary when giggling outside the window made him start. "That must be Pao-chan or Chin-kuei," he thought. "I'll pay no attention and just see what they can do."

He listened for some time. When there was no further sound, not venturing to eat any sweetmeats or drink the wine, he bolted the door and set about undressing. Then the window paper rustled. By now he was so flustered by Pao-chan's tricks that he did not know what to do. He peered at the window but could see nothing stirring and suspected that he had been imagining things. Fastening his clothes again he sat down by the lamp to think hard, then picked up a sweetmeat and scrutinized it intently. Turning his head abruptly, he saw that a patch of the window paper was wet. He went over to have a look, and jumped for fright when suddenly someone outside blew into his face. This was followed by more giggling. Hsueh Ko hastily put out the lamp and, with bated breath, lay down.

"Why don't you have some wine and a snack before turning in, Master Ko?" called the person outside.

He recognized Pao-chan's voice but made no sound, pretending to be asleep.

"How on earth could anyone be such a fool!" someone sneered after another couple of minutes.

He could not tell whether this was said by Pao-chan or Chin-kuei, but it convinced him that they were up to no good. He tossed and turned and did not fall asleep until after the fifth watch.

At daybreak, somebody knocked at his door.

"Who's there?" he called.

When there was no response, he had to get up and open the door. He found it was Pao-chan again, her hair dishevelled, her clothes loose. She had on a tight-fitting bodice with a gold border and rows of long buttons and loops in front, over which she had tied a none too new dark green sash. As she was not wearing a skirt, he could see her pomegranate-red trousers with floral designs and her new embroidered red slippers. She had evidently not yet made her toilet but come early to fetch the hamper to avoid being seen.

Her appearance in such a costume dismayed Hsueh Ko.

"You are up early," he faltered, forcing a smile.

She blushed but did not answer, simply putting the sweetmeats back into the hamper, which she then took away. Supposing that she was vexed by his behaviour the previous night, he thought, "Just as well. If they're annoyed, they'll give up and leave me in peace."

Feeling easier in his mind he called for water to wash in and decided to stay quietly at home for a couple of days, partly to rest, partly to avoid outside contacts. For Hsueh Pan's old associates were trying to cash in on the situation, now that there was only young Hsueh Ko to manage the family's affairs. Some officiously offered to run errands for him; others who could write legal plaints or knew a few clerks in government offices proffered their services to bribe the court; yet others urged him to appropriate family funds or tried to blackmail him. Each used a different approach. He steered clear of these hangers-on as far as he could, but dared not refuse them outright for fear of future trouble. So he felt constrained to lie low at home till orders came down from above. But no more of this.

Let us revert to Chin-kuei, who had sent Pao-chan with refreshments to sound out Hsueh Ko. Pao-chan on her return reported in full what had happened. As the young man had not risen to the bait, Chin-kuei feared Pao-chan might despise her for this fiasco and therefore tried to cover up, changing her tune. However, not wanting to relinquish Hsueh Ko, she sat there in silence wondering what to do.

Pao-chan did not expect Hsueh Pan back and was casting about for a lover, but had not disclosed this to Chin-kuei for fear of the consequences. Now that her mistress had made the first move, she saw it as a good chance to pre-empt Hsueh Ko herself, for then Chin-kuei could hardly raise any objection. That was why she had spoken provocatively to him. When he seemed neither entirely unresponsive nor very forthcoming either, she had hesitated to do anything more rash. Later, when he blew out the light and lay down to sleep, she went back, very disappointed, to tell Chin-kuei and see what she would do. Now that her mistress kept silent as if at a loss, she had to help her to bed and retire herself. But that night how could she sleep? She tossed and turned until she hit on a plan. She would get up first thing the next morning to fetch the hamper, alluringly dressed and with her hair uncombed to reveal her drowsy charms. While watching Hsueh Ko's reaction she would put on a show of anger and ignore him; but if he showed regret, naturally she would smooth his way and then she could get him first — she was sure of that. Such was her plan. However, when she tried to execute it, he behaved just as properly as the previous night. All she could do was act as if really affronted and take the dishes back. She deliberately left the wine-pot, though, to provide an excuse for returning.

Chin-kuei asked her, "Did anyone see you fetch those things?"

"No, madam."

"Did Master Ko ask you anything?"

"No."

Since Chin-kuei had lain awake all night unable to think of a plan she now decided, "If I go ahead with this affair, I may be able to keep it a secret from others, but how can I hide it from her? I'd better go shares with her, to keep her quiet. Besides, I can't seek out Hsueh Ko myself, I'll need her as go-between. So I may as well work out a sound plan with her."

She therefore asked with a smile, "What is your honest opinion of Master Ko?"

"He strikes me as a fool."

Chin-kuei told the young man, whose name was Hsia San, to come out to meet her mother-in-law, and he raised clasped hands to greet her. She returned his greetings and they sat down to talk.

"How long have you been in the capital?" asked Aunt Hsueh.

"My stepmother adopted me a couple of months ago, as she had no man in the house to see to things. I only came to the capital the day before yesterday; so I called on my sister today."

As he looked rather embarrassed, after sitting there for a while Aunt Hsueh got up. "Do stay longer," she urged, then turned to tell Chin-kuei, "since this is your brother's first visit here, you must keep him for a meal."

Chin-kuei assented to this and Aunt Hsueh left.

As soon as she had gone Chin-kuei told Hsia San, "Sit down. Now we're above-board, so Master Ko won't have to pry into our affairs. I want you to buy something for me today, but don't let anyone see it."

"Just leave it to me. Provided you have the money, I can get whatever you want."

"Don't boast! If you get overcharged I'm not having it."

When they had exchanged some more banter, Chin-kuei kept Hsia San to dinner, then gave him her commission and some instructions, after which he left.

Subsequently, Hsia San was a frequent visitor. And the old gatekeeper, having heard that this was Chin-kuei's brother, usually neglected to report his arrival. This led to endless trouble later on, but we need not go into that now.

One day a letter arrived from Hsueh Pan. His mother opened it and told Pao-chai to read it. He had written:

> ... I am doing all right in the county jail, so mother needn't worry. Yesterday a clerk in the county yamen told me that though the prefectural court has approved our plea — I suppose you must have squared them — the provincial court has rejected it. The chief secretary in the county was decent enough to write at once requesting a remission; but the provincial governor has reprimanded the county magistrate. Now the governor wants to try the case himself, and if that happens I'll be for it again. You can't have bought over the provincial court. So as soon as you get this, mother, ask

someone to put in a word at once with the governor; and get Hsueh Ko to come quickly. Otherwise I shall be transferred to the provincial court. Don't stint silver! This is desperately urgent!

This reduced Aunt Hsueh once more to tears. Pao-chai and Hsueh Ko while consoling her warned:

"There's no time to be lost!"

She had to send Hsueh Ko to smooth matters over with the county court. Servants were ordered to pack his luggage and weigh out silver at once so that he could set out that same night, as Li Hsiang was already in the county, one of the pawnshop assistants was sent to accompany Hsueh Ko there. In the bustle and confusion, Pao-chai helped with the packing herself in case the domestics should overlook anything, not lying down to rest till nearly dawn. Being a cosseted girl from a wealthy family, the anxiety on top of her night-long exertions brought on a fever, she was unable to eat or even drink water. Ying-erh hastily reported this to her mother.

Hurrying to Pao-chai's side, Aunt Hsueh found her fearfully flushed, burning with fever and unable to speak. She lost her head then and wept till she nearly fainted away. Pao-chin supported her and tried to console her while Hsiang-ling's tears flowed like a fountain too as she called Pao-chai's name to awaken her. For she was speechless, as if paralysed, her eyes sunken, her nose blocked. Doctors were called in to attend her and gradually, to their great relief, she recovered consciousness.

This news had alarmed both the Ning and the Jung Mansions. First Hsi-feng sent over a maid with some Ten-Spices Restorative Pills; then Lady Wang sent some Wonder-Working Powder. The old lady, Lady Hsing, Lady Wang and Madam Yu all sent maids to ask after Pao-chai; but none of them let Pao-yu know of this. For seven or eight days she took medicine with very little effect, until bethinking herself of her Cool Fragrance Pills she took three of these and finally recovered. When some time later Pao-yu heard of her illness, as she was already better he did not call to see her.

And now a letter came from Hsueh Ko which Aunt Hsueh had read to her. Instead of telling Pao-chai, for fear of worrying her, she went to enlist Lady Wang's help, then described her daughter's illness. After she had gone, Lady Wang passed on her request to her husband.

"We can ask the ministry to help, but not the provincial authorities," said Chia Cheng. "The only way is to spend money."

"That child Pao-chai is having a hard time," continued Lady Wang. "As she's betrothed to our family, I think we should fix up the wedding soon, before she ruins her health."

"I agree," he replied. "But her family's in too much of a commotion now; and as winter is nearly over, with the New Year in the offing, we have a good many affairs to attend to ourselves. Suppose we send the betrothal gifts this winter and the wedding gifts next spring — fix the date for the wedding after the old lady's birthday. You can tell Aunt Hsueh this first."

The next day, Lady Wang let her sister know this proposal, and Aunt Hsueh agreed to it. After lunch, the two of them called on the Lady Dowager. When they had taken seats she asked Aunt Hsueh:

"Have you just come over?"

"Actually I came yesterday," replied Aunt Hsueh. "But it was too late then to pay my respects."

Then Lady Wang repeated her husband's proposal, and the old lady thoroughly approved. As Pao-yu happened to come in just then, she asked him whether he had had his lunch.

"I had it as soon as I got back just now," he said. "As I'm off to school again now, I wanted to call on you first. Besides, hearing that aunty was here, I wanted to pay my respects to her as well." He asked Aunt Hsueh, "Is Cousin Pao-chai better?"

"Yes, she is," was the answer.

As their conversation had stopped at his arrival, and as Aunt Hsueh seemed less cordial to him than before, Pao-yu felt mystified.

"Even if she's upset, why should they all keep so quiet?" he asked himself as he went back to school.

On his return that evening, having paid his respects to his

elders, he went straight to Bamboo Lodge. But when he raised the portière and went in there was only Tzu-chuan there — the inner room was empty.

"Where is your mistress?" he asked.

"With the old lady," said Tzu-chuan. "When she heard that Madam Hsueh had called, she went over to pay her respects. Didn't you go too, Master Pao?"

"I did, but I didn't see your young lady there."

"She wasn't there?"

"No. Where else could she have gone?"

"That's hard to say."

He was on the point of leaving when Tai-yu returned with Hsueh-yen.

"So you're back, cousin!" He turned to follow her in.

Tai-yu invited him into the inner room and, when Tzu-chuan had brought her a housecoat into which to change, she sat down.

"Did you see aunty?" she asked.

"Yes, I did."

"Did she mention me?"

"No. And not only that, she didn't treat me as warmly as she used to. When I asked after Pao-chai's illness, she simply smiled and said nothing. Could she be annoyed because recently I haven't called to see her?"

Tai-yu smiled. "You haven't been?"

"I knew nothing about it at first. A couple of days ago I heard; but I didn't go."

"What do you expect then?"

"But, honestly," he protested, "the old lady, my mother and my father all told me not to. I could hardly defy them could I? If this were like the old days when we could slip through the small gate, I could easily call on her *ten* times a day; but now that gate's closed and going round from the front is inconvenient."

"I don't suppose that occurred to her," said Tai-yu.

"But I've always found Pao-chai most understanding."

"Don't flatter yourself. She'd be the last one to excuse you. Especially as *she* was the invalid, not aunty. Think how jolly it used to be before, when we wrote poems, enjoyed the flowers and drank in the Garden together. Now she's cut off and her family's in trouble, yet when she falls so badly ill you behave as if nothing had happened! How could she help being annoyed?"

"Does that mean we won't be on speaking-terms any more?"

"How am I to know on what terms you'll be? I was just talking about natural reactions."

Pao-yu started thinking this over, glassy-eyed, whereupon Tai-yu ignored him, just telling one of her maids to add a fresh slab of incense to the brazier while she picked up a book to read. After a while Pao-yu frowned and stamped his foot.

"Why was I born?" he exclaimed. "The world would be a better place without me!"

She commented, "When 'I' exists, so do others; and where there are people you'll have no end of worries, fears, fancies and dreams, not to mention all sorts of entanglements. I was only joking just now. Simply seeing aunty in low spirits shouldn't make you start suspecting Pao-chai, should it? Aunty called, not to entertain you, but because that lawsuit is weighing on her mind. But by letting your fancy run away with you, you end up thinking the worst."

Pao-yu laughed suddenly, as if seeing the light.

"Quite right, quite right," he cried. "You are much more perspicacious than I am. No wonder the other year when I was angry you put me through that Buddhist catechism, and I was stumped. If ever I become a real Buddha, I shall still need your guidance."

She took this chance to sound him out. "Then let me ask you something, and see how you answer."

Pao-yu crossed his legs and folded his hands as if in prayer, his eyes closed, his face solemn.

"Go on," he said.

"Suppose Cousin Pao-chai befriended you? Suppose she cold-shouldered you? Suppose she befriended you first but not later? Suppose she befriends you now but not in future? Suppose you befriend her but she cold-shoulders you? Suppose you cold-shoulder her but she befriends you? What would you do in all those different cases?"

Pao-yu thought for a while, then burst out laughing.

"However much water there is in the stream, one gourdful will suffice me," was his reply — indicating that, for him, she alone counted.

"What if your gourd is drifted off by the water?"

"No, the gourd is not drifted off by the water. The water flows where it wills and the gourd drifts of its own accord."

"What if the stream runs dry and the pearl is lost?"

"My heart is a willow-catkin caught in the mud; how can it dance like a partridge in the spring wind?" he answered — affirming that he would be true to her.

"The first Buddhist commandment is not to lie," she warned.

"The Buddhist Trinity will bear me witness!"

Tai-yu lowered her head and was silent. Then, outside the eaves, they heard a crow caw before winging off southeast.

"Is that a good omen or a bad one?" wondered Pao-yu.

" 'Good fortune or bad in the affairs of men does not depend on a bird's cry,' " she quoted.

They were interrupted by Chiu-wen who came in to say, "Please go back, sir. His Lordship sent to ask whether you're back from school, and Sister Hsi-jen said you were. You'd better go quickly."

Pao-yu sprang up in alarm and hurried out, and Tai-yu did not venture to detain him. To know what the upshot was, read the next chapter.

CHAPTER 92

Comments on the Lives of Worthy Women of Old Fill Chiao-chieh with Admiration Chia Cheng, Toying with a Mother Pearl, Discourses on the Rise and Fall of Great Houses

Pao-yu, as soon as he had left Bamboo Lodge, asked Chiu-wen, "What does my father want me for?"

"He doesn't want you," she chuckled. "Sister Hsi-jen sent me to fetch you, and for fear you wouldn't come I made that up."

In relief he cried, "It's all very well to fetch me, but why give me such a fright?"

Back in Happy Red Court, Hsi-jen wanted to know where he had been all this time.

"With Miss Lin. We got talking about Cousin Pao-chai; that's what kept me there so long."

"What were you discussing?"

He told her then about his catechism.

"You two have no sense," scolded Hsi-jen. "It's all right to chat about family affairs or discuss certain lines of poetry; but why go in for Buddhist cant? It's not as if you were a monk."

"You don't understand. We have our own esoteric talk which no one else can join in."

"If your esoteric repartee leads to squabbles, we shall have to try to guess your riddles too," she answered teasingly.

"In the past I was young and she was childish too, so if I spoke tactlessly she used to flare up. Now that I'm more careful she never takes offence. But recently she's stopped coming here so often, and I have to go to school. That's why, when we do happen to meet, we feel rather like strangers."

"That's how it should be," approved Hsi-jen. "Now that

you're both several years older, how can you go on behaving as if you were children?"

He nodded. "I know. Never mind about that now. Tell me: Has the old lady sent any message for me?"

"No, none."

"She must have forgotten. Tomorrow's the first of the eleventh month, isn't it? It used to be her rule every year to hold a 'cold-dispelling party' that day, getting everybody together to drink and have fun. Today I asked for leave from school. As no message has come, shall I go tomorrow or not? If I do, I'll have asked for leave all for nothing. If I don't, and my father knows, he'll call me an idler."

"I think you'd better go," she said. "You're just beginning to study seriously, yet here you are wanting to rest. My advice to you is to work harder. Yesterday I heard your mother praise Master Lan for really concentrating on his books. Every evening after he comes back from school, he reads and writes essays on his own, not sleeping till nearly dawn. You're much older than he is, and his uncle too. If you lag behind him the old lady will be angry. So you'd better go to school tomorrow morning."

Sheh-yueh objected, "It's so cold, and he's already asked leave. If he goes, the tutor will want to know why he asked for leave in the first place. It'll look as if he fibbed so as to play truant. Let him have a day off, I say. Even if the old lady's forgotten, can't we have our own cold-dispelling party here? Wouldn't that be fun?"

"If you take that line," complained Hsi-jen, "he'll be even less willing to go."

"Well, I like a day's fun whenever I can get it. How can I compare with you, working so hard to keep your good reputation for the sake of two extra ounces of silver a month?"

"Little bitch!" swore Hsi-jen. "We were speaking seriously, but you go talking such nonsense."

"This isn't nonsense. It's you I'm thinking of."

"What do you mean?"

"If Master Pao goes to school, you'll wait glumly longing for his return to cheer us all up again. It's no use your playing the innocent. I know you!"

Before Hsi-jen could answer back, one of the Lady Dowager's maids arrived.

"The old lady says Master Pao needn't go to school tomorrow," she announced. "She has asked Aunt Hsueh to come over to help pass the time, and most likely all our young ladies will come too. Miss Hsiang-yun, Miss Hsiu-yen and Madam Chu's cousins have been invited as well to this 'cold-dispelling party'...."

Before she could finish Pao-yu cried excitedly, "You see? The old lady always enjoyed this party. So it's on the level, my cutting school tomorrow."

Hsi-jen could say nothing to this, and the maid went back.

After a spell of hard study Pao-yu had been counting on having good fun the next day. And the news that Aunt Hsueh would be coming made him assume that Pao-chai would be present too.

He said cheerfully, "Let's turn in now, so that we can get up early tomorrow morning."

That night passed without incident.

The next day, sure enough, he went over early to pay his respects to the Lady Dowager and then to his parents. When he reported that his grandmother had exempted him from attending school today, Chia Cheng raised no objections, and Pao-yu slowly withdrew. Once outside, he ran like the wind to the old lady's quarters. None of the others had yet arrived except the nurse bringing Hsi-feng's daughter Chiao-chieh, attended by several young maids.

Chiao-chieh paid her respects to the old lady then said, "Mama told me to come on ahead, to greet you and keep you company, great-grandmama. She'll be coming presently."

"Good child!" said the Lady Dowager with a fond smile. "I got up early and all this time I've been waiting, but so far only your Uncle Pao has come."

"Pay your respects to your uncle, miss," prompted the nurse.

Chiao-chieh curtseyed to Pao-yu, who returned her greeting.

"Last night," prattled Chiao-chieh, "I heard mama say she wants to invite you over for a talk, uncle."

"To talk about what?"

"Mama says Nanny Li has been teaching me to read for several years, but she doubts if I really know many characters. I told her, 'I can read all right. Let me show you.' She thought I was making it up, though, and didn't believe me, saying I couldn't possibly have learned because I play around the whole day long. I told her I don't find learning characters hard. Even the *Book of Filial Women* is easy to read. But mama says I'm trying to fool her. She wants you to test me, uncle, when you have time."

"There's a good child!" exclaimed the old lady, laughing. "It's because your mother can't read that she thought you were fooling her. Get your uncle to test you tomorrow, and that'll convince her."

"How many characters do you know?" asked Pao-yu.

"More than three thousand. I've read the *Book of Filial Women*, and a fortnight ago I started on the *Lives of Chaste Martyrs*."

"Can you understand them?" he asked. "If not, I can explain them to you."

"Yes, as her uncle you should do that for your niece," the old lady approved.

"We can pass over King Wen's queen," began Pao-yu. "Other virtuous and able queens were Queen Chiang who took off her trinkets and blames herself for the king's indolence, and Queen Wu-yen who was plain but able to pacify the state of Chi. As for talented women, there were Tsao Ta-ku, Pan Chieh-yu, Tsai Wen-chi and Hsieh Tao-yun.

"Meng Kuang who wore a thorn hairpin and cloth skirt; Pao Hsuan's wife who fetched water herself with a pitcher; Tao Kan's mother who cut off her hair and sold it to buy wine to entertain a guest; and Ouyang Hsiu's mother who used a grass stalk to write characters on the ground to teach her son to read and write, all could put up with poverty.

"There were others who had a hard time like Princess Lo-chang who kept a broken mirror and was finally reunited with her husband, and Su Hui who wove a brocade with a palindrome on it to send to her husband and moved him. While as for such dutiful daughters as Mu-lan who went to war in her father's place and Tsao Ngo who plunged into the river to recover her father's body, they are past counting.

"Then there were many chaste ladies such as Tsao-shih, who cut off her own nose rather than remarry; that's a story of the Wei State.

"There were such famous beauties as Wang Chiang, Hsi Shih, Fan Su, Hsiao-man and Chiang-hsien. There were also jealous wives such as Jen Huai's wife who burned up two concubines' hair, and Liu Pai-yu's wife who jumped into the Lo River and died after hearing him praise the charming Goddess of the River Lo. Of course Cho Wen-chun and the girl with the red whisk[1] were known for their...."

"That's enough," put in the old lady. "No need to go on. If you list too many, how can she remember them all?"

"I've read about some of those Uncle Pao named, but not all of them," said Chiao-chieh. "What he says about those I've read about helps me understand them better."

"As you obviously know how to read, there's no need to test you on that," he observed. "Besides, I'll have to go to school myself tomorrow."

"I heard mama say too that our maid Hung-yu used to work for you, Uncle Pao; and after mama took her she's never sent you another girl instead. Now mama wants to send you one called Wu-erh from the Liu family, but she doesn't know whether you'll have her or not."

"Just listen to her!" exclaimed Pao-yu in delight. "Your mother can send anyone she likes. Why ask me if I'll have her?" He turned to say laughingly to his grandmother, "Judging by my niece's looks and intelligence, she should outdo even Cousin Hsi-feng in future. Especially as she can read as well."

"It's good when girls can read," agreed the old lady. "But

---

[1] All these were celebrated beauties.

needlework is more important for them."

"I'm learning that too from Nanny Liu," said Chiao-chieh. "Appliqué work, chain-stitch and so on.   I'm not much good at it, but I'm learning some different stitches."

"In a family like ours," said the old lady, "of course we don't have to do such chores ourselves, but still it's best to know how to, so as not to have to depend on others in future."

"Yes, great-grandmama."

Chiao-chieh would have liked Pao-yu to explain the *Lives of Chaste Martyrs* to her, but he looked so preoccupied that she refrained from making this request.

Do you know what was preoccupying Pao-yu? It was the thought of Wu-erh. When first she was to have come to Happy Red Court, she had been prevented by illness; then when Lady Wang dismissed Ching-wen, they dared not choose any maids who were good-looking.   Later Pao-yu had visited Ching-wen in Wu Kuei's house and seen Wu-erh and her mother take things to her, and on that occasion he had thought Wu-erh charming. How lucky that Hsi-feng had remembered her and was sending her to replace Hung-yu!   So the foolish youth lost himself in rapturous day-dreams.

The old lady, grown tired of waiting, now sent maids to fetch her other visitors and presently Li Wan and her girl cousins arrived, as well as Tan-chun, Hsi-chun, Hsiang-yun and Tai-yu. Having paid their respects to the Lady Dowager they greeted each other.   Only Aunt Hsueh was still missing.   Maids were sent to invite her, and she brought Pao-chin with her.   Pao-yu paid his respects to Aunt Hsueh and greeted Pao-chin but looked in vain for Pao-chai and Hsiu-yen.

"Why hasn't Cousin Pao-chai come?" asked Tai-yu.

Aunt Hsueh gave the excuse that she was unwell — and Hsing Hsiu-yen had naturally not come because her future in-laws were present.   Pao-yu was disappointed by Pao-chai's absence, but as he had Tai-yu's company he dismissed her from his mind.

Soon Lady Hsing and Lady Wang arrived too.   When Hsi-feng heard of this, as it would be remiss for her to lag behind Their Ladyships she sent Ping-erh to excuse her, saying that she had a temperature but would come a little later.

"If she's not well, she needn't come," said the old lady. "It's time now for our meal."

Maids moved back the brazier and set out two tables in front of the old lady's couch. This done, the party sat down in due order. After dinner, they chatted around the fire, but there is no need to record their conversation.

Now what had kept Hsi-feng away? In the beginning it was embarrassment at going later than Lady Hsing and Lady Wang. And then Lai Wang's wife had arrived.

"Miss Ying-chun has sent someone with her regards," she announced. "And the woman says she's not called on Their Ladyships but come straight here."

Not knowing what to make of this, Hsi-feng called the messenger in.

"Is your mistress well?" she asked.

"No, it wasn't Miss Ying-chun who sent me," was the answer. "The fact is, Ssu-chi's mother has begged me to come to ask you a favour, madam."

"Ssu-chi has already been dismissed, so what can I do to help?"

"After Ssu-chi left here she kept weeping all day long. Then, the other day, that cousin of hers turned up. At sight of him, her mother was furious — she accused him of ruining her daughter's life and grabbed hold of him to beat him. Not a word did the young fellow say in self-defence. Ssu-chi hearing this came running out, bold as brass.

"'It's because of him that I was dismissed,' she told her mother. 'I hate him too for his heartlessness. If you want to beat him now that he's come, you'd better strangle me first!'

"Her mother swore, 'Shameless slut! What do you want to do?'

"Ssu-chi said, 'A woman can only marry once. I slipped up and let him take advantage of me, so now I belong to him, and I'll never, never marry anyone else. But what makes me angry is his lack of guts. A man should be responsible for his actions.

Why run away? If he'd never shown up, I'd have stayed single all my life. If you'd tried to marry me to someone else, ma, I should have killed myself. Now that he's here, ask him what his intentions are. If he hasn't had a change of heart, I'll kowtow farewell to you, ma, and you can count me as dead, for wherever he goes I'll go too, content even if we have to beg for food.'

"Her mother wept with rage and swore, 'You're my daughter. I won't let you marry him! How dare you defy me?'

"Then the silly girl smashed her head against the wall so that her brains spilled out, and she died in a pool of blood. Her mother wept, but as it was too late to save her she wanted her nephew to pay with his own life.

"That nephew of hers was an odd fellow too. He said, 'Don't worry. I've made some money outside, and I came back because of her — I was true to her. If you don't believe me, look here.' He took from his pocket a case of jewelry.

"Her mother relented then and asked, 'If that was what you wanted, why didn't you say so?'

"He told her, 'Most women are fickle. If I'd said I had money, it might have tempted her. Now I can see she was truly one in a thousand. I'll leave you these jewels and go and buy a coffin for her.'

"Ssu-chi's mother took the jewels and let him go, not carrying on any more about her daughter. Who could have imagined, though, that he got people to carry back *two* coffins.

" 'What do you want two coffins for?' she asked.

"He said with a smile, 'One's not enough. We need two.'

"The fact that he wasn't weeping made her think he was stupefied with grief. But after laying Ssu-chi in one coffin — without so much as a whimper — before anyone could see what he was doing he whipped out a small knife and cut his own throat! Ssu-chi's mother sobbed bitterly then with remorse. And now the whole neighbourhood knows of this and they want to report it to the authorities. She's frantic, that's why she's sent me to beg you to help. She'll be coming later to kowtow her thanks."

"What a silly girl!" exclaimed Hsi-feng in amazement. "And

up against such a simpleton too — it's too bad! No wonder she
took it so calmly when they found those things during the search
that day. I'd no idea she was such a strong character! Actually
I've no time to mind other people's business, but what you've
told me really makes my heart bleed. All right then, go and
tell Ssu-chi's mother that I'll get my husband to send Lai Wang
to straighten things out for her."

Only when Hsi-feng had sent this woman away did she go
over to the old lady's place.

To return to Chia Cheng. He was playing draughts one day
with Chan Kuang, and both still had about the same number
of pieces; but in one corner the issue was not yet decided and
each was trying to enclose that sector.

A gateman came in to announce, "Mr. Feng is waiting outside
to see you, sir."

"Show him in," ordered Chia Cheng.

The man withdrew to do so, and as Feng Tzu-ying entered
Chia Cheng rose to welcome him. Having taken a seat in the
study, Feng saw that they had been playing draughts.

"Please go on with your game," he urged them. "I'd like to
watch."

"My game isn't worth watching," said Chan Kuang with a
smile.

"Don't be so modest," replied Feng. "Please carry on."

"Have you come on business?" Chia Cheng wanted to know.

"Nothing of any importance. Please go on with your game,
uncle, and I can learn by watching."

Chia Cheng told Chan, "Master Feng is a good friend of ours.
As he's in no hurry, let's finish this game and then we can have
a chat. You can watch from the side, Master Feng."

"Are you playing for stakes?"

"Yes, we are," said Chan.

"In that case I mustn't interfere."

"It doesn t matter if you do," joked Chia Cheng. "He's lost
over ten taels already. but he never pays up. I shall have to
make him stand us a meal some day instead."

"That's all right," chuckled Chan.

"Do you gentlemen both play from scratch?" asked Feng.

"We used to." Chia Cheng smiled. "But he kept losing. Now I'm handicapped by giving him two pieces at the start, yet he still loses. From time to time he revokes too, and if I challenge him he gets worked up."

"That's not true!" protested Chan Kuang laughingly.

"Just wait and see," said Chia Cheng.

They played as they chatted, and when the game was finished they counted their pieces. After deducting the one with which he had opened, Chan had lost by seven pieces.

Feng remarked, "You lost out trying to enclose uncle's pieces. And so, being less vulnerable, he got the upper hand."

"Excuse us for ignoring you," Chia Cheng apologized. "Now we can talk."

"I haven't seen you for some time, uncle, so I called in the first place to pay my respects," said Feng. "Another reason is that the vice-prefect of Kwangsi has come to the capital with four novelties from the south or overseas, all fit to present to the court. One is a carved ebony screen with twenty-four leaves. They're inlaid not with jade but with the finest marble carved with landscapes, figures, pavilions, flowers and birds. On each leaf are fifty to sixty girls in palace costume, so the screen is called 'Spring Dawn in the Han Palace.' All the girls' features, their hands and the draperies are most delicately carved. The embellishments and designs are excellent too. It seems to me just the thing for the main hall of your honourable Grand View Garden.

"Then there's a clock more than three feet high in the form of a boy holding a time-piece, which announces each hour in turn, while inside some clock-work figures play musical chimes. As both these are heavy objects, I didn't bring them. But the two things I have with me are quite intriguing too."

With that he produced a brocade box swathed in white silk floss and, having removed some padding, showed them a glass case in which was a gold stand mounted on red crepe. On the stand lay a dazzling bright pearl, as large as a dried longan.

"This is called a mother pearl," Feng told them, then asked for a plate.

Chan Kuang at once passed him a black lacquer tea-tray.

"Will this do?"

"Yes, that's fine."

Feng took a silk pouch from his pocket and emptied all the pearls in it on to the tray, then placed the mother pearl in the middle and set the tray on the table. At once, all the small pearls rolled over and over until they were close to the big one, propping it up, all without exception nestling against the big pearl.

"Fantastic!" exclaimed Chan.

"I've heard of this," said Chia Cheng. "This is how it came by its name as the mother of pearls."

Now Feng turned to the page who had accompanied him.

"Where is that box?" he called.

The page at once brought over a rosewood box. When opened it disclosed, on a lining of striped silk, some folded blue gauze.

"What is this?" asked Chan.

"A curtain of mermaid-gauze."

When Feng took it out of the box, the curtain — each fold less than five inches long — was less than half an inch thick. He unfolded it layer by layer. And by the time he had unfolded some ten layers, it was already too big for the table.

"See, there are two more folds," he said. "It can only be hung in a room with a high ceiling. This is woven of mermaid-silk. In the heat of summer, hung in the hall, it will keep out all flies and mosquitoes. It is light and transparent too."

"Don't spread it all out," interposed Chia Cheng, "or you'll have trouble folding it up again."

Then Chan helped Feng refold the curtain.

"The price for these four things isn't exorbitant," Feng said. "He's willing to sell them for twenty thousand taels: ten thousand for the mother pearl, five thousand for the curtain, and five thousand for the screen and the clock combined."

"We can't afford that!" exclaimed Chia Cheng.

"You are related to the Imperial House," said Feng. "Couldn't they use things of this sort in the Palace?"

"There are plenty of things they could use, but where is so much money to come from?" Chia Cheng retorted. "Wait, though, till I've sent these inside to show the old lady."

"Certainly," Feng agreed.

Chia Cheng ordered a servant to ask Chia Lien to take the pearl and curtain to the old lady; and Lady Hsing, Lady Wang and Hsi-feng were invited over to see them. They examined each in turn.

"He has two other novelties: a screen and a musical clock," Chia Lien informed them. "He's asking twenty thousand taels for all four."

"Of course they're good," said Hsi-feng. "But we haven't so much spare money. And we're not like those provincial governors who have to send tribute to court. In fact, for years I've been thinking that a family like ours should invest in some real estate — sacrificial land, manor houses or burial sites. Then in future, if things go badly for our descendants, they'll have something to fall back on and won't be bankrupted. This is my idea, but I don't know whether the old lady and the masters and mistresses agree or not. If the gentlemen want to buy these — that's up to them."

The old lady and the rest agreed with her.

"Then I'll take them back," said Chia Lien. "It was Lord Cheng who told me to bring these to show the old lady, thinking they could be presented to the Palace — no one spoke of buying them to keep ourselves. But before the old lady says a word you come out with all that ill-omened talk!"

He took the things away, simply telling Chia Cheng that the old lady did not want them.

Then Chia Cheng told Feng, "These are excellent things, but we haven't got the money. I'll keep my eyes open, though, and if I find someone who wants them I'll let you know."

Feng had to put pearl and curtain away and sit down again to make polite conversation, but feeling disheartened he soon rose to take his leave.

"Do stay and have dinner with us," urged Chia Cheng.

"I don't want to put you to too much trouble, uncle."

"It's no trouble at all."

Just at this point, a servant announced Lord Sheh even as he walked in, and there was the usual exchange of civilities.

Presently wine and dishes were brought in and the gentlemen started drinking. After four or five cups, mention was made again of the novelties from the south.

"Such things are hard to dispose of," remarked Feng. "Apart from distinguished families like yours, who else can afford to buy them?"

"That's not necessarily so," Chia Cheng demurred.

Chia Sheh added, "Our family isn't what it was — we're simply keeping up appearances."

"How is Master Chen of the East Mansion?" Feng inquired. "Last time I met him, in the course of conversation he mentioned that his son's second wife can't compare with his first from the Chin family. I forgot to ask which family the new young mistress comes from."

"She's from a noble family too," said Chia Cheng. "She's the daughter of old Mr. Hu, who was Governor of the Metropolitan Circuit."

"I know Mr. Hu," replied Feng. "His household isn't too well regulated. Still, that doesn't matter if the girl herself is good."

Chia Lien changed the subject by saying, "I've heard from someone in the cabinet that Yu-tsun is to be promoted again."

"Good," said Chia Cheng. "But is this news reliable, I wonder?"

"There must be something in it," insisted Chia Lien.

"I was at the Ministry of Civil Affairs earlier on, and I heard the same talk," confirmed Feng. "Is respected Master Yu-tsun a member of your honourable clan?"

"Yes, he is," said Chia Cheng.

"A close relation or a distant connection?"

"It's a long story. He's a native of Huchou Prefecture in Chekiang, who moved to Soochow and didn't make out too well there; but a certain Chen Shih-yin befriended him and helped him out. Then he passed the palace examination and was appointed a magistrate, after which he married one of the Chen family's maids — his present wife is his second. Then Chen Shih-yin lost all his money and seems to have disappeared. At the time when Yu-tsun was dismissed from his post, he didn't know our family. My brother-in-law Lin Ju-hai, who was Salt Commissioner of Yangchow then, engaged him as a tutor for his daughter. When word came that he might be reinstated, he decided to return to the capital; and as my niece happened to be coming to visit us, her father asked Yu-tsun to escort her here and wrote a letter recommending him to me. Since he made a fairly good impression on me, we saw quite a bit of each other. The strange thing was that Yu-tsun knew our whole family history from the start — all about our Jung and Ning Mansions, the inmates of each, and different happenings here. So we were soon on a familiar footing." He added with a smile, "He very soon learned how to climb the official ladder, getting himself promoted from the post of a prefect to that of a censor and then, in another few years, becoming Vice-Minister of Civil Affairs and Minister of War. After that, for some reason, he was demoted three ranks. Now it seems he is going up again."

"Prosperity and ruin," observed Feng, "are as unpredictable as success or failure in one's official career."

"Yu-tsun counts as one who has got off lightly," rejoined Chia Cheng. "There are other families much like ours, the Chen family for instance, who had the same achievements to their credit, the same hereditary honours, the same way of life, with whom we were very close. A few years ago when they came to the capital, they would send people to call on us and they cut quite a dash. Before long, though, their property was confiscated and no more has been heard of them ever since. We don't know what's become of the family and can't help worrying about them. Don't you think this must strike fear into officials?"

"Well, our family should be safe," Chia Sheh observed.

"Of course, your honourable family has nothing to fear," Feng assured him. "You have Her Highness in the Palace to watch over you, and a host of good friends and kinsmen. Besides, not one of your family from the old lady down to your young masters is grasping or niggardly."

"That may be so," said Chia Cheng. "But they have no virtue or ability either. How long can they go on just living on their capital?"

"Don't talk like that," protested Chia Sheh. "Let's have some more drinks."

They drank a few more cups, then rice was served. After they had finished the meal and drunk some tea, Feng's page came over to whisper something to him, and he asked permission to leave.

Chia Sheh asked the page what he had said.

"It's snowing outside, sir, and the first watch has sounded."

Chia Cheng sent a servant to look, who reported that more than one inch of snow had fallen.

"Have you put those valuables away?" Chia Cheng asked.

"Yes, uncle," said Feng. "If your honourable family has any use for them, we can of course negotiate the price."

"I'll keep it in mind."

"I'll wait to hear from you. It's cold; please don't see me out."

Chia Cheng and Chia Sheh told Chia Lien to see him out. If you wish to know the sequel, read the next chapter.

CHAPTER 93

A Servant of the Chen Family Offers
His Services to the Chias
A Scandal in Water Moon Convent
Is Exposed

After Feng Tzu-ying had gone, Chia Cheng summoned the gateman.

"Today the Duke of Linan sent invitations to a banquet," he said. "Do you know what the occasion is?"

"I asked, sir," replied the gateman. "It's no special celebration, but a company of young actors — a company with a fine reputation — has come to the Prince of Nanan's Mansion; and the duke is so pleased with them that he's putting on two days' performances for his friends' enjoyment. It should be very lively. There's probably no need to send presents."

Chia Sheh came over at this point to ask Chia Cheng if he would be going the next day.

"I suppose we'll have to," was the reply, "to show our appreciation."

Just then the gateman came back to report, "The secretary from your yamen has come to ask you to go there tomorrow, sir, as the minister has some business and will need you earlier than usual."

"Very well."

Then two of the family's bailiffs came in and paid their respects. After kowtowing they stood there at attention.

"Are you two from Huo Village?" Chia Cheng asked.

"Yes, sir."

Instead of inquiring their business, he chatted with Chia Sheh till the latter rose to go and was escorted home by servants with lanterns.

Chia Lien then asked the bailiffs, "Well, what have you come for?"

"We collected the rent in kind for the tenth month," they reported. "It should have arrived here tomorrow, but outside the city our carts were commandeered and, when we protested, all the things on them were dumped on the ground. We told them these weren't merchants' carts but were delivering rent to your mansions. Still they paid no attention. When we told the carters to drive on, some runners beat them up and made off with our two carts. So we've come to report this, sir, and ask you to send to the yamen to get them back. Those lawless runners should be punished too. You've no idea, sir, how hard it is on merchants. All their goods are unloaded, regardless, and their carts are driven away. If the carters so much as murmur, they get their heads smashed in."

"Outrageous!" swore Chia Lien.

He there and then wrote a note and told the servants, "Take this to the local yamen and demand the return of the carts as well as the produce. We won't stand for it if one single thing is missing! And send Chou Jui here at once!"

But Chou Jui was absent. And when they looked for Lai Wang, they found he had gone out after lunch and not yet returned.

"Not one of the bastards is here!" swore Chia Lien. "They do not work — just gorge themselves all the year round." He ordered his pages, "Go and find them, quick!" Then he went home to sleep.

The next day the Duke of Linan sent over again to invite them.

Chia Cheng told Chia Sheh, "I have business in my yamen. And Lien can't go either, he has to stay in to deal with this commandeering of our carts. For politeness' sake, you'd better take Pao-yu over for the day."

Chia Sheh nodded. "That's all right."

Then Chia Cheng sent for Pao-yu. "You're to go with Lord Sheh to the opera in the Duke of Linan's place," he told him.

Pao-yu, only too delighted, changed his clothes and went off with Pei-ming, Shao-hung and Chu-yao to present himself to Chia Sheh and pay his respects. They drove to the duke's mansion, where the gateman announced their arrival then ushered them in. Chia Sheh led Pao-yu into the courtyard in which a lively party had assembled. After they had paid their respects to the duke and greeted the other guests, everyone sat down to talk. Then the manager of the company stepped forward with an ivory tablet and a compendium of their repertoire. Falling on one knee he said:

"Please make your choice, gentlemen."

In order of seniority they selected operas. And when it came to Chia Sheh's turn, the manager caught sight of Pao-yu. He hurried straight over to him and saluted.

"Please choose a couple of scenes, Master Pao," he said.

This man with his clear complexion and red lips was fresh as lotus taken from the water, graceful as a jade tree in the breeze. Pao-yu recognized him at one glance as Chiang Yu-han. He had heard not long before that Chiang had brought a company of young actors to the capital, but his old friend had failed to come to see him. He could hardly stand up in this company to greet him.

"When did you come back?" he asked him with a smile.

Chiang pointing at himself murmured, "Surely you know, Second Master."

As they could not very well converse in public, Pao-yu just picked one item at random. After Chiang Yu-han had moved on, there was some speculation about him.

"Who is he?" someone asked.

"He used to play young ladies," another man answered. "Now that he's too old for that, he acts as manager instead and sometimes takes young men's roles. He's put aside a tidy sum of money and owns a couple of shops, but he won't give up his profession and goes on managing an opera company."

"I suppose he must have married," one guest remarked.

"No, he's not engaged yet. He's got this idea fixed that marriage is for keeps, affecting one's whole life, not something to enter into casually; so his wife, regardless of her social status, must measure up to his talent. That's why he's still unmarried."

Pao-yu wondered who the lucky girl would be to marry a man of his ability.

Then the performance started. And very lively it was too, with *Kunchu, Yiyang, Kaochiang* and *Pangtse* operas.[1] At noon tables were set out for the feast, and when they had watched a little longer Chia Sheh rose to leave.

"It's still early," said the duke, coming over to press him to stay. "And I've heard that Chi-kuan is going to play in their best item — a scene from *The Oil-Vendor and the Courtesan*."

Pao-yu hearing this was most eager to stay, and so Chia Sheh resumed his seat. Then, sure enough, Chiang Yu-han came on in the role of the oil-vendor Chin, and gave an excellent performance of how the young man cared for the courtesan when she was drunk, after which the two of them drank and sang together in affectionate intimacy.

Pao-yu was not interested in the heroine, having eyes only for the young hero. And he was quite enraptured by his singing, for Chiang Yu-han had a resonant voice, clear enunciation and good sense of rhythm. By the time this scene ended he was firmly convinced that Chiang was a romantic, completely unique. He thought, "*The Book of Music* rightly says, 'Stirred feelings find expression in sound, and when the sound follows a pattern we call it music.' So sounds, notes and music take some understanding, and a study has to be made of their origin. Poetry can convey emotions, but it can't thrill us to the marrow. In future I really must make a study of music."

His reverie was interrupted by Chia Sheh rising to leave. As their host could not prevail on him to stay, Pao-yu had no choice but to go back with him.

On their return Chia Sheh went home. And Pao-yu, paying his duty call on his father, found him just back from the ministry questioning Chia Lien about the seizure of their carts.

---

[1] Different kinds of operas from the provinces.

Chia Lien said, "I sent servants there today with my card, but the magistrate was out. His factotum said, 'His Excellency knew nothing about this, and gave no orders for the requisition of carts. It's all the fault of those trouble-making scoundrels who take unfair advantage of people outside. As these are His Lordship's carts, I'll send at once to investigate and guarantee to return them as well as the things tomorrow. If there is any delay, I shall report it to His Excellency and have them severely punished. But since he is away now, I hope His Lordship will be understanding, as it would be better not to trouble my master.' "

"Without some official order, who would dare do such a thing?" demanded Chia Cheng.

"You don't understand, sir," said Chia Lien. "It's like this everywhere outside the city. I'm sure they'll return our property tomorrow." With that he withdrew.

Then Pao-yu paid his respects to his father, who questioned him briefly before sending him to call on his grandmother.

As the stewards had been out the day before when Chia Lien sent for them, he had summoned them all and now they were ready waiting. Having cursed them roundly he told the chief steward Lai Ta, "Bring me the roster of servants and check their names; then write an announcement for them all to read. If anyone sneaks off without asking leave and isn't on hand when called, holding up our business, you're to beat him for me and drive him out forthwith!"

"Yes, sir! Yes, sir!"

Lai Ta went out to pass on this warning, and thereafter the servants were more circumspect.

Soon after this, a man came to the gate wearing a felt cap, blue cotton clothes and slippers with cloth soles and leather uppers. He saluted the servants on duty, who looked him over from head to foot before asking where he came from.

"From the Chen family in the south," he answered. "I've a letter from my master which I'd like to trouble you gentlemen to take in to His Lordship."

When they heard this they stood up and offered him a seat. "You must be tired. Sit down," they urged. "We'll see to it for you."

One gateman went in and reported this, handing Chia Cheng the letter which he opened and read:

> ... Our families have been long-standing friends sharing similar tastes, and I have the greatest admiration for you. My criminal incompetence deserved punishment by a thousand deaths, but instead the court with gracious clemency sent me to this border region. Now our fortunes have declined and our family is scattered. Our servant's son Pao Yung, who used to serve me, though he has no outstanding ability is quite honest. If you would take him on, enabling him to support himself, I should be infinitely grateful for your kindness. This is my letter's sole purpose. I shall write more fully later.

After reading this Chia Cheng smiled.

"We were thinking that our staff is too large," he said. "However, we can't turn away someone recommended by the Chen family." He told the gateman, "Bring him here. We'll keep him and find him some appropriate work."

So the gateman fetched Pao Yung, who kowtowed three times to Chia Cheng. Getting up again he said, "My master sends his respects, sir." Then he went down on one knee in salute, saying, "Pao Yung pays his respects, sir."

Chia Cheng asked after Mr. Chen's health and scrutinized Pao Yung as he stood there in an attitude of respect. Just over five feet and broad-shouldered, he had thick eyebrows, protuberant eyes and a low forehead. His face was bearded and swarthy.

"Have you always been in the Chen family or only worked there for a few years?" Chia Cheng asked.

"I have always been their man, sir."

"Then why do you want to leave them now?"

"I didn't want to, but my master insisted. He said, 'You wouldn't agree to going anywhere else, but serving the Chia family will be like serving us.' So I came, sir."

"Your master should never have got into such trouble, reducing him to these straits."

"If I may make bold to say so, it's because my master's too good. He always treats people honestly, and that landed him in trouble."

"Surely it's good to be honest."

"But because he was *too* honest, sir, nobody liked him and he offended some people."

"Well, in that case Heaven will give him his due deserts," Chia Cheng laughed. Before Pao Yung could reply he went on to ask, "Is it true, as I heard, that your younger master's name is also Pao-yu?"

"Yes, sir."

"Is he doing well?"

"As for our Master Pao, sir, that's a strange story. He's like his father — too honest. As a child, what he liked best was playing about with girls, and though his parents gave him several good beatings he wouldn't mend his ways. That year our mistress came to the capital, Master Pao fell very ill. He lost consciousness for so long that his father was frantic and had all the funeral preparations made. Then, luckily, he came round. But he started raving that he'd met a girl by an archway who took him into a temple, inside which were many cabinets filled with albums. Then going into a room he saw countless girls who'd all turned into ghosts or skeletons. That set him screaming with fright. As soon as our master saw that he'd come to he gave him good medical treatment, and gradually he recovered. After that, when our master sent him off to amuse himself with the girls, as he always used to, we discovered that he'd changed — he no longer enjoyed his old pleasures but much preferred to study. Even when they tried to coax him away from his books, he took no interest at all. So now, little by little, he's learning to help his father manage the household."

Chia Cheng digested this in thoughtful silence.

"Go off and rest now," he said presently. "When a task comes up that you can do, of course we'll assign you some duties."

Pao Yung thanked him and withdrew, going out with the gateman to rest. But no more of this.

One morning, Chia Cheng rose early and was setting off to his yamen when he noticed the servants at the gate whispering and muttering among themselves as if they had some news for him which they dared not report outright. He called them over.

"What is this hole-and-corner business?" he demanded.

"We hardly dare tell you, sir," one of them answered.

"Why not? Out with it!"

"This morning when we got up and opened the gate, we found a sheet of paper pasted on it, covered with scurrilous writing."

"The idea!" exclaimed Chia Cheng. "What was it?"

"Dirty talk about Water Moon Convent, sir."

"Bring me the paper," he ordered.

"We tried to take it down, but it was glued on too firmly; so we copied it out, then soaked the paper to get it off. Just now Li Teh brought another sheet to show us — the same as the one on the gate. We dare not hide it from you, sir."

They presented the paper, and he read:

> Chia Chin, a young supervisor,
> To Water Moon Convent came.
> One male among so many females,
> He's free to drink, whore and game.
> This worthless young master set in charge
> Is giving the Jung Mansion a bad name!

So enraged by this that his mind reeled, Chia Cheng ordered the servants to say nothing about it but to make a quiet search of the walls of the alleys in the vicinity. He then sent for Chia Lien, who came hurrying over.

Without any preliminaries Chia Cheng asked him, "Have you ever checked up on those novices in Water Moon Convent?"

"No," said Chia Lien. "Chin's always been in charge of them."

"Do you think him capable of such a trust?"

"Since you ask, sir, I suppose he must have fallen down on the job."

Chia Cheng sighed. "Look what's written on this poster!"

Chia Lien read it and exclaimed, "Could this be true?"

Just then along came Chia Jung with an envelope marked "Confidential" addressed to Chia Cheng. When they opened it, they found another copy of the same anonymous lampoon as that pasted on the gate.

Chia Cheng said, "Tell Lai Ta to go at once with three or four carriages to the convent, to bring back all those novices. Don't let word of this get out. Just tell them that they're wanted in the Palace."

Lai Ta went off to carry out these orders.

Now the young Buddhist and Taoist novices when first they went to the convent had been in the charge of an old abbess who daily taught them litanies and invocations. But because the Imperial Consort never sent for them, they gradually became lax in their devotions; and as they grew older they began to take an interest in men. Chia Chin was a romantic. In his view, it had simply been a childish whim which made these actresses enter a convent, and accordingly he went to dally with them. As Fang-kuan, genuinely devout, was deaf to his enticements, he turned his attention to the other girls. Among these were a Buddhist named Chin-hsiang and a Taoist named Ho-hsien, both of whom had seductive charm. So Chia Chin became their lover and whenever they had the time they would get together and learn how to sing and play the fiddle.

Since this was the middle of the tenth month and Chia Chin had just brought the monthly allowance for the convent, he hit on an idea.

"I've brought your allowance," he told the girls. "But as I can't get back to town today, I'll have to spend the night here. It's very cold, isn't it? So suppose we sit up together to enjoy these sweetmeats and wine that I've brought with me?"

The novices, very pleased, set tables ready and invited the older nuns too. Fang-kuan was the only one who declined to join them. After a few cups Chia Chin proposed playing some drinking games.

"We don't know how to," said Chin-hsiang and the others. "Let's just play the guessing-fingers game, and whoever loses must drink. Wouldn't that be simpler?"

The older nuns objected, "It's only just after noon, and it wouldn't look right to have a rowdy party. Let's drink a few cups, then those who like can leave first. Those who want to keep Master Chin company can drink all they please this evening, and we won't interfere."

Just then a serving-woman hurried in.

"Break this up, this minute!" she cried. "Here's Mr. Lai from the Chia Mansion!"

The novices hastily set about clearing the tables and urged Chia Chin to hide.

But emboldened by a few cups of wine he blustered, "I came to bring the monthly allowance. I'm not afraid!"

While he was still speaking, in came Lai Ta. The sight that met his eyes enraged him. But as Chia Cheng had enjoined strict secrecy, he forced himself to smile.

"So you are here too, Master Chin," he said.

"What brings *you* here, Mr. Lai?" asked Chia Chin who had risen to his feet.

"I'm glad you're here, sir. Tell these novices to get ready at once to drive to town. · They're wanted in the Palace."

This puzzled them all, but before they could question him the steward continued, "Time presses. Be quick about it, or we may be shut out."

The novices had to mount the carriages then. And Lai Ta, riding a big mule, escorted them back to the city.

Meanwhile Chia Cheng, too angry to go to his yamen, sat alone in his study sighing over this scandal, and Chia Lien felt constrained to stay with him.

Then a gateman came in to announce, "His Lordship Chang who should be on duty in the yamen this evening is ill, sir, and they would like you to take over for him."

Chia Cheng was waiting for Lai Ta's return to deal with Chia Chin. Exasperated at having to go back on duty now, he made no answer. Chia Lien stepped up to him.

"Lai Ta left after lunch, and the convent is some twenty *li* from town; so even if he hurries he can't get back till the second watch," he said. "If you are needed at the yamen, sir, you can go with an easy mind. When Lai Ta gets back, I'll tell him to detain the novices and keep the matter quiet. You can deal with them when you come home tomorrow. If Chia Chin comes, we needn't tell him anything either, but see how he accounts for himself to you tomorrow."

Chia Cheng seeing reason in this went off to his yamen, finally giving Chia Lien a chance to go home. He made his way slowly back, inwardly blaming Hsi-feng for recommending Chia Chin; but as she was ill he knew he would have to wait before reproaching her.

However, through the servants' gossiping word of this had already reached the inner chambers. Ping-erh, who heard it first, at once told Hsi-feng. After a bad night Hsi-feng was in low spirits, worried over the trouble at Iron-Threshold Temple. The news that an anonymous lampoon had been put up outside alarmed her.

"What does it say?" she asked quickly.

Here Ping-erh slipped up. "It's nothing important," she said casually. "Something to do with Steamed-Bread Convent."

Hsi-feng with her guilty conscience was so consternated by this that she could not speak. She came over dizzy and after a fit of coughing spat out a mouthful of blood.

In a fluster Ping-erh corrected herself. "It's only some problem over those Buddhist and Taoist novices in Water Moon Convent. Why should that upset you so, madam?"

"Ai! You fool!" exclaimed Hsi-feng in her relief. "Was it Water Moon Convent or Steamed-Bread Convent? Make up your mind!"

"I misheard it the first time, then discovered that it was Water Moon Convent, not Steamed-Bread Convent. Just now, by a slip of the tongue, I gave you the wrong name."

"I knew it must be Water Moon Convent. What have I to do with Steamed-Bread Convent? I did put Chin in charge of

that convent. Probably he's been helping himself to their monthly allowance."

"I didn't hear talk of that but of some scandal."

"Well, I care even less about that. Where is Master Lien?"

"They say Lord Cheng is so angry that he can't very well
leave him. When I learned there was trouble I told the maids
they mustn't blab about it; but who knows whether Their Ladyships have heard this talk or not. It seems the master ordered
Lai Ta to fetch those girls back. I've sent to find out what's
up. As you're unwell, madam, I don't think you need bother
about their affairs."

Just then Chia Lien came in. Hsi-feng wanted to question
him, but his scowling face made her pretend to know nothing
about this business.

While Chia Lien was having supper Lai Wang came in to
report, "They're asking for you outside, sir. Lai Ta is back."

"Is Chin with him?" asked Chia Lien.

"Yes, he's come too."

"Go and tell Lai Ta that the master has gone to his yamen.
The girls are to stay in the Garden for the time being. Tomor-
row, when the master comes back, they'll be sent to the Palace.
Tell Chin to wait for me in the inner study."

Then Lai Wang went off.

When Chia Chin went to the study, the way the servants
pointed at him and nudged each other made him doubt this talk
about a summons to the Palace. He asked what was afoot, but
no one would tell him. He was puzzling over this when Chia
Lien came in and, having paid his respects, Chia Chin stood at
attention.

"We don't know what Her Highness wants these girls for,"
he said. "I brought them as fast as I could. Luckily I took
them their allowance today and was still there, so I came back
with Lai Ta. I suppose you know all this, uncle."

"What do I know? *You're* the one in the know," Chia Lien
rapped out.

Chia Chin, though mystified, dared not ask his meaning.

"Fine goings-on!" Chia Lien fumed. "The master is furious!"

"I've done nothing wrong, uncle. I take them their allowance every month, and the girls keep up their devotions."

Chia Lien saw that he was in the dark, and as they had been playmates together he sighed.

"Shut up! Take a look at this."

He drew the lampoon from his boot and tossed it to him. Chia Chin picked it up and read it.

"Who's behind this?" he faltered, pale with fright. "I haven't offended anyone — why go for me like this? I only go there once a month to take them the money. These charges are sheer lies. But if the master comes back and has me beaten up, I shall die of the injustice! Worse still, if my mother hears of it she'll have me beaten to death!" As they were alone he went down on his knees to plead, "Have a heart, uncle! Save me!" He then kowtowed repeatedly, tears streaming from his eyes.

Chia Lien reflected, "This is the sort of thing the master abominates. If investigation proves that it's true, there will be a fearful scene. If the scandal gets out, our reputation will suffer and that lampoonist will become even bolder. Then we'll have a lot more trouble later on. It would be better, while the master's on duty, to fix up some way with Lai Ta to hush it up so as to avoid further trouble. So far no evidence has been produced."

His mind made up he said, "Don't try to fool me. Do you think I don't know the devilry you've been up to? If the master beats you to make you confess, your only way out is to refuse to admit it. Get up now, you shameless creature!"

Soon after this Lai Ta joined them, and Chia Lien discussed his plan with him.

"Master Chin has really behaved outrageously," said Lai Ta. "When I went to the convent just now they were drinking! The charges in that lampoon must be true."

"Hear that, Chin?" said Chia Lien. "Lai Ta wouldn't make that up, would he?"

Chia Chin blushed and dared not say a word.

Then Chia Lien urged Lai Ta, "Just say that you found Master Chin at home and so you brought him along, but you haven't seen me. Tomorrow you must try to persuade the master not to question those girls, but instead to fetch a broker to take them away and sell them. If Her Highness asks for them, we can buy some others."

Thinking this over, Lai Ta realized that a scandal would do no good but would further damage the family's reputation. Accordingly he agreed.

Then Chia Lien said to Chia Chin, "Go with Mr. Lai and do whatever he tells you." Chia Chin kowtowed his thanks and went off with the steward, to whom he kowtowed again when they came to a quiet spot.

"You're really gone too far, Master Chin," declared Lai Ta. "I don't know whom you offended to land yourself in this mess. Just think, what enemies have you?"

Chia Chin racked his brains and suddenly thought of one.

To know who it was, read the next chapter.

CHAPTER 94

The Lady Dowager Gives a Feast to Celebrate the Strange Blossoming of the Crab-Apple Trees The Loss of Pao-yu's Jade of Spiritual Understanding Heralds Trouble

After Lai Ta had taken Chia Chin off, the night passed without incident as they waited for Chia Cheng's return. The novices, overjoyed to be back in the Garden, hoped to have a good look round before going to the Palace the next day. However, Lai Ta ordered the matrons and pages there to keep watch and to supply them with food but not allow them to stir a single step. So the girls, although puzzled by this, had to stay there quietly until it was light. The maids in the different lodges in the Garden had heard of their arrival and summons to the Palace, but did not know the real facts of the case.

The next morning, Chia Cheng was about to leave his office when the minister sent him estimates of the costs for public works in two provinces, which he had to check at once before going home. He therefore sent Chia Lien instructions not to wait for his return but to make a thorough investigation as soon as Lai Ta was back, and then to take what action he thought fit.

This message pleased Chia Lien on Chin's account. He reflected, "If I hush up this business completely, uncle may smell a rat. I'd better report it to Her Ladyship and do as she suggests; for then even if it's not what he would have done he can't hold *me* to blame." Thus resolved, he went in to see Lady Wang.

"Yesterday the master was angry over that lampoon," he announced, explaining its contents. "He had Chin and the novices brought here for an investigation. Today, as he has no time to look into this scandal, he's told me to report it to you, madam, to do as you think fit. So I've come to ask you how we should deal with this."

"How disgraceful!" exclaimed Lady Wang, very shocked. "If Chin really carried on like that, our family should disown him. But what a scoundrel that lampoonist must be! How could he sling mud like that? Have you asked Chin whether there's any truth in it?"

"I did ask him just now. But think, madam, who would admit to anything so shameless even if he'd really done it? Still, I don't believe Chin would dare, for fear of the consequences, knowing that Her Highness might send for these girls any time. To my mind, it shouldn't be hard to find out the truth. But suppose it *is* true, madam, what will you do?"

"Where are those girls now?"

"All locked up in the Garden."

"Do the young ladies know about this?"

"I expect they've all heard of their summons to the Palace. There hasn't been any other gossip outside."

"That's good. These creatures mustn't be kept here a moment longer. I was in favour of packing them off before, but the rest of you insisted on keeping them — and now see what's come of it! Tell Lai Ta to take them away and carefully trace their families, if they have any. Then let him get out the bonds of those whose families can be found and draw a few dozen taels to hire a boat and send them back, with a reliable escort, to where they came from. When they've all been manumitted that will be the end of that. If we were to force them all to go back to secular life just because one or two of them have gone to the bad, that would be too heartless. And if we made them over to official brokers here, even though *we* didn't ask for any money they'd still sell them, not caring at all whether they lived or died.

"As for Chin, you must give him a good talking to. He's not to show his face here any more, except for sacrifices and celebrations. And he'd better be careful to steer clear of the master if he's in one of his tempers, or else he'll settle Chin's hash! Another thing: tell the accountants' office to cancel this allowance. And send word to Water Moon Convent that, on the master's orders, they're not to receive young gentlemen from our house except when they go to sacrifice at one of the graves there. If there's any more talk we'll drive away the whole lot, including the old abbess."

Chia Lien assented and withdrew to notify Lai Ta.

"This is how Her Ladyship wants you to handle this business," he informed him. "When it's done, let me know so that I can report to her. And better see to it quickly; then when the master comes back you can report to him that these were her instructions."

"Our mistress is really a saintly soul!" was Lai Ta's comment. "Fancy sending those creatures home, with an escort too! Well, as she's so kind-hearted, I shall have to, find some reliable man. As for Master Chin, I'll leave you to deal with him. And I'll try to track down that lampoonist so that we can crack down on him."

Chia Lien nodded and said, "Right."

He lost no time then in dismissing Chia Chin, while Lai Ta made haste to take the novices away and deal with them according to his instructions.

That evening when Chia Cheng came back, they reported this to him; and as Chia Cheng disliked trouble, on hearing this he let the matter drop. Of course rogues outside, when they heard that twenty-four girls had been dismissed from the Chia Mansion, all wanted to get their hands on them; so whether they ever reached home or not is uncertain, and we have no means of guessing.

Now that Tai-yu's health was improving, Tzu-chuan had time on her hands, and being puzzled by the report that the novices had been summoned to the Palace she went to the old lady's place for news. She happened to find Yuan-yang free too, and sitting down to chat she asked her about the nuns.

"This is news to me," said Yuan-yang in surprise. "I'll find out later on from Madam Lien."

As they were talking, two serving-women from Fu Shih's

family arrived to pay their respects to the Lady Dowager. Yuan-yang was taking them there when they heard that the old lady was having a nap, so the women delivered their message to her and left.

"Where are they from?" asked Tzu-chuan.

"They're perfect pests!" Yuan-yang told her. 'The Fus have a daughter who is not bad-looking, so they keep coming to praise her to the old lady for her good looks, good heart and good manners. They say she's no chatter-box but a skilled needle-woman, who can write and keep accounts too, most dutiful to her elders and kind to the servants. Each time they come they reel all this off, as if offering the old lady some rare treasure. I can't bear listening to them! But although they're such a nuisance, our old lady loves that kind of talk. She isn't the only one either. Even Pao-yu who can't abide most old women doesn't mind these from the Fu family. Odd, isn't it? Only the other day they came to say that lots of people are asking for their young lady, but her father won't give his consent — hinting that only a family like ours would be good enough for her. All their praise and flattery are having some effect on the old lady."

Though taken aback, Tzu-chuan asked with a show of indifference, "If she thinks it a good match for Pao-yu, then why not fix it up?"

Before Yuan-yang could explain someone inside called out, "The old lady's woken!"

Yuan-yang hurried in then and Tzu-chuan got up to leave. On her way back to the Garden she ruminated, "Is there only one Pao-yu in the world that everybody should want him? And our young lady's the one who dotes on him most. You can see by the way she behaves that she's set her heart on him: why else should she keep falling ill? There's confusion enough here already, what with gold unicorns and gold lockets, without foisting another Miss Fu on us too! I think it's our young lady that Pao-yu fancies; but judging by what Yuan-yang says, he falls in love with every girl he meets. If so, our young lady's eating her heart out for nothing."

From thinking of Tai-yu she went on to wonder what she herself should do, until she felt quite distracted. Though tempted to advise Tai-yu to stop caring so much for Pao-yu, she was afraid this would upset her; yet seeing her like this made her heart bleed. The more she brooded the more anxious she grew.

"Why worry about someone else?" she scolded herself. "Even if she really marries Pao-yu, the way she is it won't be easy to please her; and Pao-yu, for all he's good-natured, is too much of a flirt. But here I am hoping she'll stop worrying yet worrying *myself* for nothing! From now on I'll look after her as best I can and not care about anything else."

This conclusion helped to calm her down by the time she reached Bamboo Lodge, where she found Tai-yu sitting all by herself on the *kang* sorting out her old poems and essays. She looked up when Tzu-chuan came in.

"Where have you been?" she asked.

"To call on some other girls."

"Did you see Sister Hsi-jen?"

"Why should I go to see *her*?"

Tai-yu wondered how she had come to blurt out such a question, and in embarrassment she answered curtly, "I don't care *where* you go. Fetch me some tea."

Laughing up her sleeve, Tzu-chuan went out to do this and heard a clamour of voices in the Garden. As she poured the tea she sent someone to find out what had happened.

The girl came back and told her, "Some crab-apple trees in Happy Red Court had withered, and nobody watered them; but yesterday when Pao-yu had a look he claimed he saw buds on the branches. No one believed him or paid any attention. Today, all of a sudden, they burst into bloom with lovely crab-apple flowers! People were so amazed that they rushed over there to look. It's caused such a sensation that even the old lady and Her Ladyship are coming to see the flowers. So Madam Chu's given orders to have the leaves in the Garden swept up, and they were calling servants just now to do this."

Tai-yu, overhearing that the old lady was coming, at once changed her clothes and sent Hsueh-yen out to keep watch.

"Tell me as soon as the old lady comes," she said.

It was not long before Hsueh-yen came running back. "The old lady and the mistress have come with quite a party," she announced. "You'd better go right away, miss."

Tai-yu glanced at herself in the mirror and smoothed her hair, then took Tzu-chuan's arm to go to Happy Red Court, where she found the Lady Dowager seated on Pao-yu's couch. Tai-yu paid her respects to her, then to Lady Hsing and Lady Wang, after which she greeted Li Wan, Tan-chun, Hsi-chun and Hsiu-yen. The only ones absent were Hsi-feng, who was unwell; Hsiang-yun, who had been fetched home now that her uncle had a post in the capital; Pao-chin, who was staying with Pao-chai; and the two Li sisters, who had moved out to live with Aunt Li on account of all the troubles in the Garden. So Tai-yu saw only a few of the girls.

For a while they discussed this strange phenomenon of blossom out of season.

"Crab-apple should blossom in the third month," said the old lady. "Although it's now the eleventh, because the solar seasons are late this year it's actually like the tenth, and we're having an Indian summer which makes it warm enough for trees to blossom."

"You've seen so much, madam, you must be right," Lady Wang concurred. "It's not all that remarkable."

"I heard this plant had withered for a whole year," said Lady Hsing. "Why is it blossoming *now*? There must be some reason."

"I'm sure the old lady and mistress are right," put in Li Wan with a smile. "In my foolish opinion, this blossoming shows that something good is coming Pao-yu's way."

Tan-chun remained silent, thinking, "It can't be a good omen. All living things which obey Heaven's will must prosper, while all which flout it must die — even plants know that. So unseasonable blossom must be an evil omen." She could not say this, however.

Tai-yu, elated by this talk of good luck for Pao-yu, said gaily, "The Tien family of old had a redbud tree which withered when the three brothers split up the property. That made them go back in remorse to live together, and then the tree blossomed again. This shows that plants change in accordance with human beings. Now Cousin Pao is studying hard and uncle is pleased with him, so these crab-apples have blossomed again."

The old lady and Lady Wang were delighted with this explanation. "Tai-yu's made an apt comparison," they said. "Most interesting!"

As they were talking, Chia Sheh and Chia Cheng arrived with Huan and Lan to look at the flowers.

"If I were you, I'd cut them down," said Chia Sheh. "It must be some flower-monster making trouble."

Chia Cheng retorted, " 'Ignore a monster and it will destroy itself.' Just let it be. There's no need to cut it down."

"What nonsense are you talking?" his mother protested. "This is something auspicious and good; there's no monster here. If good comes of this, you can enjoy it. If bad comes of it, I'll take all the consequences. But I won't have you talking such rubbish!"

Thus silenced, Chia Cheng withdrew sheepishly with Chia Sheh.

Then the old lady in high spirits told them to order the kitchen to prepare a feast at once, so that they could enjoy the flowers.

"Pao-yu, Huan and Lan must each write a poem to commemorate this happy event," she decreed. "Tai-yu's just over her illness, so we mustn't trouble her to write; but if she's in the mood she can polish your lines." She told Li Wan, "All of you must drink with me."

Li Wan agreed to this, then said teasingly to Tan-chun, "This is all *your* fault."

"We've not even been allowed to write poems," retorted Tan-chun. "So surely this has nothing to do with *us*?"

"Didn't you start the Begonia Society? Now these crab-apples[1] want to join your club too."

At that everybody laughed.

---

[1] In north China both begonias and crab-apple trees are called *haitang*.

Presently wine and dishes were served. And as they drank they all tried to please the old lady by cheerful talk. Pao-yu poured wine for the others, then made up and wrote out a quatrain which he read to his grandmother. It was as follows:

> What made the crab-apple wither away?
> And today why have fresh blossoms come?
> To foretell a long life for our Old Ancestress
> It is flowering anew, ahead of the plum.

Huan also wrote and read out this poem:

> Crab-apples should burgeon in the spring,
> But ours were bare this year.
> The world is full of strange phenomena,
> Yet only here do winter blooms appear.

Lan wrote out his verse neatly and presented it to the old lady, who made Li Wan read it out as follows:

> Its misty charm had faded by last spring,
> But after snow and frost pink blooms unfold.
> Do not accuse this flower of ignorance —
> Good fortune at this feast it has foretold.

The old lady said, "I don't know much about poetry, but I think Lan's is the best. Huan's is no good. Now come and eat, everyone."

Pao-yu was pleased to see her in a good mood until it occurred to him, "The crab-apple died at the same time as Ching-wen. Now that it's blossoming again, of course that augurs well for us in this compound, but it can't bring Ching-wen back to life like this flower." At once his joy turned to sadness, till he remembered Chiao-chieh telling him that Hsi-feng would be sending Wu-erh to take Hung-yu's place. "This flower may be blossoming for *her*," he thought, and his spirits rising again he chatted with the rest of them as before.

After some time the old lady left, leaning on Chen-chu's arm and accompanied by Lady Wang and the others. On their way back Ping-erh accosted them.

"Our mistress heard that the old lady was enjoying the flowers here," she said with a smile. "As she couldn't come herself, she's sent me to help wait on Your Ladyships. Here are two rolls of red silk too, a congratulatory gift for Master Pao to drape over the trees."

Hsi-jen took the silk and showed it to the old lady, who commented laughingly, "Whatever Hsi-feng does is in good form, besides being original and great fun!"

Hsi-jen told Ping-erh, "When you go back please thank Madam Lien for Master Pao. If we're to have good fortune, we'll all share it."

"Aha!" chuckled the old lady. "I forgot that. Though Hsi-feng is unwell she's still so thoughtful. This was just the present to give."

She went on then and the others followed her, while Ping-erh confided to Hsi-jen, "Our mistress says this blossoming now is odd; so she wants you to cut strips of that red silk and hang them over the trees to bring good luck. And don't let anyone spread foolish talk about this being a miracle."

Hsi-jen nodded agreement and then saw her off.

Pao-yu had been resting at home that day, wearing a fur-lined gown, when he noticed that the crab-apples had blossomed and went out to look at them, sighing with admiration. So enchanted with them was he that he became quite wrapped up in their flowers, which evoked in him mixed feelings of grief and joy. At the sudden news that the old lady was coming, he changed into a fox-fur archer's jacket and black fox-fur coat, then went out so hurriedly to welcome her that he omitted to put on his Precious Jade of Spiritual Understanding. Not till the old lady had left and he had changed back into a gown did Hsi-jen see that the pendant which usually hung around his neck was missing.

"Where is your jade?" she asked.

"When I changed just now in such a hurry, I took it off and put it on the small table on the *kang* instead of wearing it."

Hsi-jen could not see it on the small table. She searched the whole room, but there was no trace of it. Dismay made her break out into a cold sweat.

"Don't worry," said Pao-yu. "It's bound to be somewhere here. Ask the others. They must know."

It occurred to Hsi-jen that one of the other girls must have hidden it to tease her. "You bitches!" she said playfully to Sheh-yueh and the rest. "What sort of joke is this to play? Where have you hidden it? If it really got lost that would be the end of us all!"

"What are you talking about?" they answered seriously. "Joking is all very well, but this is no joking matter. Don't talk nonsense. You must be crazy! Better think back to where you put it instead of accusing *us*."

"Heavens!" cried Hsi-jen anxiously, seeing them so much in earnest. "Where exactly did you put it, Master Pao?"

"I remember quite clearly putting it on that table," he assured her. "Make a good search for it."

Not daring to let outsiders know, Hsi-jen, Sheh-yueh, Chiu-wen and the other girls quietly searched the whole place. They hunted around for hours, even turning out cases and crates — but all in vain. When the jade was nowhere to be found, they wondered if one of their visitors that day could have taken it.

But Hsi-jen said, "All of them know how precious this jade is. Who'd dare take it? You mustn't, for goodness' sake, let word of this get out, but go and make inquiries at different households. If one of the other girls took it to play a trick on us, kowtow to her and beg her to return it. And if you find out that one of the little maids stole it, don't report it to the mistresses but give her something in exchange for it. This isn't just anything! If it's really lost, that's more serious than losing Master Pao!"

As Sheh-yueh and Chiu-wen were leaving, she hurried after them with a final warning: "Don't start by asking those who came to the feast. Because then, if you can't find it, that will cause more trouble and make matters worse."

Sheh-yueh and Chiu-wen agreed and went off separately to make inquiries; but nobody had seen the jade, and they were all alarmed. The two of them hurried back to eye each other blankly in consternation. By now Pao-yu was alarmed too, while Hsi-jen could only sob in desperation. The jade had vanished, and they dared not report it. All the inmates of Happy Red Court were petrified.

While they were in this state of stupefaction, along came some people who had heard of their loss. Tan-chun ordered the Garden gate to be closed and sent an old serving-woman with two young maids to make another comprehensive search, promising a handsome reward to anyone who found the jade. Eagerness to clear themselves and receive a reward made everyone search frantically high and low — they even scoured the privies. But it was like looking for a needle in a haystack. They searched all day in vain.

"This is no laughing matter," said Li Wan in desperation. "I've a blunt proposal to make."

"What is it?" the others asked.

"Things have come to such a pass, we can't be too nice. Now apart from Pao-yu all the others in the Garden are women. I'm going to ask all you girls, as well as the maids you brought with you, to take off your clothes to be searched. If the jade isn't found, we'll tell the maids to search the serving-women and the maids doing the rough work. What do you say?"

"That's an idea," they agreed. "With such a crowd of us here we're a mixed lot, and this would be a way to clear ourselves."

Only Tan-chun made no comment.

As the maids also wanted to clear themselves of suspicion, Ping-erh volunteered to be the first to be searched. Then the others stripped too, and Li Wan searched them in turn.

"Sister-in-law!" snapped Tan-chun. "Where did you learn to behave in this scandalous way? If anyone stole it she wouldn't keep it on her, would she? Besides, this jade may be treasured here but to outsiders not in the know it's quite useless, so why should anyone steal it? I'm sure that someone is up to monkey tricks."

When they heard this and noticed Huan's absence — though earlier on he had been running all over the place — they suspected him but were unwilling to say so.

"Huan's the only one who'd play such a trick," Tan-chun continued. "Send somebody to fetch him quietly and persuade him to return it; then give him a scare to make him keep his mouth shut, and that will be that."

The others nodded approval.

Li Wan told Ping-erh, "You're the only one who can get the truth out of him."

Ping-erh agreed to try and hurried off, coming back before long with Chia Huan. The rest pretended that nothing was amiss and told maids to serve him tea in the inner room. Then they excused themselves, leaving him to Ping-erh.

"Your Brother Pao has lost his jade," she told him with a smile. "Have you seen it?"

Chia Huan flushed scarlet and glared.

"When he loses something, why suspect *me*?" he protested. "Am I a convicted thief?"

He looked so worked up that Ping-erh dared not press him. "I didn't mean that," she explained with a smile. "I thought you might have taken it to scare them; that's why I simply asked if you'd seen it or not, to help them find it."

"He was the one wearing the jade, so he's the one you should ask instead of me. You all make so much of him! When there's something good going, you don't ask me to share it; but when anything's lost, I'm the one you ask about it!" He got up and marched out, and they could not stop him.

"All this trouble's due to that silly thing!" burst out Pao-yu. "I don't want it, so you needn't make such a fuss. When Huan gets back he's bound to tell everyone and raise a fearful rumpus."

Weeping in desperation Hsi-jen said, "*You* may not care that the jade's lost, Little Ancestor, but if this comes to the mistresses' ears it'll be the death of us!" She broke down and sobbed.

Now that it was clear that this could not be hushed up, feeling even more worried they discussed how best to report it to the old lady and other mistresses.

"There's no need to discuss it," expostulated Pao-yu. "Just say I've smashed it."

"How casually you're taking it, sir!" rejoined Ping-erh. "Suppose they ask why you smashed it? These girls will still be the ones to take the blame. And suppose they ask to see the broken bits?"

"Well then, say I lost it outside."

That sounded more plausible, until they remembered that Pao-yu had not been to school for a couple of days or paid any visits outside. They pointed this out.

"That's not true," he remonstrated. "Three days ago I went to see the opera in the Duke of Linan's mansion. Just say I lost it that day."

"That won't do," countered Tan-chun. "If you lost it then, why didn't you report it at the time?"

They were racking their brains to think up some good story when they heard sobbing and wailing — it was Concubine Chao approaching.

"You lose something, yet instead of looking for it you torture my Huan behind my back!" she screamed. "I've brought him here to hand him over to you arse-lickers. You can kill him or slice him to pieces just as you please!" With that she shoved Huan forward. "You're a thief!" she cried. "Own up, quick."

Then Huan started crying too from mortification.

Before Li Wan could placate them a maid announced, "Here comes the mistress!"

Hsi-jen and the other maids wished the earth would swallow them up, but they had to hurry out with Pao-yu to meet her. Concubine Chao went with them, afraid to say any more for the time being. And when Lady Wang saw the panic they were in, she realized that the news she had heard was true.

"Is the jade really lost?" she demanded.

No one dared answer.

Lady Wang went inside and sat down, then called for Hsi-jen, who fell on her knees in confusion, tears in her eyes, preparing to make her report.

"Get up," ordered Lady Wang. "Have another careful search made. It's no use losing your heads."

Hsi-jen sobbed, unable to speak.

For fear she might tell the truth Pao-yu put in, "This has nothing to do with Hsi-jen, madam. I lost it on the road the other day when I went to the duke's mansion to see the opera."

"Why didn't you look for it then?"

"I was afraid to let on, so I didn't tell them. Instead I asked Pei-ming and the rest to hunt for it outside."

"Nonsense!" his mother exclaimed. "Don't Hsi-jen and the other girls help you off with your clothes? Whenever you come back from outside, if so much as a handkerchief or pouch is missing they have to look into it, not to mention that jade! They would certainly have asked about it."

This silenced Pao-yu but pleased Concubine Chao.

"If he lost it outside why should they accuse Huan..." she began.

Before she could finish Lady Wang rapped out, "We're talking about the jade. Stop drivelling!"

With Concubine Chao crushed, Li Wan and Tan-chun told Lady Wang all that had happened, making her shed tears in dismay. She decided to report this to the old lady so that she could send people to question those members of Lady Hsing's household who had come with her to Happy Red Court that morning.

Just then, however, along came Hsi-feng, having heard about the loss of Pao-yu's jade and Lady Wang's visit to the Garden. Although still an invalid, feeling unable to hold aloof she now arrived leaning on Feng-erh's arm, just as Lady Wang was about to leave.

"How are you madam?" she faltered.

Pao-yu and the others went over and greeted her.

"So you've heard too?" said Lady Wang. "Isn't it odd? It just vanished all of a sudden and can't be found. Think now: which of the maids from the old lady's place down to your Ping-erh is unreliable and a mischief-maker? I shall have to report this to the old lady and organize a thorough-going search. Otherwise, Pao-yu's life may be cut short!"

"Our household's so big, it's a mixed lot," Hsi-feng answered. "As the proverb says, you can't judge by appearances, madam. Who can guarantee that everyone here is honest? But if we raise a hue and cry so that this becomes public knowledge, the thief will realize that if you find him out — or her, as the case may be — he will have to pay for it with his life, and in desperation he may smash the jade to destroy the evidence. Then what shall we do? In my foolish opinion, we'd better say that Pao-yu never liked it and its loss is of no consequence, so long as we all keep this secret and don't let the old lady and the master know. At the same time, we can secretly send people to search high and low and trick the thief into producing it. Once we have the jade back, we can punish the culprit. What do you think of this, madam?"

After some thought Lady Wang answered, "You're right of course, but how are we to keep this from the master?" She called Huan over and told him, "Your brother's jade is lost. Why should you raise such a row when simply asked a question? If you spread the news and the thief smashes the jade, I can't see you living it down!"

In his terror Huan sobbed, "I won't breathe a word about it!"

And Concubine Chao was too cowed to say any more.

Lady Wang now told the others, "There must be places you haven't searched. It was here all right, so how could it fly away? But the thing is to keep this quiet. I give you three days, Hsi-jen, to find it for me. If you still haven't recovered it by then, I'm afraid we shan't be able to hush it up and there will be no peace for anyone!" She told Hsi-feng to go with her to Lady Hsing's house to discuss plans for a search.

Li Wan and the others talked it over again, then summoned the servants in charge of the Garden and made them lock the gates. Next they sent for Lin Chih-hsiao's wife and told her to order the gatekeepers both at the front and the back not to let out any domestics, whether male or female, for the next three days. All were to remain in the Garden until something missing had been found again.

"Very well," said Mrs. Lin, adding, "the other day we lost something at home of no great value. But to trace it my husband went out to consult a fortune-teller, a man called Iron-Mouth Liu, who cleared up the problem for us by analysing a character. And sure enough, when Chih-hsiao came back and looked where he suggested, we found the thing at once."

"Good Mrs. Lin," Hsi-jen begged her, "do go and get your husband to consult that fortune-teller for us now."

Mrs. Lin agreed readily to this and left.

"Actually those fortune-tellers and diviners outside are no use," said Hsiu-yen. "When I was down south, I heard that Miao-yu was able to divine by writing on sand. Why don't we consult *her*? Besides, this jade is said to be supernatural, so the oracle should disclose its whereabouts."

The others rejoined in surprise, "We often see her but never heard tell of this."

"I doubt if she'll agree if we others ask her, miss," said Sheh-yueh to Hsiu-yen. "So let me kowtow to you and beg you to take this errand on yourself. If she clears up this mystery, we shall never forget your kindness as long as we live!"

She knelt down to kowtow but Hsiu-yen stopped her, while Tai-yu and the other girls also urged her to go straight to Green Lattice Nunnery.

Just then, however, Mrs. Lin came back. "Good news, young ladies!" she cried. "My husband's been to see the fortune-teller and he says the jade can't be lost: someone is bound to return it."

Most of them found this hard to believe, but Hsi-jen and Sheh-yueh were overjoyed.

"What character did he analyse?" Tan-chun asked.

"He said a whole lot, too much for me to repeat," answered Mrs. Lin. "I remember that the character he picked was *shang* meaning 'gift.' Then, without asking any questions, that Iron-Mouth Liu said, 'You've lost something, I take it.'"

"A good guess!" exclaimed Li Wan.

Mrs. Lin continued, "Then he said the upper part of the character is the *hsiao* for 'small' with the *kou* for 'mouth' below; so the thing should be small enough to put in the mouth and must be some sort of jewel."

"That's really miraculous!" they cried. "What else did he say?"

"The lower half of the character was a stroke or two short of *chien* meaning 'see,' so the object must have disappeared from sight. And as the top half was the same as in *tang* for 'pawn,' we should look for the missing object in a pawnshop. When we add *jen*, a 'man,' to *shang*, it gives *chang* meaning to 'redeem.'[1] So once we hit on the right pawnshop, we'll find whoever pawned it and then we can redeem it."

"In that case," said the others, "let's first look near by. If we search the neighbourhood pawnshops we're bound to find it. Once we have the jade, it'll be easy to question the thief."

"Provided we get the jade back, it doesn't matter whether we question the thief or not," was Li Wan's opinion. "Please go right away, Mrs. Lin, to tell Madam Lien what the fortune-teller says, and report it to Her Ladyship too so that she can stop worrying. Then ask Madam Lien to send men to investigate."

Mrs. Lin went off on this errand.

Feeling a little more reassured, they were waiting blankly for Hsiu-yen's return when they saw Pao-yu's page Pei-ming beckoning outside the door to a young maid. The girl at once went out.

"Wonderful news!" he told her. "Hurry up and tell our Master Pao and all the ladies inside."

"Tell me what it is, quick!" she retorted. "Don't drag it out."

Pei-ming clapped his hands, chuckling. "When I've told you, miss, and you go in and pass on the news, we'll both of us get tipped. Can you guess what's happened? I've got definite news about Master Pao's jade."

If you want to know the upshot, read the next chapter.

---

[1] The Chinese characters listed here are: *Shang* 賞; *hsiao* 小; *kou* 口; *chien* 見; *tang* 當; *jen* 人; and *chang* 償.

CHAPTER 95

A Rumour Comes True and the Imperial Consort
Yuan-chun Dies
A Fraud Is Perpetrated After Pao-yu
Loses His Mind

After hearing from Pei-ming that the jade had been found, the young maid hurried in to report this to Pao-yu. The others all urged him to go out to question his page, and stepped into the corridor themselves to listen. Feeling reassured, Pao-yu went to the door and asked:

"Where did you find it? Bring it here at once."

"I can't do that," said Pei-ming, "till we've found a guarantor."

"Tell me where it is then, and I'll send someone to get it."

"When I learned outside that Mr. Lin was going to consult a fortune-teller, I followed him. Then, hearing that it could be found in a pawnshop, without waiting for him to finish I rushed over to several pawnshops and gave them a description of the jade, and one shop said they'd got it. When I asked for it, though, they wanted the pawn-ticket. 'How much was it hocked for?' I asked. They said, 'We give from three hundred to five hundred cash. The other day someone brought in a jade like that and pawned it for three hundred. Today another man came with a piece and pawned it for five hundred.'"

Pao-yu cut him short with the order, "Go at once, taking money to redeem both; then we'll see whether one is the right piece or not."

"Don't listen to him, Master Pao!" scoffed Hsi-jen from inside. "When I was small my brother often told me that hawkers of small pieces of jade pawn them when they need cash. Every single pawnshop must have some."

The others had been surprised by Pei-ming's report. Now, thinking over Hsi-jen's comment, they laughed.

"Tell Master Pao to come in," they cried. "Pay no attention to that simpleton. The jade he's talking about can't be the right one."

Pao-yu was laughing too when Hsiu-yen came back.

Now Hsiu-yen on reaching Green Lattice Nunnery, as soon as she saw Miao-yu had asked her — without any preliminaries — to consult an oracle for them by writing on sand. Miao-yu laughed disdainfully.

"I've treated you as my friend," she said, "because you're not one of the vulgar herd. Why trouble me like this today on the base of some rumour? Besides, I know nothing about 'writing on sand.' " And, this said, she ignored her.

Knowing the young nun's temperament, Hsiu-yen regretted having come. Still she reflected, "After telling the others, I can hardly go back empty-handed." Since she could not very well argue with Miao-yu and affirm that she could use a planchette, she explained to her with a conciliatory smile that the lives of Hsi-jen and the other maids depended on this. When she saw her wavering, she got up and curtseyed to her several times.

Miao-yu sighed, "Why should you put yourself out for others? No one's known, since I came to the capital, that I can consult oracles. If I make an exception for you today, I'm afraid I shall have a lot of trouble in future."

"I couldn't help blurting it out, counting on your kindness," said Hsiu-yen. "If you're pestered in future, it's up to you whether you agree or not — who'd dare to force you?"

Miao-yu smiled and told the old deaconess to burn some incense, then from her case she took out a sand-board and stand and wrote an incantation. Hsiu-yen, after bowing and praying on her instructions, got up to help hold the planchette.   Presently the wand wrote swiftly:

> Ah!   Come and gone without a trace
> By the ancient pine at the foot of Blue Ridge Peak.
> To seek it, cross myriads of mountains:
> Entering my gate with a smile you will meet again.

This written, the wand stopped.

"Which deity did you invoke?" Hsiu-yen asked.

"Saint Li the Cripple."

Hsiu-yen wrote down the oracle, then begged Miao-yu to explain it.

"I can't," was the answer.   "I don't understand it myself.   Hurry up and take it back.   You have plenty of clever people over there."

Hsiu-yen went back, and as soon as she entered the courtyard the others all wanted to know how she had fared.   Without giving them the details, she handed Li Wan the oracle she had transcribed.   The girls and Pao-yu crowded round to read it and took it to mean that the jade could not be found quickly, but it would turn up some time when they were not looking.

"But where is this Blue Ridge Peak?" they asked.

"That must be some divine riddle," said Li Wan.   "We've no such peak here, have we?   I expect the thief has thrown it under some rockery with pine trees on it, for fear of detection.   But it says 'entering my gate' — whose gate would that be?"

Tai-yu remarked, "I wonder whom she invoked."

"Saint Li the Cripple," Hsiu-yen told her.

"If it's an immortal's gate, that won't be easy to enter!" exclaimed Tan-chun.

Hsi-jen hunted frantically round, clutching at shadows and searching under each rock, but there was no trace of the jade.   When she came back, Pao-yu smiled foolishly instead of asking whether she had found it.

"Little Ancestor!" cried Sheh-yueh in desperation.   "Where exactly did you lose it?   If you tell us, even if we suffer for it, we shall have something to go on."

"When I said I lost it outside, you wouldn't have it," he

reminded her. "Now how can I answer your question?"

Li Wan and Tan-chun interposed, "We've been in a flurry ever since this morning, and now it's nearly midnight. Look, Cousin Lin's already left — she couldn't last out any longer. We ought to get some rest too: we'll have our hands full tomorrow."

They all dispersed then, and Pao-yu went to bed. But poor Hsi-jen and the other maids wept and racked their brains all night, unable to sleep.

When Tai-yu, having gone home first, recalled all the earlier talk about gold and jade she told herself with inward satisfaction, "Monks and priests can't be believed, and that's a fact. If a match between the gold and the jade was predestined, how could Pao-yu lose the jade? Maybe it's because of me that this match between gold and jade has been broken up." Consoled by these reflections, she forgot the fatigues of the day and started reading again, till Tzu-chuan who was worn out urged her to sleep. But although she lay down her thoughts turned to the crab-apple trees. "He was born with that jade; it's no ordinary stone," she mused. "So its disappearance must have some significance. If the blossoming of the crab-apples was a good omen, he shouldn't have lost the jade. It looks as if the blossoming was an ill omen and he's in for a spell of bad luck." Her spirits sank again till she thought of her marriage, when it seemed right for the trees to have blossomed and for the jade to be lost. In this way, sad and happy by turns, she did not fall asleep till dawn.

Early the next day, Lady Wang sent to make inquiries at various pawnshops, and Hsi-feng also had a search made in secret. This went on for several days, but to no effect. Luckily the old lady and Chia Cheng did not know this. Hsi-jen and the other maids were on tenterhooks every day, while Pao-yu stayed away from school looking dazed and dejected, saying not a word. However, his mother did not take this to heart, attributing it to the loss of his jade.

She was brooding one day when, abruptly, Chia Lien came in to pay his respects.

Beaming, he announced, "I've just heard that Yu-tsun has sent word to the Second Master that your honourable brother has been promoted to the post of Grand Secretary and summoned to the capital. His appointment is to be proclaimed on the twentieth of the first month next year, and a despatch has been sent to his post three hundred *li* away. I expect he's on his way now, travelling day and night, and will be here in little more than a fortnight. So I've come specially to report this to you, madam."

Lady Wang was overjoyed. She had been regretting that so few of her family were left and Aunt Hsueh's family had declined, while her brother serving in the provinces could not look after them. His return to the capital now as Grand Secretary would exalt the Wang family and give Pao-yu someone to rely on in future. She stopped worrying so much about the loss of the jade, looking forward every day to her brother's arrival.

Then one day Chia Cheng burst in, tears streaming down his cheeks.

"Quick!" he panted. "Go and ask the old lady to go at once to the Palace! You can escort her there — no need for too many people. Her Highness has suddenly fallen ill. A eunuch is waiting outside. According to him, the Imperial physicians say she's had a stroke and there's no hope!"

Lady Wang at once gave way to a storm of weeping.

"This is no time for crying," he interposed. "Hurry up and fetch the old lady. But break it to her gently. Don't frighten the old soul." He then left to tell the servants to make preparations.

His wife, holding back her tears, went to tell the Lady Dowager that Yuan-chun was ill and they were to call to pay their respects to her.

Invoking Buddha the old lady exclaimed, "Is she unwell again? Last time I had a bad fright till we heard it was just a rumour. Let's hope this proves to be a false report too."

Lady Wang concurred and urged Yuan-yang and others to open the chests at once and get out the old lady's ceremonial costume. She then hurried back to her room to change herself before returning to wait on the old lady. Presently they went out and were carried by sedan-chairs to the Palace.

Now Yuan-chun, highly favoured by the sagacious sovereign since her installation as Imperial Concubine in Phoenix Palace, had grown too plump to exert herself — the least fatigue made her liable to apoplexy. A few days before this, on her way back from waiting on the Emperor at a feast, she had caught a chill which had brought on her former trouble. And this time it was serious: phlegm blocked her wind-pipe, her limbs were numb and cold. This was reported to the Emperor, and Imperial physicians were summoned. However, she was unable to take any medicine, nor could they clear up the congestion. In their anxiety the Palace officials asked permission to prepare for her death, which was why the Lady Dowager had been sent for.

Entering the Palace in response to the Imperial summons, she and Lady Wang found Yuan-chun unable to speak. At sight of her grandmother she showed signs of distress but had no tears to shed, while the old lady stepped forward to pay her respects and offer condolences. Soon the cards of Chia Cheng and the rest were sent in and presented by maids-in-waiting; but Yuan-chun's sight had failed and the colour was slowly ebbing from her face. The Palace officials and eunuchs had to report this to the Emperor and, anticipating that other Imperial concubines would be sent to see her, in which case it would not be fitting for her relatives to remain there, they asked them to wait outside. The old lady and Lady Wang could hardly bear to leave, but they had to conform to court etiquette and withdraw with aching hearts, not even daring to weep.

News was sent to the officials at the Palace gate, and presently a eunuch came out to summon the Imperial Astrologer. The old lady knew what this foreboded, but did not venture to move. Very soon a younger eunuch came out to announce:

"The Imperial Consort Chia has passed away."

As the Beginning of Spring fell on the eighteenth of the twelfth lunar month that year, and Yuan-chun had died on the nineteenth, it was already the first solar month of the next year and so her age was reckoned as forty-three.

Nursing her grief, the old lady rose to leave the Palace and go home by sedan-chair. Chia Cheng and the others, having also received the news, made their way sadly back. When they reached home, Lady Hsing, Li Wan, Hsi-feng, Pao-yu and the rest were ranged on both sides in front of the hall to meet them. After paying their respects to the Lady Dowager, then to Chia Cheng and Lady Wang, they all gave way to weeping.

Early the next day, those with official titles went to the Palace to mourn beside the coffin as etiquette prescribed. As Chia Cheng was a vice-minister of works, though there were rules concerning the construction of an Imperial consort's tomb, the minister had to consult him more specially regarding the building of this one, while his colleagues also called to ask for his instructions. This kept him doubly busy both at home and in the ministry, more so than after the deaths of the Empress Dowager and the Imperial Consort Chou some time ago. Because Yuan-chun had borne no son, her posthumous title was Virtuous and Noble Imperial Concubine, according to the rules of the Imperial House. But no more of this.

The whole Chia family, men and women alike, were kept very busy going each day to the Palace. It was fortunate that Hsi-feng's health had recently improved, as she now had to see to household affairs besides preparing to welcome and congratulate Wang Tzu-teng on his return. When her brother Wang Jen heard that their uncle was joining the Grand Secretariat, he also came with his wife to the capital. Hsi-feng was delighted, these relatives' arrival allaying some of her anxieties and contributing to her further recovery. And now that she was running the household again, Lady Wang's burden was considerably lightened, while her brother's impending arrival helped to set her mind at rest too.

As Pao-yu had no official duties and had given up studying, his tutor leaving him to his own devices in view of their family's trouble; and as Chia Cheng was too busy to check up on him, he would normally have taken this chance to amuse himself with his girl cousins every day. However, since the loss of his jade he had grown thoroughly listless and talked nonsense. When told that the old lady was back and he should go to pay his respects, he went: if not prompted, he made no move. Hsi-jen and his other maids felt deep misgivings yet dared not take him to task for fear of his anger. When his meals were set before him he would eat; otherwise he never asked for anything. Hsi-jen, suspecting that he was not sulking but ill, made time one day to slip over to Bamboo Lodge and describe his condition to Tzu-chuan.

"Do ask your young lady to come and talk some sense into him," she begged.

However, when this message was passed on to Tai-yu, she was reluctant to call on Pao-yu in the belief that the two of them were to marry. "If he came here I couldn't ignore him," she thought, "as we were together as children. But it would be quite wrong for *me* to seek him out." She therefore refused to go.

Then Hsi-jen confided in Tan-chun. But the unseasonable blossoming of the crab-apples and even stranger disappearance of the precious jade, followed by the death of Yuan-chun, had convinced Tan-chun that their family was ill-fated. She had been worrying for days and was in no mood to go to admonish Pao-yu. Besides, girls were supposed to keep a respectful distance from their brothers; and when once or twice she did call, his apathy discouraged her from paying him any more visits.

Pao-chai had also heard of the loss of the jade. However, the day that Aunt Hsueh went home having agreed to a match between her and Pao-yu she told her daughter, "Though your aunt has proposed it I've not yet given my consent, telling her we'd decide after your brother's return. But are *you* willing or not?"

Pao-chai had answered gravely, "You shouldn't ask me that, mother. A girl's marriage is arranged by her parents. As father is dead the decision's up to you, or you can consult Brother Pan; but you shouldn't ask *me*."

This only increased her mother's regard for her, for Pao-chai although much indulged since childhood had always been a paragon of virtue. From then on Aunt Hsueh never mentioned Pao-yu in her presence; and Pao-chai naturally made a point of never breathing his name. So now though shocked and disturbed by the loss of the jade she made no inquiries about it, simply listening to what others said on the subject as if this did not concern her.

Aunt Hsueh sent maids several times to ask for news. But worried as she was by the charge against her son Pan and eager for her brother's arrival to help clear him; knowing, too, that although Yuan-chun's death had thrown the Chia family into confusion Hsi-feng was now well enough to run the household, she seldom went over herself. This left Hsi-jen to bear the brunt. She waited assiduously on Pao-yu and tried to advise and console him, but still his wits wandered. Yet she had to keep her anxiety to herself.

Shortly afterwards, Yuan-chun's coffin was deposited in one of the rear temples in the Imperial Sepulchre, and while the old lady and others were away attending the funeral Pao-yu grew more deranged from day to day. He had no fever or pain but could neither eat nor sleep properly and even grew incoherent in his speech. Hsi-jen and Sheh-yueh in their alarm reported this more than once to Hsi-feng, who came over from time to time. At first she thought he was sulking because the jade had not been found; then she realized that he was losing his mind and had doctors fetched to attend him every day. Although they prescribed various medicines, his condition only grew worse. Asked whether he felt any pain, he would not answer.

After Yuan-chun's funeral was over, the old lady who had been concerned about Pao-yu came to the Garden with Lady Wang to see him. Hsi-jen and the others told him to go out to meet them and pay his respects, for though deranged he could still get about as usual. Now he paid his respects to his grandmother as before, except that Hsi-jen was beside him to prompt him.

"I thought you were ill, child," the old lady exclaimed. "That's why I came to see you. How relieved I am to find you looking all right."

Lady Wang felt reassured too. However, Pao-yu made no answer apart from tittering. Once seated inside, they questioned him and Hsi-jen had to prompt him each time with an answer. He seemed completely changed too, behaving like a moron. The old lady's misgivings increased.

"At first sight I saw nothing wrong," she said. "But now that I look at him carefully, this illness seems serious — the boy's lost his mind! How ever did this happen?"

Realizing that the truth could no longer be concealed and pitying Hsi-jen in this predicament, Lady Wang whispered to her Pao-yu's story about losing the jade when he went to hear the opera in the duke's mansion.

"We've sent to search for it everywhere," she added distractedly, hoping to stop the old lady from worrying. "We've consulted oracles too, and they all say we shall find it in a pawnshop. So we shall get it back."

At this the Lady Dowager rose frantically to her feet, tears streaming down her face.

"How could you lose that jade!" she exclaimed. "You really are too careless! Does the master also leave it at that?"

Seeing how angry she was, Lady Wang told the maids to kneel down. Then, her head bowed, she answered humbly, "For fear of worrying you, madam, and making the master angry, I dared not report it."

"This jade is the root of Pao-yu's life," sighed the old lady. "It's because he's lost it that he's out of his mind. This will never do! The whole city knows of this jade, so if someone picked it up do you expect him to let you have it back? Send for the master at once and I'll tell him this."

Lady Wang and the maids pleaded in consternation, "If *you* are so angry, madam, think what a rage the master will be in!

Now that Pao-yu's ill, just leave it to us to do our very best to find it."

"Don't be afraid of the master. I'll handle him." The old lady ordered Sheh-yueh to send to fetch him. Presently it was reported that he was out paying a call.

"We can do without him then," she said. "Say these are *my* instructions. For the time being there's no need to punish the maids. I'll get Chia Lien to write an announcement to hang up by the road Pao-yu took that day, offering a reward of ten thousand taels to anyone who picked up the jade and returns it, and five thousand to anyone who tells us who has it so that we can get it back. Provided it can be found, we won't stint our silver. In this way we're sure to recover it. If we leave it to a few of our household to search, they could search their whole lives long without finding it."

Lady Wang dared raise no objection. The old lady had these directions sent to Chia Lien with instructions to see to this quickly.

Next she ordered, "Move all the things Pao-yu uses every day to my apartments. Hsi-jen and Chiu-wen are to come over with him, leaving the other maids there in the Garden to keep an eye on his rooms."

All this time Pao-yu had said nothing, just grinning foolishly. The Lady Dowager rose then, taking his hand, and Hsi-jen and others helped them out of the Garden. Back in her own quarters, the old lady made Lady Wang sit down to supervise the rooms' arrangement.

"Do you know what I have in mind?" she asked. "It seems to me there are too few people in the Garden, and those trees in Happy Red Court have withered and blossomed suddenly in a strange way. He used to have this jade to ward off evil spirits; now that he's lost it I'm afraid he may succumb to some evil influence. That's why I've brought him here to stay with me. We won't let him out for a few days. The doctors can come here to see him."

"Of course you're right, madam," answered Lady Wang.

"Living with you, such a favourite of fortune, he can't come to any harm."

"Who's a favourite of fortune? But my rooms are cleaner, and we've plenty of Buddhist scriptures which we can read to calm him. Ask Pao-yu if he likes being here or not."

But Pao-yu only grinned. Not until prompted by Hsi-jen did he say "Yes."

Seeing this Lady Wang shed tears but could not sob aloud before the old lady.

Understanding her anxiety the latter said, "You go back now. I'll take care of him. When the master gets back this evening tell him he needn't come here. Just be sure not to complain about this."

After Lady Wang had gone, the old lady made Yuan-yang get out some tranquillizing medicines and give them to Pao-yu according to the prescription. But no more of this.

That evening Chia Cheng was coming home by carriage when he heard some passers-by talking.

"If anyone wants to make a pile, it's easy!" said one.

"How?" his companion asked.

"I heard today that some young master in the Jung Mansion has lost a piece of jade, and a notice has been posted up describing its size, shape and colour. Ten thousand taels reward has been offered for its return, and five thousand for news of its whereabouts."

Though Chia Cheng had not caught every word distinctly, he had heard enough to hurry home in amazement.

The gateman when questioned reported, "The first I heard of this, sir, was at noon today when Master Lien passed on the old lady's order and sent people to post up a notice."

"Our family must be on the decline!" Chia Cheng sighed. "For our sins we've been saddled with this degenerate. At the time of his birth he was the talk of the town, but after ten years and more the gossip died down. Now we're raising this hue and cry again to find his jade — preposterous!"

He hurried inside to question Lady Wang, who told him the whole story. As this had been done on his mother's instructions, Chia Cheng could not oppose it. He just vented his anger briefly on his wife before going out again to order the notice to be taken down without the old lady's knowledge. However, some idlers had already made off with it.

A few days later, a man came to the Jung Mansion claiming to have brought back the jade.

In great jubilation the servants at the gate said, "Hand it over and we'll go and report it for you."

The fellow reached in his pocket for the notice, pointing at it for them to see.

"Wasn't this put up by your house?" he asked. "It says clearly here that whoever returns the jade will get a reward of ten thousand silver taels. I may look poor now to you gentlemen, but once I have that silver I shall be rich; so don't be so high-handed!"

He spoke with such confidence that the gateman answered, "Well then, just show me the jade so that I can report this for you."

At first the man was unwilling, but on second thoughts he produced the jade and displayed it in the palm of one hand.

"Isn't this it?" he demanded.

These servants on duty at the gate all knew of the jade, but this was their first close look at it. They hurried in, eager to be the first with this good news. That day Chia Cheng and Chia Sheh were out. Only Chia Lien was at home.

Hearing this report, he asked, "Is it genuine?"

"We've seen it for ourselves," the servants answered. "But he won't give it to us underlings. He wants to see one of the masters, to hand over the jade to him in exchange for the money."

Chia Lien hastened in happily to report this to Lady Wang who then told the old lady, so delighting Hsi-jen that she clasped her hands together, invoking Buddha. And the Lady Dowager was as good as her word.

"Tell Lien to ask that man to wait in the study while he

brings the jade here," she said. "Once we've seen it we'll give him the silver."

Chia Lien accordingly invited the fellow in, treating him as a guest and thanking him profusely.

"I would like to take this jade in to show the young master himself," he said. "Then we'll give you your full reward."

The man handed him a red silk wrapper. Chia Lien opened it and saw indeed a fine translucent jade. He had paid scant attention to Pao-yu's jade before and now took a good look, a careful scrutiny disclosing the inscription "warding off evil." Overjoyed, he ordered servants to wait on the visitor, then hurried in to let the old lady and Lady Wang identify the stone.

By now everyone was agog to see the jade. As soon as Chia Lien came in Hsi-feng snatched it from him and, not venturing to examine it herself, presented it to the old lady.

Chia Lien chuckled, "So even over a trifle like this, you won't let me take the credit!"

When the Lady Dowager unwrapped the jade, it struck her as much more opaque than before. She rubbed it with her fingers while Yuan-yang fetched her spectacles and, putting them on, she scrutinized the stone.

"That's odd!" she exclaimed. "This is the jade all right, but how is it that it's lost all its former lustre?"

Lady Wang examined it for some time but could not give a positive opinion. She told Hsi-feng to have a look.

"It resembles it, but the colour's not quite right," Hsi-feng observed. "Better let Pao-yu look at it himself, then we shall know."

Hsi-jen beside her also had her doubts, but in her eagerness to have the stone prove authentic she did not express them. Hsi-feng took the jade from the old lady and went in with Hsi-jen to show it to Pao-yu, who had just woken from a nap.

"Here's your jade," Hsi-feng told him.

Pao-yu, his eyes still blurred from sleep, took the jade and without so much as looking at it threw it on the ground.

"You're trying to fool me again," he said with a cynical smile.

Hsi-feng hastily picked up the jade, protesting, "Strange! How can you tell without even looking at it?"

Pao-yu said nothing, just smiled.

Lady Wang had come in too and seeing this she said, "It goes without saying he must know, as that strange jade came from the womb with him. This one must be a counterfeit made from the description in the notice."

Then the truth dawned on everyone.

"If it's a fake, give it to me and I'll ask him how he dare play such tricks," cried Chia Lien, who had overheard this from the outer room.

But the old lady remonstrated, "Just return it to him, Lien, and let him go. The poor devil must have been trying to capitalize on this trouble in our family; but now he's spent money on making this for nothing and we've seen through his trick. In my view we shouldn't make things hard for him. Just return him the jade saying that it isn't ours and give him a few taels. Then when outsiders hear of it, if they pick up some clues they'll be willing to let us know; whereas if we punish this fellow, then even if the genuine jade is found no one will dare bring it to us."

Chia Lien agreed to this and withdrew. The man after his long wait was already somewhat apprehensive, and now he saw Chia Lien come out in a towering rage. But to know what happened next, read the following chapter.

CHAPTER 96

Hsi-feng Withholds Information and
Lays a Cunning Plan
Disclosure of a Secret
Deranges Tai-yu

Chia Lien stormed to the study with the counterfeit jade, and when the man there saw how angry he looked his heart misgave him. He hastily rose to greet him, but before he could speak Chia Lien laughed scornfully.

"Of all the gall!" he swore. "You scoundrel! What place is this that you dare play such devilish tricks here?"

He called for servants. Those outside answered his summons with a shout like thunder.

"Get ropes and tie him up," ordered Chia Lien. "We'll report this to the master on his return and send this rogue to the yamen."

"Very good, sir!" chorused the servants, but made no move.

Nearly paralysed with fright by this show of power, the fellow knew that there was no escape and dropping to his knees kowtowed to Chia Lien.

"Don't be angry, Your Lordship!" he begged. "It's because I was driven to it by poverty that I thought up this shameless scheme. I borrowed money to get that jade made, but I won't venture to ask for it back — I'll give it as a plaything to your young masters." He kowtowed again and again.

"You stupid fool!" Chia Lien spat out. "Who in this mansion wants your trash?"

At this point Lai Ta came in. With a smile he urged Chia Lien, "Don't be angry, sir. This wretch isn't worth it. Let him off and send him packing."

"It's disgraceful!" Chia Lien fumed.

So Lai Ta took a soft line, Chia Lien a hard one, until the servants outside called, "You stupid cur! Hurry up and kowtow to the master and Mr. Lai, then clear off. Are you waiting to be kicked out?"

Then he hastily kowtowed twice and slunk away. But this counterfeiting of Pao-yu's jade became the talk of the town.

When Chia Cheng returned that day from his round of calls, as the matter was done with and they were afraid to enrage him during the Lantern Festival, no one reported it to him. Yuan-chun's funeral had kept them busy for some time and now, with Pao-yu ill, although there were the usual family feasts the whole household was in low spirits and nothing noteworthy happened.

By the seventeenth of the first month Lady Wang was looking forward to her brother Wang Tzu-teng's arrival when Hsi-feng came in with bad news.

"Today the Second Master heard outside that uncle was travelling here posthaste, and was only two hundred *li* or so away when he died on the road!" she cried. "Did you hear this, madam?"

"Not I!" exclaimed Lady Wang in consternation. "The master said nothing about it last night either. Where did this news come from?"

"The house of Chancellor Chang."

Lady Wang was speechless, in tears.

Presently, wiping her eyes, she said, "Get Lien to check up on it and let me know."

Hsi-feng went off to do this.

Lady Wang had been reduced to weeping in secret as she mourned her daughter and worried over Pao-yu, and now this third misfortune in swift succession was more than she could bear — she came down with colic. Moreover, Chia Lien confirmed that the news was true.

"Uncle was worn out by travelling so fast and he caught a chill," he told her. "When he reached Shihlitun a doctor was sent for, but unfortunately that place has no good doctors. The wrong medicine was prescribed and one dose killed him. We don't know whether his family has arrived there or not."

Lady Wang's heart ached at this news, aggravating her pains. Unable to remain seated, she made Tsai-yun and others help her on to the *kang*, then speaking with an effort told Chia Lien to report this to Chia Cheng.

"Make ready to go there at once to help see to things," she said. "Then come straight back to let us know about it, to set your wife's mind at rest."

Unable to refuse, Chia Lien had to take his leave of Chia Cheng and set off.

Chia Cheng, who had heard the news earlier, was thoroughly disconcerted, knowing also that Pao-yu since losing his jade had grown feeble-minded and no medicine would cure him, while now Lady Wang was ill too.

That year the records of officials in the capital were examined, and the Ministry of Works ranked Chia Cheng as first class. In the second month, the Minister of Civil Affairs took him to an audience at court and the Emperor, in recognition of his frugality and circumspection, appointed him Grain Commissioner of Kiangsi. That same day, giving thanks for this favour, he reported to the throne the date of his departure. Kinsmen and friends came to offer congratulations, but disturbed as he was by his domestic problems Chia Cheng was in no mood to entertain them. Still he dared not postpone his journey.

He was in a quandary when he received a summons from the old lady and, hastening to her room, found his wife there too in spite of her illness. He paid his respects to his mother, who told him to take a seat.

"You will soon be going to your new post," she said tearfully. "There is much I want to say to you, but will you listen?"

Chia Cheng promptly rose to his feet.

"Just give me your orders, madam. How dare your son disobey them?"

"I'm eighty-one this year, yet you're going to a post in the provinces," she sobbed. "You can't ask for compassionate leave either, as you have an elder brother at home to take care of me. Once you're gone, there'll be only Pao-yu here that I care for, but the poor boy's losing his mind and we don't know what will become of him! Yesterday I sent Lai Sheng's wife to get someone to tell Pao-yu's fortune. She found a very clever fortune-teller who said, 'He must marry a bride with gold in her stars to help counteract his bad luck; otherwise there'll probably be no saving him.' I know you don't believe in such things, so I've asked you here to consult you. Your wife is here too, so the two of you can talk it over. Should we try to save Pao-yu? Or let things take their course?"

Chia Cheng answered submissively, "You were so good to your son, madam, do you think I don't love my son too? It's only because Pao-yu made so little progress that I was often exasperated with him — just a case of wanting to 'turn iron into steel.' If you wish him to take a wife, as is right and proper, how could I disobey you and show no concern for him? I am worried too by his illness. Since you kept him away from me I dared not object; but can I not see for myself just how ill he is?"

Lady Wang saw that the rims of his eyes had reddened and knew how distressed he was. She therefore told Hsi-jen to bring Pao-yu in. When the boy saw his father, prompted by Hsi-jen he paid his respects; but with his emaciated face and his lack-lustre eyes he looked like a moron. Chia Cheng told them to take him back.

He reflected, "I'm nearing sixty, and now I'm posted to the provinces with no knowing when I shall come back. If this child really doesn't recover, I shall be left heirless in my old age; for my grandson, after all, is another generation removed. Besides, Pao-yu is the old lady's favourite: if anything happens to him, I shall be guilty of a greater crime." He saw from his wife's tears how this must affect her too.

Rising to his feet he said, "Old as you are, madam, you show such concern for your grandson, how can I, your son, disobey you? I shall fall in with whatever you think best. But will Aunt Hsueh agree to this, I wonder?"

"She gave her consent some time ago," Lady Wang told him.

"We haven't spoken of it yet simply because Pan's business still isn't settled."

"This is the first problem," he answered. "With her brother in jail, how can his sister get married? In the second place, although an Imperial Consort's death does not preclude marriages, Pao-yu should mourn for nine months for a married sister, and this is hardly the time for him to take a wife. Furthermore, the date of my departure has already been reported to the throne, and I cannot postpone it. How are we to arrange a wedding in these few days?"

The old lady thought, "He's right. But if we wait till these are no longer problems, Pao-yu's father will be gone, and what shall we do if his illness gets steadily worse? We shall just have to disregard certain rules of etiquette."

Her mind made up she said, "If you're willing, I know of a way to get round these obstacles. I shall go myself with your wife to ask Aunt Hsueh's consent. As for Pan, I'll get Ko to tell him that we have to do this to save Pao-yu's life, and then he's bound to agree. Of course it wouldn't do to have a real marriage while in mourning, and Pao-yu is too ill for that anyway — we just want a happy event to ward off evil. As both our families agree and there was that prediction about the young people's 'gold' and 'jade,' there's no need to compare their horoscopes; we'll just select a good date to exchange gifts according to our family status. Then we'll choose a day for the wedding, not engaging musicians but following the example of the Palace, fetching the bride over in a sedan-chair with eight bearers and twelve pairs of lanterns. They can bow to each other as is done in the south, then sit down on the bed and let down the curtains, and won't that count as a wedding?

"Pao-chai's so intelligent, we don't have to worry. Besides, he has Hsi-jen in his chambers as well, and so much the better, as she's another reliable, sensible girl who knows how to reason with him. She and Pao-chai get on well too.

"Another thing. Aunt Hsueh once told me, 'A monk said that Pao-chai with her golden locket is destined to marry some-

one with jade.' So for all we know, once she marries into
our household her gold locket may bring the jade back. Then
he should get steadily better, and wouldn't that be a blessing
for us all?

"All that needs to be done straight away is to get their rooms
ready and furnished — it's for you to assign them a place. We
won't give any feasts, but wait till Pao-yu's better and out of
mourning before inviting relatives and friends. In this way we
can manage everything in time, and you can leave with an easy
mind, having seen the young couple settled."

Chia Cheng though averse to this could not gainsay his
mother. Forcing a smile he said, "You have thought it out well
and that would be most fitting, madam. We must order the
servants, though, not to noise this abroad or we should be cen-
sured for it. I'm only afraid Aunt Hsueh's family may not
agree. If they really do, we must manage it your way."

"Just leave Aunt Hsueh to me," she said, then dismissed him.

Chia Cheng withdrew feeling thoroughly uneasy. He had
so much to do before going to his post, what with fetching cre-
dentials from the ministry, receiving relatives and friends who
came with recommendations and entertaining a host of other people, that he left the arrangements for Pao-yu's wedding to his
mother, wife and Hsi-feng. All he did was to assign his son
a side-court with more than twenty rooms in it, adjacent to
Lady Wang's house behind the Hall of Glorious Felicity. When
the old lady sent him word of some decision, he simply replied,
"Very good." But this is anticipating.

After Pao-yu had seen his father, Hsi-jen helped him back
to the *kang* in the inner room. Since Chia Cheng was outside,
no one ventured to speak to Pao-yu, who dozed off and thus
heard nothing of the conversation in the outer room. However,
Hsi-jen, keeping quiet, heard it clearly. Talk of this had reached
her before, though only as hearsay, yet she tended to believe
it in view of the fact that Pao-chai's visits had stopped. This
confirmation today delighted her.

"The mistresses certainly have good judgement," she thought.

"This is just the match for him. And what luck for me too! If she comes, my load will be ever so much lighter. But he's set his heart on Miss Lin, so it's a blessing that he didn't hear this. If he had, Heaven knows how wildly he'd carry on!" This set her worrying.

"What shall I do?" she wondered. "Their Ladyships have no idea of their feelings for each other. They may be so pleased that they tell him, in the hope of curing him. Then suppose he acts the way he did when he first met Miss Lin and tried to smash his jade; or that summer in the Garden, when he mistook me for her and poured out his love; or when Tzu-chuan teased him later, and he nearly cried himself to death? If they tell him now that he's to have not Miss Lin but Miss Pao-chai, it may not matter if his wits are wandering; but if he's fairly lucid, far from curing his madness it may hasten his death. Unless I explain this to them I may ruin three lives!"

Having reached this resolve she waited till Chia Cheng had gone, then leaving Pao-yu in the care of Chiu-wen she slipped out and quietly asked Lady Wang to go with her to the back room. The Lady Dowager paid little attention, assuming that there was something Pao-yu wanted, and went on considering the gifts and arrangements for the wedding.

Once in the back room with Lady Wang, Hsi-jen threw herself on her knees and burst into tears.

Lady Wang pulled her up and asked in surprise, "What's come over you? What's the trouble? Get up and tell me."

"This is something a slave shouldn't say, but I see no other way out!"

"Well, take your time and tell me."

"Your Ladyships have decided to marry Miss Pao-chai to Pao-yu, and of course nothing could be better. All I'm wondering, madam, is this: which of the two, Miss Pao-chai and Miss Lin, do you think Pao-yu prefers?"

"As he and Miss Lin were together as children, he's slightly fonder of her."

"Not just 'slightly fonder,'" Hsi-jen demurred, going on to cite examples of their behaviour. "Except for the avowal he made that summer, which I've never dared tell anyone, you saw the other instances yourself, madam," she concluded.

Holding Hsi-jen's hand Lady Wang answered, "I did have some inkling from what I saw. Now you've clinched it. But he must have heard what the master said just now. Did you notice his reaction?"

"Nowadays when people talk to him he smiles; if no one talks to him he goes to sleep. So he didn't hear what was said."

"Then what's to be done?"

"I've made bold to tell you this, madam. It's for you to tell the old lady and think of some really safe plan."

"In that case, get back to your work. I won't mention it now — there are too many people there. I'll wait for a chance to tell her later on, and then we shall see."

She rejoined the Lady Dowager who was discussing Pao-yu's marriage with Hsi-feng.

"What did Hsi-jen want that she looked so secretive?" the old lady asked.

Lady Wang took this opening to give her a detailed account of Pao-yu's feeling for Tai-yu. For a while the old lady said nothing, and Lady Wang and Hsi-feng kept silent too.

"Nothing else really matters," the old lady sighed at last. "We needn't worry about Tai-yu. But if Pao-yu is really so infatuated, it's going to be difficult!"

"Not too difficult," said Hsi-feng after some thought. "I've an idea, but don't know whether Aunt Hsueh will agree to it or not."

"If you have a plan, tell the old lady," said Lady Wang. "We can discuss it together."

"To my mind," said Hsi-feng, "the only way is to 'palm off a dummy' on him."

"Palm off what dummy?" the old lady asked.

"Never mind whether Pao-yu is in his right mind or not, we must all drum it into his head that on the master's orders he is to marry Miss Lin, and see how he takes it. If he doesn't care either way, we needn't trick him. If he's pleased, we'll have to do things more deviously."

"Well, assuming he's pleased, what then?" asked Lady Wang. Hsi-feng went over to whisper something into her ear, at which she nodded and smiled.

"That should work," she said.

"Tell me what you two are plotting," urged the old lady.

In order not to give away the secret, Hsi-feng whispered in her ear too. As she had anticipated, the old lady did not understand at first and Hsi-feng, smiling, had to explain more fully.

"That's all right," agreed the old lady. "Rather hard on Pao-chai, though. And if word gets out, what about Tai-yu?"

"We'll just tell Pao-yu and forbid any mention of this outside, then how could she hear?"

At this point a maid announced Chia Lien's return. Not wanting the old lady to question him, Lady Wang signalled to Hsi-feng who went out to meet him, signing to him to go with her to Lady Wang's place. By the time they were joined by Lady Wang, Hsi-feng's eyes were red from weeping. Chia Lien, when he had paid his respects, described his trip to Shih-litun to help arrange for Wang Tzu-teng's funeral.

"An Imperial decree has conferred on him the rank of Grand Secretary and the posthumous title of Duke Wen-chin," he announced. "The family has been ordered to take the coffin back to his native district, and officials along the way are to render assistance. They set off on the journey back south yesterday. My aunt told me to convey her respects and say how sorry she is to have been unable to come to the capital — there was so much she wanted to tell you. When she heard that Hsi-feng's brother was on his way to the capital too, she promised if she met him on the road to send him here to give us all her news."

Lady Wang was naturally so upset by this account that Hsi-feng had to comfort her.

"Please have a rest now, madam," she urged. "This evening we'll come back to discuss Pao-yu's business."

Going home with Chia Lien she told him what had happened, and asked him to send servants to prepare the bridal chambers.

One morning after breakfast, Tai-yu set off to call on her grandmother to pay her respects and also by way of diversion. They had not gone far from Bamboo Lodge when she found that she had forgotten her handkerchief. She told Tzu-chuan to go back for one then catch her up — she would be walking on slowly. She had passed Seeping Fragrance Bridge and reached the rocks behind which she and Pao-yu had buried blossom, when she suddenly heard sobbing. She stopped to listen, but could not tell who was lamenting there or hear what she was saying. Very puzzled, she strolled over and found that the one crying there was an under-maid with thick eyebrows and big eyes.

Tai-yu had expected to see one of the upper-maids come here to vent some grief which she could not confide to others. But when she saw this girl she thought with amusement, "A stupid creature like this can't have been crossed in love. She's one of those doing rough work who must have got scolded by the senior maids." She looked hard at the girl but could not recognize her.

When Tai-yu appeared, the maid dared not go on crying but stood up and wiped her eyes.

"Why are you weeping here? What's come over you?" Tai-yu asked.

That set the maid off again. "Judge for yourself, Miss Lin!" she sobbed. "They knew something, but I wasn't in on it; so even if I made a slip of the tongue, sister had no call to slap me."

Tai-yu could not make head or tail of this.

"Which sister do you mean?" she asked with a smile.

"Sister Chen-chu."

Knowing from this that she worked for the old lady, Tai-yu asked again, "What's your name?"

"They call me Numskull."

"Why did she slap you? What did you say wrong?"

"Why? Just because of the marriage of our Master Pao to Miss Pao-chai."

Tai-yu felt thunderstruck. Her heart beat wildly. Composing

herself a little she said, "Come with me."

Numskull accompanied her to the quiet spot where she had buried the peach-blossom. Then Tai-yu asked, "Why should she slap you because Master Pao is marrying Miss Pao-chai?"

"Their Ladyships have settled it with Madam Lien. Because His Lordship's going to leave so soon, they're fixing up hurriedly with Aunt Hsueh to have Miss Pao-chai brought over before he goes. This will counter Master Pao's bad luck with good. And after that . . ." — she beamed at Tai-yu — "after his wedding they'll fix up a match for *you*, miss."

Tai-yu listened, half stupefied, as the maid rattled on, "I don't know how they settled this, but they won't let anybody talk about it for fear of embarrassing Miss Pao-chai if she heard. All I did was to remark to Sister Hsi-jen — the one who works for Master Pao, 'Things are going to be livelier here with Miss Pao-chai becoming Second Mistress Pao — how ought we to address her?' Tell me, Miss Lin, why should that annoy Sister Chen-chu? Yet she marched over and slapped my face, saying I was talking nonsense and should be thrown out for not obeying orders! How was I to know the mistresses didn't want this talked about? They never tell me anything, yet slap me!" She started sobbing again.

Tai-yu felt as if her heart were filled with a mixture of oil, soy, sugar and vinegar — so sweet, bitter, painful and sharp that she could not put her sensations into words.

After a pause, in a trembling voice she said, "Don't talk such nonsense. If they heard, they'd give you another slapping. Be off with you now."

She turned to go back to Bamboo Lodge. But there seemed to be a mill-stone round her neck and her legs were as limp, her steps as faltering, as if treading on cotton-wool. It seemed a long way to Seeping Fragrance Bridge, she was walking so slowly and so shakily; and moreover she added two bowshots to the distance by wandering about at random in a daze. When at last she reached the bridge, she inadvertently started back along the dyke.

When Tzu-chuan brought the handkerchief Tai-yu had gone.

Looking round for her, she saw her white-faced, her eyes fixed
in a vacant stare, wandering unsteadily this way and that.
She also glimpsed a maid walking off in front, but too far away
to make out which it was. In shocked surprise she ran over.

"Why are you going back, miss?" she asked gently. "Where
do you want to go?"

Hearing her as if in a dream, Tai-yu answered without thinking, "To ask Pao-yu what this means."

Tzu-chuan, nonplussed as she was, had to help her to the
Lady Dowager's quarters. When Tai-yu reached the door, her
mind seemed to clear. Turning to her maid who was supporting
her, she stopped to ask:

"Why have *you* come?"

"To bring your handkerchief," was the smiling answer.
"Just now I saw you by the bridge, but when I accosted you
you paid no attention."

"I thought you'd come to see Master Pao," Tai-yu laughed.
"Why else should you come this way?"

Tzu-chuan saw that her wits were wandering, and knew that
she must have heard something from that maid. She could
only nod and smile. However, this visit to Pao-yu unnerved
her, for he was already demented and now Tai-yu was bemused
too — what if they said something improper?

But for all this, she had to do as she was told and help her
young mistress inside.

Strange to say, Tai-yu was no longer as limp as before. Lifting
the portière herself instead of waiting for Tzu-chuan, she stepped in. All was quiet, for the old lady was having a nap, and
her maids had either slipped out to play or were nodding
drowsily or attending her. The clack of the portière alerted
Hsi-jen, who came out from the inner room.

"Please come in and take a seat, miss," she invited when
she saw who it was.

"Is Master Pao in?" Tai-yu asked with a smile.

Hsi-jen, being in the dark, was about to answer when Tzu-
chuan signalled to her from behind Tai-yu and, pointing at her
young mistress, waved her hand warningly. Hsi-jen was too

puzzled by this to say any more. Tai-yu, disregarding her, went on into the inner room where Pao-yu was sitting. Instead of rising to offer her a seat, he simply stared at her with a foolish grin. Tai-yu sat down and gazed back at him with a smile. They exchanged neither greetings nor civilities, just simpered at each other without a word.

Hsi-jen, at a complete loss, did not know what to do.

"Pao-yu," said Tai-yu abruptly. "Why are you ill?"

"Because of Miss Lin," he answered with a smirk.

Hsi-jen and Tzu-chuan turned pale with fright and at once tried to change the subject; but the other two ignored them, still smiling foolishly. It dawned on Hsi-jen that Tai-yu was now deranged too, exactly like Pao-yu.

She whispered to Tzu-chuan, "Your young lady's just over her illness. I'll get Sister Chiu-wen to help you take her back to rest." She turned to tell Chiu-wen, "Go with Sister Tzu-chuan to see Miss Lin back. Mind you don't say anything foolish."

Chiu-wen complied readily. In silence she and Tzu-chuan helped Tai-yu to her feet. She kept her eyes on Pao-yu, smiling and nodding.

"Go home and rest, miss," Tzu-chuan urged her.

"Of course!" said Tai-yu. "It's time for me to go now."

She turned and went out, still smiling, without their assistance and walking much faster than usual. The two maids hurried after her as once out of her grandmother's compound she forged straight ahead.

"This way, miss!" cried Tzu-chuan, catching hold of her arm.

Tai-yu allowed herself to be led back and soon they approached the gate of Bamboo Lodge.

"Gracious Buddha!" sighed Tzu-chuan in relief. "Home at last!"

But the words were still on her lips when Tai-yu staggered and fell, vomiting blood. To know what became of her, read the next chapter.

CHAPTER 97

Tai-yu Burns Her Poems to End Her Infatuation
Pao-chai Goes Through Her Wedding Ceremony

As Tai-yu reached the gate of Bamboo Lodge, Tzu-chuan's cry of relief startled her. She vomited blood. The two maids were just able to catch her as she was collapsing and carry her inside; then Chiu-wen left Tzu-chuan and Hsueh-yen to attend to her.

After a while, Tai-yu regained consciousness and saw that her maids were crying. She asked them the reason.

In relief Tzu-chuan answered, "You seemed unwell just now, miss, when you left the old lady's place, and we didn't know what to do — we cried for fright."

"Oh, I'm not going to die as easily as all that," retorted Tai-yu, panting as she spoke.

The news of Pao-yu's impending wedding to Pao-chai, a prospect which Tai-yu had dreaded for years, had so enraged her that she had lost her senses. After the hemorrhage her mind gradually cleared, but she had completely forgotten what Numskull had said. Tzu-chuan's tears brought it back to her vaguely. Instead of grieving, however, she just longed to die quickly and be done with it. Her maids felt constrained to stay with her although they wanted to go and report her condition, for they were afraid Hsi-feng would scold them again for raising a false alarm.

However, Chiu-wen had gone back panic-stricken. The old lady, just up from her nap, saw her agitation and asked her what had happened. Chiu-wen's fearful description of what she had seen made the Lady Dowager exclaim in horror and send at once for Lady Wang and Hsi-feng to communicate this bad news.

237

"I ordered all the maids to keep quiet," said Hsi-feng. "Who could have blabbed? This makes things more difficult."

"Never mind about that now," said the old lady. "Let's go and see how she is."

The three of them went to Bamboo Lodge and found Tai-yu deathly pale. She seemed comatose and her breathing was very weak. Presently she had another fit of coughing. Her maids brought over the spittoon and to their consternation her sputum was streaked with blood. Her eyelids fluttered then, and she saw the old lady by her.

"Madam," she gasped, "your love for me has been wasted."

Her heart aching, her grandmother said, "Don't be afraid, dear child. You must rest well."

Tai-yu smiled faintly, closing her eyes again as a maid came in to report the doctor's arrival to Hsi-feng. Thereupon the ladies withdrew, and Doctor Wang was led in by Chia Lien to feel the patient's pulse.

"She will be all right," he observed. "Pent-up anger has drained her liver of blood, resulting in nervous disorders. Some medicine to regulate the blood will set her right again."

This said, he went out with Chia Lien to write out his prescription and fetch medicine.

The Lady Dowager had seen that Tai-yu's state was critical. After leaving her she said to Hsi-feng, "It's not that I want to put a jinx on her but it doesn't look to me, I'm afraid, as if the child will recover. You must get ready after-life things to counter her bad luck. If she gets over this illness, that'll be a great weight off our minds. And if it comes to the worst, you won't be caught unprepared at the last minute. We've that other business to attend to these days."

When Hsi-feng had acquiesced, the old lady questioned Tzu-chuan; but the maid did not know who had told Tai-yu the news.

Dubiously, the old lady went on, "It's natural for young people who've played together as children to be partial to each other; but now that they're big enough to know the facts of life they should keep at a distance. That's how a girl should behave if she wants me to love her. To get other ideas into her head would be most improper, and all my love for her would be thrown away. I'm quite upset by what you've been telling me."

On her return to her own quarters, she called in Hsi-jen to interrogate her. Hsi-jen repeated what she had told Lady Wang, then described Tai-yu's behaviour earlier that day.

"She didn't look deranged when I saw her just now," commented the old lady. "I simply can't understand this. In a family like ours, of course there can't be any carryings-on, but even *thinking* such thoughts is taboo! If that's not the root of her illness, I'm willing to spend any sum to cure her. If it *is*, I doubt if it can be cured and I don't care!"

Hsi-feng put in, "Don't worry about Cousin Lin, madam. Lien will take the doctor to see her every day anyway. It's the other business that matters. I heard this morning that the rooms are practically ready. Why don't you and Her Ladyship call on Aunt Hsueh to discuss it with her? I'll go with you. The only snag is that with Cousin Pao-chai there it will be difficult to talk. Suppose we ask Aunt Hsueh over for a consultation here this evening? Then we can settle everything tonight."

"You're right," Their Ladyships agreed. "But it's too late today. We'll go over there tomorrow after breakfast."

As the old lady had finished her supper by now, Hsi-feng and Lady Wang went back to their own apartments.

The next day, Hsi-feng came over after breakfast and went in to sound out Pao-yu.

"Congratulations, Cousin Pao!" she greeted him gaily. "The master has chosen a lucky day for your wedding. Doesn't that make you happy?"

Pao-yu just grinned at her and nodded imperceptibly.

"Your bride will be Cousin Lin. Are you glad?"

He simply burst out laughing, and she was unclear about his mental state.

"The master says you can marry her if you're better, not if

you go on acting the fool," she warned.

"If anyone's a fool, it's you — not me!" he retorted seriously, then stood up and announced, "I'm going to see Cousin Lin to reassure her."

Hsi-feng promptly barred his way.

"She knows it already," she said. "As she's to marry you, she'll naturally feel too shy to see you."

"Will she see me after the wedding?"

Amused and perturbed Hsi-feng thought, "Hsi-jen was right. At the mention of Tai-yu, though he still raves his mind seems clearer. If he really comes to his senses and finds out that it isn't Tai-yu but we've played a trick on him, then the fat will be in the fire!"

Suppressing a smile she said, "If you're better she'll see you, not if you act crazily."

"I've given her my heart. When she comes, she's bound to bring it and put it back in my breast."

As he was raving, Hsi-feng came out and smiled at the old lady, who had been both amused and upset by their conversation.

"I heard," she said. "We can ignore him for now and leave Hsi-jen to calm him down. Let's go."

For by then Lady Wang had come too, and together they called on Aunt Hsueh, ostensibly to see how her family was faring. Aunt Hsueh was most grateful and gave them news of Hsueh Pan. When tea had been served she wanted to send for Pao-chai, but Hsi-feng stopped her.

"You needn't summon her, aunty," she said with a smile. "The old lady came partly to see how you are and partly because there's some important business which she'd like to discuss with you in our place."

Aunt Hsueh nodded and agreed to this, and after a little more idle talk they left.

That evening Aunt Hsueh came over. Having paid her respects to the old lady she called on Lady Wang, and speaking of Wang Tzu-teng's death they all shed tears.

"Just now in the old lady's place, Pao-yu came out to pay his respects," remarked Aunt Hsueh. "He looked all right, simply a little thinner. Why do you speak as if it were so serious?"

"Actually it's nothing much," replied Hsi-feng. "But the old lady is worried. Now the master is going to a provincial post and may not be back for some years. Her idea is to have Pao-yu's wedding while he's still here. Firstly, to set his father's mind at rest; and secondly, in the hope that Cousin Pao-chai's golden locket will bring Pao-yu good luck, overcoming the evil influence so that he recovers."

Aunt Hsueh wanted the match but feared Pao-chai might feel herself wronged. "That's all right," she replied, "but we must think it out more carefully."

Lady Wang told her Hsi-feng's plan, adding, "As your son is away from home now, you need not give any dowry. Tomorrow send Ko to tell Pan that while we have the wedding here we'll find some way to settle his lawsuit for him." Omitting to mention that Pao-yu had lost his heart to Tai-yu, she concluded, "Since you agree to it, the sooner the bride comes the better — the sooner we'll all feel easier in our minds."

At this point Yuan-yang arrived, sent by the old lady to hear what they had decided. Though this was treating Pao-chai shabbily, Aunt Hsueh could hardly refuse as they were so pressing. She consented with a show of readiness. Yuan-yang went back to report this to the old lady, who in elation sent her back to urge Aunt Hsueh to explain the situation to Pao-chai so that she would not feel unfairly treated. Aunt Hsueh agreed to this. Having decided that Hsi-feng and her husband should act as go-betweens, the others left. Then Lady Wang and her sister sat up half the night talking.

The next day Aunt Hsueh went home and told Pao-chai in detail all these arrangements to which she had agreed. Pao-chai lowered her head in silence, and presently shed tears. Her mother did her best to comfort her, explaining the matter at length; and when Pao-chai went back to her room Pao-chin went with her to try to cheer her up. Aunt Hsueh also told Hsueh Ko, urging him to leave the following day to find out what sentence had been passed and to give Hsueh Pan this news, then to come back immediately.

Four days later Hsueh Ko returned.

"Regarding Cousin Pan's business," he reported, "the judge has approved a verdict of accidental manslaughter, which will be pronounced at the next session; and we must have silver ready by way of compensation. As for his sister's wedding, Pan says your decision was a good one, and rushing it through will save a good deal of money. He says you shouldn't wait for his return but do as you think fit."

This news reassured Aunt Hsueh that her son would be released and her daughter's wedding could be carried through, although she could see that Pao-chai looked rather unwilling. "Still," she thought, "she's a girl who's always been submissive and a model of propriety. Knowing that I've agreed, she won't raise any objections."

She told Hsueh Ko, "Get a gilded card and write her horoscope on it, then have it sent at once to Second Master Lien and ask the date for the exchange of gifts, so that you can make preparations. We don't mean to notify relatives and friends because, as you've said, all Pan's friends are a bad lot and our only relatives are the Chia and Wang families. Now the Chias are the bridegroom's family and the Wangs have no one in the capital. When Miss Shih was engaged her family didn't invite us, so we needn't put them out either. But we must ask Chang Teh-hui here to help see to things as he's elderly and experienced."

Hsueh Ko, acting on her instructions, had a card sent to the Chia family. And the next day Chia Lien called to pay his respects to Aunt Hsueh.

"Tomorrow is a very auspicious day," he said. "So I've come to propose that we exchange gifts tomorrow. We only hope you won't think us too niggardly, aunt." He handed her the card on which was written the date of the wedding, and when she had made a polite rejoinder and nodded her consent he hurried back to report this to Chia Cheng.

"Let the old lady know," said Chia Cheng. "Suggest that as we're not notifying friends and relatives, we may as well

keep everything rather simple. Regarding the gifts, just ask her
to approve them; no need to refer to me."

Chia Lien assented and went off on this errand. Lady Wang
told Hsi-feng to take all the gifts to the old lady for her inspection, and to get Hsi-jen to let Pao-yu know as well.

"Why go to all this bother?" Pao-yu chuckled. "We send
things to the Garden, then they send them back here again —
our own people doing the sending and the accepting!"

Their Ladyships hearing this remarked cheerfully, "We say
he's weak in the head, but today he's talking sense."

Yuan-yang and the other maids could not suppress smiles
either as they showed the gifts one by one to the old lady.

"This is a gold necklet," they said. "Here are gold and
pearl trinkets, eighty of them in all. There are forty rolls of
serpent-patterned brocade, a hundred and twenty rolls of coloured silk and satin and a hundred and twenty garments for all
four seasons. As no sheep and wine have been prepared, here
is the equivalent in silver."

When the old lady had approved these gifts she quietly instructed Hsi-feng, "Go and tell Aunt Hsueh not to stand on
ceremony. Ask her to wait till Pan is released to return gifts
for his sister in his own good time. We here will prepare the
bedding for the happy occasion."

Hsi-feng assented and left to send Chia Lien to Aunt Hsueh's
place. She then instructed Chou Jui and Lai Wang, "Don't take
the presents through the main gate but by that old side-gate in
the Garden. I'll be coming over myself presently. That gate
is a good distance from Bamboo Lodge. If people from other
households notice you, warn them not to mention this to anyone
there."

The stewards went off to carry out these orders.

In the happy belief that he was to marry Tai-yu, Pao-yu's
health improved, though he still talked foolishly. The stewards
sending the presents named no names when they came back;
and though most of the household knew where they had been,
in view of Hsi-feng's instructions they dared not disclose it.

Now Tai-yu, although taking medicine, was sinking steadily. Tzu-chuan and her other maids pleaded hard with her.

"Things have come to such a pass, miss, we must speak out," they said. "We know what's in your heart. But nothing unforeseen can possibly happen. If you don't believe us, just think of Pao-yu's health — he's so ill, how could he get married? Don't listen to silly rumours, miss, but rest quietly till you're better."

Tai-yu smiled faintly without a word, then started coughing again and brought up more and more blood. Her maids saw that she was dying, and nothing they could say would save her. They remained at her bedside weeping, though sending three or four times a day to report to the old lady. But as Yuan-yang had noticed that recently Tai-yu had lost favour in her grandmother's eyes, she often neglected to pass on their messages. And as the old lady was occupied with preparations for the approaching wedding, when she had no news of Tai-yu she asked no questions. All her maids could do was send for the doctor to see her.

During Tai-yu's previous illnesses, everyone from the old lady herself down to the maids of her cousins had come to ask after her health. But now not one relative or servant came, not even sending inquiries, and when she opened her eyes there was nobody but Tzu-chuan in the room. She knew there was not the least reason for her to live on.

"Sister, you're the one closest to me," she murmured with an effort. "Ever since you were assigned to me by the old lady, I've always looked on you as my own sister. . . ." Here she had to stop for breath.

Tzu-chuan's heart ached. She was sobbing too much to speak.

"Sister Tzu-chuan!" panted Tai-yu after a while. "I feel uncomfortable lying down. Please help me to sit up."

"But you're not well, miss. If you sit up you may catch cold."

Tai-yu closed her eyes without a word but presently struggled to sit up and Tzu-chuan and Hsueh-yen had to help her, propping her up with soft pillows on either side while Tzu-chuan sat by her supporting her. Though she was so weak that she felt the bed beneath her painfully hard, she stuck it out.

"My poems . . ." she gasped to Hsueh-yen.

Hsueh-yen guessed that she wanted her manuscript book which she had been going through a few days ago. She found it and gave it to her. Tai-yu nodded, then glanced up at the case on a shelf; but this time the maid could not read her thoughts. Tai-yu's eyes dilated with exasperation till a fresh fit of coughing made her bring up more blood. Hsueh-yen hastily fetched her water to rinse out her mouth over the spittoon, then Tzu-chuan wiped her lips with a handkerchief. Taking it, Tai-yu pointed at the case, gasping for breath again so that she could not speak. Her eyes had closed.

"Better lie down, miss," urged Tzu-chuan.

When Tai-yu shook her head, Tzu-chuan realized that she must want a handkerchief and told Hsueh-yen to fetch a white silk one from the case. But at sight of it, Tai-yu put it aside.

"The one with writing . . ." she managed to whisper.

Then it dawned on Tzu-chuan that she wanted Pao-yu's old handkerchief on which she had written verses. She made Hsueh-yen get it out and passed it to her.

"For pity's sake, rest, miss!" she begged her. "Why tire yourself out? You can look at it when you're better."

But not even glancing at the poems, Tai-yu tried with all her might to tear up the handkerchief. However, her trembling fingers lacked the strength. Although Tzu-chuan knew how incensed she was by Pao-yu, she dared not disclose this.

"Don't wear yourself out again, miss, being angry!" she pleaded.

Tai-yu nodded weakly and stuffed the handkerchief up her sleeve.

"Light the lamp," she ordered.

Hsueh-yen hastily complied. After glancing at the lamp Tai-yu closed her eyes again and sat there breathing hard.

"Bring the brazier," she murmured presently.

Thinking she was cold Tzu-chuan urged, "You'd better lie

down, miss, and put on more bedding. Charcoal fumes might be bad for you."

As Tai-yu shook her head, Hsueh-yen had to light the brazier and put it on its stand on the floor. At a sign that Tai-yu wanted it on the *kang*, she moved it there, then went out to fetch a low table.

Tai-yu bent forward, supported by Tzu-chuan's two hands. She pulled out the handkerchief, looked at the fire and nodded, then dropped the handkerchief on it. This shocked Tzu-chuan, who wanted to snatch it off but could not let go of her mistress, as Hsueh-yen was still outside fetching the low table. By now the handkerchief was burning.

"Miss!" protested Tzu-chuan. "Why do such a thing?"

Turning a deaf ear, Tai-yu picked up her manuscript book and after glancing at it put it down. For fear she might burn this too, Tzu-chuan hastily leaned against her to support her, thereby freeing one of her own hands. But Tai-yu forestalled her by dropping the book on the fire out of her reach.

Hsueh-yen coming in with the table saw Tai-yu toss something on the fire and made a grab for it; but the inflammable paper was already smouldering. Not caring whether she burned her hands or not, Hsueh-yen snatched the book from the fire, threw it on the ground and trampled it with her feet. Too late — there was nothing but a charred remnant left.

Tai-yu closed her eyes and sank back, nearly knocking over Tzu-chuan who, her heart palpitating, hastily asked Hsueh-yen to help lay her down. It was too late to fetch help; yet what if they called no-one and their young mistress should die during the night with only herself, Hsueh-yen, Ying-ko and a few young maids in attendance? They sat up apprehensively till dawn, when Tai-yu seemed a little better. But after breakfast she had a sudden relapse, coughing and retching again.

Fearing the worst, Tzu-chuan left Hsueh-yen and the others in charge while she hurried to report this to the old lady. However, she found the place quiet and deserted, except for a few old nurses and some young maids of all work left there to mind the house. Asked where the old lady was, they return-

ed evasive answers. In surprise, Tzu-chuan went into Pao-yu's room and found it empty too. The young maids there also denied any knowledge of his whereabouts.

By then Tzu-chuan had a good inkling of the truth. "How cruel these people are!" she thought to herself, remembering that not a soul had called on Tai-yu during the last few days. The more she dwelt on it, the more bitter she felt. In her indignation she turned and left abruptly.

"I'd like to see how Pao-yu looks today," she fumed "Wouldn't the sight of me shame him? That year when I told him a fib he fell ill, he was so frantic; but today he blatantly does a thing like this. It shows that all men's hearts are as cold as ice — they really make you gnash your teeth!"

As she walked on brooding over this, she soon reached Happy Red Court. The gate was closed and all inside was quiet. It occurred to her then, "If he is getting married, he must have new bridal chambers. I wonder where they are?"

She was looking around when Mo-yu came flying along and she called to him to stop. The page walked over, grinning broadly.

"What brings you here, sister?" he asked.

"I heard Master Pao's getting married so I came to watch the fun, but apparently the wedding's not here. When exactly is it to be?"

"I'll tell you in strict confidence, sister," he whispered. "But don't let Hsueh-yen know. Our orders are not even to let *you* know. The wedding will take place this evening. Of course it won't be here. His Lordship made Second Master Lien fix up new quarters for them. Well, is there anything you want me to do?"

"No, nothing. Off you go."

Mo-yu darted off.

Tzu-chuan remained lost in thought until she remembered Tai-yu — was she still alive?

"Pao-yu!" she swore through clenched teeth, her eyes swimming with tears. "If she dies tomorrow, you'll get out of seeing her. But after you've had your pleasure, how are you going to brazen it out with *me*?"

She walked on in tears towards Bamboo Lodge and saw two young maids at the gate looking out for her.

At sight of her one cried, "Here comes Sister Tzu-chuan!"

With a sinking heart she signalled to them to keep quiet. Hurrying to Tai-yu's bedside, she found her feverish, her cheeks hectically flushed. Knowing that this was a bad sign, Tzu-chuan called for Tai-yu's old nurse Nanny Wang, who took one look then started sobbing and wailing.

Tzu-chuan had hoped that old Nanny Wang with her experience would lend her courage; but the nurse's reaction threw her into a tizzy till she bethought herself of someone else and sent a young maid quickly in search of her. Do you know who this was? Li Wan. As a widow, it was out of the question for her to attend Pao-yu's wedding; besides, she was the one in charge in the Garden. So Tzu-chuan sent to ask her over.

Li Wan was correcting a poem for Lan when a young maid burst in.

"Madam!" she cried. "It looks as if Miss Lin's done for! They're all weeping and wailing there."

Li Wan was horrified. Not stopping to ask any questions she sprang up and hurried out, followed by Su-yun and Pi-yueh. And on the way she reflected tearfully, "We've been as close as sisters here. Her looks and talents are truly so outstanding, one can only compare her to some goddess in heaven. But poor girl, fated to die so young and be buried far from home! I didn't like to visit her all because of Hsi-feng's underhand plan to fob off a different bride on Pao-yu — so I've let my cousin down. How tragic this is!"

Now, reaching the gate of Bamboo Lodge, she was unnerved not to hear a sound inside. "Perhaps she's already dead and they've finished lamenting her," she thought as she hurried inside. "I wonder if they had clothes, bedding and shroud ready."

A young maid by the door of the inner room at sight of her announced, "Here's Madam Chu!"

Tzu-chuan hastily came out as Li Wan walked in.

"How is she?" she asked urgently.

Tzu-chuan choked with sobs and could not get a word out. Her tears falling like pearls from a broken string, she could only point at Tai-yu.

The maid's grief distressed Li Wan even more. Asking no further questions she went over to look at the dying girl, already past speaking. She called her softly twice. Tai-yu opened her eyes slowly and seemed to recognize her. She was still breathing faintly, but though her eyelids fluttered and her lips quivered, she could not utter a single word or shed a single tear.

Turning away, Li Wan saw that Tzu-chuan had vanished and asked Hsueh-yen where she was.

"In the outer room," was the answer.

Li Wan hurried out and found her lying on the divan there, her face pale, tears flowing so fast from her closed eyes that a big patch of the silk-bordered flowered mattress was wet with tears and mucus. At Li Wan's call she opened her eyes slowly and got up.

"Silly creature!" scolded Li Wan. "This is no time for weeping. Hurry up and get Miss Lin's clothes ready. How long will you wait to change her? Are you going to expose an unmarried girl to set out naked to the other world?"

At this, Tzu-chuan broke down and sobbed bitterly. Li Wan though weeping too was impatient as well. Wiping her own eyes, she patted the maid on the shoulder.

"Good child, your crying is driving me distracted! Prepare her things quickly before it's too late," she urged.

She was startled just then by someone rushing in. It was Ping-erh. Bursting in on this scene she stood rooted to the spot, speechless.

"Why aren't you over there now? What brings you here?" asked Li Wan as Lin Chih-hsiao's wife also joined them.

Ping-erh said, "Our mistress was worried and sent me to have a look. But as *you're* here, madam, I shall tell her that she need only attend to affairs over there."

Li Wan nodded.

"I'll go in to see Miss Lin too," added Ping-erh, already in tears as she entered the inner room.

"You've come in the nick of time," Li Wan told Mrs. Lin. "Go out quickly and get some steward to prepare Miss Lin's after-life things. When everything's ready he's to report to me — there's no need to go over there."

Mrs. Lin assented but made no move.

"Do you have other business?" Li Wan asked.

"Just now Madam Lien consulted the old lady and they want to have Miss Tzu-chuan to help out there."

Before Li Wan could answer, Tzu-chuan interposed, "Please don't wait for me, Mrs. Lin. When she's dead, of course we'll leave her. They needn't be in such a hurry. . . ." Embarrassed by this outburst she went on more mildly, "Besides, nursing an invalid here I'm not clean. Miss Lin is still breathing and wants me from time to time."

Li Wan helped her out by explaining, "It's true. The affinity between Miss Lin and this girl must have been predestined. Though Hsueh-yen's the one she brought with her from the south, she doesn't care for her much. I can see that Tzu-chuan is the only one who can't leave her for a second."

Mrs. Lin had been put out by Tzu-chuan's reply, but she was unable to rebut Li Wan. Seeing Tzu-chuan dissolved in tears, she smiled at her faintly.

"It's all very well for Miss Tzu-chuan to talk like that," she rejoined. "But what am I to say to the old lady? And how can I repeat this to Madam Lien?"

At these words, Ping-erh came out wiping her eyes.

"Repeat what to Madam Lien?" she wanted to know.

Mrs. Lin explained the situation, and Ping-erh lowered her head to think it over.

"In that case," she suggested, "let Hsueh-yen go instead."

"Will she be suitable?" Li Wan inquired.

Ping-erh stepped closer to whisper something to her, at which she nodded.

"Very well, then. Sending Hsueh-yen will do just as well."

Mrs. Lin asked Ping-erh if she agreed, and the answer was: "Yes, it's the same."

"Then please tell her to come with me immediately. I'll report to the old lady and Madam Lien that this was your idea, madam, and Miss Ping-erh's too. Later you can explain to Madam Lien yourself, miss."

"All right," said Li Wan. "But why should someone of your seniority be scared to answer for such a little thing?"

"It's not that." Mrs. Lin smiled. "But we can't be sure what plan the old lady and Madam Lien have; and besides you and Miss Ping-erh are here, madam."

Ping-erh had already called out Hsueh-yen, who had been holding aloof these last few days as the others had been taunting her as a careless child; and in any case she would never dream of ignoring a summons from the Lady Dowager and Madam Lien. She hastily smoothed her hair and on Ping-erh's instructions changed into colourful clothes, then went off with Mrs. Lin. Li Wan, after a brief discussion with Ping-erh, sent her to tell Mrs. Lin to urge her husband to get a coffin ready without delay.

Ping-erh left to attend to this and, rounding a bend, saw Mrs. Lin walking ahead of her with Hsueh-yen. She called to them to stop.

"I'll take her there," she said. "You go first to tell your husband to get Miss Lin's things ready. I'll report this for you to my mistress."

Mrs. Lin agreed and went off, while Ping-erh took Hsueh-yen to the bridal chambers and, having made her report, left to see to her own business.

Now that things had come to such a pass, Hsueh-yen could not but grieve for Tai-yu, though she dared not show her feelings to the old lady and Hsi-feng. "What do they want me for?" she wondered. "I'll wait and see. Pao-yu used to be so devoted to our young lady, why doesn't he come out? Is he really ill or just shamming? He may be trying to put her off by pretending to have lost his jade and to be out of his mind,

so that she'll lose interest in him and he can marry Miss Pao-
chai. I'll slip in and see whether he's really crazy or not. He
can hardly be shamming today."

She tiptoed to the door of the inner room and peeped in.

Now though the loss of his jade had deranged Pao-yu, the
news that he was to marry Tai-yu seemed to him the most
wonderful thing that had ever happened, and at once his health
had improved, though he seemed less quick in the uptake than
before. So Hsi-feng's cunning scheme had succeeded completely.
He could hardly wait to see Tai-yu and go through with his
wedding today. Beside himself with joy, although he sometimes
talked nonsense he behaved quite differently from when he
was demented. Hsueh-yen saw this with indignation and distress,
not knowing what was in his heart, then she slipped away.

Pao-yu, seated in Lady Wang's room, was pressing Hsi-jen
to help him into his wedding clothes and watching busy Hsi-
feng and Madam Yu as he longed for the auspicious hour to
arrive.

"Cousin Lin's only coming from the Garden," he said to
Hsi-jen. "Why should it take so long?"

Suppressing a smile she answered, "She has to wait for the
appointed hour."

Then he heard Hsi-feng say to Lady Wang, "Although we're
in mourning and won't have musicians outside, according to
us southerners' rule they must bow to each other and utter
silence won't do. So I've ordered our troupe of house musicians
to play some tunes and liven things up a little."

"Very well," said Lady Wang, nodding.

Presently a big sedan-chair entered the courtyard and the
family musicians went out to meet the bride, while in filed
twelve pairs of maids in two rows with Palace lanterns — a
novel and distinctive sight. The Master of Ceremonies invited
the bride to alight from the chair, and Pao-yu saw a maid with
a red sash help her out — her face was veiled. And who do
you think the other maid assisting the bride was? No other
than Hsueh-yen!

"Why Hsueh-yen and not Tzu-chuan?" he wondered, then told himself, "Of course. She brought Hsueh-yen with her from her home down south. Tzu-chuan is one of *our* household; so naturally she needn't bring her." Reasoning like this, he felt as jubilant as if seeing Tai-yu herself.

The Master of Ceremonies announced the procedure. Bride and bridegroom paid their respects to Heaven and Earth, then invited the old lady to come out and receive four bows from them, after which they bowed to Chia Cheng and Lady Wang. Next they ascended the hall and paid their respects to each other before being ushered into the bridal chamber where they went through other ceremonies such as "sitting on the bed" and "letting down the bed curtains," in accordance with the old rules of Chinling.

Chia Cheng had never believed that this wedding could cure Pao-yu, but he had to go along with his mother's decision. Today, however, he was pleased because Pao-yu looked as if he had really recovered.

After the bride sat down on the bridal bed, she had to be unveiled. To be on the safe side, Hsi-feng had asked the old lady and Lady Wang there to keep an eye on things. Pao-yu fatuously stepped over to the bride.

"Are you better, Cousin Lin?" he asked. "It's so long since I've seen you! Why keep your face covered with that rag?"

He reached out to take off the veil, making the old lady break out in a cold sweat. But then Pao-yu reflected, "Cousin Lin's very sensitive; I mustn't offend her." So he waited till he felt he could wait no longer, then stepped forward and removed the veil, which the bridesmaid whisked away. At the same time Hsueh-yen withdrew, and Ying-erh came in to wait upon her young mistress.

Pao-yu looked at his bride and could not believe his eyes — she seemed to be Pao-chai. He shone the lamp on her face and rubbed his eyes. There was no doubt about it — it was Pao-chai! Splendidly dressed, soft and plump, her hair slightly dishevelled, fluttering her eyelashes and holding her breath she looked as alluring as lotus dripping with dew, as bashful as apricot blossom moistened by mist.

Pao-yu was stupefied by the realization that Hsueh-yen had disappeared and Ying-erh had taken her place. At a loss, he thought he must be dreaming and stood there in a daze till they took the lamp from his hand and made him sit down. Staring vacantly, he uttered not a word. The old lady, afraid he had lost his senses again, took charge of him herself while Hsi-feng and Madam Yu led Pao-chai to the inner room to rest. She, of course, remained silent too, lowering her head.

Soon Pao-yu calmed down sufficiently to notice the presence of his grandmother and mother.

"Where am I?" he whispered to Hsi-jen. "Is this a dream?"

"This is your wedding day," she answered. "Don't let the master hear you talking such nonsense. He's just outside."

"Who's that beautiful girl sitting there?" he asked, pointing inside.

Hsi-jen put a hand to her mouth to hide her laughter, so amused that she could not speak.

"That's the new Second Young Mistress," she finally told him.

The others also turned their heads away, unable to keep from smiling.

"Don't be silly!" cried Pao-yu. "What Second Young Mistress do you mean?"

"Miss Pao-chai."

"Then where is Miss Lin?"

"It was the master's decision that you should marry Miss Pao-chai, so why ask in that foolish way about Miss Lin?"

"But I saw her just now, and Hsueh-yen too. How can you say they're not here? What game are you all playing?"

Hsi-feng stepped forward to whisper, "Miss Pao-chai is sitting in the inner room; so don't talk foolishly. If you annoy her, the old lady won't like it."

This bewildered Pao-yu still more. Already deranged, after the mysterious apparitions and vanishings of this evening he knew even less what to think. Ignoring all else he just clamour-

ed to go and find Cousin Lin. The ladies did their best to pacify him, but he would not listen to reason; and as Pao-chai was inside they could not speak out plainly. Indeed, they knew that explanations were useless now that his wits were wandering again. They lit benzoin incense to calm him and made him lie down. No one made a sound and presently, to the old lady's relief, he fell into a lethargic sleep. She decided to sit up with him till dawn and sent Hsi-feng to urge Pao-chai to rest too. Pao-chai, behaving as if she had heard nothing, lay down then fully dressed in the inner room. As for Chia Cheng, being outside he had no knowledge of these happenings and, in fact, felt relieved by what he had seen. Since the next day was the auspicious date to start his journey, he too rested for a while before receiving the congratulations of those who had come to bid him farewell. And when Pao-yu was sound asleep, the old lady also returned to her room to sleep.

The next morning Chia Cheng bowed farewell in the ancestral temple, then came over to take his leave of his mother.

"Your unfilial son is going far away," he said. "My one wish, madam, is that you will take care of your health at different seasons. As soon as I reach my post, I shall write to pay my respects. Please don't worry about me. And Pao-yu's wedding has been carried out in accordance with your wishes. I beg you, madam, to admonish him from time to time."

In order not to worry him on his journey, she did not tell him of Pao-yu's relapse.

"All I have to say is this," she answered. "Though Pao-yu was married last night he didn't share the same room with his bride, so today we should make him see you some way on your journey. But as his wedding was to cure his illness and he's only just slightly better, and as yesterday was a tiring day for him, I'm afraid he might catch cold if he went out. So I'd like to know your opinion. If you want him to see you off, I'll send for him at once; but if you're concerned for him, I'll just have him fetched here to kowtow to you by way of farewell."

"Why should he see me off? Provided he studies hard from now on that will please me more than having him escort me."

In relief, the old lady told him to sit down while she sent Yuan-yang to fetch Pao-yu and Hsi-jen.

Presently Pao-yu came. Told to pay his respects, he complied. Luckily his mind cleared for a while at sight of his father, and he made no gaffes, assenting to Chia Cheng's instructions. Then his father dismissed him and went to his wife's room to stress the need to discipline their son.

"You must on no account go on spoiling him," he warned her. "Next year he must sit for the provincial examination."

Lady Wang heard him out without mentioning what had passed and had Pao-chai fetched to wish her father-in-law a good journey. The other female members of the family saw him off at the inner gate, but she as a new bride could not leave the house. Chia Chen and the other young men listened respectfully to his admonitions. Then having drunk a parting goblet with him, the younger male relatives and his old friends accompanied him ten *li* beyond the capital, then bid him farewell.

We shall now leave Chia Cheng travelling to his new post and return to Pao-yu. After coming back he had a sudden relapse, becoming so deranged that he could not even take any nourishment. To know whether he lived or died, read the next chapter.

CHAPTER 98

Unhappy Vermilion Pearl's Spirit
Returns in Sorrow to Heaven
Deranged Shen Ying[1] Sheds Tears
in the Lodge of His Loved One

Pao-yu returned to his room after seeing his father more dizzy, confused and listless than before. Without even eating his meal he drifted off to sleep. Doctors were called in again but their remedies proved ineffectual — he could not even recognize those around him, although when helped to sit up he looked normal enough. And this state of affairs continued for several days.

The ninth day after the wedding had now come — the day on which newly-weds should visit the bride's family. If they stayed away, Aunt Hsueh might well feel slighted; but how could they go with Pao-yu so distraught on account of Tai-yu? On the other hand, they feared that if told of her death he might die himself of chagrin. His bride could hardly reason with him either — for that, her mother was needed there. Yet if they neglected to pay this courtesy call, Aunt Hsueh would take offence.

The Lady Dowager consulted Lady Wang and Hsi-feng and proposed, "Pao-yu may have lost his mind, but I can't see that going out would hurt him. Let's order two small sedan-chairs and have them escorted over through the Garden to keep up appearances; then we can invite Aunt Hsueh here to comfort

[1] See Chapter I. The Goddess of Disenchantment granted her attendant Shen Ying's wish to assume human form, and gave the Vermilion Pearl Plant this chance to repay her debt of gratitude to him by a lifetime of tears in the world of men. Shen Ying was reincarnated as Pao-yu, Vermilion Pearl as Tai-yu.

Pao-chai, while we give our whole minds to curing Pao-yu. Wouldn't that be best on both scores?"

Lady Wang agreed and had preparations made without delay. As Pao-chai was a new bride and Pao-yu was crazed, neither objected to being taken over; for although Pao-chai knew how things stood and at heart blamed her mother for this injudicious match, it was too late now to protest.   True, Aunt Hsueh reproached herself bitterly when she saw Pao-yu's condition; still, they had to go through with the ceremonies in a perfunctory way.

On their return Pao-yu took a turn for the worse. The next morning he could not sit up, and he wasted away day by day until he could not even take liquid nourishment.   In panic Aunt Hsueh and the others searched everywhere for good doctors, but not one was able to diagnose his illness until a certain Pi Chih-an, a poor physician who lived in a ruined temple outside town, ascribed it to both internal and external factors: sudden transports of joy and grief depriving him of his senses and appetite, and pent-up indignation resulting in congestion. He made out his prescription accordingly, and Pao-yu took the first dose that evening. After the second watch, sure enough, he came to and asked for a drink of water. Their Ladyships in relief invited Aunt Hsueh and Pao-chai to the old lady's room to rest.

Pao-yu, now that his mind had cleared, was convinced that he was dying. As the others had gone, leaving only Hsi-jen there, he called her over to him and clasped her hand.

"Tell me," he sobbed, "what is Cousin Pao-chai doing here? I remember my father choosing Cousin Lin to marry me, so how did she get driven out by Cousin Pao-chai? Why should *she* force her way in here? I don't like to ask her for fear of offending her. And what news have you of Cousin Lin? Is she crying her heart out?"

Hsi-jen prevaricated, "Miss Lin is ill."

"I'll go and see her then."

He tried to get up, but after several days without nourishment of any kind he was too weak to move.

"I'm dying!" he exclaimed. "But I've one request which I beg you to pass on to the old lady. Cousin Lin will be sobbing herself to death too and I'm done for now anyway, so that's two of us mortally ill in different places. If we die apart that'll make more trouble for you, so why not turn out a spare room and move the two of us there? You can nurse us both together while we're still living, and when we're dead you can lay us out together. For the sake of our friendship these years, please do this for me!"

Hsi-jen was so affected by his words that she sobbed convulsively. And Pao-chai, coming back then with Ying-erh, heard him too.

"Why talk in that unlucky way instead of resting well so as to recover?" she asked. "The old lady's just feeling a bit easier in her mind, yet here you are starting fresh trouble. You've always been the old lady's favourite, and now she's over eighty. Though she's not expecting you to win her honours, if you turn out well that will please her and the pains she's taken over you won't be wasted. As for your mother, it goes without saying she's given her heart's blood to bring you up, and if you die young what's to become of her? And I, though I may be ill-fated, don't deserve this. Because of the three of us, even if you want to die Heaven won't allow it! So just rest quietly for four or five days till you're over this chill and your vital forces are restored; then this disorder will naturally disappear."

This silenced Pao-yu for some minutes. Then he sniggered, "You stopped talking to me for so long, why start haranguing me now?"

"Let me tell you the truth," she continued. "While you were in a coma for two days Cousin Lin died."

He sat up abruptly.

"Is that true?" he demanded.

"Of course it is. I wouldn't say such a fearful thing if it wasn't. The old lady and your mother, knowing how fond of her you were, were afraid the news would kill you too. That's why they didn't tell you."

Pao-yu burst out sobbing and fell back on his pillows. All before him was black and he could not make out where he was. He was feeling lost when he saw a figure approaching.

"Excuse me," he blurted out. "What is this place?"

"The way to Hell," was the answer. "But what are *you* doing here? Your span of life has not ended."

"I just heard that a friend had died, and looking for her here I lost my way."

"What friend?"

"Lin Tai-yu of Soochow."

"Lin Tai-yu in life was no ordinary mortal; in death she is no ordinary ghost," said the apparition with a scornful laugh. "As she has no ghost, where can you find her? The spirits of men assume a form only when concentrated; when dissipated they change into vapour. In life they have a form; after death they scatter. So even ordinary mortals cannot be traced after death, let alone Lin Tai-yu. You had better go back at once."

Nonplussed by this Pao-yu asked, "If you say the spirit is dissipated after death, why should there be a Hell?"

"Hell exists for those who believe in it," was the disdainful answer. "Because the vulgar herd are afraid of death they tell cautionary tales about the wrath that Heaven visits on fools who are not content with their lot or senselessly cut short their lives by indulging in lust or running amok, making away with themselves for no good reason. So Hell has been dreamed up as a prison where such ghosts will suffer endless torments to expiate their crimes during their lifetime. By searching for Tai-yu, you are courting death unjustifiably. The more so, as she has already returned to the Illusory Land of Great Void. If you want to find her, you must cultivate virtue and you will have occasion to meet again. If you chafe at your lot and commit the crime of cutting short your life, you may see your parents again — but never Tai-yu!" This said, he took a stone from his sleeve and aimed it at Pao-yu's heart.

Terrified by this warning and a pain in the region of his heart, Pao-yu longed to go home but did not know the way. He was hesitating when he heard his name and turned to find that the old lady, Lady Wang, Pao-chai and Hsi-jen had gathered round, tearfully calling him, and he himself was still lying in his bed. The red lamp on his desk, the bright moon outside the window showed that he was still in this vain world, in the lap of luxury. Calming down, he realized that he had been dreaming. Though drenched with cold sweat he felt refreshed and clear-headed. Reflecting that there was in truth no way out for him, he heaved sigh after sigh.

Now Pao-chai had known from the start of Tai-yu's death, but the Lady Dowager forbade any mention of it to Pao-yu for fear of making his illness worse, though she herself knew that his breakdown was due to his longing for Tai-yu, the loss of his jade being only secondary. She had taken her opportunity to tell him to end his torment and bring him back to his senses, so that he could be cured. The old lady and Lady Wang, not knowing her motive, blamed her for her impetuosity; but when Pao-yu came to they felt relieved and at once summoned Doctor Pi from the outer study to examine him.

"Strange!" observed the physician after feeling his pulse. "His pulse is steady and there is no sign now of melancholia. We'll give him a restorative tomorrow, and can hope for a cure." Then he left and the others dispersed, much easier in their minds.

Hsi-jen, too, had been shocked by Pao-chai's disclosure, though she could not very well say so. But Ying-erh in confidence had taken her to task for her indiscretion.

"You don't understand," said Pao-chai. "Come what may, I'll take the responsibility."

She paid no attention to ill-natured gossip, but carefully probed Pao-yu's psychology and quietly needled him for his own good. And little by little he was growing more lucid, only lapsing into senselessness when he remembered Tai-yu. It was Hsi-jen who reasoned with him most frequently.

"The master chose Miss Pao-chai for you because she's so affable and good," she told him patiently. "He thought Miss Lin eccentric and suspected that she hadn't long to live. As for the old lady, she was afraid you might get worked up as you'd taken leave of your senses, so she had Hsueh-yen brought over here to trick you."

Still Pao-yu's heart ached and he often shed tears, tempted to kill himself. But he checked this impulse, remembering the warning in his dream and reluctant to hurt his grandmother and his mother. He took comfort too from the thought that, although Tai-yu was dead, Pao-chai was a girl in a thousand and there might be something in the prophecy of a "match between gold and jade." As he seemed unlikely to do anything drastic, Pao-chai felt easy enough in her mind to wait dutifully on Their Ladyships, devoting the rest of her time to amusing him. Though Pao-yu was too weak to sit up for long, the sight of Pao-chai sitting by his bed rekindled his amorous proclivity. But she would urge him gravely:

"That can wait. We're already husband and wife, but the main thing now is to recover your health."

Reluctantly, he had to fall in with her wishes, for during the day his grandmother, mother and Aunt Hsueh took it in turns to keep him company, and at night Pao-chai slipped away to sleep elsewhere, leaving nannies sent by the old lady to wait on him. So he had to convalesce quietly. Moreover, Pao-chai's gentle ways made him gradually transfer to her some of the love he had felt for Tai-yu. But this is anticipating.

On the day of Pao-yu's wedding Tai-yu lay in a coma, her life hanging by a thread, while Li Wan and Tzu-chuan wept as if their hearts would break. That evening she recovered consciousness and feebly opened her eyes. She seemed to want something to drink. As Hsueh-yen had gone, leaving only Li Wan and Tzu-chuan there, the latter brought her a bowl of pear juice and dried-longan syrup and gave her two or three sips with a small silver spoon, after which Tai-yu closed her eyes to rest again. Li Wan knew that this lucid interval and slight rallying were the prelude to the end, but thinking that still a few hours away she went back to Paddy-Sweet Cottage to see to some business.

Meanwhile Tai-yu opened her eyes and saw only Tzu-chuan,

her old nanny and some young maids. Clasping Tzu-chuan's hand she addressed her with an effort.

"I'm done for! You've served me for several years, and I'd hoped that the two of us could always stay together. But now. . . ." Stopping to catch her breath, she closed her eyes in exhaustion.

Tzu-chuan, whose hand she was still gripping, dared not move. Because Tai-yu seemed better than earlier on she was still hoping for her recovery, and so these words struck chill into her heart.

"Sister!" continued Tai-yu presently. "I have no dear one here, I have lived chastely. . . . Get them to send me home!"

Closing her eyes again, she clasped Tzu-chuan's hand even more tightly as she panted silently, breathing out more than she breathed in — at her last gasp.

Tzu-chuan was frantically sending to fetch Li Wan when luckily Tan-chun arrived.

"Look at Miss Lin, miss!" whispered Tzu-chuan, her tears falling like rain.

Tan-chun came over and felt Tai-yu's hand — it was chill and her eyes were glazed. Weeping, they called for water with which to wash her. Then Li Wan hurried in. The three of them had no time for civilities. They were washing Tai-yu when she raised a sudden cry:

"Pao-yu, Pao-yu! How. . . ."

Those were her last words. She broke out in a cold sweat. Tzu-chuan and the others, holding her as she sweated, felt her body grow colder and colder. Tan-chun and Li Wan bade her maids dress her hair and change her clothes. But her eyes turned up — alas!

> Her sweet soul gone with the wind,
> They sorrow at midnight, lost in fragrant dreams.

It was in the very same hour in which Pao-yu and Pao-chai were married that Tai-yu breathed her last. Tzu-chuan and the other maids wept bitterly while Li Wan and Tan-chun, recalling her lovable ways, lamented her fate and sobbed too with distress. As Bamboo Lodge was far from the bridal chambers, their wailing could not be heard there. Presently they caught the sound of distant music, but as soon as they pricked up their ears it vanished. When Li Wan and Tan-chun stepped into the courtyard to listen, they saw only the wind-tossed bamboos and the shifting moonlight on the wall — a scene of loneliness and desolation.

They sent for Lin Chih-hsiao's wife, had Tai-yu laid out and assigned maids to watch by her corpse, not notifying Hsi-feng till the next morning.

As Their Ladyships were so busy with Chia Cheng leaving home that morning and Pao-yu's increased derangement making the whole household frantic, Hsi-feng decided not to report Tai-yu's death for fear Their Ladyships would fall ill under this fresh burden of grief. So she went herself to the Garden. On reaching Bamboo Lodge, she could not hold back her tears. Then she was told by Li Wan and Tan-chun that all preparations had been made for the funeral.

"Well done," she said. "But why didn't you let me know before to save me worrying?"

Tan-chun answered, "How could we, when seeing the master off?"

"At least the two of you took pity on her," commented Hsi-feng. "Very well then, I must go back to cope with the lovesick one over there. What a to-do! Not to report it today would be wrong; but if I report it I'm afraid it may be too much for the old lady."

"Do as you think fit," said Li Wan. "If possible, you should report it."

Nodding, Hsi-feng hurried away.

When she reached Pao-yu's quarters and heard that the doctor had pronounced him out of danger, to Their Ladyships' relief, she broke the news to them about Tai-yu without letting Pao-yu know. The old lady and Lady Wang were consternated.

"I have her death on my conscience," sobbed the old lady. "But the child was really too foolish!"

She was in a dilemma, wanting to go to the Garden to mourn

Tai-yu, yet reluctant to leave Pao-yu. Lady Wang, suppressing her own grief, persuaded her to remain to look after her health, and the old lady agreed to her going instead.

"Tell her spirit from me," she instructed, "it's not because I'm heartless that I'm not coming to see you off, but there's someone closer here whom I have to see to. As my daughter's daughter you are dear to me; but Pao-yu is closer to me even than you. If any harm comes to *him*, how am I to face his father?" She wept again.

"You were very good to her, madam," said Lady Wang soothingly. "But each one's span of life is fixed by Heaven, and now that she's dead there's nothing we can do except give her the best funeral possible. That will show our feeling for her, and her mother's spirit and hers can rest in peace."

This made the old lady weep still more bitterly. And not wanting her to grieve too much, as Pao-yu was still bemused Hsi-feng quietly sent someone with the trumped-up message, "Pao-yu is asking for you, madam."

"Has anything happened?" she asked, no longer weeping.

"No, nothing," Hsi-feng assured her. "I expect he just wants to see you."

The old lady hurried out attended by Chen-chu and followed by Hsi-feng. Half-way there they met Lady Wang, whose report on her visit to Bamboo Lodge naturally caused the old lady fresh distress; but she swallowed back her tears because she was going to see Pao-yu.

"As all the preparations are made, I won't go over for the time being," she said. "Do as you think fit. Seeing her would make my heart ache. But mind you give her a handsome funeral."

When Lady Wang and Hsi-feng had agreed to this, she went on to see Pao-yu and asked what he wanted her for.

"Last night I saw Cousin Lin," he said with a smile. "She wants to go back south. I'm sure you're the only one who can keep her here for me, madam. Don't let her go!"

"All right. Don't worry," she answered.

Then Hsi-jen made Pao-yu lie down again.

After leaving him the old lady went in to see Pao-chai, who having been married less than a week behaved shyly in company. She noticed that the old lady's face was tear-stained. After she had served tea, she was told to take a seat and perched respectfully on the edge of a chair.

"I heard that Cousin Lin was unwell," she remarked. "Is she any better?"

Bursting into tears the Lady Dowager answered, "I'll tell you, child, but don't let Pao-yu know. It's all because of your Cousin Lin that you've been so unfairly treated. Now that you're married I can tell you the truth: your Cousin Lin died a couple of days ago — at the very hour of your wedding. This illness Pao-yu has is because of her. You used to live together in the Garden, so I'm sure you know what I mean."

Pao-chai blushed, then shed tears at the thought of Tai-yu's death. And after chatting with her a little longer, the Lady Dowager left.

After this, Pao-chai weighed the pros and cons carefully before hitting on a plan; but not wanting to act rashly she had waited till after her visit home on the ninth day after their wedding before breaking the news to Pao-yu. And now that, sure enough, he was on the mend, they no longer had to keep things secret from him.

But though Pao-yu was recovering steadily, he had not overcome his infatuation and he insisted on going to mourn for Tai-yu. Knowing that the cause of his illness was not yet uprooted, his grandmother forbade him to give way to foolish fancies, but that only deepened his gloom and brought on a relapse. The doctor, however, saw that he was ill with longing and advised them to allow him to vent his feelings, for then the medicine would be more efficacious. Hearing this, Pao-yu at once clamoured to go to Bamboo Lodge. They had to send for a bamboo chair and help him on to it, after which they set off, the old lady and Lady Wang leading the way.

The sight of Tai-yu's coffin in Bamboo Lodge made the old lady weep till she had no more tears to shed and was out of breath. Hsi-feng and the others urged her to desist. Meanwhile

Lady Wang had wept too. And they shed tears anew even after Li Wan invited them to rest in the inner room.

Pao-yu on his arrival thought back to his visits here before his illness. Now the lodge remained but its young mistress was gone. He gave way to a storm of grief. How close they had been, yet today they were parted by death! He felt his heart would break. Alarmed by his frenzied anguish, all tried to comfort him, but already he had almost fainted away. They helped him out to rest. Pao-chai and the others who had come with him also mourned bitterly.

Now Pao-yu insisted on seeing Tzu-chuan to ask her what Tai-yu's dying words had been. Tzu-chuan had a deep grudge against him, but his misery softened her heart and in the presence of Their Ladyships she dared take no liberties. So she reported in detail how her young mistress had fallen ill again, how she had burned his handkerchief and her poems, and what her last words had been. Pao-yu wailed again until he was hoarse and breathless, and Tan-chun seized this chance to repeat Tai-yu's dying request to have her coffin taken back to the south, reducing Their Ladyships to tears again. It was Hsi-feng with her persuasive tongue who succeeded in consoling them a little and urged them to go back. When Pao-yu refused, his grandmother had to override his wishes.

Because the Lady Dowager was old and had been on tenterhooks day and night ever since Pao-yu fell ill, this fresh access of grief made her so dizzy and feverish that although still worried about him she had to retire to her room to lie down. Lady Wang went back too in even greater anguish, leaving Tsai-yun to help Hsi-jen, with the instructions:

"If Pao-yu breaks down again, send us word at once."

Knowing that his grief must run its course, instead of trying to console him Pao-chai made some cutting remarks; and suspecting that she was jealous he swallowed back his tears. So the night passed without mishap.

The next morning when others came to see how he was, they found him debilitated but less distracted. They nursed him devotedly till he slowly recovered. Luckily the old lady had not fallen ill; only Lady Wang was still suffering from her heart trouble. When Aunt Hsueh called she was relieved to find her son-in-law looking better, and she kept the young couple company for a while.

Some time after this, the Lady Dowager asked Aunt Hsueh over for a consultation.

"We owe Pao-yu's life to you," she said. "Now he seems out of danger, but we've wronged your daughter. As he's convalesced for the prescribed hundred days and recovered his health, and as the mourning for Her Imperial Highness is over too, it's time for them to consummate their marriage. Please make the decision and choose a lucky day for this."

"You know best, madam. Why ask me?" replied Aunt Hsueh. "Pao-chai may look stupid but she has good sense — *you* know what she's like, madam. I only hope the young couple will live in harmony to spare you worry, and then my sister and I can be easy in our minds too. You settle on a date, madam. . . . Is there any need to notify relatives?"

"For Pao-yu and your daughter, this is the biggest event in their whole lives. Besides, think of all the trouble we had before things turned out well. We must celebrate for a few days and invite all our relatives. For one thing, it'll be a thanksgiving for Pao-yu's recovery; for another, drinking on this happy occasion will make up to us for all the worries we've had."

Aunt Hsueh was naturally pleased by this proposal. She described the dowry she meant to give Pao-chai.

"I don't think that's necessary," said the old lady, "as we were relatives before this marriage. Their rooms already fully furnished; but if there are any things Pao-chai specially likes you can bring them over, aunt. The child has never struck me as narrow-minded like Tai-yu — that was what made her die so young." At this both of them shed tears.

Just then Hsi-feng came in and asked with a smile, "What are you ladies discussing?"

"We were speaking about your Cousin Lin," Aunt Hsueh told her. "That's what upset us."

"Well, don't be upset," Hsi-feng urged them. "I've just

heard a good joke which I mean to tell you."

The old lady wiped her tears and said with a smile, "Whom are you making fun of this time I wonder? Go ahead and tell us. But if it isn't funny, look out!"

Hsi-feng, before she even started to speak, gesticulated with both hands and doubled up with laughter. If you want to know what she told them, read the next chapter.

CHAPTER 99

An Upright Official Has Venal Underlings
A Perusal of the "Court Gazette" Fills Chia Cheng
with Concern for His Nephew

Hsi-feng offered to tell a joke to stop the Lady Dowager and Aunt Hsueh from grieving over Tai-yu.

"Can you ladies guess whom this joke is about?" she asked, laughing herself before embarking on it. "Our new bridegroom and his bride!"

"What's happened?" the old lady wanted to know.

"One was sitting like this, one standing like this," began Hsi-feng, miming. "One turned away like this, one wheeled round like this. Then one. . . ."

The Lady Dowager burst out laughing. "Tell us properly!" she scolded. "You've named no names yet, but already you have us in stitches."

"Yes, just tell us straight out," urged Aunt Hsueh. "No need to act it."

Then Hsi-feng expatiated, "Just now I went to Cousin Pao's place and heard laughter in his room. I wondered who was there and peeped through the window. Cousin Pao-chai was sitting on the edge of the *kang*, with Cousin Pao standing in front of her. He pulled her sleeve and pleaded, 'Do talk to me, cousin! One word from you would cure me completely — I swear it!' But Pao-chai turned her head away, refusing to meet his eyes. He bowed to her then and tugged at her jacket. When she wrenched away, of course his legs were so weak after his illness that he toppled over and fell on top of her. Then blushing scarlet she scolded, 'You're getting more and more undignified!' "

The old lady and Aunt Hsueh laughed.

"Pao-yu got up then," Hsi-feng went on.   "He said with a grin, 'It's lucky I toppled over — that loosened your lips.' "

"How strange of Pao-chai," remarked Aunt Hsueh.   "What's wrong with having a bit of fun now that they're married? Hasn't she seen how you and Lien carry on?"

"What way is that to talk?" protested Hsi-feng, flushing. "I was telling you a joke to cheer you up, aunt, but you make fun of me instead."

The old lady chortled, "Quite right and proper too.   Of course a husband and wife are fond of each other; still, they ought to keep within bounds.   What I like about Pao-chai is her sense of dignity.   I only worry because Pao-yu is still such a simpleton; but judging by what you say, his mind is much clearer now.   What other jokes can you tell us?"

"Soon Pao-yu will have consummated his marriage, and then Aunt Hsueh will have a grandson to dandle — won't that be a still better joke?"

"You monkey!" laughed the old lady.   "It was all very well for you to cheer us up when we were grieving over your Cousin Lin, but now you're getting cheeky.   Do you want us to forget your Cousin Lin?   You've no call to gloat, because she hated you; so don't go to the Garden all alone or her ghost may pounce on you to have her revenge!"

"She bore *me* no grudge," replied Hsi-feng.   "It was Pao-yu who made her grind her teeth with rage just before she died."

Thinking she was still joking they paid no attention to this.

"Stop talking nonsense," the old lady said.   "Go and get people outside to choose the most auspicious day for Pao-yu to round off his marriage."

Hsi-feng assented and after a little more chat went off on this errand.   Then invitations were sent out to a feast with operas; but no more of this.

Now although Pao-yu had recovered, when Pao-chai happened to discuss with him some books she had been reading, he remembered those with which he was most familiar but had quite lost his former intelligence, and he himself could not account for this.   Pao-chai attributed it to the loss of his jade of "spiritual understanding." Hsi-jen, however, frequently reproached him.

"How come you've lost that ready wit you used to have?" she would ask. "If you'd forgotten your foolish ways that would be fine; but you're just as bad as before — the only change is that you've grown more dim-witted."

Pao-yu never flared up at these strictures, simply grinned. If he carried on wilfully, Pao-chai reasoned with him and managed to restrain him to some extent. Thus Hsi-jen did not have to scold him so often and could devote herself to serving him well. The other maids also admired Pao-chai for her goodness and gentleness, and out of respect for her they all behaved well.

Pao-yu, by nature restless, hankered after a stroll in the Garden. However, his grandmother was afraid that he might get over-heated there or catch cold, and that the place might upset him; for though Tai-yu's coffin had been deposited in a nunnery outside town, the sight of Bamboo Lodge might bring back his earlier grief for its dead mistress. So they would not allow him to go. Besides, most of his girl cousins had left the place. Hsueh Pao-chin had gone back to live with Aunt Hsueh. Shih Hsiang-yun had been fetched home after Marquis Shih's return to the capital, and as a date for her marriage had been fixed she seldom paid them visits, coming only for Pao-yu's wedding and the later celebration, on both of which occasions she stayed with the old lady. And as Pao-yu was now a married man and she would soon be married herself, she could not joke and laugh with him as before; so sometimes she just talked with Pao-chai, merely greeting Pao-yu if they happened to meet. After Ying-chun's marriage, Hsing Hsiu-yen had gone to live with Lady Hsing. The Li sisters were also living outside at present, and when they came with their mother they simply called on Their Ladyships and their girl cousins, then stayed for a couple of days with Li Wan. Thus the only inmates of the Garden now were Li Wan, Tan-chun and Hsi-chun. The old lady had meant to move them out, but after Yuan-chun's death a succession of domestic troubles had left her no time to attend to this. Moreover, now that it was growing warmer, it was pleasant in the Garden and they decided not to move till autumn. We will return to this later.

Now Chia Cheng had set off from the capital with several secretaries. Travelling by day and resting at night, he finally reached his provincial post and presented himself to his superior. He then went to his office, and when the official seal had been ceremoniously made over to him he started checking up on the granaries in the districts and counties under his jurisdiction. Most of his previous posts had been in the capital, and he thought all official tasks the same, for even when appointed as examiner outside he had had no dealings with the local administration. And therefore, although he had heard of such abuses as appropriating a percentage of the grain collected and squeezing money out of the local people, he had no direct experience of such matters and was determined to be a good official. So in discussions with his secretaries he issued stern prohibitions, threatening to report in detail any instances of corruption that were discovered.

At the start, his subordinates were apprehensive and tried in all manner of ways to ingratiate themselves with him. However, Chia Cheng was inflexible. There had been no perquisites for his servants in the capital working for such a master, and when he was posted here they had borrowed money and made new clothes to put up a better appearance, sure that once in the provinces they would make their fortunes — the money would just roll in. But this master of theirs was so stubborn that he carried out serious investigations and refused all gifts sent by the local officials.

The yamen secretaries and scriveners made a mental calculation. "Another fortnight like this," they said, "and we'll have to pawn all our clothes. And when our creditors dun us, what shall we do? There's all this glittering silver under our noses, but we can't lay hands on it."

The attendants and runners also complained, "You gentle-

men at least didn't sink any capital into landing your posts.
We're the ones who've been sold out: we spent pots of silver
to get these jobs, but after more than a month here we haven't
made a single cent! If we stick to this master, we shall probably never recoup our capital. Tomorrow we're going in a
group to resign."

The following day they did this. And Chia Cheng not
knowing the reason said, "You wanted to work here; now you
want to leave. Since you dislike these posts, do as you please."

The runners went off then, complaining loudly, leaving only
some family stewards who talked the matter over.

"Those able to leave have gone," they said. "But as we
can't, we must think of some way out."

One of them, a gateman called Li Shih-erh, scoffed, "What
a useless lot you are, getting so het-up! While those runners
were around, I couldn't be bothered to give them a tip-off.
Now that they've been starved out, I'll show you what I can
do. Our master will have to listen to me! If we just work
together to make some money, we can enjoy ourselves when
we get home. If you won't do as I say, I shall wash my hands
of you — I can get the better of you any day."

"The master trusts you, Mr. Li," said the others. "If you
won't help, we're done for."

"Well, after I've shown the way and we've got money, don't
complain that I've taken the lion's share; because if we fall out
among ourselves it will go hard with us all."

"Don't worry," the rest replied. "We'd never do that. However little we get, it will be better than dipping into our own
pockets."

Just then a clerk from the granary office arrived, asking for
Chou Jui. Li Shih-erh sat down crossing his legs, his chest
thrown out, and demanded:

"What do you want him for?"

Standing at respectful attention the clerk answered, "The
Grain Commissioner has been here for over a month, and in
view of his strict orders the local magistrates know they can't
ask for favours, so none of them has opened the granaries yet.

But once the time is up for grain to be shipped out, what will you gentlemen have come here for?"

"Don't talk nonsense," retorted Li. "Our master is most systematic and always keeps his word. These last two days he has been meaning to expedite the delivery. He only put it off because I asked for a few days' delay. What do you want Mr. Chou for anyway?"

"Just to ask about the order to expedite the delivery — that's all."

"Stop talking rot! You made that up because of what I just said. Don't try any hanky-panky, or I'll get the commissioner to have you beaten and dismissed!"

"My family has worked in this yamen for three generations," said the clerk. "We're respected hereabouts and not badly off; so we can afford to serve this commissioner on the level until his promotion. We're not like those waiting for rice to put in their pan." This said, he added formally, "I'll take my leave of you now, sir."

Li Shih-erh stood up then, smiling.

"Can't you take a joke?" he chuckled. "Don't be so thin-skinned."

"It's not that. But if I say any more, won't I be damaging your good reputation?"

Li stepped over to take his hand and asked, "What's your honourable name?"

"Chan Hui, sir. In my young days I worked in the capital for a few years."

"Mr. Chan! I've long heard of you. We brothers here are in accord. If you have some proposal, come over this evening and we can talk it over."

"We all know how sharp you are, Mr. Li. You had me scared stiff just now!"

They all laughed then and dispersed. But that evening Li had a long talk with the clerk.

The next morning Li Shih-erh made some suggestions to sound out Chia Cheng, who reprimanded him sternly.

The day after, Chia Cheng gave orders for attendants to

escort him out to pay calls, and the servants outside assented. Some time went by during which the gong sounded three times, but they had trouble finding a man to beat the drum in the hall, and when Chia Cheng stepped out of the vestibule, there was only one runner on duty to clear the way. Letting this pass, he mounted his sedan-chair in the porch; but again he had to wait quite a while for the bearers to assemble; and when they carried him out of the yamen gate the gun fired only one salute, moreover on the bandstand there were only one drummer and one trumpeter. At this Chia Cheng lost his temper.

"Things used to be orderly enough," he exclaimed. "Why are there so many absentees today?"

He took a look at his retinue — the men were slouching and straggling. None the less he went through with his round of calls, on his return ordering the absentees to be summoned and given a beating. Some pleaded that they had mislaid their hats, pawned their uniforms, or were too weak to carry his chair because they had eaten nothing for three days. In anger he had one or two of them flogged, then let the matter drop.

A day later, when the steward in charge of the kitchen came with a request for money, Chia Cheng had to pay him out of his own pocket. But after that things went from bad to worse — compared with this, it had been plain sailing in the capital. In desperation he summoned Li Shih-erh.

"What's come over those servants who accompanied me here?" he asked. "It's your job to discipline them. The silver we brought was spent days ago, and it's not yet time to draw the allowance from the provincial treasury. We shall have to send to the capital for more."

"Not a day has passed without my pulling them up," replied Li. "But somehow or other they're all so dispirited there's nothing I can do about it, sir. How much money does Your Lordship want us to fetch from home? I've heard that the governor will be celebrating his birthday in a few days, and all the other officials are sending him thousands of taels. How much shall we send?"

"Why didn't you tell me earlier?"

"You know how it is, sir. We're new here and haven't had much to do with those other gentlemen; so why should they send us word? They're only hoping you won't call to congratulate him, sir; so that when you're dismissed they can get your lucrative post."

"Nonsense!" Chia Cheng retorted. "I was appointed by His Majesty. The governor can't dismiss me just because I fail to congratulate him on his birthday."

"You're right, of course, sir," replied Li with a smile. "But the capital is far away, and it's the governor who reports on everything here. If he commends you, you are a good official; if he finds fault, you're likely to lose your job. By the time the court learns the truth, it is too late. Our old lady and the other mistresses are all longing for you to have a magnificent success here."

Chia Cheng of course understood his drift.

"Why didn't you tell me earlier?" he repeated.

"I dared not, sir. Now that you ask me, it's my duty to speak; but if I do, most likely you will be angry."

"Not if what you say makes sense."

"Those clerks and runners all bribed their way into this yamen; so of course they all want to feather their nests," Li explained. "They have families to support. Since you came to this post, sir, and before you've achieved anything for the state, there's already been talk."

"What are people saying?"

"The common folk say, 'The stricter the orders a new official gives, the more grasping he will be. The more frightened the county officials, the bigger the bribes they'll send in.'

"When the time comes to levy grain, your yamen officials say they have orders from the new commissioner not to accept any money, and this makes it difficult for those country people who'd rather grease their palms and be done with it. So instead of praising you, sir, they complain that you don't understand the situation. But your close friend and kinsman has climbed to the top in just a few years, simply because he has the good sense to please both his superiors and his inferiors."

"Rubbish," protested Chia Cheng. "Are you implying that I lack sense? As for pleasing both superiors and inferiors, do you want me to connive with rogues — to be 'a cat sleeping with rats'?"

"I spoke frankly, sir, out of concern for you, not wanting to keep anything back," Li answered. "If you were to go on like this till you had no achievements to your credit and your reputation was damaged, you could accuse me of disloyalty for not putting the facts before you."

"What would you do in my place?"

"Just this, sir. While you're in your prime, with friends at court and the old lady in good health, look after your own interests. Otherwise, in less than a year you'll have spent all your family's money and made those above and below resent you too. They'll all assume that in this provincial post Your Lordship must be salting money away. So if some trouble crops up, who's going to help you? By then it will be hard to clear yourself and too late to regret!"

"Are you advising me to become a corrupt official? Forfeiting my life would be of less consequence, but would you have my ancestors deprived of their noble titles?"

"A gentleman of your discernment, sir, must surely have noticed which officials have landed in trouble in recent years. All old friends of Your Lordship's they were, and you often remarked on their probity; but now what has become of their good name? On the other hand, some relatives whom you have always run down have been promoted. It all depends on how well one handles things. You must understand the need, sir, to care for the local officials as well as for the people. Why, if you had your way, sir, and wouldn't let the local magistrates make a cent, who would handle all the work in the provinces? All you need to do is keep up appearances, living up to your good name as an honest official, while in private we underlings get the job done and take whatever blame there may be without involving Your Lordship. We have been so long in your service, sir, you can surely rest assured of our loyalty."

Chia Cheng did not know what rejoinder to make to this.
"I can't risk my life!" he exclaimed. "If you get into trouble.
I won't be responsible." He then retired to his room.

After that Li Shih-erh assumed great airs, conniving with
others inside and outside the yamen to handle affairs unbe-
known to Chia Cheng, who felt so satisfied that all was going
smoothly that, far from suspecting Li, he trusted him completely. Certain accusations were brought against his office, but in
view of Chia Cheng's austerity and honesty his superiors made
no investigations. Only some of his secretaries who were well
informed warned him what was happening; and when he did
not believe them some resigned while those on good terms with
him remained to help out. So the government grain was collected and shipped off without any scandal.

One day Chia Cheng was reading at leisure in his study
when a clerk brought in a missive. It bore an official seal and
the inscription: Urgent Despatch from the Garrison Command
of Haimen to the Yamen of the Grain Commissioner of Kiangsi.
Chia Cheng opened it and read:

Your old friend and fellow-provincial from Nanking, I was posted
to the capital last year, delighted to be near you; and you did
me the honour, for which I shall ever be grateful, to agree to link
our families by marriage. But after my transfer to this coastal
district I did not venture to pursue the matter, and with deep
regret lamented my misfortune. Now that you have luckily travelled
all this distance, my lifelong wish is fulfilled. I was about to send
my congratulations when your gracious letter arrived, shedding
lustre on our camp and on me, a mere soldier; for though we
are separated by the ocean I am still favoured by your protection.
Trusting that you will not spurn my low position, I aspire to con-
nect myself with your family; as you have looked upon my son
with favour and we have always admired your refined daughter.
If you condescend to honour your earlier promise, I shall send the
go-between immediately. Though the journey is far, it can be made
by boat; and though we cannot welcome the bride with a hundred
chariots, we have a barque ready for the fairy maid. So I write
this short letter to wish you further promotion and beg for your
gracious consent. Eagerly awaiting your reply!
                              Your younger brother Chou Chiung.

Having read this, Chia Cheng reflected, "One's children's
marriages do seem to be fated. I met him last year when he

took up a metropolitan post, and as he was a fellow-provincial and an old friend and I was struck by his son's handsome appearance I proposed this match at a feast, but said nothing about it to the family as it was not finally settled. When he was transferred to the coast we let the matter drop. Now I have been assigned here and he has sent this request. I consider our families well matched and think this should be a good marriage for Tan-chun. However, since the family is not here I must write back to consult them."

As he was mulling this over, the gatekeeper brought him a summons to the provincial capital to discuss some business with the governor. He had to make ready at once and proceed to the city to await the governor's orders.

Resting in his hostel one day, Chia Cheng started reading through a pile of *Court Gazettes* on his desk and found a report from the Board of Punishments which dealt with "the merchant Hsueh Pan of Nanking."

"This is disastrous!" he exclaimed. "They've referred the matter up!"

He read carefully through the account of how Hsueh Pan had killed Chang San in a brawl, then bribed the witnesses to make it out a case of manslaughter.

"He's done for!" he cried, pounding the desk with his fist. He then read on as follows:

The Garrison Commander of the capital reported: "Hsueh Pan, a native of Nanking, while travelling through Taiping County put up in Li Family Hostel. He had no previous acquaintance with the waiter Chang San. On the day in question, Hsueh Pan ordered the inn-keeper to prepare wine and invited Wu Liang of Taiping County to drink with him. He sent Chang San for the wine, but it was sour and he called for something better. Chang San said that once he had bought it they could not change it and, annoyed by his insolence, Hsueh Pan dashed the wine in the waiter's face so fiercely that his hand slipped and the bowl hit Chang San's temple just as he was stooping to pick up some chopsticks. The skin was broken, blood spurted out, and very soon he died. When the inn-keeper could not revive him, he informed Chang San's mother, who finding her son dead called in the local bailiff and reported the matter to the county yamen. The report of the post-mortem which they sent to the prefecture omitted to mention that the blow on the temple cracked the skull, making a gash one-third of an inch deep, and that there was another bruise in the small of his back. Apparently Hsueh Pan's hand did slip when he threw the wine, and the blow from the bowl accidentally killed Chang San. So Hsueh Pan was convicted of manslaughter during a quarrel, and kept in custody until the payment of an indemnity."

A careful study of all the statements made by the culprits, witnesses and dead man's relatives reveals that they are full of discrepancies. Furthermore, there is this proviso to the ruling on death through brawls: When two men grapple together, it is a brawl; only when there is no brawl and the one killed is a stranger to his slayer can it be considered as manslaughter. So we ordered the Garrison Commander to ascertain the true facts and report back.

Now we hear from the Garrison Commander that it was because Chang San refused to change the wine that Hsueh Pan, who was tipsy, seized his right hand and struck him first in the small of the back. When Chang San cursed him for this, Hsueh Pan threw the bowl at him, gashing his temple and cracking his skull so that his brains spilled out and he died on the spot. This means that Hsueh Pan killed Chang San by striking him with the wine bowl and he should pay with his life. For this crime, the law decrees death by strangulation, pending Imperial review. Wu Liang should be flogged and sentenced to hard labour. The prefectural and county magistrates who sent in false reports. . . .

Below this was appended: To be continued.

Since Aunt Hsueh had enlisted Chia Cheng's help and he had appealed to the magistrate, if the court was asked to punish these officials he might find himself involved. He was very worried. He picked up the next issue of the gazette, but it was not the right one; and although he looked through the whole pile he could not find the sequel to this report. His heart misgave him. He was brooding over this with growing apprehension when Li Shih-erh entered.

"Will Your Lordship please go to the government office," he said. "The drum has sounded twice in the governor's yamen."

As Chia Cheng was too lost in thought to hear him, Li had to repeat his message.

"What am I to do?" muttered Chia Cheng.

"Have you something on your mind, sir?"

Chia Cheng told him what he had read in the gazette.

"Don't worry, sir," Li rejoined. "If this is how the Board's handled it, Master Hsueh has got off lightly! Back in the capital, I heard that Master Hsueh fetched a lot of women to the inn, all drunk and disorderly, and he beat the waiter to death. Not only was the magistrate bribed, they told me, but Master Lien had to spend a lot of money squaring the different yamens before the case was sent up. I can't think why the Board didn't get it straight.

"But even if it's come out now, officials protect each other. At most they'll admit that they didn't get the facts right, for which they will simply be dismissed or penalized. They'll never own up to having taken bribes. Don't let it weigh on your mind, sir. I'll find out more for you presently, but don't keep the governor waiting."

"You don't understand," said Chia Cheng. "It'll be too bad if the magistrate loses his post, and may even be otherwise penalized too, just for doing us a favour."

"Well, worrying won't help. They've been waiting outside for a long time; please go now, sir."

To know what the governor wanted with Chia Cheng, you must read the following chapter.

CHAPTER 100

By Frustrating Chin-kuei Hsiang-ling
Makes a Worse Enemy of Her
Pao-yu Grieves Over Tan-chun's Departure
to Marry Far from Home

Chia Cheng remained so long with the governor that the attendants outside started speculating what the reason could be; and when Li Shih-erh could get hold of no information, he remembered the ominous report in the *Court Gazette* and began to be really worried. At last Chia Cheng emerged, and Li escorted him back. On the way, when no one else was near, he asked:

"Was it urgent business that kept you there so long, sir?"

"Nothing of consequence," replied Chia Cheng with a smile. "The garrison commander of Haimen is related to the governor and has written recommending me to him. For this reason, the governor paid me some compliments and said, 'Now we are relatives too.'"

Pleased and emboldened by this, Li urged him to agree to the garrison commander's proposal. However, Chia Cheng was still afraid that he might be implicated in Hsueh Pan's case. Being so far away, cut off from news and in no position to cope with emergencies, on his return to his office he lost no time in sending a servant to the capital to find out the situation and tell the Lady Dowager about the garrison commander's proposal. If she agreed to it, Tan-chun could be sent to him.

The servant travelled post-haste to the capital. Having made his report to Lady Wang, he found out from the Ministry of Civil Affairs that Chia Cheng was in no trouble — only the magistrate of Taiping County had been dismissed from his post.

He sent word of this to Chia Cheng to relieve his mind, then stayed on to await further developments.

Now Aunt Hsueh had spent huge sums bribing the yamens dealing with Hsueh Pan's case to bring in a verdict of man-slaughter, not murder. She had planned to sell a pawnshop to raise the ransom for him; but now that the Board of Punish-ments had unexpectedly reversed the verdict, she had to spend still more on bribes, all in vain — Hsueh Pan remained sentenced to death and immured in prison pending the Major Sessions in the autumn. Aunt Hsueh wept day and night for rage and grief.

"Brother was born ill-fated," Pao-chai kept telling her to com-fort her. "Inheriting so much property, he should have lived quietly, minding his own business. Instead he carried on scandalously down south, behaving so disgracefully over Hsiang-ling. It was only because of his powerful connections and money that he got away with killing that young gentleman. He should have turned over a new leaf then, and taken good care of you; but here in the capital he carried on just as before. Goodness knows how often he's provoked you, mother, how many tears he's made you shed.

"Then you got him a wife, and we thought we could all live in peace; but it was his fate to marry such a shrew that he left home to avoid her. As the proverb says, 'Foes are fated to meet' — before very long he killed a man again!

"You and Cousin Ko have done all you could for him: spending money and begging this one and that one to help. But there's no escaping fate, and he brought this on himself. People bring up children as props for their old age, and even the son of a poor family will work to support his mother. What good is one who squanders his whole inheritance and breaks his old mother's heart?

"Maybe I shouldn't say this, but the way brother behaves he isn't your son but your enemy. If you don't wake up to this, you'll keep crying from dawn till dusk, from dusk till dawn, and have more to put up with from sister-in-law as well. As for me, I can't always be here to smooth things over, for though Pao-yu's a simpleton he won't let me stay here. But it makes me so worried seeing you like this!

"The other day the master sent to tell us how alarmed he was after reading the *Court Gazette*: that's why he sent a servant to see to things. I'm sure lots of people are anxious over this trouble brother's made. I'm lucky to be so close to you still. If I heard this news far away, I'd worry myself to death thinking about you! So do calm down, mother, and while brother's still alive check up on the various accounts. Get the old accountant to reckon up how much is owed to us and how much we owe, so as to see how much money there is left."

"These days we've been so upset about your brother," said Aunt Hsueh tearfully, "whenever you came, if you weren't consoling me I was telling you what had happened in the yamen; so I didn't let you know. We've already lost the title of Court Purveyor in the capital, and we've sold two of our pawnshops — the proceeds went long ago. We still have one pawnshop left, but its manager has absconded with several thousand taels, for which we're suing him. Your Cousin Ko outside asks every day for more money, and we must have spent tens of thousands from our funds in the capital. We can only make up the deficit by drawing silver from our clan funds down south and by selling our houses there. But only the other day we heard a rumour that our clan pawnshop in Chinling has been confiscated too, because it went bankrupt. If this is true, what's your poor mother to live on?" She broke down and sobbed.

"It's no use worrying about money matters, mother," said Pao-chai, in tears herself. "Cousin Ko will see to them for us. But how hateful of those assistants! When they see us come down in the world they strike out on their own; and some of them, so I've heard, help other people to squeeze us. This shows that all these years the only friends brother has made are wine-and-meat ones, not one of whom stands by him in time of trouble.

"If you're fond of me, mother, take my advice and now that

you're old take better care of your health. I can't believe you'll ever go cold or hungry. What little clothing and furniture there is here, you'll simply have to let sister-in-law do as she likes with. I don't suppose the servants want to stay on, so if they ask to leave just let them go. Poor Hsiang-ling has had a hard life; you'll have to keep her with you. If you're short of anything, I'll provide it if I can — I don't imagine Pao-yu will object. Hsi-jen is a good sort too. When she heard of our family trouble she spoke of you with tears. *He's* not upset, not knowing that anything's amiss. If he knew, he would be frantic...."

"Don't tell him, there's a good child," Aunt Hsueh cut in. "He nearly died because of Tai-yu, and he's only just recovering. If he's upset and anything happens to him, you'll have more to worry about and I shall have fewer people to whom to turn."

"That's what I think," answered Pao-chai. "That's why I never told him."

Just then they heard Chin-kuei storm into the outer room.

"I want to die and be done with it!" she shrieked. "My man's as good as dead! We may as well make a scene, all going to the execution ground for a show-down!"

She banged her head on the partition until her hair was all tousled. Aunt Hsueh could only glare in rage, unable to get a word out. It was Pao-chai who begged Chin-kuei to be reasonable.

"Dear sister-in-law!" sneered Chin-kuei. "You're no longer part of this household. You're living in comfort with that husband of yours, but I'm all on my own — I needn't care about appearances!"

She threatened to rush out, back to her mother's home. Fortunately there were enough of them there to restrain her and talk her round so that, eventually, she left off storming. But Pao-chin was so terrified that she kept out of her way.

Whenever Hsueh Ko was at home, Chin-kuei would rouge and powder her face, paint her eyebrows, deck her hair and dress up like a vamp. She kept passing his room, coughing deliberately; and though well aware that he was inside, she would make a point of asking who was there. When they met, she would ogle him and ask coyly after his health, simpering and pouting by turns. The maids who saw her hastily scurried away. But disregarding appearances, she set her whole heart on enticing Hsueh Ko, to carry out Pao-chan's plan.

Hsueh Ko did his best to avoid her, but when they happened to meet he made a show of cordiality for fear that otherwise she might make a scene. And Chin-kuei, besotted by her infatuation, indulged in the wildest fantasies which blinded her to his real attitude to her. She noticed, though, that Hsueh Ko left his things in Hsiang-ling's keeping and that she was the one who washed and made clothes for him; while if Chin-kuei chanced to find them talking together, they hastily parted company. This made her jealous. Not liking to vent her anger on Hsueh Ko she focused it on Hsiang-ling. But afraid to offend him by quarrelling openly with her, she hid her resentment.

One day Pao-chan came to her, smiling all over her face.

"Have you seen Master Ko, madam?" she asked.

"No," said Chin-kuei.

"I told you not to believe that strait-laced pose of his," chuckled Pao-chan. "That time we sent him wine, he said he couldn't drink; but just now I saw him going to see the mistress, red in the face and tipsy. If you don't believe me, wait at our courtyard gate for him to come out. You can intercept him then and challenge him to see what he has to say."

Provoked by this Chin-kuei answered, "He won't be coming out yet a while; and he's such a cold fish, why should I challenge him?"

"That's no way to look at it, madam. If he's well-disposed, we'll know what to do. If not, we'll make other plans."

Convinced by this, Chin-kuei sent her off to keep watch till he came out, then opened her dressing-case and eyed herself in the mirror. Having rouged her lips and selected a flowered silk handkerchief she left her room, rather flustered, as if she had overlooked something.

She heard Pao-chan outside saying, "You're in high spirits, Master Ko, today. Where have you been drinking?"

Taking her cue, Chin-kuei lifted the portière and stepped out.

"Today is Mr. Chang's birthday," Hsueh Ko was telling Pao-chan. "They forced me to drink half a goblet. Even now my face is still burning. . . ."

Chin-kuei interposed, "Of course other people's wine tastes better than ours at home!"

At this taunt, Hsueh Ko blushed even redder. Stepping over quickly he countered with a smile, "How can you say such a thing, sister-in-law!"

Seeing them talking together, Pao-chan slipped inside.

Chin-kuei had meant to make a show of annoyance, but now his flushed cheeks, sparkling eyes and appealing expression had melted her anger away.

"You mean you were forced to drink?" she asked with a smile.

"Of course. I can't drink," he said.

"It's best not to drink — much better than landing in trouble through drinking like your cousin, so that when you take a wife she becomes a lonely grass widow like me, poor thing!" She shot him a sidelong glance, blushing as she spoke.

Shocked by these improper advances, Hsueh Ko decided to leave her; but she forestalled him by seizing hold of him.

"Sister-in-law!" he spluttered, trembling from head to foot. "Remember who you are!"

"Just come on in," she answered brazenly. "I've something important to tell you."

This clash was cut short by the announcement behind them: "Madam! Hsiang-ling is here."

With a start Chin-kuei turned to see Pao-chan watching them from under the raised portière. She had called out this warning at sight of Hsiang-ling. The shock made Chin-kuei let go of Hsueh Ko, who took this chance to escape.

Hsiang-ling had not noticed them until Pao-chan called out. Horrified by the sight of Chin-kuei trying desperately to tug Hsueh Ko into her room, her heart went pit-a-pat and she wheeled away, leaving Chin-kuei rooted to the spot in furious consternation as she stared after Hsueh Ko's retreating figure.

With a curse she went back to her room then in frustration, and from that day on she hated Hsiang-ling to the marrow of her bones. Hsiang-ling had just passed the inner gate on her way to call on Pao-chin when this sight frightened her away.

That same day Pao-chai, in the Lady Dowager's room, heard Lady Wang tell of Tan-chun's marriage proposal.

"It's good that his family comes from our district," the old lady commented. "But you say that boy visited our house — why didn't your husband mention this before?"

"We didn't know it ourselves at the time," said Lady Wang.

"It's a good match but too far away. Though the master is in the south now, if he gets transferred in future won't the child be lonely there all by herself?"

"We're both official families, with no knowing where the next post will be. Their family may be transferred to the capital. Anyway, 'Leaves that fall return to their root in the end.' As the master's been posted there, and this was proposed by his superior, how can he refuse? I think he must approve, but not presuming to make the decision himself he sent the servant to ask your consent, madam."

"It's all right if you're both willing. But once Tan-chun's gone who knows how long it'll be before she can come home. Any later than two or three years and I may never see her again!" She shed tears.

"When our girls grow up we have to marry them off," replied Lady Wang. "Even if the other family's from our own district, we can't be sure of always being together — unless they're not officials. All we can hope for is that the girls will be happy. Take Ying-chun: she's married into a family near by, yet we keep hearing how her husband ill-treats her — sometimes they even give her nothing to eat. And anything we send never reaches her. Recently, they say, it's gone from bad to worse and her in-laws won't let her come home. When she and her husband have words, he jeers that we're in debt to his family. Poor child, never able to hold up her head!

"The other day I was so worried about her, I sent some

maids to see her. Ying-chun hid herself in a side-room and
wouldn't come out. When they insisted on going in they saw
that, cold as it was, she was still wearing thin, shabby clothes.
With tears in her eyes she pleaded, 'When you go back, don't
tell them what a wretched time I'm having; this is my fate.
And don't send me clothes or things. I wouldn't get them.
Instead, they'd accuse me of complaining and give me another
beating.' Just think, madam, because she's close enough for
us to know what's going on, when she has a bad time we feel
even worse. Not that her mother pays any attention, and her
father does nothing either, so poor Ying-chun's worse off now
than one of our third-grade maids.

"Though Tan-chun's not my child, since the master's agreed
to this match after seeing the boy, I feel sure it must be all right.
So please give your consent, madam, then we'll choose a good
day to send her off, well escorted, to join her father. He'll see
that everything is done in style."

"Very well, as her father approves, get everything ready and
choose a day for setting off on this long journey," said the old
lady. "That will be another business settled."

"Very good, madam."

Pao-chai who had heard all this did not say a word, although
inwardly she was lamenting, "Of all the girls in our family
she's the best, yet now she's going so far away to get married —
there are fewer and fewer of us here every day."

When Lady Wang rose to leave, she went out with her.
Back in her room, she did not tell Pao-yu this news; but finding
Hsi-jen sewing alone she confided it to her, distressing her too.

But when word reached Concubine Chao she started gloating, "This daughter of mine has never shown me any respect
in this household. She treats me not like her mother but worse
than her maids! She sucks up to those who have influence and
sides with others against me. With her taking first place, Huan
doesn't stand a chance. Now that the master's fetching her
away, I'll have a freer hand. I can't expect her to look after me,
but only hope she ends up like Ying-chun — yes, that would
please me."

With these thoughts in mind, she went over as fast as she could to congratulate Tan-chun.

"You're going up in the world, miss," she said. "You'll be better off in your husband's home than here; so I've no doubt you're agreeable to this marriage. Though I brought you up, you've not done me any favours. But even if I'm seven-tenths bad, I'm still three-tenths good; so don't forget all about me once you get there."

Tan-chun went on sewing with lowered head throughout this rigmarole, not saying a word. Finding herself ignored, Concubine Chao left in dudgeon.

Mixed anger, amusement and grief made Tan-chun shed tears when she was alone again. After a while she went off in low spirits to call on Pao-yu.

"Third Sister," he said, "I heard that you were there when Cousin Lin died and that, far off in the distance, there was the sound of music. For all we know, she may have been an immortal."

"You're imagining things!" laughed Tan-chun. "But there *was* something strange about that evening, and it didn't sound like any mortal music. Perhaps you're right."

This confirmed Pao-yu's belief. He recalled how, when he was out of his mind, an apparition had told him that Tai-yu in life was no ordinary mortal, and after death no ordinary spirit. She must have been a goddess come down to earth. This reminded him of the Moon Goddess in an opera he had seen, so lovely, ethereal and charming!

After Tan-chun had left, he insisted on having Tzu-chuan to work for them and at once despatched a maid to ask the old lady to send her.

Tzu-chuan was unwilling to come, but she could only comply with Their Ladyships' orders. In Pao-yu's presence, however, she did nothing but exclaim in dismay and sigh. When he quietly took her hand and softly questioned her about Tai-yu, she gave him offhand answers. But Pao-chai did not blame her for this, secretly approving her loyalty to her young mistress.

As for Tai-yu's other maids, though Hsueh-yen had helped

out at Pao-yu's wedding that night, thinking her rather stupid he had asked Their Ladyships to send her away, and she had been married off to one of the servants. Nanny Wang had been kept on to escort Tai-yu's coffin back south later on, while Ying-ko and the other young maids had gone back to work for the Lady Dowager.

Pao-yu's grief for Tai-yu deepened as it led him to reflect on the dispersal of all her attendants. He brooded helplessly till the sudden recollection that she had died fully conscious convinced him that she had returned to the realm of immortals. His spirits rose again.

Just at that moment, however, he heard Hsi-jen and Pao-chai discussing Tan-chun's marriage. With a cry of dismay he threw himself on the *kang*, sobbing. In alarm they helped him up and asked what was wrong, but he could not speak for tears.

Presently, when he was calmer, he blurted out, "I can't live on like this! All my girl cousins and sisters are leaving one by one. Cousin Lin has become an immortal. First Sister's dead — but I don't miss her so much, as we weren't always together. Second Sister has married a scoundrel. Now Third Sister is going to marry far from home, so we'll never meet again! Where Hsiang-yun will be going I don't know. And Pao-chin is engaged to be married too. Why shouldn't *one* of them at least stay here? Why leave me all alone?"

Hsi-jen started to reason with him, but Pao-chai waved her aside.

"It's no use trying to persuade him," she said. "Let me ask him a few questions." Turning to Pao-yu she demanded, "Do you expect all these girls to keep you company here to the end of your life, and never to get married? You may have something else in mind for some of them, but how about your own sisters? Never mind whether they leave to marry far away or not; once your father's made the decision, what can *you* do? Are you the only one in the world who is fond of his cousins and sisters? If everyone were like you, I wouldn't be able to keep you company either. People study to increase their understanding; how is it then that, with you, the more you study the more muddled you get? You talk as if Hsi-jen and I should both go away, so that you can invite all your sisters and cousins here to stay with you."

"I understand," he cried, clutching hold of them both. "But why part so soon? Why not wait till I've turned to ashes?"

Hsi-jen put her hand over his mouth and scolded, "You're talking nonsense again. The last two days you've just taken a turn for the better, and your young lady's eating a bit more too. If you make another rumpus, I'll wash my hands of you."

"I know, I know!" cried Pao-yu in desperation, aware that they were right. "But my mind's in a ferment."

Pao-chai ignored him, secretly telling Hsi-jen to give him a sedative and talk him round little by little. Hsi-jen for her part suggested telling Tan-chun not to come to take leave of him.

"Why not?" retorted Pao-chai. "In a few days when his mind's clearer they should have a good talk. After all, his third sister's very sensible, not one of those who just make a pretence of shrewdness. She's bound to give him good advice, so that he doesn't behave like this again."

At this point Yuan-yang arrived, sent by the old lady to say that she had heard of Pao-yu's relapse and Hsi-jen must comfort him and talk him round — he must stop having foolish fancies. Hsi-jen agreed to this, and not long after that Yuan-yang went back.

Soon Tan-chun would be setting off on her long journey and, though they did not have to give her a complete dowry, the old lady felt they should provide her with all necessities. She sent for Hsi-feng, told her the master's decision, and asked her to see to things. Hsi-feng accepted this task. But to know how she carried it out, read the next chapter.

CHAPTER 101

A Ghostly Warning Is Given One Moonlit Night
in Grand View Garden
A Fearful Omen Is Issued by the Oracle
in Scattering Flowers Temple

On Hsi-feng's return home, because Chia Lien was still out, she assigned servants to prepare Tan-chun's dowry and baggage. After dusk, on the spur of the moment, she decided to call on her accompanied by Feng-erh and two other young maids, one going in front with a lantern. But when they went out, as the moon had already risen and was casting a shimmering, liquid light, she sent the girl with the lantern back again.

As they passed the window of the boiler house, they heard the babble of voices inside and what sounded like a half tearful half laughing discussion. In annoyance, Hsi-feng told Hung-yu to go in casually but keep her ears open to find out what the women in there were gossiping about. The girl left them to do her bidding.

Then Hsi-feng went on with Feng-erh to the Garden. The gate was closed but not yet locked. They opened it and entered. The moonlight here seemed brighter than outside, the ground was covered with the dark shadows of trees and not a voice could be heard in that lonely stillness. As they made for the path to Autumn Freshness Studio, the soughing wind brought leaves rustling down from the trees on every side, while the creaking of their branches startled the chilly crows roosting there so that they winged off in alarm. Hsi-feng had been drinking, and this wind made her shiver. Feng-erh behind her hunched her shoulders too.

"My, it's cold!" she exclaimed.

"Run back and fetch me that sleeveless ermine jacket. I

can't stand this," ordered Hsi-feng. "I'll be waiting for you in Miss Tan-chun's place."

The maid agreed with alacrity, eager to go back to put on more clothes herself. She set off at a run.

Hsi-feng was just walking on when a snuffling and sniffing behind her made her hair stand on end. She turned to look. A creature black as coal was sniffing at her with out-stretched nose, its two eyes shining like lamps. Scared out of her wits, she let out a little scream as she saw that it was a hound. Trailing its bushy tail, the great dog bounded off up a hillock, where it turned and folded its front paws to salute her.

Trembling with fright she hurried on towards Autumn Freshness Studio, and was passing some rocks near its gate when a shadowy figure flitted in front of her. She wondered which apartment this maid belonged to.

"Who's there?" she called out.

No one answered even when she repeated the question, and she was frightened out of her wits. Then, indistinctly, she heard a voice behind her:

"Aunty, don't you recognize me?"

She swung round to see a pretty, well-dressed young woman who looked extremely familiar, though she could not identify her.

"Aunty," the other continued, "you're so set on enjoying wealth and luxury, you've thrown to the winds my advice to you that year to lay a foundation that will last for ever."

Hsi-feng lowered her head to think, but could not for the life of her place this young woman.

"Aunty, you used to be so fond of me, how is it that now you've forgotten me completely?" the other asked her with a cynical laugh.

Only then did Hsi-feng realize that this was Chia Jung's first wife Chin Ko-ching.

"Mercy!" she exclaimed. "You're dead — how did you get here?"

She spat at the apparition and turned to run, but tripped over a stone and fell down, drenched with sweat as if awaken-

ing from a nightmare. Though convulsed with fear, she was
clear enough in her mind to see the blurred figures of Feng-
erh and Hung-yu approaching. Not wanting to be laughed at,
she scrambled up.

"What have you been doing that kept you so long?" she
asked. "Hurry up and help me into that jacket."

Feng-erh came over to do this, after which Hung-yu took
Hsi-feng's arm to help her forward.

"I've just been there and they're all asleep," Hsi-feng
prevaricated. "Let's go back." With that she hurried home
with her two maids.

By this time Chia Lien had returned, and she saw from his
worried face that he was not his usual self. Though tempted
to ask what was wrong, knowing his temper she refrained and
simply went to bed.

The next day Chia Lien rose at dawn, meaning to call on
the chief eunuch Chiu Shih-an who was in charge of the
Audience Hall, to find out what news there was. As it was
too early to leave, he picked up from the desk a copy of the
Court Gazette delivered the previous day and started to read
it.

The first item was a report from Wang Chung, Governor
of Yunnan, that eighteen felons had been apprehended in an
attempt to smuggle muskets and gun-powder over the frontier.
The ringleader Pao Yin was a servant in the household of
Chia Hua, Duke of Chenkuo and Senior Imperial Tutor.

He then read the second item. Li Hsiao, Prefect of Soochow,
had impeached a man for condoning the crimes of one of his
stewards, who had bullied soldiers as well as civilians, and
had killed a chaste wife and two others of the family after
failing to rape her. The culprit, Shih Fu, admitted that he
served the family of Chia Fan who had a third-rank hereditary
title. These two items made Chia Lien uneasy.

He wanted to read on, but feared that might make him too
late to see Chiu Shih-an; so putting on formal clothes and not
stopping for breakfast, he took two sips of the tea Ping-erh
had just brought in, then went out, mounted his horse and

rode off. Ping-erh put away the clothes out of which he had changed.

Hsi-feng was still in bed, and Ping-erh suggested, "I heard you tossing and turning during the night. Let me massage you now so that you can have a good nap."

Construing Hsi-feng's silence as consent, Ping-erh sat on the *kang* beside her and pummelled her gently. Hsi-feng was dozing off when the cries of her small daughter in the next room made her open her eyes again.

Ping-erh called out, "Nanny Li, what are you doing? If baby cries, you should pat her. What a glutton for sleep you are!"

Nanny Li, waking up with a start, was annoyed by this scolding. She gave Chiao-chieh several hard spanks.

"Die and be done with it, you little wretch!" she grumbled. "Why don't you sleep? Is your mother dead that you're wailing like this in the middle of the night?" Grinding her teeth, she pinched the child so that she burst out howling.

"This is the limit!" cried Hsi-feng. "Listen to the way she's taking it out on the child! Go and wham that black-hearted bitch, and bring Chiao-chieh in here."

"Don't be angry, madam," said Ping-erh. "She wouldn't dare. I expect she bumped into her by accident. If I were to give her a few whacks, they'd start accusing us behind our backs of beating people at midnight."

Hsi-feng was silent for some time, then she sighed, "Look what happens while I'm still alive and kicking. If I die tomorrow what will become of this imp?"

"What a way to talk, madam!" chuckled Ping-erh. "First thing in the morning too."

"You don't understand." Hsi-feng gave a cynical laugh. "I know I shan't last very long. Though I've lived only twenty-five years, I've seen and tasted things not given to others to see or taste, and had the best of food and clothing as well as of all the good things in this world. I've vented my spite fully too, and done enough others down. So if I'm a bit short on 'longevity' what does it matter?"

At this, Ping-erh's eyes brimmed with tears.

"Don't put on that soft-hearted act," scoffed Hsi-feng. "Once I'm dead, the two of you will be only too pleased. You can live in peace and harmony, without me as a thorn in your side. All I ask of you, come what may, is to take good care of my child."

Ping-erh was weeping now.

"Don't be such a fool," jeered Hsi-feng. "I'm not dying yet a while. Why start mourning so early? Are you trying to hasten my death with your wailing?"

Ping-erh hastily dried her eyes.

"It's the way you talk, madam, that upset me," she said, then went on massaging her until Hsi-feng dropped off.

Ping-erh had no sooner got down from the *kang* than she heard footsteps outside. For Chia Lien had left too late to see the chief eunuch, who had gone to court. And so he had come back in a bad temper.

"Are they still not up?" he asked Ping-erh.

"Not yet," she said.

He came in, banging the portière behind him. "Fine!" he swore. "Not up at this hour, just to make things more difficult for me!"

He called for tea, and she promptly poured him a cup. But the maids had gone back to bed after Chia Lien went out, not expecting him home so quickly, and had therefore not prepared tea; so what Ping-erh brought him was not freshly brewed. In a fury he raised the bowl and — crash! — smashed it to smithereens.

Hsi-feng, startled from sleep, woke up in a cold sweat. She opened her eyes and gave a cry of dismay at sight of her husband sitting there in a rage while Ping-erh stooped to pick up the broken pieces.

"Why are you back so soon?" she asked.

She waited in vain for an answer and then repeated the question.

"Don't you want me back?" he bellowed. "Want me to die outside?"

"Why talk like that?" she said gently. "You don't usually come back so quickly, that's why I asked. You've no call to lose your temper."

"Since I didn't find him, why shouldn't I come straight back?" he bellowed again.

"If you didn't find him, you'll just have to be patient and go earlier tomorrow; then he'll be in."

"Why should I run errands for other people?" he roared. "I've plenty of work of my own here, with no one lifting a finger to help; yet for no reason at all I've had to run right and left for other people. Why the hell should I? The ones in hot water are taking it easy at home, not giving a damn; and I hear they're laying on feasts and operas to celebrate some birthday with gonging and drumming! Why should I run these pointless errands for them?" He spat in disgust and swore at Ping-erh again.

Hsi-feng swallowed her anger and, on second thoughts, refrained from arguing with him.

"Why get so worked up?" she said, forcing a smile. "Why yell at me like that first thing in the morning? Who told you to take on jobs for other people? Since you have, you must just have patience and do as they ask. It's news to me that anyone in trouble should feel in the mood for feasts and operas."

"That's what *you* say! Tomorrow you can ask him."

"Ask whom?" she exclaimed in surprise.

"Whom? Your brother!"

"Is he the one you've been talking about?"

"Of course. Who else?"

"What business is it that he wants you to see to for him?" she demanded hastily.

"Are you still in the dark?"

"This is really very strange! I haven't heard a word."

"How could you hear? Even the mistress and Aunt Hsueh haven't heard. Because I didn't want to worry them, and because you're always complaining of bad health, I hushed the business up outside and didn't let the family know either. The mere mention of this really makes me livid! If you hadn't asked me today, I couldn't very well have told you. You may think that brother of yours a gentleman; but do you know what people outside call him?"

"What do they call him?"

"Wang Jen (忘仁 — forgetting humanity)."

She burst out laughing. "Of course, that's his name — Wang Jen (王仁)."

"It's not the Wang Jen you think, but the Wang Jen meaning that he's lost all sense of decency and propriety."

"What backbiters have been slandering him like that?"

"It isn't slander. I may as well tell you now, because you ought to know what your fine brother's like. It's your second uncle's birthday he's celebrating — did you know that?"

Hsi-feng thought for a second, then exclaimed, "Oh! But tell me — isn't his birthday in the winter? I remember it was Pao-yu who went every year. When the master was promoted, second uncle sent an opera troupe to perform here, and I told the family in confidence, 'Second uncle's very tight-fisted, not like our elder uncle. The two families keep bickering over money. When our elder uncle died, didn't his younger brother try to grab his property?' That's why I advised them, when his birthday came round, to pay back the opera so that we wouldn't be beholden to him. But what's the idea, celebrating his birthday in advance this year?"

"You're still in the dark," said Chia Lien. "As soon as your brother came to the capital, he held a requiem for your elder uncle. For fear that we might stop him, he didn't tell us; and he made thousands of taels out of the donations. Later, your second uncle bawled him out for grabbing the whole lot. Then, under pressure, he thought up another trick. He's invited guests on the pretext that it's second uncle's birthday, fishing for more money from them to pacify him. What does he care whether it's summer or winter, or whether relatives and friends know the date of the birthday or not? That's how shameless he is!

"Do you know why I got up so early? The censors have

investigated the business by the coast and discovered a deficit during your elder uncle's term of office. As he's dead, his younger brother Wang Tzu-sheng and his nephew Wang Jen have to make it good. In desperation, the two of them came to enlist my help; and because they looked scared stiff, and because they're related to you and our mistress, I agreed. I wanted to get Old Chiu who's in charge of the inner court to fix it up by transferring the deficit to some earlier or later account. Unfortunately I got there too late, after he'd gone to the Palace. So I went to all that trouble for nothing. But your brother's still ordering operas and giving feasts. Isn't that maddening?"

Although Hsi-feng knew that Wang Jen was in the wrong, it was not her way to admit it.

"Whatever he's like, he's your brother-in-law," she said. "Besides, both the elder uncle who's dead and the second uncle who's alive should be grateful for what you're doing. It goes without saying that as this is our Wang family business, I must beg you humbly to help; otherwise other people will get blamed on my account and curse me behind my back."

In tears, she threw back her bedding and sat up, gathering her hair into a loose knot and slipping on some clothes.

"You don't have to take on like that," said Chia Lien. "It's your brother who's so disgusting. I didn't blame *you*. When I was out and you were poorly, these maids were still sleeping even after I was up — since when has that been the rule in our family? You let it go, to show how kind-hearted you are. When I say a word against someone, you get up. If I find fault with them tomorrow, will you take all the blame on yourself? This is so pointless!"

"It's high time for me to get up now," answered Hsi-feng, drying her eyes. "If that's how you feel, I'll be grateful if you'll fix things up for them. Not only for my sake either. When the mistress hears about it, she'll be pleased too."

"All right. I know. You don't have to teach me that."

"Why get up so early, madam?" asked Ping-erh. "Don't you have a fixed time for getting up every day? Master Lien's in a bad temper over something and taking it out on us. That's just too bad!" She turned to challenge him, "Madam's done enough for you, hasn't she, always bearing the brunt for you? It's not my place to say this, sir, but you've taken advantage of her all this time, and it's not much you're doing for her now — not just for her sake either — yet you make such a song and dance about it. Don't you mind hurting her feelings?

"Besides, you can't pin this on *her*. If we get up late, you've a right to be angry with us — after all, we're only slaves. But madam's ruined her health by wearing herself out. Why treat her so unkindly?" She was on the verge of tears.

Chia Lien had been bursting with rage, but he was floored by these sharp yet gentle reproaches from his lovely wife and beautiful concubine.

"All right, all right!" he laughed. "She's quite enough for me to cope with, without your taking her side. Anyway I'm not wanted here: the sooner I die the better off you'll be."

"Don't talk like that," Hsi-feng retorted. "Who knows what will happen? I may die before you. The earlier I do, the sooner I'll have some peace." She wept again, and Ping-erh had to console her.

By now the sun was shining through the window and Chia Lien, having no more to say, rose and left. Hsi-feng had just got up to make her toilet when a young maid came in with a message from Lady Wang:

"The mistress wants to know whether you're going to call on your uncle, madam. If you are, she'd like you to take Madam Pao along."

Hsi-feng was depressed after her husband's disclosure and resented the way her family had let her down; on top of which she really felt very limp after her fright the night before in the Garden.

"Tell Her Ladyship I still have one or two things to attend to, so I can't go today," was her answer. "Besides, it isn't an important occasion. If Madam Pao wants to go, she can go by herself."

The girl assented and went back to report this.

After Hsi-feng had finished her toilet, she reflected that even if she did not go she ought to send some message; besides, Pao-chai, still a new bride, should be accompanied if she paid a visit. So she went to see Lady Wang, then made some excuse to look in on Pao-yu. She found him lying fully dressed on the *kang*, raptly watching Pao-chai as she combed her hair. Pao-chai was the first to see Hsi-feng in the doorway. She hastily rose to offer her a seat, and Pao-yu got down from the *kang*. Hsi-feng seated herself with a smile.

"Why didn't you announce Madam Lien?" Pao-chai scolded Sheh-yueh.

"As soon as she came in, she signed to us to keep quiet," the maid replied with a smile.

Hsi-feng asked Pao-yu, "Why are you still here? You're grown up now, yet you still behave like a child. Do you have to stick around watching her doing her hair? Together all day long, don't you see enough of each other? Aren't you afraid the maids will make fun of you?" She laughed and smacked her lips.

Pao-yu, though rather sheepish, paid no attention. Pao-chai blushed all over her face, feeling she should not let this pass but not knowing what to say. At this point Hsi-jen brought in tea, and to hide her confusion Pao-chai passed their guest a tobacco-pipe, which Hsi-feng stood up to accept with a smile.

"Never mind us, sister," she said. "Hurry up and get dressed."

Pao-yu, too, tried to pass off his embarrassment by rummaging around.

"You go on ahead," Hsi-feng urged him. "Who ever heard of gentlemen waiting to go with the ladies?"

"I just feel these clothes I'm wearing aren't very good, not up to that peacock-feather cape the old lady gave me that year."

"Why don't you wear it then?" she asked mockingly.

"It's too early in the season."

Thus reminded, Hsi-feng regretted having spoken. Luckily Pao-chai was related to the Wangs, still she felt rather put out in front of the maids.

But then Hsi-jen interposed, "You don't realize, madam, that he wouldn't wear it even if the weather was cold."

"Why not?" asked Hsi-feng.

"Because our young master's behaviour is really fantastic. That year the old lady gave him this cape to wear on your second uncle's birthday, but that very same day he burnt it. My mother was very ill, so I was away; but Sister Ching-wen was still here at the time. Though she was unwell, I heard she sat up all night mending it for him, so that the next day the old lady didn't notice the burn. One cold day last year when he was going to school, I told Pei-ming to take that cape for him, but the sight of it reminded him of Ching-wen and he said he'd never wear it again. He told me to keep it for him all his life. . . ."

"Speaking of Ching-wen," Hsi-feng cut in, "it really was a shame! She was a pretty child with clever hands, only rather sharp-tongued. It was too bad that the mistress heard some rumour which cost the girl her life.

"That reminds me: I noticed one day that Wu-erh, the daughter of Mrs. Liu in the kitchen, was the image of Ching-wen, and I decided to take her on. When I asked her mother she was only too willing. Then it occurred to me that since Hung-yu had left Pao-yu's service for mine, I ought to give him Wu-erh in exchange; but Ping-erh told me the mistress had given orders that no girl looking like Ching-wen was to work in Pao-yu's place. So I dropped the idea. However, now that he's married what does it matter? I'd better tell her to come — that is, if Pao-yu would like it. If he misses Ching-wen, he can look at this Wu-erh instead."

Pao-yu who was on his way out stopped when he heard this.

Hsi-jen answered for him, "Of course he would like it. He wanted to get her here long ago, only the mistress was so strongly against it."

"In that case I'll send her over tomorrow," said Hsi-feng. "I can square it with the mistress."

Pao-yu, delighted by this, went to call on his grandmother while Pao-chai got dressed.

Pao-yu's obvious affection for Pao-chai upset Hsi-feng when she contrasted it with Chia Lien's behaviour to her earlier on. Not wanting to stay there, she stood up and suggested to Pao-chai, "Let's go to see the mistress."

They went off cheerfully together to call on the old lady, and found Pao-yu there explaining that he was going out to visit his uncle.

The old lady nodded. "Go along then," she said. "But don't drink too much, and come home early. You're only just over your illness."

Pao-yu assented and left, coming back again from the courtyard to whisper a few words in Pao-chai's ear.

"All right," she replied with a smile. "Off you go now." She urged him to hurry.

The old lady chatted with Hsi-feng and Pao-chai until, presently, Chiu-wen came in to say, "Master Pao has sent Pei-ming back with a message for Madam Pao."

"Has he forgotten something again?" Pao-chai wondered. "Why send his page back?"

"I told one of the girls to ask Pei-ming," Chiu-wen answered. "He said, 'Master Pao forgot to tell Madam Pao this, so he sent me back with the message: If she's going, she'd better go soon; if not, she mustn't stand too long in a draught.'"

The old lady, Hsi-feng, the serving-women and maids all burst out laughing at this.

Pao-chai, flushing crimson, spat in disgust at Chiu-wen. "You silly creature!" she scolded. "Bursting in so wildly just to tell us this!"

Chiu-wen went off, giggling, to tell the girl outside to curse Pei-ming.

He ran off, calling back over his shoulder, "Master Pao *insisted* that I must dismount and bring back this message. If he found out I hadn't delivered it, he'd have sworn at me. Now I've been sworn at all the same just for doing as I was told!"

The girl laughed and ran back to report this.

"Off you go then," said the old lady to Pao-chai. "That'll stop him from worrying about you."

Pao-chai hardly knew which way to look, with Hsi-feng teasing her too. She left in a fluster.

Just then, Abbess Ta-liao of Scattering Flowers Temple arrived. Having paid her respects to the Lady Dowager and Hsi-feng, she sat down and had some tea.

"Why haven't you been to see us for so long?" the old lady asked her.

"These days we've been having sacrifices in our temple," said the abbess. "We had visits too from several noble ladies, so I didn't find time before. I've come today specially, Old Ancestress, to let you know that tomorrow we are holding another mass. If you'd care to join us, it would be a little outing for you."

The old lady asked the nature of the mass.

"Last month evil spirits appeared in the Wang mansion, contaminating it," the abbess explained. "One night Madam Wang saw the ghost of her dead husband; so yesterday she came to our temple saying that she wanted to offer incense to the Flower-Scattering Saint and to have sacrifices made for forty-nine days to ensure the family peace, so that the dead may ascend to Heaven and the living enjoy good fortune. This is what kept me from coming to pay my respects before."

Hsi-feng normally had no patience with such proceedings, but since seeing a ghost the night before she had been filled with misgivings. This had changed her attitude, making her inclined to believe what the abbess said.

She asked, "Who is this Flower-Scattering Saint? How can he ward off evil and exorcise devils?"

Seeing that she was open to conviction, the abbess said, "Since you ask, madam, let me tell you. This saint's extraordinary powers are deep-founded. He was born in the Country of Great Trees in the Western Paradise. His parents were woodcutters. He came into the world with three horns on his head and four eyes, eight feet in height, with arms reaching to the ground. Because his parents thought he was a monster, they abandoned him behind the Icy Mountain. But an old monkey there with magic powers, coming out in search of food, saw a white vapour rising from this saint's head and noticed that tigers and wolves kept away from him. He knew then that this was no ordinary child, so carried him back to his cave and brought him up. Now this saint had been born so quick of understanding, he was able to discuss the Way and Buddhism with the monkey. They did this every day, until flowers rained down from the skies.

"A thousand years later the saint ascended to Heaven. But even now on the mountain you can see the place where he expounded the canons, scattering flowers. All prayers to him are granted, and he often manifests his divinity by saving those in distress. That is why this temple was built and offerings are made to his image."

"What proof have you of this?" Hsi-feng wanted to know.

"You're cavilling again, madam! What proof is needed? If this were false it could only fool one or two people. How could so many people with good sense have been fooled from old times till now? Just think, madam, the reason why Buddhist sacrifices have been made throughout the centuries is because they have proved efficacious in safeguarding the country and enriching the people — that's why men believe in them."

Convinced by this reasoning, Hsi-feng replied, "In that case, I'll go tomorrow and try. Do you have divination lots in your temple? I'd like to draw one. If it solves my problem, I shall become a believer!"

"Our lots are infallible," Ta-liao assured her. "You'll know that when you draw one tomorrow, madam."

"Better wait till the day after that — the first of the month," said the old lady.

When Ta-liao had finished her tea, she went to pay her respects to Lady Wang and those in other apartments, after which she returned to the temple.

Hsi-feng bore up as best she could till the morning of the first; then she ordered a carriage and horses to be made ready and, attended by many servants, went with Ping-erh to the temple. Ta-liao came out at the head of all the nuns to welcome her; and after tea had been served, Hsi-feng washed her hands and entered the main hall to offer incense. In no mood to gaze at the image, she kowtowed devoutly and picked up the bamboo container holding the lots. First she offered up a silent prayer about the apparition and her bad health, then she shook the container three times. A bamboo slip shot out. With another kowtow she picked it up and saw the inscription: "Number 33. Most auspicious."

Ta-liao looked up that number in the oracle book and found the entry: "Wang Hsi-feng returns home in splendour."

In amazement Hsi-feng asked her, "Was there another Wang Hsi-feng in olden times?"

Ta-liao answered with a smile, "Why, madam, with your broad knowledge of past and present, haven't you heard the story of how Wang Hsi-feng of the Han Dynasty found an official post?"

Chou Jui's wife beside them chuckled, "The other year, we wouldn't let that story-teller, Mrs. Li, tell this story because that was *your* name, madam."

"That's right," agreed Hsi-feng. "I had forgotten."

She then read the words below:

> The one who for a score of years left home
> Now in fine raiment will return again.
> The honey culled from blossoms by the bee
> Is seized by others — all its toil is vain.

> > The traveller arrives.
> > Word comes too late.
> > Settle the lawsuit.
> > Reconsider the match.

Hsi-feng could not make much of this, but the abbess cried, "Congratulations, madam! What a coincidence! You have been here since childhood, never going back to Nanking. Now that His Lordship has a provincial post he may send for his family, which will give you a chance to 'return in splendour' as the oracle says." While speaking she had copied out the prediction and handed it to the maid.

Hsi-feng was still only half convinced. When Ta-liao served

her a meal, she simply toyed with the food then made ready to leave, first donating some silver for incense, and the abbess could not prevail on her to stay longer.

When she reached home, the old lady and Lady Wang asked what the oracle had said. Once it had been explained to them they were delighted.

"The master may really have such a plan!" they exclaimed. "It would make a pleasant trip for us."

As one and all said this, Hsi-feng too accepted this interpretation.

When Pao-yu woke from his siesta that day, Pao-chai was not in the room; but before he could ask her whereabouts she came in.

"Where have you been all this time?" he wanted to know.

"I was explaining an oracle for Cousin Hsi-feng," she told him with a smile.

He asked her what it had been and she read it out to him.

"Everyone declares it's a good omen," she told him. "But I think 'returns home in splendour' may mean something else. Well, time will show."

"You're too sceptical, trying to twist the saint's meaning," he protested. "Everybody has always known that this is a good omen. Why read some other meaning into it? How else would you explain it anyway?"

Before Pao-chai could tell him, a maid came from Lady Wang to summon her and she had to go over at once. To know the reason for this summons, read the next chapter.

CHAPTER 102

Powers of Darkness Derange the Inmates
of the Ning Mansion
Priests Exorcise Evil Spirits
in Grand View Garden

Summoned by Lady Wang, Pao-chai hurried over to pay her respects to her.

"Tan-chun is going to be married," her mother-in-law said. "As her sister-in-law, you should give her some good advice to show your affection. After all, she's an intelligent child too, and I know how well both of you get on together. But I hear the news of her marriage set Pao-yu crying bitterly — you should reason with him as well.

"These days I'm constantly ailing, and Hsi-feng is unwell three days out of five. As you have good sense you ought to take things in hand, not holding back for fear of giving offence. In future you'll be responsible for this whole household."

"Yes, madam."

"Another thing," continued Lady Wang. "Your sister-in-law Hsi-feng brought Mrs. Liu's daughter here yesterday and said, as you're one maid short, the girl's to join your staff."

"Ping-erh brought her over just now, saying that both you and Hsi-feng had agreed to it, madam."

"Yes, Hsi-feng proposed it to me and I raised no objection — I could hardly turn her down. Only, judging by the look in that girl's eyes, she's not the kind to keep quiet. I dismissed some of Pao-yu's maids before because they were such vixens; but of course *you* know that — that was why you moved out of the Garden. Now with you here things are different. I'm telling you just so that you'll be on the look-out. The only reliable girl in your place is Hsi-jen."

Pao-chai expressed agreement and after a little more chat
she took her leave. After her meal, she called on Tan-chun
and they had a good heart-to-heart talk which we need not
record in detail.

The next day before setting off on her journey, Tan-chun
came to say goodbye to Pao-yu who was, of course, most reluctant to see her go. She held forth, however, on the moral
principles governing human relations and, though at first he
hung his head in silence, he gradually brightened up and showed
signs of seeing sense. Then, relieved in her mind, she bade
farewell to the whole household, mounted her sedan-chair and
set off to journey south by boat and by carriage.

Formerly all the girls had stayed in Grand View Garden;
but after the Imperial Consort's death the place was not kept
up. By the time of Pao-yu's marriage and Tai-yu's death, as
Hsiang-yun had also left and Pao-chin had moved home, very
few people remained there. Then, when the weather grew
colder, Li Wan and her cousins as well as Tan-chun and Hsi-
chun moved back to their former quarters, only returning sometimes by common consent to enjoy the flowers and moonlight.
Now that Tan-chun had gone and Pao-yu was staying indoors
to recuperate, there were even fewer pleasure-seekers left. So
the Garden was very quiet, with only a few caretakers in residence.

After Madam Yu had gone over to see Tan-chun off that
day, as it was already dark and she did not want to take a
carriage, she decided to walk through the side-gate which had
been made in the Garden to give access to the Ning Mansion.
She found the place desolate, its pavilions and lodges deserted,
with vegetables growing in the former flower-beds. The sight
filled her with nostalgia.

By the time she reached home she had a slight fever and,
after bearing up for a couple of days, she had to take to her bed.
During the daytime she was not too feverish, but at night her
temperature shot up and she became delirious. The doctor
summoned by Chia Chen to attend her diagnosed a chill which
had upset her digestion, making her delirious and subject to

delusions. A bowel movement should set her right.

However, two doses of medicine failed to cure her — she raved more wildly than ever. In his anxiety Chia Chen sent for Chia Jung.

"Find out what other good doctors there are outside and ask some of them here to see her," he ordered his son.

"This doctor we had is the best-known," was the answer. "Maybe my mother's illness is one that medicine can't cure."

"Nonsense! Stop giving her medicine, just leaving her to get over it herself?"

"That's not what I meant, sir. But the other day, when she went to the West Mansion, she came back through the Garden and as soon as she got home she had this fever, so something there may have put a jinx on her. There's a very good diviner here from the south, a man called Mao Pan-hsien. Why not ask him here to consult him? If it seems that's what happened, we'll follow his advice. If it doesn't work, we can look for other good doctors."

Chia Chen immediately sent to invite this man. He was offered a seat in his study and served with tea.

"You sent for me, sir," the diviner said to Chia Jung. "What do you want me to prognosticate?"

"My mother is ill. We'd like you to divine the reason."

"In that case," said Mao, "bring me clean water to wash my hands and set incense on the table. I'll see what I can do."

When the servants had done as he asked, he took out from his pocket a bamboo tube and, stepping forward, made a reverent bow.

He shook the tube, intoning, "The Yin and Yang of the Primal Order have interacted; sacred symbols have appeared with infinite changes; divine manifestations must answer the prayers of the pious.

"Now here is a devout gentleman named Chia whose mother is ill. We piously beseech the four great sages Fu Hsi, King Wen, the Duke of Chou and Confucius to hear our supplication, that manifestations may appear for the faithful and bad or good fortune be truthfully predicted. First vouchsafe the three inner signs."

He emptied three coins from the tube on to a plate, then announced, "A true manifestation: the first toss shows three obverses."

Then he picked up the coins and poured them out again. The second toss was two obverses and one reverse, the third another three obverses.

Picking up these coins he intoned, "Now the inner signs have been revealed; we vouchsafe the three outer signs to make up the answer."

These came out as two obverses and one reverse for the first toss, two reverses and one obverse for the second, while the third was the same as the first.

Thereupon Mao Pan-hsien put away the tube and the coins and resumed his seat.

"Please sit down while I study this carefully," he said. "This is an irrelevant diagram. The third sign indicates plundering of brothers and certain misfortune. But since you are asking about your honourable mother's illness, it is the first sign that counts; and in that parents' sign there is a hostile ghost. The fifth sign shows another ghost; hence I fear your mother's illness is quite serious.

"However, there is a compensating factor, namely that the water element is now in the ascendant, and next comes wood which leads in turn to fire. Then there is a progeny sign which subdues ghosts. Besides, in another two days the water will subside and all will be well.

"But I fear from the ghost in the parents' sign that your father's health may be affected too. The manifestations also show serious contradictions and destruction, and there will be trouble when water is in the ascendant and earth is weak." With this he sat down, thrusting forward his goatee.

Chia Jung had at first been laughing up his sleeve at this rigmarole, but now he felt there might be something in it and in this prediction that his father would fall ill too.

"This is brilliantly divined, sir," he said. "But what caused my mother's illness?"

"The signs indicate fire counteracted by water, therefore it must be a case of a cold congestion combined with a hot humour. Even divination by milfoil would be unable to determine this more clearly — for that you would need to resort to the method of the Duodecimal Cycle."

"Are you expert in that too, sir?"

"I know something about it."

Chia Jung asked him to demonstrate and gave him the two-hour period. Then Mao Pan-hsien drew a board, set the deities in due order and found that it was the hour of the White Tiger.

"This is called the 'dissolution of animal spirits,'" he said. "White tigers are evil. When controlled by a spirit in the ascendant they cannot run amok; but now that disaster has befallen the house, at a time of misfortune and death, tigers grow ravenous and must prey on people. The portent acquired this name because animal spirits dissipate when alarmed.

"This sign indicates the loss of animal spirits attended by deaths, sicknesses and alarms. Since, according to the portent, tigers appear at dusk, she must have been taken ill in the evening. It also says, 'All who cast this lot must have a tiger spirit lurking in an old house to cause trouble. It may take form and utter sounds.' You asked to have your parents' fortunes told, sir. This coincides with the saying that a tiger appearing in the daytime harries men, seen at night it harries women. This is very ominous!"

Before Chia Jung had heard him out he was pale with fright. "No doubt, sir," he agreed. "But this doesn't altogether accord with that other prediction. Just how serious is it?"

"Don't panic. Let me study it carefully again." He lowered his head and muttered to himself for a while.

"Good!" he cried presently. "There is hope. I have worked out that a noble spirit will come to the rescue. This sign is known as the 'dissolution of the sentient soul with the return of the spiritual soul.' Anxiety will be followed by joy. All will be well, but you must take precautions."

Chia Jung presented him with his fee and saw him out.

He then reported to Chia Chen, "Mother caught this illness in the old house at dusk, when she met a white tiger spirit."

"You told me that the other day your mother came back through the Garden; she must have run into it there. Remember how your aunt Hsi-feng fell ill after going to the Garden? Though she didn't see anything herself, later on all the maids and nurses with her declared they had seen a furry creature on a rock with eyes as big as lanterns, and able to speak. It drove her back, making her fall ill from fright."

"Yes, I remember," replied Chia Jung. "I also heard from Uncle Pao's page Pei-ming that Ching-wen had become the Spirit of the Hibiscus in the Garden, and that after Miss Lin died music sounded high above, so she must have been put in charge of some flowers there too. What a dreadful thing — all those monsters in the Garden! Before, with all those people coming and going and the place so full of life, it didn't matter. But now it's very lonely, and when my mother went there she may have trodden on some flowers or had some jinx put on her. So it seems the divination was correct."

"Did he say there was any danger?" asked Chia Chen.

"According to him, in another two days she'll be better — but I hope it doesn't all happen as he predicted."

"What do you mean?"

"If that fortune-teller was right, sir, I'm afraid you'll be out of sorts too."

Just then, someone called out from the inner quarters, "The mistress wants to get up and go over to the Garden. Her maids can't stop her!"

Her husband and son went in to pacify her.

"The one in red's calling me! The one in green's hurrying me!" Madam Yu was raving.

All present were both frightened and amused. Chia Chen sent to buy paper money to burn in the Garden. And, sure enough, that night she sweated and calmed down, while after another two days she gradually recovered.

This story spread until everyone was talking of the devils

in the Garden, and the servants in charge there were too scared to cut flowers, prune trees or water the vegetables. At first, they dared not venture out at night, so that birds and beasts ran wild; then, even in the daytime, they would only go there in groups and armed with weapons.

Later, indeed, Chia Chen also fell ill, but instead of consulting a doctor or taking medicine he made certain vows and had paper money burnt in the Garden and prayers offered to the stars. No sooner had he recovered than Chia Jung and the others fell ill in turn. This went on for several months, so that both households were appalled — the sough of the wind and the cry of cranes caused panic, while people saw monsters in each tree or tuft of grass. As all income from the Garden stopped, the monthly expenses of different compounds increased and the Jung Mansion was harder pressed for money. The servants in the Garden, eager to leave the place, kept making up stories and stirring up trouble with their tales of flower spirits and tree monsters. So finally the Garden gate was sealed up and no one dared to go there any more. The fine towers, pavilions, lodges and terraces were each and all taken over by birds and beasts.

Now Ching-wen's cousin Wu Kuei lived just outside the Garden gate. Since Ching-wen's death and the story that she had turned into a flower spirit, his wife dared not go out at night. One day she had a cold and took the wrong medicine while Wu Kuei was out shopping, so that on his return late that evening he found her dead on the *kang*. Outsiders, knowing her bad reputation, claimed that a monster had climbed over the wall to enjoy her until she died of exhaustion.

The old lady, scandalized by this talk, posted guards outside Pao-yu's house who sounded the watch as they patrolled in turn. And these young maids alleged that they had seen a red-faced figure as well as a ravishing beauty, raising such a ceaseless commotion that Pao-yu went in terror every day. Luckily, Pao-chai had sense and she managed to curb these rumours to some extent by threatening to beat any maids whom she heard talking wildly. Still, all who lived there were so apprehensive that they hired extra watchmen, adding to the household's expenses.

Chia Sheh alone was sceptical.

"How could there be monsters in such a fine garden?" he scoffed.

Choosing a fine sunny day and ignoring the others' warnings, he led a troop of armed servants to investigate.

Inside the Garden there was indeed a sinister atmosphere. Chia Sheh braced himself to proceed, while his followers flinched with fear. One young servant, already afraid, heard a whizzing noise and looked round to see a gaudy creature fly past. With a cry of terror, his legs gave way and he fell down. Chia Sheh turned to ask what had happened.

"I saw a monster!" gasped the boy. "Yellow in the face with a red beard, dressed in green. It flew into a cave behind the trees."

Shaken by this, Chia Sheh asked, "Did the rest of you see it?"

Some servants seized this chance to chime in, "Yes, we did, sir. But as you were ahead, we didn't like to alarm you. So we kept quiet about it. We slaves can control ourselves."

Afraid to go any further, Chia Sheh beat a hasty retreat, instructing the servants not to mention this but to say that a thorough search of the Garden had revealed nothing amiss. At heart, however, he believed the boy's story and decided to go to the Taoist Patriarch to invite some priests to exorcise evil spirits. And when they saw his fear, those servants who never let slip a chance to make trouble not only did not hush it up but embroidered on the story, so that all who heard it gaped in consternation.

Chia Sheh felt he had no choice but to call in Taoists to exorcise the spirits haunting the Garden. An auspicious day was selected, and on the altar set up in the Hall of Reunion were placed the images of the Three Taoist Gods with, beside them, the Twenty-eight Constellations, the Four Great Generals Ma, Chao, Wen and Chou and, below these, the Thirty-six Heavenly Officers. Incense, flowers, lamps and candles filled the hall, on either side of which were ranged bells, drums and other sacred vessels, as well as five flags denoting north, south, east, west and centre. The Board of Taoist Sacrifices sent forty-nine attendants who spent a whole day purifying the altar. Then three high priests offered incense and sprinkled water, after which the sacred drum was beaten. The priests wore seven-star chaplets, nine-coloured robes with Eight Diagrams designs, and cloud-ascending sandals. Holding ivory wands, they presented a memorial begging the gods to descend.

Then for a whole day they chanted the *Primal Void Canon* to wipe out evil spirits and bring good fortune. This done, they issued the order to summon the heavenly generals. On it was written in large characters, "The Grand Monad, using the holy signs of the Three Sacred Realms, convokes all the deities of these realms to the altar for service."

The masters and the men-servants of both mansions had gone to the Garden that day to watch the priests catch monsters.

"What an impressive order!" they commented. "This commotion to summon heavenly generals here should frighten any number of monsters away."

They crowded round the altar to watch the acolytes raising flags and taking up their positions north, south, east, west and centre to await orders. Next, the three high priests took their places before the altar, the first holding a sword and pitcher of holy water, the second the seven-starred black flag, and the third the peach-wood rod for beating monsters. As soon as the music stopped, the magic tablet was rapped three times and they chanted incantations while the acolytes with their flags circled round them. Then the high priests, leaving the altar, made members of the family lead them to the various pavilions, lodges, rocks and streams so that they could sprinkle them with holy water and brandish the sword at each. Returning, they rapped the tablet again several times and raised high the seven-starred flag. Next, the priests held the flags together and the rod beat the air three times.

The onlookers, sure that by now the monsters must have been caught, pressed forward to see them; but there was no sign of them. They saw nothing but the high priests sending for a bottle in which to imprison the monsters, and when this had been sealed up they wrote a charm in vermilion on the seal, then put the bottle away with instructions that later it should be taken back and kept securely under their temple pagoda. Finally, the altar having been cleared, they offered up thanks to the heavenly generals.

Chia Sheh expressed respectful gratitude to the priests, but Chia Jung and some other younger men of the family were secretly most amused.

"What a great to-do!" they scoffed. "We expected them to show us the monsters they'd caught, to let us see what they were really like after all that hunting round. Heaven knows whether they caught anything or not!"

"You fools!" swore Chia Chen. "Monsters take shape or vanish into thin air just as they please. With all the heavenly generals here, how dare they show themselves? Now that the evil has been exorcised, they'll have to stop making trouble — such is the power of the sacred doctrine."

The young men waited sceptically to watch for further developments. The servants, however, did not question the claim that the monsters had been captured. They stopped panicking and let the matter drop. The recovery of Chia Chen and the other invalids was also attributed to the Taoists' magic.

Only one page chortled, "I don't know what happened earlier on, but I went to the Garden that day with Lord Sheh, and it was a big pheasant that flew past — that was plain as daylight. But Shuan-erh took fright, thought he'd seen an apparition and described it to the life! We all backed him up by fibbing, so Lord Sheh took his story seriously. That's why we had this grand show to watch today!"

But none of his hearers believed him, and still no one had the courage to live in the Garden.

One day, when Chia Sheh was at leisure, he thought of ordering some servants to move into the Garden as caretakers to prevent bad characters from hiding there at night. Before he could give this order, Chia Lien came in and paid his respects.

"Today, in Uncle Wang's place, I heard that Second Uncle has been impeached by the governor," he announced. "He's accused of not keeping a check on his subordinates and of levying too much grain. The court has been petitioned to dismiss him."

"It must surely be a rumour!" replied Chia Sheh, very shocked. "Only the other day, he wrote to tell us the date of Tan-chun's arrival and the auspicious day chosen for seeing her off to the coast. She'd had a smooth journey, he said, so the family need not worry. He also wrote that the governor was treating him as a relative and had given him a congratulatory feast. How could anyone related to him impeach him? But let's not waste time talking. Go straight to the Ministry of Civil Affairs to find out the facts, then come and let me know."

Chia Lien left at once.

On his return a few hours later he said, "I've just heard in the ministry that he *has* been impeached. A report has been sent to the court, but thanks to His Majesty's clemency it hasn't been referred to the ministry. It has been decreed: 'Since he failed to keep his subordinates in check and levied too heavy a grain tax, cruelly exploiting the people, he should be dismissed. But in view of the fact that he was new to this provincial post and inexperienced in administration, enabling his subordinates to deceive him, he is to be demoted three ranks and, by the gracious favour of the Emperor, can still serve as assistant minister of the Ministry of Works. He is to return forthwith to the capital.'

"This news is reliable. We were just discussing it in the ministry when a magistrate from Kiangsi, newly summoned to court, arrived. He has a high opinion of Second Uncle. Says he's a good official but doesn't know how to handle subordinates, so those servants of his made trouble outside, bullying and cheating people and spoiling his reputation. The governor, knowing this all along, also thinks well of Second Uncle. It's puzzling that he should have impeached him now.

Maybe things were getting so out of hand he was afraid there might be some big scandal and therefore accused him of negligence to get him off more lightly."

Cutting him short, Chia Sheh instructed him, "Go and tell your aunt about this, but don't let the old lady know."

Chia Lien went to report this news to Lady Wang. To know her reactions you must read the next chapter.

CHAPTER 103

Chin-kuei Plots Murder and Destroys Herself
Chia Yu-tsun, Blind to the Truth,
Meets an Old Friend in Vain

Chia Lien went to tell Lady Wang all that had happened. The next day he returned to the Ministry of Civil Affairs for fuller information, then reported back to her.

"Is this news reliable?" she asked. "If so, the master will be pleased and our minds will be set at rest too. Those provincial posts are too risky. If he hadn't been recalled like this, those scoundrels might have been the death of him!"

"How did you know that, madam?" he inquired.

"Since your Second Uncle went to this provincial post, instead of sending home a single cent he's spent a whole lot of the family's money. And look at those men who went with him: They hadn't been gone long before their wives started dolling themselves up with gold and silver trinkets. Obviously they've been raking in money outside without the master knowing. And he's let them get away with such goings-on. If there'd been a scandal, not only would he be dismissed — our ancestors might even be deprived of their titles!"

"You're quite right, madam. When I first heard he'd been impeached I had the fright of my life, but after I got the facts clear I felt relieved. I hope he'll pass some years quietly as an official in the capital, keeping his good reputation as long as he lives. Even if the old lady hears this she needn't worry, provided you reassure her."

"I know what to say. But go and see what more you can find out."

Chia Lien assented and was on the point of leaving when in hurried one of Aunt Hsueh's old serving-women in a fluster.

Not stopping to pay her respects she blurted out:

"Our mistress has sent me, madam, to tell you that another dreadful thing has happened in our family!"

"What is it?"

"Something too awful for words!"

"You silly creature!" scolded Lady Wang. "If it's so serious, tell me properly."

"Master Ko is away, we've no man in the house; so how are we to cope? She wants you, madam, to send some gentlemen over to help us out."

"But what do you want them for?" asked Lady Wang impatiently, having no idea what she was talking about.

"Madam Pan is dead!"

"Pah! Good riddance to bad rubbish! Why get so worked up?"

"It wasn't a natural death — there's been foul play. Please, madam, send someone over at once to cope!" With that she turned to go back.

Both angry and amused Lady Wang exclaimed, "What a fool this old woman is! You'd better go and see what's happened, Lien. Pay no attention to that stupid creature."

Not catching the instruction to him to go over, all the old woman heard was "pay no attention." She hurried off in a huff.

Aunt Hsueh was waiting anxiously for her return. When at last the servant came back she asked her, "Well, whom is she sending?"

"It's no use!" The old woman sighed. "When you're in a fix, the kindest of kin will do nothing. Her Ladyship not only refuses to help us, she swore I was a fool!"

"If *she* won't help," cried Aunt Hsueh in exasperation, "what did the young mistress say?"

"If Her Ladyship won't lift a finger, how can her daughter-in-law do anything? I didn't go to tell her."

"Her Ladyship isn't one of our family, but how can the daughter whom I brought up ignore me?" demanded Aunt Hsueh irately.

"Of course!" exclaimed the old woman, catching on. "Well then, I'll go again."

But just then Chia Lien arrived. Having paid his respects to Aunt Hsueh and offered his condolences he said, "My aunt has heard that Pan's wife is dead, but she couldn't get any sense out of your servant and so she's very worried. She's sent me to find out what's happened and told me to help. What can I do for you, aunt?"

Aunt Hsueh had been sobbing with rage, but on hearing this she said quickly, "I'm sorry to put you out, Master Lien. I know how good my sister is to me, but this old creature can't give a message clearly and nearly held matters up. Please take a seat and I'll tell you all about it. The thing is — she didn't die a natural death."

"Did she kill herself in a pique because of Pan's trouble?"

"I only wish she had! These last few months she made scenes every day, going barefoot with tousled hair like a crazy creature. Although at the news of Pan's death sentence she did cry, she soon started making up again with rouge and powder; and had I protested she would have made a big row, so I ignored her. Then one day, for some reason, she came and asked to have Hsiang-ling to keep her company. I told her, 'You have Pao-chan, so what do you want Hsiang-ling for? It's not as if you liked her; why let her provoke you?' As she insisted, however, I had to tell Hsiang-ling to move in with her. The poor girl dared not disobey me and, bad as her health was, she went there. I was pleasantly surprised when Chin-kuei treated her very well, but when Pao-chai knew she said, 'Do you suppose Chin-kuei is plotting something?' I paid no attention, though.

"A few days ago Hsiang-ling fell ill, and Chin-kuei made some soup for her herself. But Hsiang-ling was out of luck: as Chin-kuei took it to her she scalded her own hand and the bowl was smashed. I'd have expected her to blame it on Hsiang-ling, but instead of losing her temper she swept up the pieces herself then mopped the floor, and they remained on good terms.

"Last night, she told Pao-chan to make two more bowls of soup for her to drink with Hsiang-ling. After a while, I heard a great commotion in her room: first Pao-chan was screaming like mad, then Hsiang-ling joined in and staggered out, leaning against the wall, to call for help.

"I hurried in and found my daughter-in-law thrashing about on the floor. Blood was gushing from her nose and eyes, and she was clawing with both hands at her stomach. I was frightened to death! When I asked what had happened she couldn't speak, and presently she died in agony. It looked to me as if she had taken poison.

"Then Pao-chan tearfully seized hold of Hsiang-ling, accusing her of poisoning her mistress. I don't believe Hsiang-ling would do such a thing. In any case, confined to her bed, how *could* she? But Pao-chan insisted she'd done it. So what could I do, Lien? I had to harden my heart to tell the matrons to tie Hsiang-ling up and leave her in Pao-chan's charge. Then we locked them into the room, and I sat up all night with your cousin Pao-chin waiting for your gate to open so that we could send you word. You have good sense, Lien. Tell me, how should we handle this?"

"Does the Hsia family know about it?" he asked.

"No. We must clear up the business before we tell them."

"I think we'll have to go through official channels to get the matter settled. Naturally it's Pao-chan whom we suspect, but other people will ask what reason she had to poison her own mistress. To them, Hsiang-ling would seem more likely to do it."

As they were talking, maids from the Jung Mansion came in to announce their young mistress. Although Chia Lien was Pao-chai's elder cousin-in-law, as they had known each other since childhood he did not withdraw when she entered. Pao-chai paid her respects to her mother and him, then went into the inner room to sit with Pao-chin. Aunt Hsueh followed her in and told her what had happened.

Pao-chai pointed out, "If we have Hsiang-ling bound, it will look as if we too believe she was the poisoner. You say the soup was prepared by Pao-chan, mother. In that case, you should tie her up and question her, at the same time sending to tell the Hsia family and to report this to the authorities."

Aunt Hsueh thought this reasonable and consulted Chia Lien.

"Pao-chai is quite right," he agreed. "When we have reported this, I must also go and ask some men in the Board of Punishments to help see to things at the inquest and interrogation. But I think it may make things awkward if we tie up Pao-chan and set Hsiang-ling loose."

"I didn't want to tie up Hsiang-ling," Aunt Hsueh told him. "But I was afraid that, ill as she is, this false accusation might make her so desperate she'd try to kill herself — then we'd have another death on our hands. That's why I decided to have her tied up and put in Pao-chan's charge."

"Still, this is strengthening Pao-chan's case," he objected. "They should either both be set free or both bound up, as the three of them were together. Well, just get somebody to comfort Hsiang-ling."

Aunt Hsueh ordered the door to be opened and went in, while Pao-chai sent the maids she had brought with her to help tie up Pao-chan, who had been gloating over the sight of Hsiang-ling crying her heart out. When Pao-chan saw them coming with ropes to bind her she screamed, but the maids from the Jung Mansion silenced her and trussed her up. The door was left open with people on watch outside.

By then they had sent to inform the Hsia family which had only recently moved to the capital, as in the last few years they had gone bankrupt and Mrs. Hsia, a widow, missed her daughter. She had an adopted son, a scoundrel who had squandered all their money and who often called on the Hsueh family. Chin-kuei was too amorous to live without a man and had long been hankering after Hsueh Ko, but hers was a case of "beggars can't be choosers." However, this foster-brother of hers was dense. Though he knew pretty well what she wanted he had not yet made love to her; and so Chin-kuei, on her frequent visits home, would help him out with money. Today he was looking forward to a visit from her, when the arrival of a Hsueh family servant convinced him that here was another gift for him. At the news that she had died of poison, he set up an angry outcry. His mother raised an even bigger uproar.

"My daughter was doing all right there!" she screamed. "Why should she poison herself?"

Weeping and wailing, she set off on foot with her son without waiting for a carriage, for the Hsias being bankrupt tradesmen did not trouble to keep up appearances. The son walked on ahead while his mother, accompanied by an old slattern, sobbed and snivelled in the street as she hired a carriage. As soon as she entered the Hsuehs' gate, without greeting anyone she started loudly bewailing her "darling daughter," and clamouring for revenge.

Chia Lien had gone to the Board of Punishments to enlist help, leaving only Aunt Hsueh, Pao-chai and Pao-chin at home. They had never seen such goings-on before and were too frightened to speak. Indeed, even had they reasoned with her, Mrs. Hsia would not have listened.

"What good treatment did my daughter ever get in your family?" she ranted. "Her husband beat and cursed her all the time; then you wouldn't let the young couple stay together. You plotted to have my son-in-law imprisoned, so that she'd never set eyes on him again. Mother and daughter, you enjoy yourselves with your fine relatives' backing, but you still couldn't bear the sight of Chin-kuei and got someone to poison her, then accused her of killing herself! Why should she take poison?"

She charged at Aunt Hsueh, who fell back protesting, "Madam! First go and look at your daughter and question Pao-chan, before making such allegations."

As Mrs. Hsia's adopted son was there, Pao-chai and Pao-chin were unable to come to Aunt Hsueh's rescue. They could only wring their hands in the inner room.

Then, as luck would have it, Lady Wang sent Chou Jui's wife to help out. She came in to see an old woman wagging a finger at Aunt Hsueh and screaming at her. She knew this must be Chin-kuei's mother.

"Are you Mrs. Hsia, madam?" asked Mrs. Chou stepping

forward. "The young mistress has poisoned herself. It wasn't Madam Hsueh's doing. How can you abuse her like this?"

"And who may *you* be?" Mrs. Hsia retorted.

This reinforcement emboldened Aunt Hsueh to say, "She is one of the household of our Chia relatives."

"We all know you have powerful relatives," sneered Mrs. Hsia. "That's why you can keep my son-in-law in jail. But does that mean that my child's death can go unavenged?" Seizing hold of Aunt Hsueh she demanded, "Just how did you murder my daughter anyway? Show me!"

Mrs. Chou interposed, "Just go and see for yourself. Stop tugging at other people." She gave her a shove.

The adopted son ran over to protest, "Are you banking on your masters' power to beat up my mother?" He threw a chair at Mrs. Chou, but missed her.

Pao-chai's maids inside on hearing this commotion hurried out, afraid Mrs. Chou might get hurt. They crowded forward to intervene, expostulating and warning the fellow off. But that only made Mrs. Hsia and her son set up a still greater clamour.

"We know how powerful your Jung Mansion is!" they yelled. "Now our girl has been killed, you may as well kill us too!"

Again they charged Aunt Hsueh. The maids, for all there were so many of them, were powerless to stop them for as the saying goes, "Ten thousand men are no match for one desperado."

Things had just taken this ugly turn when Chia Lien arrived with seven or eight men-servants. Sizing up the situation, he ordered his men to drag Mrs. Hsia's son away.

"Stop this brawling and talk reasonably," he said. "This place must be straightened up at once. Officers from the Board of Punishments are coming to hold an inquest."

The arrival of this gentleman with attendants before him to clear the way made all the servants present stand at attention, and Chin-kuei's mother realized that this must be one of the Chia family. Then her son was seized and she heard there was to be an official inquest. She had been meaning to raise a great ballyhoo over her daughter's corpse, then appeal to the court for justice, little thinking that the others would inform the authorities first. This took the wind out of her sails. Aunt Hsueh was still too stunned to speak, and it was Mrs. Chou who reported to Chia Lien:

"This woman came here not to look at her daughter but to abuse Madam Hsueh. We were remonstrating with her when a wild man burst in to raise pandemonium. In the presence of ladies too — it was simply outrageous!"

"We needn't argue with them now," said Chia Lien. "Later we can have him beaten and interrogated. Men should keep to themselves and not intrude on ladies. His mother could surely have seen her daughter by herself. Why should he rush in if not to loot the place?"

Meanwhile his servants had secured the young man.

"What a way to behave, Mrs. Hsia!" cried Chou Jui's wife now that she had more support. "Since you came, you should have asked the facts of the matter. Either your daughter committed suicide, or Pao-chan poisoned her. Why try to blackmail people before finding out the facts and seeing the corpse? Would Madam Hsueh let her daughter-in-law die and do nothing about it? We've tied Pao-chan up. Because your daughter was always making trouble, she asked Hsiang-ling to keep her company and they slept in the same room. That's why both she and Pao-chan are under guard there. We were waiting for you to come and attend the inquest, at which we'll find out just what happened."

Aware that her position was weak, Mrs. Hsia had to go with Chou Jui's wife to her daughter's room. The sight of Chin-kuei lying stark on the *kang,* her face covered with clotted blood, set her wailing aloud.

When Pao-chan saw Mrs. Hsia she sobbed, "Our young lady was kind to Hsiang-ling, getting her to move in with her, yet Hsiang-ling seized this chance to poison her!"

By now the whole Hsueh household had gathered there. "Nonsense!" they protested. "She died after drinking that soup yesterday. Weren't you the one who prepared it?"

"Yes, I was. But after bringing it in I went out to see to something else. Then Hsiang-ling must have put some poison in it."

Before she had finished speaking, Chin-kuei's mother dashed towards Hsiang-ling, but the others barred her way.

Aunt Hsueh said, "It looks as if she was poisoned by arsenic. We certainly have none here. No matter whether it was Hsiang-ling or Pao-chan, someone must have bought it for her. After investigation the authorities are sure to find out. The culprit can't get away. Now let's lay her out properly ready for the inquest."

As the women-servants set about doing this, Pao-chai proposed, "You should clear away those feminine articles — there will be men coming in."

Then, under the mattress on the *kang*, they discovered a crumpled paper packet. Chin-kuei's mother pounced on this and opened it, but finding nothing in it threw it away.

"There's the evidence all right!" exclaimed Pao-chan. "I recognize this packet. A few days ago, when we were plagued by rats, my mistress went to ask her brother for some arsenic and on her return put it in her jewel case. Hsiang-ling must have seen it and used it to poison her. If you don't believe me, look in the jewel case."

Chin-kuei's mother did so, but found nothing there except a few silver hairpins.

"Where have all her trinkets gone to?" wondered Aunt Hsueh.

Pao-chai made servants open the cases and cabinets, but all were empty.

"Who took my sister-in-law's things?" she asked. "Pao-chan must answer for this."

"How should she know?" asked Chin-kuei's mother uneasily.

"Don't say that, madam," put in Mrs. Chou. "I know Pao-chan was with her all the time. Of course she must know."

Under such pressure, Pao-chan could not deny it and had to confess, "My mistress always took something each time she went home. How could I stop her?"

"A fine mother you are!" the rest jeered at Mrs. Hsia. "Squeezing your daughter till she had nothing left, then making her kill herself so that you could blackmail us! Very well, we'll report this at the inquest."

Pao-chai ordered a maid, "Go and ask Master Lien outside not to let any of the Hsia household get away."

In the inner room Mrs. Hsia was on pins and needles.

"You bitch!" she swore at Pao-chan. "Stop blabbing! When did my daughter ever take things home?"

"The things don't matter," countered Pao-chan. "What's important is to find out who murdered her."

"Once we've found those things, we shall know who murdered her," Pao-chin declared. "Hurry up and ask Cousin Lien to check up on the arsenic her son bought, then report it to the authorities."

"This Pao-chan must have lost her mind, talking such rubbish," protested Chin-kuei's mother frantically. "My daughter never bought any arsenic. If Pao-chan says this, *she* must have poisoned her!"

In desperation Pao-chan started shouting, "Other people may accuse me falsely, but how can *you*? Many's the time I heard you tell your daughter not to take things lying down but to raise a rumpus and ruin their family, then move out bag and baggage and marry a better man. Did you tell her that or not?"

Before Mrs. Hsia could speak Chou Jui's wife chimed in, "When one of your own servants bears witness against you, how can you deny it?"

Gnashing her teeth Mrs. Hsia swore at Pao-chan, "I never treated you badly! Do you want to be the death of me talking that way? When the officers come, I'll tell them *you* were the one who poisoned my daughter!"

Pao-chan's eyes nearly started out of her head for fury. "Madam," she begged Aunt Hsueh, "please let Hsiang-ling go. We shouldn't wrong innocent people. I know what to say when I'm interrogated."

Hearing this, Pao-chai told them to untie Pao-chan instead.

"An easy-going girl like you, why get yourself involved need-lessly?" she asked. "If you know something, speak out and be done with it so that we can get this straight."

Afraid that if it came to an interrogation she might be tortur-ed, Pao-chan told them, "My mistress was for ever complaining, 'With my looks, why did I have to have such a senseless mother, who instead of marrying me to Master Ko gave me to that stupid ruffian! If I could spend a day with Master Ko, I'd die content!' That's what made her hate Hsiang-ling. At first I didn't realize this, and later when she was good to Hsiang-ling I supposed it was because Hsiang-ling had won her round. I thought she ordered that soup out of kindness. . . ."

"This is even greater nonsense!" fumed Chin-kuei's mother. "If she wanted to poison Hsiang-ling, why should she get poisoned herself?"

Pao-chai asked, "Hsiang-ling, did you drink that soup yesterday?"

"A few days ago I was too ili even to raise my head," Hsiang-ling replied. "When the mistress told me to drink I dared not refuse; but before I could struggle up the soup was spilt and she had to clean up the mess — I felt very bad about it. Yesterday, again, she told me to drink some soup. I didn't want to, but I had to. Before I could start on it, though, I came over dizzy and to my relief Sister Pao-chan took the bowl away. I was dozing off when the mistress drank her own soup and told me to try mine, so I forced myself to take a couple of sips. . . ."

Pao-chan broke in, "That's it! I'll tell you the truth. Yester-day the mistress told me to make two bowls of soup for her to drink with Hsiang-ling. I was furious! I thought: Who is Hsiang-ling that I should make soup for *her*? So, on purpose, I put an extra handful of salt in one of the bowls and marked it secretly, meaning that one for Hsiang-ling. But as I carried it in the mistress stopped me and sent me to tell a page to order a carriage, as she wanted to go home. When I came back from this errand, I saw the bowl I'd marked in front of the mistress. I was afraid she'd scold me for over-salting it, and didn't know what to do; but then she moved to the back of the room, and while she wasn't looking I changed the bowls round. Well, it served her right! She came back and carried the soup to Hsiang-ling's bed, saying while she drank her bowl, 'You must at least taste this.' Hsiang-ling didn't seem to find it too salty, and they both finished their bowls while I laughed up my sleeve at Hsiang-ling for not noticing the salt. How was I to know that my devilish mistress wanted to poison her? She must have put in the arsenic while I was out, then didn't know that I'd changed the bowls around. Truly, 'Heaven is just, and each reaps as he has sown.' "

The others thought over the sequence of events and could find no flaw in her story. They untied Hsiang-ling too and made her lie down in bed.

But in spite of these incriminating facts Chin-kuei's mother went on protesting, whereupon Aunt Hsueh and the others, all talking together, insisted that her son must pay with his life for the murder.

Chia Lien called from outside, "There's no need to argue. Get everything cleared up quickly. The officers from the Board of Punishments are coming."

This flustered Mrs. Hsia and her son, who foresaw dire consequences.

"It's all the fault of my dead daughter," Mrs. Hsia had to plead with Aunt Hsueh. "She brought this on herself. If we let them hold an inquest, it will reflect badly on your family too. Do hush the business up, madam!"

"That's impossible," said Pao-chai. "We've already reported it; how can it be hushed up?"

Chou Jui's wife intervened, "The only way to hush the matter up is for Mrs. Hsia herself to call off the inquest, in which case we shall say no more about it."

Chia Lien outside had also intimidated the son so that he was only too willing to go to the Board of Punishments to sign a statement that no inquest was needed as the cause of death was clear and to promise not to bring any suit later on. And to this the others agreed. Aunt Hsueh sent to buy a coffin for Chin-kuei — but no more of this.

Let us return to Chia Yu-tsun, who had now been promoted to be prefect of the capital in charge of taxation. One day he went out of the city to check on the acreage of arable land, and passing through the County of Esoteric Understanding he reached the ford in the Stream of Rapid Reversal. He made his chair-bearers stop there to wait for his retinue. And seeing a small temple by the village, its crumbling walls revealing some hoary pines, he sauntered towards it. The gold had flaked off the images inside, and the hall was rickety. On one side was a broken tablet, but he could not decipher the half-obliterated inscription on it.

He decided to stroll to the back. In the shade of a green cypress there he saw a thatched hut in which a Taoist priest was sitting cross-legged, his eyes closed in meditation. As Yu-tsun went closer, the man's face struck him as familiar and he suspected that they had met before, though he could not remember where. His attendants wanted to rouse the priest by shouting, but he stopped them. Walking slowly towards him he called out a greeting.

The Taoist opened his eyes a crack and asked with a smile, "What brings you here, Your Honour?"

"I have come from the capital on a tour of inspection, and happened to pass this way. Seeing you meditating so tranquilly, I felt sure you must have a profound understanding of the Way and would therefore like to make so bold as to ask for your instructions."

"Our coming and our going — each has its predestined place," was the Taoist's reply.

Sensing that this was no ordinary priest, Yu-tsun bowed low and asked, "Where have you been practising virtue, venerable master? And why are you staying here? What is the name of this temple? How many inmates has it? Are there not holy mountains where you could cultivate Truth?

Or if you want to do virtuous deeds, why not choose somewhere more accessible?"

The Taoist replied, "A gourd is shelter enough for me, I need no holy mountains. The name of this temple has long been lost, but the broken tablet remains; and since the shadow follows the form, why should I ask for alms to have the temple repaired? 'The jade in the box hopes to fetch a good price; the pin in the casket longs to soar on high' — that doesn't apply to me."

Yu-tsun was quick-witted. The mention of "gourd," "jade" and "pin" at once reminded him of Chen Shih-yin, and looking more intently at the Taoist he recognized him.

"Aren't you old Mr. Chen, sir?" he asked, after motioning his attendants to withdraw.

With a faint smile the Taoist answered, "Why talk about *chen* (true) and *chia* (false)? They are the same."

The word *chia*, a homonym for Yu-tsun's surname, confirmed his conjecture. He bowed again and said, "Since you generously helped me to go to the capital, I was lucky enough to pass the examination and was assigned to your honourable district. Only then did I learn that you, venerable sir, had left the dusty world and become an immortal. Although I longed to trace you, I feared that as a mundane, vulgar official I would never see your saintly countenance again. I am overjoyed at this encounter here! I beg you, venerable saint, to instruct the ignorant. If you do not spurn me, my house in the capital is near at hand and I would count it an honour to entertain you there so that I can hear your instructions every day."

The Taoist rose to return his bow and replied, "I know of nothing in this world but my hassock. What Your Honour just said completely passes this poor priest's understanding." With that he sat down again.

Yu-tsun thought dubiously, "If he isn't Chen Shih-yin, how is it that he looks and talks just like him? We haven't met for nineteen years, yet he appears unchanged. It must be because he has achieved immortality that he's unwilling to disclose his past. But now that I have found my benefactor, I can't let slip this opportunity. Evidently he's not to be tempted by wealth or rank, much less by mention of his wife and daughter."

"How can I bear it, saintly teacher," he said, "if you draw a veil over your past?"

He was about to bow again when one of his servants came to report, "It is growing dark, sir, high time to cross the ford."

As Yu-tsun hesitated the Taoist said, "Pray lose no time in crossing, Your Honour. We shall meet again. If you delay, a storm may spring up. If you really wish to see me, I shall wait for you some other day at the ford." With that he sat down again and closed his eyes.

Chia Yu-tsun had no choice but to say goodbye to the priest and leave the temple. He was about to cross the ford when someone came rushing towards him. If you want to know who it was, read the next chapter.

CHAPTER 104

The Drunken Diamond Brags That Small Fry
Can Stir Up Big Billows
A Crazy Lordling Grieves Over the Past

As Chia Yu-tsun was about to cross the ford someone rushed up to him.

"Your Honour!" this man, one of his runners, exclaimed. "That temple you just visited is on fire!"

Yu-tsun turned to see flames leaping skyward and the sun blotted out by smoke and dust.

"How extraordinary!" he thought. "I've barely left the place. How could this blaze have started? I hope this hasn't done for Chen Shih-yin!"

He felt an urge to go back but did not want to delay his tour of inspection; yet he could not set his mind at rest without investigating. After a moment's reflection he asked, "Did you see that old Taoist leave the temple?"

"I followed you out, Your Honour," said the man. "Then I had the gripes and had to relieve myself. When I turned I saw flames — the temple had caught fire — so I hurried here to report it. I didn't see anybody leaving the place."

Although Yu-tsun was worried, his own career was his first concern and he did not want to turn back.

"You stay here till the fire burns out," he ordered. "Then go in to see whether the old priest was trapped or not, and come back to report to me."

The man assented and remained behind while Yu-tsun crossed the river to carry on with his inspection. After checking up on a few districts, he put up in a hostel for the night.

The following day he journeyed another stage and re-entered the capital, runners before him clearing the way while others of his attendants followed behind. Then, seated in his sedan-chair, he heard the men in front shouting angrily and asked them what had happened. One of the runners dragged over a man and made him kneel down before the prefect's chair.

"This drunkard didn't get out of the way but came charging at us," he reported. "When ordered to stop, he put on a drunken act and flopped down in the middle of the road, then accused me of knocking him down."

"I am in charge of this district," Yu-tsun announced. "All citizens here come under my jurisdiction. When you saw your prefect coming, you were too drunk to make way yet had the nerve to make false accusations!"

"I buy drink with my own money," retorted the fellow. "When I'm tipsy it's the Emperor's land I lie down on. Not even high officials can interfere."

"Lawless scoundrel!" Yu-tsun fumed. "Ask him his name."

"I am Ni Erh the Drunken Diamond."

Yu-tsun was furious. "Have this wretch beaten," he ordered. "We'll soon see whether he's hard as a diamond!"

The runners pinned Ni Erh down and gave him some hard lashes till, sobered up by the pain, he begged for mercy.

Yu-tsun from his chair scoffed, "So that's the rough diamond you are! I won't have you beaten now but taken to the yamen for a thorough interrogation."

The runners shouted assent, tied Ni Erh up and dragged him off, ignoring his entreaties.

Yu-tsun went to court to make his report, and by the time he returned to his office this incident had slipped his mind completely. But men in the street who had witnessed it commented to one another, "Ni Erh, in his cups, counts on his strength to throw his weight about; but now he's fallen into Prefect Chia's clutches he's not likely to get off lightly!"

This talk reached the ears of Ni Erh's wife and daughter, who waited in vain that night for him to come home. The girl went to search different gambling-houses for him, and when everyone there confirmed the report she wept.

"Don't worry," they said. "Prefect Chia is connected with

the Jung Mansion, and a certain Second Master Chia of that family is one of your father's friends. If you and your mother ask him to put in a word, your father will be let off."

Ni Erh's daughter thought, "Yes, I've often heard father say that Mr. Chia Yun next door is his friend, so why not get him to help?"

She hurried home to propose this to her mother, and together they called on Chia Yun. He happened to be in that day and promptly offered them seats while his mother ordered tea. Then Ni Erh's wife and daughter told him their story.

"We've come to beg you to put in a word, Second Master, to get him set free," they entreated.

"That's easy," Chia Yun bragged. "As soon as I mention this to the West Mansion he'll be released. This Mr. Chia Yu-tsun owes his high post to the help of the Jung Mansion, so once they send him a message the thing will be settled."

Mother and daughter went joyfully home, then took word to Ni Erh in the lock-up that he need not fret because Chia Yun had promised to see about his release. Ni Erh's spirits rose again.

However, since the embarrassing occasion when Hsi-feng had declined his presents, Chia Yun had seldom called at the Jung Mansion. For the gatemen there watched their masters' behaviour to visitors and acted accordingly. Welcome guests who were treated with favour they announced; but those who were cold-shouldered they turned away, even if they were relatives, fobbing them off with excuses.

Today Chia Yun went to the gate saying that he had come to pay his respects to Chia Lien.

"The Second Master is out," the gatemen told him. "We'll tell him when he comes back that you called."

Chia Yun thought of asking to see Hsi-feng instead, but for fear of another snub he refrained and went home, where Ni Erh's wife and daughter importuned him again.

"You always said that not a single yamen, no matter which, dared disobey your family," they said. "Now this prefect is one of your clan, and it's not a big favour to ask. If you can't even do this, you're one of the Chias in vain!"

"Yesterday I was too busy to send a message, but today I'll tell them and he'll be released," he boasted to cover up his discomfiture. "You've nothing to worry about!"

So mother and daughter waited again for news. As for Chia Yun, unable to gain admission through the main gate, this time he went round to the back, meaning to go through the Garden to find Pao-yu. But the back gate was locked. He retraced his steps dejectedly, telling himself, "I wangled a tree-planting job from her that year because Ni Erh lent me money and I sent in that gift of aromatics. Now that I've no money for gifts she won't let me in. It's not as if she's a decent sort. She simply loans out the family's funds left by our ancestors at exorbitant interest, but won't let us poor relations have even one ounce of silver! Can they count on remaining rich all their lives? Why, their name stinks outside! I'm not one to blab — if I were, they would be involved in plenty of murder cases!"

Occupied by these reflections he reached home, where Ni Erh's wife and daughter were waiting for him. Unable to put them off again he told them, "The West Mansion sent a message but Prefect Chia has ignored it. You had better get Leng Tzu-hsing, who's related to their steward Chou Jui, to put in a word."

Mother and daughter objected, "If a gentleman like you failed, how could a servant succeed?"

"You don't understand," he blurted out in embarrassed exasperation. "Nowadays servants have much more say than their masters."

Seeing that he was unable to help, Mrs. Ni laughed sarcastically.

"Sorry to have troubled you for nothing these days," she said. "We shall thank you again when that man of mine comes out."

They left to ask others to intercede, and finally Ni Erh was let off with only a few strokes, not convicted of any crime.

On his return, his wife and daughter told him how the Chia family had refused to help. Ni Erh, who was drinking, flared up and wanted to seek Chia Yun out.

"The bastard, the ungrateful beast!" he fumed. "When he was starving and wanted to worm his way into that house to wangle a job, I was the one who helped him. Now when I land in trouble he leaves me in the lurch. Fine! If Ni Erh raises a row, both the Chia Mansions will be dragged through the mud!"

"Ai! You're drunk again, talking so wildly," they objected. "Weren't you beaten the other day for making a drunken scene? Before you've got over it, here you are starting again!"

"Do you think a beating makes me afraid of them? I was only afraid of not finding a handle against them. In jail, I palled up with quite a few decent fellows. According to them, apart from all these Chias here in the city there are plenty of others in the provinces too, and not long ago a number of their servants were put in clink. I'd always known the younger Chia men and their servants here were a bad lot but thought the older generation all right, so I was surprised to hear they'd landed in trouble. After asking around I heard that those in trouble belong to branches of the clan in other provinces. Now they are on trial, brought here to wait for the verdict. So I no longer need worry.

"As this puppy Chia Yun has let me down for all I was so good to him, my friends and I can spread word that their family's ridden roughshod over people, practised usury and abducted other men's wives. When the scandal spreads and reaches the censor's ears they'll catch it! Then they'll get to know Ni Erh the Diamond!"

"Go to bed and sleep it off," urged his wife. "Whose wives have they abducted? You're making it up. You mustn't talk such nonsense."

"Staying at home, what do *you* know about what goes on outside? The year before last I met a young fellow called Chang in a gambling-den, and he told me that his betrothed had been bagged by the Chias. He asked my advice, and I stopped him from making a row. I don't know where he is now, I haven't seen him for the last couple of years. If I knock into him, I'll fix up a plan to do in that young bastard Chia Yun! I won't let him off unless he offers me rich gifts! How dare he refuse to help me?"

He lay down, muttered for a while to himself, then dozed off. His wife and daughter paid no attention, considering these threats mere drunken talk. The next morning Ni Erh went back to his gambling-house, and there we can leave him.

Upon Chia Yu-tsun's return home, after a night's rest he told his wife of his encounter with Chen Shih-yin.

"Why didn't you go back to have a look?" she asked reproachfully, shedding tears. "If he got burnt to death, won't we seem too heartless?"

"He's outside the mundane world now and wouldn't have anything to do with us," Yu-tsun assured her.

Just then a servant outside announced, "The man Your Honour left at the temple after the fire the other day has come back."

Yu-tsun went out and that runner, having paid his respects, reported, "After going back on Your Honour's orders, I didn't wait for the fire to burn out but went in through the flames to look for the priest. The fire had burnt the place where he had been sitting and the back wall had collapsed, so I expected to find him dead, but there was no sign of him, although a hassock and gourd there were undamaged. I looked everywhere for his corpse, yet found not a single bone. For fear that you might not believe me, I decided to bring back the hassock and gourd as evidence; but when I touched them they both turned to ashes!"

Yu-tsun realized that Chen Shih-yin had vanished by magic, being an immortal. He dismissed the runner and went back to his room but did not repeat this message to his wife for fear that she as an ignorant woman might grieve, simply telling her that there was no trace of the priest so most likely he had escaped.

Then he went out and sat alone in his study to mull over Chen Shih-yin's conversation with him, when a servant suddenly brought him a summons to court to read some edicts. He

hastily mounted his chair to go to the Palace, where he heard
that Chia Cheng, recalled from his post as Grain Commissioner
of Kiangsi, was to acknowledge his fault today at court.

He hurried to the cabinet and found the ministers assembled
there reading an Imperial edict deploring the maladministration
of the coastal provinces. Coming out, he went at once to find
Chia Cheng, expressed his sympathy over his impeachment, then
congratulated him on his return and asked about his journey.
Chia Cheng described his experiences since last they met.

"Have you sent in your acknowledgement of culpability?"
asked Yu-tsun.

"Yes. After lunch I shall learn the Emperor's will."

That very moment he was summoned to an audience and hurried in, while the ministers concerned for him waited there.

It was some time before Chia Cheng emerged, his face streaming with sweat. The others crowded round to ask what had
happened. He stuck out his tongue in dismay.

"I had the fright of my life!" he gasped. "Thank you,
gentlemen, for your concern. Luckily nothing serious has happened."

They asked him what the Emperor had said.

"His Majesty wanted to know about the smuggling of firearms
in Yunnan," Chia Cheng told them. "It was reported that the
culprit was a servant of the former Senior Imperial Tutor Chia
Hua, which reminded His Majesty of my ancestor's name, and
he asked me what it was. At once I kowtowed and replied
that it was Chia Tai-hua. Then the Emperor asked with a smile,
'Wasn't that former Minister of War who was later demoted to
be prefect of the capital also called Chia Hua?'"

Yu-tsun beside him gave a start. "What was your reply, sir?"
he asked.

"I explained distinctly that the former Senior Imperial Tutor
Chia Hua came from Yunnan, the present prefect from Huchow
in Chekiang. Then His Majesty asked, 'Is that Chia Fan impeached by the prefect of Soochow one of your family?' Kowtowing again I said, 'Yes, sir.' Then the Emperor demanded
angrily, 'How can your family allow your servants to abduct

a good citizen's wife?' I dared say nothing. 'What is Chia Fan's relation to you?' was the next question. 'He's a distant kinsman,' I said. The Emperor snorted at that and dismissed me. It was touch-and-go!"

"Quite a coincidence that," they commented, "these two cases one after the other."

"That's not so strange," said Chia Cheng. "What's bad is both men being Chias. Our poor clan is such a large one that after all these years we have relatives everywhere. Though no trouble came of it this time, the name Chia will stick in the Emperor's mind — and that's bad."

"Truth will always prevail," they assured him. "You've nothing to fear."

"I would give anything not to be an official, but I dare not retire. Besides, our family has two hereditary titles. This is something that can't be helped."

"You are still in the Ministry of Works, sir," pointed out Yu-tsun. "A metropolitan post should be quite safe."

"Even so, that's hard to say after two provincial appointments."

"We admire your character and your conduct, sir," the other officials told him. "Your brother is a man of honour too. All you need do is control your nephews more strictly."

"I am seldom at home to check up on them and can't be too easy in my mind about them. Since you've brought this up and we are close friends, please tell me — have my nephews in the East Mansion been misconducting themselves?"

"Not really, but a few vice-ministers — some Imperial eunuchs too — are not on very good terms with them. It's nothing to worry about if you just warn them to be more circumspect in future."

They saluted him and left, and Chia Cheng went home. All his nephews and sons had turned out to welcome him, and when he had asked after the old lady's health and the young men had paid their respects, together they entered the house. Lady Wang and the other womenfolk had assembled in the Hall of Glorious Felicity to meet him, but first he went to the old lady's apartments to pay her his respects and report to her all that had happened since his departure. Asked for news of Tan-chun, he described the marriage arrangements.

"I had to leave in too much of a hurry to wait for the Double Ninth Festival," he explained. "But though I didn't see her, I heard from the other family that everything went very well. Her father- and mother-in-law send their regards to you, madam. They hope, this winter or next spring, to be transferred to the capital, which would of course be still better. But I hear there is trouble in the coastal regions, so the transfer may be delayed."

The old lady had been depressed by Chia Cheng's demotion and Tan-chun's marrying so far from home; but his explanation of his recall and the good news of Tan-chun cheered her up again and with a smile she urged him to go and rest. Chia Cheng saw his brother, sons and nephews next, and when the younger ones had paid their respects he informed them that the next morning he would sacrifice in the ancestral temple.

After Chia Cheng's return to his quarters, when Lady Wang and others had greeted him, Pao-yu and Chia Lien paid their respects again. Chia Cheng was relieved to see Pao-yu looking better than at the time of his departure and, knowing nothing of his son's mental illness, he did not regret his demotion but was pleased to think how well the old lady had managed things. When, moreover, he observed that Pao-chai appeared still more quiet and composed and Lan quite cultured and handsome, he fairly beamed. Only Huan was unchanged, and his father could feel no real affection for him.

After a short rest, however, he asked abruptly, "Isn't there someone missing?"

Lady Wang knew he had noticed Tai-yu's absence. As they had not written to him about her death and he was only just home and in high spirits, she did not like to break the news at once. She just said that Tai-yu was unwell. Pao-yu felt as if his heart had been pierced by a dagger, but as his father was back he had to repress his grief and wait on him. Lady Wang ordered a feast of welcome at which Chia Cheng's sons and

grandsons poured him wine; and though Hsi-feng was the wife
of a nephew, since she was running the household she joined
Pao-chai and the others in passing the wine. After one round of
toasts, Chia Cheng sent them away to rest and dismissed the
servants too with instructions that the domestics could come
to meet him after the ancestral sacrifice the next day.

When the others had gone, he and his wife talked of the
happenings since their separation. Certain subjects Lady Wang
did not venture to broach, and when he brought up the death
of her brother Wang Tzu-teng she dared not show her grief.
When he mentioned Hsueh Pan, she said simply that he had
brought this trouble on himself, then she took this occasion to
tell him about Tai-yu's death. In consternation, Chia Cheng
shed tears and sighed. Then Lady Wang gave way to weeping
too until Tsai-yun who was attending her tugged her sleeve.
She controlled herself then and talked of more cheerful topics,
after which they retired for the night.

The next morning Chia Cheng worshipped in the ancestral
temple, accompanied by all the younger male members of the
family. This done, he took a seat in the temple annex and
called Chia Chen and Chia Lien in to ask about family affairs.
Chia Chen gave him a carefully edited account.

"Since I've just come home I can't make a detailed check-up,"
Chia Cheng told him. "But I've heard outside that your household isn't doing as well as before. You must be more circumspect in everything. You are no longer young, and you should
discipline those youngsters so that they don't offend people
outside. You take this to heart too, Lien. It's not that I want
to find fault as soon as I get back, but I've heard talk. You
must take extra care."

Chia Chen and Chia Lien flushed red, not venturing to answer
more than "Yes, sir." Then Chia Cheng dismissed them and
went back to the West Mansion. After all the men-servants
had kowtowed to him he entered the inner quarters where the
women-servants paid their respects in turn — we need not dwell
on this.

Chia Cheng's question about Tai-yu the previous day and Lady Wang's reply that she was unwell had set Pao-yu brooding again. After his father dismissed him he went back, shedding tears all the way. As Pao-chai was chatting in his room with Hsi-jen and others, he sat gloomily by himself in the outer room. Pao-chai told Hsi-jen to take him tea then came out to cheer him up, imagining that he was worried that his father might question him about his studies.

"You go to bed first," said Pao-yu. "I want to collect my thoughts a bit. My memory's not what it was, and if I keep forgetting what to say it'll make a bad impression on my father. If you go to sleep first, Hsi-jen can keep me company here."

Pao-chai could not refuse and nodded agreement.

In the outer room, Pao-yu softly begged Hsi-jen to fetch Tzu-chuan.

"I've something to ask her," he said. "But as she always looks so angry and cold-shoulders me when she sees me, you must do some explaining for me before she'll come."

Hsi-jen answered, "I was pleased to hear that you wanted to collect your thoughts, but what's this you're thinking about? If you've something on your mind, why not ask her tomorrow?"

"I'm only free this evening. Tomorrow the master may give me something to do and keep me busy. Dear sister, please fetch her quickly!"

"She won't come unless Madam Pao sends for her."

"That's why I want you to go and persuade her."

"What should I say?"

"You understand how I feel and how she feels — both of us because of Miss Lin. Tell her that I wasn't faithless to her. It was you people who made me look faithless." He glanced towards the inner room and pointing at it continued, "I never wanted to marry *her*, but they tricked me into it — the old lady and others — and that was the death of poor Cousin Lin. But even so, they should have let me see her and clear myself — then she wouldn't have died with such a sense of grievance! You must have heard from Miss Tan-chun and the others that, at the last, she reproached me angrily. And Tzu-chuan hates me like poison because of her.

"But how can you think me so heartless? Ching-wen was only a maid who didn't mean so much to me, yet the truth is that when she died I wrote an elegy for her and sacrificed to her. Miss Lin saw that for herself. Now that Miss Lin is dead, would I treat her worse than Ching-wen? But I can't even sacrifice to her. Besides, her spirit is living on; so when she thinks about this won't she blame me still more?"

"You can sacrifice to her if you like," said Hsi-jen. "What do you want of me?"

"Since my health started improving I've been wanting to write an elegy but somehow I've grown dim-witted. I can sacrifice any old way to other people, but there mustn't be anything the least bit crude about a sacrifice to *her*. So I want to find out from Tzu-chuan what her mistress was thinking and how she detected it. Before my illness I could have figured it out, but now I can't remember a thing. You told me that Miss Lin was getting better; how did she come to die so suddenly? What did she say when she was well and I didn't go to see her? She didn't call when I was ill, and how did she explain that? And why is it your mistress never lets me touch those things of hers which I managed to get hold of?"

"She's afraid they might upset you, that's all."

"I don't believe it. If Miss Lin felt for me, why did she burn her poems before she died instead of leaving them to me as a memento? I heard tell that music sounded in the sky, so she must have become a goddess or an immortal. I saw her coffin, it's true, but who knows whether she was in it or not?"

"You're talking more and more nonsensically. How could anyone announce a death simply by displaying an empty coffin?"

"I didn't mean that!" he cried. "But when people become immortals, some retain their bodily form, others shed their mortal frame. Good sister, *please* fetch Tzu-chuan for me!"

"You'll have to wait till I've explained to her just how you feel. If she's willing to come, all right; if she refuses it may take time to talk her round. But even if she comes, at sight of *you* she's bound to hold certain things back. It seems to me I'd better question her tomorrow after Madam Pao has gone to see the old lady. That way I may find out more. Then when there's time to spare, I'll tell you about it."

"That's all very well, but I'm too impatient to wait!"

At this point Sheh-yueh came out. "The young mistress says it's already the fourth watch and she wants the young master to go to bed," she announced. "And Sister Hsi-jen must have been enjoying her chat so much that she lost track of the time."

"That's right!" exclaimed Hsi-jen. "It's time to go to bed. We can talk again tomorrow."

Though distressed, Pao-yu had to comply, but as he was leaving he whispered, "Mind you don't forget tomorrow!"

Hsi-jen smiled and said, "All right."

"You two are up to some tricks again," Sheh-yueh teased. "Why not ask the mistress to let you sleep with Hsi-jen, then you can talk all night for all we care."

Pao-yu waved his hand saying, "There's no need for that."

"You bitch, talking such rot!" scolded Hsi-jen. "Tomorrow I'll pinch your lips." She turned to Pao-yu. "Look at all the trouble you've caused. Sitting up so late talking but without so much as a word about this." They escorted him to the inner room then went to bed themselves.

Pao-yu could not sleep that night, and he was still thinking of Tai-yu the next day when a servant brought in the message, "Relatives and friends have offered to send over operas and feasts to celebrate the master's return; but the master has declined. He says there's no need for operas, but we'll have a simple meal at home to invite them all for a chat. The date fixed is the day after tomorrow, so I've come to notify you."

To know what visitors came, turn to the next chapter.

CHAPTER 105

Imperial Guards Raid the Ning Mansion
A Censor Brings a Charge Against
the Prefect of Pingan

Chia Cheng was entertaining his guests in the Hall of Glorious Felicity when in burst Lai Ta.

"Commissioner Chao of the Imperial Guards and several of his officers are here to see you, sir," he announced. "When I asked for their cards the commissioner said, 'No need: we are old friends.' He dismounted from his carriage and came straight in. Please make haste to meet them, sir, with the young gentlemen."

Chia Cheng, who had had no dealings with Commissioner Chao, could not understand why he should have come uninvited. As he had guests he could hardly entertain him, yet not to ask him in would be discourteous.

He was thinking it over when Chia Lien urged, "Better go at once, uncle, before they all come in."

That same moment a servant from the inner gate announced, "Commissioner Chao has entered the inner gate."

Chia Cheng and others hastily went to meet him. The commissioner, smiling, said not a word as he walked straight into the hall. Behind him were five or six of his officers, only a few of whom they recognized, but none of these answered their greetings. At a loss, Chia Cheng had to offer them seats. Certain of the guests knew Commissioner Chao, yet with his head in the air he ignored them all, simply taking Chia Cheng's hand as he made a few conventional remarks. This looked so ominous that some of the guests slipped into the inner room while all the rest stood at respectful attention.

Chia Cheng, forcing a smile, was about to make conversation

when a flustered servant announced the Prince of Hsiping.
Before he could hasten to meet him the prince had entered.

Commissioner Chao stepped forward at once to salute him,
then ordered his officers, "Since His Highness has arrived, you
gentlemen can take runners to guard the front and back gates."

His officers assented and went out. Chia Cheng, knowing
that this spelt trouble, fell on his knees to welcome the prince,
who helped him to his feet with a smile.

"We wouldn't presume to intrude without special reason,"
he said. "We have come to announce an Imperial decree to
Lord Sheh. You have many feasters here, which is somewhat
inopportune, so I'll ask your relatives and friends to disperse,
leaving only your own household to hear the decree."

Commissioner Chao put in, "Your Highness is very gracious,
but the prince officiating at the East Mansion takes his duties
so seriously that the gates are doubtless already sealed up."

Hearing that both mansions were involved, the guests were
desperate to extricate themselves.

"These gentlemen are free to go," the prince said affably.
"Have attendants see them out and notify your guards that there
is no need to search them as they are all guests. Let them leave
at once."

Then those relatives and friends streaked off like lightning,
leaving Chia Cheng, Chia Sheh and their households livid and
trembling with fear. Meanwhile runners had swarmed in to
guard all the doors, so that no one — whether master or man —
could stir a foot from his place.

Commissioner Chao turned to request the prince, "Please read
the decree, Your Highness, then we can start the search."

The runners hitched up their tunics and rolled up their sleeves,
ready to go into action.

The Prince of Hsiping proclaimed slowly, "His Majesty has
ordered me to bring Chao Chuan of the Imperial Guards to
search Chia Sheh's property."

Chia Sheh and the rest prostrated themselves on the ground.

The prince, standing on the dais, continued, "Hear the Imperial decree: Chia Sheh has intrigued with provincial officials

and abused his power to molest the weak, showing himself unworthy of Our favour and sullying his ancestors' good name. His hereditary rank is hereby abolished."

Commissioner Chao thundered, "Arrest Chia Sheh! Keep guard over the others."

At that time, all the men of both Chia Mansions were in the hall except for Pao-yu, who had slipped off to join the old lady on the pretext of indisposition, and Chia Huan who was seldom presented to guests. So all the rest were now under surveillance.

Commissioner Chao told his men to dispatch officers and runners to search the different apartments and draw up an inventory. This order made Chia Cheng's household exchange consternated glances, while the runners gleefully rubbed their hands, eager to ransack the place.

The prince interposed, "We hear that Lord Sheh and Lord Cheng keep separate accounts, and according to the decree we are to search the former's property. The rest is to be sealed up pending further orders."

Commissioner Chao rose to his feet. "May it please Your Highness," he said, "Chia Sheh and Chia Cheng have not divided the family property, and we hear that Chia Cheng has put his nephew Chia Lien in charge of his household affairs. We shall therefore have to search the whole premises." When the prince made no comment he added, "I must go in person with my officers to search the houses of Chia Sheh and Chia Lien."

"There is no hurry," demurred the prince. "Send word first so that the ladies inside may withdraw before you start to search."

But already the commissioner's attendants and runners, making the Chias' servants show them the way, had set off in different directions to ransack both mansions.

"No disorder now!" called the prince sternly. "I shall come in person to supervise the search!" Then getting up slowly he ordered, "None of those who came with me are to move. Wait here. Later we shall check up on the property and make an inventory."

Just then a guard came in and knelt to report, "In the inner apartments we have found some clothes from the Palace and other forbidden things which we haven't presumed to touch. I have come, Your Highness, to ask for your orders."

Presently another group gathered round the prince to report, "In Chia Lien's house we have found two cases of title-deeds and one of promissory notes — all at illegally exorbitant rates of interest."

"Good!" cried Commissioner Chao. "So they are usurers too. All their property should certainly be confiscated! Please rest here, Your Highness, while I supervise the search before coming back for your instructions."

Just then, however, the prince's steward announced, "The guards at the gate say that His Majesty has sent the Prince of Peiching to proclaim another decree and they ask the commissioner to receive him."

As Commissioner Chao started out to meet the Prince of Peiching he told himself, "I was out of luck having that crabbed prince foisted on me. Now, with this other one here, I should be able to crack down on them hard!"

The Prince of Peiching had already entered the hall. Standing facing the doorway he announced, "Here is a decree. Let Chao Chuan, Commissioner of the Imperial Guards, pay heed." He then proclaimed, "The commissioner's sole task is to arrest Chia Sheh for trial. The Prince of Hsiping will determine what other measures to take according to the earlier decree."

Elated by this, the Prince of Hsiping seated himself beside the Prince of Peiching and sent the commissioner back to his yamen with Chia Sheh. This development disappointed all his officers and runners, who had come out on hearing of the second prince's arrival. They had to stand there awaiting Their Highnesses' orders. The Prince of Peiching selected two honest officers and a dozen of the older runners, sending away the rest.

The Prince of Hsiping told him, "I was just losing patience with Old Chao. If you hadn't brought that decree in the nick of time, sir, they'd have been really hard hit here."

"When I heard at court that Your Highness had been sent to search the Chia Mansions I was relieved, knowing you would let them off more lightly," the Prince of Peiching replied. "I never thought Old Chao was such a scoundrel. But where are Chia Cheng and Pao-yu now? And how much damage has been done inside?"

His men reported, "Chia Cheng and the rest are under guard in the servants' quarters, and the whole place has been turned upside-down."

At the Prince of Peiching's orders, the officers fetched Chia Cheng for questioning. He fell on his knees before Their Highnesses and with tears in his eyes begged for mercy. The prince helped him up and urged him not to worry, then informed him of the terms of the new decree. With tears of gratitude, Chia Cheng kowtowed towards the north to thank the Emperor then turned back for further instructions.

The prince said, "When Old Chao was here just now, Your Lordship, his runners reported finding various articles for Imperial use and some promissory notes for usurious loans — this we cannot cover up. Regarding those forbidden articles, as they were for Her Imperial Highness' use it will do no harm to report them. But we must find some way to explain those IOU's. Now I want you, sir, to take the officers and honestly hand over to them all your brother's property, to end the matter. Don't on any account conceal anything, or you will be asking for trouble."

"I would never dare," answered Chia Cheng. "But we never divided up our ancestral estate, simply considering the things in our two houses as our own property."

"Very well," they said. "Just hand over everything in Lord Sheh's house." They sent the two officers off with orders to attend only to this and nothing else.

Let us return now to the ladies' feast in the Lady Dowager's quarters. Lady Wang had just warned Pao-yu that unless he went out to join the gentlemen his father might be angry.

Hsi-feng, still unwell, said faintly, "I don't think Pao-yu's

afraid of meeting them, but he knows there are plenty of people there to entertain the guests, so he's waiting on us here instead. If it occurs to the master that they need more people there to look after the guests, you can trot out Pao-yu, madam. How about that?"

"This minx Hsi-feng!" the old lady chuckled. "She still has the gift of the gab for all she's so ill!"

The fun was at its height when one of Lady Hsing's maids came rushing in crying, "Your Ladyships! We're done for! A whole lot of robbers have come, all in boots and official caps. . . . They're opening cases, overturning crates, ransacking the whole place! . . ."

The old lady and the others had not recovered from this shock when Ping-erh, her hair hanging loose, dashed in with Chiao-chieh.

"We're ruined!" she wailed. "I was having lunch with Chiao-chieh when Lai Wang appeared, in chains, and told me to lose no time in warning you ladies to keep out of the way, as some prince has come to raid our house! I nearly died of fright! Before I could go in to fetch any valuables, a band of men drove me out. You'd better make haste to get together the clothes and things you need."

Lady Hsing and Lady Wang were completely flummoxed, frightened out of their wits. Hsi-feng who had listened wide-eyed now collapsed in a faint. The old lady was crying with terror, unable to utter a word.

Pandemonium reigned as the maids tried to attend to their mistresses. Then they heard shouts, "The women inside must make themselves scarce! The prince is coming!"

Pao-chai and Pao-yu looked on helplessly as the maids and nurses attempted desperately to hustle the ladies out. Then in ran Chia Lien.

"It's all right now!" he panted. "Thank goodness the prince has come to our rescue!"

Before they could question him, he saw Hsi-feng lying as if dead on the floor and gave a cry of alarm. Then the sight of the old lady, terror-stricken and gasping for breath, made him even more frantic. Luckily Ping-erh and others managed to revive Hsi-feng and help her up. The old lady recovered consciousness too, but lay back dizzily on the couch sobbing and choking for breath, while Li Wan did her best to soothe her.

Taking a grip on himself, Chia Lien explained to them how kindly the two princes had intervened. But fearing that the news of Chia Sheh's arrest might make the old lady and Lady Hsing die of fright, he withheld it for the time being and went back to his own quarters.

Once over the threshold, he saw that all their cases and wardrobes had been opened and rifled. He stood speechless in consternation, shedding tears, till he heard his name called and had to go out. Chia Cheng was there with two officers drawing up an inventory, which one of the officers read out as follows:

One hundred and twenty-three gold trinkets set with jewels; thirteen strings of pearls; two pale gold plates; two pairs of gold bowls; two gilded bowls; forty gold spoons; eighty big silver bowls and twenty silver plates; two pairs of ivory chopsticks inlaid with gold; four gilded pots; three pairs of gilded cups; two tea-trays; seventy-six silver saucers; thirty-six silver cups; eighteen black fox furs; six deep-grey fox furs; thirty-six sable furs; thirty yellow fox furs; twelve ermine furs; three grey fox furs; sixty marten furs; forty grey fox-leg furs; twenty brown sheep-skins; two raccoon furs; two bundles of yellow fox-leg furs; twenty pieces of white fox fur; thirty lengths of Western worsted; twenty-three lengths of serge; twelve lengths of velveteen; twenty musk-rat furs; four pieces of spotted squirrel fur; one bolt of velvet; one piece of plum-deer skin; two fox furs with ornamental cloud patterns; a roll of badger-cub skin; seven bundles of platypus fur; a hundred and sixty squirrel furs; eight male wolf-skins; six tiger-skins; three seal-skins; sixteen otter furs; forty bundles of grey sheep-skins; sixty-three black sheep-skins; ten sets of red fox-fur hat material; twelve sets of black fox-fur hat material; two sets of sable-fur hat material; sixteen small fox furs; two beaver-skins; two otter-skins; thirty-five civet-cat furs; twelve lengths of Japanese silk; one hundred and thirty bolts of satin; one hundred and eighty-one bolts of gauze; thirty-two bolts of crepe; thirty bolts of Tibetan serge; eight bolts of satin with serpent designs; three bales of hemp-cloth; three bales of different kinds of cloth; one hundred fur coats; thirty-two Tibetan serge garments; three hundred and forty padded and unpadded garments; thirty-two jade articles; nine jade buckles; over five hundred utensils of copper and tin; eighteen clocks and watches; nine chaplets; thirty-two lengths of different kinds of satin with

serpent designs; three satin cushions with serpent designs for Imperial use; eight costumes for Palace ladies; one white jade belt;
twelve bolts of yellow satin; seven thousand and two hundred
taels of silver; fifty taels of gold; seven thousand strings of cash.

Separate lists were made of all the furnishings and the mansions conferred on the Duke of Jungkuo. The title-deeds of
houses and land and the bonds of the family slaves were also
sealed up.

Chia Lien, listening at one side, was puzzled not to hear his
own property listed.

Then the two princes said, "Among the property confiscated
are some IOU's which are definitely usurious. Whose are they?
Your Lordship must tell the truth."

Chia Cheng knelt down and kowtowed. "I am guilty of
never having managed the household affairs and that is the
truth," he said. "I know nothing about such transactions. Your
Highnesses will have to ask my nephew Chia Lien."

Chia Lien hastily stepped forward and knelt to report, "Since
those documents were found in my humble house, how can I
deny knowledge of them? I only beg Your Highnesses to be
lenient to my uncle who knew nothing about this."

The two princes said, "As your father has already been found
guilty, your cases can be dealt with together. You did right
to admit this. Very well then, let a guard be kept over Chia
Lien; the rest of the household can return to their different
quarters. Lord Cheng, you must wait prudently for a further
decree. We shall go now to report to His Majesty, leaving
officers and runners here to keep watch."

They mounted their sedan-chairs, Chia Cheng and the others
kneeling at the inner gate to see them off. The Prince of Peiching, on leaving, stretched out one hand with a look of compassion and said, "Please set your minds at rest."

By now Chia Cheng felt slightly calmer, although still dazed.

Chia Lan suggested, "Grandfather, won't you go in to see
the old lady first? Then we can send for news of the East
Mansion."

Chia Cheng hastily did so, and found serving-women from

different apartments all milling about in confusion. In no mood to check what they were doing he entered his mother's room, where one and all were in tears. Lady Wang, Pao-yu and others had gathered silently around the old lady, tears streaming down their cheeks. Lady Hsing was shaken by sobs. At his arrival they exclaimed in relief.

"The master has come back safely," they told the old lady. "Don't worry any more, madam."

The Lady Dowager, apparently at her last gasp, feebly opened her eyes and quavered, "My son, I never thought to see you again!"

She burst out weeping and all the others joined in until Chia Cheng, fearing these transports of grief might be too much for his mother, held back his tears.

"Set your heart at rest, madam," he urged. "It is a serious matter, but His Gracious Majesty and the two princes have shown us the kindest consideration. The Elder Master has been taken into custody for the time being; but once the matter is cleared up the Emperor will show more clemency. And our property is not being confiscated."

Chia Sheh's arrest distressed the old lady anew, and Chia Cheng did his best to comfort her.

Lady Hsing was the only one who ventured to leave, going back to her apartments. She found the doors sealed up and locked, the serving-women confined in a few rooms. Unable to get in she burst out wailing, then made her way back to Hsi-feng's apartments. The side-gate there was also sealed, but Hsi-feng's room was open and from it came the sound of continuous sobbing. Entering, she saw Hsi-feng lying with closed eyes, her face ashen-pale, while Ping-erh wept beside her. Thinking her dead, Lady Hsing started sobbing too.

"Don't cry, madam," said Ping-erh, stepping forward to greet her. "We carried her back just now in a dead faint, but presently she came to and cried a little. Now she is quieter. Please calm down, madam. How is the old lady now?"

Lady Hsing made no answer but went to rejoin the Lady Dowager. The only people there were members of Chia Cheng's household, and she could not hold back her grief at the thought that both her husband and son had been arrested, her daughter-in-law was at death's door, and her daughter was ill-treated by her husband, so that she had nowhere to turn. The others tried to console her. Li Wan told servants to clear out some rooms for her for the time being, and Lady Wang assigned maids to look after her.

Chia Cheng outside was on tenterhooks, tweaking his beard and wringing his hands as he waited for the Emperor's next decree.

"Which house do you belong to anyway?" he heard the guards outside shouting. "As you've come butting in here, we'll put you down on our list and chain you up to hand over to the officers inside."

Chia Cheng went out and saw it was Chiao Ta.

"Why did you come here?" he asked.

Chiao Ta stamped his foot and wailed, "I warned those degenerate masters of ours all along, but they treated me as their sworn enemy! Even you don't know, sir, what hardships I endured serving the old duke. Now things have come to a pretty pass with Sir Chen and Jung arrested by some princes' officers! The ladies' trinkets were looted by the officers and runners and they were shut up in an empty room! And those useless slaves cooped up like pigs and dogs! Everything has been confiscated, furniture broken in pieces, porcelain smashed — they even want to put *me* in chains too! I've lived eighty to ninety years and trussed people up for the old duke; how can I let myself be trussed up instead? I told them I belonged to the West Mansion and broke out, but those fellows wouldn't let me go. They hauled me here, where I find things are just as bad. I'm sick of life — I'll have it out with them!" With that he butted the runners.

As he was so old and their orders were not to make trouble, the runners simply said, "Pipe down, old man. This is done by Imperial decree. You'd better take it easy and wait for news."

Although Chia Cheng tried to ignore this, he felt as if a

knife had been plunged in his heart. "We're done for, done for!" he sighed. "To think that we should be reduced to this!"

As he was waiting impatiently for news from court, Hsueh Ko came running in. "What a time I had getting in here!" he panted. "Where is uncle?"

"Thank Heaven you've come!" Chia Cheng exclaimed. "How did you gain admittance?"

"By pleading hard and promising them money."

Chia Cheng described the raid to him and asked him to make inquiries. "I can't very well send messages to other relatives and friends now that we're under fire," he explained. "But you can deliver messages for me."

"It never occurred to me that you'd have trouble here, sir; but I've heard something about the East Mansion's business."

"What exactly are the charges against them?"

"Today I went to the yamen to find out what Cousin Pan's sentence is, and I heard that two censors have accused Cousin Chen of corrupting young nobles by getting them to gamble — that isn't so serious. The more serious charge is of abducting the wife of an honest citizen, who was forced to kill herself rather than submit. To bring this charge home, the censors got our man Pao Erh and a fellow called Chang as witnesses. This may involve the Court of Censors too, as that fellow Chang had brought a suit before."

Chia Cheng stamped his foot. "Terrible! We're done for!" he sighed, tears streaming down his cheeks.

Hsueh Ko tried to reassure him then went off to find out more news, returning a few hours later.

"It looks bad," he informed him. "When I asked at the Board of Punishments, I didn't hear the result of the two princes' report but was told that this morning Censor Li brought another charge against the prefect of Pingan, accusing him of pandering to an official in the capital and oppressing the people to please his superior — there were several serious charges."

"Never mind about other people," said Chia Cheng impatiently. "What did you hear about *us*?"

"That charge against the prefect of Pingan involves us too, sir. The official in the capital referred to by the censor was Lord Sheh, who's accused of tampering with lawsuits. This adds fuel to the flames! All your colleagues are trying hard to keep out of this, so who would send you word? Even those relatives and friends at your feast either went home or are keeping well away until they know the upshot. Some clansmen of yours — confound them! — have been saying openly, 'Their ancestors left them property and titles. Now that they're in trouble who knows whom the title may go to. We all ought to take steps....'"

Without hearing him out Chia Cheng stamped his foot again. "What a fool my brother is!" he groaned. "It's a scandal, too, the way they've carried on in the East Mansion! For all we know this may be the death of the old lady and Lien's wife! Go and see what more you can find out while I look in on the old lady. If there's any news, the sooner we know it the better."

Just then a great commotion broke out inside and they heard cries of "The old lady's dying!" Chia Cheng hurried anxiously in. To know whether she lived or died, you must read the next chapter.

CHAPTER 106

Hsi-feng Is Conscience-Smitten
at Causing Calamity
The Lady Dowager Prays to Heaven
to Avert Disaster

The cry that the Lady Dowager was dying made Chia Cheng speed over to see her. She had in fact fainted from shock, but Lady Wang, Yuan-yang and the rest had revived her and given her a sedative which had gradually restored her, though she was still crying for grief.

In the hope of soothing her he said, "Your unfilial sons have brought this trouble upon our family, alarming you, madam. If you will take comfort, we can still handle the situation outside; but if you fall ill our guilt will be even greater!"

"I'm four score years and more," was her reply. "Ever since my girlhood when I married your father, thanks to our ancestors I've lived in the lap of luxury and never even heard tell of a nightmare like this. Now, in my old age, seeing you come to grief — it's too bad! I wish I could die and be done with worrying about you!" She broke down again.

Chia Cheng was at his wit's end when a servant outside announced a messenger from the court. He went out at once and saw that it was the Prince of Peiching's chamberlain.

"Good news, sir!" were the chamberlain's first words.

Chia Cheng thanked him and offered him a seat. "What instructions has His Highness for me?" he asked.

"Our master and the Prince of Hsiping reported to the Emperor your trepidation, sir, and your gratitude for His Majesty's magnanimity. As it is not long since the Imperial Consort's passing, His Majesty, being most merciful, cannot bring himself to condemn you. You are to retain your post in the Ministry of Works. Regarding the family property, only Chia Sheh's share is to be confiscated; the rest will be restored to you and you are enjoined to work well. As for those promissory notes, our master has been ordered to examine them. All those at usurious, illegal rates of interest are to be confiscated according to regulations. Those on which the standard rates are charged are to be returned to you, together with your title-deeds. Chia Lien is dismissed from his post, but will be released without further punishment."

Chia Cheng rose to kowtow his thanks to the Emperor, then bowed his thanks to the prince.

"I beg you, sir, to report my gratitude now," he said. "Tomorrow I shall go to court to express my thanks, then go to your mansion to kowtow to His Highness."

Soon after the chamberlain had left the Imperial edict arrived and was put into force by the officers in charge, who confiscated certain things, returning the rest. Chia Lien was released, while all Chia Sheh's men and women bondservants were registered and sequestrated.

Unhappy Chia Lien had lost virtually all his possessions apart from some furnishings and those legitimate promissory notes which were returned to him. For though the rest of his property was not confiscated, the runners during their raid had carried it off. He had dreaded being punished and rejoiced at his release, but the loss overnight of all his savings as well as Hsi-feng's money — seventy or eighty thousand taels at least — was naturally galling; on top of which he was afflicted by his father's imprisonment by the Imperial Guards and Hsi-feng's critical condition. And now Chia Cheng reproached him with tears in his eyes.

"Because of my official duties, I turned over the supervision of our family affairs to you and your wife," he said. "Of course you could hardly keep a check on your father, but who is responsible for this usury? Such conduct is most unbefitting a family like ours. Now that those notes of yours have been confiscated, the financial loss is of secondary importance, but think of the damage to our reputation!"

Chia Lien fell on his knees to reply, "In running the household I never presumed to act on selfish interests. All our income and expenditure were entered in the accounts by Lai Ta, Wu Hsin-teng and Tai Liang, and you can check on them by asking them, sir. In the last few years, our expenditure has exceeded our income; and as I haven't made good the difference there are certain deficits in the accounts. If you ask the mistress, sir, she will confirm this. As for those loans, I myself have no idea where the money came from. We shall have to find out from Chou Jui and Lai Wang."

"According to you, you don't know even what is going on in your own apartments, to say nothing about family affairs! Well, I won't cross-examine you now. You've got off lightly yourself, but shouldn't you go to find out about the cases of your father and Cousin Chen?"

Wronged as he felt, Chia Lien assented with tears and went away.

Heaving sigh after sigh Chia Cheng thought, "My ancestors spared no pains in his sovereign's service, winning fame and two hereditary titles; but now that both our houses have got into trouble these titles have been lost. As far as I can see, none of our sons or nephews amounts to anything. Merciful Heaven! Why should our Chia family be ruined like this? Though His Gracious Majesty has shown extraordinary compassion by restoring my property, how am I — alone — to meet our two households' expenses? Chia Lien's admission just now was even more shocking: it seems that not only is our treasury empty but there are deficits in the accounts, so we've made a mere show of affluence all these years, and I can only blame myself for being such a fool! If my son Chu were alive he would have been my right hand. Pao-yu, though he's grown up, is a useless creature." By now tears had stained his clothes, and he reflected, "My mother is so old yet not for a single day have we, her sons, provided for her out of our own earnings. Instead of that we've made her faint for terror. How can I shirk the blame for all these misdeeds?"

He was sunk in self-abasement when a servant announced

some relatives and friends who had called to condole with him. Chia Cheng thanked each in turn.

"I am to blame for this family disaster," he said. "I failed to bring up my sons and nephews well."

One of them replied, "I have long known of your brother Lord Sheh's unseemly conduct, and Master Chen of that mansion was even more profligate. If they are blamed for their malpractices, it is no more than they deserve. Unfortunately, this scandal they've created has involved you as well, sir."

Another said, "Plenty of others kick over the traces without being impeached by the censors. This must be because Master Chen offended some of his friends."

"It's not the censors' fault," put in another. "We heard that one of your servants connived with some rogues outside to raise a hue and cry against your house. Then for fear there wasn't sufficient evidence, the censors tricked others of your men into talking. I always had the impression that your family treated its servants most generously, so why should such a thing happen?"

"No slaves are any good," someone else declared. "We're all relatives and friends here and can speak frankly. Even at that post in the provinces, sir, scrupulous as you are yourself, I suspect that those grasping servants of yours damaged your reputation; so you had better watch out. Though your property hasn't been touched, if the Emperor's suspicions are aroused it may be troublesome."

In consternation Chia Cheng asked, "What talk against me have you gentlemen heard?"

"There's no evidence of this, but it was said that when you served as Grain Commissioner you allowed your subordinates to feather their nests."

"I swear to Heaven I never dared to think of such a thing!" Chia Cheng protested. "But if those slaves of mine fleeced and swindled people, and trouble comes of it, I shall be done for!"

"It's no use panicking," they said. "You must make a serious check-up of your stewards, and if you find any of them insubordinate you should crack down on them hard."

Chia Cheng nodded. Then a gateman came in to report, "The Elder Master's son-in-law Young Master Sun has sent word that he is too busy to call in person and so has sent a messenger instead. He says that the Elder Master owed him money and wants you to pay him back, sir."

"Very well," answered Chia Cheng with a sinking heart.

The others sneered, "No wonder your kinsman Sun Shao-tsu is said to be a scoundrel. Now that his father-in-law's house has been raided, instead of coming to help out he loses no time in demanding his money back. This is truly fantastic!"

"Let's not talk about him," said Chia Cheng. "My brother should never have agreed to that match. My niece has already paid dearly for his mistake, and now her husband has started dunning me!"

As they were talking Hsueh Ko brought back the news, "Commissioner Chao of the Imperial Guards insists on pressing the charges made by the censors. I'm afraid things look black for the Elder Master and for Master Chen."

"You must go and beg the princes to intervene, sir," Chia Cheng's friends urged him. "Otherwise both your families will be ruined."

He agreed and thanked them, after which they dispersed.

It was already time to light the lamps. Chia Cheng went inside to pay his respects to his mother and found her better. Returning to his own quarters, he brooded resentfully over the folly of Chia Lien and his wife, whose usury — now that it had come to light — had landed the whole family in trouble. He was most put out by this disclosure of Hsi-feng's misdoings. But since she was so ill and must be distraught too by the loss of all her possessions, he could hardly reprimand them for the time being. Thus the night passed without further incident.

The next morning Chia Cheng went to court to express his gratitude for the Imperial favour, then called on both princes to kowtow his thanks and beg them to intervene on behalf of his brother and nephew. After they had agreed to do this, he went to enlist the help of other colleagues.

Let us return to Chia Lien. Unable to extricate his father and cousin from the straits they were in, he returned home. He found Ping-erh sitting weeping by Hsi-feng, who was being abused by Chiu-tung in the side-room. Chia Lien walked over to Hsi-feng, but as she seemed at her last gasp he had to hold back his reproaches.

"What's done is done," sobbed Ping-erh. "We can't get back what we've lost. But the mistress is so ill, you must send for a doctor for her."

"Pah!" spat out Chia Lien. "My own life is still at stake; why should I care about *her*?"

At this Hsi-feng opened her eyes and, without a word, shed tears. As soon as Chia Lien had left she said to Ping-erh, "Stop being so dense. Now that things have come to this pass, why worry about me? I only wish I could die this very minute! If you have any feeling for me, just bring up Chiao-chieh after my death and I shall be grateful to you in the nether regions!"

This only made Ping-erh sob more bitterly.

"You've sense enough to see," Hsi-feng continued, "that even if they haven't come to complain he must hold me to blame. Though the trouble was sparked off outside, if I hadn't been greedy for money I'd have been in the clear. Now after scheming so hard and trying all my life to get ahead, I've ended up worse off than anyone else! If only I hadn't trusted the wrong people! I heard something vaguely too about Master Chen's trouble and how he abducted the wife of an honest citizen named Chang to be his concubine, forcing her to kill herself rather than submit. Well, we know, don't we, who that fellow Chang was? If that business comes out, Master Lien will be involved too and I shall lose face completely. I'd like to die this instant, but I haven't the courage to swallow gold or take poison. And here you are talking of getting a doctor for me! That's not doing me a kindness but a bad turn."

This upset Ping-erh even more. She was at her wit's end. For fear that Hsi-feng might try to take her own life, she kept a close watch over her.

Luckily the Lady Dowager was ignorant of these developments. Now that her health was improving, she was relieved that Chia Cheng had kept out of trouble and Pao-yu and Pao-chai stayed by her side every day. As Hsi-feng had been her favourite she told Yuan-yang, "Give some of my things to Hsi-feng, and take Ping-erh some money so that she can look after her well. Once she's better I'll see what else can be done for her." She also told Lady Wang to help Lady Hsing.

Since the whole estate of the Ning Mansion had been confiscated, all its bondservants registered and taken away, the Lady Dowager sent carriages to fetch Madam Yu and her daughter-in-law over. Alas for the Ning Mansion, once so grand! All that remained of it was these two ladies and the concubines Pei-feng and Hsieh-luan, without a single servant. The old lady placed at their disposal a house next to Hsi-chun's, sent four women-servants and two maids to wait on them, had food prepared for them by the main kitchen, and provided them with clothing and other necessities. She also allotted them the same monthly allowances as were issued by the accountants' office to members of the Jung Mansion.

As for the expenses incurred by Chia Sheh, Chia Chen and Chia Jung in prison, the accountants' office was quite unable to meet them. Hsi-feng had no property left; Chia Lien was heavily in debt; while Chia Cheng who had no head for affairs simply said:

"I have asked friends to see that they are looked after."

Chia Lien in desperation thought of appealing to their relatives; but Aunt Hsueh's family was bankrupt, Wang Tzu-teng was dead, and none of the rest was in a position to help. All he could do was send some stewards in secret to raise a few thousand taels by selling certain country estates to defray the prison expenses. As soon as he did this, however, the servants realized that the family was on the rocks and seized this chance for hanky-panky, filching money from the rents of the eastern manors too. But this is anticipating.

To revert to the old lady, she had not a moment's peace of mind but kept weeping as she wondered what was to become of them all. Their hereditary titles had been abolished, one of her sons and two younger kinsmen were in jail awaiting trial, Lady Hsing and Madam Yu were disconsolate, and Hsi-feng was at death's door. Though Pao-yu and Pao-chai kept her company to console her, they could not share her worries.

One evening, after sending Pao-yu away, she struggled to sit up and told Yuan-yang and the other maids to burn incense in the various shrines and then to light a censerful in her courtyard. Leaning on her cane she went out there. Hu-po, knowing that she meant to worship Buddha, had placed a red felt cushion on the ground. The old lady offered incense and knelt down to kowtow and invoke Buddha several times.

She prayed to Heaven then with tears in her eyes, "Born a Shih, I married into the Chia family, and I earnestly implore holy Buddha in Heaven to have mercy on us! For generations our Chia family has never dared transgress or abuse our power. A devoted wife and mother, though unable to do much good I have never done anything wicked. But some of the Chia descendants must have offended Heaven by their arrogance and dissipation; thus our family has been raided, its property confiscated. Now my son and grandsons are in jail and fortune is frowning on them. I alone am responsible for these misfortunes because I failed to give them the proper training. Now I entreat Heaven to save us, turning the sorrow of those in jail to joy, and curing those who are ill. Even if the whole family has sinned, let me alone take the blame! Spare my sons and grandsons! Have pity, Heaven, on a pious woman! Grant me an early death, but spare my children and grandchildren!" Her voice faltered here from distress and she burst out sobbing. Yuan-yang and Chen-chu as they helped her back inside did their best to comfort her.

Lady Wang had just brought Pao-yu and Pao-chai to pay their evening respects. The old lady's grief set the three of them crying too. The saddest of all was Pao-chai as she reflected that her brother was imprisoned in the provinces, with no knowing whether his death sentence would be commuted or not; and though her father-in-law was not in trouble, the Chia family was declining, while Pao-yu was still deranged and showed no sign of trying to make good. Anxiety over her future made her weep still more bitterly than Their Ladyships. And her grief infected Pao-yu.

He mused, "My grandmother can't be at peace in her old age, and that naturally upsets my father and mother. All the girls have scattered like clouds before the wind, with fewer left every day. How jolly it was, I remember, when we started that poetry club in the Garden; but ever since Cousin Lin's death I've felt gloomy, yet with Pao-chai by me I can't cry too often. And now *she's* so worried about her brother and mother, she hardly smiles all day." The sight of her now so overcome with grief was more than he could bear. He broke down and sobbed.

At this, Yuan-yang, Tsai-yun, Ying-erh and Hsi-jen, each of whom had her own cares, started sobbing too. This moved the other maids to tears as well, and nobody restrained them. So the wailing in the room grew louder and louder till the women-servants keeping watch outside hurried off in alarm to report this to the master.

Chia Cheng was sitting gloomily in his study when this message from his mother's servants was announced. He hurried over frantically and while still at a distance heard the whole household crying, which convinced him that the old lady must be dying. Running distractedly in, he was relieved to see her sitting there sobbing.

"When the old lady is upset, the rest of you should comfort her," he chided the others. "Why are you all weeping too?"

They hastily dried their tears and stared blankly around. Chia Cheng stepped forward to console his mother, then once more briefly reprimanded the rest, all of whom were wondering how they could have forgotten themselves and broken down when they had come meaning to soothe the old lady.

Just then a serving-woman brought in two maids from Marquis Shih's family. They paid their respects to the Lady Dowager and the rest of the company.

· "We've been sent by our master, mistress and young mistress," they announced. "They've heard that your trouble here isn't serious, nothing more than a passing alarm. For fear Your Lordship and Ladyships might be worried, they sent us to say that the Second Master here has nothing to fear. Our young mistress wanted to come herself but couldn't, because soon she'll be getting married."

"Give them our regards when you go back," responded the old lady, as it was inappropriate to thank these underlings. "This misfortune must have been fated. It was kind of your master and mistress to think of us, and another day we'll go over to express our gratitude. I take it they've found your young lady a good husband — what's his family's position?"

"They are not too well-off," the maids answered. "But he's a handsome young man, and, from what we've seen of him, very easy-going. He looks rather like your Master Pao, and is said to have literary talents too."

"That's good," said the old lady cheerfully. "Being southerners, though we've lived here so long we abide by the customs of the south, so we haven't seen him yet. The other day I was thinking of my old family, and your young mistress is the one I love most — I used to have her here for the best part of the year. When she was old enough I meant to find a suitable husband for her, but because her uncle was away I couldn't arrange a match. If she's lucky enough to have found a good young man, that sets my mind at rest. I'd wanted to attend the wedding feast this month, but my heart is burning over this terrible upset here, so how can I possibly go? When you get back, give them my best regards. All of us here send our greetings. And tell your young lady not to worry about me. I'm more than eighty years old, and even if I die today I shall have had a good life. I just hope that she and her husband will live happily together till old age; then I'll rest content in my grave." By now she was weeping again.

"Don't grieve, madam," said the maids. "Nine days after

the wedding you may be sure she'll come here with her husband to pay her respects. Then how pleased you'll be to see them!"

The old lady nodded and the two maids left.

Others dismissed this from their minds, but Pao-yu started brooding, "What a life, with things going from bad to worse every day! Why must a girl marry into another family when she grows up? Marriage seems to change her into a different person. Now our dear Cousin Shih is being forced by her uncle to get married, so when next she sees me she's bound to keep at a distance. What is there to live for if everybody shuns you?" His heart ached again, but since his grandmother was just calming down he dared not weep and simply sat brooding instead.

Presently Chia Cheng returned, as he still had misgivings about the old lady. Finding her better, he went back and sent orders to Lai Ta to bring him the register of the servants in charge of the various household tasks. He checked the names. There were more than thirty families left — two hundred and twelve men and women in all — not counting Chia Sheh's bondservants who had been sequestrated.

Chia Cheng summoned the twenty-one men-servants then working in the mansion to question them about the family's income and expenditure in the past. When the stewards in charge presented the accounts for recent years, he saw that their expenditure had exceeded their income, in addition to which there had been yearly expenses in the Palace, and there were many entries of sums borrowed from outside too. He then looked into their land rents in the east province, which of late amounted to less than half the rent delivered to their ancestors, whereas the family expenses had increased tenfold. This discovery made him stamp in desperation.

"This is scandalous!" he exclaimed. "I put Lien in charge to keep a check on things; but it seems that for years we've been spending our rents a year in advance, yet insisted on keeping up appearances! Setting no store by our hereditary titles and emoluments, how could we fail to be ruined? Even if I retrench now it will be too late." He paced up and down, hands clasped behind his back, unable to hit on any way out.

The stewards knew that their master was worrying to no purpose, as he had no idea how to manage the household. "Don't worry, sir," they said. "This happens to every family. Why, even the princes, if you work out their expenses, don't have enough to live on. They just keep up appearances and get by for as long as they can. You at least have this small property thanks to the Emperor's favour, sir; but even if it had been confiscated too, wouldn't you still manage somehow?"

"You're farting!" swore Chia Cheng. "You slaves have no conscience! When your masters prosper you throw money around; when they're done for you take off, leaving them to their fate. You say it's good that our property hasn't been confiscated, but with a grand reputation while unable to hold on to our capital, how can we stand your putting on airs outside, boasting and cheating people? And when trouble comes of it, you shift the blame to your masters! This charge against the Elder Master and Master Chen is said to have come of our servant Pao Erh blabbing; but this register lists no Pao Erh — why is that?"

"This Pao Erh was not on our roster. His name used to be on the Ning Mansion register. Because Master Lien thought him an honest fellow he had him and his wife transferred here. When later his wife died, Pao Erh went back to the Ning Mansion. Then when you were busy in your yamen, sir, and Their Ladyships and the young gentlemen were away mourning for the Imperial Consort, Master Chen took over the management of the house and reinstated Pao Erh. But afterwards he left. Since you haven't run the household all these years, sir, how could you know such things? You may think this is the only name not on the roster, but actually each steward has quite a few of his relatives under him as under-servants."

"Disgraceful!" was Chia Cheng's comment, and with that he dismissed them. Aware that he could not set his house in order overnight, he postponed taking action until Chia Sheh's case was settled.

One day he was thinking things over in his study when one of his men rushed in. "Your Lordship, you are wanted at once at court for questioning!" he announced.

With some trepidation Chia Cheng obeyed this summons. To know whether it boded well or not, read the next chapter.

CHAPTER 107

The Lady Dowager Impartially
Shares Out Her Savings
Chia Cheng's Hereditary Title Is
Restored by Imperial Favour

Chia Cheng found the whole Privy Council as well as the princes assembled in the Palace.

The Prince of Peiching announced, "We have summoned you today on His Majesty's orders for an interrogation."

Chia Cheng at once fell on his knees.

"Your elder brother connived with provincial officials to oppress the weak, and allowed his son to organize gambling parties and abduct another man's wife, who took her own life rather than submit. Were you cognizant of these facts?" the ministers asked him.

"After my term of office as Chief Examiner by His Majesty's favour, I inspected famine relief," replied Chia Cheng. "I returned home at the end of winter the year before last and was sent to inspect some works, after which I served as Grain Commissioner of Kiangsi until I was impeached and came back to the capital to my old post in the Ministry of Works. Never, day or night, did I neglect my duties. But in my folly I paid insufficient attention to household affairs and failed to train my sons and nephews correctly. I have proved unworthy of the Imperial favour and beg His Majesty for severe punishment."

The Prince of Peiching reported this to the Emperor, who soon issued an edict which the prince proclaimed:

> We have ordered a strict investigation of Chia Sheh, who has been impeached by the censors for conniving with local officials to oppress the weak and, in league with the prefect of Pingan, subverting the law. Chia Sheh admits that he and the prefect were connected by marriage but denies intervening in a lawsuit, and the

375

censors have no evidence of this. It is true that he took advantage of his power to extort antique fans from the Stone Idiot; but fans are mere trifles and this offence is less serious than robbery with violence. Though the Stone Idiot committed suicide, it was because he was deranged, not because he was hounded to death. Chia Sheh is to be shown lenity and sent to the frontier to expiate his crime.

As for the charge that Chia Chen abducted another man's wife and she killed herself rather than be his concubine, a study of the censorate's original report reveals that Second Sister Yu was betrothed to Chang Hua but he, being poor, consented to break the engagement, and her mother agreed to marry her to Chia Chen's younger cousin as his concubine. This was not a case of abduction. Regarding the charge that Third Sister Yu's suicide and burial were not reported to the authorities, it transpires that she was the sister of Chia Chen's wife and they engaged her to a man who demanded the betrothal gifts back because of talk of her loose morals. She killed herself for shame; Chia Chen did not hound her to death.

However, Chia Chen deserves harsh punishment because, although he inherited a title, he flouted the law by a clandestine burial; but in view of his descent from a meritorious minister We will forbear from inflicting punishment and in Our clemency will revoke his hereditary title and send him to serve at the coast to expiate his crime. Chia Jung, being young and not involved, is to be released. Since Chia Cheng has undeniably worked diligently and prudently for many years outside the capital, his reprehensible mismanagement of his household is condoned.

Chia Cheng, moved to tears of gratitude, had kowtowed repeatedly while listening to this edict. He now begged the Prince of Peiching to petition the Emperor for him.

"You should kowtow your thanks for the Imperial favour," replied the prince. "What other petition have you?"

"Although I am guilty, His Majesty in His great favour has not punished me severely and my property has been returned to me. Overwhelmed with shame as I am, I would like to make over to the state my ancestral estate, emoluments and savings."

"His Majesty, ever merciful to His subjects, disciplines them with perspicacity, meting out unerring rewards and punishments," replied the prince. "Since you have been shown such clemency and had your property restored, it would be inappropriate to present any further petition."

The other ministers also dissuaded him. Then Chia Cheng

kowtowed his gratitude and having thanked Their Highnesses withdrew, hurrying home to reassure his mother.

All the men and women, high and low, in the Jung Mansion had been wondering what this summons to the Palace meant and had sent out for news. Chia Cheng's return relieved them but none dared question him. He hastened to the old lady's side to explain to her all the details of his pardon; but although this set her mind at rest, she could not help grieving over the loss of the two hereditary titles and the banishment of Chia Sheh and Chia Chen to such distant regions. As for Lady Hsing and Madam Yu, this news reduced them to tears.

"Don't worry, madam," said Chia Cheng, hoping to comfort his mother. "Though Elder Brother is going to serve at the frontier, he will be working for the government too and isn't likely to undergo any hardships. Provided he handles matters well, he may be reinstated. Chen is young, it is only right for him to work hard; otherwise he won't be able for long to enjoy the fortune left us by our ancestors."

The old lady had never been too fond of Chia Sheh, while Chia Chen being of the East Mansion was not one of her descendants. Only Lady Hsing and Madam Yu were sobbing as if they would never stop.

Lady Hsing was thinking, "We've lost everything and my husband is going so far away in his old age. Though I still have my son Lien, he always listens to his Second Uncle, and now that we have to live on him naturally Lien and his wife will take their side. What's to become of me left all on my own?"

Madam Yu had been in sole charge of household affairs in the Ning Mansion, second only to Chia Chen, and they were a well-matched couple. Now he was to be banished in disgrace, all their property had been confiscated, and she would have to live in the Jung Mansion where, though the old lady was fond of her, she would be a poor dependent saddled with Pei-feng and Hsieh-luan into the bargain; for her son Jung and his wife were in no position to restore the family's fortunes.

She thought, "Lien was the one to blame for my two sisters'

deaths; yet he's in no trouble now, not parted from his own wife, while we're left stranded. How are we to cope?" These reflections made her sob.

The old lady's heart ached for them. She asked Chia Cheng, "Can't your elder brother and Chen come home now that they've been sentenced? And as Jung is not involved, shouldn't he be released as well?"

"According to the rules, elder brother can't come home," he told her. "But I've asked people to put in a word so that he and Chen can come back to get their luggage together, and the ministry has agreed. I expect Jung will return with his grand-uncle and father. Please don't worry, madam. I shall see to this."

"These years I've grown so old and useless that I haven't checked up on our family affairs," she said. "Now the East Mansion has been confiscated. Not only the house either, but your elder brother and Lien have lost all their property too. Do you know how much is left in our West Mansion's treasury? And how much land in our eastern estates? You must give them a few thousand taels for their journeys."

Chia Cheng was in a dilemma. He reflected, "If I tell her the truth she may be very worried; but if I don't, how am I to manage now — to say nothing of the future?"

Accordingly he answered, "If you hadn't questioned me, madam, I wouldn't have ventured to report this. But since you ask — and Lien is here too — I must tell you that yesterday I investigated. Our treasury is empty. Not only is all the silver gone but we have debts outside too. Now that elder brother is in this predicament, if we don't bribe people to help, then in spite of His Majesty's kindness they may be hard put to it. But I can't think where the money is to come from. We've already used up next year's rent from our eastern estates, so can't raise any sums there for the time being. We shall just have to sell those clothes and trinkets which thanks to Imperial favour weren't confiscated, to cover the travelling expenses of elder brother and Chen. As to what to live on ourselves, we can worry about that later."

The old lady shed tears in her consternation.

"Is our family reduced to this?" she exclaimed. "I didn't see it for myself, but in the old days my family was ten times richer than this one, yet after a few years of keeping up appearances — though we were never raided like this — it went downhill and in less than two years was done for! Do you mean to say we shan't be able to manage even for a couple of years?"

"If we'd kept those two hereditary stipends we could still manoeuvre outside. But whom can we expect to help us now?" In tears he continued, "All those relatives whom we helped before are poor, and the others we didn't help won't be willing to come to our rescue. I didn't investigate too carefully yesterday, but simply looked at the register of our servants. Quite apart from the fact that we can't meet our own expenses, we can't afford to feed such a large staff."

The old lady was distraught with anxiety when Chia Sheh, Chia Chen and Chia Jung came in together to pay their respects to her. At sight of them she clasped Chia Sheh with one hand, Chia Chen with the other, and sobbed. Her grief made them blush for shame and fall to their knees.

"We are reprobates who have forfeited the honours accorded to our ancestors and brought you grief, madam," they said tearfully. "We don't even deserve a piece of ground in which to bury our bones after death!"

All present seeing this gave way to weeping.

Chia Cheng interposed, "The first thing to do is make ready for their journey. The authorities will probably not agree to their staying at home for more than a couple of days."

Holding back her tears the old lady dismissed Chia Sheh and Chia Chen to see their wives. Then she told Chia Cheng, "There's no time to be lost! I'm afraid it's no use trying to raise money outside, and it will be bad if they fail to leave by the appointed time. So I had better settle this for you. But the household is topsy-turvy — this won't do!" She sent Yuan-yang off to restore order.

After Chia Sheh and Chia Chen had withdrawn with Chia

Cheng, weeping again they deplored their past excesses and spoke of their grief at parting. Then they went to lament with their wives. Chia Sheh being old did not mind leaving Lady Hsing; but Chia Chen and Madam Yu could not bear to be parted, and Chia Lien and Chia Jung wept beside their fathers. For though their banishment was less harsh than service in the army, the exiles might never again see their families. However, since things had come to such a pass they had to make the best of the situation.

The old lady made Lady Hsing, Lady Wang, Yuan-yang and the others open up her cases and take out all the things she had stored away since coming here as a bride. Then she summoned Chia Sheh, Chia Cheng and Chia Chen to share out her belongings.

Chia Sheh received three thousand taels of silver with the instructions, "Take two thousand for your journey and leave your wife one thousand."

"This three thousand is for Chen," the old lady continued. "You are only to take one thousand, leaving your wife two thousand. She and your concubines can go on as before, sharing the same house but eating separately; and I shall see to Hsi-chun's marriage in future. Poor Hsi-feng has put herself out for us all these years yet now she has nothing left; so I shall give her three thousand too, on condition that she keeps it herself and doesn't let Lien use it. As she's still only half-conscious, tell Ping-erh to come and take it. And here are clothes left by your grandfather and costumes and trinkets I wore when I was young, which I have no further use for. The Elder Master, Chen, Lien and Jung can divide his clothes between them; the rest are to be shared out by the Elder Mistress, Chen's wife and Hsi-feng. This five hundred taels of silver is for Lien, for when he takes Tai-yu's coffin back south next year."

Having made this apportionment she told Chia Cheng, "You spoke of debts outside; well, they must be cleared. Take this gold to settle them. It's the others' fault that I have to part with all my possessions like this; but you're my son too, and I can't show favouritism. Pao-yu is already married. The gold, silver and other things which I have left must be worth a few thousand taels, and that will go to him. Chu's wife has always been dutiful to me, and Lan's a good lad, so I'll give them something too. This is all that I can do."

Impressed by her sound judgement and fair treatment, Chia Cheng and the rest knelt down and said with tears, "You are so advanced in years, Old Ancestress, and your sons and grandsons have failed in their duty to you. Your goodness to us makes us doubly ashamed!"

"Stop talking nonsense," she answered. "If not for this trouble I'd have kept everything to myself. But our household is too large now, with only the Second Master holding a post, so we can manage with just a few servants. Tell the stewards to summon them all and make the necessary retrenchment. Provided each house has someone, that's enough. What should we have done, anyway, if they'd all been sequestrated? The maids should be re-assigned too, and some of them married off, some given their freedom. And though this mansion of ours wasn't taken over by the authorities, you should at least give up the Garden. As for our other estates, let Lien investigate to see which should be sold and which kept up. We must stop putting on an empty show. I can speak bluntly: the Chen family down south still has some money in the Elder Mistress' keeping, which she should send back. Because if any other trouble should happen to us in future, wouldn't they be 'out of the frying-pan into the fire'?"

Chia Cheng had no head for family affairs and readily agreed to all her proposals. "The old lady certainly is a good manager!" he reflected. "It's her worthless sons who have ruined the family." Then, as his mother looked tired, he urged her to go and rest.

"I haven't much else," she continued. "What there is can be spent on my funeral, and anything left over can go to my maids."

Distressed to hear her talk like this, Chia Cheng and the others knelt down again and pleaded, "Don't take it so hard, madam! Sharing in your good fortune, we can hope later on for more marks of Imperial favour; and then we shall exert ourselves to set our house in order, and atone for our faults by caring for you until you are a hundred."

"I certainly hope it turns out like that, so that I can face our ancestors after death. But you mustn't imagine I'm someone who enjoys riches and rank and can't endure poverty. These last few years you seemed to be doing fine, so I didn't interfere, content to laugh and chat and nurse my health, never dreaming that our family was doomed to ruin like this! I knew all along that we were putting on an empty show, but everyone in the household was so used to luxury that we couldn't cut down expenses all of a sudden. Well, here's a good chance to retrench, to keep the family going, if we don't want to become a laughing-stock. You expected me to be worried to death on hearing that we're bankrupt. But in fact I was upset because, recalling the honours conferred on our ancestors for their splendid services to the state, I kept wishing that you might do even better, or at least manage to keep what you'd inherited. Who knows what dirty business they got up to, uncle and nephew!"

As she was haranguing them like this, a flustered Feng-erh ran in to tell Lady Wang, "This morning our mistress cried and cried when she learned about our trouble. Now she's at her last gasp. Ping-erh sent me to report this to you, madam."

Before she could finish the old lady asked, "Just how is she?"

"Not too well, they say," Lady Wang replied for Feng-erh.

"Ah!" exclaimed the old lady rising to her feet. "These wretched children won't give me a moment's peace!" She told maids to help her over to see Hsi-feng, but Chia Cheng barred the way.

"Madam, you've been so upset and attended to so much business, you ought to rest now. If your grandson's wife is unwell, your daughter-in-law can go and see to her; there's no need to go yourself. If you were to be upset again and fall ill, how could your sons bear it?"

"You're all to leave now and come back presently — I've more to say to you."

Not venturing to raise any further objections, Chia Cheng went to help prepare for his brother's and nephew's journeys, instructing Chia Lien to choose servants to accompany them.

Meanwhile the old lady made Yuan-yang and the others go over with her to see Hsi-feng, taking her gifts for her. Hsi-feng's breath was coming in gasps, and Ping-erh's eyes and cheeks were red from weeping. When Their Ladyships were announced, Ping-erh hurried out to meet them.

"How is she now?" asked the old lady.

Not wanting to alarm her Ping-erh said, "She's a little better. Since you're here, madam, please step in and see for yourself."

She followed them inside, then darted over and quietly raised the bed-curtains. Hsi-feng, opening her eyes, was overcome with shame at sight of the old lady, for she had assumed that the Lady Dowager must be angry with her erstwhile favourite and would leave her to die — she had never expected this visit. Relief eased her choking sensation and she struggled to sit up; but the old lady made Ping-erh hold her down.

"Don't move," she said. "Are you feeling a bit better?"

"Yes, madam," answered Hsi-feng with tears in her eyes. "Since I came here as a girl, Your Ladyships have been so good to me! But it was my misfortune to be driven out of my mind by evil spirits so that I couldn't serve you dutifully and win my father- and mother-in-law's approval. You treated me so well, letting me help run the household; and after turning everything upside-down how can I look you in the face again?" Here she broke down and sobbed, "Now Your Ladyships have come in person to see me, quite overwhelming me! Even if I had another three days to live, I deserve to have two days docked!"

"That trouble started outside," said the old lady. "It had nothing to do with you. And even though you were robbed it doesn't matter. I've brought you a whole lot of things, to do just as you like with." She told the maids to show Hsi-feng her gifts.

Hsi-feng was insatiably acquisitive. The loss of all her possessions had naturally cut her to the quick, in addition to which she had dreaded being held to blame and felt life was not worth living. Now it seemed she was still in the old lady's good books, and Lady Wang instead of reproaching her had come to comfort her, while she knew that Chia Lien had kept out of trouble too. In relief she kowtowed to the old lady from her pillow.

"Please don't worry, madam," she said. "If I recover thanks to your good fortune, I'll gladly be your menial and serve Your Ladyships with all my heart!"

Her obvious distress made the Lady Dowager give way to tears. Pao-yu was accustomed to comfort and enjoyment, and had never known genuine anxiety. This was his first experience of disaster. Now that sobbing and wailing assailed him wherever he turned, his mind became more unhinged and when others wept he joined in.

All of them seemed so upset that Hsi-feng raised her head from the pillow and made an effort to comfort the old lady. "Please go back, Your Ladyships," she urged. "When I'm a bit better I'll come to kowtow my thanks."

The old lady told Ping-erh, "Mind you look after her well. If you're short of anything, come to me for it."

On her way back with Lady Wang, they heard weeping in several apartments. Once home, unable to check her grief any longer, the old lady dismissed Lady Wang and sent Pao-yu to see off his uncle and cousin. She then lay down on her couch and burst into tears. Luckily Yuan-yang and the other maids finally succeeded in consoling her, so that she fell asleep.

Chia Sheh and Chia Chen were by no means the only ones to be distressed at leaving. None of the servants escorting them wanted to go. Simmering with resentment they cursed their fate, for separation in life is harder to bear than separation by death, and saddest of all were the people seeing them off. The once splendid Jung Mansion resounded with lamentations.

Chia Cheng, a model of propriety with a strong sense of moral obligation, clasped his brother's hand in farewell then rode ahead out of the city to offer them wine at the Pavilion of Parting and wish them a good journey. He reminded them of the government's concern for meritorious ministers, and exhorted them to work hard to repay this compassion. Shedding tears then, Chia Sheh and Chia Chen went their different ways.

When Chia Cheng returned with Pao-yu, they found messengers outside their gate clamouring that an Imperial edict had just been issued bestowing the title of Duke of Jungkuo on Chia Cheng. These men wanted largesse for bringing such good tidings.

The gatemen argued, "This is a hereditary title which our master already possesses; so how can you claim to be bringing us good tidings?"

The messengers retorted, "Hereditary titles are a great honour, harder to come by than an official appointment. Your Elder Master has lost his and will never get it back. But now His Sagacious Majesty has shown kindness greater than Heaven and restored this title to your Second Master — such a thing only happens once in a thousand years. So why don't you tip us for bringing the good news?"

Chia Cheng arrived in the middle of this dispute. When the gatemen reported the news to him he was pleased, although this reminded him of his brother's offence. Shedding tears of gratitude he hurried in to report this to the old lady. She was naturally delighted and, taking him by the hand, urged him to work diligently to repay the Emperor's kindness. Lady Wang, arriving just then to comfort the old lady, rejoiced too at this news. Lady Hsing and Madam Yu, the only ones sick at heart, had to hide their feelings.

Those relatives and friends outside who had fawned on the Chias when they were powerful had steered clear of them since hearing of their disgrace. Now that Chia Cheng had inherited the title and apparently still enjoyed the Emperor's favour, they hurried over to offer congratulations. To their surprise, Chia Cheng felt genuine embarrassment at inheriting his brother's title, despite his gratitude to the Emperor. The next day he went to court to offer thanks, and asked permission to make over to the state the houses and Garden which had been returned to him. When an edict declared this petition unwarranted, he went home in relief and continued to work steadily at his post.

But the family was now impoverished, its income falling short of its expenditure, and Chia Cheng was unable to take advantage of his social connections. The servants knew that though he was a worthy man, while Hsi-feng was too ill to run the household Chia Lien was piling up debts from day to day which forced him to mortgage houses and sell land. The wealthier of the stewards were afraid Chia Lien might appeal to them for help, and therefore made a pretence of poverty or kept out of his way. Some even asked for leave and did not return, for each was looking around for a new master.

The sole exception was Pao Yung, who had only recently come to the Jung Mansion just as disaster struck it. This honest fellow was filled with indignation by the way the rest cheated their masters; but being a newcomer his words carried no weight, so in anger he just went to sleep after supper each day. The other servants resented his lack of compliance, and slandered him to Chia Cheng as a drunken trouble-maker and a slacker.

"Let him be," said Chia Cheng. "He was recommended by the Chen family; we can hardly send him away. We may be in difficulties, but feeding one extra mouth won't make any difference."

As he would not dismiss Pao Yung, the servants complained about him to Chia Lien; but the latter no longer dared act high-handedly and took no action either.

One day, feeling disgruntled, Pao Yung had a few drinks then strolled out to the road outside the Jung Mansion, where he saw two fellows talking.

"See there!" said one. "That fine mansion was raided the other day. I wonder what's become of its owners."

"How could a family like theirs be ruined?" the other said. "I heard that one of their daughters was an Imperial Consort, and even though she's dead they should be well entrenched. I've seen them hobnobbing with princes and nobles too, so they must have plenty of backing. Why, even the present prefect, the last War Minister, is related to them. Couldn't these people have protected them?"

"You live here but don't know the first thing about it! The others weren't so bad, but that Prefect Chia was the limit! I've often seen him calling on both mansions, and after the censors impeached them the Emperor ordered him to investigate before any decision was made. What do you think he did? Because he'd been helped by both mansions, for fear of being accused of shielding them he gave them a vicious kick — that's why they were raided. Friendship docsn't mean a thing nowadays."

Pao Yung beside them overheard this idle gossip. "Are there such people in the world with no sense of gratitude?" he thought. "I wonder what relation he is to our master. If I meet the scoundrel I'll knock him off — and to hell with the consequences!"

He was letting his drunken fancy run wild when he heard runners shouting, "Clear the way!" Although some distance off, he stood still and heard one fellow whisper, "It's Prefect Chia coming."

Pao Yung was furious. Emboldened by drink he yelled, "Heartless slave! How could you forget our Chia family's goodness to you?"

Chia Yu-tsun peered out from his chair at the sound of the name Chia, but seeing a drunkard he ignored him and went on.

Pao Yung, being drunk and reckless, swaggered back to the house to question his fellow servants, who confirmed that Chia Yu-tsun owed his promotion to the Chia family.

"Instead of remembering their kindness, he kicked them down," Pao Yung fumed. "When I cursed him just now he dared not answer back."

The servants in the Jung Mansion had always disliked Pao Yung, but their masters would not take any action against him. Now that he had made this row outside, they seized the chance when Chia Cheng was free to report that Pao Yung had been drunk and disorderly. This news angered Chia Cheng, who was afraid of fresh trouble. He summoned Pao Yung and reprimanded him; but not liking to punish him ordered him to keep watch in the Garden and not to leave the place. Pao Yung was a loyal, straightforward fellow who safeguarded his master's interests. Chia Cheng had berated him on the basis of hearsay, but not venturing to justify himself he packed up his things and moved into the Garden to keep watch there and water the plants.

To know what happened later, read the next chapter.

CHAPTER 108

Pao-chai's Birthday Is Celebrated
with Forced Mirth
Pao-yu, Longing for the Dead, Hears Ghosts
Weeping in Bamboo Lodge

When Chia Cheng s petition to make over to the state his mansion and Grand View Garden was rejected by the court, as there was no one staying in the Garden he had the place locked up. Later, as it adjoined the quarters of Madam Yu and Hsi-chun and its vast grounds were deserted, to punish Pao Yung he sent him there to keep watch.

Chia Cheng was regulating the household now in accordance with his mother's instructions, gradually cutting down the staff and economizing in all possible ways; but still he could not manage. Luckily for him, Hsi-feng was the old lady's favourite — although no love was lost between her and Lady Wang and the rest — and as she was an able manager the household affairs were once more entrusted to her. Since the raid, however, for lack of funds she had no scope to manoeuvre and because the mistresses and maids of the different apartments were used to luxury, with their income less than a third of what it had been she found it impossible to satisfy them. Inevitably there were endless complaints. But Hsi-feng, in spite of her illness, dared not relinquish her task and did her best to please the Lady Dowager.

After Chia Sheh and Chia Chen reached their destinations, having money they settled down there for the time being, writing home that they were comfortably off and the family need not worry. This relieved the old lady's mind, and Lady Hsing and Madam Yu took comfort too.

One day, Shih Hsiang-yun arrived on her first visit after her marriage. The old lady, to whom she paid her respects, complimented her on her husband; and Hsiang-yun told her that her whole family was well and she need have no anxiety on that score. Then, speaking of Tai-yu's death, they both shed tears; and the thought of Ying-chun's hard lot made the old lady even sadder. After trying to console her, Hsiang-yun paid a round of calls on the others, returning to rest in the old lady's room. And now they spoke of the Hsueh family and how it had been ruined by Hsueh Pan; for though this year he had been granted a reprieve, there was no knowing whether his sentence would be commuted next year or not.

"You haven't heard the latest," said the old lady. "The other day Pan's wife died in mysterious circumstances, nearly causing another scandal. Thanks to the mercy of Buddha, the maid she had brought with her made a clean breast of the business, so that old Mrs. Hsia couldn't raise a row and stopped them from holding an inquest. The trouble your aunt had getting rid of the Hsias! So you see the truth of the saying 'All kinsmen share the same fate.' The Hsuehs are in a bad way. Now the only one she has staying with her is Ko. He's a good-hearted lad who says he won't marry while Pan is still in jail, his case not settled; that's why your Cousin Hsiu-yen is staying with the Elder Mistress and having a thin time. Pao-chin hasn't married yet either, because Academician Mei's son is still in mourning for him. The Second Mistress' elder brother has died, Hsi-feng's elder brother is a nincompoop, and that niggardly Second Uncle of theirs has embezzled public funds; so they're in hot water as well. As for the Chen family, we've had no news of them since their house was raided."

"Has Cousin Tan-chun written home since she left?" asked Hsiang-yun.

"After her marriage your uncle came back with the news that she was happily settled at the coast. We've had no letter from her, though, and I miss her the whole time; but what with all the troubles our family's had, there's nothing I can do. Now Hsi-chun's marriage still has to be fixed. As for Huan, who has time for him? We're harder up now than we used to be when you stayed here. Poor Pao-chai hasn't passed a single day in comfort since she came to our family. And your Cousin Pao's still so crazy — what can we do?"

"I grew up here so I know all my cousins well," Hsiang-yun replied. "They've all changed since last I was here. I thought at first they were holding aloof because I'd stayed away so long; but on thinking it over I realize it isn't that. When we met, I could see they meant to be as free-and-easy as in the old days; but, somehow, once we got talking they grew depressed. That's why after sitting with them for a bit I came back here to you, madam."

"The way we're living now is all right with me, but how can those young people stand it? I've been wondering how to give them a day's fun, but I haven't the energy for it."

"I have an idea!" cried Hsiang-yun. "It's Pao-chai's birthday, isn't it, the day after tomorrow? I can stay an extra day to congratulate her, and we'll all have a day's fun. What do you think, madam?"

"Anger must have addled my wits. If you hadn't reminded me, I'd have forgotten. Of course, the day after tomorrow is her birthday. I'll get out some money to celebrate it tomorrow. We had several parties for her in the past, but not since she married into the family. Pao-yu used to be such a clever, mischievous boy, but our family misfortunes have left him speechless. Chu's wife is still a good daughter-in-law, quietly bringing Lan up and behaving the same whether things go well or badly — it's hard on her."

"The one who's changed most is Cousin Hsi-feng," put in Hsiang-yun. "She's lost her good looks and her old gift of the gab. Wait till I tease them tomorrow and see how they react. But I'm afraid, though they won't say so, they'll secretly resent the fact that now I have. . . ." She broke off at this point blushing.

"Don't worry," said the old lady seeing her embarrassment. "You and your cousins used to have a good time chaffing each other. You mustn't have such scruples. People should make the best of what they've got, able to enjoy rank and riches or to put up with poverty. Your Cousin Pao-chai has always been broad-minded. When her family was well-off she wasn't the least bit conceited; later, when they got into trouble, she kept cheerful. Now that she's one of our family, when Pao-yu treats her well she takes it calmly, and if he's bad to her it doesn't provoke her. I think that's her good fortune. Your Cousin Tai-yu, on the other hand, was narrow-minded and hyper-sensitive; that's why she didn't live long. Hsi-feng, being more experienced, shouldn't let upsets influence her behaviour. If she's so foolish, that's rather petty too. Well, as the day after tomorrow is Pao-chai's birthday, I'll get out some silver for a lively celebration, to give her a happy day."

"You're quite right, madam. And while you're about it, why not invite all her girl cousins too? Then we can have a good chat."

"I certainly will." More cheerful now, the old lady told Yuan-yang to get out a hundred taels and order the servants to prepare two days' feasts, starting from the next day.

Yuan-yang sent one of the matrons off with the money, after which the night passed uneventfully.

The next day, servants were sent to fetch Ying-chun home. Aunt Hsueh and Pao-chin were invited too, and asked to bring Hsiang-ling. Aunt Li was also invited, and Li Wen and Li Chi with her.

Pao-chai was still in the dark when one of the old lady's maids arrived with the message, "Aunt Hsueh has come, and you're asked to go over, madam."

Without stopping to change her clothes, she went over happily to see her mother. She found assembled there her cousin Pao-chin and Hsiang-ling, as well as Aunt Li and others. Ascribing their visit to the news that the Chia family was no longer in trouble, she paid her respects to Aunt Li and to the old lady, said a few words to her mother, then greeted the Li sisters.

"Please take seats, ladies," urged Hsiang-yun, "while we girls wish Cousin Pao-chai a long life."

Pao-chai stood amazed, then thought, "Yes, of course tomorrow is my birthday."

"It's right and proper for you girls to come and see the old lady," she protested. "I can't have you saying that it's on *my* account."

Pao-yu, come to greet Aunt Hsueh and Aunt Li, arrived in time to hear her modest rejoinder. He had been wanting to celebrate his wife's birthday, but had not ventured to suggest it to his grandmother because the household was at sixes and sevens. Now that Hsiang-yun and the rest were about to congratulate Pao-chai, he was delighted.

"It's tomorrow, her birthday," he said. "I was meaning to remind the old lady."

"For shame!" retorted Hsiang-yun playfully. "The old lady doesn't need any reminding. Do you suppose these visitors would have come if she hadn't invited them?"

Pao-chai could hardly believe this, but now she heard the old lady tell her mother, "Poor Pao-chai has been married for a year, but with one thing after another cropping up here we've not celebrated her birthday. I'm giving this party for her today, and have asked you ladies over for a good chat."

"You shouldn't have put yourself out, madam," said Aunt Hsueh. "You've been having such an anxious time, and the child hasn't been dutiful enough."

"The old lady's favourite grandchild is Cousin Pao," quipped Hsiang-yun. "So why shouldn't his wife be a favourite too? Besides, Pao-chai deserves a birthday party."

Pao-chai lowered her head and said nothing.

Pao-yu told himself, "I thought marriage was bound to turn Cousin Shih into a different person, so I was afraid to approach her and she ignored me too; but it seems from the way she talks that she hasn't changed. In that case, why has Pao-chai grown so bashful since we married? She can hardly get a word out."

As he was wondering about this, a young maid came in to report Ying-chun's return. Then Li Wan and Hsi-feng arrived too, and greetings were exchanged.

Ying-chun mentioned that at the time of her father's departure she had wanted to see him off, but her husband had forbidden her. "He said that our family was having a run of bad luck and I mustn't be tainted by it," she explained. "I couldn't talk him round so I didn't come, just cried for days on end."

"Then why did he let you come today?" asked Hsi-feng.

"He says it's all right to keep up the connection now that our Second Master has inherited the title." She wept again.

"I was feeling very depressed," complaind the old lady. "That's why I invited you all here today to celebrate my grand-daughter-in-law's birthday. I thought some fun and laughter would cheer us up, but here you are provoking me by bringing up those tiresome things again."

Then Ying-chun and the others dropped the subject.

Though Hsi-feng forced herself to crack a joke or two, she was less witty and amusing than before; but the old lady egged her on, in the hope of diverting Pao-chai. And Hsi-feng, understanding this, did her best.

She said, "Today the old lady's feeling more cheerful. And look at all these people who haven't foregathered for so long, here today all together." There she broke off for, glancing round, she realized that her mother-in-law and Madam Yu were absent.

The two words "all together" reminded the old lady of them too, and she sent to invite them. Lady Hsing, Madam Yu and Hsi-chun had perforce to come, although much against their wishes, reflecting that if the Lady Dowager was in the mood to celebrate Pao-chai's birthday — with the family half ruined — it showed her favouritism. Hence they arrived looking listless and apathetic. When asked about Hsiu-yen, Lady Hsing made the excuse that she was unwell and the old lady said no more, knowing that Aunt Hsueh's presence made it embarrassing for Hsiu-yen to come.

Soon sweetmeats and wine were served. "We won't send any to the gentlemen outside," said the Lady Dowager. "Today's party is just for us womenfolk."

Pao-yu, though a married man now, still had the freedom of the inner quarters because he was his grandmother's favourite. Being unable to sit with Hsiang-yun and Pao-chin, he took a seat by the old lady and started toasting the guests one by one on Pao-chai's behalf.

"Sit down now and let's all drink," proposed the old lady. "You can go round and pay your respects to them later. If you do that now, everyone will be formal and that would spoil my fun."

Pao-chai complied and sat down.

"Today we may as well let ourselves go," continued the old lady. "We'll just keep one or two maids to wait on us, and I'll tell Yuan-yang to take Tsai-yun, Ying-erh, Hsi-jen and Ping-erh to the back to drink by themselves."

The maids protested, "We haven't yet kowtowed to Madam Pao. How can we go off to drink?"

"Just do as I say," she answered. "We'll call you when we need you."

After Yuan-yang had gone off with the other maids, the old lady urged Aunt Hsueh and the others to drink. But none of them behaved as they had in the old days.

"What's wrong with you?" she demanded frantically. "I want everyone to have fun!"

"We're eating and drinking — what more should we do?" asked Hsiang-yun.

"They used to be young and gay," explained Hsi-feng. "Now they're standing too much on their dignity to talk wildly; that's why you find them rather quiet, madam."

Pao-yu whispered, "There's nothing we can talk about, madam, because any talk's bound to lead to something depressing. Why don't you get them to play a drinking game?"

The old lady had inclined her head to listen. Now she remarked with a smile, "If we're to play drinking games we must call Yuan-yang back."

Needing no further instructions, Pao-yu went to the back to give her this message.

"Won't you let us drink a cup in peace, young master?" she protested. "Why come and disturb us?"

"It's true," he insisted. "The old lady wants you there. This isn't *my* doing."

Yuan-yang had to tell the others, "Just go on drinking, I'll be back before long." With that she rejoined the old lady.

"So here you are, eh?" said the Lady Dowager. "We want to play drinking games."

"I came because Master Pao told me you wanted me, madam. What game would you like to play?"

"Those literary games are terribly dull, but rowdy ones are no good either. You must think of something fresh."

After a moment's reflection Yuan-yang said, "Aunt Hsueh at her age doesn't like to cudgel her brains, so why don't we fetch the dice-pot and toss for the names of melodies, making the losers drink?"

"Very well." The old lady sent for the dice-pot and had it put on the table.

"We'll throw four dice," Yuan-yang announced. "Anyone who fails to produce a name must drink one cup as forfeit. If a name is thrown, the others will have to drink according to the pips."

"That sounds simple," said the rest. "We'll do as you say."

They made Yuan-yang drink a cup and toss to see who should start, counting from herself — and it happened to be Aunt Hsueh, who threw four ones.

"The name for this," said Yuan-yang, "is 'The Four Elders of Shangshan.' Those getting on in years should drink." This meant the old lady, Aunt Li, Lady Hsing and Lady Wang. But as the old lady raised her cup Yuan-yang continued, "Since Aunt Hsueh threw this, she must give the name of a melody corresponding to it, and the one whose turn is next must follow with a line of poetry. The forfeit if either of them fails is one cup."

"You're having me on!" objected Aunt Hsueh. "How can I possibly answer?"

"It's too tame if you don't," said the Lady Dowager. "So better make a try. It's my turn next, and if I can't think of a line I'll drink with you."

Then Aunt Hsueh said, "The melody's called *Retreating into Flowers as Old Age Approaches*."

The old lady nodded and quoted:

"Men may say that in idle moments I ape children."

Then the dice-pot was passed to Li Wen, who tossed two fours and two twos.

Yuan-yang said, "This has a name too. It's 'Liu Chen and Yuan Chao Go to Mount Tientai.' "

Li Wen named the melody *Two Scholars Go to Peach-blossom Stream,* and Li Wan who was next to her quoted:

> "Finding Peach-blossom Stream to escape from Chin."

All took a sip of wine, after which the dice-pot went to the old lady, who tossed two twos and two threes. "I suppose I shall have to drink," she said.

But Yuan-yang told her, "There's a name for this: 'The Swallow on the River Leads Its Fledgelings.' Everybody has to drink."

"Many of the fledgelings have flown," began Hsi-feng, when glances from the others silenced her.

"Well, what shall I say?" the old lady went on. *"The Grandfather Leads His Grandchildren."*

Li Chi, the next, quoted:

> "Idly watching children catching willow-catkins."

And this won general approval.

Pao-yu was eager to try his hand but had to wait for his turn. While he was thinking the pot was set before him and he threw one two, two threes and a single one. He asked, "What is this called?"

Yuan-yang smiled and replied, "It's no good. Drink up and throw again."

This time he threw two threes and two fours.

"This is called 'Chang Chang Paints His Wife's Eyebrows,' " Yuan-yang announced.

Pao-yu knew that she was teasing, and Pao-chai blushed scarlet. But Hsi-feng, not catching on, urged him, "Answer quickly, Cousin Pao, so that we can pass on to the next."

He gave up then, saying sheepishly, "I'll pay the forfeit. There's no one after me either."

Then the dice-pot went to Li Wan who made her toss.

Yuan-yang said, "You've thrown 'The Twelve Girls with Golden Hairpins.'"

Pao-yu at once hurried over to have a look and saw that half the pips were red, half green. "Very pretty!" he exclaimed. Suddenly recalling his dream of twelve girls he went back to his seat in a daze. "Those twelve girls were supposed to be from Chinling," he mused. "How is it that of all those in our family only these few are left?" Seeing Hsiang-yun and Pao-chai there but not Tai-yu, he felt tears well up in his eyes and, to escape detection, excused himself on the pretext that he was hot and wanted to take off some clothes. Hsiang-yun, who noticed him slip away, supposed that he was sulking because he had tossed less successfully than the rest. She was rather vexed herself too because the game was so dull.

Then Li Wan said, "I'm stumped. There are people missing too. I'd better pay the forfeit."

"This game isn't much fun, let's give it up," suggested the old lady. "Let Yuan-yang have a try. See what she gets."

A young maid put the dice-pot before Yuan-yang, who did as she was told, throwing two twos and one five. While the fourth dice was still rolling in the pot she cried, "Not a five!" But a five it was. "Too bad!" she exclaimed. "I've lost."

"Doesn't this count as anything?" asked the old lady.

"Well, it has a name, but I can't think what melody goes with it."

"Tell me its name and I'll think up something for you."

"It's 'Water-weeds Swept by Waves.'"

"That's not difficult. Here you are: *Autumn Fish Amid Caltrops.*"

Hsiang-yun who came next recited:

> "I sang white water-weeds on the southern river in autumn."

"Very apt," approved the others.

"This game's finished. Let's drink a few cups, then have rice," proposed the Lady Dowager, then noticed that the place beside her was empty. "Where has Pao-yu gone? Why isn't he back yet?" she asked.

Yuan-yang told her he had gone to change his clothes.

"Who went with him?"

Ying-erh stepped forward to report, "When I saw Master Pao going out I told Sister Hsi-jen to go with him."

Their Ladyships felt reassured, but after waiting for a while Lady Wang sent a young maid in search of him. She went to the bridal chamber where Wu-erh was setting out candles.

"Where is Master Pao?" asked the maid.

"Over with the old lady, drinking."

"I've just come from there, sent by Her Ladyship to find him. If he were there, why should she send me?"

"In that case I don't know where he is," said Wu-erh. "You'd better try somewhere else."

On her way back the maid met Chiu-wen. "Have you seen Master Pao?" she asked her.

"I'm looking for him too," was the reply. "The mistresses are waiting for him to start dinner. Wherever can he have got to? Hurry back and tell the old lady, not that he's not at home but that he's feeling out of sorts after drinking and doesn't want any food. After resting for a little he'll rejoin them. He hopes Their Ladyships will start without him."

The young maid ran meekly off to give this message to Chen-chu, who reported it to the Lady Dowager.

"He never eats much," the old lady said. "So missing a meal doesn't matter. Tell him to have a good rest and not to trouble to come back today as we have his wife here instead."

Chen-chu asked the younger maid, "Did you hear that?"

Replying in the affirmative and not liking to tell them the truth, the girl went out for a stroll then came back to report that she had delivered this message. The others paid no attention and after their meal broke up into groups to chat. But enough of this.

Pao-yu who had left the feast in a fit of distress was at a loss what to do. Hsi-jen overtook him to ask what was amiss.

"Nothing," he answered. "I'm just bored. While they're drinking, suppose we stroll over to Madam Yu's place."

"She's with the old lady," Hsi-jen pointed out. "How can you call on her?"

"I'm not thinking of calling on anyone, just of seeing what her place is like."

Hsi-jen had to follow him, chatting as they made their way to Madam Yu's lodge, near which they saw a small gate left ajar. Instead of going in, Pao-yu accosted two matrons in charge of the Garden who were sitting on the threshold gossiping.

"Is this small gate always open?" he asked.

"No, it's usually kept shut," they answered. "Today, hearing that the old lady might be wanting fruit from the Garden, we opened it in readiness."

He strolled over and looked at the half open gate. Before he could step through it Hsi-jen stopped him.

"Don't go in there," she warned. "The Garden's unclean after being deserted for so long, and you might see another apparition."

Rather tipsily he boasted, "I'm not afraid of such things!"

Hsi-jen tried hard to restrain him, but the old women butted in, "This Garden's been quiet ever since the priests haled off the evil spirits that day, and we often go in alone to pick flowers or fruit. If Master Pao wants to go in we'll keep him company. There's safety in numbers!"

Pao-yu was pleased and Hsi-jen, unable to stop him, had to go along with them.

When Pao-yu stepped into the Garden, it struck him as a scene of desolation. The plants were withering, and the paint was flaking off the lodges in various places. In the distance, however, he saw a clump of bamboo which was still luxuriant. After a second's thought he said, "Since moving out of the Garden because of my illness, I've been living in the back and haven't been allowed to come here for months. How quickly the place has run wild! Look, the only green things left are those bamboos. Isn't that Bamboo Lodge?"

"After a few months away, you've even lost your bearings," Hsi-jen told him. "We were so busy chatting, you didn't notice passing Happy Red Court." She turned and pointed behind. "Bamboo Lodge is over there."

He looked in the direction in which she was pointing. "Have we really passed it?" he asked dubiously. "Let's go back and have a look."

"It's getting late, time to go home. The old lady must be waiting for you to start dinner."

Pao-yu made no answer but found the path and walked on. You may wonder, Reader, how he could possibly have forgotten the way, even after an absence of nearly a year. The fact is that Hsi-jen had tried to fob him off for fear that the sight of Bamboo Lodge, reminding him of Tai-yu, would distress him again. When she saw him heading straight there and was afraid that he might be bewitched, she had pretended that they had passed the place. But Pao-yu had set his heart on visiting Bamboo Lodge. He strode swiftly ahead and she had to follow him, till he froze in his tracks as if watching or listening to something.

"Do you hear anything?" she asked.

"Is there anybody staying in Bamboo Lodge?"

"I shouldn't think so."

"I distinctly heard sobbing inside, so there must be someone."

"That's just your imagination. Because you often used to come here before and find Miss Lin weeping."

Pao-yu did not believe her and wanted to go closer to hear better.

The matrons overtaking them urged, "Better go back, Master Pao. It's growing dark. Other places aren't scary, but this is out of the way and they say that since Miss Lin's death weeping has often been heard here, so everybody gives the place a wide berth."

Pao-yu and Hsi-jen were startled.

"So it's true!" he exclaimed, shedding tears. "Cousin Lin! Cousin Lin! There was nothing the matter with you, but I killed you! Don't hold it against me — my parents made the decision. It's not that I was untrue!" Feeling broken-hearted he burst into loud sobbing.

Hsi-jen was at her wit's end when Chiu-wen and some others hurried towards them.

"Whatever possessed you?" Chiu-wen asked Hsi-jen. "Why bring Master Pao *here* of all places? Their Ladyships are so frantic, they've sent out search parties. Just now someone at the side-gate said the two of you had come here, so frightening Their Ladyships that they lashed out at me and ordered me to bring people here at once. Hurry up and go back!"

Pao-yu was still weeping bitterly. Ignoring his sobs, Hsi-jen and Chiu-wen dragged him off, wiping his tears as they told him how worried his grandmother was. He had no choice but to go back.

To allay the old lady's anxiety Hsi-jen took him straight to her room, where the others were still waiting.

"Hsi-jen!" stormed the Lady Dowager. "I entrusted Pao-yu to you thinking you had some sense. How could you take him to the Garden today, with him just over his illness? If something had given him a turn and brought on another fit, what should we have done?"

Not venturing to justify herself, the maid hung her head in silence. Pao-chai was appalled too by Pao-yu's unhealthy colour, thus it was left to him to exonerate Hsi-jen.

"What does it matter in broad daylight?" he asked. "It's so long since I've had a stroll in the Garden that I went there after drinking to clear my head. How could anything there possibly give me a turn?"

Hsi-feng, who had been so terrified in the Garden, shivered with fright at this. "Cousin Pao's too reckless!" she cried.

"Not reckless but loyal," put in Hsiang-yun. "He must have gone to find the Hibiscus Spirit, or in search of some other goddess!"

Pao-yu made no reply, and Lady Wang was too worried to get a word out.

"Did anything frighten you in the Garden?" the old lady asked him. "Well, don't talk about it now. If you want to stroll there in future, you must take more people with you. If not for this rumpus you made, our party would have broken up long

ago. Go and have a good night's sleep now, everyone, and mind you come early tomorrow. I want to make it up to you all by giving you another day of fun. Don't let this rumpus he kicked up upset you."

Then they all took their leave, Aunt Hsueh going to spend the night with Lady Wang while Hsiang-yun stayed with the Lady Dowager, and Ying-chun went with Hsi-chun. The others all returned to their own quarters.

Pao-yu, back in his room, heaved sigh after sigh but Pao-chai, knowing the reason for this, ignored him. However, for fear that his grief might bring back his old illness, she called Hsi-jen into the inner room to ask her just what had happened in the Garden. If you want to know Hsi-jen's answer, read the next chapter.

CHAPTER 109

Pao-yu Waits for a Fragrant Spirit and
Wu-erh Is Loved by Default
Ying-chun Pays Her Mortal Debt and Returns
to the Primal Void

After Pao-chai had heard Hsi-jen's story, for fear lest Pao-yu should fall ill from grief she spoke to her, as if casually, of Tai-yu's death.

"People feel for each other while on earth," she said. "But after death they go their separate ways, no longer the same as in life. Even if the one still living remains fond, the one who is dead can't know it. Besides, Miss Lin is said to have become an immortal, so to her all men on earth must be unbearably vulgar and she'd never stoop to coming back. To imagine otherwise is to invite evil spirits to take possession of you."

Aware that these remarks were intended for Pao-yu's ears, Hsi-jen chimed in, "That's true, her coming back is out of the question. I was on good terms with her too, so if her spirit were still in the Garden how is it I've never seen her once in my dreams?"

Pao-yu eavesdropping outside thought to himself, "Yes, this *is* strange! Though I've thought of her time and again each day since her death, why has she never appeared to me in dreams? She must have gone up to Heaven, I suppose, and because I'm too vulgar to have any communication with the divine I've not once dreamed of her. Well, tonight I'll sleep in the outer room and maybe, now that I've visited the Garden, she'll know my heart and let me dream of her. I must ask her where she's actually gone and offer regular sacrifices to her. If she'll really have nothing to do with a lout like me and won't let me dream of her, then I'll stop thinking about her."

His mind made up, he announced, "Tonight I'm going to sleep in the outer room, and you can just let me be."

Pao-chai made no attempt to dissuade him, only saying, "Don't go imagining all sorts of things. Didn't you see how worried your mother was — too worried to speak — because you went to the Garden? If you don't look after your health and the old lady hears of it, she'll blame us for not taking better care of you."

"I just said that for fun," he answered. "I'll join you after sitting here awhile. You must be tired; you'd better turn in first."

Believing him, Pao-chai prevaricated, "I'll go to bed and let Hsi-jen wait on you."

This was just what Pao-yu wanted. After Pao-chai had retired he told Hsi-jen and Sheh-yueh to make up a bed for him outside, then sent them in several times to see whether she was sleeping yet or not. She pretended that she was, but in fact stayed awake all night.

When he thought Pao-chai was asleep he told Hsi-jen, "I want you all to turn in. I've stopped feeling upset. If you don't believe me you can wait till I've dropped off before going inside, but mind you don't disturb me."

Hsi-jen helped him to bed, made his tea then went inside, closing the door behind her, to attend to other things, after which she lay down fully dressed, ready to go out if summoned.

As soon as she had gone, Pao-yu dismissed the two matrons who were sitting up to keep watch. Then he quietly sat up to pray below his breath before lying down once more. At first he could not sleep; but once he had calmed himself he dozed off and slept soundly all night, not waking until dawn. He sat up, rubbing his eyes, and thought back — no, he'd had no dream. With a sigh he recited the lines:

> One living and one dead, sundered for years,
> Her spirit never appeared to him in his dreams.[1]

---

[1] A couplet from Pai Chu-yi's *Song of Eternal Sorrow.*

Pao-chai who had passed a sleepless night herself heard this from the inner room. "That's a wild way to talk!" she called out. "If Cousin Lin were alive she'd take offence again."

Pao-yu got up in embarrassment and went sheepishly in to tell her, "I meant to come in but somehow or other I happened to fall asleep."

"What's it to me whether you come in or not?" she retorted.

Hsi-jen had not slept either. At the sound of their voices she promptly came in to pour tea. Then a young maid arrived, sent by the old lady, to inquire whether Pao-yu had passed a good night or not and to tell him that, if he had, he should go over with Madam Pao as soon as they were dressed.

Hsi-jen sent her back with the message that Pao-yu had slept well and would soon be going over.

After a hasty toilet, Pao-chai went ahead with Ying-erh and Hsi-jen to pay her respects to the Lady Dowager, then to Lady Wang and Hsi-feng. By the time she rejoined the old lady Aunt Hsueh had arrived.

When asked if Pao-yu had slept well, Pao-chai told them, "He's quite all right. He went to sleep as soon as we got back." Then, their minds relieved, they chatted.

And now a young maid came in to report, "Miss Ying-chun has to go home. They say Mr. Sun sent servants to complain to the Elder Mistress, who sent word to Miss Hsi-chun to let her go back. Miss Ying-chun's weeping in the Elder Mistress' room. She should be coming soon to say goodbye."

The others, sad to hear this, deplored Ying-chun's fate.

"Such a brute of a husband has ruined her life," the old lady sighed.

Then Ying-chun, her face tear-stained, came in to take her leave. As this was Pao-chai's birthday she had to choke back her grief, and knowing how strictly she was controlled her grandmother could not detain her.

"All right, you'd better go back," she said. "But don't be so upset. It's no use crying over spilt milk. I'll send for you again in a few days' time."

"You've always been goodness itself to me, madam," sobbed

Ying-chun. "But now there's nothing you can do. And I'm afraid this is the last time I shall see you!"

"What's to stop you from coming again?" the others remonstrated. "Your third sister's worse off, so far away that she's hardly any chance of coming home." The thought of Tan-chun reduced them all to tears.

But as this was Pao-chai's birthday, the old lady tried to strike a more cheerful note. "It's not impossible," she said. "Once peace is restored along the coast and her father-in-law is transferred to the capital, we shall see each other again."

"That's true," the rest agreed.

Then Ying-chun had to leave disconsolately. Having seen her out the others rejoined the old lady, who entertained them till the evening when as she looked tired they dispersed.

Aunt Hsueh went back with Pao-chai to whom she said, "Your brother's got by this year. When there's an Imperial amnesty and his sentence is commuted, we can try to ransom him. But how am I to manage these next few years on my own? I'd like to get Hsueh Ko married. Do you think that a good idea?"

"You had doubts about it before, mother, because you were horrified by my sister-in-law," Pao-chai answered. "I think it's high time that you saw to this. You know Hsiu-yen and what a thin time she's having here. Once she marries into our family, though we're poor, at least she'll be much better off than staying here as a dependent."

"Then find a chance to mention it to the old lady. Tell her I need someone to help out, and so I want to fix the wedding day."

"Why not just discuss it with Cousin Ko? When you've chosen a good day you can come and tell the old lady and Elder Mistress, then take her over and be done with it. The Elder Mistress here is eager to get her married off."

"I heard today that your Cousin Shih's going back too. The old lady wanted to keep Pao-chin for a few days and she's staying. As I think that sooner or later she'll be leaving home to get married, you'd better take this chance to have some good talks."

"Yes, mother, I will."

After sitting there for a while Aunt Hsueh said goodbye to the others and went home.

When Pao-yu returned to his quarters that evening he thought, "The fact that I didn't dream of Tai-yu last night may be because she has become an immortal and doesn't want to meet vulgar oafs like me; or it may be because I'm too impatient."

That gave him an idea and he told Pao-chai, "Last night I happened to doze off outside, and slept so much more soundly than in here that I woke up this morning feeling refreshed. So — if you've no objection — I'd like to sleep outside for a couple more nights."

Pao-chai knew from the poetry he had recited that morning that he was thinking of Tai-yu, and that there was no reasoning with such a simpleton. She decided she might as well let him have his own way until he himself lost hope, especially as he had slept well the previous night.

"What's that got to do with me?" she asked. "You can sleep wherever you like; why should we stop you? But don't let your fancy run wild or put a jinx on yourself."

"What an idea!" he chuckled.

"Take my advice, Master Pao, and sleep inside," put in Hsi-jen. "If you're not well looked after outside and catch cold, that will be bad." Before he could answer, Pao-chai tipped Hsi-jen a wink and she continued, "Very well then. We'll get somebody to keep you company, to pour you tea during the night."

"In that case, *you* stay with me," he said with a smile.

Hsi-jen flushed crimson with embarrassment and did not answer him.

Knowing how staid she was Pao-chai proposed, "She's used to staying with me, so let her do that. Sheh-yueh and Wu-erh can look after you. Besides, she's tired out after dancing attendance on me all day; we should let her have a good rest."

Pao-yu went out gleefully.

Pao-chai told Sheh-yueh and Wu-erh to make a bed for him in the outer room and to sleep lightly themselves and see to his

tea. Assenting to this, they went out and found Pao-yu seated
bolt upright on the bed, his eyes closed and his hands folded
just like a monk. Not daring to speak, they stared at him in
amusement. Hsi-jen, sent out by Pao-chai to see that he had all
he wanted, was amused by this sight too.

"It's time to sleep," she said softly. "Why are you practising
yoga?"

Pao-yu opened his eyes and seeing who it was replied, "You
all go to bed. I'll sit here a bit then sleep."

"The way you behaved yesterday kept Madam Pao awake
all night. Are you starting all over again?"

Knowing that none of them would sleep if he stayed up, Pao-
yu lay down. Hsi-jen gave the two other girls some final instructions then went inside, closing the door, and retired for the
night.

Sheh-yueh and Wu-erh spread out their quilts too, and when
Pao-yu had lain down they went to bed. But Pao-yu could not
sleep. As he watched them unfolding their quilts he had recalled the time during Hsi-jen's absence when Ching-wen and
Sheh-yueh had waited on him. Sheh-yueh had gone out in the
night and Ching-wen, to frighten her, had slipped out in her
night clothes and caught cold — it was that illness that later
carried her off. At this memory his heart went out to Ching-wen.
And mindful, suddenly, of Hsi-feng describing Wu-erh as the
image of her, he shifted his longing for Ching-wen to her double.
While shamming sleep he peeped at Wu-erh, and more and more
she looked to him like Ching-wen, making him quite enraptured.
There was no sound now from the inner room and he assumed
that the occupants were asleep. Not knowing whether Sheh-yueh
was awake or not, he called her a couple of times but received
no answer.

Wu-erh hearing him asked, "Do you want something, Master
Pao?"

"I want to rinse my mouth."

Since Sheh-yueh was asleep, Wu-erh had to get up. Having
trimmed the candle she poured him a cup of tea, holding ready
the spittoon in her other hand. She had got up in a hurry wear-

ing only a peach-red silk shift, her hair loosely knotted. To Pao-yu she appeared the reincarnation of Ching-wen. He bethought himself abruptly of Ching-wen's saying, "If I'd known I was going to get a bad name, I'd have committed myself." He gaped at Wu-erh, neglecting to take the cup.

Now after Fang-kuan's dismissal, Wu-erh had lost interest in coming into service here. But when later she heard that Hsi-feng was sending her to work for Pao-yu, she was more eager for this than Pao-yu himself. After her arrival, however, she was overawed by Pao-chai and Hsi-jen and found Pao-yu deranged and less handsome than before; moreover she heard that Lady Wang had dismissed certain maids for playing around with him, and so she gave up her girlish infatuation. Yet tonight her witless master, taking her for Ching-wen, was attracted to her. Wu-erh blushed all over her face. Not venturing to raise her voice she said softly:

"Rinse your mouth, Master Pao."

He took the tea with a smile, but forgetting to rinse his mouth asked with a grin, "You and Sister Ching-wen were on good terms, weren't you?"

In bewilderment she answered, "We were like sisters; of course we were on good terms."

"When Ching-wen was dying and I went to see her, weren't you there too?" he asked softly.

She smiled and nodded.

"Did you hear her say anything?"

"No." She shook her head.

Forgetting himself, he took her hand. Wu-erh blushed furiously, her heart beating fast.

"Master Pao!" she whispered. "Say what you have to say, but keep your hands to yourself."

He dropped her hand then and told her, "She said to me, 'If I'd known I was going to get a bad name, I'd have committed myself.' Did you hear that?"

Wu-erh felt this was a challenge, yet dared not rise to it. "That was a shameless thing to say," she answered. "How can young girls talk like that?"

"Are you such a moralist?" he cried frantically. "It's because you look just like her that I confided this to you. Why run her down in that way?"

Not knowing what was in his mind she said, "It's late. You'd better sleep, Master Pao. If you keep sitting up you may catch cold. What did Madam Pao and Sister Hsi-jen tell you?"

"I'm not cold." Suddenly remembering that she was in her night clothes, he was afraid she might catch cold like Ching-wen. "Why didn't you put more on before bringing my tea?" he asked.

"You sounded in such a hurry, what time did I have for that? If I'd known you'd keep talking so long, I'd have put on something warmer."

At once he offered her the pale grey silk padded jacket which was lying over his quilt, and urged her to put it on.

She refused, saying, "Keep it yourself, Master Pao. I'm not cold. Anyway, I have clothes of my own."

She went back to her bed and slipped into a long gown, listening to make sure that Sheh-yueh was still sound asleep, then came back slowly and asked, "Don't you want to have a good rest tonight, Master Pao?"

"Not a bit of it!" he answered with a smile. "To tell you the truth, I'm hoping to meet a goddess."

"What goddess?" she asked, even more bewildered.

"If you want to know, it's a long story. Sit down next to me and I'll tell you."

"How can I sit down with you lying there?" she asked blushing.

"Why shouldn't you? It was very cold that year when Ching-wen played a trick on Sheh-yueh, and for fear she might catch cold I tucked her under my quilt. What does it matter? It's hypocritical to be so prudish."

It sounded to Wu-erh as if he were flirting with her. Little did she know that this foolish master of hers was speaking from his heart. She was at a loss, equally averse to leaving, standing there or sitting down.

"Don't talk such nonsense," she said playfully. "Suppose

someone was to hear? No wonder people say you waste all your time on girls! You have Madam Pao and Sister Hsi-jen, both as pretty as goddesses, yet you insist on fooling around with others. If you go on talking that way I'll report it to Madam Pao — then what face will you have left?"

Just then they were startled by a sound outside. Pao-chai in the inner room coughed. Pao-yu at once pursed his lips, and at this signal Wu-erh put out the light and tiptoed back to bed. Actually, because Pao-chai and Hsi-jen had not slept the night before and today had been a busy day for them both, they had slept through the conversation. The sound in the courtyard made them wake with a start and prick up their ears, but nothing more could they hear. Pao-yu in bed wondered, "Could Cousin Lin have come? Maybe hearing me talk she decided to give us a fright." He tossed and turned, giving way to foolish fancies, not falling into a troubled sleep till dawn.

Because Pao-yu had fooled about with her half the night and then Pao-chai had coughed, Wu-erh had a guilty conscience and was afraid her mistress had overheard them. Filled with misgivings she could not sleep all night. When she got up the next morning, as Pao-yu was still dead to the world she tidied the room.

"Why get up so early?" Sheh-yueh asked. "Couldn't you sleep last night?"

Suspecting from this that Sheh-yueh knew what had happened, Wu-erh smiled sheepishly and made no reply. Presently Pao-chai and Hsi-jen got up too. When they opened the door and saw Pao-yu still slumbering, they wondered how he had managed to sleep so soundly the last two nights outside.

Pao-yu woke to find them all up. He sat up quickly, rubbing his eyes, and thought back. No, he had not dreamed last night either. So it must be true that "The ways of immortals and mortals never meet." Getting slowly out of bed he recalled Wu-erh's remark during the night that both Pao-chai and Hsi-jen were as pretty as goddesses. Indeed they were! He stared at Pao-chai as if stunned. She assumed he was thinking of Tai-

yu, but could not tell whether he had dreamed of her or not.
Put out by his stare she asked:

"Did you meet a goddess last night?"

Imagining that she must have overheard them he faltered,
"What do you mean?"

Wu-erh, too conscience-stricken to speak, waited for Pao-
chai to go on.

"Did you hear Master Pao talk with someone in his sleep?"
Pao-chai asked her with a smile, making Pao-yu beat a discom-
fited retreat.

Red in the face, Wu-erh mumbled, "He did say something —
I couldn't catch it clearly — in the first part of the night. Something about 'getting a bad name' and 'not committing herself.'
I couldn't make it out and begged Master Pao to sleep. Then I
fell asleep myself, so I don't know whether he said anything
more."

Pao-chai lowered her head and thought, "He obviously had
Tai-yu in mind. If we let him stay outside, he may get more
deranged and some flower fairy or tree spirit may take possession of him. Besides, his illness was brought on by his strong
feeling for her. If only there were some way to divert his affection to me, he'd get over it." At this idea, she blushed up to
her ears and went sheepishly back to her room to do her hair.

The old lady's improved spirits these last two days had
made her overeat, and that evening she was out of sorts. The
next day her chest felt constricted; however, she would not let
Yuan-yang report this to Chia Cheng.

"I've been rather greedy these two days and had too much
to eat," she said. "Missing a meal will set me right. Don't
make a fuss about it." So Yuan-yang and the others kept quiet.

When Pao-yu went home that evening, Pao-chai had just
come back from paying her respects to the old lady and Lady
Wang. The sight of her reminded him of her remarks that morning, making him rather ashamed. Seeing how put out he looked

and knowing what a sentimentalist he was, she decided to use his infatuation to cure him.

"Are you going to sleep outside again tonight?" she asked.

"Outside or inside — it's all the same to me," he answered glumly.

She wanted to say more but could not get the words out.

"Well, just what does *that* mean?" asked Hsi-jen. "I don't believe you slept so well outside."

Wu-erh seized this chance to add, "When Master Pao sleeps outside, the only snag is that he talks in his sleep in a way we can't understand, yet we dare not talk back."

"I'll move my bed outside tonight to see whether *I* talk in my sleep or not," said Hsi-jen. "You two move Master Pao's bedding back to the inner room."

Pao-chai said nothing. Pao-yu, too ashamed to argue, let them move his bedding inside.

Now Pao-yu in his contrition wanted to set Pao-chai's mind at rest, while she, for fear lest longing might drive him distracted, thought it best to show affection to win him over — to take Tai-yu's place in his heart. So that evening when Hsi-jen moved out, he made abject advances which Pao-chai naturally did not reject. And thus that night at last their marriage was consummated. Later she conceived, but that need not concern us now.

When next day husband and wife had got up together, after Pao-yu had dressed he set off first to see his grandmother. As she was so fond of him and thought Pao-chai dutiful too, it suddenly occurred to her to make Yuan-yang open a case and get out a Han-Dynasty jade, an heirloom of hers. Though less precious than Pao-yu's jade, it was a rare pendant.

Yuan-yang found the jade and handing it over remarked, "I don't believe I've ever seen this before. Fancy you remembering so clearly, madam, the exact case and box it was in after all these years! By looking where you told me I found it in a jiffy. But what do you want this for, madam?"

"I'll tell you. This jade was given by my great-grandfather

to my father. Since I was my father's favourite, just before I married he sent for me and gave me this himself, saying, 'This jade is a pendant of the kind worn in the Han Dynasty; it's very precious. Keep it to remind you of me.' I was young at the time I took it and didn't set much store by it, so I left it in the case. And after I came to this house and saw how many knick-knacks we had here, this seemed nothing special so I never wore it, and there it's lain for more than sixty years. Now seeing how dutiful Pao-yu is to me, as he's lost his own jade I decided to get this out and give it to him, just as my father gave it to me."

Just then Pao-yu arrived to pay his respects.

The old lady said gaily, "Come here, I've something to show you."

He walked up to her bed and she handed him the Han jade. A close scrutiny revealed that it was some three inches square, shaped like a musk-melon, pinkish, and very well carved. Pao-yu was loud in his praise.

"You like it?" asked the old lady. "This was given me by my great-grandfather. Now I'm passing it on to you."

Smilingly Pao-yu bowed his thanks and wanted to take the jade to show his mother.

"If your mother sees it," the old lady said, "she'll tell your father and he'll say that I love my grandson more than my son! They've never even seen this."

Pao-yu went off cheerfully, leaving Pao-chai and the others to talk a little longer before taking their leave.

After this the Lady Dowager fasted for two days, yet the congestion of her chest persisted and she had dizzy spells and fits of coughing. When Lady Hsing, Lady Wang and Hsi-feng came to pay their respects and saw that she looked quite cheerful, they simply sent to notify Chia Cheng, who immediately came over. On leaving, he sent for a doctor to examine her. Before long the doctor arrived and felt her pulses. He diagnosed that the old lady had caught a chill as a result of not eating regularly, but some medicine to help the digestion and expel the cold would cure her. He wrote out a prescription. Chia Cheng,

noting that the ingredients were ordinary medicines, told
servants to prepare this for his mother. He himself came each
morning and evening to inquire after her health. When three
days had passed and there was no improvement, he told Chia
Lien to make haste to find some better doctor.

"I don't think those doctors we usually have are much good,"
he explained. "That's why I want you to find one to diagnose
her illness correctly."

Chia Lien reflected and said, "I remember that year when
Cousin Pao fell ill, we got a man who wasn't a professional
to cure him. We'd better call him in again."

"Medicine is abstruse, and the least celebrated physicians
are often the best," Chia Cheng agreed. "Send to ask him over."

Chia Lien assented and left, returning to report, "That Doctor
Liu has recently left town to teach. He only comes back every
ten days or so. As we can't wait, I've invited another man who
should be here presently." Then they had to wait.

All the ladies of the house called daily to ask after the old
lady's illness. They were all assembled there one day when in
came the old woman in charge of the Garden's side-gate.

She announced, "Sister Miao-yu of Green Lattice Nunnery
has heard of the old lady's illness and come to pay her respects."

"She's a rare visitor," they said. "Since she's called today,
hurry up and show her in."

Hsi-feng went to the old lady's bedside to tell her this, while
Hsiu-yen — Miao-yu's old friend — went out to meet her.
Miao-yu was wearing a nun's cap, a pale grey plain silk tunic
under a long, sleeveless checked jacket with dark silk borders,
a yellow silk sash and a white skirt with dark designs. Holding
a whisk and her beads she swept gracefully in, attended by a
maid.

Having greeted her Hsiu-yen said, "When I stayed in the
Garden I could often drop in to see you; but now that it's so
deserted I don't like to go in on my own, and the side-gate is
usually closed, so I haven't seen you for ages. I'm so glad
you've come!"

"You were all of you so lively in the old days that even

when you were living in the Garden I didn't feel it appropriate
to call too often," Miao-yu replied. "Now I know their family
isn't doing too well and I hear the old lady is ill; so I've been
thinking of you and would like to see Pao-chai too. What do
I care whether you lock the gate or not? I come and go as I
please. If I didn't want to come, you couldn't get me here even
by invitation."

"I see you haven't changed in the least," Hsiu-yen chuckled.

Chatting together they entered the old lady's room. When
the others had greeted Miao-yu, she approached the old lady's
bed to ask after her health and exchange civilities.

"Can you, who are saintly, tell me whether I shall get over
this illness or not?" asked the Lady Dowager.

"A kindly old lady like you is bound to live to a great age,"
Miao-yu assured her. "You've just caught cold, and a few doses
of medicine should set you right. Old people shouldn't worry."

"I'm not the worrying sort," replied the old lady. "I always
try to have fun. And I'm not feeling too bad, simply rather
bloated. Just now the doctor said it's because I was vexed,
but you know very well that nobody here would dare vex me.
He can't be much good at diagnosis, can he? As I told Lien,
the first doctor was right when he diagnosed a chill and indigestion. Tomorrow we're going to ask him over again." She
told Yuan-yang to order the kitchen to prepare Miao-yu some
vegetarian dishes.

"I've had my lunch," said the nun. "I won't eat anything,
thank you."

"That's all right," said Lady Wang. "But stay a little longer
to chat."

"Yes, I haven't seen you all for so long, today I had to come."

They talked for a while until Miao-yu rose to leave. Turning
round she saw Hsi-chun standing there and asked, "Why are
you so thin, Fourth Sister? Don't let your fondness for painting
wear you out!"

"I haven't painted for ages," Hsi-chun told her. "I don't feel
like it because my present rooms aren't as light as those in
the Garden."

"Where are you living?"

"In that house east of the gate you came through. It's very close if you care to drop in."

"I'll call when I'm in the mood," Miao-yu promised her.

Then Hsi-chun and the others saw her out. On their return, hearing that the doctor had arrived they dispersed.

The Lady Dowager's illness grew daily worse, no medicine proving effective, and later she developed diarrhoea too. Worried because she was not likely to recover, Chia Cheng sent to ask leave from his yamen and he and his wife attended her day and night. One day she took some nourishment, and they were feeling relieved when they saw an old woman peeping through the door. Tsai-yun, told by Lady Wang to see who she was, recognized her as one of the serving-women who had accompanied Ying-chun to the Sun family.

"What brings you here?" she asked.

"I've been waiting outside for some time but couldn't find a soul, and I dared not burst in — I was frantic!"

"Why, what's wrong? Has Mr. Sun been bullying your young lady again?"

"My young lady's dying! The day before yesterday they had a row and she cried all night long. Yesterday she was choking, her throat blocked up with phlegm, yet they wouldn't get a doctor. Today she's worse!"

"The old lady's ill; don't kick up such a shindy."

Lady Wang inside had heard their conversation. Fearing that the old lady would be upset if she knew this, she ordered Tsai-yun to take the woman away. But the Lady Dowager lying there quietly had overheard them too.

"Is Ying-chun dying?" she asked.

"No, madam," said Lady Wang. "These women are all alarmists. She says Ying-chun hasn't been well the last couple of days and may take some time to recover. They want us to get her a doctor."

"My doctor's a good one. Have him fetched at once."

Lady Wang told Tsai-yun to send the woman to report this to Lady Hsing.

When the woman had left, the old lady lamented, "Of my three grand-daughters, one died after enjoying great good fortune; the third has married so far from home that I shan't be able to see her again; Ying-chun had a hard time but I thought she might pull through, never dreaming she'd die so young! What is there for an old woman like me to live for?"

Lady Wang, Yuan-yang and the rest consoled her at length. Pao-chai and Li Wan were absent at the time and Hsi-feng had recently fallen ill again. Now Lady Wang sent for them to keep the old lady company, for fear lest grief should aggravate her illness. Returning then to her own quarters, she sent for Tsai-yun.

"What a fool that woman is!" she scolded. "In future when I'm with the old lady and you have something to report, it can wait." The maids agreed to this.

Just as the serving-woman reached Lady Hsing's apartments, word came that Ying-chun was dead. Her mother wept. In Chia Sheh's absence, she had to send Chia Lien to the Sun family to find out the situation. Since the old lady was so ill, nobody dared tell her the news. Alas, that this girl fair as a flower or the moon should be hounded to death by the Sun family after little more than a year of marriage! As the old lady was at death's door the others could not leave her, but had to let the Sun family arrange the funeral in perfunctory fashion.

The Lady Dowager, failing from day to day, longed to see her grand-daughters and nieces. Her thoughts turned to Hsiang-yun and she sent to fetch her. The servant on her return slipped in to find Yuan-yang, but could not enter the old lady's room where Yuan-yang happened to be with Lady Wang and others Instead she went to the back where she found Hu-po.

"The old lady wanted to see Miss Shih and sent us to ask her to come," she told her. "But we found her crying her heart out, because her husband's desperately ill, and the doctors say he's not likely to recover unless it turns into consumption — in which case he may drag on for another four or five years. So Miss Shih is frantic. She knows the old lady is ill, but she can't

come. She told me, too, not to mention this to her grand-aunt.
If the old lady asks, she hopes you'll make up some excuse
for her." Hu-po exclaimed in dismay but did not answer. After
some time she told the other to go. Not liking to report this,
she decided to tell Yuan-yang and ask her to make up some
story. She went to the old lady's bedside then and found her
in a critical condition. As there were many people standing
round murmuring that it seemed there was no hope, Hu-po had
to hold her tongue.

Chia Cheng quietly drew Chia Lien aside and whispered
some instructions to which he assented softly. He then went
out to summon all the stewards at home.

"The old lady's sinking fast," he said. "You're to send at
once to make the necessary preparations. First, get out the
coffin and have it lined. Then get the measurements of the
whole household and order tailors to make mourning for them.
The funeral retinue must be arranged too, and more hands will
be needed to help in the kitchen."

Lai Ta told him, "You needn't worry, Second Master. We've
got it all figured out. But where is the money to come from?"

"You needn't raise money outside," replied Chia Lien. "The
old lady has kept a sum in readiness. Just now the master told
me that it must be handsomely done — we want a good show."

The stewards assented and went off to see to these matters
while he returned to his own quarters.

"How is your mistress today?" he asked Ping-erh.

Ping-erh pouted towards the inner room. "Go in and see
her."

He did so and found Hsi-feng, exhausted by dressing, leaning against the small table on the *kang*.

"I'm afraid you can't rest now," he told her. "The old lady
will be gone by tomorrow at the latest, so you can't keep out
of it. Hurry up and get somebody to clear up here, then make
the effort to go over there. If it comes to the worst, we shan't
be able to come back today."

"What is there here to clear up?" retorted Hsi-feng. "We've
only these few things left, so what does it matter? You go first;

the master may want you. I'll come when I've changed my clothes."

Chia Lien went ahead to the old lady's place and whispered to Chia Cheng that all the preparations had been made. Chia Cheng nodded. Then the doctor was announced. Chia Lien invited him in to feel the old lady's pulse. After some time he withdrew and quietly told Chia Lien, "The old lady's pulse is very weak. Be prepared. . . ."

Chia Lien understood and told Lady Wang, who signalled to Yuan-yang and, when she came over, sent her off to make ready the garments in which to lay out the old lady. At this point the Lady Dowager opened her eyes and asked for some tea. Lady Hsing gave her a cup of ginseng broth but after tasting it she said:

"Not this. Give me a cup of tea."

Forced to humour her, they brought it immediately. She took two sips, then said, "I want to sit up."

"If you want something, madam, just tell us," urged Chia Cheng. "There is no need to sit up."

"After a little drink I feel better," she answered. "Prop me up on the pillow so that I can talk to you."

Chen-chu gently propped her up, and they saw that she did look better. To know whether she lived or died, read the next chapter.

CHAPTER 110

The Lady Dowager Passes Away Peacefully
Hsi-feng Is Powerless and Loses Support

Sitting up the old lady said, "I've lived in your family sixty years and more, from girlhood to old age, and had more than my share of good fortune. Reckoning from your father down, all my sons and grandsons are good. But Pao-yu whom I've been so fond of...." She broke off here and looked round. Lady Wang pushed Pao-yu to her bedside and the old lady reaching out one hand from the quilt took his hand.

"You must make good, child!" she exhorted him.

"Yes, madam." He felt a pang but dared not cry, simply standing there while his grandmother continued, "I shall be content if I can see another great-grandson born. Where is my Lan?"

As Li Wan pushed him forward, the old lady let go of Pao-yu and took Lan's hand.

"You must be a dutiful son," she said. "Make your mother feel proud of you when you grow up! Where is Hsi-feng?"

Hsi-feng, standing near the bed, stepped forward saying, "Here I am."

"You're too clever, child; you must do more good works. I haven't done many myself, simply letting others take advantage of me. I never went in much for fasting or chanting Buddhist scriptures, except that year when I had all those copies of the *Diamond Sutra* made. Have they all been distributed?"

"Not yet," was Hsi-feng's reply.

"Then hurry up and have them all given away. Our Elder Master and Chen are enjoying themselves outside, but the most heartless one of all is that little wretch Hsiang-yun who still hasn't come to see me!"

422

Yuan-yang and those who knew the reason said nothing. Next the old lady looked at Pao-chai and sighed. Her face was flushed now, a sign as Chia Cheng knew that the end was near. He offered her some ginseng broth, but already her jaws were locked and her eyes closed. She opened them, however, for a last look round the room. Lady Wang and Pao-chai stepped forward and gently propped her up, while Lady Hsing and Hsi-feng changed her clothes. Meanwhile serving-women had prepared the bier and spread bedding over it. Now they heard a rattling in her throat, and a smile overspread her face as she breathed her last — at the age of eighty-three. The women hastily laid her on the bier.

Chia Cheng and the other men knelt down in the outer room, Lady Hsing and the other ladies inside, and together they lamented. The stewards' preparations outside were complete. As soon as they heard the news, all the gates of the Jung Mansion were thrown wide open and pasted with white paper. Funeral sheds were erected as well as an archway in front of the main gate. The family and the domestics lost no time in putting on mourning.

Chia Cheng reported his mother's death, and the Ministry of Rites petitioned the Emperor for leave for him. The Most High in deep compassion, in view of the Chia family's past achievements and the fact that the old lady was the Imperial Consort's grandmother, bestowed on Chia Cheng one thousand taels of silver and ordered the Ministry of Rites to take charge of the sacrifice. The stewards spread word of the old lady's death and, though the Chia family had declined, when their relatives and friends saw the favour shown them by the Emperor they all came to offer their condolences. An auspicious day was chosen for coffining the dead and the coffin was deposited in the hall.

In the absence of Chia Sheh, Chia Cheng was the head of the house. Pao-yu, Chia Huan and Chia Lan, as young descendants, had to keep watch by the coffin. Chia Lien, though a grandson too, undertook with Chia Jung's assistance to assign the men-servants' tasks. Certain kinsmen were also invited to help out.

As for the ladies, Lady Hsing, Lady Wang, Li Wan, Hsi-feng and Pao-chai were to lament by the coffin. Madam Yu should by rights have helped organize the household, as since Chia Chen's departure she had been staying in the Jung Mansion; but she had never shown any initiative and had little knowledge of its management. Chia Jung's wife, it goes without saying, was even less competent while young Hsi-chun although she had grown up in the Jung Mansion knew nothing about its domestic affairs. So none of these could take charge.

Hsi-feng was the only one capable of undertaking the task, and indeed with Chia Lien in charge outside it seemed appropriate to have her helping him inside. Emboldened by her previous experience of superintending Chin Ko-ching's funeral, she was confident that here was another chance to display her ability; and Their Ladyships both thought her the best choice. When, therefore, she was asked to superintend, she accepted readily.

"I ran this household before and the staff here obey me," she thought. "The servants of Lady Hsing and Madam Yu used to be troublesome, but now they've gone. Though we haven't used a tally to get money from the treasury, we have ready cash in hand for this purpose which is even better; and my husband is in charge of affairs outside. So even if my health isn't what it was, I don't think I'll fall down on the job as it's bound to be simpler than that time in the Ning Mansion."

She decided to wait another day till the first three days had passed, then assign the servants tasks first thing in the morning. She told Chou Jui's wife to announce this to the staff and to bring her the register. Looking through this she found twenty-one men-servants in all and only nineteen women, not counting the maids in the various apartments. As this made a total of barely forty people, they were going to be short-handed. "We've fewer hands now for the old lady's funeral than that time in the East Mansion," she reflected. Even if she transferred a few servants from their farm, they still would not have enough.

As she was mulling this over a young maid came to report, "Sister Yuan-yang would like you to go over, madam."

Hsi-feng went and found Yuan-yang weeping bitterly. She caught hold of Hsi-feng and cried, "Please sit down, madam, and let me kowtow to you. Mourners can dispense with ceremony, they say, but I must kowtow to you now!" She fell on her knees.

Hsi-feng hastily stopped her. "What does this mean? Just tell me what you want," she said, pulling her up.

"All the arrangements, inside and outside, for the old lady's funeral are being made by Master Lien and you, madam. The silver for this was put aside by the old lady, who never squandered money in her whole life; so now I beg you, madam, to give her a fine, handsome send-off. Just now I heard the master quote a classical tag — I didn't understand it — something like 'In mourning, grief counts for more than appearances.' I asked Madam Pao, who told me he meant that the most filial way to mourn the old lady is to show our grief, instead of wasting money to make a good show. But it seems to me that surely things should be done more impressively for someone like the old lady. I'm only a slave, though, so what can I say? But the old lady was so good to us both, won't you do the thing handsomely? I know you're an able organizer, madam; that's why I asked you here to decide. I've served the old lady all my life, and now that she's dead I mean to follow her still. If I don't see her given a good funeral, how shall I be able to face her?"

Puzzled by this outburst Hsi-feng replied, "Don't worry. It's not difficult to prepare a fine funeral. Though the master wants us to economize, we've a position to keep up. Even if we spend the whole sum on this, that's only right."

"The old lady's last words were that anything she had left was for us. If you don't have enough, madam, just use this to make up the deficit. Whatever the master says, he can't go against her last wishes. Besides, he was there, wasn't he, and heard how the old lady shared things out."

"You've always been a sensible girl. Why are you carrying on like this now?" Hsi-feng asked.

"I can't help worrying, because the Elder Mistress lets things slide and the master's afraid of being ostentatious. If *you* share his view, madam, that for a family that's been raided to have a splendid funeral may lead to another raid, and don't care about the old lady, what's to be done? I'm just a bondmaid and this doesn't concern me; but our family's reputation is at stake!"

"I understand. Don't worry. I'll see to it."

Then Yuan-yang thanked Hsi-feng profusely for her goodness.

Hsi-feng left thinking, "What an odd creature Yuan-yang is! I wonder what's on her mind? By rights the old lady should have a handsome funeral. Well, never mind her. We'll do it according to our family tradition." She sent for Lai Wang's wife to ask Master Lien to come in.

"What do you want me for?" inquired Chia Lien when presently he entered. "Just look after your end of things inside the house. All decisions will be made anyway by the Second Master. It's up to us to do whatever we're told."

"So you take that line too?" said Hsi-feng. "Apparently Yuan-yang guessed right."

"What did she say?"

Hsi-feng described how Yuan-yang had asked her over and what she had said.

"What they say doesn't count," scoffed Chia Lien. "Just now the Second Master sent for me and said, 'Of course we must do things in style for the old lady. People in the know are aware that she provided for her own funeral; those not in the know may think that we kept some money tucked away and are still well-off. But if this silver of hers isn't used, who wants it? It should still all be spent on her. The old lady's from the south, where there is a graveyard but no houses for offering sacrifices. As her coffin's to go back to the south, we should keep some money to build houses in the ancestral graveyard and use the remainder to buy a few acres of fields to provide for sacrifices. Even if we don't return south ourselves we can let some poor relations live there, to sacrifice to her during festivals and to see to the upkeep of the grave.' Don't you agree that that's a sound idea? So how can we spend the whole sum on the funeral?"

"Have they issued the silver yet?"

"Who's seen any silver? All I know is that after my mother

heard this she thoroughly approved, telling the Second Master and Mistress that it was a good idea. So what can *I* do? Now the men putting up the funeral sheds outside want several hundred taels, but no silver has been issued. When I went to draw some, they said they had the money but we should get the workmen to finish the job before settling accounts with them. Just think, all those servants with money have skedaddled. When we call the roll, some are said to be on sick leave, others to have gone to the farm. Those few left here, unable to leave, are just out to make money. Who's going to advance us any?"

Hsi-feng was struck speechless. Eventually she asked, "Then how are we to manage?"

Just then a maid came in and said, "The Elder Mistress wants to ask you, madam, why everything's still topsy-turvy though today is the third day. After the sacrifice, why keep relatives waiting around? She called several times for the meal before the dishes came — without any rice. What way is this to manage?"

Hsi-feng at once went to expedite the servants and manage to get a meal of sorts served to the guests. As ill luck would have it, many guests had come, but all the servants were so apathetic that Hsi-feng had to see to things herself. Then in her concern she hurried out and made Lai Wang's wife summon all the serving-women to assign them different tasks. The women accepted these but made no move.

"What time is it?" Hsi-feng demanded. "Why haven't you prepared the sacrificial offerings?"

"That's easily done," they answered. "But first we have to be issued with supplies."

"You stupid creatures!" fumed Hsi-feng. "Of course you'll get what you need for the jobs you're given."

The women went off then reluctantly, while Hsi-feng hurried to the main apartment to ask Their Ladyships' permission to fetch what would be needed. She could hardly do this, however, in front of so many guests. As it was nearing sunset, she had to find Yuan-yang and tell her which of the old lady's things she wanted.

"Why ask me?" replied Yuan-yang. "Didn't Master Lien pawn them that year? Has he ever redeemed them?"

"We don't need gold or silver, just an ordinary dinner service."

"Hasn't that gone to Lady Hsing and Madam Yu?"

Hsi-feng realized that this was so and went to Lady Wang's quarters to find Yu-chuan and Tsai-yun. Having got what she required from them she hastily made Tsai-ming list these things, then handed them over to the serving-women.

Hsi-feng had looked so flustered that Yuan-yang did not like to call her back. She wondered, "Why is she bungling things like this now when she used to be such a good manager? In the last few days things have been at sixes and sevens. The old lady's love for her was thrown away!"

She was unaware that Lady Hsing had concurred with Chia Cheng's proposal because she had been worrying about her family's future and was eager to put something by. Besides, as the old lady's funeral should have been superintended by the senior branch of the family, although Chia Sheh was away, each time there was some decision to make punctilious Chia Cheng would say, "Ask the Elder Mistress."

Lady Hsing had always considered Hsi-feng extravagant and Chia Lien unreliable and would therefore not let any money out of her hands. Yuan-yang, assuming that the funeral expenses had already been issued, suspected Hsi-feng of floundering because she did not take the business seriously. Accordingly she kept weeping and wailing before the old lady's coffin.

When Lady Hsing heard these implied reproaches, instead of blaming herself for not facilitating Hsi-feng's work she said, "It's true, Hsi-feng isn't putting herself out."

That evening Lady Wang summoned Hsi-feng and told her, "Though our family's in these straits, we must keep up appearances. I've noticed that in the last few days our visitors haven't been properly looked after. I suppose you didn't give instructions for this. You must bestir yourself a bit more for us!"

Hsi-feng was at a loss for words. She wanted to explain that there was no silver to meet their expenses, but the silver was not her concern while this charge against her was one of negligence. Not venturing to defend herself she remained silent.

Lady Hsing put in from the side, "By rights we daughters-in-law, not you young people, should see to these things. But as we can't leave the coffin we entrusted them to you. You mustn't trifle with your task."

Hsi-feng flushed crimson and was about to answer when music struck up outside — it was time for the dusk burning of sacrificial paper. As everyone had to mourn now she could say nothing; and later, when she came back to explain the real situation to them, Lady Wang urged her to go and see to things.

"We'll hold the fort here," she said. "Run along to make preparations for tomorrow."

Hsi-feng had to withdraw then, bottling up her resentment, and summoned all the matrons to give them instructions.

"Take pity on me, nannies!" she pleaded. "I've been scolded by Their Ladyships because you've not pulled together, making our family look ridiculous. You must try a bit harder tomorrow!"

"This isn't the first time you've run things, madam," they said. "We wouldn't dream of disobeying you. But this time our mistresses are too pernickety! Just take the question of meals: some want to eat here, others in their own quarters; when we fetch in one lady, another refuses to come. What with all this, how can we see to everything? Do persuade those ladies' maids, madam, not to pick so many faults."

"The most troublesome are the old lady's maids," said Hsi-feng. "Their Ladyships' are a difficult lot too — how can I tell them off?"

"When you took charge in the East Mansion, madam, you beat or cursed anyone you pleased," they countered. "You were so sharp, who dared to disobey you? Can't you control these minxes today?" Hsi-feng sighed, "When I was given that East Mansion job, though the mistress was there she didn't like to find fault. Now this business concerns the others as well as ourselves, so everyone feels free to criticize. Besides, the money outside isn't issued promptly. When something's needed, for example, for the funeral sheds and we send out for it, it isn't forthcoming — what can *I* do about it?"

"Isn't Master Lien in charge outside?" they countered. "Can't he attend to such things?"

"Don't tell me he's in charge! He's in a fix too. In the first place, the silver isn't in his hands and he has to put in a request for every purchase. He has no ready money."

"Isn't the sum the old lady left in his hands?"

"Go and ask the stewards presently — they'll tell you."

"No wonder then!" they said. "We've heard the men outside complain, 'A big do like this, yet there's nothing in it for us except hard work!' So how can you expect people to pull together?"

"Never mind that now but concentrate on the work in hand. Any more complaints from above and I shan't let you off!"

"How dare anyone grumble, whatever you want done, madam? But it's really hard for us to please everyone with each of the mistresses giving different orders."

At a loss, Hsi-feng pleaded, "Good nannies, at least help me out tomorrow! We'll talk things over again after I've made the ladies' maids see sense."

Then the serving-women left.

Hsi-feng, seething with resentment, brooded with mounting anger till dawn, when she wanted to discipline the maids of the various apartments, yet feared that might offend Lady Hsing; and she could not complain to Lady Wang, whom Lady Hsing had turned against her. When the maids saw that Their Ladyships were not backing Hsi-feng up, they treated her with even less respect.

Ping-erh alone spoke up for her, explaining, "Of course Madam Lien wants to do things in style, but the master and Their Ladyships have forbidden any extravagance, which makes her unable to satisfy everybody." By stressing this she calmed them down a little.

Now they had Buddhists chanting sutras and Taoists saying masses, with endless mourning, sacrifices and meals for guests; but they were so niggardly that no one would buckle to and the service was slipshod. Although titled ladies kept arriving, Hsi-feng had no time to attend to them, so busy was she supervising the servants. As soon as she summoned one, another slipped away. She would first fume at them then appeal to their better nature; and in this way she managed to send off batch after batch of guests after entertaining them all anyhow. Of course Yuan-yang and the others thought it disgraceful, and even Hsi-feng herself was mortified.

Though Lady Hsing was the elder daughter-in-law, she turned a blind eye to everything else, simply displaying her filial piety by an appearance of overwhelming grief. Lady Wang had to follow suit, and naturally so did the rest. Li Wan, the only one to appreciate Hsi-feng's dilemma, dared not speak up for her.

She just sighed to herself, "As the saying goes, though the peony is lovely it needs the support of green leaves. With Their Ladyships letting her down, who else is going to help poor Hsi-feng? If Tan-chun were here it wouldn't be so bad. Now she has only a few of her own servants to make shift as best they can, and they keep complaining behind her back that they're not making a cent or getting any credit! The master harps on filial piety but doesn't know much about management. How can a big affair like this be properly conducted without a certain outlay? Poor Hsi-feng! She's been to such pains these few years to win a reputation, and now it looks as if she's going to lose it over this funeral!"

She made time to summon her own maids and told them, "Don't follow the example of those others and start plaguing Madam Lien too. You mustn't think you can get by by wearing mourning and keeping watch by the coffin for a few days. If you see them unable to cope, you should lend a hand. This is the affair of us all: it's everybody's duty to help out."

Some of the servants who had genuine respect for Li Wan agreed, "You're quite right, madam, and we'd never dream of making trouble. But Sister Yuan-yang and the others seem to hold Madam Lien to blame."

"I've spoken to Yuan-yang too," replied Li Wan. "I've explained to her that it's not that Madam Lien doesn't take the old lady's funeral seriously, but she doesn't control the money, and how can the smartest daughter-in-law make gruel without rice? Now that Yuan-yang understands she's stopped blaming her. Still, it's extraordinary the way Yuan-yang has altered. When she was the old lady's favourite, she didn't try to take advantage of it; now that the old lady's gone and she has no backing, she seems to have changed for the worse. I used to worry what would become of her. Luckily the Elder Master isn't at home now, so she's escaped his clutches. Otherwise, what could she have done?"

At this point Chia Lan came up and said, "Mother, it's time to go to bed. So many visitors all day long must have tired you; do have a rest now. I haven't touched my books these days, so I'm very glad that today grandfather told me to sleep at home — I must review one or two books, so as not to have forgotten everything by the time the mourning is over."

"Good child!" said Li Wan. "Of course it's good to study, but today you'd better rest. Wait till after the funeral."

"If you're going to sleep, mother, I'll curl up in my quilt too and think over my lessons."

The others all approved, "There's a good boy! Such a little lad, yet when he's a moment to spare he thinks of his books. How different from Master Pao who's still so childish even after his marriage. How uneasy he looks these days kneeling by his father; and the moment the master leaves he rushes off to find Madam Pao and whisper some nonsense to her. When she ignores him he looks for Miss Pao-chin, who tries to steer clear of him too. Miss Hsing hardly ever talks to him either. The only ones nice to him are his cousins Hsi-luan and Ssu-chieh, for ever calling him 'cousin' this and 'cousin' that. We don't believe Master Pao thinks of anything except fooling about with young ladies. He hasn't lived up to the old lady's expectations. She always doted on him, yet he can't hold a candle to our Master Lan. You won't have to worry about *his* future, madam!"

"It's too early to say," replied Li Wan. "And who knows

what will have become of our family by the time he grows up? But what's your opinion of young Master Huan?"

"That one's even worse!" they exclaimed. "He has eyes like a real monkey, darting shiftily this way and that. Though he's supposed to wail by the coffin, when the ladies come he spends all his time peeping at them round the curtain before it."

"Actually he's no longer a child," she said. "The other day I heard they were thinking of finding him a wife, but now that will have to wait. Still, our family's too big for us to sort out everyone's problems, so let's not gossip about them. And there's something else I meant to ask. The funeral procession is to be the day after tomorrow. Are carriages ready for all the different households?"

"Madam Lien seems so distracted these days that we haven't seen her issuing instructions. Yesterday we heard from the men outside that Master Lien told Master Chiang to see to this. As our family doesn't have enough carriages or drivers, he says we'll have to borrow some from relatives."

"Can carriages be borrowed?" asked Li Wan with a smile.

"You must be joking, madam! Of course they can. But that day all our relatives will be using theirs, so borrowing may be hard and we'll probably have to hire some."

"We shall have to hire some for the servants, but how can the ladies take hired mourning carriages?"

"The Elder Mistress has no carriage now. Neither have Madam Yu and Master Jung's wife from the East Mansion," they reminded her. "What can they do but hire some?"

Li Wan sighed, "In the old days, when female relatives called on us in hired carriages, we all thought it scandalous. Now it's our turn. Tell your husbands tomorrow to get our carriages and horses ready as early as possible, to avoid a jam."

The serving-women assented and withdrew.

Since Shih Hsiang-yun's husband was ill, she had called only once after the old lady's death; but she felt she must attend the funeral which she reckoned would be held in two days' time. In any case, her husband's illness had proved to be consumption, so that he was in no immediate danger. She therefore came over the day before the wake, when she recalled the old lady's goodness to her, then thought of her own wretched fate. She had only just married a talented, handsome husband with a cheerful disposition, but then he had contracted this fatal illness which might any day carry him off. In distress she wept half the night, despite the attempts of Yuan-yang and the others to console her.

Pao-yu, seeing this, grieved for her too but was in no position to comfort her. He noticed that in her white mourning, her face bare of rouge and powder, she looked even lovelier than before her marriage. He turned then to eye Pao-chin and the other girls in white and found them all very charming. Pao-chai, who was in deep mourning, had an air of greater distinction than in the coloured clothes she normally wore.

Pao-yu told himself, "The men of old said that of all flowers the plum-blossom ranks first. That must be not only because it's the first to bloom, but because its pure white and its fine fragrance are matchless. If only Cousin Lin were here now, dressed like this, how beautiful she would be!" At this thought, he felt a pang and could not hold back his tears; and as they were mourning the Lady Dowager he did not restrain himself but sobbed aloud.

The others were trying to make Hsiang-yun stop crying when Pao-yu suddenly burst out sobbing too. They assumed that he was upset by the memory of the old lady's kindness to him, little knowing that he and Hsiang-yun were weeping for different reasons. Their storm of grief brought tears to the eyes of all. It was Aunt Hsueh and Aunt Li who finally stopped them.

The next day, the day of the wake, was still more strenuous. Hsi-feng felt too exhausted to bear up, yet she had no choice but to exert herself until she was hoarse from shouting. That morning she managed to cope. By the afternoon, however, more relatives and friends arrived, entailing even more work, and she could not see to everything at once. She was frantic when a young maid ran up to her.

"So here you are, madam!" she cried. "No wonder our Elder Mistress says, 'There are too many visitors for me to look after, but Madam Lien has sneaked off to take it easy.' "

At this, Hsi-feng thought she would burst with anger. She held back her rage, but tears welled up in her eyes, everything turned dark and she tasted something sweet. Then red blood spurted from her mouth, her knees buckled and she collapsed. Ping-erh ran to support her as she went on vomiting whole mouthfuls of blood. To know what became of her, read the following chapter.

CHAPTER 111

Yuan-yang Dies for Her Mistress and Ascends to the Great Void A Despicable Slave Leads Robbers into the Mansion

The young maid's taunt so enraged and wounded Hsi-feng that she vomited blood and fainted. Ping-erh held her up and called for help to carry her back to her room, where they laid her gently on her bed and ordered Hung-yu to give her a drink of warm water. After one sip, however, Hsi-feng relapsed into unconsciousness. Chiu-tung came over to glance at her then went off, and Ping-erh did not call her back. Instead she told Feng-erh who was standing near by to take word of this at once to Their Ladyships.

When Feng-erh explained Hsi-feng's inability to entertain the guests, Lady Hsing suspected her of shamming and shirking, but did not like to say this in the presence of so many relatives.

She simply replied, "All right, let her take a rest." And the others made no comment.

That evening, naturally, they had a stream of visitors. It was lucky that certain close relatives helped entertain them, for some of the staff took advantage of Hsi-feng's absence to play truant or slack and pandemonium reigned — it was most unseemly.

After the second watch, when the guests living at a distance had left, they prepared to farewell the dead and the women behind the mourning curtain began to wail. Yuan-yang wept so bitterly that she fainted away. They raised her up and massaged her till she came round.

"The old lady was so good to me, I must follow her!" she cried.

Thinking her beside herself with grief, the others paid no attention. When the ceremony started, there were over a hundred mourners high and low present, but Yuan-yang had disappeared. In the general confusion her absence passed unnoticed until it was time for Hu-po and the other maids to kowtow to the dead; however, supposing that Yuan-yang worn out by weeping must be resting somewhere, they let it go at that.

The ceremony at an end, Chia Cheng called Chia Lien outside to ask about the cortège the next day and whom he meant to leave in charge at home.

"Of the masters, I've told Chia Yun to stay behind," Chia Lien reported. "Of the servants, I've ordered Lin Chih-hsiao's family to see to the dismantling of the sheds. But which of the ladies should stay to keep an eye on the inner apartments?"

"I hear from your mother that your wife is too unwell to go. She can stay at home. And your Sister-in-law Yu suggests that since she is so ill, Hsi-chun should keep her company and get a few maids to look after the mistresses' quarters."

Chia Lien knew that Madam Yu had made this proposal because she was not on good terms with Hsi-chun, who could not take effective charge; and Hsi-feng was too ill to cope. After some consideration he replied, "Please have a rest, sir, while I go in to settle it with them before reporting back."

Chia Cheng nodded and Chia Lien went to the inner quarters.

Now Yuan-yang after a bout of weeping thought, "I've been with the old lady all my life, and I've found no niche for myself. Although the Elder Master isn't at home now, I don't think much of the Elder Mistress either. And with the Second Master letting things slide, there'll be such chaos in future that there's no knowing who else may take over. Then we shall be at their mercy, whether they decide to make us concubines or marry us off to some servants. I couldn't stand that. Better die and be done with it! But how shall I kill myself?"

By now she had entered the old lady's annex. As she stepped over the threshold in the dim lamplight, she saw the shadowy figure of a woman who appeared to be about to hang herself with the scarf in her hand. Yuan-yang felt no fear but wondered, "Who is she? She has the same idea as mine, but is a step ahead of me."

"Who are you?" she asked. "Since we're both of the same mind, let's die together."

The other made no reply, and Yuan-yang approaching her saw that it was not one of their household. When she tried to look closer, the air struck chill and the apparition vanished. In stupefaction she left the room and sat down on the *kang*.

"Ah, I know," she murmured after a moment's reflection. "That was Master Jung's first wife from the East Mansion. She died so long ago, what brought her here? She must have come to summon me. But why should she hang herself?" She thought it over and decided, "That's it. She's showing me the way."

This train of thought enabled an evil spirit to take possession of her and standing up, weeping, she opened her dressing-case to take out the lock of hair which she had cut off when she swore never to leave the old lady's service. Having tucked it inside her tunic, she undid her sash and looped it over the beam indicated by Chin Ko-ching. Then she wept again until the sound of guests dispersing outside made her afraid that someone might come in. She made haste to close the door, moved over a footstool and stood on it, tied the sash into a noose, slipped it round her throat and kicked the stool away. Then, alas, strangled to death, her sweet spirit took flight!

Her wraith was wondering where to go when she saw Chin Ko-ching's shadowy form in front. She overtook her crying, "Wait for me, Madam Jung!"

"I am not Madam Jung," was the reply, "but the sister of the Goddess of Disenchantment."

"I can see quite clearly that you're Madam Jung — why should you deny it?"

"Let me tell you the reason, then you'll understand. I was

the Arbiter of True Love in the palace of the goddess, and all romantic affairs were in my charge; then I descended to the dusty world as the most amorous of mortals, to lead all lovesick maidens back betimes to the Board of Love. This is why it was my lot to hang myself. Now that I have seen through earthly love, passed over the sea of love and returned to heaven, there is no one in charge of the Board of Infatuation in the Illusory Land of Great Void. The Goddess of Disenchantment has appointed you in my place to head this Board, and has therefore ordered me to lead you there."

"I have never known passion," replied Yuan-yang's spirit. "How can I count as amorous?"

"You don't understand. Mortals mistake carnal appetite for love, and justify their immorality by calling themselves romantics and passing it off lightly. In fact, before the expression of joy or anger, grief or happiness, love is latent in each one's nature; once these feelings are expressed then we have passion. *Our* love is as yet unexpressed like a flower in bud. If once expressed, it would cease to be true love."

Yuan-yang's wraith nodded agreement, then followed Ko-ching's spirit.

After Hu-po had bid farewell to the dead and heard Their Ladyships designate caretakers, she decided to go and ask Yuan-yang what carriage they would be taking the next day. Unable to find her in the old lady's room, she approached the smaller room which opened off it. The door was closed, but peeping through a crack she was startled by the dim lamplight and flickering shadows, though she could hear not a sound.

She went away exclaiming, "Where can the wretch have run off to?" Bumping into Chen-chu she asked, "Have you seen Sister Yuan-yang?"

"I'm looking for her too," was the answer. "Their Ladyships want her. Is she asleep in the annex?"

"I had a peep and didn't see anyone. The lamp hasn't been trimmed, and it was too dark and scary to go in. But now we can go in together, to make sure there's no one inside."

As they went in to trim the lamp Chen-chu exclaimed, "Who put the stool here? It nearly tripped me up!"

Happening to look up, she let out a little scream and fell backward, knocking hard against Hu-po, who by then had also seen the fearful sight. She shrieked, rooted to the spot. People outside hearing their cries rushed in and, after exclaiming in horror, went to report this to Their Ladyships.

At this news, Lady Wang, Pao-chai and the rest shed tears and went to take a look.

Lady Hsing remarked, "I never imagined Yuan-yang had it in her! We must send word of this at once to the master."

Pao-yu kept silent, gaping in consternation, till Hsi-jen anxiously took his arm and urged him, "Cry if you want to, but don't suppress your feelings."

Then Pao-yu burst out wailing. "Only someone like Yuan-yang would choose this way to die!" he thought. "The subtlest elements in the universe are truly concentrated in such girls! She died a splendid death. Which of the old lady's sons or grandsons can compare with her, filthy creatures that we are?" This reflection raised his spirits.

Pao-chai had heard Pao-yu wailing, but by the time she reached his side he was smiling.

"This is a bad sign!" cried Hsi-jen. "He's losing his mind again."

"Don't worry," said Pao-chai. "He has his reason."

This delighted Pao-yu, who thought, "After all *she* understands me. The others don't."

As Pao-yu was letting his fancy run wild, Chia Cheng and some others came in.

"What a good girl!" declared Chia Cheng approvingly. "The old lady's love for her wasn't thrown away." He told Chia Lien, "Go and send to buy a coffin immediately and give her a good funeral. Tomorrow her coffin can go in the old lady's cortège and be left in the temple behind the old lady's coffin. This is what she wished for."

Chia Lien withdrew to attend to this, while orders were

given to cut down Yuan-yang's corpse and lay it out in the inner room.

Word of this brought Ping-erh, Hsi-jen, Ying-erh and the other maids to the scene, where they mourned bitterly. Tzu-chuan. who could see no future for herself, wished she had followed Tai-yu to her grave to repay her mistress' kindness, thinking that would have been a good death. As it was, she was hanging about for nothing in Pao-yu's quarters; for though he treated her affectionately, nothing would come of it. So she wept even more heart-rendingly than the rest.

Lady Wang now summoned Yuan-yang's sister-in-law to attend to the coffining. After some discussion with Lady Hsing, she also presented her with a hundred taels of the old lady's money, promising to give her all Yuan-yang's belongings later. The sister-in-law kowtowed her thanks and withdrew.

"She really had spirit, the lucky girl!" she exulted. "Winning herself a good name like this and a fine send-off!"

"What a way to talk!" said a matron standing near by. "You're so tickled at selling her life for a hundred taels, you'd have been even better pleased that year to have given her to the Elder Master for a still bigger sum."

This home-thrust made the sister-in-law blush. She had just reached the inner gate when Lin Chih-hsiao led in men carrying the coffin, obliging her to return to help lay out the corpse and make a pretence of wailing.

Because Yuan-yang had died for the Lady Dowager, Chia Cheng called for incense, lighted three sticks, and bowed before her coffin.

"Since she immolated herself she can't be treated as a bondmaid," he said. "All you youngsters should pay homage to her."

Pao-yu, only too glad to comply, came over and kowtowed respectfully. Chia Lien, mindful of her past goodness to him, wanted to follow suit but Lady Hsing stopped him.

"It's enough for one of the masters to kowtow to her," she reasoned. "If we overdo it she'll lose her chance of reincarnation."

Then Chia Lien desisted.

Pao-chai put out by this officiousness said, "By rights I shouldn't pay homage to her, but after the old lady's death we dared do nothing rash because of all the business we had to attend to; and as she showed true filial piety in our place, we should entrust to her the task of serving the old lady in our stead when she enters paradise. So it's only right for us to express our thanks."

Then leaning on Ying-erh's arm she went up to the coffin and poured a libation of wine, tears flowing down her cheeks. After that she bowed several times with clasped hands and wept bitterly. Some of those present thought Pao-yu and his wife both rather crazed, others that they were compassionate, yet others that they understood etiquette; and Chia Cheng approved of their conduct. They agreed to leave Hsi-feng and Hsi-chun in charge of the house while the rest joined the funeral cortège. There was little sleep for anyone that night.

At the fifth watch the cortège could be heard assembling outside. At seven it set off, headed by Chia Cheng in deep mourning and weeping as befitted a filial son. Then the coffin was borne out of the gate and sacrifices were offered at the roadside by different families — we need not go into detail. Eventually they reached Iron Threshold Temple, where both coffins were deposited and all the men were required to stay. But no more of this.

Meanwhile in the Jung Mansion Lin Chih-hsiao supervised the dismantling of the sheds, refitted the doors and windows, had the courtyards swept clean and then assigned night-watchmen. According to the rules of the house, after the second watch the three gates were closed and no man was permitted to enter the inner apartments, where only women kept watch.

Hsi-feng felt a little clearer in her mind after a night's rest, although too limp to get up. So Ping-erh and Hsi-chun inspected the various apartments, then issued instructions to the women on watch and retired to their own quarters.

Let us turn back now to Chou Jui's godson Ho San. The previous year when Chia Chen was in charge, he had been thrashed and driven out because of his brawl with Pao Erh, and he spent most of his time in a gambling-den. Recently, hearing of the old lady's death and assuming that there must be odd jobs going, he had gone there to make inquiries day after day — but all to no effect. He went back grumbling to the gambling-house and sat down dejectedly.

His cronies asked, "Why not play to recoup your losses?"

"I would if I could," said Ho San, "but I've no money."

"You've been with your godfather for several days and must have got pots of money from the Jung Mansion. Don't go telling us you're broke."

"Shut up!" he snapped. "They've got millions all right, but they're hanging on to it. It'll serve them right if one of these days there's a fire or thieves break in."

"You're lying again," said the others. "After their place was raided they can't have much left."

"A fat lot you know. It was only things from the Palace that got confiscated. The old lady left masses of gold and silver, but they won't touch it — it's all tucked away in her room waiting to be shared out after the funeral."

One of the gamesters made a note of this and after a few more throws remarked, "I've lost quite a bit but won't try to win it back now. I'm for bed." As he left he pulled Ho San out too. "Come on," he said, "I want a word with you."

Ho San went out with him.

"You're a smart fellow yet now you're broke," said the man. "I think it's a shame."

"It's my fate to be poor. What can I do about it?"

"You just said there's pots of silver in the Jung Mansion. Why don't you get hold of some?"

"Brother, they may be rolling in gold and silver, yet when the likes of us ask for a cent or two will they part with it for nothing?"

"If they won't, what's to stop us from helping ourselves?"

Catching his implication Ho San demanded, "Then what do you suggest?"

"I call you pretty dumb. If I were you I'd have taken it long ago."

"How would you go about it?"

"If you want to make a pile," the other whispered, "all you need do is act as guide. I have plenty of friends who are dabs at this. Not to say the Chias are away at the funeral, with only a few women left in the house; no matter how many men were there we wouldn't be afraid! All I'm afraid of is that you haven't the guts."

"Of course I have! Do you think I'm scared of that godfather of mine? I only put up with him for my godmother's sake. He doesn't count. As for your idea, I'm afraid it may be a flop and land us in trouble instead. They have connections, you know, in all the yamens. So quite apart from the fact that we may not pull it off, even if we do they'll raise a hullabaloo."

"If that's all that's worrying you, you're in luck! I've palled up with some men from the coast, who are on the look-out here for some opening. If we get the loot, there's no point in staying here — we'd better go to sea to have a good time, eh? If you don't want to ditch your godmother, we can take her along as well to share the fun. How about it?"

"You must be drunk, old man, to talk such rubbish!" With that Ho San pulled him to a quiet spot to discuss the matter further. Then they went their different ways, and there we will leave them.

Let us now revert to Pao Yung, who had been berated by Chia Cheng and sent to keep watch in the Garden. After the Lady Dowager's death, although the whole household was busy while he was assigned no job that did not disturb him. He cooked his own meals, went to sleep when bored, and in his waking hours would exercise with a sword or staff in the Garden, left to his own devices. That morning he knew that the funeral cortège had left, but as no assignment had been given him he rambled round as his custom was till he saw a nun with an old deaconess go up to the side-gate and start knocking on it.

Pao Yung went over and asked, "Where are you going, reverend sister?"

The deaconess said, "We heard today that the services for the old lady have ended, but didn't see Miss Hsi-chun with the cortège, so we think she must be at home minding the house. For fear she may feel lonely, my mistress has come to call on her."

"The family are all away and I'm the gateman here," was Pao Yung's reply. "I must ask you to go back. If you want to call, wait till the masters are back."

"What upstart scavenger are you," she asked, "that you try to interfere with our coming or going?"

"I've no use for the likes of you," was his retort. "I won't let you in, so you'll just have to lump it."

"The impertinence!" she screeched. "Even when the old lady was alive, no one ever stopped us from coming. Who are *you*, you lawless brigand? We're going this way, so there!" With that she beat a tattoo with the door-rapper.

Miao-yu, speechless with anger, was about to turn back when the woman in charge of the inner gate heard them quarrelling and hastily opened the gate. Seeing Miao-yu turning away, she guessed that Pao Yung must have offended her. As all the women-servants knew how fond their mistresses and Hsi-chun were of Miao-yu, she feared that if they came to learn that she had been refused admittance there would be trouble.

She hurried over calling, "We didn't know you were here, sister, and were late in opening the gate. Miss Hsi-chun is at home, longing to see you. Please come back. This caretaker is new here and doesn't know our ways. We'll report him later to Her Ladyship and see that he's given a whipping and thrown out."

When Miao-yu pretended not to hear, the woman chased after her and pleaded with her. Finally she voiced her own fear of punishment, all but going down on her knees, she was so frantic. So Miao-yu had to follow her through the gate. Pao

Yung glared but, unable to bar the way, went off fuming.

Miao-yu, attended by the old deaconess, called on Hsi-chun and after expressing her condolences they started chatting.

Hsi-chun told her, "I'm to stay and look after the house, and shall have to manage as best I can for a few nights; but Madam Lien is ill and I find it boring and scaring all on my own. If I had company I'd feel easier, for there isn't a single man in the house now. As you've done me the honour of calling today, won't you spend the night with me? We can play draughts and chat."

Miao-yu had no wish to stay but gave her consent because Hsi-chun looked so pathetic, and a game of draughts appealed to her too. When she had sent back the deaconess to get her maid to bring over her tea things, night-clothes and bedding, they settled down for a good talk; and Hsi-chun in her delight told Tsai-ping to fetch some rain water kept from the previous year to brew some choice tea. Miao-yu would not drink out of any cups but her own; however, before long her maid brought over her things and Hsi-chun herself made the tea. They chatted happily until the first watch, when Tsai-ping got out the draughts board and they played draughts. Hsi-chun lost twice in succession, then managed to win the third game by half a point only because Miao-yu ceded her four pieces.

In no time it was the fourth watch. The night was still, with not a sound outside.

"I must meditate at the fifth watch," Miao-yu remarked. "My maid will look after me. You'd better rest."

Hsi-chun felt reluctant to part with her, but could hardly interfere with her devotions. She was about to go to bed when the women keeping watch in the Lady Dowager's quarters on the east side set up a sudden commotion. At once the matrons attending Hsi-chun joined in.

"Help!" they screamed. "Men have broken in!"

In a panic, Hsi-chun and Tsai-ping heard the night-watch outside shouting too.

"Mercy!" gasped Miao-yu. "They must be robbers!"

She promptly locked the door, shrouded the lamp and peeped

out through the window. There were men standing in the yard. Too terrified to utter a sound, she turned, signalling for silence, then crept back and whispered, "What shall we do? There are some rough fellows outside."

That same instant they heard a great clattering on the roof, and watchmen came running to their compound to catch the thieves.

One called, "The old lady's room has been ransacked, but there's nobody there. We have men at the east side; let's search the west ourselves."

When Hsi-chun's serving-women heard that these were their own family retainers, they called out, "There are lots of them on our roof!"

The watchmen yelled, "Look! There they are!" and raised a clamour; but as tiles were raining down from the roof they dared not clamber up. Just as they were at a loss, the side-gate of the Garden banged and through it rushed a hefty fellow wielding a staff. At sight of him they took cover in alarm.

"Don't let one of them get away!" the newcomer yelled. "All follow me!"

The servants were too consternated to move — their bones seemed turned to water. They stared at that fellow standing there bellowing till the most keen-sighted among them identified him as Pao Yung, recommended to their house by the Chen family. That reassured them.

"One has gone," they faltered. "Some others are up on the roof."

Pao Yung ran and vaulted on to the roof to give chase.

The thieves had known that there were no men in the house. While in Hsi-chun's courtyard they had peeped through the window and been inflamed by the sight of a ravishing nun. As there were only terrified women inside, they were about to kick down the door when they heard the night-watch rushing in after them and promptly climbed up the roof. When they saw that their pursuers were few they thought of putting up a fight, but just then someone leapt on to the roof and charged them. As he was alone the thieves were not alarmed and went for him

with knives; but when Pao Yung with his staff knocked one of
them off the roof, the rest fled over the Garden wall with him
in hot pursuit. Accomplices hidden in the Garden to receive
the loot had already carried most of it off. When they saw the
thieves fleeing they drew weapons to defend them, and as Pao
Yung was one against many they swarmed round him.

"You bandits!" he swore. "Dare you take me on?"

One thief reminded the rest, "He knocked down one of our
mates whom, dead or alive, we'd better carry off."

Pao Yung hit out and four or five of the ruffians, all armed,
surrounded him and fought back wildly. But now the night-
watchmen plucked up courage to join in, and seeing that they
could not get the upper hand the thieves had to run for it. Pao
Yung, pursuing them, tripped over a case. When he regained
his balance he thought: If the things are still here and the thieves
have got away, there's no point in chasing them. He told the
other servants to search with their lanterns, but all they found
on the ground were a few empty cases which he asked them to
put away while he himself went to the mistresses' quarters. As
he did not know the way, he arrived first at Hsi-feng's house
which was lit up.

"Do you have thieves here?" he asked.

Ping-erh inside quavered, "We haven't opened the gate. We
only heard them shouting that there were thieves in the old
lady's rooms. You'd better go there."

Pao Yung was wondering what path to take when some
watchmen turned up and led the way. They found all the doors
open and the women on night duty weeping and wailing.

Presently Chia Yun and Lin Chih-hsiao arrived, frantic at
having learned of the robbery. They went in to investigate.
The door to the old lady's room was wide open, and they saw
by their lanterns that the lock was broken. Going in, they
found all the chests and cases empty.

They swore at the women who had been on duty, "Are you
all dead? Didn't you know when thieves broke in?"

The women sobbed, "We took turns keeping watch, and *our*
shifts were before midnight. We never stopped making our

rounds from front to back. Those thieves came well after midnight when we'd gone, so we just heard shouting but didn't see anybody. You must ask the women in charge of the later shifts, sir."

"You all deserve to die!" fumed Lin Chih-hsiao. "We'll deal with you later. Let's go first to the different quarters to have a look."

The watchmen took them to where Madam Yu lived. The gate was locked, but some women inside called out, "Oh, what a fright we had!"

"Did you lose anything here?" asked Lin Chih-hsiao.

They opened the door saying, "Nothing."

Next Lin Chih-hsiao led the way to Hsi-chun's quarters.

"Mercy on us!" they heard a woman inside exclaiming. "Our young lady's fainted for fright. Quick, bring her round!"

He told them to open the door and asked what had happened.

The woman who admitted them reported, "Thieves were fighting here, and our young lady passed out for terror. Luckily Sister Miao-yu was here, and she and Tsai-ping revived her. We haven't lost anything."

"What were the thieves fighting over?"

A watchman told him, "We have to thank Pao Yung for jumping on the roof to chase them away. We heard that he knocked down one of the thieves too."

"He's by the Garden gate," volunteered Pao Yung. "You'd better go quickly to have a look at him."

Chia Yun and the others did so. They found a man lying there dead. Looking at him closely, to their surprise they recognized Chou Jui's godson. They assigned one man to guard the corpse and two others to watch the front and back gates, both still locked. Lin Chih-hsiao told men to open the gate and report this robbery to the police. At once an investigation was made, and it was discovered that the thieves had climbed up to the roof from the back passage. Following their tracks to the roof of the west courtyard, they found many broken tiles and other tracks leading to the back and the Garden.

The watchmen insisted, "They were brigands, not thieves."

The constable protested, "If they didn't break in openly with torches and clubs, how can you call them brigands?"

"When we gave chase, they pelted us with tiles from the roof so that we couldn't get near them. Then one of our household, a man called Pao, managed to get on the roof and beat them off. When he chased them to the Garden, a whole bunch of them attacked him. They only ran away after they started getting the worst of it."

"That proves it," the constable said. "If they'd been brigands, couldn't they have beaten you people? Never mind that now. Quickly check on what has been stolen and send in a list so that we can report it to our superiors."

Chia Yun and the others went back to the main apartments, where Hsi-feng had come, ill as she was, and Hsi-chun. Chia Yun paid his respects to Hsi-feng and greeted Hsi-chun, then together they tried to find out what was missing. But as Yuan-yang was dead and Hu-po and the old lady's other maids had gone to the funeral, no one knew exactly how many things she had had, since they had been kept locked up. So how could they make a check?

They said, "There were many things in these cases and chests, and now they're all empty. It must have taken quite a time to ransack them. What were those women on night duty doing? And the thief killed was Chou Jui's godson. So it must have been partly an inside job."

"Have all those women locked up," ordered Hsi-feng, glaring at them furiously. "Then take them to the police to be cross-examined!"

The women fell on their knees, wailing, to beg for mercy. How they were dealt with and whether or not the lost property was recovered is recorded in the next chapter.

CHAPTER 112

A Terrible Disaster Befalls Miao-yu
Nursing Enmity Concubine Chao Is
Haled Off to Hell

When Hsi-feng ordered the women on night duty to be bound and sent to the police for interrogation, they threw themselves on their knees to beg for mercy.

"It's no use pleading," said Lin Chih-hsiao and Chia Yun. "The master left us in charge here. If nothing had happened, well and good; as it is, high and low alike we're all in trouble so who can get you off? If the dead man is Chou Jui's godson, then from Her Ladyship down the whole household is involved."

"This is our fate," gasped Hsi-feng. "Why talk to them? Just turn them in. As for what was stolen, assure the police that it was the old lady's property and we must find out from the masters just what she had. After this is reported to them and they come back, we shall certainly send in the list of stolen goods and notify the civil authorities too."

Chia Yun and the steward assented and withdrew.

Hsi-chun, who had given no orders, simply lamented, "I've never heard of such a thing before! Why did this have to happen to *us* of all people? How can I face the master and mistress when they come back? They'll say: We entrusted the house to you, and you let this dreadful thing happen. How can I live on?"

"We didn't wish it on ourselves, did we?" said Hsi-feng. "Anyway, it's the night-watchers who are responsible."

"You have some justification because you're ill; but I have no excuse. It's my elder sister-in-law who did for me by getting the mistress to make me mind the house! How can I look anyone in the face again?" She broke down anew and wept.

"Don't take it so hard," said Hsi-feng. "We've all lost face equally. If you take this silly attitude I shall feel worse."

Just then someone in the yard started bellowing, "I've always said those nuns, bawds, go-betweens and the like are no good! Our Chen family never let such creatures cross our threshold. Who would have thought *this* house would put up with them? Yesterday, the moment the old lady's cortège left, that nun from some small temple was dead set on coming over here. When I refused to admit her, the old woman at the side-gate bawled *me* out and fairly grovelled to invite her in. The side-gate kept opening and shutting — heaven knows what they were up to! I was too worried to sleep, and at the fourth watch bedlam broke loose inside. They wouldn't let me in when I saw a fellow standing in the west courtyard I charged over and killed him. Today I've discovered that this is where Miss Hsi-chun lives, and where that nun came. She sneaked off this morning before it was light. Stands to reason it was the nun who led the thieves in!"

"Who is this mannerless wretch?" demanded Ping-erh. "How dare he shout so wildly outside when there are ladies in here?"

"Didn't you hear him talk of the Chen family?" Hsi-feng said. "He must be that pesky creature they recommended." She asked Hsi-chun, now even more upset by Pao Yung's diatribe, "What nun was he ranting about? Did you have some nun staying with you?"

Hsi-chun explained how Miao-yu had called and how she had kept her for the night to play draughts.

"So that's who it was. And she was willing? Well, wonders will never cease! But if this tiresome wretch keeps yelling about it and the master hears, there may be trouble."

Nervous about the possible consequences, Hsi-chun stood up to leave. Hsi-feng urged her to stay for, although she could hardly bear up, she was afraid that Hsi-chun in her alarm might do something desperate.

"Wait till we've seen them put away the things left by the thieves and assigned people to keep an eye on the place," she said. "Then we can go."

Ping-erh interposed, "How can we put anything away till officers have come to investigate? We'll just have to stay and keep watch here. But has anyone gone to report this to the master?"

Hsi-feng told her to send a matron to find out, and the latter came back to announce, "Lin Chih-hsiao can't get away, and some servants will have to stay to wait on the officers while the others can't take a clear message. So young Master Yun has gone."

Hsi-feng nodded and, with Hsi-chun, went on sitting there anxiously.

To return to the gang of thieves roped in by Ho San, after they had carried off the old lady's gold, silver and other valuables and seen how feeble their pursuers were, they decided to rob the houses on the west side. Looking through a lighted window there they saw two beauties: a young lady and a nun. Then these wicked desperadoes would have broken in had not Pao Yung's arrival made them run off with their loot, although Ho San was missing. They hid for the time being with their fence, and the next day learned that Ho San had been killed and the theft reported to the authorities — which meant they could not stay in the capital. They decided to make haste to join some pirates at sea, for if they delayed until warrants were out against them they would be unable to pass the customs stations.

"Of course we must clear out," said the boldest among them. "But I can't bear to leave that nun behind. She's certainly a beauty! I wonder from which nunnery this chick comes."

"I know!" exclaimed another. "She must be from that Green Lattice Nunnery in the Chia Mansion. Wasn't there talk some years ago of an affair between her and their Master Pao? She was said to be so lovesick that a doctor was called in to give her some potion."

Thereupon the other proposed, "Let's lie low for one more day while our chief buys what we need for the journey. Tomorrow when the dawn bell strikes, you can leave the city gate separately and wait for me at Twenty-*li* Slope outside."

Having agreed to this, the thieves divided out the loot and dispersed.

Meanwhile Chia Cheng and the others had escorted the coffin to Iron Threshold Temple and deposited it there, after which the relatives and friends went back. Chia Cheng kept vigil in the outer hall of the temple, Lady Hsing and Lady Wang within, lamenting the whole night long.

The next day another sacrifice was to be held and the offerings were being set out when Chia Yun arrived. Having kowtowed before the Lady Dowager's coffin he ran over to kneel to Chia Cheng and pay his respects, then blurted out the news of last night's robbery — how everything in the old lady's rooms had been stolen, how Pao Yung had given chase and killed one of the thieves, and how they had reported this to the authorities. Chia Cheng listened dumbfounded. Their Ladyships overhearing this inside were frightened out of their wits. Speechless, they could only sob.

After a while Chia Cheng asked, "How did you draw up the list of stolen property?"

"As no one at home knew what was there, we haven't drawn it up yet," was Chia Yun's reply.

"So much the better. As our house was searched, to list any valuables would be reprehensible. Tell Lien to come here at once."

He sent for Chia Lien, who had taken Pao-yu and some others to sacrifice elsewhere. And Chia Lien was so frantic when he heard the news that, regardless of Chia Cheng's presence, he cursed Chia Yun.

"You worthless wretch!" he fumed. "When I trusted you with such an important job, you should have seen to it that the place was patrolled at night. What are you — a zombie? I wonder you have the nerve to come and report it."

He spat repeatedly in Chia Yun's face while the young man stood at respectful attention, not daring to say a word.

"It's no use swearing at him," objected Chia Cheng.

Then Chia Lien knelt to ask him, "What shall we do, sir?"

"All we can do is report this to the authorities and hope they will apprehend the thieves. The trouble is that we didn't touch the old lady's legacy. When you asked for money I thought it wrong to use her silver so soon after her death, meaning to settle accounts and pay the workmen after the funeral. I intended to use what was left to buy land here and in the south near the ancestral graveyard to provide for sacrificial expenses. I don't really know how much she had left. Now that the authorities want a list of what's lost, it may cause further trouble to mention valuables. In any case, we don't know the exact amount of her gold and silver or her clothes and trinkets, and we can't fake it up. It's ridiculous, I must say, the way you've bungled affairs. What's come over you? What use is it kneeling there?"

Not venturing to answer, Chia Lien stood up to leave.

"Where are you going?" snapped Chia Cheng.

He turned back to reply, "I'm going to hurry home to straighten things out, sir."

When Chia Cheng simply snorted, Chia Lien hung his head again.

"Go in and tell your mother first," ordered Chia Cheng. "Take one or two of the old lady's maids with you. Tell them to think carefully then make out a list."

Chia Lien knew perfectly well that all the old lady's things had been in the charge of Yuan-yang who was dead; so to whom could he apply for information? Chen-chu and the others would certainly not know. However, afraid to argue, he assented. Then he went inside where he was taken to task again by Their Ladyships, who told him to hurry back and ask the caretakers, "How will you have the face to meet us tomorrow?"

Chia Lien agreed and withdrew to order a carriage for Hupo and the maids. Mounting a mule himself he galloped home accompanied by a few pages. Chia Yun, too cowed to say any more to Chia Cheng, withdrew slowly with lowered head to mount his horse and follow. We can pass over their journey.

When Chia Lien reached home, Lin Chih-hsiao paid his respects and followed him in to the old lady's quarters where Hsi-feng and Hsi-chun were. Though seething with anger Chia Lien could not vent it on them.

He asked Lin Chih-hsiao, "Have officers been sent to investigate?"

With a guilty conscience the steward knelt down and reported, "The civil authorities have investigated the tracks made by the thieves, and also examined the corpse, sir."

"What corpse!?"

Told how Pao Yung had killed one of the thieves who looked like Chou Jui's godson, Chia Lien immediately summoned Chia Yun, who came in and knelt down too to hear his orders.

"Why didn't you report to the master that Chou Jui's godson was one of the thieves and he was killed by Pao Yung?" Chia Lien demanded.

"The night-watchmen thought it looked like him, but as we couldn't be sure I didn't report it."

"You idiot!" swore Chia Lien. "If you'd reported it, I would have brought Chou Jui back to identify him, to clear the matter up."

Lin Chih-hsiao informed him, "The police have taken the corpse to the market-place to see who claims it."

"Then they're idiots too!" cried Chia Lien. "Who's going to ask to have justice done if one of his family has been killed as a robber?"

"Actually, they don't have to identify him," said the steward. "I recognized him all right."

Chia Lien replied thoughtfully, "Yes, wasn't it Chou Jui's godson whom Master Chen wanted to punish that year?"

"He had a fight with Pao Erh, and you saw him yourself, sir."

This made Chia Lien more furious. He wanted to have all the night-watchmen beaten.

The steward begged him, "Please don't be angry, sir. Which of those watchmen would dare shirk his duty? But the rule of our house is that none of them can enter the inner gate — even *we* don't go in unless sent for. Master Yun and I kept a careful check outside and saw that the inner gate was firmly locked. None of the outer gates was opened either. The thieves came from the back passage."

"Then how about those women inside who were watching during the night?"

He was told that on Hsi-feng's orders they had been bound to await his questioning.

"Where is Pao Yung now?" he asked.

"He has gone back to the Garden."

"Bring him here."

When servants had fetched him Chia Lien said, "It's a good thing you were here; otherwise most likely they'd have robbed all our houses."

Pao Yung said nothing to this, while Hsi-chun was on tenterhooks for fear lest he mention Miao-yu. Hsi-feng did not dare to speak either.

Then someone outside announced the return of Hu-po and the other maids. When they came in all wept together again. Ordered by Chia Lien to ascertain what had been left by the thieves, all they could find were some clothes, some lengths of silk and a money-box — everything else had gone. He thought with desperation of the workmen and the cooks who had not been paid — how to settle with them all tomorrow? He was bemused.

After Hu-po and the others had had their cry and discovered all the chests and cases open, unable to remember what they had contained they made up a list at random to send in to the authorities. Then Chia Lien reassigned the night-watch and Hsi-feng and Hsi-chun retired to their own quarters. Chia Lien could not presume to rest at home and had no time to remonstrate with Hsi-feng. He mounted a horse and rode back out of the city while she, afraid Hsi-chun might commit suicide, sent Feng-erh to comfort her.

At the second watch that night, all the inmates of the house were on their guard, too scared to sleep, locking the stable door after the horse had been stolen. But the thieves were set on kidnapping Miao-yu, knowing that there were only weak women in the nunnery. By the third watch when all was still, armed with daggers and narcotic incense they climbed on to the high wall and saw from the distance that there were still lights in Green Lattice Nunnery. One of them slithered down and hid himself beside it.

He waited till the fourth watch, when there was only one lamp left burning inside, and saw Miao-yu on her hassock sitting cross-legged in meditation.

After a while she sighed, "I came from Hsuanmu to the capital hoping to make a name; but then I was invited here and couldn't go anywhere else. Yesterday out of kindness I called on Hsi-chun only to be abused by that lout, and during the night I had another bad fright. Coming back today I still feel on tenterhooks, unable to concentrate."

As a rule she meditated in solitude and she was therefore reluctant to call in someone today to keep her company. But by the fifth watch, shivering with cold, she had just decided to summon her maid when a sound outside the window startled her, recalling what had happened the previous night. She called for her women, but not one of them answered. As she sat there, she smelt a whiff of scent which seemed to seep into her brain; and a numbness overcame her, making her unable to move or utter a sound. Panic-stricken then, she saw a man climb in with a gleaming dagger. Although still conscious she could not stir and, thinking that he must be going to kill her, she resigned herself to her fate and her fear left her. However, the intruder tucked his knife in the back of his belt to free his hands, then quietly took her in his arms and trifled with her a while. He then picked her up and slung her on to his back. Miao-yu felt as if drunk or deranged. So, alas, this pure-minded girl was drugged by the robber and ravished!

Carrying Miao-yu to the back wall of the Garden, this thief fixed up a rope-ladder and climbed over to where his mates had a carriage waiting. They laid Miao-yu inside it, then carrying lanterns inscribed with official titles called upon the guards to open the street gates and hurried to the city gate just as it was due to open. The officers there, assuming that they were going out on official business, did not even challenge them. They whipped their horses on to Twenty-*li* Slope to join the rest of their gang, then made their way by different routes to the south coast.

Whether Miao-yu lived on in shame after being kidnapped, or whether she resisted and was killed we cannot venture to say, not knowing the sequel.

Another of Miao-yu's attendants in Green Lattice Nunnery had been sleeping in the back room at the fifth watch when she heard a call from in front and supposed that her mistress was too restless to meditate. Next, she heard what sounded like a man's footsteps and a window being opened. She wanted to get up and investigate, but felt too listless even to call out. Hearing no summons from Miao-yu she waited till dawn by which time her head had cleared. Throwing on some clothes she got up then and called the deaconess to prepare tea and water. When she went to the front, however, Miao-yu had vanished without a trace and the window was wide open. Remembering the noises during the night, she had misgivings and wondered, "Where can she have gone so early?"

Going out of the courtyard to have a look, she found a rope-ladder by the wall and on the ground a pouch and dagger sheath.

"Mercy on us!" she cried. "Some thief must have drugged us last night!" She frantically called to the others to get up and make a search. The gate of the nunnery was still locked.

"We must have been overcome by charcoal fumes so that none of us could get up," said the serving-women. "But what do you want us for so early in the morning?"

"Our mistress has disappeared."

"She'll be meditating in the hall."

"You're still dreaming! Come and look!"

In bewilderment they opened the nunnery gate and made a search of the whole Garden. Drawing a blank and assuming that Miao-yu had gone to see Hsi-chun, they knocked at the inner gate and were once more roundly abused by Pao Yung.

They explained, "Sister Miao-yu disappeared last night so we've come looking for her. Please be good enough to open the gate to let us ask whether she's here or not."

"That mistress of yours brought in thieves to rob our family," he swore. "Now she's gone off with them to enjoy the loot."

"Amida Buddha! What a thing to say! Aren't you afraid of going to the Hell Where Tongues Are Cut Out?"

"Shut up!" he fumed. "If you go on making a row I'll beat you up."

"Please tell them to open the gate," they begged. "We just want to have a look. If she isn't there we won't trouble you again, sir."

"If you don't believe me, go ahead and look. But if you don't find her you'll have to answer for it."

With that he called people to open the gate and Miao-yu's attendants trooped into Hsi-chun's compound.

Hsi-chun was feeling anxious and depressed. She wondered, "After Miao-yu left so early, can she have heard what that fellow Pao said? If she's offended she may never come back, and I shall be left friendless. I'm really in a fix now, with my parents dead and my sister-in-law against me. The old lady used to be good to me but now she's gone too, leaving me all alone. What's to become of me?"

She mused, "Cousin Ying-chun died through cruel treatment; Cousin Hsiang-yun's husband is dying of consumption; and Cousin Tan-chun has gone so far away. This was their fate, they had no say in the matter. Miao-yu's the only one who's completely free, free as a cloud or wild crane. How I do envy her! But how can the daughter of an official family do as she pleases? I'm in disgrace now because of this robbery. How can I look people in the face again? And I doubt whether Their Ladyships understand me, so I've no idea what the future holds for me."

She decided to cut off her hair and become a nun. When Tsai-ping and the others saw what she was doing they hastily intervened, but not before half of it had been snipped off.

"Before one trouble ends, another starts!" exclaimed Tsai-ping frantically. "What shall we do?"

As they were crying out in consternation, Miao-yu's attendants arrived in search of her. When Tsai-ping knew their errand she gave a start.

"She left first thing yesterday morning and hasn't been back," she told them.

Hsi-chun inside asked hastily, "Where has she gone?"

Then the women described the noises during the night, the charcoal fumes which had overcome them and Miao-yu's disappearance this morning, as well as the sheath and rope-ladder they had found. Hsi-chun was alarmed, not knowing what to make of this. Recalling what Pao Yung had said, she felt sure the thieves had seen Miao-yu and returned last night to kidnap her. If that were so, proud and chaste as she was, she would surely take her own life.

"Did none of you hear anything else?" she asked.

"We did. But though we were awake we couldn't utter a sound. Those thieves must have drugged us with narcotic incense. Most likely Sister Miao-yu was drugged too and unable to cry out. In any case, with all those thieves threatening her with swords and clubs, she wouldn't dare make a sound."

At this point Pao Yung bawled from the inner gate, "Hey, you there! Drive out those dirty nuns, quick! Hurry up and lock the gate."

Tsai-ping, afraid she might be blamed for admitting them, urged the women to leave and ordered servants to lock the inner gate. By now Hsi-chun was feeling more wretched than ever. However, Tsai-ping and the rest reasoned with her and persuaded her to dress her half-shorn hair. They agreed to keep this to themselves and feign ignorance of Miao-yu's kidnapping, not taking any action till the return of the masters and mistresses. Hsi-chun was even more determined now to enter a convent, but no more of this for the moment.

Chia Lien on his return to Iron Threshold Temple reported how he had cross-examined the night-watch, made out a list of the lost property and notified the police.

"What did you list?" asked Chia Cheng.

Chia Lien showed him a copy of the list of things which Hu-po remembered.

"Regarding the gifts from the Imperial Consort, we have noted them," he said. "We left out certain other things which ordinary families are not supposed to have. As soon as it's time for me to stop wearing mourning I shall go and get people to make a careful search, and we should be able to recover them."

Chia Cheng nodded his approval but said nothing. Chia Lien went in then to see Their Ladyships.

"Better urge the master to go home early," he suggested. "Or everything will be at sixes and sevens."

"That's right," agreed Lady Hsing. "Staying here we're on tenterhooks."

"We juniors can't propose this," he added. "But if you do, madam, the Second Master is bound to fall in with your wishes."

Lady Hsing and Lady Wang talked it over and decided to go back.

The next morning Chia Cheng, who was also worried, sent Pao-yu to request Their Ladyships to go home that day and return a few days later. He had assigned stewards to take charge in the temple and hoped they would assign their serving-women different duties. Then Lady Hsing instructed Ying-ko and some other maids to keep watch by the coffin, and put Chou Jui's wife and some matrons in overall charge. All the rest of the servants were to accompany them home. Carriages and horses were hastily made ready while Chia Cheng and the others bid farewell with lamentations to the old lady's coffin.

As they rose to leave, Concubine Chao remained prostrate. Thinking she was still mourning, Concubine Chou went to help her up and found that she was foaming at the mouth, her eyes staring blankly, her tongue lolling out. They were staggered by the sight and Huan started howling.

Concubine Chao regaining consciousness cried, "I'm not going home! I'm going south with the old lady."

"There's no need for that," the others expostulated.

"I've served the old lady all my life," she said. "The Elder Master wouldn't take no for an answer, and tried all sorts of tricks to get hold of me. So I asked the sorceress Ma to help me get my own back, spending all that silver for nothing — neither of them was killed. Now I'm going back, I don't know who'll plot against me again!"

All knew that Yuan-yang's spirit must have taken possession of her. Their Ladyships stared at her speechlessly. It was Tsai-yun who interceded, "Sister Yuan-yang, you died of your own accord and Concubine Chao had nothing to do with it. Please let her be." In Lady Hsing's presence she dared not say any more.

"I'm not Yuan-yang," protested Concubine Chao. "She's long since gone to the immortals' realm. The King of Hell has sent to arrest me, to try me for practising witchcraft with that priest-ess Ma." Then she screamed, "Good Madam Lien! Don't denounce me to the King of Hell! Bad as I was I must have done a bit of good as well. Dear madam, kind madam! I didn't mean to kill you. I was muddled for a while and did what that old bitch said."

While she was raving like this, Chia Cheng sent for Chia Huan. Serving-women reported to him, "Concubine Chao is bewitched and Master Huan is looking after her."

"What nonsense!" scoffed Chia Cheng. "We shall go first then." So the gentlemen set off.

Concubine Chao went on raving in the temple and they did not know how to bring her to her senses. For fear of further disclosures Lady Hsing said, "Leave some people here to look after her. We'll go back first. When we reach the city we'll send a doctor to see her."

Lady Wang who had never liked Concubine Chao also washed her hands of her. But Pao-chai was too kind-hearted to do this, despite the attempt on Pao-yu's life which she remembered, and so she secretly told Concubine Chou to stay and look after her. The latter, being a good soul, agreed. Li Wan volunteered to stay too but Lady Wang overrode her.

"Do *I* have to stay here?" asked Chia Huan in desperation as they were leaving.

"Stupid creature!" snapped Lady Wang. "Your mother may be dying. How can you leave?"

This silenced Chia Huan, and Pao-yu told him, "Good brother, you mustn't leave. When I get back to town I'll send people to see you."

Then they all went home by carriage, leaving only Concubines Chao and Chou, Chia Huan, Ying-ko and a few others in the temple.

After Chia Cheng, Lady Hsing and the others reached home, they went to the old lady's room and wept. Lin Chih-hsiao led in the servants to kneel and pay their respects.

"Get out!" ordered Chia Cheng sternly. "We'll question you tomorrow."

Hsi-feng had been feeling too faint that day to come out to welcome them. Hsi-chun met them blushing with shame. Lady Hsing ignored her, while Lady Wang treated her as if nothing had happened and Li Wan and Pao-chai took her hand and said a few words to her.

Only Madam Yu sneered, "Thank you, miss, for looking after the house the last few days."

Hsi-chun made no answer, her face flushing crimson as Pao-chai pulled Madam Yu's sleeve and shot her a glance. Then they all dispersed to their own quarters.

Chia Cheng after a cursory look round heaved a sigh but made no comment. He went to sit in his study and summoned Chia Lien, Chia Jung and Chia Yun to give them certain instructions. Pao-yu's offer to keep him company there he declined; and Lan remained with his mother.

After an uneventful night, Lin Chih-hsiao came to the study first thing in the morning to kneel before his master. Questioned about the theft, he mentioned Chou Jui's involvement.

"The police have arrested Pao Erh," he said. "They found on him some of the things listed as stolen. Now they are interrogating him to find out the whereabouts of that gang of thieves."

"What ingratitude!" thundered Chia Cheng. "Family slaves bringing thieves to rob their masters! Outrageous!" He at once sent men out of the city to tie up Chou Jui and take him to the police to be cross-examined. Lin Chih-hsiao remained kneeling before him in trepidation.

"Why are you still kneeling there?" Chia Cheng demanded.

"I deserve death. I beg you, sir, to be merciful!"

Just then Lai Ta and other senior servants came in to pay their respects and present the accounts for the funeral.

"Give those to Master Lien to check and report back to me." This order given, Chia Cheng dismissed the stewards.

Chia Lien going down on one knee whispered something to him.

"Rubbish!" replied Chia Cheng sternly. "Though the money for the old lady's funeral has been stolen, how can we punish our slaves by making them pay instead?"

Chia Lien flushed but dared not argue, and stood up but dared not leave.

"How is your wife?" Chia Cheng asked.

Chia Lien knelt again to reply, "It looks as if she's past saving."

"I never guessed our family could go downhill so fast!" Chia Cheng sighed. "Huan's mother has fallen ill too in the temple, and we have no idea what the trouble is. Do you know?"

Chia Lien did not venture to answer.

"Go and send servants to take a doctor to attend her."

Chia Lien promptly assented and went off to see that a doctor was despatched to Iron Threshold Temple. To know whether Concubine Chao lived or died, you must read the chapter which follows.

CHAPTER 113

Repenting Her Sins Hsi-feng Seeks Help
from a Village Woman
Relinquishing Her Resentment Tzu-chuan Is
Touched by Her Besotted Master

Concubine Chao, throwing a fit in the temple, babbled even more wildly once the main party had left, to the consternation of the few who remained there. When two serving-women tried to lift her up she insisted on kneeling, raving and weeping by turns. Then, grovelling, she begged for mercy.

"You're beating me to death, Master Red Beard!" she cried. "I shall never dare do such a thing again!"

Presently, wringing her hands, she shrieked with pain, her eyes nearly starting from her head, blood trickling from her mouth, her hair dishevelled. The attendants were afraid to go near her.

By nightfall her voice was so hoarse that she sounded like a ghost wailing. The women, not daring to stay with her, called in a few bold men to keep her company. Sometimes she fainted away then after a while came round, keeping up a commotion all night. The next day she was speechless but with her face contorted kept tearing her clothes and baring her breasts, as if someone were stripping her. Though unable to utter a sound, the poor creature's agony was painful to witness.

At this critical juncture a doctor arrived. He dared not go near her to feel her pulse but warned them to prepare for the funeral.

As he rose to leave, the steward who had brought him pleaded, "Please examine her pulse, sir, so that I can report it to our master."

When the doctor complied the pulse had already stopped

beating. Chia Huan hearing this burst out howling, and the others turned all their attention to him, ignoring Concubine Chao as she lay there dead. Only kindly Concubine Chou thought to herself, "So this is the end of a concubine! Though *she* at least had a son. Heaven knows what it will be like when *I* die!" This reflection pained her.

The steward hurried back to inform Chia Cheng, who sent people to attend to Concubine Chao's funeral and keep Huan company there for three days before bringing him back. After the steward's return the news spread like wildfire that Concubine Chao had been tortured to death by the King of Hell because she had plotted murder.

Some predicted, "Madam Lien must be done for too, if Concubine Chao said it was she who denounced her."

This talk reached Ping-erh's ears, increasing her worry, for she saw that Hsi-feng's illness really looked fatal. And Chia Lien had recently lost his affection for her — busy as he was, he might at least have shown some concern for her health. Ping-erh tried to comfort her mistress; but Their Ladyships, though they had been back several days now, merely sent servants to ask after her instead of coming themselves, adding to Hsi-feng's wretchedness. And Chia Lien, when he came home, never had a kind word for her.

By now Hsi-feng's sole wish was to die and be done with it, and in this state of mind she was assailed by spectres — she saw Second Sister Yu walking over from the back of the room towards her *kang*.

"How long it's been since last I saw you, sister!" said Second Sister Yu. "I missed you badly but was unable to see you. Now that you've worn yourself out by all your scheming, my chance has come at last. Our husband's too foolish to feel obliged to you and blames you instead for stinginess and for ruining his career, so that now he can't hold up his head. This is so unfair that my heart bleeds for you!"

In a daze Hsi-feng replied, "And I'm sorry now that I was

so narrow-minded. Yet instead of bearing a grudge you come to see me!"

Ping-erh beside her heard this and asked, "What's that you're saying, madam?"

Then Hsi-feng woke up and remembered that Second Sister Yu was dead and must have come to demand her life. She felt afraid but, not liking to disclose this, forced herself to say, "My mind was wandering. I must have been talking in my sleep. Massage my back for me."

As Ping-erh was doing this a young maid came in to announce the arrival of Granny Liu, whom a serving-woman had brought to pay her respects.

Ping-erh immediately left the *kang* asking, "Where is she?"

"She won't presume to come in unless madam sends for her."

Ping-erh nodded. Thinking Hsi-feng too ill to receive visitors she said, "Madam is resting. Tell her to wait outside. Did you ask her business?"

"The others did," answered the maid. "She's not here for anything special. She says she only heard the other day about the old lady's death, or she'd have come earlier."

Hsi-feng overhearing them called, "Ping-erh, come here! Since she's kind enough to call we mustn't cold-shoulder her. Go and ask Granny Liu in. I want to chat with her."

While Ping-erh went off on this errand Hsi-feng was about to close her eyes when she saw a man and a woman approaching as if they meant to get on to her *kang*. At once she called out to Ping-erh, "Where has this man burst in from?"

She called twice, and Feng-erh and Hung-yu came running in.

"Do you want something, madam?" they inquired.

Opening her eyes she saw no strangers there and realized what had happened, though unwilling to admit it.

She asked Feng-erh, "Where is Ping-erh?"

"Didn't you tell her to go and fetch Granny Liu, madam?"

Hsi-feng forced herself to keep calm and said nothing as Ping-erh and Granny Liu came in with a little girl.

"Where is Madam Lien?" asked the old woman. And when

Ping-erh led her to the *kang* she announced, "I've come to pay my respects, madam."

Hsi-feng opened her eyes and felt a pang of distress. "How are you, granny?" she responded. "Why haven't you been to see us for so long? How big your grand-daughter's grown!"

Granny Liu was grieved to see how wasted Hsi-feng had become, and how unclear in her mind. "Madam!" she exclaimed. "It's only a few months since last I saw you, and now you look so ill! It was very bad of me not to call earlier to pay my respects."

She told Ching-erh to curtsey, but she simply giggled. Hsi-feng took a fancy to the little girl and handed her over to the charge of Hung-yu.

"We villagers don't fall ill," said Granny Liu. "When we feel poorly we just pray and make pledges to the gods — we never take medicine. I daresay, madam, this illness of yours was brought on by evil spirits."

At this tactless remark Ping-erh nudged her secretly. Granny Liu took the hint and said no more; however, this coincided with Hsi-feng's own view.

"Granny," she said with an effort. "You're old and experienced. What you said is quite true. Did you hear of the death of Concubine Chao whom you met here?"

"Amida Buddha!" exclaimed Granny Liu in surprise. "She was in good health — what did she die of? I remember she had a young son. What will happen to him?"

"He'll be all right," said Ping-erh. "The master and mistress will take care of him."

"Well, miss, you never know. However bad your child may be, he's your own flesh and blood; it's different if he's a stepson!"

This touched Hsi-feng on the raw and set her sobbing. They all tried to comfort her. Chiao-chieh came to the *kang* when she heard her mother weeping and took her hand, shedding tears too.

"Have you greeted granny?" sobbed Hsi-feng.

"Not yet," said the child.

"She's the one who gave you your name, so she's your godmother in a way. You should pay your respects to her."

Chiao-chieh went over to do this but the old woman hastily stopped her.

"Amida Buddha!" she cried. "You mustn't do that to the likes of me! I haven't been here for over a year, Miss Chiao-chieh. Do you still remember me?"

"Of course I do. When I saw you that year in the Garden I was still small. The year before that when you came, I asked you for some green crickets but you didn't bring me any. You must have forgotten."

"Ah, miss, I'm in my dotage. If it's green crickets you want, our village is swarming with them, but you never go there. If you did, you could easily get a whole cartful."

Hsi-feng suggested, "Well, take her back with you."

Granny Liu chuckled, "A delicate young lady dressed in silks and brought up on the fat of the land, how could I amuse her in our place? And what could I give her to eat? Do you want to ruin me?" Laughing at the idea she went on, "I know what: I can arrange a match for her. Though we live in the country, we have big money-bags there too who own thousands of acres of land and hundreds of cattle, not to mention pots of silver. They just don't have gold and jade knick-knacks like yours. Of course, madam, *you* look down on such families. But to us farming folk they seem to be living in heaven!"

"Go and fix a match then," said Hsi-feng. "I'll agree to it."

"You must be joking! Why, a lady like you would most likely turn down even big official families; how could you agree to marry her to country folk? Even if *you* did, the mistresses wouldn't agree."

Chiao-chieh, not liking this talk, went off to chat with Ching-erh. Finding each other's company congenial, they soon became good friends.

Fearful that Granny Liu might tire Hsi-feng out with her loquacity, Ping-erh tugged at her sleeve and said, "You mentioned Her Ladyship whom you haven't seen yet. I'll go and

find someone to take you there, to make your trip here more worthwhile."

As the old woman rose to leave, Hsi-feng asked, "What's the hurry? Sit down. Let me ask you: how are you making out these days?"

Her heart brimming over with gratitude Granny Liu answered, "If not for you, madam. . . ." She pointed at her granddaughter then went on, "Her dad and mum would have starved. Now, though life on a farm is hard, we've bought quite a few *mu* of land and sunk a well. We grow vegetables and fruit too, and make enough from them to feed ourselves. The last couple of years, besides, you've given us clothes and material from time to time so that in our village we count as quite well-off. Amida Buddha! The other day when her dad came to town and heard that your family here had been raided, I nearly died of fright! Luckily others told me it wasn't *this* house, and that set my mind at rest. We learned later that the master had been promoted, and I was so pleased I wanted to come to offer congratulations, but what with all the field work I couldn't get away.

"Then yesterday we heard that the old lady had passed away. I was getting in beans when they brought me word, and it shocked me too much to go on. I broke down there in the field and cried my heart out! I told my son-in-law, 'I shall have to leave you to your own devices. Whether it's true or not, I must go to town to have a look.' My daughter and son-in-law aren't lacking in gratitude either. They both cried over the news, and this morning before dawn they sped me on my way. I didn't know anyone in town to ask, so came straight to your back gate and saw that even the door gods were pasted over. That gave me another fright! When I came in and looked for Chou Jui's wife she was nowhere to be found, and a little girl told me she'd been driven out for doing something wrong. I had to wait around till I met someone who knew me before I could get in. I'd no idea that you were so ill too, madam." By now she was shedding tears.

Ping-erh, concerned for her mistress, pulled Granny Liu to her feet before she could finish.

"After talking so long you must be parched," she said. "Let's go and have some tea." She took her to the maids' quarters, leaving Ching-erh with Chiao-chieh.

"I don't need any tea," Granny Liu assured her. "But please, miss, get someone to take me to pay my respects to Her Ladyship and to weep at the old lady's shrine."

"There's no hurry," Ping-erh replied. "You can't leave town today anyway. Just now I was afraid you might say something tactless and set our mistress weeping again: that's why I hustled you out. I hope you don't mind."

"Amida Buddha! I know how thoughtful you are, miss. But what's to be done about madam's illness?"

"Does it look serious to you?"

"Maybe it's wrong to say so, but it does."

Just then they heard Hsi-feng calling, yet when Ping-erh went to her bedside she remained silent. As Ping-erh was questioning Feng-erh, Chia Lien came in. After a cursory glance at the *kang* he entered the inner room without a word and plumped himself down, glowering. Chiu-tung alone went in to serve him tea and wait on him, but the others could not hear what they were saying. Then Chia Lien called for Ping-erh.

"Isn't your mistress taking medicine?" he asked.

"What if she isn't?"

"How should I know?" he retorted. "Bring me the key of the chest."

As he was in a temper she did not venture to question him but went out and whispered something to Hsi-feng. When the latter said nothing, Ping-erh brought in a casket and put it before Chia Lien, then turned to go.

"What the devil's your hurry?" he demanded. "Who's going to give me the key?"

Suppressing her annoyance she took it out of the casket and opened the chest. "What do you want taken out?" she asked.

"What is there?"

"Say plainly what you want," she sobbed angrily. "Then we can die content!"

"What is there to say? You were the ones who brought all the trouble on us. Now we're four or five thousand taels short for the old lady's funeral, and the master told me to raise some money from the title-deeds of the family land — but what is there left? Do you want us to default? I should never have taken on this job! All I can do is sell the things the old lady left me. Are you against that?"

Ping-erh was sulkily turning out the chest when Hung-yu darted in.

"Quick, sister!" she cried. "Madam's in a bad way!"

Ignoring Chia Lien, Ping-erh hurried out to discover Hsi-feng clawing the air with both hands. Restraining her, she wept and cried for help. Chia Lien coming out to have a look stamped his foot.

"Now this!" he groaned with tears. "I'm finished!"

Just then Feng-erh announced, "They're asking for you outside, sir." And Chia Lien had to leave.

Hsi-feng was now so delirious that her maids set up a great wailing which drew Chiao-chieh to the room. Granny Liu also hastened to the *kang*, to invoke Buddha and mutter incantations till Hsi-feng grew slightly calmer. Then Lady Wang arrived, alerted by one of the maids, and was relieved to find Hsi-feng quieter. Greeting Granny Liu, she asked when she had come; but after paying her respects the old woman could talk of nothing except Hsi-feng's illness.

Then Tsai-yun came in to report, "The master wants you, madam." So after giving Ping-erh a few instructions Lady Wang went away.

Hsi-feng had come to her senses now. At the sight of Granny Liu, whose prayers she had faith in, she sent her maids away and asked the old woman to sit beside her. Told of her qualms and the ghosts she had seen, Granny Liu assured her that the Buddhist deities in her village temple could work miracles.

"Please offer prayers for me!" begged Hsi-feng. "If you need money for a sacrifice, I have some." She slipped off a golden bracelet and held it out to her.

"There's no call for this, madam. When we villagers recover after making pledges, we just spend a few hundred coppers. What need is there for all this? I shall pray for you and make some pledge, and once you're better you can spend as much as you like."

Aware that she was in earnest, Hsi-feng could not insist. "Granny, my life is in your hands!" she said. "And my little Chiao-chieh is always ailing too; I entrust her to you as well."

Granny Liu assented readily and proposed, "In this case, as it's still early, I'll go back now. When you recover, madam, you can go to thank the gods."

Haunted by the ghosts of those she had wronged, Hsi-feng in her terror was eager for her to set off. "If you'll do this for me so that I can have a good night's sleep, I'll be very grateful," she said. "You can leave your grand-daughter here."

"She's a country girl with no manners, and may make trouble. I'd better take her back with me."

"Don't worry about that. We're all one family, so what does it matter? Though we're poor now, one extra mouth to feed is nothing."

Seeing that Hsi-feng meant this, Granny Liu wanted to leave Ching-erh for a few days to save them food at home; but she did not know whether the child would be willing. She decided to sound her out and questioned her. Ching-erh was now on such good terms with Chiao-chieh that they were reluctant to part; so Granny Liu, having given her some instructions, said goodbye to Ping-erh and went with all speed out of town. Enough of this.

Now Green Lattice Nunnery belonged to the Chia family but had been incorporated into the Garden built for the Imperial Consort's visit home. However, it had its own income and needed no allowance from the Chia Mansion. After the nuns had notified the police of Miao-yu's abduction, they did not like to leave until the thieves were arrested and they knew what had happened to their mistress. They simply reported the business to the Chia Mansion.

But though the Chia family stewards all knew of the kidnapping, they thought it too trifling a matter with which to trouble Chia Cheng now that he was in mourning and disturbed in his mind. Hsi-chun was the only one who fretted day and night because of this. Before long, however, the news reached Pao-yu's ears and it was insinuated that, tempted by desire, Miao-yu had run off with some man. "She must have been kidnapped," he told himself. "As it wasn't in her nature to submit, she must have died resisting." In the absence of news of Miao-yu he kept brooding.

"She used to call herself the 'one outside the threshold.' How could a chaste girl like that come to such an end?" he wondered. "How lively we were in the old days in the Garden! After my second sister's marriage, though, all the girls died or were married off. I thought *she* at least, unsullied by dust, would stay here; yet this sudden storm carried her off even more unexpectedly than Cousin Lin." His thoughts wandering, he recalled Chuang Tzu's saying about the illusory nature of life and felt that men were born to drift with the wind and scatter like clouds. He burst out weeping. Hsi-jen and the rest thought he was deranged again and tried in every way to comfort him.

At first Pao-chai reasoned with him too, not understanding his distress. But Pao-yu went on moping, his mind wandering. In her perplexity she made inquiries, and when she heard that Miao-yu had been kidnapped and vanished without a trace that upset her too. Still, to counteract Pao-yu's depression she lectured him, "Though Lan hasn't gone back to school I hear he's studying hard day and night. He's the old lady's great-grandson. The old lady always hoped that you, her grandson, would do well; and the master worries about you all the time. If because of some whimsy you ruin your health, what's to become of us all?"

Pao-yu did not know how to answer. After a while he said,

"Why should I worry about other people? What upsets me is the decline in our family fortune."

"There you are!" she cried. "Your parents want you to do well so as to carry on the family line. If you stick to your silly ways what good will come of it?"

Put out by this, Pao-yu laid his head on his desk as if to sleep. Ignoring his sulkiness, Pao-chai told Sheh-yueh and the other maids to keep an eye on him while she went to bed.

When he was alone in the room it occurred to Pao-yu, "I've never had a heart-to-heart talk with Tzu-chuan since she came here and feel bad the way I've cold-shouldered her, especially as she's not like Sheh-yueh and Chiu-wen whom I can keep in their place. I remember how she kept me company all that time while I was ill, and I still have that little mirror of hers — she was really good to me then. But now for some reason or other she's treating me coldly. It can hardly be because of Pao-chai, who was good friends with Cousin Lin and who isn't bad to Tzu-chuan either. When I'm out, Tzu-chuan chats quite happily with her; but as soon as I come in she goes away. I suppose it must be because after Cousin Lin died I got married. Ah, Tzu-chuan, Tzu-chuan! Can't an intelligent girl like you understand how wretched I am?" It struck him then, "They're sleeping or doing needlework this evening: here's my chance to go and find her. I'll sound her out. If I've offended her I'll beg her pardon." His mind made up, he slipped out to look for Tzu-chuan.

Tzu-chuan's room was on the west side of the courtyard. Tiptoeing up to her window, Pao-yu saw that there was still a light inside. He licked the window-paper and, peeping through the hole made in this way, saw Tzu-chuan sitting all alone in the lamplight. She was doing nothing, lost in thought.

"Sister Tzu-chuan," he called softly. "Aren't you asleep yet?"

Tzu-chuan gave a start then sat as if stunned. "Who is it?" she finally asked.

"It's me."

"Is it Master Pao?" she asked, recognizing his voice.

"Yes," he answered softly.

"What do you want?"

"I've something to tell you in private. Please let me in."

After a pause she replied, "If you've something to tell me, young master, please wait until tomorrow. It's late now; you'd better go back."

This sent a chill down Pao-yu's spine. He knew Tzu-chuan was unlikely to let him in, yet if he were to go back now he would feel even worse after her rebuff.

"I haven't much to say," he faltered. "I just want to ask you one question."

"Well then, out with it."

But for a long time he said nothing.

When he remained silent, Tzu-chuan inside was afraid that by snubbing him she had unhinged him again. She stood up and listened carefully, then asked, "Have you gone or are you standing stupidly there? If you've something to say, fire away. You've already goaded one to death; is it *my* turn now? Isn't this futile?"

She peeped through the hole he had made in the window-paper and saw Pao-yu standing there woodenly listening. In silence then she turned to trim the lamp.

Pao-yu sighed, "Sister Tzu-chuan! You used not to be so hard-hearted. How is it that nowadays you won't even say a single kind word to me? Of course I'm a lout, beneath your notice; but I do wish you'd tell me what I've done wrong so that even if you ignore me from now on I shall at least die knowing why."

"Is that all, young master?" she asked sarcastically. "Have you nothing else to say? If this is all, I tired of hearing it when my young lady was alive. If we do anything wrong, I was sent here by Her Ladyship and you can report me to her. What are we bondmaids anyway but slaves?" She broke off, choking, here and blew her nose.

Pao-yu outside realized that she was weeping and stamped in desperation. "How can you say such things!" he cried.

"After all these months here, surely you understand me? If no one else will tell you how I feel, won't you let *me* explain? Do you want me to die of frustration?" He started sobbing too.

As Pao-yu was blubbering, someone behind him remarked, "Who do you want to tell her for you? Whose slaves are we anyway? If you've offended her, it's up to you to apologize. Whether she'll accept your apologies or not is up to her. Why shift the blame to people like us who aren't involved?"

The two of them, one inside one outside, started. It was Sheh-yueh. Her intervention embarrassed Pao-yu.

"Well, what's going on?" Sheh-yueh continued. "Here's one making apologies and one ignoring him. Hurry up and plead with her! Ai! Our sister Tzu-chuan is too cruel. It's freezing outside, and he's begged you so long, yet you show no sign of relenting." Then she told Pao-yu, "Just now our mistress remarked that it's rather late and she wondered where you were. Why are you standing here all alone under the eaves?"

"Yes, what's the idea?" called Tzu-chuan from her room. "I asked the young master to go back. If he has something to say it can wait till tomorrow. This is so pointless!"

Pao-yu still wanted to speak, but not in front of Sheh-yueh. So he had to go back with her, telling himself, "Confound it! I shall never as long as I live be able to bare my heart. Only Old Man Heaven understands me!" His tears fell like rain.

"Take my advice, young master, and give up," Sheh-yueh said. "You're crying for nothing."

Pao-yu did not answer but went into his room where he saw that Pao-chai was pretending to be asleep.

Hsi-jen however scolded, "If you have something to say, can't you wait till tomorrow? Why rush there to make such a scene? What if. . . ." She left this sentence unfinished. Presently she asked, "Are you feeling all right?"

When Pao-yu said nothing and simply shook his head, she helped him to bed. But naturally he passed a sleepless night.

After being provoked and further upset by Pao-yu, Tzu-chuan wept the whole night long. She thought, "It's common knowledge that Pao-yu got married when he was out of his mind, and they tricked him into it. Later he came to his senses but then fell ill again and often wept with longing — it's not as if he were heartless. The feeling he showed today was really touching. What a pity our Miss Lin didn't have the good fortune to marry him! This shows that everybody's fate is predestined. Right up to the end they cherish foolish fancies; then when the blow strikes and there's no help for it, blockheads let it go at that while sensitive souls can only shed tears and lament to the breeze or moon. The dead may have no consciousness but, alas, there is truly no end to the anguish of the living. So it seems we are worse off than rocks or plants which can rest at peace, having no knowledge or feeling."

This reflection eased her, chilling her fevered passions, and she was getting ready to sleep when a clamour broke out in the eastern courtyard. To know its cause, read the next chapter.

CHAPTER 114

Hsi-feng Has Hallucinations and
Goes Back to Chinling
Chen Ying-chia, Pardoned by the Emperor,
Returns to Court

When Pao-yu and Pao-chai heard that Hsi-feng was mortally ill, they hastily got up and the maids brought in candles to wait on them. They were on the point of leaving when some of Lady Wang's servants arrived to report, "Madam Lien is in a bad way, but not yet at her last gasp. The second master and mistress had better not go there just yet. There is something very strange about her illness, for she has been delirious since midnight, calling for a boat and sedan-chair so that she can hurry back to Chinling to fill in some register. Nobody knows what she means, and she keeps on crying and wailing. So Master Lien has had to order a paper boat and paper chair for her. They haven't been delivered yet, and Madam Lien is still waiting, panting for breath. Her Ladyship sent us to tell you not to go over till she has passed away."

"That's odd!" exclaimed Pao-yu. "Why should she go to Chinling?"

Hsi-jen reminded him softly, "I seem to remember you had a dream one year about some registers, didn't you? Perhaps that's where she's going."

He nodded. "That's right. It's a pity I can't remember what was written there. It goes to show that all mortals' fates are predestined. But where can Cousin Lin have gone, I wonder? Now that you've reminded me, I feel I have an inkling. If I ever have that dream again I must read those registers carefully so as to be able to foretell the future."

"You're impossible to talk to!" protested Hsi-jen. "How can

you take a casual remark of mine so seriously? Even if you
were able to foresee the future, what could you do about it?"

"I'm afraid it's out of the question. But if I knew in advance
I wouldn't have to worry about you all."

Pao-chai came over at this point to ask, "What are you two
discussing?"

Not wanting her to question him Pao-yu said, "We were talking about Cousin Hsi-feng."

"Why gossip about somebody who's dying? In the past you
blamed me for putting a jinx on people, but that prediction came
true, didn't it?"

Recalling the incident Pao-yu clapped his hands. "Quite right,
quite right!" he exclaimed. "So *you* can predict the future. In
that case let me ask you to tell my fortune."

"What nonsense!" Pao-chai laughed. "I simply guessed at
what the oracle meant. How can you take it seriously? You're
as bad as my second sister-in-law. When you lost your jade,
she asked Miao-yu to consult the planchette; and when nobody
could understand what it wrote she assured me secretly that
Miao-yu could foretell the future and had attained enlightenment. How is it, then, that Miao-yu didn't know of the terrible
thing that has happened to her now? Can this count as foretell-
ing the future? Even if I hit upon the truth about Hsi-feng,
I didn't really know what was going to happen to her. I don't
even know what's going to happen to me, so how can I tell about
you? All such auguries are bogus. How can you believe in
them?"

"Never mind her. Let's talk about Cousin Hsing," he said.
"What with one trouble after another here, we've forgotten about
her marriage. It was such an important event in your family,
how could you handle it so sloppily, not even inviting relatives
and friends?"

"You're wide of the mark again. Our closest relatives are
your family and the Wangs. There are no respectable Wangs
left now, and we couldn't invite people from this house just after
the old lady's funeral; so only Cousin Lien helped out a little.
Of course a few other relatives attended, but since you didn't

go you didn't know that. My second sister-in-law's fate seems rather like mine. When she was betrothed to my Cousin Ko, mother meant to hold the wedding in style; but with Pan in prison Ko didn't want a big show, and then there was that trouble in our house. However, Cousin Hsing was having a thin time of it with the Elder Mistress, the more so as their property had been confiscated; and she found it hard to put up with Lady Hsing's harshness. That's why I asked mother to hold the wedding — but to do it quietly. Now she seems quite contented and very dutiful to my mother too, ten times better than her real daughter-in-law ever was. She makes an excellent wife for Cousin Ko and is good to Hsiang-ling as well. When he's away the two of them get on famously together. So though our family is poorer now, mother feels quite comfortable these days and only grieves whenever she thinks of Pan. Besides, he keeps sending home for money, and it's Ko who copes by raising cash outside. I hear that all but one of our houses in towns are mortgaged, and they're planning to move over there."

"Why move house?" asked Pao-yu. "With them here, it's more convenient for you to drop in. If she moves far away a visit will take a whole day."

"Even though we are mother and daughter, it's still better for each to have her own establishment. How can she stay with relatives all her life?"

Pao-yu was about to dispute this when Lady Wang sent a maid to announce, "Madam Lien has breathed her last and everyone's gone over there. Her Ladyship wants the young master and young mistress to go too now."

Hearing this Pao-yu stamped his foot, on the verge of tears. Pao-chai although upset too tried to restrain him.

"Why mourn here?" she demurred. "We'd better go over."

They went straight to Hsi-feng's quarters, and found many mourners assembled there. When Pao-chai saw Hsi-feng already laid out, she gave way to loud weeping. Pao-yu, taking Chia Lien's hand, sobbed bitterly; and Chia Lien too wailed again. As there was no one else present to remonstrate, Ping-erh stepped forward sadly to urge them to desist; but still they went on lamenting.

Chia Lien, unable to cope, summoned Lai Ta and told him to see to the funeral, then reported this to Chia Cheng and obtained his approval. But having little money in hand, he was hard put to it. The thought of Hsi-feng's help in the past increased his wretchedness; and the sight of Chiao-chieh beside herself with grief made his heart ache even more. He wept till dawn, then sent to ask Hsi-feng's brother Wang Jen to come over.

Since the death of Wang Tzu-teng, as Wang Tzu-sheng was so incompetent Wang Jen had done as he pleased and alienated all his relatives. When he heard of his younger sister's death he had to come and mourn; but the shabby way things were being done provoked him.

"My sister worked hard for years running your household, and did nothing wrong," he said. "So your family ought to take her funeral seriously. Why is nothing ready yet?"

Chia Lien who had never liked him ignored this foolish, injudicious talk. Then Wang Jen called Chiao-chieh over.

"When your mother was alive," he said, "she neglected some of her duties and was so set on pleasing the old lady that she paid very little attention to *us*. Now, niece, you are growing up. Have you ever seen me take any advantage of your family? Now that your mother's dead you must be guided in everything by your second grand-uncle and me — we're your only kinsmen left in her family. I know what your father is like: all he cares about is other people. That year his concubine Yu died, although I wasn't in the capital I heard you spent pots of money; yet now that your mother's dead he's skimping things like this. Why don't you protest?"

"My father would be only too glad to do things handsomely," Chiao-chieh replied. "But we're not as well-off as before. Having no money in hand, we have to economize wherever we can."

"Haven't you plenty of valuables?" he asked.

"How could we after that raid?"

"So *you* take that line too? I heard that the old lady gave you lots of things. Now is the time to use them."

Not liking to say that her father had already sold those heir-looms, Chiao-chieh denied any knowledge of the matter.

"Ha, I know!" he sneered. "You want to keep them all for your dowry!"

Chiao-chieh dared not retort and could only sob with rage. But Ping-erh remonstrated angrily, "If you have any complaints, sir, wait till our master comes back. What does the child under-stand?"

"You were looking forward to your mistress' death so that you could take her place!" he retorted. "I don't want anything for myself; but you owe it to yourselves to keep up appearances." He sat down glowering.

Seething with resentment Chiao-chieh told herself, "It's not that my father is heartless. When mama was alive, uncle made off with ever so many of our things; but now he talks as if he had clean hands!" He went down in her estimation.

Wang Jen for his part was convinced that his sister must have sizable savings, so that even after the raid they could hardly be short of silver. He thought, "My niece must be afraid I'll cadge on them; that's why she's taking her father's side. This minx is no good either!" This made him take a dislike to Chiao-chieh too.

Chia Lien, unaware of this, was preoccupied with raising money. He had put Lai Ta in charge of outside business; but their home expenses were going to be heavy too, and he had no idea where the money was to come from. Ping-erh appreciated his anxiety.

"Don't ruin your health by worrying too much," she urged him.

"To hell with my health!" he exploded. "I haven't even the money for daily expenses. What's to be done? And to make matters worse, this fool has come butting in. What do you expect me to do?"

"Don't worry, Second Master. If you're short of money, I

still have some things which luckily weren't confiscated. Take them, sir, to be going on with."

Chia Lien was most relieved. "That's splendid," he answered with a smile. "It'll save me the trouble of borrowing right and left. I'll pay you back when I'm in funds again."

"All I have was given me by the mistress, so why talk about paying me back? I just want this funeral to be properly managed."

Feeling immensely grateful, Chia Lien raised money on these things of Ping-erh's, and thereafter he consulted her on all matters, much to Chiu-tung's annoyance.

"Now that the mistress is gone, Ping-erh wants to take her place," she kept complaining. "I was the Elder Master's maid, so how can she outrank *me*?"

Ping-erh paid no attention to such remarks, but when Chia Lien learned of them he was disgusted and each time he lost his temper would swear at Chiu-tung. But when Lady Hsing knew this she took Chiu-tung's side, and he had to control his anger. No more of this.

After the corpse had been laid out for more than ten days, the funeral took place. All this time Chia Cheng, still in mourning for his mother, was staying in the outer study. By now all his protégés and secretaries had left with the exception of Cheng Jih-hsing who often kept him company.

Chia Cheng told him, "Our family's gone downhill! with so many dying one after the other, and the Elder Master and Master Chen away. We are more hard pressed every day, and I don't know what's become of our farm at East Village. All in all, we're in a bad way!"

"Yes, after all these years here I know the situation," said Cheng Jih-hsing. "Which of your servants hasn't been battening on you by filching things from your mansion year after year? Naturally you're running shorter every year. On top of that you have to meet the expenses of the Elder Master and Master Chen, not to mention your debts outside; besides, recently you were robbed, and the police aren't likely to catch the thieves or recover your stolen property. If you want to set your house in order, sir, you will have to summon your stewards and send one whom you trust to check up everywhere. Some servants should be dismissed; and if there is a deficit anywhere, make the one responsible pay for it. Then you will know where you are. As for that big Garden of yours, no one would dare sell it; but you haven't put anyone in charge of all its produce. During those years when you were away, these people got up to their tricks pretending the place was haunted so that everybody was afraid to go there. Better check up on your staff and keep on only the servants loyal to you, sending the rest away."

Chia Cheng nodded. "I don't mind telling you, sir," he said, "that quite apart from the servants even my own nephews aren't to be relied on! If I start investigating, how am I to see to everything myself? Besides, being still in mourning, I can't attend to these things. And never having paid much attention to family affairs, I'm not clear what the situation is."

"You are the soul of goodness, sir. If other families owned such a property and fell on hard times, they would be able to get by for five or ten years by applying to these stewards. Some of them, I hear, have had themselves made magistrates."

"It's unthinkable to ask one's servants for money," objected Chia Cheng. "We shall just have to be more frugal. If the properties entered in our books really exist, then we should be all right. I only fear they may be empty names."

"Quite true, sir. That's why I humbly suggest a check-up."

"I suppose you have heard some talk?"

"Though I have an idea what these stewards are capable of, sir, I wouldn't dare voice my suspicions."

Aware that there was something behind this, Chia Cheng sighed, "Since our grandfather's time we have always been kind masters, never treating our underlings harshly. But they seem to be getting more out of hand every day. If I try to act the stern master now, people will laugh at me!"

Just then one of the gatekeepers announced, "Master Chen from the Yangtze Valley has arrived."

"What brings him to the capital?" Chia Cheng asked.

"I inquired, sir, and they say he has been reinstated through the Emperor's favour."

"Very well, then. Invite him in at once!"

The man went off to usher in Chen Ying-chia, whose secondary name was Yu-chung, the father of Chen Pao-yu. He too was a native of Chinling of noble ancestry and related to the Chia family, with whom he had been on close terms. Two years before this, having committed a fault, he had been degraded, his property confiscated. Now the Emperor, out of concern for subjects who had performed meritorious service, had restored his hereditary title and summoned him to the capital for an audience. Learning of the Lady Dowager's recent death, he had prepared sacrificial gifts and come today to pay his respects at her shrine, first calling on Chia Cheng.

Chia Cheng, still in mourning, could not go out to meet him but waited by his study door. Their reunion filled Mr. Chen with mixed joy and sorrow. As they could not greet each other formally while Chia Cheng was in mourning, they took hands and exchanged a few civilities, then sat down as host and guest and while tea was served described their experiences since their last meeting.

"When did you go to court, sir?" Chia Cheng asked.

"The day before yesterday."

"I presume the Most High must have given you certain instructions since he was gracious enough to summon you."

"Yes, the Sovereign's kindness surpasses heaven. He issued several decrees."

"What is your good news?"

"Recently pirates have been raiding the southeast coast, giving the people no rest, and the Duke of Ankuo is being sent to wipe them out. Since our Sovereign knows that I am familiar with that locality, he has ordered me to pacify the people and to set off straight away. Yesterday I heard of the old lady's passing, so to express my condolences I have brought incense to pay my respects at her shrine."

Chia Cheng bowed his thanks and rejoined, "By going on this mission, sir, you will certainly relieve the Emperor's anxiety and bring peace to the people. You are bound to achieve great deeds. As I shall be unable to witness them, I can only wait far off for news of your triumph. The garrison commander there happens to be related to me; I hope you will think well of him when you meet."

"What is your relationship, sir?"

"When serving as Grain Commissioner in Kiangsi, I betrothed my young daughter to his son. They've been married for three years now. But as pirates have been raiding the coast and some cases there are still under litigation, I have had no news of them. My daughter is much in my thoughts. After your work of pacification, sir, I hope you will spare time to see them. I shall write a few lines to her, and if I may trouble you to pass on my letter I shall be extremely grateful!"

"Who doesn't feel for his children?" replied Chen Ying-chia. "That reminds me of a favour I'd like to ask of you. When His Majesty graciously summoned me to court, because my son is young and there is no one in charge at home I decided to bring my whole household here as well. But having to travel post-haste I came on ahead, leaving them to follow more slowly, and they have not yet arrived. I have orders to go straight to my post and dare not procrastinate. When my worthless son arrives, I shall certainly leave word for him to come and pay his respects to you, sir. I hope you will give him good advice, and if there is a chance to arrange a suitable match I would be most grateful if you would keep him in mind."

Chia Cheng assented to these requests, and after a little more talk Chen Ying-chia rose to leave.

"I'll see you tomorrow outside the city," he said.

Since he was in too much of a hurry to stay, Chia Cheng saw him out of his study. Chia Lien and Pao-yu were waiting outside to see the guest off for him, not having presumed to enter as they had not been summoned. They both stepped forward now to pay their respects. The sight of Pao-yu astounded Chen

Ying-chia, who thought, "Why, he's the image of my Pao-yu, except that he's in mourning!"

He greeted them and said, "Though we are close relatives, young gentlemen, we haven't met for so long that we don't recognize each other."

Chia Cheng indicated Chia Lien and said, "This is my elder brother Sheh's son, my second nephew Lien." Then he pointed at Pao-yu. "This is my second son, Pao-yu."

Chen Ying-chia clapped his hands in amazement. "How extraordinary!" he exclaimed. "I heard at home that you had a son born with a piece of jade in his mouth, whose name was Pao-yu. And I was amazed because he had the same name as *my* son. Later it seemed nothing unusual, so I thought no more about it. Now that I see him, though, they look exactly alike and bear themselves in the same way as well. This is most extraordinary!" He inquired Pao-yu's age and remarked, "My boy is one year younger."

Chia Cheng thanked him then for recommending Pao Yung, and referred back to how he had asked the servant about his young master having the same name as his son. Since Chen Ying-chia was so struck by Pao-yu, he did not ask about Pao Yung but kept exclaiming "Truly extraordinary!" He took Pao-yu attentively by the hand. However, as the Duke of Ankuo was about to set out on his journey, he had to go at once to get ready himself and reluctantly took his leave. He asked Pao-yu many questions as the two young men saw him out, then left in his carriage. When Chia Lien and Pao-yu came back, they reported what the guest had said to Chia Cheng, who then dismissed them. Chia Lien went off to work out the accounts for Hsi-feng's funeral.

When Pao-yu returned to his own quarters he told Pao-chai, "I've never had a chance to meet that Chen Pao-yu whom they're always talking about, but today I've seen his father. He says Pao-yu will be arriving here any day now and wants to call on my father. He also says his son looks exactly like me, but I can hardly believe it. If he does come, you must all take a look at him to see whether he's really my double or not."

"Oh!" scoffed Pao-chai. "What nonsense you talk! Claiming that some man is your double and even asking us to look at him!"

Aware of his gaffe Pao-yu blushed, wanting to explain. To know how he justified himself, read the next chapter.

CHAPTER 115

Personal Prejudice Strengthens
Hsi-chun's Conviction
Pao-yu Fails to Find a True Friend
in His Double

Pao-yu, challenged by Pao-chai because of his gaffe, was trying to cover it up when Chiu-wen came in to announce that the master wanted him in his study. He went there, glad of this chance to slip away.

"I'll tell you why I sent for you," said Chia Cheng. "You can't go to school as long as you are in mourning, but while staying at home you must review those essays you studied before. I am fairly free at present, so I want you to write a few essays to show me a couple of days from now, to see what progress if any you've made recently." When Pao-yu had assented he went on, "I have told your brother Huan and your nephew Lan to do some revision too. If your essays are poor, not even up to theirs, that will be disgraceful."

Not daring to protest Pao-yu answered, "Yes sir," and stood there motionless till his father dismissed him On his way out he met Lai Ta and other stewards coming in with ledgers. He streaked back to his room.

When Pao-chai ascertained that he had been told to write essays she was delighted and, though reluctant himself, he could not refuse this assignment. As he was sitting down to collect his thoughts, two nuns arrived from Ksitigarbha Nunnery and paid their respects to Pao-chai, who greeted them coldly then told maids to serve tea. Pao-yu would have liked to chat with the nuns but refrained in view of her evident aversion to them. And they, aware that they were being cold-shouldered, very soon took their leave.

"Won't you stay?" said Pao-chai.

"We have been chanting sutras in Iron Threshold Temple," they replied. "That's why we've not come for some time to pay our respects. Today, after calling on Their Ladyships, we want to see Miss Hsi-chun too."

Then she nodded and let them go.

Proceeding to Hsi-chun's quarters the nuns asked Tsai-ping, "Where is your young lady?"

"You may well ask," Tsai-ping answered. "These days she won't eat a thing, just curls up on the *kang*."

"What's the matter?"

"That's a long story. When you see her, she'll probably tell you."

Hsi-chun who had overheard them promptly sat up. "How are you?" she cried. "When our family's hard up you don't come near us!"

"Amida Buddha!" they exclaimed. "Whether well or badly off you're still our patrons, not to say that our nunnery belongs to your family and the old lady was always so good to us. During her funeral we saw all the mistresses except you. It's because we missed you that we've come today especially to see you, miss."

Hsi-chun inquired after the nuns in Water Moon Convent.

"There was some scandal there; so now your gatemen won't let them in," they told her. "Is it true, as we heard the other day, that Sister Miao-yu of Green Lattice Nunnery ran off with someone too?"

"What nonsense! Whoever gossips like that should have her tongue cut off! She was kidnapped by bandits. Why spread such wicked rumours?"

"That crankiness of hers — was she putting on an act? Mind, we don't want to run her down to you, miss. She's not like us rough creatures who can only chant Buddhist canons or masses for others, and pray to come to a good end ourselves."

"What do you mean by a good end?"

"Of course a virtuous family like yours has nothing to worry about; but ladies of other houses, however noble, can't be sure of living in luxury all their lives. When trouble comes, they've no way to save themselves. But the Bodhisattva Avalokitesvara is most kind and compassionate: when she sees anyone in distress she takes pity on her and finds a way to save her. That's why we all say, 'All-merciful Avalokitesvara saves souls in distress!' Those of us in holy orders, though we have a much harder life than ladies, are not in any danger. Even if we can't attain sainthood, we can at least hope for a better future by being reincarnated as men. Then we shan't have to suffer in silence as we do now, born as women. You don't realize it, miss, but if you get married you'll be tied to your husband all your life, worse off than at present. But you have to be in earnest about renouncing the world. Sister Miao-yu, now, with her intelligence, thought herself a cut above us and looked down on us as vulgar. Little did she know that we vulgar ones would come to a good end while she met with such a fearful calamity."

As these words touched the right chord, ignoring the presence of her maids Hsi-chun told them how Madam Yu had treated her and how she had been left to watch the house. Pointing at her shorn head she asked, "Do you think me so weak-willed as to hanker after this wretched life? I made up my mind long ago to renounce the world, but just didn't know how to do it."

In simulated alarm the nuns demurred, "You mustn't talk like that, miss. If Madam Yu heard, she'd drive us away from our nunnery with curses! A lovely young lady like you, from such a fine family too, is bound to make a good match and enjoy a life of luxury and splendour...."

Flushing crimson Hsi-chun cut them short. "If Madam Yu can drive you away, can't I?"

Knowing then that she was in earnest, they deliberately goaded her on by saying, "Don't be angry, miss, if we speak out of turn. But the mistresses would never let you, would they? It wouldn't be good if trouble came of this. It's you we're thinking of, miss."

"Just wait and see."

This sounded so ominous that Tsai-ping signalled to the nuns to go. They took the hint, being afraid to incite Hsi-chun any

further.   When they took their leave she did not try to detain
them, simply saying sarcastically, "Do you think your nunnery
is the only one in the world?"

Without venturing to answer, the nuns left.

As this development looked serious and Tsai-ping feared she
would be held to blame, she quietly went and reported it to
Madam Yu.

"Our young lady still wants to cut off her hair," she said.
"These last few days she's been unwell or else lamenting her
fate.   You'd better be careful, madam, that she doesn't make
away with herself or we shall get the blame."

"*She* doesn't want to be a nun!" scoffed Madam Yu.   "She
just likes to provoke me while the master's away.   Well, let
her."

Then Tsai-ping could only try to talk Hsi-chun round; but her
young mistress went on fasting every day and remained set on
cutting off her hair.   Her maids, unable to cope, reported this
to the other mistresses.   Their Ladyships did their best to dissuade Hsi-chun, but she was adamant.

They were thinking of telling Chia Cheng when the arrival
of Lady Chen and her son Pao-yu was announced.   All hurried
out to welcome her, then ushered her into Lady Wang's room
to sit down.   After an exchange of amenities Lady Wang sent
to invite Chen Pao-yu in too, having heard that he was the image
of *her* Pao-yu.

The messenger came back to report, "Master Chen is talking
with the master in the study.   His Lordship is so struck by him
that he's sent for our Master Pao and Master Huan and wants
Master Lan to have his meal there too.   They'll come over after
they've eaten."   By this time dinner had also been served inside.

When Chia Cheng saw that Chen Pao-yu did indeed look
exactly like his son, he tested his literary talents and was so impressed by the youth's fluent answers that he sent for his sons
and grandson to meet this prodigy, also meaning Pao-yu to compare himself with him.   Thus summoned, Pao-yu came out in
mourning with his younger brother and nephew.   At sight of
Chen Pao-yu he felt as if they were old acquaintances, while

young Chen too had the impression that they had met before. After they had greeted each other, Huan and Lan stepped forward in turn to pay their respects.

Chia Cheng, being in mourning, had been sitting on the floor. When he offered Chen Pao-yu a seat the lad felt it would be presumptuous to take it as he belonged to the younger generation. He placed a mattress on the floor and sat on that. Pao-yu and the two other boys could not sit with Chia Cheng; on the other hand, since the visitor belonged to their generation, Chia Cheng could hardly make his sons stand in his presence. In this dilemma he rose after a few remarks and ordered the meal to be served.

"Please excuse me," he said. "My sons will keep you company. They can profit by your edifying conversation."

"Don't let me keep you, sir," rejoined Chen Pao-yu politely. "I am the one hoping to learn from them."

After a few further words Chia Cheng went to his inner study, not letting young Chen escort him. Pao-yu, Huan and Lan, who had left the room first, stood respectfully outside the door until Chia Cheng had gone before returning to ask the guest to sit down. Then they told each other how long they had been looking forward to this meeting — no need to record their conversation in detail.

Now the sight of Chen Pao-yu had reminded Pao-yu of his dream. Sure that they must share the same views, he felt he had found a friend after his own heart; but since this was their first meeting he had to hold himself in check, the more so as Chia Huan and Chia Lan were present.

He complimented the visitor by saying, "I have long known of your fine reputation, but never had the chance to meet you in person. Now that I see you, sir, you truly seem an immortal descended from heaven!"

Chen Pao-yu had also heard of Pao-yu, and felt that he lived up to his reputation. "We can study together, but we may not be travelling the same road,"[1] he thought. "Since we have the

---

[1] A quotation from *The Analects* of Confucius and his disciples.

same name and look alike, we must be predestined to be kindred spirits. Now that I am beginning to know what is right, why shouldn't I pass my knowledge on to him? But as we've only just met, I don't know whether we are of the same mind. I mustn't be too hasty." So he said, "I have long known of your talents. You are one in ten thousand — so pure and refined. Being nothing but a vulgar fool myself, I am well aware that I disgrace the name which we both share."

Hearing this Pao-yu thought, "He really does think as I do. But as both of us are men who can't compare with chaste girls, how can he attribute their qualities to me?" He answered, "Indeed, I don't deserve such praise. I am a foolish lout, a mere block of stone. How can I compare with your pure nobility? It is you who live up to the name 'precious jade.' "

"When I was young I was very cocksure," replied Chen. "I thought myself jade which only needed polishing; but after our family got into trouble, for some years I ranked lower than a pebble or tile. Though I can't claim to have experienced prosperity and adversity in full, I've nevertheless reached a slightly better understanding of human affairs. You have all the luxuries you can desire while your literary talent and grasp of affairs must be outstanding, so naturally your father treasures you. This is why I think *you* deserve to be called 'precious jade.' "

This seemed to Pao-yu sycophantic talk, and he did not know how to answer. Chia Huan was rather unhappy at being ignored. Chia Lan, however, approved of what Chen had said.

"You are too modest, sir," he chimed in. "Regarding literary talent and the ability to manage affairs, the only way to amass genuine knowledge is through experience and study. Though I am too young to know much about literature, when I carefully think over what I have read, a good reputation and honour rank a hundred times higher than wealth and luxury."

Pao-yu wondered irritably when the boy had picked up this pedantic twaddle. He said to Chen, "I have heard that you too are against all that is vulgar and have a superior understanding of life. I am very lucky to have met you today and would like to hear some of your transcendent views to cleanse my heart of vulgarity and enable me to see things in a new light. I didn't think you would take me for such a fool as to fob me off with mundane talk of that kind."

Chen Pao-yu thought, "He knows what I was like as a boy, so he suspects me of shamming. I had better made myself clear in the hope that then we may become close friends." So he replied, "You have spoken very sincerely, and the fact is that when I was younger I did detest those old truisms too. As I grew older, though, and my father retired from official life, he couldn't be troubled to entertain guests and gave the task to me. Then I saw that all those mandarins had brought glory to their families, while of men of letters not one but spoke of loyalty and filial piety, concerned to win fame for their virtue and learning in order not to have lived in vain under such a sagacious reign or fall short of the expectations of their fathers and the tutors who brought them up. So gradually I rid myself of some of the foolish notions I had as a boy. Now I want to seek out teachers and friends to help enlighten me. I am fortunate to have met you who can certainly edify me. What I said just now was truly from my heart."

By now Pao-yu was thoroughly exasperated, but for politeness' sake he made an evasive answer. Luckily a message now came from the inner quarters: "If the young gentlemen have finished dinner, Master Chen is invited over for a chat."

Pao-yu seized this chance to urge Chen Pao-yu to go in and the latter accordingly went ahead, accompanied by the others to Lady Wang's apartments. There Pao-yu saw Lady Chen in the seat of honour and paid his respects to her. Chia Huan and Chia Lan followed suit, while Chen Pao-yu paid his respects to Lady Wang. So the two mothers confronted each other's sons. Though Pao-yu was already a married man, as Lady Chen was advanced in years and an old relative too, she showed a great interest in him when she saw his close resemblance to her son. Lady Wang, it goes without saying, when she took young Chen by the hand to question him found him better mannered than her own Pao-yu. She glanced at Chia Lan who, although more handsome than most, could not compare with either of them in looks. As for Chia Huan, he was so uncouth that she could not hide to whom she felt most partial.

All the maids came in to look at the two Pao-yu's. "But how extraordinary!" they commented. "It's not so strange their having the same name, but they are the image of each other! It's a good thing our Master Pao is in mourning, because if they were dressed alike there'd be no telling them apart."

Tzu-chuan suddenly thought back fondly to Tai-yu, telling herself, "What a pity Miss Lin is dead! Otherwise she might have been willing to marry this Chen Pao-yu." Then she heard Lady Chen say, "The other day I heard from my husband that since our son is growing up he has begged your husband to take care of his marriage."

Lady Wang who had taken to the boy answered readily, "I'd like to act as go-between myself. Our house had four daughters, but three are either dead or already married, and the only one left, the younger sister of our nephew Chen, is a few years too young; so it wouldn't be a good match. However, my elder daughter-in-law has two girl cousins, both nice-looking. One is already betrothed; the other would be just right for your honourable son. After a day or so I'll propose the match. The only snag is that her family is not so well-off nowadays."

"Madam, don't stand on ceremony with us!" protested Lady Chen. "What have *we* to boast about? I'm afraid her family may think us too poor."

"Now that your husband has been entrusted with a mission, your fortunes will not only be restored — you're bound to prosper even more than before."

"I only hope so," replied Lady Chen with a smile. "In that case, I beg you to be the go-between."

When they started discussing his marriage Chen Pao-yu had taken his leave, and Pao-yu escorted him back to the outer study where Chia Cheng had returned. They stood talking there for a while until the Chens' servant announced that his mother was leaving and wanted him to go home. Chia Cheng told the three boys to see him out. No more of this.

To revert to Pao-yu, ever since he had met Chen Pao-yu's father and learned that his son was coming to the capital, he had been longing to meet him, sure that he would prove a kindred spirit. However, their talk had shown him that they were as incompatible as ice and charcoal. He went back dejectedly to his own quarters to brood in gloomy silence.

"Is that Chen Pao-yu really like you?" Pao-chai asked him.

"In looks, yes; but judging by the way he talks he doesn't have much understanding. He's just a place-seeker of the lowest sort."

"There you go running people down again! How can you be sure of that?"

"He talked and talked but said not a word about seeking for truth, just holding forth on scholarship and the management of affairs, as well as loyalty and filial piety. Isn't such a person a toady? It's too bad that we look alike! The thought of him makes me wish I could change my looks!"

As this sounded nonsensical to Pao-chai, she said, "The way you talk is really laughable! How can you change your looks? Besides, he was quite right. A man should establish himself and make a name. Who else is as soft and sentimental as you? Yet instead of admitting your weak character you call other people place-seekers."

Pao-yu had been thoroughly exasperated by Chen Pao-yu's homily, and this rebuff from Pao-chai rankled still more. His dejection made his old illness flare up again, and instead of answering he grinned inanely. Pao-chai, not knowing the reason, thought he was scoffing at her to show disapproval and therefore paid no attention. But that day he was so distracted that when Hsi-jen and others teased him, he said nothing. The next morning he got up looking as vacant and stupid as during his past derangement.

Since Hsi-chun was set on cutting off her hair and becoming a nun and Madam Yu was unable to talk her round, it seemed that unless they let her have her way she would commit suicide. Though she was under constant watch that did not solve the

problem.   So one day Lady Wang reported this to Chia Cheng.
Her husband stamped his foot.

"What has our East Mansion done to be reduced to this?" he
sighed.

Sending for Chia Jung to admonish him, he told him to get
his mother to have a serious talk with Hsi-chun.   "If she insists
on this course, she'll no longer be a daughter of our house," he
warned.

However, Madam Yu's exhortations only made Hsi-chun more
eager to kill herself.

"As a girl, I can't stay with the family all my life," she said.
"If my marriage proved like Second Sister's, the master and
mistress would have more cause to worry, and besides she died
too in the end.   So if you have any real affection for me, just
count me as dead and let me become a nun to live a clean life.
Especially as I don't have to leave the house.   Green Lattice
Nunnery is in our own grounds and I can practise my devotions
there, while if I need anything you can see to it. Miao-yu's maids
are still there too now.   If you'll agree to this you'll be saving
my life; if you don't, I have no option but to die and be done
with it!   If I can have my wish, when my brother comes back
I shall explain to him that you didn't force me to do this; but
if I die he's bound to think it was you who drove me to it."

Madam Yu, who had always been on bad terms with Hsi-chun,
felt there was reason in this argument and went off to report
it to Lady Wang; but the latter had gone to Pao-chai's apartments.

Horrified to find Pao-yu out of his mind, Lady Wang reprimanded Hsi-jen, "How careless you all are!   Why didn't you
tell me that Pao-yu was ill again?"

"This illness of his is chronic," replied Hsi-jen.   "He gets
better for a while, then has a relapse.   He's been going to pay
his respects to you every day, with nothing wrong with him,
madam, and it's only today that his wits have wandered again.
Madam Pao was just thinking of letting you know, but was
afraid you might scold us for raising a false alarm."

When Pao-yu heard his mother rebuking them, his mind cleared for a moment and to defend them he said, "Don't worry, madam. There's nothing wrong with me except that I feel rather gloomy."

"This is an old trouble of yours. You should tell me as soon as you feel unwell, so that we can get a doctor to prescribe medicine. What an ado there'd be if you had another bad relapse like that time when you lost your jade!"

"If you're worried, madam, you can send for a doctor and I'll take some medicine," he answered.

Lady Wang despatched maids to see to this and, as her whole concern was Pao-yu, she forgot about Hsi-chun's problem, not returning to her own quarters until the doctor had come and made out a prescription.

A few days later Pao-yu was more feeble-minded and, to everyone's consternation, he would not eat. As the termination of mourning was keeping the others busy, Chia Yun was instructed to receive the doctor; and Chia Lien, being short-handed, asked Wang Jen to help attend to outside affairs Chiao-chieh was ill too after crying day and night for her mother. So once again the Jung Mansion was in a tumult.

On the day that they returned from terminating the mourning, Lady Wang came to see Pao-yu. He was unconscious, and the whole household was frantic.

Weeping she told Chia Cheng, "The doctor refuses to prescribe any medicine. All we can do is prepare for the last rites."

Sighing bitterly Chia Cheng went over in person, and when he saw that Pao-yu was indeed dying he told Chia Lien to have preparations made. Chia Lien had to pass on his orders, but lacking money he was in a dilemma.

Just at this juncture a servant rushed in crying, "More trouble, Master Lien!"

Staggered, staring at the servant, Chia Lien demanded, "What now?"

"A monk has come to our gate bringing the jade which Master Pao lost. He's asking for a reward of ten thousand taels.'

Chia Lien spat in the fellow's face. "Is that any reason to panic? Don't you know last time it was a fraud? Even if this is genuine, Pao-yu is dying, so what good will the jade do him?"

"I told the monk that. But he says if we give him the silver Master Pao will recover."

Just then they heard shouts outside, "This monk has run amuck! He rushed in and no one could stop him."

"Preposterous!" cried Chia Lien. "Throw him out, quick!"

They heard another commotion, and Chia Cheng was wondering what to do when a wailing went up inside, "Master Pao is dying!"

Feeling still more distraught, he heard the monk shouting, "If you want him to live, give me the money!"

He thought, "Last time it was a monk who cured Pao-yu; now another has turned up who may be able to save him. But even if it's the genuine jade, how are we to raise so much money?" On second thoughts he decided, "Never mind. We can worry about that if Pao-yu really recovers." He was sending for the monk when in the man came and, without so much as paying his respects or saying a word, ran towards the inner apartments.

Chia Lien grabbed his arm protesting, "There are ladies inside; how can you charge in so wildly?"

"Any delay and I'll be too late to save him!"

Then Chia Lien went over yelling, "Stop crying, everyone inside! A monk is coming in!"

Lady Wang and the others were sobbing too bitterly to pay any attention. As Chia Lien entered, still shouting, they turned to see a hulking monk. Although terrified, they had no time to hide as the monk marched straight to Pao-yu's *kang*. Pao-chai slipped away then, but Hsi-jen dared not move as Lady Wang had remained standing there.

"Benefactresses," cried the monk, "I've brought the jade." Holding it up he added, "Hurry up and bring out the silver, then I'll save him."

Panic-stricken Lady Wang could not tell whether it was genuine or not. "Provided you save his life, you'll get the silver," she promised.

"Hand it over then!" the monk insisted.

"Don't worry. We can raise that much silver anyway," Lady Wang assured him.

The monk roared with laughter and, holding the jade, lent over the *kang* to cry, "Pao-yu, Pao-yu! Your precious jade has come back."

Lady Wang and the rest saw Pao-yu open his eyes, at which Hsi-jen cried out for joy.

"Where is it?" Pao-yu asked.

The monk placed it in his hand and he grasped it tightly, then slowly held it up to examine it closely. "Ah!" he exclaimed. "At last!"

All there invoked Buddha in elation, even Pao-chai forgetting the monk's presence.

Chia Lien coming over too now saw that Pao-yu had indeed regained consciousness. Although delighted he made off hastily. The monk, however, overtook and grabbed him without a word, and Chia Lien had to go with him to the front of the house where he lost no time in reporting this to Chia Cheng. Overjoyed, Chia Cheng bowed his thanks to the monk, who bowed in return then sat down, making Chia Lien suspect that he would not leave until he received his reward. Chia Cheng, looking closely at him, saw that this was not the same monk as last time.

He asked, "Where is your monastery, and what is your name in religion? Where did you find this jade? How is it that the sight of it restored my son to life?"

"That I don't know," answered the monk with a smile. "All I want is ten thousand taels of silver."

He looked so boorish that Chia Cheng dared not offend him and simply replied, "You shall have it."

"If you have it, hurry up and bring it. I must be going."

"Please wait a little while I go inside to have a look."

"Go on then. Don't be long about it."

Chia Cheng went inside without having himself announced and walked to Pao-yu's bedside. At sight of him his son wanted to sit up but was too weak to do so, and Lady Wang made him lie down, telling him not to move.

With a smile Pao-yu showed his father the jade and said, "The precious jade has come back."

Chia Cheng glanced at it but did not examine it closely, knowing there must be some mystery about it. "Now that Pao-yu has recovered," he said to his wife, "how are we to raise the reward?"

"We must just give the monk all we possess," she answered.

"I can't believe this monk came for the money, did he?" asked Pao-yu.

Chia Cheng nodded. "I find it strange too, yet he keeps demanding silver."

Lady Wang suggested, "Go and entertain him first, sir."

After his father had left, Pao-yu said he was hungry. He finished a bowl of congee then asked for rice, and the serving-women brought him a bowl. His mother did not want him to eat too much, but he assured her, "It's all right, I'm better now." He propped himself up to finish the bowl, and very soon felt well enough to sit up.

Sheh-yueh helped him gently up, and in her jubilation remarked tactlessly, "This really is a treasure! Just the sight of it cured him. How lucky it wasn't smashed that time before!"

Reminded of his quarrel with Tai-yu, Pao-yu changed colour, let fall the jade and toppled over backwards. To know whether he lived or died, read the next chapter.

CHAPTER 116

Pao-yu, His Divine Jade Recovered,
Attains Understanding in the Illusory Realm
Chia Cheng Escorts His Mother's Coffin Home
to Fulfil His Filial Duty

At Sheh-yueh's reference to his jade, Pao-yu fell backwards and fainted away again. Lady Wang and the others cried out in consternation, and although they did not reproach her Sheh-yueh knew that her ill-considered comment was to blame. Weeping, she resolved that if Pao-yu died she would follow him to the grave. When the others failed to revive him, his mother sent to ask the monk to save him; but when Chia Cheng looked for him, the monk had disappeared. Taken aback and hearing a fresh commotion from the inner apartments, he hurried in and found Pao-yu once more in a coma. His teeth were clenched and his pulse had stopped, though when they felt his heart it was still warm. In desperation Chia Cheng summoned a doctor to administer medicine and restore him to life.

By then Pao-yu's spirit had taken flight. Do you think he was really dead? As if in a dream he sped to the front hall where he paid his respects to the monk who was seated there. The monk at once rose to his feet and led him away. Pao-yu felt as light as a leaf floating through the air, and somehow without passing through the main gate they left the mansion.

After a while they came to a desolate region with a distant archway which struck Pao-yu as familiar; but before he could ask the monk their whereabouts, the nebulous figure of a woman approached them. "How could there be such a beauty in a wilderness like this?" he wondered. "She must be a goddess come down to earth." Going closer and gazing at her more intently, he thought he knew her yet could not identify her. The woman greeted the monk, then disappeared, and as she did so he realized that it was Third Sister Yu. Marvelling at her presence there, he was again about to question the monk when the latter pulled him through the archway. On it was inscribed in large characters "Happy Land of Truth" flanked by the couplet:

> When false gives way to true, true surpasses false.
> Though nothingness exists, being differs from nothingness.

Once through the archway they came to a palace gate, on its lintel the inscription "Fortune for the Good, Calamity for the Licentious." Another couplet on the two sides read:

> Even sages cannot change the past and future;
> Causes and effects tear the closest kin apart.

Having read this, Pao-yu thought, "So here is my chance to find out about karma, past and future." At this point he saw Yuan-yang standing there beckoning to him. "Apparently after coming all this way I'm still in the Garden," he mused. "But why is it so changed?" He wanted to accost her, but to his astonishment in a flash she was gone. Going over towards where she had stood, he saw a row of side courts with tablets over their gates. In no mood to read their inscriptions, he hurried to the place where Yuan-yang had vanished. The gate of this court was ajar, but not liking to intrude he decided to ask permission from the monk. When he turned round, however, the monk was nowhere to be seen. He gazed abstractedly at the magnificent hall which he had certainly never seen in the Garden, and halted to look up at the inscription "Enlightenment for the Infatuated." The couplet on both sides read:

> Joy and sorrow alike are false;
> Desire and longing are folly.

Pao-yu nodded to himself, sighing, and wanted to go in to ask Yuan-yang what this place was. Then realizing that it looked familiar he summoned up courage to open the gate and step in. Yuan-yang was nowhere in sight and the whole building was so eerily dark that he was about to slip away when his eye fell on a dozen or so large cabinets, their doors half open. It suddenly occurred to him, "When I was young, I dreamed that

I came to a place like this. What a stroke of luck my coming here again today!"

In a daze he forgot his search for Yuan-yang and boldly opened the first cabinet, in which he found several albums. Elatedly he told himself, "Most people think dreams are false, but this one was based on fact! I never expected to have the same dream again, yet today I've recaptured it. I wonder whether these albums are the same as those I saw last time?"

He took the topmost album entitled *First Register of Twelve Beauties of Chinling*. Holding it he thought, "I have a faint recollection of this; it's too bad that I can't remember clearly." He opened it at the first page and saw a picture, too blurred to make out distinctly. On the back were a few lines of indistinct writing, but by straining his eyes he deciphered a few words about a jade belt, and over these what seemed to be the word *lin*. "Could this refer to Cousin Lin?" he wondered, then read about a golden hairpin in the snow and marvelled at the resemblance to Pao-chai's name. But when he reread the four lines consecutively, he could make no sense of them except that they seemed to suggest Tai-yu and Pao-chai, which in itself was nothing extraordinary. Only the words "pity" and "sighing" were ominous. How to interpret this? Then he rebuked himself, "I'm doing this on the sly. If I rack my brains too long and somebody comes, I shan't be able to read the rest." So he leafed through the register without paying much attention to the pictures, and finally found the lines:

> When Hare and Tiger meet,
> From this Great Dream of life she must depart.

At that, the truth dawned on him. "Right! This prediction came true! It must mean Sister Yuan-chun. If all the others were equally clear and I could copy them down to study them, I'd be able to find out the life-spans and fortunes of all these girls. When I went back I'd keep it secret, but knowing in advance would save me worrying so much for nothing."

He looked round but could see no writing-brush or ink, and for fear of being disturbed he read rapidly on. One of the pictures showed a shadowy figure flying a kite, but he did not trouble to examine it carefully. Instead he read hastily through all the twelve verses. Some he understood at a glance, some after reflection; others baffled him and he tried to memorize them. Then, sighing, he picked up the third register of the beauties of Chinling. At first he did not understand the lines:

> This prize is borne off by an actor,
> And luck passes the young master by.

But when he saw the picture of flowers and a mat, he wept in consternation.

Before he could read on he heard someone calling, "You're playing the fool again. Your Cousin Lin wants you."

It sounded like Yuan-yang's voice, yet when he turned he could see no one. While he was vacillating she suddenly beckoned to him from outside the gate and he hurried joyfully over. Yuan-yang's shadowy figure walked ahead so fast that he could not overtake her.

"Good sister, wait for me!" he cried.

She paid no attention, continuing on her way, so that Pao-yu was forced to put on a spurt. Then he saw another fairyland with high pavilions, stately mansions with hanging eaves, and among them the indistinct figures of palace maids. As he feasted his eyes on this scene he forgot Yuan-yang and his legs carried him through a palace gate. Inside were all manner of exotic flowers and herbs unknown to him, while in a flower-bed surrounded by a white stone balustrade grew a green plant, the tips of its leaves a light red. He wondered what rare plant this could be that it was so specially treasured, observing that the faintest breeze set it swaying incessantly, and that though it was so small and had no blossoms its delicate grace was utterly enchanting.

He was looking on raptly when someone beside him demanded, "Where did this oaf come from to spy on our fairy plant?"

He swung round in dismay to see a fairy maid and explained to her with a bow, "While looking for Sister Yuan-yang I blundered into this fairy realm. Please pardon my presumption!

May I ask what place this is? Why did Sister Yuan-yang come here to tell me that Cousin Lin wants me? I beg you to enlighten me."

"Who knows your cousins?" the fairy maid retorted. "I am keeping watch over this fairy plant, and no mortals are allowed to loiter here."

Reluctant to leave he pleaded, "Sister Fairy, if you are in charge of these fairy plants you must be the Goddess of Flowers. Do tell me what makes this plant unique!"

"That's a long story," she answered. "This plant, Vermilion Pearl, used to dwell on the shore of the Sacred River and was withering away until it was revived by being watered every day with sweet dew by the attendant Shen Ying. Because of this, it went down to the world of men to repay Shen Ying's kindness. Now that it has returned to the realm of truth, the Goddess of Disenchantment has ordered me to watch over it and not let butterflies or bees molest it."

Pao-yu could not fathom this. Convinced that he had met the Goddess of Flowers and determined not to let slip this chance, he persisted, "If you are in charge of this plant, Sister Fairy, there must be others in charge of those countless rare flowers. I won't trouble you to tell me who all of them are, but which fairy is in charge of the hibiscus?"

"That I can't tell you, but my mistress may know."

"Who is your mistress, sister?"

"The Queen of Tear-stained Bamboos."

"That's it!" Pao-yu exclaimed. "The Queen of Bamboos, I'd have you know, is my cousin Lin Tai-yu."

"Nonsense! This is the celestial abode of goddesses. Even if you call your cousin the Queen of Bamboos she's no Ngo-huang or Nu-ying[1] — how could *my* mistress be related to mortals? If you go on talking so wildly, I'll call guards to drive you out!"

In abashed dismay Pao-yu was just withdrawing when a messenger arrived to announce, "The attendant Shen Ying is invited to enter."

---

[1] See the note on p. 535, Vol. II.

The fairy maid said, "I've been waiting all this time, but he hasn't put in an appearance. So how can I send him in?"

"Isn't that him leaving now?"

Then the fairy maid hurried out calling, "Please come back, Shen Ying!"

Pao-yu, thinking it was somebody else she wanted and afraid of being driven away, made off as fast as he could.

Suddenly his way was barred by a sword and he was ordered to halt. In panic he looked up and saw Third Sister Yu. Slightly reassured he pleaded, "Sister, why should you threaten me too?"

"All the men of your house are a bad lot, spoiling people's reputations and breaking up marriages! Now that you're here I'm not going to let you off!"

Reduced to despair by this threat, Pao-yu heard a voice behind him call, "Sister, stop him! Don't let him get away!"

"On my mistress' orders," Third Sister Yu told Pao-yu, "I've been waiting for a long time. Now that we've met, with one stroke of my sword I'm to cut through your involvements in the mundane world!"

This made Pao-yu even more frantic, not that he fully understood her meaning. Turning to run, he found Ching-wen behind him and torn between sorrow and joy appealed to her, "I've lost my way all on my own, and run into enemies. I want to go back but have none of you with me. Thank goodness you're here, Sister Ching-wen! Do take me home at once."

"Don't be so alarmed, sir," she said. "I'm not Ching-wen but have come on our Queen's orders to take you to her. No one is going to harm you."

Nonplussed he replied, "You say your Queen wants to see me. Who is she?"

"This is no time to ask questions. You'll know when you meet."

Pao-yu had no choice but to follow her, and watching her carefully he felt certain she was Ching-wen. "No doubt about it, that's her face and her voice," he told himself. "So why should she deny it? Well, I'm too confused to bother about

that now. When I see her mistress I'll beg her to forgive me
for anything I've done wrong. After all, women are so kind-
hearted, she's bound to excuse my presumption."

By now they had reached a fine palace blazing with colour,
with a clump of bamboos in the courtyard, outside the door
several pines. Under the eaves stood maids dressed like palace
attendants who at sight of him murmured, "Is this the attendant
Shen Ying?"

The maid who had brought him there said, "Yes, it is. Go
in quickly to announce him."

One of the waiting-maids beckoned Pao-yu with a smile, and
he followed her through several buildings to the main apartment
which had a pearl curtain over its lofty door.

"Wait here till you're sent for," she told him, and in abject
silence he did so while she went in, reappearing soon to say,
"You may go in to pay your respects."

Another maid rolled up the portière, and Pao-yu saw a gar-
landed young lady in embroidered robes seated inside. Raising
his eyes to her face he saw it was Tai-yu.

"So here you are, cousin!" he blurted out. "How I've been
longing for you!"

The waiting-maids outside expostulated, "This attendant has
no manners! Out you go, quick!" One of them lowered the
portière again.

Pao-yu longed to go in but dared not, yet was reluctant to
leave. He wanted to question the waiting-maids, but none of
them knew him and they drove him out. Ching-wen, when he
looked round for her, was nowhere to be seen. Filled with misgivings he left disconsolately, still with no one to guide him,
unable to find the way by which he had come. He was in a
quandary when he caught sight of Hsi-feng under the eaves of
a house beckoning to him.

"Thank goodness!" he exclaimed. "I'm home again! What
flummoxed me so just now?" He ran towards her crying, "So
this is where you are, sister. The people here have been plaguing
me, and Cousin Lin refused to see me, I don't know why."

As he reached her he saw it was not Hsi-feng but Chin Ko-ching, the first wife of Chia Jung. He halted and asked where Hsi-feng was. Instead of answering, Ko-ching went inside.

Not venturing to follow her, he stood there woodenly in a daze and sighed, "What have I done wrong to make them all cut me like this?" He burst out crying.

At once guards in yellow turbans with whips in their hands bore down on him demanding, "Where is this fellow from that he dares intrude into this fairy realm of bliss! Off you go!"

Afraid to protest, Pao-yu was trying to find a way out when in the distance he saw a group of girls approaching, chatting and laughing. He was pleased to see that one of them looked like Ying-chun.

"I've lost my way," he called to her. "Come to my rescue!"

At once the guards behind gave chase, and as he dashed off headlong the girls changed into demons too and joined in the pursuit.

Pao-yu was desperate when along came the monk who had returned his jade. Holding up a mirror he declared, "I have come on orders from the Imperial Consort to save you."

The demons instantly vanished — all left was the desolate plain.

Seizing the monk by the arm, Pao-yu implored him, "I remember you were the one to bring me here, but then you disappeared. I met many people dear to me, but they all ignored me and suddenly turned into demons. Was that a dream or did it really happen? Please explain this to me, father."

"Did you pry into any secrets here?" asked the monk.

Pao-yu thought, "Since he brought me to this fairy realm, he himself must be an immortal; so how can I hide anything from him? Besides, I want him to elucidate this." He therefore answered, "Yes, I saw some registers."

"There you are! After reading them can't you understand? All earthly ties of affection are bewitchments. Just bear what has happened carefully in mind, and I shall explain it to you later on." He gave him a violent shove. "Now go back!" Pao-yu lost his balance and fell with a cry of dismay.

His whole household was in tears when Pao-yu regained consciousness. At once they called out to him. He opened his eyes to find himself on the *kang* and, seeing that the eyes of Lady Wang, Pao-chai and the rest were red and swollen from weeping, he calmed himself and thought, "Why, I must have died and come to life again!" Recalling all that had befallen his spirit, and pleased that he could still remember it, he laughed aloud and exclaimed, "That's it, that's it!"

His mother summoned a doctor, thinking he was deranged again, at the same time sending maids to report to Chia Cheng that their son had recovered from his heart attack and now that he could talk there was no need to prepare for the last rites. At this, Chia Cheng hurried over and saw that Pao-yu had indeed regained consciousness.

"You luckless fool!" he cried. "Trying to frighten us to death!" All unwittingly he shed tears. Then, sighing, he called in the doctor to examine Pao-yu's pulse and administer medicine.

Sheh-yueh, who had been thinking of suicide, was equally relieved by his recovery. Lady Wang sent for a longan cordial, and when he had taken a few sips he felt calmer. In the general relief no one blamed Sheh-yueh, but Lady Wang had the jade given to Pao-chai to hang on Pao-yu's neck.

"I wonder where that monk found the jade," she remarked. "It's odd the way one moment he was asking for silver and the next he vanished. Could he be an immortal?"

Pao-chai said, "Judging by the way he came and left, he can't have *found* the jade. When it was lost before, it must have been this monk who took it away."

"But it was here in our house," objected Lady Wang. "How could he have taken it?"

"If he could bring it back, he could have taken it too."

Hsi-jen and Sheh-yueh reminded them, "That year when the jade was lost, Lin Chih-hsiao consulted a fortune-teller; and after Madam Pao married into our house we told her that the character he came up with was the *shang*[1] meaning reward. Do

---

[1] *Shang* (尚) meaning "monk" bears a resemblance to the upper half of *shang* (赏) meaning "reward."

you remember, madam?"

"Yes," said Pao-chai thinking back. "You all said it meant we should look for the jade in a pawnshop. Only now is it clear that it meant that the jade had been taken by a monk, as the upper part of that character is the *shang* for 'monk.' "

"I just can't get over that monk!" remarked Lady Wang. "When Pao-yu fell ill that time, another monk came and said we had a treasure in our house — meaning this jade — which could cure him. Since he knew that, there must be more to this jade than meets the eye. Besides, your husband was born with it in his mouth. Have you ever heard of such a thing before? But who knows after all what this jade can do or what will become of him? It was this jade that made him fall ill, this jade that cured him, this jade that he was born with. . . ." She broke off here in a fresh fit of weeping.

Pao-yu, who had been following their conversation, was better able now to understand what had happened when his spirit took flight. He said nothing, however, just fixing it in his mind.

Then Hsi-chun joined in, "When the jade was lost, we asked Miao-yu to try the planchette and it wrote 'By the ancient pine at the foot of Blue Ridge Peak . . . entering my gate with a smile you will meet again.' I think 'entering the gate' is most significant. Buddhism is the gate to sainthood; I'm only afraid Second Cousin can't enter that gate."

Pao-yu laughed sarcastically at this but Pao-chai knitted her brows, lost in thought.

"There you go harping on Buddhism again!" scolded Madam Yu. "Haven't you dropped your idea of becoming a nun?"

Hsi-chun smiled. "The truth is, sister-in-law, I've been abstaining from meat for some time now."

"Good gracious, child!" exclaimed Lady Wang. "You mustn't have these notions."

Hsi-chun said nothing, but Pao-yu could not help sighing as he recollected the verse "By the dimly lit old shrine she sleeps alone." Then suddenly recalling the inscription for the painting of a mat and flowers, he glanced at Hsi-jen and tears started to his eyes. His abrupt transitions from smiles to tears puzzled the others, who could only assume that he was unhinged again, not knowing that his agitation arose from the verses he had memorized from the registers into which he had pried. Though unwilling to speak of them, he was convinced of the truth of these predictions. But we can return to this later.

The others saw that after Pao-yu's revival his mind had cleared, and by taking medicine every day he steadily recovered his health. This being the case, Chia Cheng turned his mind to other matters. As there was no knowing when Chia Sheh would be pardoned, and he did not like to leave the old lady's coffin in the temple for too long, he decided to escort it back to the south for burial and called in Chia Lien to consult him.

"Your decision is quite correct, sir," said Chia Lien. "Not being in office now you are free to see to this important business, whereas once you take off your mourning you will probably have other demands on your time. In my father's absence I couldn't presume to suggest this; but although your decision is excellent, this is going to cost several thousand taels and it's useless to expect the police to recover our stolen property."

"I have made up my mind," said Chia Cheng, "but since the Elder Master is away I wanted to consult you on how to handle this. You can't leave home or there would be no one in charge here. In my opinion all those coffins should be conveyed to the ancestral graveyard, and as I can't cope single-handed I'm thinking of taking Chia Jung along, the more so as his wife's is one of the coffins. Then there is your Cousin Lin's. The old lady left instructions that it should go south with hers. I suppose we shall have to borrow a few thousand taels to cover these expenses."

"Nowadays we can't count on others helping us out," replied Chia Lien. "As you are not in office, sir, and my father is away, we're in no position to raise a loan at present. All we can do is mortgage some properties."

"How can we, when this mansion of ours was built by the government?"

"I don't mean this mansion we live in, but there are houses outside which can be mortgaged and redeemed again after you resume office, sir.   If in future my father returns and is given a post, that will make it easier.   My one regret is that you should have to exert yourself in this way at your advanced age, sir."

"I'm simply doing my duty by the old lady.   But you must be more prudent in running the household!"

"You can rest assured about that, sir.   I shall certainly do my best, incompetent as I am.   Besides, you will need to take quite a few servants south, and as that will leave fewer here I can cut down on expenses and get by.   If you should find yourself short of funds on the way, sir, since you will be passing Lai Shang-jung's place you can enlist his help."

"It's my own mother's funeral.   Why should I ask other families to help?"

"Yes, sir," muttered Chia Lien, then withdrew to raise the money.

Chia Cheng told Lady Wang his plans and asked her to take charge of domestic affairs, then chose an auspicious day to start this long journey.   By now Pao-yu had completely recovered his health, while Chia Huan and Chia Lan were studying hard. Chia Cheng entrusted all three to the care of Chia Lien.

"This is a year for the triennial examination," he told him. "Huan can't sit for it while in mourning for his mother.   Lan is only a grandson, so after the mourning is over he's still entitled to take the examination and you must send Pao-yu there too with his nephew.   If he is a successful candidate, it will help to atone for our faults."

Chia Lien and the boys assented.   After giving further instructions to other members of the family, Chia Cheng bade farewell to the ancestral shrine, had sutras chanted for a few days at the temple outside the city, then boarded a boat with Lin Chih-hsiao and others.   He did not take leave of his friends and relatives, not wanting to put them out; thus only family members saw him off.

Lady Wang reminded Pao-yu from time to time of his father's instructions, and checked up on his studies.   Pao-chai and Hsi-jen too, it goes without saying, encouraged him to work hard. Though he was in better spirits after his illness, he took more fantastic notions into his head: not only was he averse to rank and an official career, he had lost much of his former interest in girls. But this was not too apparent to other people as he did not voice these views.

One day, after returning from seeing off Tai-yu's coffin, Tzu-chuan stayed disconsolately in her room to weep. "How un-feeling Pao-yu is!" she thought. "When he saw Miss Lin's cof-fin taken south he showed no sadness, shed not a tear, and in-stead of consoling me when I sobbed he actually laughed at me. So all this heartless fellow's honeyed talk before was to fool us! It's a good thing I didn't take him seriously the other night, or I'd have been taken in by him again. One thing I can't make out, though, is his coolness towards Hsi-jen nowadays as well. Madam Pao has never liked too much show of feeling, but don't Sheh-yueh and the rest resent his behaviour? What fools most of us girls must be to have cared so much for him all that time — what can come of it in the end?"

Just then Wu-erh came in to see her. Finding Tzu-chuan in tears she asked, "Are you crying for Miss Lin again? I see now that it's no good basing your opinion of somebody on hearsay. Because we'd always heard how good Master Pao was to girls, my mother tried time and again to get me into his service; and since coming here I've nursed him devotedly each time he was ill, yet now that he's better he hasn't a single kind word for me — he doesn't even so much as look at me!"

Tickled by this, Tzu-chuan laughed. "Bah, you little slut!" she spat out. "How do you want Pao-yu to treat you? A young girl should have some shame! When he shows so little interest in all those who belong to his household by rights, what time has he to waste on *you*?" Laughing again, she drew one finger over her cheek to shame her. "Tell me, what's the rela-tionship between you and Pao-yu?" she demanded.

Aware that she had given herself away, Wu-erh blushed furiously. She was about to explain that *she* wanted no special consideration from Pao-yu but he had recently shown too little to his maids, when someone outside the courtyard gate shouted, "That monk is back again. He wants ten thousand taels of silver! The mistress is worried and wanted Master Lien to talk to him, but Master Lien isn't at home! That monk is ranting crazily outside. The mistress asks Madam Pao to go and discuss what to do."

To know how they got rid of the monk, read the next chapter.

CHAPTER 117

Two Maids Protect Pao-yu's Jade Lest
He Renounce the World
A Worthless Son, Taking Sole Charge
of the House, Revels in Bad Company

When Lady Wang sent to ask for Pao-chai, and Pao-yu knew that the monk was outside, he hurried all alone to the front crying out, "Where is my master?"

He called repeatedly but could not find him and, reaching the gate, saw Li Kuei barring the way, refusing the monk admission.

"The mistress has sent me," said Pao-yu, "to invite this holy man in."

Then Li Kuei let go of the monk who swaggered in and, seeing that he looked like the monk in his trance, Pao-yu had an inkling of the truth. Bowing he said, "Excuse my tardiness in welcoming you, master."

"I don't want you to entertain me," the monk replied. "Just hand over the silver and I'll be off."

This did not sound to Pao-yu the way a saint would talk; moreover, the monk had a scabby head and was wearing filthy rags. He reflected, "The ancients said, 'One who has attained the Way makes no show of it; one who makes a show of it has not attained the Way.' I mustn't let slip this chance, but agree to give him the reward so as to sound him out."

He replied, "Please have patience, master, and sit down to wait while my mother gets it ready. May I ask if you are from the Illusory Land of Great Void?"

"What 'illusory land'? Whence I came, thither shall I depart. I'm here to return you your jade. Can you tell me where it comes from?" When Pao-yu could not answer the monk chuckled, "You don't even know your own origin yet question me!"

Pao-yu had the intelligence after all he had experienced to have seen through the vanity of this earth, being simply ignorant of his own antecedents. The monk's question awoke him to the truth.

"You don't need any silver," he cried. "I'll return you the jade."

"And so you should!" laughed the monk.

Without a word Pao-yu raced in to his own compound, which Pao-chai and Hsi-jen had left to see Lady Wang. He snatched the jade up from his bed and dashed out, running full tilt into Hsi-jen who started with fright.

"The mistress said it was very good of you to entertain the monk, and she means to give him some silver," she informed him. "What brings you back?"

"Go straight and tell her there's no need to raise any money. I'll return him the jade instead."

"Not on any account!" She caught him by the arm. "This jade is your life. If he takes it away your illness will come back!"

"Not any more. Now I'm in my right mind again, what do I need the jade for?" He wrenched himself free and made off.

Hsi-jen ran frantically after him calling, "Come back! I've something to tell you."

He cried over his shoulder, "There's nothing we need talk about."

She chased after him regardless, expostulating, "Last time you lost the jade it nearly cost me my life! You've just got it back, and if he takes it away that will be the death of us both! You can only give it back over my dead body!" With that, overtaking Pao-yu, she caught hold of him.

"Whether you die or not I must give it back," was his desperate retort.

He pushed her with all his might, but she seized his belt with both hands and would not let go, weeping and screaming as she sank to the ground. The maids inside hearing this darted out and found them both distraught.

"Tell the mistress, quick!" Hsi-jen sobbed. "Master Pao

wants to give his jade back to the monk."

When the maids ran to report this, Pao-yu grew even angrier and tore at Hsi-jen's hands to free himself; but mindless of the pain she would not let go. And when Tzu-chuan inside heard what Pao-yu meant to do, even more frantic than the rest she completely forgot her resolve to remain aloof and ran out to help restrain him. Though he was a man and struggling hard, he could not free himself from their desperate clutches.

"So you're hanging on to this jade for dear life!" he sighed. "What would you do if I went away myself?" At that they burst into uncontrollable sobbing.

They were still locked together when Lady Wang and Pao-chai hurried over. "Pao-yu!" wailed his mother. "You've gone crazy again!"

At sight of her Pao-yu knew he could not escape. With a sheepish smile he said, "Why all this fuss? Why upset the mistress for no reason at all? I thought it unreasonable of the monk to insist on ten thousand taels, not one tael less; so in a pique I came back meaning to return him the jade, saying that it was a fake and we didn't want it. If he saw that we didn't value it, he'd be willing to accept whatever we offered."

"I thought you really meant to give it back," scolded Lady Wang. "All right then, but why didn't you tell them clearly? Why make them raise such a rumpus?"

Pao-chai put in, "If that's the case, well and good. If you really gave the jade back, that monk is so odd that he could cause fresh trouble for our family and that would never do. As for the reward, you can raise it by selling my jewels."

"Yes," agreed Lady Wang. "Let's do that."

Pao-yu made no objection as Pao-chai stepped forward to take the jade from his hand. "There's no need for you to go out," she said. "Her Ladyship and I will give him the money."

"I don't mind not giving him the jade," he replied, "but I must see him once more."

Hsi-jen and Tzu-chuan were still keeping hold of him. Pao-chai, having sized up the situation, told them, "Let go of him. He can go if he wants to."

Then Hsi-jen released Pao-yu, who said with a smile, "You people think more of the jade than you do of me! Now that you're not stopping me, suppose I go off with the monk and leave you the jade?"

In renewed alarm Hsi-jen wanted to seize him again, but in the presence of the mistresses she could not take liberties, and Pao-yu had already slipped away. She at once sent a maid to Pei-ming at the inner gate with the message, "Tell the servants outside to keep an eye on Master Pao; he's not in his right mind." The girl went off on this errand.

Lady Wang and Pao-chai went in now and sat down to ask Hsi-jen just what had happened, and she related in detail all Pao-yu had said. This so worried them that they sent word to the servants outside to wait on Pao-yu and hear what the monk had to say.

The maid on her return informed Lady Wang, "Master Pao is really rather crazed. The pages outside say he was at a loss because you wouldn't let him have the jade. Now he's gone out and begged the monk to take him with him."

Lady Wang exclaimed in horror, then asked what the monk had replied.

"He said he wants the jade, not it's owner," the girl said.

"Doesn't he want the money then?" asked Pao-chai.

"I didn't hear anything about that, madam. Later the monk and Master Pao were laughing and chatting together about many things, but the pages couldn't understand a word."

"Stupid creatures!" cried Lady Wang. "Even if they don't understand, they can memorize it." On her orders the maid hurriedly fetched one of the pages and, standing outside the window, he paid his respects.

"Though you didn't understand the talk between the monk and Master Pao, can't you repeat it to me?" asked Lady Wang.

"All we caught were phrases like 'the Great Waste Mountain,' 'Blue Ridge Peak,' 'the Land of Great Void' and 'severing mortal entanglements,'" he told her.

Lady Wang could not make head or tail of this either, but Pao-chai's eyes widened in alarm and she could not get a word out. They were about to send to fetch Pao-yu back, when in he came grinning and saying to himself, "Fine, fine!"

Pao-chai remained speechless while his mother asked, "What is this crazy talk?"

"I'm in earnest," protested Pao-yu, "yet you call me crazy! That monk and I knew each other before and he simply wished to see me. He never really wanted a reward but was just doing a good deed. After he'd explained that, he vanished. Isn't that fine?"

His mother, not believing him, sent the page to question the gateman.

"The monk has really gone," he came back to report. "He left word that Your Ladyships needn't worry. He wants no silver, simply wants Master Pao to pay him occasional visits. 'Just submit to fate and things will take their natural course,'" he said.

"So he was a good monk after all! Did you ask where he lives?"

"The gateman said he told Master Pao, so he knows."

But Pao-yu when questioned answered with a smile, "That place is far or near, depending on how you look at it. . . ."

"Wake up!" cut in Pao-chai. "Stop dreaming! The master and the mistress dote on you, and the master told you to study hard to advance yourself."

"What I have in mind will advance us all, won't it? Don't you know the saying, 'When one son renounces the world, seven of his ancestors will go to heaven'?"

Lady Wang lamented, "What's to become of us? First Hsi-chun insists on renouncing the world, and now here's another. How can I live on like this?" She broke down and wept.

Pao-chai tried hard to console her and Pao-yu said, "I was joking, madam. Don't take it seriously."

His mother stopped weeping to retort, "Is this a joking matter?"

Just then a maid came in to announce, "Master Lien is back, quite unlike his usual self. He hopes you'll go back, madam, so that he can report something to you."

"Tell him to come in here," ordered Lady Wang in fresh alarm. "He's known his sister-in-law since they were children, so he doesn't have to avoid her."

When Chia Lien had entered and paid his respects to her, Pao-chai stepped forward to greet him.

He reported, "I have just had word from my father that he's seriously ill. He's sent for me. Any delay and I may never see him again!" Tears coursed down his cheeks.

"What illness did he say he had?" asked Lady Wang.

"It started as influenza but turned into consumption, and now he's dying. He sent a messenger posthaste with the news, warning that if I delay for so much as two days I shall be too late to see him. So I've come to ask your permission to leave at once, madam. But there's no one at home to see to things unless we rope in Chiang and Yun. Though they aren't much good at least they are men, and if business crops up outside they can report it.

"My own household is no problem. Because Chiu-tung kept weeping and wailing that she didn't want to stay, I told her family to fetch her back and that has saved Ping-erh a good deal of vexation. Though Chiao-chieh has no one to look after her, Ping-erh is kind to her and she's an intelligent girl though even more wilful than her mother, madam, so I hope you will discipline her from time to time." The rims of his eyes were red now and he dabbed at them with the silk handkerchief attached to the sachet at his waist.

"The child has her grandmother here," demurred Lady Wang. "Why should you entrust her to me?"

"If you bring that up, madam," he muttered, "I may say something outrageous. I can only beg you anyway to be kind, as you always are, to your nephew." He fell on his knees.

"Get up quickly!" she said, her own eyes reddening. "We are all one family, of course I'll help. Only one thing: the child is growing up, and if anything should happen to your father her marriage would be delayed. If some suitable family makes a proposal, should we wait for your return or let her grandmother decide what to do?"

"Since Your Ladyships are at home, naturally you can decide without waiting for me."

"Before you go, write to the Second Master telling him there is no one responsible at home and you don't know whether your father will recover, so we hope he will have the old lady buried quickly and come back as fast as he can."

Chia Lien assented and started out, then turned back. "We have enough servants here for the house," he said. "But there's not one in the Garden since Pao Yung went back to his master. And Master Hsueh Ko has vacated that compound where Aunt Hsueh lived to move to their own house. It's not good having no caretakers for all those empty lodges in the Garden, so I hope you'll send people from time to time to keep an eye on them. Green Lattice Nunnery belongs to us too, and since Miao-yu's disappearance the nuns who attended her dare not take charge and want us to assign someone to see to things there."

"We can't set our own house in order, so how can we handle other people's affairs? But mind you don't mention this to Hsi-chun, or she'll plague us again to let her be a nun. How can a family like ours allow one of our daughters to become a nun?"

"If you hadn't raised this, madam, I wouldn't have ventured to. But after all Cousin Hsi-chun belongs to the East Mansion, and because she has no parents, her elder brother's away and she's hardly on speaking terms with her sister-in-law, I hear that she's often threatened to take her own life. Since her mind is made up, if we thwart her and she really kills herself, won't that be worse than entering a nunnery?"

Lady Wang nodded. "This business is really too much for me. I can't make the decision; that's up to her sister-in-law."

After a few further words Chia Lien went out, summoned the stewards to give them their instructions, then wrote to Chia Cheng and packed up for his journey. Ping-erh naturally gave him some parting advice. It was Chiao-chieh, however, who was most distressed. Her father wished to entrust her to Wang Jen, but she was most unwilling; and it upset her even more, although she could hardly say this, to learn that Yun and Chiang

would be in charge of outside business. She said goodbye to
her father and settled down to live quietly with Ping-erh, for
after Hsi-feng's death Feng-erh and Hung-yu had asked leave
on the pretext of illness. Ping-erh would have liked to get a
girl from the Chia family to keep Chiao-chieh company and look
after her, but there was no one available; nor could she get Hsi-
luan or Ssu-chieh — former favourites of the old lady — for the
latter had recently married and the former was engaged and
shortly to wed.

Chia Yun and Chia Chiang, having seen Chia Lien off, came
in to pay their respects to Their Ladyships. They stayed in the
outer study by turns, and during the day would fool around
with the servants or assemble friends to feast, taking it in turn
to stand treat. They even held gambling parties; but this was
kept secret from the inner apartments.

One day Lady Hsing's brother and Wang Jen called and
discovered Chia Yun and Chia Chiang staying there. As they
were boon companions, on the pretext of helping with family
affairs they often joined in the gambling and drinking parties.
The few reliable stewards had gone away with Chia Cheng and
Chia Lien, leaving only some sons and nephews of Lai Ta and
Lin Chih-hsiao. These young fellows, used to taking advantage
of their parents' positions to enjoy themselves, had no idea of
how to manage a household and in their elders' absence ran
wild like unbridled colts. Egged on by their two masters who
were only kinsmen they did just as they pleased. So the Jung
Mansion was turned upside-down.

Chia Chiang thought of roping in Pao-yu, but Chia Yun dissuaded him saying, "Don't ask for trouble. Uncle Pao was
born under an unlucky star. One year I proposed an excellent
match for him: the girl's father was a provincial tax-collector,
the family owned several pawnshops, and she herself was pret-
tier than a fairy. I went to the trouble of writing him the full
particulars, but he wasn't cut out for such luck." Glancing
round at his companions he continued, "He'd already fallen for
Aunt Pao! And didn't you hear too — everyone must know

it — that he made Miss Lin die of a broken heart? Oh well, each one's romance is fated by heaven. Yet he was annoyed with me because of this and since then has cold-shouldered me. He must have imagined I wanted to make him indebted to me."

Chia Chiang nodded and did not press the point. Neither of them knew that since meeting that monk Pao-yu was eager to sever all worldly ties, and though he dared not break with his mother he was already holding aloof from Pao-chai and Hsi-jen. When the younger maids, unaware of this, still tried to attract him he paid no attention. He did not care about the family either. Lady Wang and Pao-chai kept urging him to study and while he made a pretence of doing so he remained preoccupied with the fairyland to which the monk had led him, thinking all those around him vulgar creatures. Since his own household irked him, when at leisure he would go to talk with Hsi-chun and, seeing eye to eye, they strengthened each other's convictions.

Chia Huan and Chia Lan were left to their own devices. Chia Huan, because his father was not at home, his own mother had died and Lady Wang paid little attention to him, joined Chia Chiang's group; and when Tsai-yun reproached him she only got cursed for her pains. Yu-chuan, having seen how unbalanced Pao-yu was growing, had also asked her mother to take her home. So Chia Huan and Pao-yu, each in his different way, were making themselves shunned by all. Only Chia Lan stayed with his mother and studied hard, writing compositions which he took to school for Chia Tai-ju to correct; but as recently the tutor had been confined to his bed the boy had at present to study on his own. Li Wan had always been sedate and now, apart from duty calls on Lady Wang and visits to Pao-chai, she did not stir from her rooms, just watching her son study. So although there were not a few inmates in the Jung Mansion, they kept to themselves, not imposing their will on others. Thus Chia Huan and Chia Chiang went from bad to worse, going so far as to steal things to pawn or sell. And Chia Huan in particular stopped at nothing, even frequenting brothels and gambling-dens.

One day when Uncle Hsing and Wang Jen were drinking with them in the outer study, being in high spirits they sent for some singsong girls to join them and propose toasts.

"The racket you make is too vulgar," objected Chia Chiang. "I suggest we recite some verses while we drink."

"All right," agreed the rest.

"Start with the word 'moon,'" he went on. "I'll recite a line first, and we'll count round to see who has to drink when I reach the word 'moon.' Then he must recite another line on my orders and, if he fails, must drink three big cups as a forfeit."

When they acquiesced he tossed off a cup and declaimed:

"Winged goblets fly as we drink to the moon."

This made it Chia Huan's turn. "Recite a line ending with 'oleander,'" he was ordered.

"Silently the cold dew wets the oleander."

After this quotation he asked, "What's the other line?"

"One containing the word 'fragrance.'"

"Heavenly fragrance wafts down from the clouds."

"How deadly dull!" protested Uncle Hsing. "A fat lot of literature you know, yet you pose as literati! This isn't fun; it's downright exasperating! Let's drop it and play a finger-game instead with the loser drinking and singing a song — 'a double dose of gall' this is called. If someone can't sing he can tell a joke, provided it's amusing."

"Right!" cried the rest.

They started playing wildly. Wang Jen lost, drained a cup and sang a song which was applauded. Then they began again and the singsong girl who lost sang *Such a Pretty Young Lady*. The next loser was Uncle Hsing, who when asked for a song said, "I can't sing. I'll tell you a joke instead."

"If it doesn't make us laugh," warned Chia Chiang, "you must pay the forfeit."

Uncle Hsing emptied his cup. "Listen, gentlemen," he began. "In a certain village stood a temple to Emperor Yuan-ti, with next to it the shrine of the tutelary god whom the Emperor often called over for a chat. One day Yuan-ti's temple was robbed, and he told the tutelary god to investigate.

"The tutelary god reported, 'There are no thieves in this locality. Your officers must have slipped up and allowed thieves from outside to break in and rob you.'

" 'Nonsense!' said Yuan-ti. 'As the local deity, you're responsible for any thefts; yet instead of catching the robbers you're accusing my officers of negligence!'

"The other said, 'If they weren't negligent, there must be something unlucky about your temple.'

"Yuan-ti asked, 'Do you know anything about geomancy?'

" 'Let me have a look round,' the other replied. He did this, then reported, 'You're running a risk with those double red doors behind you. Behind *my* shrine is a wall, so naturally I don't lose things. Once you build a wall behind yourself all will be well.'

"Emperor Yuan-ti was convinced and ordered his officers to fetch masons to build a wall.

"His officers objected, 'Nowadays no one comes to offer incense, so how are we to get the bricks and mortar and masons to build a wall?'

"Not knowing what to do, he told them to use magic but they were powerless.

"Then General Tortoise at Yuan-ti's feet stood up to say, 'You fellows are useless, but I have a plan. Just pull down those red doors, and when night falls I'll stop up the doorway with my belly. Wouldn't that do as well as a wall?'

"The other officers approved, 'Good. This costs no money and should be very solid.'

"So General Tortoise undertook this task and for a few days all was quiet. Then, however, things started disappearing again. They summoned the tutelary god and told him, 'You said that once we had a wall these thefts would stop. Now, with a wall, we're still losing things; how is that?'

"He answered, 'Your wall can't be solid enough.'

" 'Go and see for yourself,' they retorted.

"He examined it and it was certainly solid. So why were

things still disappearing? However, when he felt it he exclaimed, 'I thought it was a real wall, but this is just a fake wall!' "[1]

All hooted with laughter, even Chia Chiang joining in.

"Fine, Foolish Uncle!" he cried. "Why should you abuse me without any provocation? Hurry up and drink a big cup as punishment."

Although already tipsy Uncle Hsing did so, and the others went on carousing until they were all rather drunk. Then Uncle Hsing ran down his elder sister and Wang Jen his younger, in the most virulent terms. Chia Huan in his cups also spoke scathingly of the way Hsi-feng had bullied his mother and him, trampling all over them.

"People should be more considerate," said the others. "Hsi-feng was so ruthless when she had the old lady's backing that now she's died sonless, leaving only one daughter. She's suffering for her sins!"

Chia Yun, recalling how shabbily Hsi-feng had treated him and how Chiao-chieh had cried at the sight of him, joined in the general abuse till Chia Chiang said, "Let's drink! Why gossip about other people?"

The two singsong girls asked, "How old is this daughter of hers? What does she look like?"

"She's very good-looking," answered Chia Chiang, "and nearly fourteen already."

"It's too bad she was born into such a rich family," said one of the girls. "If she were from a humble family, she could help her parents and brothers get official titles and make pots of money." Asked what she meant she explained, "There's a borderland prince not related to the Imperial House, a very gallant noble who is looking for a concubine. If she took his fancy, her whole family could move into his palace. Wouldn't that be fine?"

The others paid little attention as they went on drinking, but Wang Jen made a mental note of this.

At this point they were joined by two youngsters from the families of Lai Ta and Lin Chih-hsiao. "What a jolly party

---

[1] The characters for "fake wall" are *chia chiang*.

you gentlemen are having!" they said.

The others stood up to rejoin, "Why are you so late? We've been waiting for you for some time."

"This morning we were worried by a rumour about more trouble for our family. We hurried off to investigate; but it's not true."

"If it has nothing to do with us, why didn't you come earlier?"

"Though we're not directly concerned there *is* a connection. You know who's in trouble? Mr. Chia Yu-tsun. This morning we went there and saw him in chains and were told he was to be taken to court for trial. Knowing what a frequent visitor he was here, we were afraid our house might be involved and therefore went to make inquiries."

"That was thoughtful of you, brothers," said Chia Yun. "Yes, you were right to find out. Sit down and drink a cup, then tell us about it."

After some polite deferring they sat down to drink and said, "This Chia Yu-tsun is an able gentleman and clever climber, who holds quite a high post but is too grasping; so several charges of extorting money from his subordinates have been brought against him. Our most sagacious, benevolent Emperor is angered by nothing so much as reports of venal officials who abuse their power to oppress good citizens; He therefore issued a decree for his arrest and trial. If he is found guilty he will be in trouble; if the charges prove groundless, those who impeached him will suffer. This is a really good reign, if only we had the luck to be officials!"

"Your elder brother's in luck," the others told Lai Ta's son. "Isn't he sitting pretty as a magistrate?"

"I'm only afraid he may not remain a magistrate for long, the way he's carrying on," was the reply.

"Does he fleece people too?"

The young man nodded, then raised his cup to drink.

"What other news did you hear?" they were asked.

"Nothing much," the two of them answered. "Only that a number of brigands captured at the coast have been tried, and during their interrogation they revealed the whereabouts of many more, some of them lying low here in town and looking out for a chance to break into more houses. But now all our high officials are good administrators and strategists, exerting themselves to repay the Emperor's favour, so wherever they go they quickly wipe out brigands."

"You spoke of some brigands in town. Have they found out who robbed our family?"

"That we haven't heard. There was some vague talk about a man from the provinces who robbed a house here and kidnapped a girl to take her to the coast; because she resisted him the brigand killed her, and before he could leave the capital he was caught and executed on the spot."

"Wasn't Miao-yu in our Green Lattice Nunnery kidnapped? Could she be the girl who was killed?"

"Yes, it must be her!" said Chia Huan.

"How do *you* know?" they asked him.

"That creature Miao-yu was disgusting, the airs she gave herself! She was all smiles to Pao-yu, yet never cast so much as a glance at *me*. If it turns out to be her I'll be only too glad!"

"Women are being kidnapped all the time. This doesn't have to be her."

"There's some indication that it is," said Chia Yun. "The other day we heard that her serving-woman dreamed that she saw Miao-yu murdered."

The others chuckled, "A dream doesn't count!"

"Never mind about her dream," said Uncle Hsing. "Let's have supper now. We must play for high stakes tonight."

The rest were willing and after their meal started betting heavily. They were still at it after midnight when they heard a clamour from the inner apartments.

A servant reported, "Miss Hsi-chun has quarrelled with Madam Yu, then cut off all her hair and rushed to kowtow to Their Ladyships, begging them to let her enter a nunnery and threatening that if they won't she'll kill herself on the spot. Their Ladyships don't know what to do and want Master Chiang and Master Yun to go in."

Chia Yun knew that Hsi-chun had taken this into her head

when left in charge of the house, and they had little chance of dissuading her. He proposed to Chia Chiang, "Though Their Ladyships have sent for us we can't — and indeed we shouldn't — make any decisions. We'll have to try to talk her round and, failing that, leave it to them to decide. After discussing it we can write to report this to Uncle Lien so that we won't be held responsible."

Having agreed on this they went inside to see Their Ladyships, and made a show of dissuading Hsi-chun. She, however, was determined to renounce the world and begged them, if they would not let her leave, to give her a couple of clean rooms in which she could chant sutras and worship Buddha. Since the two young men were unwilling to make a decision and Hsi-chun might really commit suicide, Madam Yu had to decide the matter herself.

"All right," she announced. "I'll take the blame. We'll just say that I couldn't stand my young sister-in-law and forced her to become a nun. Of course we mustn't let news of this get out. Here at home, with Their Ladyships as witnesses, let me take the responsibility. Chiang will have to write to Master Chen and your Uncle Lien."

The two young men assented. To know whether Their Ladyships agreed or not, you must read the next chapter.

CHAPTER 118

A Disgruntled Uncle and Cousin Delude
a Helpless Girl
Alarmed by His Cryptic Talk, Wife and Concubine
Reprove Their Witless Husband

Madam Yu had convinced Their Ladyships that Hsi-chun's case was hopeless.

"If you're set on worshipping Buddha," said Lady Wang, "it must be predestined* and we really can't stop you. It doesn't seem proper, though, for a girl from a family like ours to become a nun. Now your sister-in-law has agreed to it and your piety is commendable, but I've one condition to make: Don't shave your head. So long as you're sincere, what does your hair matter? Just think of Miao-yu — she became a nun with long hair — but who knows what change of heart she had to come to such a bad end! Since you're set on this, we'll count your present quarters as your convent. We'll also have to question all your maids, and if some are willing to stay with you we won't find husbands for them; for the rest we'll make other arrangements."

At this, Hsi-chun stopped weeping and kowtowed her thanks to Their Ladyships, Li Wan and Madam Yu.

Then Lady Wang asked Tsai-ping and the other maids, "Which of you want to join in your young lady's devotions?"

"Whichever of us you choose, madam," they replied. And, inferring that they were unwilling, she started casting about for someone else.

Hsi-jen standing behind Pao-yu expected him to burst into tears and have another relapse. But to her surprise, upsetting her even more, he simply sighed, "How sublime!"

Though Pao-chai said nothing, not yet having fathomed his

534

meaning, her heart ached to see him a victim still of delusions.

Before Lady Wang could question any more maids, Tzu-chuan came forward and knelt down before her. "Just now you asked who would stay with Miss Hsi-chun," she said. "Whom do you have in mind, madam?"

"How can I choose anyone against her will?" was Lady Wang's reply. "If anyone wants to, she can volunteer."

"Of course Miss Hsi-chun's doing this of her own free will, but the girls in her service aren't willing to do the same," said Tzu-chuan. "I have a request to make, madam. It's not that I want to separate the other girls from Miss Hsi-chun, but we each have our own ideas. I waited on Miss Lin all that time and Your Ladyship knows how good she was to me. I can truly never repay her tremendous kindness. When she died I longed to follow her to the grave, but as she belonged to another family and I'm a bond-slave of this house I could hardly kill myself. Now that Miss Hsi-chun wants to enter holy orders, I beg Your Ladyships to assign me to wait on her all my life. If you will agree to this, I shall count it my good fortune!"

Before Lady Hsing or Lady Wang could answer, Pao-yu felt a pang at the thought of Tai-yu and shed tears. The others were about to ask the reason when he burst out laughing again.

"It wasn't my place to propose this," he said, stepping forward. "But as you assigned Tzu-chuan to my service, madam, I'm emboldened to ask you to agree so that she can realize her aspirations."

His mother objected, "When Tan-chun married you nearly cried your heart out; yet now that Hsi-chun wants to become a nun, instead of trying to dissuade her you approve. What do you mean by this? I can't understand you."

"You've already agreed to her becoming a nun, and I assume her mind's made up on the subject. If that's the case, there's something I'd like to tell you; but if she hasn't decided yet I dare not speak out of turn."

"How ridiculous you are, cousin," protested Hsi-chun. "If

I hadn't made up my mind, how could I have won round the mistresses? I agree with what Tzu-chuan just said. If you let me have my way I shall count it my good fortune. Otherwise I can always die — I'm not afraid! So just say what you have in mind."

"It can't count as disclosing any secret, as this was fated. I'm going to recite you a poem."

The others expostulated, "Why pester us with your poems when we're all so upset?"

"It's not *my* poem, but one I read somewhere. Listen."

"All right," they conceded. "Recite it, but stop talking nonsense."

Without further argument Pao-yu declaimed:

> She sees through the transience of spring,
> Dark Buddhist robes replace her garments fine;
> Pity this child of a wealthy noble house
> Who now sleeps alone by the dimly lit old shrine.

Li Wan and Pao-chai exclaimed, "Oh dear! He's bewitched."

Lady Wang, however, nodded and asked with a sigh, "Tell me truly, Pao-yu, where you saw this poem?"

Not liking to disclose his dream he answered, "Don't ask me the place, madam."

Having digested the meaning she burst out sobbing, "I thought at first you were joking, but then you came out with this poem. All right, I understand. What do you expect me to do? I shall simply have to let you do as you choose; but just wait till I'm dead before you each go your own way!"

Pao-chai, trying to console her, felt such a stab of anguish that she could not help sobbing too, while Hsi-jen was so prostrated with grief that Chiu-wen had to support her. Pao-yu neither wept nor attempted to comfort them, simply remaining silent. And at this point Chia Lan and Chia Huan slipped away.

To soothe Lady Wang, Li Wan said, "Pao-yu must have been so upset by Hsi-chun's decision that he started raving.

Don't take his nonsense seriously, madam. Why not give Tzu-chuan an answer, so that she can get up?"

"What does my consent count for?" replied Lady Wang. "When someone's made up her mind there's no stopping her. As Pao-yu said, this was fated."

Tzu-chuan kowtowed. Hsi-chun also thanked Lady Wang. Then Tzu-chuan kowtowed to Pao-yu and Pao-chai too.

"Amida Buddha! Fine!" cried Pao-yu. "You've stolen a march on me!"

Pao-chai, for all her self-control, was finding it hard to bear up. And Hsi-jen despite the presence of Lady Wang sobbed, "I want to be a nun with Miss Hsi-chun too."

"You mean well," Pao-yu told her gently. "But you're not fated to enjoy this pure happiness."

"Do you mean I'm going to die?" she cried.

Grieved as he was for her he could not tell her more, and since it was nearly dawn he urged his mother to rest, whereupon Li Wan and the others dispersed. Tsai-ping escorted Hsi-chun back as usual, but was later married off; and then Tzu-chuan waited on Hsi-chun as long as she lived, without any change of heart. But this is anticipating.

Let us now return to Chia Cheng who was escorting the old lady's coffin south. On his way, boatloads of troops withdrawing upstream jammed the river and held him up, much to his anxiety. Luckily he learned from some officials from the coast that the garrison commander there had been recalled to the capital, and it relieved him to think that Tan-chun must be going home. However, he was upset, not knowing when she would be starting on her journey. Estimating that his funds would be running out, he had no choice but to write to Magistrate Lai Shang-jung, the son of Lai Ta, to ask for a loan of five hundred taels of silver, instructing the messenger to overtake him with the requisite sum.

Some days passed, during which his boat proceeded only a few dozen *li*; then his servant overtook them and, coming aboard, delivered Lai Shang-jung's letter. It pleaded poverty, and the silver sent was a paltry fifty taels.

In a rage Chia Cheng ordered the man, "Take this back at once with his letter, and tell him not to trouble."

The servant had to go back to Lai Shang-jung. Worried by the return of his letter and the silver, and aware that he had bungled things, Lai added another hundred taels and begged the servant to take this back and put in a good word for him. The man refused, however, and left without the money.

Lai Shang-jung in dismay at once wrote home to his father, urging him to ask for leave and to buy his freedom. The Lai family requested Chia Chiang and Chia Yun to beg Lady Wang to be kind enough to release him; but Chia Chiang knew that this was out of the question and told them a day later that she had refused. Thereupon Lai Ta asked for leave and sent to advise his son to resign on the pretext of illness. Lady Wang, however, knew nothing of all this.

Now Chia Chiang's lie that Lady Wang had refused to let Lai Ta redeem himself had dashed Chia Yun's hope of bettering his position in the Jung Mansion. While gambling outside he lost heavily for several days in succession and, unable to pay up, applied to Chia Huan for a loan. But Chia Huan had not a cent, having already squandered his mother's savings, and was unable to help anyone else. Resenting his harsh treatment at Hsi-feng's hands, he decided now that Chia Lien was away to vent his spite on Chiao-chieh, using Chia Yun as his cat's paw.

He jeered at him, "You're a grown man, yet for lack of guts you let go a chance to make money, and instead come begging from a pauper like me!"

"That's ridiculous talk, Third Uncle," protested Chia Yun. "Being on the spree together all the time, what chance have we to make money?"

"Didn't someone say the other day that a prince in a border province wants to buy a concubine? Why not discuss this with Uncle Wang and marry Chiao-chieh off?"

"Don't take offence, uncle," retorted Chia Yun. "But if that prince were to buy her, how could he keep on good terms with our family?"

Chia Huan whispered something into his ear, but although Chia Yun nodded he thought this too childish a notion to entertain seriously.

Just then Wang Jen turned up. "What are you two plotting behind my back?" he asked.

Chia Yun told him what Chia Huan had just whispered to him.

Wang Jen clapped his hands crying, "This is a fine idea! There's money in it! I'm only afraid you won't be able to pull it off. If you have the nerve to, as her maternal uncle I can authorize it. If Huan will propose it to Lady Hsing I'll have a word with Uncle Hsing; then if the other mistresses ask about it you can speak up in favour and it should go through."

Once they had agreed to this, Wang Jen went to find Uncle Hsing while Chia Yun made this proposal — in an embroidered form — to Their Ladyships. Lady Wang was somewhat sceptical, but when Lady Hsing heard that her brother approved she sent to sound him out.

Uncle Hsing, who had been won round by Wang Jen and hoped to share the proceeds, told his sister, "That prince is most distinguished. If we agree to this match, even though she's not his principal wife, once she goes to his palace my brother-in-law's rank is bound to be restored and you'll be in a good position again."

Lady Hsing had no mind of her own. Taken in by Foolish Uncle's fabrications she consulted Wang Jen, who gave her even more blarney. Then she sent to urge Chia Yun to make the proposal, and Wang Jen lost no time in despatching a messenger to the prince's palace.

Not knowing the truth of the matter, the prince ordered some of his household to inspect the girl. Chia Yun informed them, "We've kept this secret from most of the family, just telling them that His Highness is proposing marriage. But once it's settled, as her grandmother approves and the girl's own uncle is the guarantor, we have nothing to fear."

When they agreed to this arrangement, he sent word to Lady Hsing and reported the proposal to Lady Wang. Li Wan, Pao-chai and the others who were ignorant of the real facts thought it a good match and were all delighted.

On the appointed day, two ladies in magnificent costumes called. Lady Hsing welcomed them in and civilities were exchanged, the visitors treating her with due respect as she was a lady of rank. Since the matter was not yet decided, Lady Hsing instead of telling Chiao-chieh about it sent for her to come and meet some relatives who had called. Chiao-chieh, too young to suspect anything, came over with her nurse. And Ping-erh accompanied them as she had certain misgivings. She saw these two visitors dressed like ladies-in-waiting look Chiao-chieh over from head to foot, after which they got up and took her hand to examine her once more; then after sitting a little longer they left. Chiao-chieh, most embarrassed by this scrutiny, went back to her room very puzzled and, not having heard of these relatives before, asked Ping-erh who they were.

Ping-erh had more or less guessed from their behaviour that they were looking over a prospective bride; but in Chia Lien's absence, with Lady Hsing in charge, she could not find out which family they came from. Their close scrutiny was uncalled for if it was a match between families of equal status; and the two visitors had not behaved like members of any of the royal households with which the Chias were connected, but rather like provincials. She decided not to tell Chiao-chieh this but to make certain inquiries, which she did by discreetly questioning the maids and serving-women under her, who told her everything they had heard outside. Ping-erh was consternated. Though she kept this from Chiao-chieh, she hurried over to tell Li Wan and Pao-chai, begging them to inform Lady Wang.

Lady Wang knew that this was a bad business and warned

Lady Hsing against it; but the latter, taken in by her brother and Wang Jen, suspected Lady Wang's motives.

"My grand-daughter has reached marriageable age," she said. "With Lien away the decision is up to me. Besides, her own grand-uncle and maternal uncle have made inquiries, and *they* must surely know the facts of the case better than other people. So I'm quite willing. If things turn out badly, Lien and I won't hold anyone else to blame."

Lady Wang, secretly angered by such talk, forced herself to chat for a while on other matters before going off to confide tearfully to Pao-chai what had happened.

"Don't let this upset you, madam," said Pao-yu. "I don't think it will go through. If it does, it's Chiao-chieh's fate, so you needn't intervene."

"You can't open your mouth without raving!" his mother retorted. "Once the matter is fixed they'll come and take her away. And then, as Ping-erh says, won't your cousin Lien hold me to blame? Not to say that she's my own grand-niece, even if she were some distant relative we'd want something better for her. We arranged that match between Miss Hsing and your cousin Hsueh Ko, and isn't it good the way they're living happily together? Then there's Pao-chin who's made an excellent marriage into the Mei family, which by all accounts is very comfortably off. As for Hsiang-yun's marriage, that was her uncle's idea and all went well to start with, but now her husband's died of consumption and she's made up her mind never to marry again, poor thing. How can I have the heart to let Chiao-chieh marry into the wrong family?"

As she was talking, Ping-erh called on Pao-chai to find out Lady Hsing's intentions, and Lady Wang told her what the latter had said. Ping-erh, speechless at first, fell on her knees then implored, "Chiao-chieh's whole future is in your hands, madam! If we trust *them*, not only will the girl have a wretched life, but how are we to account for it to Master Lien when he comes home?"

"You're a sensible girl," Lady Wang replied. "Get up and listen to me. The Elder Mistress, after all, is Chiao-chieh's grandmother. If *she* decides on this, how am I to stop her?"

Pao-yu insisted, "It doesn't matter, if only you're clear-headed."

For fear that in his madness he might disclose her appeal to Lady Wang, Ping-erh did not remonstrate with him but left soon afterwards.

Lady Wang's anxiety made her heart palpitate. She told maids to help her to her room to lie down but would not let Pao-yu and Pao-chai attend her, saying, "A little rest will set me right." However, she was so troubled in her mind that when word was brought that Li Wan's aunt had called she did not feel up to entertaining her.

Chia Lan came in then to pay his respects and reported, "This morning a letter came from my grandfather, which the servants at the gate brought in to my mother. She wanted to bring it to you, but then my grand-aunt arrived, so she told me to deliver it instead, madam. My mother will be coming presently and so will my grand-aunt, she says." He presented the letter.

"What has your grand-aunt come for?" asked Lady Wang.

"I don't know," he answered. "I only heard her mention some letter from my aunt Li Chi's future in-laws."

Lady Wang realized that since a match had been arranged and betrothal gifts exchanged between Chen Pao-yu and Li Wan's cousin Li Chi, the Chen family must be wanting to go ahead with the marriage and Aunt Li had come to discuss this. She nodded and opened the letter, in which she read:

> My journey has been delayed by the ships all along the river re-turning from their successful coastal campaign. I hear that Tan-chun is coming to the capital with her father-in-law and husband, and wonder if you have any news of her. I received Lien's letter about the Elder Master's illness, but do not know if there is more definite news. Pao-yu and Lan will shortly be taking the examina-tion; they must study hard and not slack. It will be some time before the old lady's coffin can be conveyed to our native place. My health is good; have no worry on that score. Tell Pao-yu and the others what I have written. Jung will write separately.

To this were appended the date and Chia Cheng's signature.

Lady Wang returned the letter to Lan saying, "Take this

to show your Uncle Pao, then give it back to your mother."

Just then, however, Li Wan brought over her aunt to pay their respects, and Lady Wang offered them seats. Aunt Li told her of the Chen family's wish to expedite Li Chi's wedding, and they talked this over.

Then Li Wan asked Lady Wang, "Have you read the master's letter, madam?"

"Yes, I have."

Chia Lan showed it to his mother, whose comment was, "Tan-chun hasn't been back once in all these years since her marriage. Now that she's coming to the capital you can feel much easier in your mind, madam."

"Yes," said Lady Wang. "I had palpitations of the heart just now; but this news has made me feel better. I only wonder when she will arrive."

When Aunt Li had asked whether Chia Cheng had had a good journey, Li Wan said to her son, "Did you read the letter? It's nearly time for the examination and your grandfather has it very much on his mind. You must take his letter to show Uncle Pao."

"They haven't passed the first degree; how can they sit for the provincial examination?" Aunt Li inquired.

Lady Wang explained, "When his grandfather was Grain Commissioner he bought him and Pao-yu the rank of Imperial College Student."

Aunt Li nodded and Chia Lan went off with the letter to find Pao-yu.

After seeing his mother to her room, Pao-yu had gone back to amuse himself by reading the chapter "Autumn Water" in *Chuang Tzu*. Pao-chai, coming out from the inner room and finding him utterly absorbed in a book, went over to have a look and was dismayed to discover what it was. "He takes that talk about 'leaving the world of men' seriously," she reflected. "No good will come of it in the long run." But thinking it useless to try to dissuade him, she sat down beside him lost in reverie.

Pao-yu noticing this asked, "What's on your mind now?"

"Since we are man and wife, you're the one I have to rely on all my life; this isn't a question of my personal feelings. Of course wealth and honour are 'transient as drifting clouds'; but the sages of old set store by moral character and a firm foundation. . . ."

Without waiting for her to finish, Pao-yu laid his book aside and said with a faint smile, "So you talk about 'moral character and a firm foundation' and the 'sages of old.' Don't you know that one ancient sage taught that we 'should not lose the heart of a child'? What's special about a child? Simply this: it has no knowledge, no judgement, no greed and no taboos. From our birth we sink into the quagmire of greed, anger, infatuation and love; and how can we escape from earthly entanglements? I've only just realized that mortal men are like water weeds drifting together and then apart again. Though the ancients spoke of this, no one seems to have awakened to the fact. If you want to talk about character and foundation, tell me who has achieved the supreme primeval state?"

"Since you speak of the heart of a child," she countered, "the sages of old took it to mean loyalty and filial piety, not leaving the world and giving up all human relationships. The constant concern of Yao and Shun, Yu and Tang, the Duke of Chou and Confucius was to save the people and benefit the world; so what they meant by the heart of a child was simply love for humanity. What would the world come to if everyone took your advice and disregarded all natural relationships?"

Pao-yu nodded and chuckled, "But Yao and Shun didn't force Tsao Fu and Hsu Yu[1] to take up office, nor did King Wu and the Duke of Chou force Po Yi and Shu Chi[2] to serve them."

---

[1] Legend had it that the sage kings Yao and Shun wanted to make over the country to these men, but they declined.

[2] Po Yi and Shu Chi refused to cooperate with King Wu and the Duke of Chou, becoming hermits instead.

Before he could finish, Pao-chai interposed, "What you're saying now is even more wrong. If all the men of old had been like Tsao Fu, Hsu Yu, Po Yi and Shu Chi, why should Yao and Shun, the Duke of Chou and Confucius be considered as sages today? It's even more ridiculous to compare yourself with Po Yi and Shu Chi. They lived when the Shang Dynasty was in decline, and because they couldn't cope with the situation found some pretext to run away. But we live under a sage Emperor, our family is deeply indebted to the state, and our ancestors have lived in luxury; while in your case, particularly, since your childhood you've been treasured by the old lady while she was alive and by your parents. Just think over what you said. Was it right or wrong?"

Pao-yu made no answer, just looked up and smiled.

Pao-chai went on to plead, "Since you've run out of arguments, my advice to you is to take a grip on yourself and study hard; because if you can pass the triennial examination, even if you stop at that, you'll be paying back your debt of gratitude for your sovereign's favour and your ancestors' virtue."

Pao-yu nodded and sighed, then said, "Actually it isn't difficult to pass. And what you said about stopping there and repaying my debt is not far wide of the mark."

Before she could answer, Hsi-jen joined in, "Of course, *we* don't understand those old sages whom Madam Pao was talking about. I just feel that those of us who've been hard at it since we were small serving Master Pao, and told off ever so often — though of course that was only right — all hope he will show more consideration for us. Besides, it's for *your* sake that Madam Pao has been such a dutiful daughter-in-law; so even if you haven't much family feeling you shouldn't let her down. All those legends about gods and spirits are lies — who ever saw an immortal come down to earth? Yet when that monk from goodness knows where talked some nonsense to you, you believed it! How can someone with book-learning like you, Master Pao, take his advice more seriously than your parents'?"

Pao-yu bowed his head and said nothing.

Before she could continue, they heard footsteps in the courtyard and someone outside the window asked, "Is Uncle Pao in?"

Recognizing Chia Lan's voice, Pao-yu stood up and called cheerfully, "Come in!"

Pao-chai also rose to her feet as Chia Lan entered, beaming, to pay his respects to them both, after which he and Hsi-jen exchanged greetings. Then he presented the letter to Pao-yu.

After reading it Pao-yu said, "So Tan-chun's coming back?"

"According to grandfather, she must be," he answered.

Pao-yu nodded and seemed lost in thought.

"Did you read the end of the letter, uncle, where grandfather urges us to study hard? Have you written any compositions these days?"

Pao-yu smiled and said, "Yes, I must write a few to keep my hand in, so that I can wangle a pass."

"In that case, uncle, won't you set some subjects for us both, so that I can muddle through this examination too? Otherwise I may have to hand in a blank paper, making a fool of myself, which would reflect badly on you, uncle, as well."

"No, you should do all right."

Pao-chai invited Chia Lan to take a seat, and as Pao-yu was still sitting in his own place the boy sat down respectfully beside him. They cheerfully discussed writing essays; and Pao-chai, observing this, withdrew to the inner room. "Judging by Pao-yu's present behaviour," she thought, "he appears to have seen reason. Yet just now he stressed that this was where he would stop — what did he mean by that?"

Though Pao-chai still had her doubts, Hsi-jen was delighted to hear how animatedly Pao-yu was talking about essay-writing and the examination. "Merciful Buddha!" she thought. "He seems to have come to his senses at last after that lecture we gave him!"

As Pao-yu and Chia Lan were talking, Ying-erh brought them tea and Chia Lan stood up to take it. He then consulted Pao-yu about the examination rules and suggested that they might invite Chen Pao-yu over. Pao-yu appeared very willing.

Presently Chia Lan went home, leaving the letter with Pao-yu, who went in cheerfully and handed it to Sheh-yueh for safe keeping. Coming out again he put away the volume of *Chuang Tzu*, then gathered together some of his favourite books on Taoism and Zen Buddhism and told Sheh-yueh, Chiu-wen and Ying-erh to take them all away. Wondering what he was up to, Pao-chai sounded him out playfully, "It's quite right and proper to stop reading those, but why have them taken away?"

"It's just dawned on me that these books count for nothing. I'm going to have them burnt to make a clean sweep!" Hearing this she was beside herself with joy. But then he chanted softly to himself:

> Buddha's nature is not to be found in sacred canons,
> The fairy barque sails beyond the realm of alchemy.

She could not hear too clearly, but caught the words "Buddha's nature" and "fairy barque" which caused her fresh misgivings. As she waited to see what he would do next, Pao-yu ordered Sheh-yueh and Chiu-wen to prepare a quiet room for him, and got out all his collections of the sayings of past sages as well as other famous works and poems written during examinations, which he had put in this room. Then, to Pao-chai's relief, he set to work in good earnest.

Hsi-jen was amazed by these developments. She quietly told Pao-chai, "The talking-to you gave him did the trick after all, madam. The way you kept refuting him made him see reason. Too bad, though, that it's rather late in the day — so close to the examination!"

Pao-chai nodded and answered with a smile, "Success or failure in examinations is fated, regardless of how soon or late one starts to study. We can only hope that from now on he'll stick to the right path and never be influenced again by those evil spirits!" Since they were alone in the room she went on softly, "Of course it's good that he's seen the light at last; but I'm afraid he may revert to his bad old ways and start fooling about with girls."

"Exactly, madam. After Master Pao put his trust in that monk he cooled off towards the girls here; now that he's lost faith in him, his old trouble may very well flare up again. I don't think he ever cared much for you or me, madam. Now Tzu-chuan's gone, leaving just four senior maids and the only vamp among them is Wu-erh. They say her mother has asked Their Ladyships to let her go home to get married; however, for the time being she's still here. Sheh-yueh and Chiu-wen are all right, but in the old days Master Pao used to fool about with them too; so it looks as if Ying-erh is the only one in whom he's shown no interest, and she's a steady girl. I suggest that pouring his tea and fetching his water can be left to her, with some younger girls to help her. What do you think of that, madam?"

"This is what I've been worrying about. Your idea's a good one." So from then on Ying-erh was assigned to wait on Pao-yu with some younger maids.

Pao-yu, however, never left his compound, just sending someone every day to pay his respects for him to Lady Wang. And she, it goes without saying, was pleased to know how hard he was studying.

The third day of the eighth lunar month was the old lady's birthday. Pao-yu went that morning to kowtow to her shrine before going to his study. After lunch, Pao-chai, Hsi-jen and some of the maids were chatting in the front room with Their Ladyships while he remained in his quiet room deep in thought, when suddenly Ying-erh brought in a tray of fruit and sweetmeats.

"Her Ladyship told me to bring you this, Master Pao," she announced. "It's a sacrifice to the old lady."

Pao-yu stood up to express his thanks, then resumed his seat saying, "Put it down there."

As Ying-erh did so she whispered, "Her Ladyship's praising you." When he smiled she added, "Her Ladyship says, now you're working hard and will soon pass the examination; and next year you'll get your third degree and an official post, living up to your parents' hopes!"

He still merely nodded and smiled.

Ying-erh suddenly recalled what he had said when she made him a net before. "If you really pass, Master Pao, Madam Pao will be in luck! Remember that year in the Garden, when you told me to make you a plum-blossom net? You said he'd be a lucky man, whoever got the pair of us, mistress and maid. Now you're the one in luck."

Hearing this, Pao-yu felt a stirring of desire, but quickly suppressing it said with a faint smile, "You say I'm in luck and your mistress too. How about you?"

Ying-erh blushed. "What luck is there for the likes of me — bondmaids for life?"

"If you can really remain a bondmaid all your life, you'll be luckier than us," he chuckled.

She was afraid he was raving again on account of what she had said, and decided to leave.

"You silly girl!" he laughed. "I've something to tell you."

To know what this was you must read the next chapter.

CHAPTER 119

Pao-yu Passes the Examination with Honours and Severs Earthly Ties
The Chia Family Retains Its Wealth and Titles Thanks to Imperial Favour

Bewildered by Pao-yu's talk, Ying-eah was about to leave.

"You silly girl!" he said. "I've something to tell you. Since your young mistress is in luck, of course you as her maid will be lucky too, which is more than your sister Hsi-jen can count on. You must work hard in future, so that when your mistress prospers she may repay you for your faithful service."

The first half of this made sense to Ying-erh, not the last. However all she said was, "I understand. Madam Pao is expecting me. When you're ready to taste the sweetmeats just send a maid to call me."

Pao-yu nodded and she left. Presently Pao-chai and Hsi-jen also went back to their rooms, where we will leave them.

A few days later it was time for the examination. Everyone else simply hoped that the two young masters would write good compositions and pass with honours; but Pao-chai had noticed that Pao-yu, though studying hard, seemed strangely detached and indifferent. As this was the first examination for which he and Chia Lan had entered, she feared they might meet with some mishap in the throng of people and horses; moreover ever since the monk's departure Pao-yu had stayed indoors, and though she had rejoiced to see him studying she was sceptical about his sudden conversion and afraid of some new misfortune. And so, the day before the examination, she sent Hsi-jen with some maids to help Su-yun pack the young gentlemen's things; and when she had made sure that everything needed was ready, she went with Li Wan to ask Lady

Wang to send more than the usual number of experienced stewards with them, ostensibly to prevent their being jostled in the crowd.

The next day Pao-yu and Chia Lan, in clothes neither new nor shabby, presented themselves cheerfully to Lady Wang.

"This is your first examination," she warned them. "The first time in all these years that you've ever left me. Even when I wasn't keeping an eye on you, you were surrounded by maids and serving-women, never sleeping for a single night alone. Today, entering for the examination, you're going to be entirely on your own, so you'll have to take care of yourselves! Come out as soon as you've finished your compositions to find our family servants, then come straight back to set the minds of your mothers and wife at rest." She was moved to grief as she spoke.

Chia Lan had assented to each sentence, whereas Pao-yu had said nothing. But when his mother finished he came over to kneel before her, shedding tears. After kowtowing three times he said, "I can never repay the mother who gave birth to me. But I shall do as well as I can in the examination, to obtain a good *chu-jen* degree and make you happy, madam. Then I shall have done my duty as a son and atoned for all my faults."

This upset Lady Wang even more. "It's good, of course, for you to feel that way," she said. "If only the old lady could have lived to see you now!" Weeping she tried to raise him to his feet, but Pao-yu refused to get up.

"Even if the old lady can't see me, she'll know and be pleased," he answered. "So it's all the same whether she sees me or not. We're separated in form only, not in spirit."

This exchange made Li Wan afraid that Pao-yu was losing his mind again, besides striking her as inauspicious. She made haste to say, "Madam, why grieve over such a happy occasion? Especially as Brother Pao-yu has recently been so sensible and dutiful, studying hard as well. When he and his nephew have taken the examination and written some good compositions, they'll come straight back to show what they wrote to our seniors, after which we can wait for news of their success." She told maids to help Pao-yu up.

He turned to bow to her saying, "Don't worry, sister-in-law. We're both of us going to pass. Later on, your Lan is going to do so well that you'll wear the costume of a high-ranking lady."

She chuckled, "I only hope it works out as you say, so that it won't have been in vain. . . ." She broke off there, afraid to upset Lady Wang.

"Provided you have a good son to continue our ancestors' line," rejoined Pao-yu, "even though my brother hasn't lived to see it, it means he has done his duty."

Li Wan simply nodded, reluctant to say any more as it was growing late.

Pao-chai was most dismayed. For not only had Pao-yu's words struck her as ill-omened, so had everything said by Lady Wang and Li Wan. Still, trying not to take it seriously she just held back her tears and kept silent. And now Pao-yu walked over to make her a deep bow. All present, though mystified by his strange behaviour, did not like to laugh. They were even more amazed when Pao-chai wept.

Pao-yu told her, "I'm going now, cousin. Take good care of the mistress and wait for my good news!"

"It's time you were off. There's no need to maunder like this," she answered.

"So you're hurrying me? I know it's time to be off." He turned to look round and noticed two people missing. "Send word for me to Hsi-chun and Tzu-chuan," he added. "Well, all I want to say is I shall be seeing them again."

As he sounded half rational, half crazy, the others attributed this to the fact that he had never left home before and was affected by what his mother had said. They thought it best to speed him on his way. "People are waiting outside," they reminded him. "If you delay any longer you'll be late."

Pao-yu threw back his head and laughed. "I'm going now! No more ado! This is the end!"

The others answered cheerfully, "Go quickly."

Only Lady Wang and Pao-chai behaved as if this were a separation for life. Their tears coursed down and they nearly burst out sobbing as Pao-yu, laughing like a maniac, went out. Truly:

> Taking the only approach to fame and wealth,
> He breaks through the first door of his cage.

Let us leave Pao-yu and Chia Lan for the time being. When Chia Huan saw them set off to take the examination he was furious. Regarding himself as the master now, he decided, "Here's my chance to avenge my mother. All the other men of the family have gone, and as the Elder Mistress listens to me whom else do I have to fear?" His mind made up, he called on Lady Hsing, flattering her to get into her good graces.

Very gratified she said, "Now you're talking like a sensible boy! Chiao-chieh's marriage is something I should decide; but your cousin Lien is a fool and instead of leaving it to me, the child's own grandmother, he's entrusted it to other people!"

"That family says this branch of our house is the only one they recognize," Chia Huan told her. "Now that it's settled, they'll be sending you rich presents, madam; and once your grand-daughter's married to a prince, the Elder Master will get a high post for sure. It's not my place to speak ill of our mistress, but after one of her daughters was made an Imperial Consort she became too overbearing! I hope that in future Chiao-chieh won't be so heartless. I must make her promise that."

"Yes, you should talk to her to let her know whom she has to thank for this. Why, even if her father were at home, he wouldn't be able to find her a better husband. It's only that silly Ping-erh who thinks this match no good and says your mistress is against it too. I suppose she begrudges us this satisfaction. If we put this off till your cousin Lien comes back, he may listen to them and it may fall through."

"The other side has agreed. They're just waiting for you to send her horoscope, madam. According to the rules of the prince's house they'll fetch her three days after receiving it. There's one thing, though, which may not please you: They say since it's forbidden to marry the grand-daughter of a cashiered official, they can only carry her over quietly and the celebration will have to wait till after our Elder Master is pardoned and back in office."

"Why should I object to that? It's only correct."

"In that case you can send the horoscope, madam."

"Don't be a fool! We've only women at home. You must tell Chiang to write it."

Chia Huan assented with gleeful alacrity and hurried off to give Chia Yun this message, after which they urged Wang Jen to go to the prince's residence to draw up the contract and bring back the money.

However, one of Lady Hsing's maids — one recommended by Ping-erh — had overheard them and now slipped away to repeat the whole of their conversation to her. Ping-erh had known that they were up to no good and had explained this to Chiao-chieh, with the result that the girl wept all night, insisting that they must wait for her father's return instead of accepting Lady Hsing's decision. This fresh news made her cry more bitterly, and she wanted to appeal to Lady Wang.

Ping-erh hastily stopped her saying, "Steady on, miss! The Elder Mistress is your grandmother, so in your father's absence she's the one who has the say. Besides, your uncle is acting as guarantor, and they're in cahoots, so how can *you* override them? I'm only a servant, what I say doesn't count. We must think of some way out but on no account act rashly!"

"You'd better be quick about it," said Lady Hsing's maid. "Otherwise a sedan-chair will be coming to fetch her!" With that she left.

When Ping-erh had seen her off, she found Chiao-chieh prostrated with grief. Helping her up she said, "It's no use crying, miss. We're not in touch with your father, and judging by what they said. . . ."

Before she could finish, a maid arrived from Lady Hsing to announce, "The young lady's marriage is fixed! Ping-erh is to get together all the things she'll be needing. Her dowry can wait till Master Lien comes back."

Ping-erh had to agree. On her return to the room she found that Lady Wang had called and Chiao-chieh was weeping in her arms.

"Don't worry, child," said Lady Wang tearfully. "Your grandmother gave me a good ticking-off because I spoke up for you; so I can't see myself talking her round. We shall have to agree but put it off while we send a servant posthaste to tell your father."

"You haven't heard the latest, madam," said Ping-erh. "This morning Master Huan told Lady Hsing it's the rule of the prince's house to fetch the girl there within three days of receiving her horoscope. She's already asked Master Yun to write it out; so how can we wait for Master Lien?"

The news that Chia Huan was behind this made Lady Wang speechless with rage. When she found her tongue again she gave furious orders to have him fetched; but after a long search her maids reported that he had gone out that morning with Chia Chiang and Wang Jen.

"Where is Chia Yun?" she demanded.

"He's nowhere to be found either."

They stared at each other in dismay, at a loss. As Lady Wang could hardly take issue with Lady Hsing, all they could do was weep.

A serving-woman came in at this point to announce, "The servants at the back gate say that Granny Liu's here again."

"In a family crisis like this we've no time to entertain visitors," said Lady Wang. "Put her off with some excuse."

But Ping-erh demurred, "Better invite her in, madam. As Chiao-chieh's godmother she should be told about this."

As Lady Wang raised no objection, the erving-woman brought in Granny Liu and greetings were exchanged. Puzzled to find them all with red eyes, Granny Liu presently asked, "What's wrong? You must have been grieving for Madam Lien again."

This mention of her mother made Chiao-chieh weep even more bitterly.

Ping-erh said, "Let's not beat about the bush. Since you're her godmother you ought to know this." She drew her aside to explain the situation.

Granny Liu was flabbergasted too. After a while, however, she laughed and said, "A clever young lady like you must surely have listened to drum-ballads? They describe plenty of ways and means. It's not hard to find a way out."

"What way out have you, granny?" asked Ping-erh eagerly. "Do tell us quickly."

"It's very simple. Don't say a word to a soul; just up and leave, and that's that."

"That's easier said than done. A young lady from a house like ours, where's she to go?"

"If you want to spirit her away and don't mind her coming to my village, *I'll* hide the young lady. I'll get my son-in-law to find a messenger, and she can write a letter in her own hand for him to take to her father, so that he comes back at once. How about that?"

"What if the Elder Mistress finds out?"

"Do they know that I'm here?"

"As her quarters are in the back and she's such a tartar, nobody passes on any news to her. If you'd come by the front gate she'd have known about it, but not now that you've come in by the back."

"Then let's fix a time, and I'll get my son-in-law to come with a carriage to fetch her."

"That would take too long," said Ping-erh. "Just wait here a moment." She hurried in and took Lady Wang aside to pass on Granny Liu's proposal.

Lady Wang after thinking it over decided it would not do.

"It's the only way!" pleaded Ping-erh. "I wouldn't dare propose this to anyone else. You can pretend to be in the dark, madam, and later ask the Elder Mistress where Chiao-chieh has gone. We'll send to get Master Lien to hurry back."

Lady Wang said nothing but sighed.

Chiao-chieh who had overheard them begged, "Please come to my rescue, madam! When my father comes home he's bound to be grateful to you!"

"That's settled then," said Ping-erh. "You'd better go back, madam. We'll just ask you to send someone to look after our house."

"Keep it hushed up!" urged Lady Wang. "And mind you both take clothes and bedding with you."

"We can only pull it off if we leave at once," replied Ping-erh. "If they come back with everything fixed, then we're sunk!"

"All right. Go and get ready quickly. I'll see to things here." With that Lady Wang went over to see Lady Hsing, engaging her in conversation to keep her at home while Ping-erh sent servants to make preparations.

"Don't sneak out!" she instructed them. "If anybody sees you, just say that the Elder Mistress has ordered a carriage to take Granny Liu home."

So the servants at the back were told to hire a carriage, while Ping-erh dressed Chiao-chieh up to look like Ching-erh and hurried her out. She herself, pretending to be seeing off Granny Liu, slipped into the carriage too when no one was looking; and so they left the mansion. Though the back gate had been open recently, there were only a couple of gatekeepers on duty; and though there were a few other servants around, as the place was so big and practically deserted how could they keep an eye on everything? Besides, Lady Hsing had never shown them the least consideration whereas they were all indebted to Ping-erh; so although aware that this was wrong they connived at Chiao-chieh's escape. Lady Hsing, still talking with Lady Wang, had no inkling of what was afoot.

Lady Wang, however, was on tenterhooks. After making conversation for a while she slipped over to see Pao-chai, who observing her distracted air asked what was worrying her. Lady Wang told her in confidence what had happened.

"How dangerous!" exclaimed Pao-chai. "We must hurry up and stop Yun from going there."

"But I can't find Huan."

"You had better pretend to know nothing about this, madam, while I find someone to inform Lady Hsing."

Lady Wang nodded and left it to her; but no more of this for the time being.

Now that prince from the provinces wanted to buy some serving-maids, and on the strength of the go-between's description he sent some of his household to look Chiao-chieh over. When they reported back to him he asked about her family, and not daring to deceive him they told him the truth.

On learning that she came from an old noble family, the prince exclaimed, "Out of the question! This is strictly forbidden: it would have been a fiasco! Since I have already paid homage at court I must choose a day now to return to my post. If anyone comes to broach this again, send him packing!"

So today when Chia Yun and Wang Jen arrived to present Chiao-chieh's horoscope, the prince's attendants blustered, "His Highness has given orders: Anyone who tries to pass off ·a daughter of the Chia family as a common citizen must be arrested and tried! In this reign of peace who dares do such a thing?"

This so terrified Wang Jen and Chia Yun that they scuttled off, complaining that this had not been made clear at the start. They parted crestfallen.

Chia Huan, back at home waiting for news, was flustered to hear of Lady Wang's summons. When Chia Yun came back alone his first words were, "Is it settled?"

Chia Yun stamped his foot. "The fat's in the fire! Someone's let the cat out of the bag!" He described the dressing-down they had been given.

In consternation Chia Huan said, "Now what's to be done? After I made it sound so good to the Elder Mistress this morning. You lot have landed me in a proper mess!"

As they were wondering what to do, they heard servants inside calling that Their Ladyships wanted them. Very sheepishly they went in.

Lady Wang looked blackly at them and exclaimed, "A fine

thing you've done, hounding Chiao-chieh and Ping-erh to death! Hurry up and bring me their bodies!"

The two young men fell on their knees. Chia Huan was too afraid to say a word. Chia Yun with bowed head protested, "We would never have dared, but Grand-Uncle Hsing and Uncle Wang proposed this match for Chiao-chieh, as we reported to Your Ladyships. The Elder Mistress was willing, and told me to write out the horoscope. But that family has turned her down, so how did we hound her to death?"

"Huan told the Elder Mistress she'd be fetched away in three days," snapped Lady Wang. "And that her relatives were the guarantors. Isn't that what you said? Well, I shan't question you now. Hurry up and bring Chiao-chieh back. You'll have to answer for this when the master returns!" Lady Hsing being now reduced to tearful silence, Lady Wang swore at Chia Huan, "Concubine Chao was a bitch, and she left behind her a misbegotten scoundrel!" She called her maids to help her back to her own quarters.

Chia Huan, Chia Yun and Lady Hsing indulged in mutual recriminations, then said, "Well, let's stop blaming each other. They can't really have killed themselves. Ping-erh must have hidden her in some relative's house."

Lady Hsing sent for the gatemen from the front and the back of the house and berated them. "Do you know where Chiao-chieh and Ping-erh have gone?" she demanded.

They answered in the same vein, "Don't ask *us*, madam. Ask the gentlemen in charge. You've no call to storm at *us*. When our mistress questions us we know what to say. She can have us all beaten or dismissed; but since Master Lien left there've been fine goings-on in the outer quarters! We haven't been issued our monthly allowances. They gamble, get drunk, fool about with young actors, and even bring women from outside into the house. Isn't that so, gentlemen?"

Chia Yun and Chia Huan had nothing to say for themselves, and when Lady Wang sent to order them to find Ping-erh and Chiao-chieh immediately they only wished the earth would swallow them up. They did not venture to question Chiao-chieh's household, knowing that all the maids there, detesting them, would keep her whereabouts secret. Not daring to admit this to Lady Wang, they sent round to other relatives to ask, but in each case drew a blank. So Lady Hsing inside and Chia Huan and the others outside were given no peace for several days in a row.

Soon came the day for the examination to end, and Lady Wang was eager for the return of Pao-yu and Chia Lan. By the afternoon when there was no sign of them, she, Li Wan and Pao-chai sent servants out to make inquiries, but they did not come back, having no news. Others were sent, and when these did not return either the three women felt quite distraught.

That evening, to their delight Chia Lan came back.

"Where is your Uncle Pao?" he was asked.

Without stopping to pay his respects he sobbed, "Uncle Pao has disappeared!"

Lady Wang, dumbfounded, collapsed. Luckily Tsai-yun and others were at hand to carry her to her bed and revive her; but at once she started wailing. Pao-chai remained speechless, dazed.

Hsi-jen, dissolved in tears, reproached Chia Lan, "Stupid creature! You were with him, how could you lose him?"

"In the hostel we ate and slept in the same place," he told them. "And in the examination grounds our cells weren't too far apart, so we kept in close touch. This morning, Uncle Pao finished his papers first and waited for me to hand them in together. Then we came out together; but in the crowd at the Dragon Gate he disappeared. The servants who'd come to meet us asked me where he was and Li Kuei said he'd seen him, just a few yards away, but he'd vanished in the crowd. I sent Li Kuei and others to search in different directions while I took some men with me to search all the cells. But he wasn't there. That's why I'm so late back."

Lady Wang was crying too much to speak, Pao-chai had a fair idea of the truth of the matter, while Hsi-jen was sobbing as if she would never stop. So Chia Chiang without waiting for orders went out with others in different directions to search. In the Jung Mansion, plunged in gloom and half deserted, the banquet to welcome the candidates back went untouched. Forgetting his own exhaustion, Chia Lan wanted to make another search for Pao-yu, but Lady Wang restrained him.

"Child, your uncle has disappeared," she said. "We can't have *you* getting lost too. Go and rest now, there's a good boy!"

Still Chia Lan insisted on going, till Madam Yu and the rest managed to dissuade him.

Hsi-chun, the only one to grasp the truth, could not divulge it. She asked Pao-chai, "Did Cousin Pao-yu take his jade with him?"

"Of course, he always wore it," was the answer, to which Hsi-chun made no reply.

Hsi-jen, recalling her attempt to snatch the jade from Pao-yu, suspected the monk of spiriting him away. Her tears fell like pearls as, sobbing and broken-hearted, she remembered Pao-yu's past kindness. "Sometimes when I provoked him he lost his temper," she thought. "But he always had the grace to make it up later, to say nothing of his warm-hearted consideration. When I provoked him too much, he swore he'd become a monk. For all we know he may have kept his word!"

By now it was already the fourth watch and there was still no news. Afraid Lady Wang would wear herself out with grief, Li Wan urged her to go and rest, and the others attended her, only Lady Hsing going back to her own quarters while Chia Huan skulked out of sight. Lady Wang sent Chia Lan to bed but herself passed a sleepless night.

At dawn, the servants came back to report that they had searched high and low without finding a trace of Pao-yu. Then Aunt Hsueh, Hsueh Ko, Hsiang-yun, Pao-chin and Aunt Li called in turn to pay their respects and ask for news. This went on for several days, with Lady Wang too grief-stricken to eat.

She was at death's door when a servant announced, "A messenger from the coast says he comes from the Garrison Commander, and our Miss Tan-chun will be arriving tomorrow."

This news relieved Lady Wang's mind, although she still grieved for Pao-yu. And the next day, sure enough, Tan-chun came home. They all went out some distance to welcome her and saw that, splendidly dressed, she looked lovelier than ever. At sight of Lady Wang's haggard looks and the red, swollen eyes of the others, she too broke down and wept before greeting them. It distressed her to see Hsi-chun dressed like a Taoist nun; and when she learned of Pao-yu's disappearance and the family's many misfortunes they all wept again. Fortunately, with her persuasiveness and good sense she succeeded little by little in consoling Lady Wang to some extent.

The following day Tan-chun's husband also called and, when informed what had happened, urged her to stay for a while to comfort the household. The maids who had accompanied her at the time of her marriage, reunited with their old friends, talked of all that had taken place since their departure; but day and night high and low alike were waiting for word of Pao-yu.

One day, after the fifth watch, servants from the outer apartments came to the inner gate to announce good tidings. A few young maids rushed in, without waiting for the senior maids' permission, and burst out, "Such good news, madam!"

Jumping to the wrong conclusion, Lady Wang stood up elatedly to ask, "Where did they find him? Bring him in at once!"

"He's come seventh of the successful candidates."

"But where is he?" When there was no answer she sat down again.

"Who came seventh?" asked Tan-chun.

"Master Pao," they told her.

Then another shout went up outside, "Master Lan has passed too!" The maids hurried out and came back with the announcement that Chia Lan's name was the hundred-and-thirtieth on the list. Li Wan was naturally overjoyed, but while Pao-yu was missing she dared not show it. Lady Wang too was pleased that Chia Lan had passed but thought, "If only Pao-yu were to come back how happy we all should be!"

Pao-chai, the only one still overcome with grief, had to hold back her tears.

All who offered congratulations said, "Since Pao-yu was fated to pass, he's bound to turn up. Besides, now as a successful candidate, he's too well-known to remain lost."

Lady Wang half convinced by this gave a wan smile, whereupon they urged her to take some nourishment.

Pei-ming outside the third gate was clamouring, "Now that Master Pao has passed, we're certain to find him!" Asked what he meant he explained, "The proverb says: 'A successful candidate's fame spreads throughout the world.' Wherever he goes now, people will know about him and will have to send him back."

Those in the inner apartments commented, "That young fellow has no manners, yet he talks sense."

Hsi-chun, however, countered, "How could a grown man like him get lost? I suspect he's seen through the ways of the world and taken monastic vows, in which case it will be difficult to find him."

This set Lady Wang and the others weeping again.

Li Wan agreed, "Yes, since ancient times many men have given up rank and wealth to achieve Buddhahood and become immortals."

"If he's so unfilial as to abandon his parents, how can he become a Buddha?" sobbed Lady Wang.

"People shouldn't have anything unique about them," Tan-chun remarked. "We all thought it a good thing, Brother Pao-yu being born with that jade; but now it seems all this trouble stems from it. Don't be angry, madam, at what I'm going to say, but if he doesn't turn up in the next few days then there must be some reason, and you'd better consider him as never having been born. If there really is some mystery about him and he becomes a Buddha, this must be owing to your virtue in some previous existence."

Pao-chai said nothing, but Hsi-jen could not bear her mental anguish — her head reeled and she collapsed. Lady Wang compassionately told some maids to help her back to her room.

Chia Huan was thoroughly mortified by the success of his brother and his nephew on top of Chiao-chieh's disappearance, for which he held Chia Chiang and Chia Yun to blame. He knew that with Tan-chun back this matter would not be dropped, yet he dared not hide himself. These days he felt on thorns.

The next day when Chia Lan went to offer his thanks at court, he learned that Chen Pao-yu had also passed and so they ranked as classmates. Young Chen, told of Pao-yu's mysterious disappearance, expressed his sympathy.

The officer in charge of recommendations presented the papers of the successful candidates to the Emperor, who perused each in turn and found them all perspicuous. Observing that the seventh candidate Chia Pao-yu was a native of Chinling, as was the hundred-and-thirtieth Chia Lan, he asked, "Is either of these Chias from Chinling from the same family as the late Imperial Consort?"

His ministers sent for them to question them, then repeated Chia Lan's account of Pao-yu's disappearance as well as of their antecedents. Thereupon our sagacious, compassionate Emperor recalled the Chia family's services to the state and ordered his ministers to draw up a detailed memorial on the subject. His Majesty in his great goodness then ordered the bureau in charge to re-investigate Chia Sheh's case and submit their findings to him. He also read in the report "On the Successful Conclusion of the Compaign Against Brigands at the Coast" that "the whole empire is at peace and the people are content." In his delight he ordered his ministers to reward those officials responsible and to proclaim a general amnesty.

After Chia Lan had left the court and thanked his examiner, he heard of the general amnesty and reported it to Lady Wang. The whole family rejoiced and only hoped that Pao-yu would now return home. Aunt Hsueh, even more overjoyed, made ready to ransom Hsueh Pan.

Then one day it was announced that old Mr. Chen and Tan-chun's husband had called to offer congratulations. Lady Wang sent Chia Lan out to entertain them. Presently he returned to her beaming.

"Wonderful news, madam!" he told her. "Mr. Chen has heard at court that our Elder Master has been pardoned; and Uncle Chen has not only been pardoned but is to inherit the Ning Mansion's noble title. Grandfather will keep the title of Duke of Jungkuo, and after the period of mourning is to be made vice-minister of the Ministry of Works. All the property confiscated will be returned. The Emperor was impressed by Uncle Pao's essays, and discovered that he is the Imperial Consort's younger brother, whose good character the Prince of Peiching has vouched for. His Majesty summoned him to court and when it was reported that according to his nephew Chia Lan he had disappeared after the examination and a search was being made for him everywhere, the Emperor decreed that all the garrisons of the capital must do their utmost to find him. This decree should set your mind at rest, madam. Now that the Emperor has shown us such favour, Uncle Pao is bound to be found!"

Lady Wang and the rest of the family exchanged jubilant congratulations. Only Chia Huan was frantic as he searched high and low for Chiao-chieh, who had left the city with Granny Liu and Ping-erh. In the village Granny Liu treated her with respect, cleaning out the best rooms for her and Ping-erh to stay in; and though she could only offer them country fare the food was fresh and clean, while with Ching-erh to keep her company Chiao-chieh felt quite at home.

When the few well-to-do families in the village heard that a young lady from the Chia Mansion was staying with Granny Liu, they flocked to see her and thought her a goddess come down to earth. Some sent presents of vegetables and fruit, others of game, making quite a commotion. The richest family among them, named Chou, were millionaires owning a vast estate of good land. Their only son, a handsome, intelligent lad of fourteen for whom his parents had procured a tutor, had just passed the county examination. When his mother saw Chiao-chieh she thought enviously, "Country folk like us aren't good enough for such a young lady from a noble house."

Granny Liu guessed what she was thinking. "I know what's

in your mind," she said. "Let me propose the match."

"Don't make fun of me!" laughed Mrs. Chou. "Such grand people would never agree to marry her to a family like ours."

"We'll see about that," was the reply. And there the matter rested.

Concerned to know how the Chia family was faring, Granny Liu sent Pan-erh to town to make inquiries. As it happened, he found Jungning Street lined with carriages and sedan-chairs, and people in the neighbourhood informed him, "The heads of the Ning and Jung Mansions are getting back their official posts and their confiscated property. They're going up in the world again. Only that Pao-yu of theirs who passed the examination has disappeared."

Pan-erh was about to go happily home when some horsemen galloped up and alighted before the gate. The gateman went down on one knee to salute the foremost. "So you're back, Second Master," he cried. "Congratulations! Is the Elder Master better?"

"He is," was the smiling answer. "Thanks to the Imperial favour, he will be home very soon. Whose are all these carriages?"

The gateman reported, "Imperial envoys have been sent to order us to fetch back the family property." Then the gentleman went in as if walking on air, and Pan-erh guessed that he must be Chia Lien. Without making further inquiries, he hurried back to tell his grandmother.

When Granny Liu heard this news, beaming with smiles she passed it on to Chiao-chieh with her congratulations.

Ping-erh exclaimed, "What a lot we owe you, granny! If not for the way you fixed things, our young lady wouldn't be so happily placed today." Chiao-chieh was still more delighted.

As they were chatting, the messenger who had taken her letter to Chia Lien came back to report, "Master Lien is extremely grateful and told me, as soon as I reached home, to escort the young lady back. He rewarded me too with several taels of silver."

Granny Liu, gratified to hear this, had two carts prepared

for them and urged Chiao-chieh to mount one. But by now she felt so at home here that she was reluctant to leave, while Ching-erh burst into tears, unwilling to part with her. Seeing this, Granny Liu told Ching-erh to go with them, and together they drove straight back to the Jung Mansion.

Earlier on, when Chia Lien had heard that his father was mortally ill and sped to his place of exile, they had wept on meeting again; but gradually Chia Sheh recovered. When Chiao-chieh's letter arrived, Chia Lien told his father what had happened at home and promptly started back. On the way he heard of the general amnesty, and pressing on for another two days he reached home just as the Imperial decree had been brought. Lady Hsing was worried because there was no one to receive it, Chia Lan being too young. Now Chia Lien's return was announced, and both joy and sadness attended this reunion, but having no time to stop and talk he hurried to the front hall to pay homage.

The Imperial envoys asked after his father and instructed him, "Come tomorrow to the Imperial Treasury to receive your bounty. The Ning Mansion is yours to live in again." With that they took their leave.

When Chia Lien escorted them out, he saw several coun- trified carts which the servants were forbidding to draw up there. He knew from the altercation going on that Chiao-chieh had come back.

"Stupid bastards!" he swore at the servants. "When I was away you swindled us, forcing my daughter to flee, and now that they're bringing her back you bar the way! What grudge have you got against me?"

The servants had been afraid that Chia Lien on his return would bring them to book, not grasping the situation; but to their surprise he knew more about it than they did. Standing at respectful attention they reported, "After you left, sir, some of us fell ill, some had to ask for leave. Master Huan, Master Chiang and Master Yun were in charge — we had nothing to do with this."

"You scoundrels!" he swore. "When I'm through with my business I'll deal with you. Let those carts in at once!"

When Chia Lien went inside again he ignored Lady Hsing. Going instead to Lady Wang's apartments he knelt down and kowtowed to her. "Chiao-chieh is back safe and sound, all thanks to you, madam!" he said. "I'll leave Cousin Huan out of this, but Yun is a rascal who made trouble before when left in charge of the house. Now I've only been away a couple of months, yet look at the chaos here! A fellow like this, I suggest we drive him away and have no more to do with him!"

"That wretch Wang Jen is just as bad," she complained.

"Don't worry, madam. I know how to deal with them."

As they were talking, Tsai-yun announced Chiao-chieh, and the girl paid her respects to Lady Wang. They had not been parted long, yet the thought of her narrow escape moved them both to tears, Chiao-chieh weeping bitterly. Chia Lien lost no time in thanking Granny Liu, and Lady Wang made the old woman sit beside her to talk over recent events. When Chia Lien saw Ping-erh he shed tears of gratitude, although he could not express his feelings in public. And so much had she risen in his estimation that he decided, after his father's return, to ask to have her promoted to be his wife. But this is anticipating.

Lady Hsing had feared ructions when Chia Lien found Chiao-chieh missing. The news that he had gone to see Lady Wang alarmed her even more, and she sent a maid to find out what was afoot. When the girl came back to report that Chiao-chieh and Granny Liu were talking there too, Lady Hsing at last re-alized the trick played on her and suspected Lady Wang of setting her son against her. "But who could have sent Ping-erh word?" she fumed.

Just then Chiao-chieh came in with Granny Liu and Ping-erh, followed by Lady Wang who laid the whole blame on Chia Yun and Wang Jen.

"When you heard their proposal, you naturally thought it a good one," she said. "How were you to know what they were up to outside?"

Abashed, Lady Hsing admitted to herself that Lady Wang had made the right decision. After this, these two mistresses were on better terms.

Upon leaving Lady Wang, Ping-erh took Chiao-chieh to see Pao-chai, and each confided her troubles to the other.

Ping-erh told them, "The Emperor has shown us such favour that now our family should prosper again. I'm sure Master Pao will come back."

Just then Chiu-wen came running in frantically. "Hsi-jen is dying!" she cried. If you want to know what had happened, read the next chapter.

CHAPTER 120

Chen Shih-yin Expounds
the Illusory Realm
Chia Yu-tsun Concludes the Dream
of Red Mansions

On hearing from Chiu-wen that Hsi-jen was dying, Pao-chai hurried to her bedside with Chiao-chieh and Ping-erh. Finding her unconscious after a heart attack they revived her with a drink of boiled water, then laid her down again and sent for a doctor.

"How did Sister Hsi-jen fall so ill?" Chiao-chieh asked.

Pao-chai explained, "The other evening she wept so bitterly that she fainted away. The mistress made people help her back to sleep; but because of that commotion outside we didn't get her a doctor."

The doctor arriving just then, they withdrew. After taking her pulse he attributed her illness to anxiety and anger, and made out a prescription accordingly.

Now Hsi-jen had heard it rumoured that if Pao-yu failed to return all his maids would be dismissed, and anxiety on this score aggravated her illness. After the doctor had gone Chiu-wen brewed medicine for her, but lying there alone she had no peace of mind. She seemed to see Pao-yu before her, then had a hazy vision of a monk who was leafing through an album and who told her, "Don't make a wrong decision. I'm having nothing more to do with you."

Before she could question him, Chiu-wen came over saying, "Here's your medicine. Drink it up, sister."

Hsi-jen opened her eyes and kept to herself what she now knew had been a dream. When she had drunk the medicine she reflected, "Pao-yu must have left with the monk. That

time when he tried to take the jade out, he looked as if he
wanted to escape. When I stopped him he wasn't his usual
self, the rough way he pushed and shoved me without any
feeling at all; and later he had less patience with Madam Pao
and not the least feeling for the other girls either, as if he'd
awoken to the Truth. But even so, how can you abandon
your wife? I was sent by the mistress to wait on you, and
though I've been getting the monthly allowance of a concubine,
this was never publicly announced to the masters and mistresses. If they dismiss me and I insist on staying, people will
laugh at me; yet if I leave I shan't be able to bear it, remembering how good Pao-yu was to me." She could not resolve this
dilemma until recalling her dream in which it had been implied
that she and Pao-yu were destined to part she decided, "Better
die and be done with it."

The medicine had eased the pain in her heart, yet she had
to lie there in discomfort for several days before getting up again
to wait on Pao-chai. The latter secretly shed tears of longing
for Pao-yu, lamenting her wretched fate; however, since her
mother was preparing to ransom her brother, there was much
to attend to and she had to help out. But no more of this
for the present.

Chia Cheng escorting the old lady's coffin, and Chia Jung
those of Ko-ching, Hsi-feng and Yuan-yang, had now reached
Chinling where they had them interred. Then Chia Jung took
Tai-yu's coffin to be buried in her ancestral graveyard, leaving
Chia Cheng to supervise the building of the tombs. One day
he received a letter from home, and the news that Pao-yu and
Chia Lan had passed the examination delighted him; but Pao-
yu's disappearance so perturbed him that he felt constrained
to hurry back at once. On the way he heard of the general
amnesty and received another letter from home confirming his
pardon and official reinstatement. Much heartened, he pressed
on rapidly day and night.

The day they reached the Kunlu post station, it suddenly
turned cold and began to snow, and their boat moored in a

secluded spot. Chia Cheng sent servants ashore to deliver cards to friends in that locality, and to explain that he had no time to call and they should not trouble to call on him either, as the boat would be leaving again immediately. Only one page remained to wait on him as he wrote a letter to send home by a messenger travelling ahead by road. Before broaching the subject of Pao-yu he paused. Looking up through the snow, he glimpsed at the prow of the boat a figure with a shaven head and bare feet, draped in a red felt cape. This man prostrated himself before Chia Cheng, who hurried out of the cabin, meaning to raise him up and see who he was, but the man had already kowtowed four times, then stood up and made him a Buddhist salutation. Chia Cheng was about to bow in return when he recognized his son.

"Is it Pao-yu?" he asked in amazement.

The other made no answer, looking torn between grief and joy.

"If you are Pao-yu, what are you doing here, and in this costume?" Chia Cheng asked again.

Before Pao-yu could reply, a monk and a Taoist priest appeared, each taking one of his arms. "Your worldly obligations have been fulfilled," they declared. "Why delay your departure?" Then all three of them glided ashore.

Though it was slippery underfoot, Chia Cheng hurried after them but could not overtake them. However, he heard one of them chant:

> My home is Blue Ridge Peak,
> I roam the primeval void.
> Who will go with me to keep me company,
> Returning to the Great Waste of infinity!

Chia Cheng pursued them round a slope, only to find they had vanished. Limp and out of breath, his heart misgave him. Turning, he found that the page had followed him.

"Did you see those three men just now?" Chia Cheng asked.

"Yes, sir. As you were running after them I came too. But then I lost sight of those three."

Chia Cheng was tempted to go on, but in the white wilder-

ness there was no one in sight. Marvelling, he had to turn back.

When the servants returned and found their master gone, the boatman told them that he had gone ashore in pursuit of two monks and a Taoist priest. They followed his footprints in the snow and, seeing him approaching in the distance, went to meet him and escorted him back to the boat. After he had sat down and caught his breath he told them of his encounter with Pao-yu. They suggested searching the vicinity.

"You don't understand," he sighed. "I saw them with my own eyes, they were not apparitions. And I heard them chanting a most occult poem. When Pao-yu was born with jade in his mouth, I knew it was uncanny and boded no good; but because the old lady doted on him we brought him up all these years. As for the monk and the priest, I have seen them three times. The first time was when they came to explain the miraculous nature of the jade; the second time, when Pao-yu was so ill and the monk took the jade in his hand and intoned some incantation to cure him; the third time, when he brought back the jade and I saw him sitting in the front hall, then all of a sudden he vanished. Although that increased my misgivings, I thought Pao-yu fortunate to have the protection of these Buddhist and Taoist saints. Little did I know that Pao-yu was a spirit who had come to earth to undergo certain trials, and who managed to fool the old lady for nineteen years! Only now is it clear to me." He shed tears.

"If Master Pao was really a Buddhist saint, he shouldn't have become a *chu-jen*," they objected. "Why take the official examination then leave?"

"You don't understand that all the stars in the heavens, the saints in the mountains and the spirits in caves have each their own different nature. Pao-yu never showed any inclination to study, yet he'd only to glance at a book to master it. By temperament, too, he was different from other people." He sighed again.

They consoled him with talk of Chia Lan's success and the improvement in the family's fortunes. Then Chia Cheng went on with his letter, describing this incident and urging the family not to grieve. He sealed the letter and sent it off with a servant, then continued on his way. No more of this.

Aunt Hsueh, after hearing of the amnesty, told Hsueh Ko to raise loans in various quarters until she had enough to ransom her son. The Board of Punishments sanctioned this and after receiving the money issued an order for Hsueh Pan's release. We need not dwell on their family reunion with its natural intermingling of joy and sorrow.

"If I ever run amuck again," swore Hsueh Pan, "may I be killed and disembowelled!"

His mother stopped his mouth. "Just make up your mind to it instead of raving. Why must you swear such a blood-curdling oath?" she scolded. "Now I've a proposal to make. Hsiang-ling's had so much to put up with since becoming your concubine, that now that your wife has killed herself and poor though we are we can still make ends meet, I suggest making her my daughter-in-law. What do you think?"

Hsueh Pan nodded his agreement.

"Quite right and proper," agreed Pao-chai and the rest.

Hsiang-ling flushing crimson protested, "I shall go on serving the master as his maid. There's no need to raise my status."

Thereupon they started addressing her as the young mistress, and none of the household objected.

Then Hsueh Pan went to thank the Chia family, and Aunt Hsueh and Pao-chai went over too. When all were assembled and they had talked for a while, Chia Cheng's messenger arrived and presented his letter, announcing that the master would soon be home. Lady Wang made Chia Lan read the letter out, and when he reached the passage describing the encounter with Pao-yu the whole family wept, Lady Wang, Pao-chai and Hsi-jen being the most affected. They discussed Chia Cheng's injunction to them not to mourn for Pao-yu because he was a reincarnated spirit.

One said, "If he'd become an official then had the misfortune to get into trouble and ruin the family, that would have been worse. It's better to have produced a Bodhisattva, thanks to the virtue of our master and mistress. In fact, Lord Ching of the East Mansion practised alchemy for more than ten years yet never became an immortal. It's harder still to become a Bodhisattva! If you look at it this way, madam, you'll feel better."

Lady Wang confided tearfully to Aunt Hsueh, "I don't blame Pao-yu for deserting me, it's my daughter-in-law's cruel fate that upsets me most. When they'd only just been married a couple of years, how heartless it was of him to abandon her!" This made Aunt Hsueh's heart ache too.

Pao-chai, weeping, was oblivious to all around her; and as the men of the family had withdrawn to the outer apartments, Lady Wang went on, "He kept me on tenterhooks all those years, till he got married and passed the examination and I was pleased to hear that Pao-chai was pregnant. To think it should end like this! If I'd known, I wouldn't have found him a wife or ruined your daughter's life!"

"This was their fate," Aunt Hsueh answered. "What else could families like ours have done? It's lucky that she's with child. If she gives birth to a son, he's bound to make good and all's well that ends well. Look at your elder daughter-in-law: now Lan's a *chu-jen* and next year he'll be a court scholar — doesn't that mean that he'll become an official? After all that bitterness, she's having a taste of sweetness now to reward her for her goodness. You know my daughter, sister. She's not flighty or petty-minded; you needn't worry about her."

Lady Wang, convinced of the truth of this, reflected, "Pao-chai was always a quiet, unassuming child with simple tastes; that's why this has happened to *her*. It seems that everyone's lot in life is predestined! Though she wept so bitterly, she retained all her dignity and even tried to console me — she's really one in a thousand. What a pity, though, that a boy like Pao-yu lost out on his share of good fortune in this dusty world!" Comforted by these reflections she went on to consider Hsi-jen's case and thought, "The other maids are easily disposed of: the older ones can be married off and the younger ones kept here to wait on Pao-chai. But what's to be done about Hsi-jen?" As there were others present, she decided to discuss this with Aunt Hsueh that evening.

Aunt Hsueh did not go home that day, staying with her heart-broken daughter to comfort her. However, Pao-chai showed her usual good sense, saying that it was no use complaining as Pao-yu had been someone quite unique and this had been fated to happen. When she spoke so reasonably her mother, much relieved, went over to tell Lady Wang what she had said.

Lady Wang nodded. "I wouldn't deserve such a good daughter-in-law if I hadn't done some good deeds!" she sighed, giving way to grief again.

Aunt Hsueh consoled her for a while then raised another question. "Hsi-jen's only the shadow of her old self, what with pining for Pao-yu," she said. "The proper wife should stay at home as a widow, and sometimes a concubine wants to do the same; but in Hsi-jen's case, her relationship with Pao-yu was never made public."

"Exactly," said Lady Wang. "This is just what I wanted to talk over with you. If we dismiss her, I'm afraid she'll be unwilling, or threaten to kill herself; but I doubt whether my husband would agree to keeping her on. That's our dilemma."

"I'm sure he would never agree, especially as he doesn't know her position and thinks her simply a maid, with no reason to stay on here. You'll have to get one of her family to come, insist on them finding her a respectable husband, then give her a generous dowry. Being a sensible girl and still young, she should realize that she hasn't served you for nothing and that you've treated her quite handsomely, sister. I shall have a good talk with her too. Even after you've sent for one of her family, you needn't tell her about it until a good match has been fixed up and we've made sure that the family's well-off and the man's presentable. Then we can send her away."

"That's an excellent idea. Otherwise, if I let the master dispose of her off-hand wouldn't that be the ruin of her?"

Aunt Hsueh nodded her agreement and after some further talk went to see Pao-chai. Finding Hsi-jen still in tears there she tried to console her; and the good-hearted girl, not being acrimonious, agreed to all she said.

"It's good of you to talk like this to a serving-maid, madam," said Hsi-jen. "I should never dream of disobeying the mistress."

Aunt Hsueh felt even more drawn to her, finding her so submissive. Pao-chai also spoke of a woman's duties in life, and so they found themselves in complete accord.

A few days later, Chia Cheng arrived home and all the men went out to welcome him. By now Chia Sheh and Chia Chen were also back and, meeting again, they described their experiences since parting. But the women of the house, when they saw Chia Cheng, could not help grieving at the thought of Pao-yu.

Chia Cheng urged them not to be distressed, telling Lady Wang, "This was fated. From now on those of us outside will have to manage the family affairs with your assistance inside, on no account letting things slide as we did before. The different households can see to their own affairs; there is no need for a general manager. You can decide, as you think right, on everything done in our family's inner apartments."

When Lady Wang told him that Pao-chai was with child and suggested dismissing Pao-yu's former maids, he simply nodded in silence.

The next day Chia Cheng went to court to ask the chief ministers how he should express his gratitude for the Imperial favour while still in mourning. They petitioned the Emperor on his behalf, and the Sovereign in his great goodness granted him an audience. When Chia Cheng had expressed his thanks and received various instructions, the Emperor asked what had become of Pao-yu and marvelled at the account which Chia Cheng gave him.

The Emperor decreed, "The brilliance of Pao-yu's writing must be due to his being an immortal. Were he at court we could have promoted him. Now, since he would never accept a noble rank, let him be given the title 'The Immortal of Literary Genius.' "

Chia Cheng kowtowed his thanks and withdrew, to be welcomed home by Chia Lien and Chia Chen. When told of the Emperor's decree, the whole household was overjoyed.

Chia Chen reported, "The Ning Mansion has been cleaned up, and with your permission we shall move over now. Sister Hsi-chun can have Green Lattice Nunnery in the Garden for her devotions."

Chia Cheng made no comment, but after a pause he urged them to do their best to repay the Imperial favour.

Then Chia Lien informed him that his parents were willing to marry Chiao-chieh to the Chou family. Chia Cheng, who had heard the previous night of all that had happened to her, said, "That's for the Elder Master and Elder Mistress to decide. We shouldn't despise country people, providing they are honest folk and their son is studious and seems promising. Not all the officials at court are city bred, are they?"

"No, sir," agreed Chia Lien. "But as my father is growing old and suffers from chronic asthma, he hopes to live quietly for a few years, leaving you in overall charge."

"I only wish I could live as a recluse in the country myself," Chia Cheng answered. "But I haven't yet repaid our Sovereign's great kindness." With that he went inside.

Chia Lien sent for Granny Liu to tell her the match was agreed on, after which she called on Lady Wang to predict that now they would win official promotion and all the family's sons and grandsons would prosper.

Just then, a maid announced Hsi-jen's sister-in-law, from whom Lady Wang elicited that some relatives had proposed a match for Hsi-jen with a certain Chiang family in the south city who owned houses, land and shops. The prospective bridegroom was a few years older but he had never been married and, as far as appearances went, was one in a hundred.

Lady Wang was favourably inclined and replied, "You can agree to it. Come back in a few days' time to fetch your sister-in-law." She also sent to make inquiries and, on being assured that it would be a good match, informed Pao-chai and asked Aunt Hsueh to break the news gently to Hsi-jen.

Hsi-jen was desolated yet dared not disobey. She remember-ed, that year Pao-yu called on her family, she had sworn to them that she would rather die than be redeemed and go home. "Now the mistress is set upon this," she thought. "If I ask to stay they'll say I have no sense of shame; yet I really don't want to leave here!" She started sobbing. When Aunt Hsueh and Pao-chai reasoned with her she reflected, "If I died here that would be a poor return for Her Ladyship's kindness. I'd better die at home." So suppressing her grief she bade them all farewell, heart-rending as she found it to leave the other maids.

She mounted the carriage determined to kill herself, and when she saw her brother and sister-in-law she could not speak for sobbing. Her brother showed her one by one the betrothal gifts sent by the Chiang family as well as the dowry he had prepared, telling her which items had been given by Lady Wang, which they had bought themselves, so that Hsi-jen was even more at a loss for words. After a couple of days at home she thought, "My brother's done things so handsomely, how can I cause him trouble by killing myself in his house?" In a dilemma, she felt her heart would break yet had to bear up.

The day came to fetch the bride, and not being the type to make a scene however wronged she felt, she let herself be carried off in the sedan-chair, deferring her decision till her arrival. However, once over their threshold, she found that the Chiangs had made scrupulous preparations according to all the correct wedding etiquette, and as soon as she entered the house she was addressed by the maid-servants as "Mistress." All treated her so well that, once again, she did not like to bring trouble on them by committing suicide there. That night she wept and refused her husband's advances, yet he very ten-derly deferred to her wishes.

The next day when her chests were opened and he saw his old scarlet sash, he realized that this was Pao-yu's maid. At first he had thought her one of the old lady's attendants, never dreaming that she was Hsi-jen. Now, abashed by the memory of Pao-yu's past friendship with him, he treated her even more kindly, deliberately showing her the pale green sash which Pao-yu had given him in exchange. Only then did Hsi-jen understand that he was Chiang Yu-han. Convinced that their marriage must have been predestined, she told him how she had meant to kill herself. Deeply impressed by her loyalty, Chiang Yu-han showed her even more consideration so that Hsi-jen felt she had really nowhere to die.

Now, Honourable Readers, though certain things are predestined and "cannot be helped," it is wrong for sons of concubines or ministers of vanquished states as well as for men of principle and chaste women to keep using this phrase as a handy excuse. That was why Hsi-jen was ranked in the *Third Register*. As a former poet passing the Temple of Lady Peach-blossom wrote:

> Since time immemorial, the hardest thing is to die;
> It is not the Lady of Hsi[1] alone who was broken-hearted.

But let us leave Hsi-jen embarking on a new life and return to Chia Yu-tsun, who had been found guilty of embezzlement and condemned to punishment. He was pardoned under the general amnesty, but ordered back to his native place and reduced to the status of a common citizen. Having sent his family home first, he was making his way there with a baggage-cart and a page when, by the Ford of Awakening in the Stream of Rapid Reversal, he saw a Taoist priest emerge from a thatched shed to greet him. Recognizing his old friend Chen Shih-yin, he promptly returned the greeting.

"How have you been, worthy Mr. Chia?" asked Shih-yin.

"So you are Master Chen, Immortal One!" replied Yu-tsun. "How is it that last time we met you refused to recognize me? Later I was very worried to hear that your temple had been

---

[1] Lady Wei of Hsi who was captured in 683 B.C. by King Wen of the State of Chu when he conquered the Hsi State. She bore him two sons, but regretted not having killed herself, saying, "If a woman serves two husbands, she should die!"

burned down. Now that I am lucky enough to meet you again, I am sure your virtue must be even greater. As for me, owing to my own inveterate folly, I've now been reduced to this."

"Last time you were a high official, so how could a poor priest claim acquaintance with you? As an old friend I ventured to offer you some advice, but you ignored it. However, wealth and poverty, success and failure are predestined. How amazing that we should meet again today! My humble temple is not far from here. Would you care to come for a chat?" Yu-tsun agreed willingly.

They walked off hand in hand, followed by the page with the cart till they reached a thatched temple. Shih-yin invited Yu-tsun in to sit down, and a boy served tea.

Asked how he had come to renounce the world, Shih-yin said with a smile, "It's easily done, with the speed of thought. Coming from the great world, sir, don't you know of a certain Pao-yu who used to live in the lap of luxury?"

"Of course I do! Recently it has been rumoured that he has entered Buddhist orders too. I met him several times, but never dreamed he would take such a decision."

"That's where you were wrong! I knew his strange story in advance, and had already met him at the time when the two of us talked before the gate of my old house in Jenching Lane."

"How could that be?" exclaimed Yu-tsun in surprise. "With the capital so far from your honourable district!"

"I met him in spirit a long time ago."

"Then you know, no doubt, where he is now?"

"Pao-yu means 'divine jade.' Before the raid on the Jung and Ning Mansions, on the day when Pao-chai and Tai-yu separated, that jade had already left the world of men to escape from calamity and effect a reunion. Then, former ties of affection severed, form and essence once more became one. It further showed its miraculous origin by passing the examination with distinction and begetting a noble son, proving that this jade is a treasure tempered by the divine powers of nature, not to be compared with ordinary objects. It was taken to the mortal world by the Buddhist of Infinite Space and the Taoist of Boundless Time. Now that its mortal course is run, they have carried it back to its original place: this is what has happened to Pao-yu."

Yu-tsun, though he understood barely half of this, nodded and marvelled, "So that's the way it was! I was too ignorant to know. But why, with such a spiritual origin, was Pao-yu so enamoured of girls before he became so enlightened? Would you explain that?"

"This may be hard for you to grasp fully, sir. The Illusory Land of Great Void is the Blessed Land of Truth. By reading the registers twice, he saw the beginning and the ending too all set down there in detail. How could that fail to enlighten him? Since the fairy herb has reverted to her true form, shouldn't the jade of 'spiritual understanding' do the same?"

Yu-tsun was mystified, but knowing that this was some divine secret he did not press for a fuller explanation. "You have told me about Pao-yu," he said. "But there are many ladies in our humble clan; how is it that apart from the Imperial Consort all the others came to such undistinguished ends?"

"You must allow me to speak bluntly, sir. All noble ladies come from the realm of love and retribution. From time immemorial, carnal desire has been their cardinal sin, and they must not even immerse themselves in love. Thus Tsui Ying-ying and Su Hsiao-hsiao[1] were immortals with earthly desires, while Sung Yu and Ssuma Hsiang-ju[2] were writers of genius whose works were wicked. Anyone ensnared by love can come to no good end!"

Yu-tsun absently stroked his beard and sighed. "I have one more question, Reverend Immortal," he ventured. "Will the Jung and Ning Mansions be restored to their former prosperity?"

"It is an immutable law that the good are favoured by fortune while the dissolute meet with calamity. In these two

---

[1] The first was a talented and beautiful girl in a well-known Chinese romance and the second a courtesan in Hangchow at the end of the sixth century.

[2] Brilliant and romantic poets of ancient times.

mansions now, the good are laying up virtue, the bad repenting their crimes; so naturally their houses will prosper again with the orchid and fragrant osmanthus blooming together."

Yu-tsun lowered his head in thought, then suddenly laughed, "I get it! One of the sons of their house called Lan[1] has passed the examination; so that prediction of yours has come true. But just now, Reverend Immortal, you spoke of 'the orchid and fragrant osmanthus blooming together,' and you mentioned that Pao-yu has begotten a noble son. Is this as yet unborn son going to advance rapidly in his official career?"

"This belongs to the future," said Shih-yin with a smile. "It's not for me to predict."

Yu-tsun had more questions on the tip of his tongue but the other, unwilling to answer them, ordered his servant to prepare food and invited Yu-tsun to share it. After the meal, Shih-yin forestalled further questions about Yu-tsun's own future by urging him to have a rest in his temple.

"I still have some worldly affairs to settle and must attend to them today," he explained.

"What worldly affairs can you have, Immortal One, you whose life is given to cultivating virtue?" asked Yu-tsun in surprise.

"Simply some private business concerned with family affection."

"What do you mean?" Yu-tsun was yet more amazed.

"You are unaware, sir, that my daughter Ying-lien met with misfortune as a child, and at the start of your official career you judged a case in which she was involved. She has married into the Hsueh family, but is dying now in childbirth leaving behind her a son to carry on the Hsuehs' line. Since the time has come for her to sever all mortal ties, I must go to guide her spirit." With a flick of his sleeve he rose.

Yu-tsun, left dazed, fell asleep in this thatched temple by the Ford of Awakening in the Stream of Rapid Reversal, while Shih-yin went to conduct Hsiang-ling to the Illusory Land of

---

[1] Lan means "orchid."

Great Void to enter her name in the record of the Goddess of Disenchantment. As he passed the archway, he saw a monk and a priest come drifting towards him.

"Congratulations, holy men!" he called. "Have you severed all their entanglements of love?"

"Not completely," they replied. "But we have brought that stupid object back with us. We still have to return him to his original place and record his experiences in the world, so that he won't have descended there for nothing."

Shih-yin saluted and left them, whereupon the monk and the priest took the divine jade to Blue Ridge Peak and left it in the place where Nu Wa had melted down stones to repair heaven. This done, they went their different ways. Thus:

> A book not of this world records events not of this world;
> A man with two lives reverts to his first form.

One day the Taoist immortal the Reverend Void, coming to Blue Ridge Peak again, found there the stone left unused when heaven was repaired, with the same inscription on it that he had seen before. On reading it carefully once more, he discovered that appended to the epilogue-poem were more accounts of the denouement.

He nodded and sighed, "When I first read this strange story of Brother Stone, I said that it could be made known to the world and therefore had it transcribed. But at that time I hadn't read how he returned to his original form and place. This is quite a story — I wonder when it was added? Apparently Brother Stone after his descent to the world of men was burnished and awoke to the truth, which is highly gratifying! If too many years pass and the inscription is blurred, it may be misconstrued. I had better transcribe it again and find someone with the leisure to circulate it, to show the illusory nature of marvels, mundane matters, truth and falsehood. Then perhaps some men tired of mortal vanity may return to the truth, or some friendly mountain spirit may enable the Stone to descend again to the world."

Thereupon he copied out the inscription again, tucked it into his sleeve and searched the haunts of splendour and wealth; but he found there only men striving to advance their careers or to feed and clothe themselves — not one had time for the story of the Stone. However, when he reached the thatched temple by the Ford of Awakening in the Stream of Rapid Reversal, he discovered a man sleeping there and felt that here was someone sufficiently leisured to be given this *Story of the Stone*. The sleeper did not wake when called, but when the Reverend Void tugged at him he sat up slowly and opened his eyes, then leafed through the manuscript before putting it down again.

"Yes, I witnessed this whole business myself," he said. "The account you have copied out is quite correct. I'll tell you someone who will circulate it, so that this extraordinary case can be concluded."

The Reverend Void at once asked whom he had in mind.

"Wait till such-and-such a year, month, day and hour, then go to Mourning-the-Red Studio where you will find a certain Mr. Tsao Hsueh-chin," was the answer. "Just give him Chia Yu-tsun's name, and tell him what you want of him." With that he lay down and went to sleep again.

The Reverend Void bore these instructions in mind and, after no one knows how many generations or aeons, sure enough he found Mourning-the-Red Studio, where Mr. Tsao Hsueh-chin was reading an ancient history. He gave him Chia Yu-tsun's message and handed him the *Story of the Stone*.

Tsao Hsueh-chin laughed, "This certainly sounds like Chia Yu-tsun!"[1]

"How did you come to know him, sir?" asked the Reverend Void. "What makes you willing to pass this tale on for him?"

Mr. Tsao chuckled, "They call you Void, and you really are devoid of sense! Since this is a fictitious rustic tale, provided it contains no clerical errors or perverse contradictions, it will serve to while away the time with a couple of friends after wine and food, or to dispel loneliness some rainy evening under

---

[1] Homophone for "fiction in rustic language."

the lamp by the window. It doesn't have to be vouched for or launched by men of consequence. All these questions you ask show that you're a pig-headed pedant and won't get you anywhere!"

The Reverend Void threw back his head and laughed, then tossed him the manuscript and left saying to himself, "So it's all hot air — fantastic! Neither author, transcriber, nor readers can tell what it is about. It is nothing but a literary diversion to entertain readers."

When this tale later came to be read, someone wrote four lines of verse to elucidate the author's meaning, as follows:

> A tale of grief is told,
> Fantasy most melancholy.
> Since all live in a dream,
> Why laugh at others' folly?

Acknowledgment

The publishers and translators gratefully acknowledge the expert advice and assistance they received from Professor Wu Shichang of the Literary Research Institute of the Academy of Social Sciences, who collated the different Chinese editions of Volumes I and II and helped to improve the accuracy of the English version. Thanks are also due to their colleague Cheng Wen who carefully checked all three volumes of the translation.

图书在版编目(CIP)数据

红楼梦　第三卷:英文/(清)曹雪芹,(清)高鹗著.
北京：外文出版社，1995
ISBN 7－119－01548－6

Ⅰ.红… Ⅱ.①曹…②高… Ⅲ.古典小说:章回小说:长篇小说
—中国—古代—英文 Ⅳ.I242.4

中国版本图书馆 CIP 数据核字（95）第 08463 号

红楼梦

（三）

曹雪芹　高　鹗　著

杨宪益　戴乃迭　译

*

ⓒ外文出版社

外文出版社出版

（中国北京百万庄路 24 号）

邮政编码 100037

北京外文印刷厂印刷

中国国际图书贸易总公司发行

（中国北京车公庄西路 35 号）

北京邮政信箱第 399 号　邮政编码 100044

1980 年(28 开)第一版

1995 年第一版三次印刷

（英）

ISBN 7－119－01548－6 /I·302(外)

12700

10－E－1424SC